Virginia Woolf, the War Without, the War Within

UNIVERSITY PRESS OF FLORIDA

Florida A&M University, Tallahassee
Florida Atlantic University, Boca Raton
Florida Gulf Coast University, Ft. Myers
Florida International University, Miami
Florida State University, Tallahassee
New College of Florida, Sarasota
University of Central Florida, Orlando
University of Florida, Gainesville
University of North Florida, Jacksonville
University of South Florida, Tampa
University of West Florida, Pensacola

Virginia Woolf,

THE WAR WITHOUT, THE WAR WITHIN

Her Final Diaries & the Diaries She Read

Barbara Lounsberry

UNIVERSITY PRESS OF FLORIDA
Gainesville/Tallahassee/Tampa/Boca Raton
Pensacola/Orlando/Miami/Jacksonville/Ft. Myers/Sarasota

Copyright 2018 by Barbara Lounsberry
All rights reserved
Published in the United States of America

First cloth printing, 2018
First paperback printing, 2020

25 24 23 22 21 20   6 5 4 3 2 1

Library of Congress Cataloging-in-Publication Data
Names: Lounsberry, Barbara, author.
Title: Virginia Woolf, the war without, the war within : her final diaries and the diaries she read / Barbara Lounsberry.
Description: Gainesville : University Press of Florida, 2018. | Includes bibliographical references and index.
Identifiers: LCCN 2017055317 | ISBN 9780813056937 (cloth : alk. paper) ISBN 9780813068077 (pbk.)
Subjects: LCSH: Novelists, English—20th century—Diaries. | Woolf, Virginia, 1882–1941—Diaries.
Classification: LCC PR6045.O72 Z8118 2018 | DDC 828/.91203 [B]—dc23
LC record available at https://lccn.loc.gov_2017055317

The University Press of Florida is the scholarly publishing agency for the State University System of Florida, comprising Florida A&M University, Florida Atlantic University, Florida Gulf Coast University, Florida International University, Florida State University, New College of Florida, University of Central Florida, University of Florida, University of North Florida, University of South Florida, and University of West Florida.

University Press of Florida
2046 NE Waldo Road
Suite 2100
Gainesville, FL 32609
http://upress.ufl.edu

Contents

Acknowledgments   vii
List of Abbreviations   ix

Introduction   1

1. THE WAR WITHIN   5
    Virginia Woolf's June 1929 to September 1930 Diary   6
    Dorothy Wordsworth's Journals   11

2. THE MARCH OF HEADLINES   24
    Virginia Woolf's 1930–1931 Diary   25
    John Skinner's *Journal of a Somerset Rector*   38
    James Woodforde's *Diary of a Country Parson*   48
    The *Private Diary* of Princess Daisy of Pless   55

3. ADEPT SAILING BEFORE THE STORM   68
    Virginia Woolf's 1932 Diary   69
    Virginia Woolf's 1933–1934 Diary   79
    Michael Field's *Works and Days*   87

4. WARNINGS   101
    Virginia Woolf's Second 1934 Diary   102
    André Gide's *Journals*   110
    Guy de Maupassant's Travel Journal *Sur l'eau (Afloat)*   118
    Alice James' *Journal*   126

5. TIGHTNESS & STRUGGLE   138
    Virginia Woolf's 1935 Diary   138
    Dr. John Salter's *Diary*   150
    John Bailey's *Diaries*   160

6. MISGUIDED GENERAL   168

   Virginia Woolf's 1936 Diary   168
   The Diaries of Lord & Lady Amberley: *The Amberley Papers*   177
   Journal of a Governess: Ellen Weeton   198
   Stephen MacKenna's *Journal*   210

7. STORM-TOSSED & EXPOSED   221

   Virginia Woolf's 1937 Diary   222
   The Late Diaries of Leo & Countess Tolstoy   231

8. HITLER DARKENS THE WATERS   249

   Virginia Woolf's 1938 Diary   250
   The *Diary* of the Reverend Francis Kilvert   257

9. WAR SHADES LIFE & WORK   272

   Virginia Woolf's 1939 Diary   273
   F. L. Lucas' *Journal under the Terror, 1938*   282
   Charles Ricketts' *Journals*   292

10. ENCIRCLED BY WAR   302

    Virginia Woolf's 1940 Diary   303
    Virginia Woolf's 1941 Diary   315

Epilogue   324

Appendix: The Diaries Virginia Woolf Read   331
Notes   337
Works Consulted   365
Index   379

Acknowledgments

Melancholy hovers as I write the last words of my trilogy on Virginia Woolf's diary and the many diaries she read. Still, what a privilege and joy to live with Woolf's prose for more than two decades.

My first and greatest thanks must go to Shannon McCarthy, longtime acquisitions editor for the University Press of Florida, who first saw merit in the prospectus for *Becoming Virginia Woolf: Her Early Diaries and the Diaries She Read* and invited me to send the book. Little did she know what would follow. Shannon's kind, yet firm, counsel helped me shape all three books; indeed, she offered the title to volume 2: *Virginia Woolf's Modernist Path*.

Thanks, too, go to the poet Kathleen Kelly, who, from the start, expressed keenest interest in Woolf's final diaries and years. I hope this book will fulfill her hopes, for Kathleen's probing questions led me to see that I could write a book on each of Woolf's three diary stages. Poet and novelist Nancy Price was also there from the start, pointing to the many threads I was trying to weave in my first manuscripts and helping me to pare strands, yet also to deepen the weave.

I can never express sufficient gratitude to Anne Olivier Bell, whose accurate, helpful, and (sometimes even) droll editing of Woolf's 1915 to 1941 diaries sets the standard for such work. Without her labors, our understanding of Woolf would be greatly impoverished—and my books could not exist. Olivier Bell's help extended beyond the precious print editions of Woolf's diaries, for in 2001 she allowed me to interview her in her home. She offered me a delicious lunch on the long wooden table where the diary work unfurled; showed me the huge photocopies she had made of Woolf's handwritten diary pages; and then drove me to see Charleston. That same year, Andrew McNeillie, Bell's assistant editor of the 1920 to 1941 diaries, took time to describe to me those "heady" days in Sussex and how funny Quentin Bell could be when McNeillie helped him compile the indexes to the diaries. Before his death,

Quentin Bell promptly and fully answered all questions I had regarding his aunt and her diaries.

In 2003, scholar Sybil Oldfield continued this English largesse. She drove me to the bridge over the River Ouse. (Nothing was green on that cold April Sunday, all bare and brown.) Then she boosted me up to look over the wall at Monk's House, the Woolf's Sussex home. Most of all, Sybil shared with me her own important work, which I've drawn on most fully in this final book, *The War Without, the War Within*.

In the United States, biographer Panthea Reid generously gave of her time to read and offer suggestions that have greatly improved this book and the two previous volumes. Woolf scholar Beth Rigel Daugherty did the same with this final volume, offering helpful guidance on matters large and small.

Over more than a score of years, the curators of the Henry W. and Albert A. Berg Collection of English and American Literature in the New York Public Library have also shared their expertise during my hours of work with Woolf's manuscripts. This access was vital, particularly for this final book. My thanks also go to Dorothy Sheridan, head of Special Collections at the University of Sussex, for allowing me to work with the Monk's House papers.

I am indebted as well to many arms of the University of Northern Iowa. The Graduate College and the College of Humanities and Fine Arts provided grants and leaves that allowed the books to grow. Special thanks go to Rosemary Meany and others in the Rod Library who helped me locate many of the obscure diaries Woolf read.

The poet Penelope Cray also deserves the highest endorsement as the copyeditor supreme for all three volumes. Although we've never met in person, I've come over the years to think of her as the best kind of friend. I also thank the press designers for their striking covers, type styles, and page designs.

Final thanks to members of the International Virginia Woolf Society—and to members of the many Woolf societies in specific nations—who are so welcoming and generous with their knowledge and support.

Abbreviations

CH   *Carlyle's House and Other Sketches* [Woolf's 1909 Diary]. Ed. David Bradshaw.
CR   *The Common Reader.* 2 vols.
D   *The Diary of Virginia Woolf.* Ed. Anne Olivier Bell. 5 vols.
E   *The Essays of Virginia Woolf.* Ed. Andrew McNeillie and Stuart N. Clarke. 6 vols.
L   *The Letters of Virginia Woolf.* Ed. Nigel Nicolson and Joanne Trautmann. 6 vols.
MOB *Moments of Being.* Ed. Jeanne Schulkind.
PA   *A Passionate Apprentice: The Early Journals, 1897–1909.* Ed. Mitchell A. Leaska.
ROO *A Room of One's Own*
RN   *Virginia Woolf's Reading Notebooks.* Ed. Brenda Silver.
SF   *The Complete Shorter Fiction of Virginia Woolf.* Ed. Susan Dick
TG   *Three Guineas*

Introduction

When their last house in London is bombed in the war... [Virginia Woolf] makes sure, first, of the twenty-four volumes of diaries.[1]

From her first tiny diary, written at age fourteen, Virginia Woolf personifies her diary as a living, breathing *life*. This explains her urgent rescue of her diary books from the rubble in 1940. It adds poignancy to her moves to upgrade her diaries in the last years of her life. The third and final stage of Woolf's diary life, from mid-1929 to her suicide in March 1941, shows the diary's late bloom. At the same time, we see there unfold—more clearly than any biographer has yet shown—her artistic *inner wars* as they interact with the ever-nearing *war without*.

By 1929, Woolf has become an established and famous writer; at age forty-seven, the author of books widely read and admired. But she is the author of another kind of book, as well: semiprivate diaries, which mark a writer's progress in years and skill, a very rare sort of book indeed. Woolf's diary first reached the public (tantalizingly abridged) in 1953. It belongs, all agree, among the world's great diaries. Diary scholar Anna Jackson even suggests that Woolf may be "the Shakespeare of the diary genre" (151). Woolf's nephew and biographer, Quentin Bell, calls her diary "a literary achievement equal to though very different from *The Waves* or *To the Lighthouse*, having the same accurate beauty of writing but also an immediacy such as one finds only in diaries" (*D* 1: xiii). Biographer Alexandra Harris writes of the "glittering and moving diaries" that offer "one of the most intricate records of a life ever made" (7, 151). These diary books, shared with only a few, are also the door to Woolf's public fiction and nonfiction.

In writing of the *three* stages of Woolf's diary career, I seek to counter the view—fostered by the six published diary volumes—that her diary-writing breaks into two neat phases: her "apprentice" early diaries, from 1897 to 1909 (published in 1990 as *A Passionate Apprentice*), and her later diaries, from 1915 to 1941 (edited by Anne Olivier Bell and published in five volumes under the title *The Diary of Virginia Woolf*). Close reading of the thirty-eight diary books themselves reveals that Woolf's diary-keeping evolves in three stages.

Woolf's experimental first stage, from 1897 to mid-1918, covers her first thirteen diary books.[2] It begins when Woolf is fourteen and ends in her thirty-sixth year. The early diaries differ vastly from each other—a noteworthy fact in itself. Woolf tries out travel diaries, a natural history diary, journals with titled entries (and tables of contents), and even an occasional life diary. Here is fascinating *diary experiment*: these early diaries show how the young girl becomes the extraordinary public writer Virginia Woolf.

A crisis in November 1918, involving female support, propels Woolf toward a new audience and purpose for her diary and, with it, the start of her second diary stage: her mature, lean, modernist diaries of 1919–1929.[3] Woolf creates "Old Virginia" and begins to mother herself.

The unexpected recurs in June 1929. Suddenly, halfway through the year, Woolf abandons her two-and-a-half-year experiment with a loose-leaf diary (meant to catch more "stray" or "loose" thoughts) and starts a new diary in a bound diary book. She says she does this to save her diary's life. She seeks now the greater solidity and permanency of a bound diary book as she begins her "attack" on her most difficult work to date: *The Waves*. French diary theorist Philippe Lejeune calls diaries "life insurance" (189). Woolf now turns to a bound diary book for support, as if she senses danger ahead.

Her final diary stage, from 1929 to 1941, is distinguished by three traits. Most obviously, she increases her *number of entries per year* from that in her second, lean, modernist diary stage. Thirteen diary books cover that second stage (July 1918 through June 1929), with an average of forty entries per year. In the 1920s, Woolf pares the *periodic diary* about as far as it can go and still convey a life. Twelve diary books unfold across Woolf's third diary stage. However, she now averages almost eighty-four entries per year—more than double the number of annual entries in the 1920s.

She also turns to more *morning* diary-writing than before. In 1919, diary-keeping fit nicely into Woolf's "casual half hours after tea" (*D* 1: 266). In the 1930s, the diary becomes increasingly a morning prop, as well. A battle plays out across Woolf's diaries: her fierce fight for freedom. As Woolf becomes caught in extended revision in the 1930s—of *The Waves* and, particularly, of

The Years and *Roger Fry: A Biography*—the diary becomes a welcome new and "free page." There, she can fly free. She uses her diary as a morning prop but also as a bridge from (and to register) her inner artistic fights.

Woolf turns more often to her diary in her final diary stage, and she also turns more to *other diaries* than she does in her first two stages. She seems to need diaries more in her final years. Woolf was better read in Western diaries than any well-known diarist before her—and likely even since.[4] She gravitated to diaries, I believe, to hear the natural human voice. This voice became more and more vital to her in the growing blare and welter of war. For Woolf, diaries represented not only *life* and its natural human voice but also life regularly renewed—in fact, life beyond death. The following pages will show how nineteen diaries, written by others, aided Woolf's battles without and within and also that certain diaries, most unluckily, undermined her in her final years.

I hope also to add to the growing trend that sees Woolf's whole body of work across the 1930s, to her death in 1941, as one interrelated, yet multiform, foray against tyranny and war.[5] Woolf herself gave first impetus to this view in her repeated insistence in her diary that her 1931 public lecture "Professions for Women," her novel *The Years* (1937), and her nonfiction antiwar volume *Three Guineas* (1938) were all part of the same work. The following pages will show that Woolf's *diary* also played a key role in her magnum fight against war.

I hope these pages will also contribute to the current reassessment not only of Woolf's own writing arc but also of the literary significance of the 1930s. For decades, as Valentine Cunningham notes, a "knee-jerk division" has been made between Modernism and the 1930s that "denies anything written in the 1930s 'the highest *literary* merit'" (Joannou 195). This tack, of course, ignores the fact that *The Waves* was published in 1931. One doesn't need to lower one's view of Woolf's 1920s modernist classics to recognize that she may have been on to something beyond in the 1930s, a larger project. "Oh yes, between 50 & 60 I think I shall write out some very singular books, if I live," Woolf tells her diary in 1931. "I mean I think I am about to embody, at last, the exact shapes my brain holds" (*D* 4: 53). As we begin to see Woolf's 1930s books—including her 1929–1941 diary books—as one huge, multiform, battle against the advancing war, we must re-figure our sense of her final years and may reach a new assessment of the 1930s' literary strength.[6]

In the following pages, I trace Woolf's movement as a diarist across her final stage—something never as yet attempted in depth. I offer close readings of each of Woolf's twelve final diary books, treating each (1) as a work of art itself; (2) as it relates to her other diaries; and (3) as it intersects with her public works (letters and published essays, reviews, fiction, and nonfiction). This method lays bare Woolf's final development as a *diarist* and—an extra dividend—as a public writer, as well. Close study of Woolf's diaries also allows me to offer a new reading of her suicide, a reading based on her diaries.

1

The War Within

The *outer* world touches profoundly Virginia Woolf's *inner* life in 1929: her war within. In 1929, Winston Churchill, Neville Chamberlain, and Rudyard Kipling all express admiration for Benito Mussolini, the Italian dictator (Pawlowski, *Virginia Woolf and Fascism* 5). The years 1929 to 1932 see fascism's "gathering stage in Britain" (Berman 106). The international financial crisis and its rising unemployment spur Oswald Mosley, the British Labour Party insider, to resign and found the New Party in 1930. In only a few years, it grows into the (renamed) British Union of Fascists. "But in 1930, when Woolf was writing *The Waves*," Jessica Berman stresses, "Mosley's politics were not yet openly fascist, and the claims of his followers were that they were continuing the work" the Labour Party had abandoned (108).

Meanwhile, in Germany, a policy of deflation from 1928—to ensure the German mark would retain a high value so that the country could more efficiently pay its World War I reparations and debts—causes massive unemployment and huge wage decline (Skidelsky 336). The percentage of votes cast for the Nazis grows from 2.6 percent in 1928 to 18.3 percent in 1930 (Skidelsky 336n4). A new invention, radio, has also entered the scene. As never before, the outer world begins to penetrate the inner, private home.

Virginia Woolf was neither deaf nor blind to these outer events. Biographer Hermione Lee notes that she was "an addicted reader of newspapers" (671). In 1929, Woolf begins to create a series of scrapbooks that collect materials on tyranny and war. As her husband, Leonard Woolf, explains in his autobiography, Virginia was "highly sensitive to the atmosphere which surrounded her.... She was therefore the last person who could ignore the political menaces under which we all lived" (*Downhill all the Way* 27).

As Woolf seeks out a bound diary book in June 1929 and embarks on her third and final diary stage, her mind also turns inward to the lonely artistic battle she foresees with *The Waves*. Both her diary and this novel reveal what she will argue in *Three Guineas*: that the private and the public are inseparably linked. In October 1929, Woolf publishes a tribute to "Dorothy Wordsworth's Journals," a vivid illustration of her ability to choose diaries and to find in them just what she needs to assist her public prose.

Virginia Woolf's June 1929 to September 1930 Diary

"& when I wake early I say to myself, Fight, fight."

(October 11, 1929; *D* 3: 260)

Across her 1929–1930 diary book, Virginia Woolf fights to free herself of outer distractions, so she can turn inward to "attack" *The Waves* (*D* 3: 219). Live-in servants disrupt her inward turn; so, too, the need to "see" others. On November 5, 1929, Woolf notes that improved appliances and a *non*-live-in servant, Annie, assist her: "what with oil stoves & Annie, [I am] battling my way to freedom" (*D* 3: 265). Thirteen days later, learning that Leonard will soon be freed from *his* work as literary editor of the *Nation & Athenaeum*, she writes: "And so, what with the oil stove, Annie, giving up the Nation ... the new year will be one of the most interesting—a great advance towards freedom which is the ideal state of the soul. Yet it must not be thought that I have suffered acutely from servitude. My one claim ... is that, directly I feel a chain, I throw it off" (*D* 3: 267).

Woolf wants to turn inward to write *The Waves*. She calls this novel "[u]nlike all my other books in every way" (*D* 3: 303). Should it surprise us, therefore, that it evokes a different diary? Woolf's first diary book of 1929 (covering January 4 through June 15) brings to a close her second, spare, modernist diary stage. On June 15, Woolf abandons the loose-leaf diary she has begun, after only ten entries. She replaces it with a large blank book with a sturdy burgundy spine, its front and back covers a burgundy-on-beige print of tiny diamonds, dots, and squares.[1]

She also *increases* her diary entries. Seventy-four entries preserve the 445 days from June 15, 1929, to September 2, 1930—an entry now about every six days, as opposed to every sixteen days, as in the first 1929 diary. Woolf now summons support to navigate *The Waves*. As she has done before, she paints *diary portraits*—often contrasting ones—to probe her struggles. In 1919, she projected "Old Virginia" at the start of her second diary stage: a new audience for her diary and a vision of vigorous, productive old age. In 1929 and 1930, seventy-one-year-old composer Ethel Smyth becomes a further model of valiant senior life. Smyth falls in love with *A Room of One's Own* in 1929, and then with its author. Hermione Lee writes that "[u]nlike Vita [Sackville-West], Ethel Smyth greeted *A Room of One's Own* as a heroic addition to the history of the liberation movement" (577).

I believe that Smyth's life as a *battler*—as well as her ardent admiration—enhanced Woolf's interest and regard. Smyth was the daughter of an army general, after all, and had to fight for her musical career. As Olivier Bell notes, she became "an inveterate campaigner"; indeed, she "was a militant (and imprisoned) suffragist" (*D* 3: 286n2). Writer Vera Brittain called Smyth's "March of Women" the "Battle Song of the Suffragettes," while Lee describes her cantata, *The Prison,* as the "story of the soul bursting its bonds" (580). How fortifying this would be to Woolf as she begins her own march.

Woolf also could link Smyth to her Fanny Burney–inspired image of a horse leaping its fences. "[Smyth] was . . . brave as befitted a General's daughter," Quentin Bell writes, "one who would ride . . . tumble, remount, ride on regardless of either pain or ridicule—a gallant figure whom it was impossible not to admire, perhaps to love" (2: 151). Lee believes that Woolf draws on Smyth for the "battle-scarred suffragette Rose Pargiter" in *The Years*—and also for the lesbian playwright and director Miss La Trobe in her final novel, *Between the Acts* (581). Both fictional characters, Lee notes, are "resilient figures who are also vulnerable, troubled—and ridiculed" (581).

In her February 1930 diary, Woolf contrasts Smyth with her sister Vanessa's artist friend Margery Snowden, whose "preserved look seems to indicate lack of experience; as if life had put her in a refrigerator. . . . [Snowden] seemed to be saying inwardly 'I have missed everything. . . . I am fifty & it has all slipped by'" (*D* 3: 289). "Lord," Woolf exclaims to her diary, for she herself now is forty-eight, "how I praise God that I had a bent strong enough to coerce every minute of my life since I was born!" Acknowledging, however, that Snowden lacks money, beauty, and artistic gifts, Woolf then asks: "How could one battle? How could one leap on the back of life & wring its scruff?" (*D* 3: 290).

She begins her next entry, February 21: "No two women could be more extravagantly contraposed than Marjorie [sic] Snowden & Ethel Smyth. I was lying here at four yesterday when I heard the bell ring . . . & then behold a bluff, military old woman . . . bounced into the room" (*D* 3: 290). Woolf captures Smyth's talk: "I am said to be an egoist. I am a fighter" (*D* 3: 291). She then links Smyth to freedom. In the next months, Woolf compares Smyth to her earlier elderly supporters, Margaret Llewelyn Davies and Lilian Harris, who are "somehow rejected by active life" (*D* 3: 297). "Must old age be so shapeless?" Woolf asks herself. "The only escape is to work the mind" (*D* 3: 297). Smyth, in contrast, "has ridden post haste through life.... She is a game old bird—an old age entirely superior in vitality to Margaret's" (*D* 3: 306).

The Waves is, perhaps, helped by these diary probes of vigor, battle, and freedom. The novel "forms very slowly," Woolf tells her diary on September 16, 1929 (*D* 3: 253). She decides to broach it by writing "a few phrases here at my window in the morning" (*D* 3: 253). She turns then to morning diary-writing to fill out the time. Her September 22 entry opens: "And it is ten minutes past ten in the morning, & I am not going to write a word. I have resolved to shut down my fiction for the present. My head aches too easily at the moment; I feel The Moths [*The Waves*] a prodigious weight which I can't lift yet. And yet, so odd a thing is the mind, I am never easy, at this early hour, merely reading or writing letters. Those occupations seem too light & diffused. Hence, though write letters I will & must... I will canter here a moment" (*D* 3: 256). Her diary will keep her in trim, and we see the sacred place diary-keeping still holds. Nineteen days later, she again "snatch[es] at the idea of writing here in order not to write Waves or Moths or whatever it is to be called" (*D* 3: 259).

The result is both *more* diary entries and more indulgent diary turns. On August 22, 1929, Woolf gives herself the pleasure of recording a specimen day. It offers a clear window on her country life:

> I get up at half past eight & walk across the garden.... I wash & go into breakfast which is laid on the check table cloth. With luck I may have an interesting letter; today there was none. And then bath & dress; & come out here [her writing lodge] & write or correct for three hours, broken at 11 by Leonard with Milk, & perhaps newspapers. At one luncheon—rissoles today & chocolate custard. A brief reading & smoking after lunch; & at about two I change into thick shoes, take Pinker's [their dog's] lead & go out—up to Asheham hill this afternoon, where I sat a minute or two, & then home again, along the river. Tea at four, about; & then I come out here & write several letters, interrupted by the Post, with another invitation to lecture; & then I read one book of [Wordsworth's] Prelude. And soon the bell will ring, & we shall dine & then we shall have some music, & I shall smoke a cigar; & then we shall read—La Fontaine I think tonight & the papers—& so to bed. (*D* 3: 247)

She nods to Pepys' diary with the last four words, one of her oldest diarist friends.[2]

From the start, Woolf uses war imagery in her diary for *The Waves*.[3] As early as March 28, 1929, as she finishes the first draft of *A Room of One's Own*, Woolf sees her next novel in terms of attack: "I am going to enter a nunnery these next months; & let myself down into my mind. . . . It is going to be a time of adventure & attack, rather lonely & painful I think. . . . I shall be external outwardly. I shall buy some good clothes & go out into new houses. All the time I shall attack this angular shape in my mind" (*D* 3: 219). This language persists in October 1929, when she actually starts *The Waves*. She speaks of "some inner loneliness" in her October 11, 1929, entry. She says to herself: "How I suffer, & no one knows how I suffer, walking up this street, engaged with my anguish, as I was after Thoby died—alone; fighting something alone. . . . Here is something to fight: & when I wake early I say to myself, Fight, fight.[4] If I could catch the feeling, I would: the feeling of the singing of the real world, as one is driven by loneliness & silence from the habitable world; the sense that comes to me of being bound on an adventure; of being strangely free now, with money & so on, to do anything" (*D* 3: 259–60).

At the end of the year, she tries fierce "shots" at the work. "I write variations of every sentence; compromises; bad shots; possibilities; till my writing book is like a lunatic's dream," she confesses on December 26. "I incline now to try violent shots—at London—at talk—shouldering my way ruthlessly—& then, if nothing comes of it—anyhow I have examined the possibilities" (*D* 3: 275).

Her violent shots break through, for seventeen days later she tells her January 12, 1930, entry: "Thanks to my pertinacity & industry, I can now hardly stop making up The Waves" (*D* 3: 282). She now feels greater control, for she declares on January 26: "I have at last, by violent measures—like breaking through gorse—set my hands on something central" (*D* 3: 285).

She reads poets as she writes the most poetic of her works: Dante, Shakespeare, Byron, and Wordsworth.[5] In February 1930, she copies into her diary lines from Byron's *Childe Harold* that reflect her own current inner war for artistic freedom and reach:

Hereditary Bondsmen! Know ye not
Who would be free *themselves* must strike the blow?
By their right arms the conquest must be wrought?
Will Gaul or Muscovite redress ye? No! . . .

She follows, however, these militant lines by copying other lines from the poem that "ring . . . to [her] truer" (*D* 3: 288). These lines reflect her lifelong sustenance from nature as woman:

> Dear Nature is the kindest mother still!
> Though always changing, in her aspect mild;
> From her bare bosom let me take my fill,
> Her never-weaned, though not her favoured child.[6]

Woolf thus summons poets as aid across these lonely, battling months, and she also calls on other diarists. She refers to eleven diarists, more than in any other of her thirty-eight diary books, and turns more than once to her diary parents, Sir Walter Scott and Fanny Burney. She evokes her other early diary favorites, Samuel Pepys and James Boswell, as well.[7] In her fourth entry, June 30, 1929, her joy when eighteen Boswell journals surface in Ireland reveals, again, that she sees diaries as breathing "lives." "I feel as if some dead person were said to be living after all," she tells her diary (*D* 3: 237–38). On August 22, she salutes Pepys as she pens her own specimen day, and earlier in the month she wonders why Pepys wrote *his* diary—if not to confide. During this month, Woolf also salutes (and channels) Dorothy Wordsworth's journals.

In February 1930, as *The Waves* comes more fully in hand, Woolf's desire to write on her diary father, Sir Walter Scott, gives birth to a vision of a new Hogarth Press publication—a simple broadsheet—for that purpose. Woolf longs to reinvigorate Scott in 1930, for his renewal reinforces hers. In late April, the moment she finishes her first draft of *The Waves*, she rushes once more to Scott. She cables her *Times* editor that she will review *The Private Letter-Books of Sir Walter Scott*, but when the book arrives she finds his letter-books won't do.

Intriguingly, in this May 1, 1930, entry, she replaces Scott's letters with Fanny Burney's diary. What shall her "critical brain" be set to, she asks her diary, with her first draft of *The Waves* complete? "Perhaps Miss Burney's half sister's story" (*D* 3: 303). And across the summer, as Woolf revises her own novel, she writes this long essay in which she enters imaginatively, even extends, Burney's diary world. Burney, "the mother of English fiction" (as Woolf twice calls her) and her diaries thus attend the birth of Woolf's most difficult book to date. Revealingly, on August 19, 1930, Woolf asks Ethel Smyth if she can "one day" read *her* diary (*L* #2222, 4: 203).

Woolf's 1929–1930 diary launches the final stage in her diary life, where she will turn to her diary—and to other diaries—more and more for support.[8] Save for occasional battles with her servant Nelly, with Vita Sackville-West, and with the noisy Imperial Hotel, all signs point to success. On October 2, 1929, Woolf can boast to her diary that "all the Americans write & cable for articles" and, in mid-December, that 5,500 copies of *A Room of One's Own* have sold and "our next years[9] income is made" (*D* 3: 259, 273). "[O]h & we are very successful—& there is—what I most love—change ahead," she exalts (*D* 3: 260). Free from the *Nation*, Leonard installs a new printing press in May 1930. He passes on the old one to Vita, whose "flamboyant [radio] broadcast" boosted *A Room of One's Own* in November 1929 and whose own novel, *The Edwardians*, becomes a surprise best seller for the Hogarth Press in May and June 1930.[10] So secure is Woolf that she closes her 1929–1930 diary on September 2 with a "map of [her] world.... [e]ase & shabbiness & content... all ensured" (*D* 3: 315, 316).

But *The Waves* would not exist without the intense inward war and without Woolf's diary and the community of diarists she evokes in support. "I make these notes waiting in vain for that very interesting remark to occur wh. was on the tip of my tongue; & will not now emerge, though I bait & wait," Woolf explains in an August 1930 entry. "If one writes little notes, suddenly one thinks of something profound."[11] Poets and diarists—and her own diary—aid her lonely inner fight. Wordsworth's lines from "The Prelude," which she copies into her diary, reveal what transpires:

> The matter that detains us now may seem,
> To many, neither dignified enough
> Nor arduous, yet will not be scorned by them,
> Who, looking inward, have observed the ties
> That bind the perishable hours of life
> Each to the other, & the curious props
> By which the world of memory & thought
> Exists & is sustained. (*D* 3: 247)

Dorothy Wordsworth's Journals

Dorothy Wordsworth, *diarist*, likely first caught Virginia Woolf's eye in the pages of John Lockhart's *Memoirs of the Life of Sir Walter Scott*, her father's birthday gift to her at age fifteen. To introduce Scott's happy 1803 meeting with the Wordsworth siblings, Lockhart explains that he draws the account "partly

[from] Mr Wordsworth's conversation—partly from that of his sister's charming 'Diary,' which he was so kind as to read over to me on the 16th May, 1836" (1: 405n). That diaries could be charming and of such value might have buoyed teenage Virginia, who had just begun her own diary.

Dorothy Wordsworth rose again for Woolf in 1918—in the pages of Henry Crabb Robinson's ebullient *Diary*. This literary lawyer, who circled round Goethe and the Wordsworths, diarized along with Dorothy during their well-documented 1820 continental tour.[12] Robinson urged Dorothy to publish her Continental diary, but (to our loss) she refused. In early 1921, Woolf took reading notes on Dorothy Wordsworth and thought to write on her. She copied into her reading notebook three passages from William Wordsworth's poetic tributes to his sister—"She gave me eyes, she gave me ears"; "She in the midst of all preserved me still / A poet . . ."; and "Thy wild eyes" (*RN* 195). Even more intriguing are the four pages of further notes Woolf made from *William Wordsworth: His Life, Works, and Influence*, beginning with the words, "My sister when she first heard the voice of the / sea" (*RN* 195). But Woolf failed to write on Wordsworth's sister in 1921. "I can't begin Dorothy Wordsworth, nor start Jacob's travels to the East," Woolf laments in her March 13, 1921, diary entry during this year when Russian lessons usurp her diary and other creative life (*D* 2: 100).

In the fall of 1926, Thomas Cobden-Sanderson's journals recalled Dorothy Wordsworth to Woolf, for this artist of *The Book Beautiful*, this seeker for mystic truth, records reading Dorothy's journals at Grasmere, with Dove Cottage in view.[13] Perhaps, however, it took Katherine Mansfield's *Journal* jeer at Dorothy and William to move Woolf to mount a defense. (Woolf reviewed Mansfield's *Journal* in 1927.) In her 1914 diary, Mansfield quoted these words from Dorothy's journal, "A calm, irresistible well-being—almost mystic in character, and yet doubtless connected with physical conditions." Mansfield followed Dorothy's words with this poem of her own, mocking the pair:

Writes Dorothy:
William (P[raise]. G[od].) is very well,

. . .

He rises and breakfasts sharp at seven,
Then pastes some fern-fronds in his book,
Until his milk comes at eleven
With two fresh scones baked by the cook.
And then he paces in the sun

Until we dine at half past one.
"God and the cook are very good,"
Laughs William, relishing his food.
(Sometimes the tears rush to my eyes:
How kind he is, and oh, how wise!)
After, he sits and reads to me
Until at four we take our tea.
My dear, you hardly would believe
That William could so sigh and grieve
Over a simple, childish tale
How "Mary trod upon the Snail,"
Or "Little Ernie lost his Pail."
And then perhaps a good half-mile
He walks to get an appetite
For supper, which we take at night
In the substantial country style.
By nine he's in bed and fast asleep,
Not *snoring*, dear, but very deep,
Oh, very deep asleep indeed. . . .

"And so on *ad lib*. What a Pa man!" Mansfield exclaims (3–4). This jibe may have stayed in Woolf's mind as she finished her own essay tribute to "Dorothy Wordsworth's Journals" in mid-August 1929, for her August 22 diary entry offers her own specimen country day: *her* milk at 11, *her* walk, *her* tea at four, her reading Wordsworth's "Prelude," "& so to bed."[14] By identifying herself with the Wordsworths, Woolf counters Mansfield's poem.

And no wonder Woolf links arms across a century. Many facets of Dorothy Wordsworth's life resembled her own—her own but *intensified*. Dorothy lost her adored mother at age six; Virginia at thirteen. Dorothy's less-loved father died when she was twelve, a loss Virginia did not face until age twenty-two. The mother's death, however, changed everything for little Dorothy. She lost her mother, home, and beloved brothers all at one stroke, for the grieving father sent Dorothy to relatives, her brothers away to school. Dorothy was the third child (like Virginia) and worshiped her older brother, William, who (like Thoby Stephen to Virginia) was fewer than two years older than she.

Dorothy's educational plight also mirrored Virginia's. While William went off to Cambridge (as did Thoby), Dorothy's learning was rarely supervised.[15]

A rapid reader like Virginia—"It is natural to me to do everything as quick as I can," she wrote a friend—teenage Dorothy upset her grandparents, who called her "wild and intractable."[16] Like Fanny Burney before her and (diarist) Beatrice Webb soon to come, Dorothy needed to hide her books from her guardians. "My Grandmr sits in the shop in the afternoons and by working particularly hard for one hour I think I may read the next, without being discovered," Dorothy confided to her friend Jane Pollard, "and I rise pretty early in a morning" (Gunn 24). In this way, she learned to read French, German, and Italian.

Like Woolf, Dorothy found herself in *movement*, in "saunters" and "rambles" and every sort of country walk. She cared nothing for looks or for clothes, but in her "woodland dress" (as her brother poetically called it) sauntered forth in all seasons and weathers. Rather like Woolf's 1905 and 1907 diary "Walks by Night" that signal Woolf's embrace of the unconscious, Dorothy relished evening moonlit walks as well as daytime strolls.

Dorothy also never forgot the sea, and she adored birds and the moors. "I can always walk over a moor with a light foot," she writes in her wonderful 1803 travel diary, her *Recollections of a Tour Made in Scotland* with her brother and Samuel Taylor Coleridge. "I seem to be drawn more closely to nature in such places than anywhere else; or rather I feel more strongly the power of nature over me, and am better satisfied with myself for being able to find enjoyment in what unfortunately to many persons is either dismal or insipid" (Knight 1: 184). The vacant moors drew Woolf as well, as her 1906 Giggleswick diary so clearly shows. Woolf writes of Dorothy in her 1929 tribute: "But it was out of doors, on the road or on the moor, not in the cottage parlour, that her imagination had freest play" (*CR* 2: 154).

Dorothy Wordsworth, in short, anticipated Woolf's love for untrammeled nature, a fact Woolf recognized. Dorothy savors in her diary "the Coniston Fells, in their own shape and colour—not man's hills, but all for themselves."[17] At age thirty-one, with her brother and Coleridge in Scotland, Dorothy writes of Dumbarton rock:

> Above our heads the rock was perpendicular for a considerable height, nay, as it seemed, to the very top, and on the brink of the precipice a few sheep, two of them rams with twisted horns, stood, as if on the look-out over the wide country. At the same time we saw a sentinel in his red coat, walking backwards and forwards between us and the sky, with his firelock over his shoulder. . . . As will be easily conceived, the fearlessness and

stillness of those quiet creatures, on the brow of the rock, pursuing their natural occupations, contrasted with the restless and apparently unmeaning motions of the dwarf soldier, added not a little to the general effect of this place, which is that of wild singularity. (Knight 1: 214)

Woolf summarizes this passage in her salute. And did she see the two quiet sheep standing at lookout on the brink of the precipice as the two Wordsworths, in their wild singularity, or, being "rams with twisted horns," as William and Coleridge, Dorothy grazing—and gazing—more anonymously by?

In her journals, Dorothy calls herself and William "willing gazers"—an apt and moving phrase (Knight 1: 248). Dorothy caught the changing light, which Woolf sought to do from age seventeen and her 1899 diary. On her Scottish tour in 1803, Dorothy writes of Rose Castle: "We . . . stood some minutes watching the swallows that flew about restlessly, and flung their shadows upon the sunbright walls of the old building; the shadows glanced and twinkled, interchanged and crossed each other, expanded and shrunk up, appeared and disappeared every instant . . . seeming more like living things than the birds themselves."[18]

In Woolf's tribute, Dorothy becomes an emblem of woman and Nature as one, Woolf's own goal in *The Waves*. "[N]ow they could address themselves undisturbed to the absorbing occupation of living in the heart of Nature and trying, day by day, to read her meaning," Woolf explains. "Thus giving to Nature, thus receiving from Nature, it seemed, as the arduous and ascetic days went by, that Nature and Dorothy had grown together in perfect sympathy" (*CR* 2: 150, 153).

But Dorothy's gaze rayed beyond the swallows and the traveling fields of light. "I was much amused by the various employments and dresses of the people who passed before us," she writes at age twenty-six on her German study tour with William and Coleridge in 1798 (Knight 1: 23). She exclaims in her Continental diary at age forty-eight: "But every object connected with animated nature (and human life especially) is interesting on such a road as this; we meet no one with a stranger's heart!" (Knight 2: 251).

De Quincey prized Dorothy's empathetic heart. He described her as "the quickest and readiest in her sympathy with either joy or sorrow, with laughter or with tears, with the realities of life or the larger realities of the poets."[19] Beyond the journals' precise views of the natural world, Woolf admired Dorothy's human portraits, which, like Woolf's, were often accented with talk. For all Dorothy's quiet life in nature, "taciturnity," Elizabeth Gunn notes, "was never her strong point, talk always a vital outlet" (28). Tracking William's poem on Alice Fell, the little girl whose cloak catches in a wheel, Pamela Woof reports that a Mr. Graham told the story to William, William to Dorothy, and Dorothy to her journal, and shortly afterward William retold the story in verse. "It is a reminder of how many of the stories in the Journal seem to have begun in conversations," Woof observes. "Among other things, the Journal is a collection, a deliberate collection, of oral stories" (124).

The famous preface to *Lyrical Ballads* (1802) stressed the advantages of writing of "low and rustic life" among the "beautiful and permanent forms of nature," the very traits Dorothy modeled in her journals. Woolf saw this in her 1929 essay. Dorothy "searched into the lives of the poor as if they held in them the same secret as the hills," Woolf explained, noting Dorothy's "indefatigable" curiosity.[20] "And then as they rambled on with their talks of seafaring and the pressgang and the Marquis of Granby, she never failed to capture the one phrase that sounds on in the mind after the story is forgotten" (CR 2: 154).

Dorothy's ear, in short, was as good as her eye, and her senses and sympathies led her to preserve in her journals moving portraits of women as well as of men.[21] She compares the lives of the young boy and girl she meets in Lanark, Scotland. "What a difference between the manner of living and education of boys and of girls among the lower classes of people in towns!" she exclaims in her precise way. "[S]he [the eight-year-old girl] had never seen the Falls of the Clyde, nor had ever been further than the porter's lodge; the [six-year-old] boy, I daresay, knew every hiding-place in every accessible rock, as well as the fine 'slae bushes' and the nut trees" (Knight 1: 192). Observing one Scottish woman after another forced to spend her day following a single cow, Dorothy reflects, "It is indeed a melancholy thing to see a full-grown woman thus waiting, as it were, body and soul devoted to the poor beast; yet even this is better than working in a manufactory the day through" (Knight 1: 188). A few pages later, an amused Dorothy records how a Scotswoman views *her*. Faced again with the question, "the old one over again, if I was married ... when I told her that I was not, she appeared surprised, and, as if recollecting herself, said to me, with a pious seriousness and perfect simplicity, 'To be sure, there is a great promise for virgins in Heaven'" (Knight 2: 121). Woolf quotes this in her salute.

Dorothy also preserved journal portraits of women more distressed. She appears to admire the female traveler who sells mustard, hardware, and thread: "She is very healthy; has traveled over the mountains these thirty years. She does not mind the storms, if she can keep her goods dry. Her husband will not travel with an ass, because it is the tramper's badge; she would have one to relieve her from the weary load" (Knight 1: 52). On the road two years later, Dorothy and William meet a woman with two small girls: "[O]ne in her arms, the other, about four years old, walking by her side, a pretty little thing, but half-starved.... Alas, too young for such cares and such travels. The mother, when we accosted her, told us how her husband had left her, and gone off with another woman, and how she *'pursued'* them. Then her fury kindled, and her eyes rolled about. She changed again to tears. She was a Cockermouth woman, thirty years of age—a child at Cockermouth when I was. I was moved, and gave her a shilling" (Knight 1: 117).

The same year Dorothy reports in her Grasmere journal that "[a] funeral came by of a poor woman who had drowned herself, some say because she was hardly treated by her husband; others that he was a very decent respectable man, and *she* but an indifferent wife" (Knight 1: 88). Then Dorothy adds her own view: "However this was, she had only been married to him last Whitsuntide and had had very indifferent health ever since. She had got up in the night, and drowned herself in the pond. She had requested to be buried beside her mother, and so she was brought in a hearse.... Molly says folks thinks o' their mothers. Poor body, *she* has been little thought of by any body else" (Knight 1: 88–89).

If Woolf saw a kindred soul in Dorothy Wordsworth, another "willing gazer," Dorothy's journals also brought back that earlier diary friend Henry Crabb Robinson, but now from Dorothy's point of view. (Woolf read the *Diary, Reminiscences, and Correspondence of Henry Crabb Robinson* in 1918.) Robinson's jovial presence in Dorothy's journals may have brought to Woolf's mind his *Diary*'s haunting views of Dorothy's later days. In 1829, nine years after their continental tour, Dorothy suffered an attack of gallstones at age fifty-seven. This led to hardening of the arteries, which, by 1835, made the avid walker unable to move her legs and eventually damaged her mind.

Woolf had already read, in Robinson's *Diary*, William Wordsworth's moving April 1829 letter following the first attack. "Were she to depart," William wrote to Robinson, "the phases of my moon would be robbed of light to a degree that I have not courage to think of" (2: 95). In his "Reminiscence" of his Christmas visit to the Wordsworths in 1835, Robinson writes: "[B]ut already her health had broken down. In her youth and middle age she stood in somewhat the same relation to her brother William as dear Mary Lamb to her brother Charles. In her long illness, she was fond of repeating the favorite small poems of her brother, as well as a few of her own. And this she did in so sweet a tone as to be quite pathetic. The temporary obscurations of a noble mind can never obliterate the recollections of its inherent and essential worth" (2: 217–18).

When Coleridge's son Hartley dies in 1849, Robinson tells his diary, "Poor Miss Wordsworth I thought sunk still further in insensibility. By the by, Mrs. Wordsworth says that almost the only enjoyment Wordsworth seems to feel is in his attendance on her, and that her death would be to him a sad calamity" (2: 385–86). However, it is William who will die the next year at age eighty. Dorothy languishes on for five more years, to die at eighty-three.

This specter of walks ended, mind blighted, and lingering ill health loomed before Woolf even as she read Dorothy's earliest journal. However, she ignores these losses in her 1929 essay, affirming instead Dorothy's bond with Nature and rare sister-brother tie. Surely this aids her as she begins herself to reach for the fin and the moth and for her own dead brother, Thoby, in *The Waves*. Dorothy's early loss of William for more than a decade, their joyous reunion, and then union in pursuit of art might have seemed to Woolf almost a magic tale, a Shakespearean resurrection to be found in literature, perhaps, but hardly in real life. The siblings' bond engaged Woolf long before her 1929 tribute to Dorothy's journals. In 1908, a year-and-a-half from Thoby's death, Virginia reviewed the *Letters of the Wordsworth Family* for the *Times Literary Supplement* and chose to quote a passage from twenty-one-year-old Dorothy's letter to a friend. William possessed, Dorothy confided, a "violence of affection . . . which demonstrates itself every moment of the day . . . in a sort of restless watchfulness which I know not how to describe, a tenderness that never sleeps" (*E* 1: 185). "[T]heir companionship, so equal, so simple, and so sincere," twenty-six-year-old Virginia declared in 1908, "continued throughout their lives . . . every letter hints at the exquisite relationship. They walk together, notice the same buds and clouds, read at the same table; and Dorothy, when she has given her criticisms, bids him, in fine words, trust the rest to posterity. 'His writing will live,' is her valiant assertion, 'when we and our little cares are all forgotten'" (*E* 1: 185). No wonder Woolf balked when Mansfield mocked Wordsworth's "exquisite sister" (as Coleridge called her) and the "exquisite relationship" of the pair.

Dorothy Wordsworth and her journals exemplified for Woolf communion with brother, nature, and art: her own goals in August 1929 as she starts on *The Waves*. Woolf's sense of a diary as shared art rose from her own first days as a fourteen-year-old diarist, when she, Thoby, her older sister Vanessa, and her younger brother Adrian all kept diaries or notebooks—along with her half-sister and her father. On her honeymoon in August 1912, Woolf sent a postcard to Lytton Strachey of Alfoxden House. There, Dorothy began to write a diary and to share it with *her* brother—and also with Coleridge, who lived close by. "Here we are in the middle of divine country, literary associations," Woolf writes to Strachey, hinting, perhaps, at the prospect of three *twentieth-century* writers (she, Leonard, and Lytton) in similar union and literary pursuit (*L* #641, 2: 2). Twelve years later, in her *Vogue* essay "Indiscretions," Woolf declares emphatically that William Wordsworth "should have had no wife" (*E* 3: 461).

Instead, sister and brother, diarist and poet, must unite in search of Nature for the offices of art. "William and Nature and Dorothy herself, were they not one being?" Woolf asks in her 1929 salute to Dorothy's journals. "Did they not compose a trinity, self-contained and self-sufficient and independent whether indoors or out?" (*CR* 2: 153). Dorothy's journals, Woolf saw, came to life to serve art—as did Woolf's diaries. No one questions today that William and Coleridge drew from Dorothy's diaries sights and sounds, figures and stories, for their poems.[22] Both men read her 1798 Alfoxden journal. Her celebrated 1800–1803 Grasmere journal rose only in William's absence and "because I shall give William pleasure by it when he comes home again" (Knight 1: 32). The word *pleasure*, Levin reminds us, held rich meaning for both Wordsworths, well beyond mere "enjoyment," for in the preface to *Lyrical Ballads*, the "grand elementary principle of pleasure" is the force by which one "knows, and feels, and lives, and moves"—bold aspiration for a journal (20).

Dorothy's 1803 *Recollections of a Tour Made in Scotland* with Coleridge and William was nothing if not a journey *with* poets in pursuit of poets (and poetry). On August 18, they stop in the Dumfries churchyard to pay homage to Robert Burns. "We looked at the grave with melancholy and painful reflections, repeating to each other his own verses," Dorothy records and then writes out the Burns poems. "We were glad to leave Dumfries," she continues, "which is no agreeable place to them who do not love the bustle of a town that seems to be rising up to wealth. We could think of little else but poor Burns, and his moving about on that unpoetic ground" (Knight 1: 167, 168).

At Brownhill, the empathetic Dorothy writes, "we talked of Burns, and of the prospect he must have had, perhaps from his own door, of Skiddaw and his companions [mountains], indulging ourselves in the fancy that we *might* have been personally known to each other, and he have looked upon those objects with more pleasure for our sakes" (Knight 1: 170). She then includes William's four-stanza "Address" to Burns' sons. They visit the Falls of Bruar, "for the sake of Burns," and, on September 7, see the gardens at Blair Athol. "We rested upon the heather seat which Burns was so loth to quit that moonlight evening when he first went to Blair Castle," Dorothy writes, "and had a pleasure in thinking that he had been under the same shelter, and viewed the little waterfall opposite with some of the happy and pure feelings of his better mind" (Knight 2: 87, 86).

And then they meet Walter Scott, Woolf's diary father, in the first years of his fame. On September 17, 1803, Dorothy and William arrive at Lasswade.[23] Coleridge has split from them by now, too ill to tolerate the siblings and their open Irish jaunting cart, but William and Dorothy breakfast with the Scotts and stay until two, when "Mr. Scott accompanied us back almost to Roslin, having given us directions respecting our future journey, and promised to meet us at Melrose two days after" (Knight 2: 126). Dorothy's praises surely pleased Woolf. "Mr. Scott is respected everywhere: I believe that by favour of his name one might be hospitably entertained throughout all the borders of Scotland," Dorothy marvels (Knight 2: 131).

Scott offers himself as tour guide to Melrose Abbey. "He pointed out many pieces of beautiful sculpture in obscure corners which would have escaped our notice," a grateful Dorothy reports, and at Jedburgh, the innkeeper's wife will not show Dorothy the bedrooms until Scott himself assures her he does not mind sharing a room with William (Knight 2: 134, 135). In this town, when free from his court duties as Selkirk sheriff, Scott recites to them from his *Lay of the Last Minstrel*. In fact, Scott seems loath to leave them—but then why wouldn't he be drawn to the pair? How often did he meet one who would exclaim in the Ferniehurst forest, as Dorothy did, "What a life there is in trees!" (Knight 2: 142)?

His court duties met, Scott abandons his own gig to his servant and travels to Hawick with the Wordsworths in their open cart. "Mr. Scott pointed out to us Ruberslaw, Minto Crags, and every other remarkable object in or near the vale of Teviot," Dorothy reports, "and we scarcely passed a house for which he had not some story" (Knight 2: 146). When they finally must part, they do it with "great regret," for "he would gladly have gone with us to Langholm, eighteen miles further" (Knight 2: 147).

If the 1803 tour of Scotland is travel for poetry, in 1810 William draws on Dorothy's 1805 "Journal of a Mountain Ramble" (with him) for his own published prose work *A Description of the Scenery of the Lakes in the North of England*. This is "another curious instance of their literary copartnery," Knight writes, coining a most congenial word (1: xii). And what was the 1820 continental tour but

Dorothy's and William's chance to relive his 1790 tour, but now together and with *her* eyes and ears?[24]

Woolf's tribute to "Dorothy Wordsworth's Journals" appears the same month as her own *A Room of One's Own* and should be read as an extension of it. With her linked 1929 essays on Mary Wollstonecraft and Dorothy Wordsworth, Woolf expands *A Room*'s history of literary foremothers to embrace nonfiction (essays and diaries) as well as fiction. In May 1929, as she read the fullest text then available of Dorothy's journals, Woolf took nine pages of reading notes and discovered two links between Wollstonecraft and Dorothy Wordsworth (*RN* 114). Both women saw the Elbe River at Altona in the 1790s and recorded it. And then came Dorothy's offhand 1798 Alfoxden journal words: "Mary Wollstonecraft's life, etc., came"—and not a syllable more (Knight 1: 16). Here was a vacancy Woolf could fill. What did Dorothy Wordsworth think of Mary Wollstonecraft, for Woolf notes in her reading notebook the profound difference between the two. Wollstonecraft "branches out to reform the world," Woolf observes. "D[orothy] W[ordswor]th here & now; the thing before one. Eno' to realise it" (*RN* 114). In May 1929, these two writers represent Woolf's own two books-in-progress: the soon-to-be-published *A Room of One's Own* (her *Vindication of the Rights of Women*) and the long-pending poetic *Moths/Waves*.

Woolf recognizes the instructive, even medicinal, role of Dorothy's journals as she moves from *A Room* to *The Waves*. "So you see I am recovered, and have, more or less, finished my articles," she writes to Vita Sackville-West on August 18, 1929: "The last was Dorothy Wordsworth, and if the written word could cure rheumatism, I think her's [*sic*] might—like a dock leaf laid to a sting; yet rather astringent too. Have you ever read her diaries, the early ones, with the nightingale singing at Alfoxden, and Coleridge coming in swollen eyed—to eat a mutton chop? Wordsworth made his head ache, thinking of an epithet for cuckoo. I like them very much" (*L* #2057, 4: 79–80).

Dorothy's journals offered an antidote to ego, a trap that worried Woolf as she turned to *The Waves*, just as she feared ego at the start of *Jacob's Room*, her earlier novel evoking Thoby.[25] In her tribute to Dorothy's journals, Woolf twice notes that Dorothy subordinates "I" to nature in order to see:

Dorothy never railed against "the cloven hoof of despotism." Dorothy never asked "men's questions." . . . Dorothy never confused her own soul with the sky. . . . For if she let "I" and its rights and its wrongs and its passions and its suffering get between her and the object . . . she would be soaring into reveries and rhapsodies and forgetting to find the exact phrase for the ripple of moonlight upon the lake. It was like "herrings in the water"—she could not have said that if she had been thinking about herself. (CR 2: 149)

Woolf is contrasting Dorothy with Mary Wollstonecraft here, but she could as easily be lecturing herself.

Woolf's 1929 "Journals of Dorothy Wordsworth" helped light the trail to today's increasing regard for Dorothy Wordsworth, not only as essential to the Romantic movement but also as an arresting diarist and prose poet herself. Woolf remarks how oddly vivid Dorothy's journals become: "[C]onsidering that the diary is made of brief notes such as any quiet woman might make of her garden's changes and her brother's moods and the progress of the seasons. . . . Even in such notes one feels the suggestive power which is the gift of the poet rather than of the naturalist, the power which, taking only the simplest facts, so orders them that the whole scene comes before us, heightened and composed, the lake in its quiet, the hills in their splendour" (CR 2: 150–51).

This heightened, composed quality causes us again and again to feel not just the sudden shock of beauty in certain lines but also that Dorothy's nature scenes become elemental, become emblematic of the *human* state—particularly her own interior state. We feel the two quiet sheep on the precipice as *more* than sheep, and the same of this 1802 scene of swallows whose nest, built in Dorothy's window, falls to the ground: "I watched them one morning, when William was at Eusemere, for more than an hour. Every now and then there was a motion in their wings, a sort of tremulousness, and they sang a low song to one another" (Knight 1: 134). A page is torn out here in Dorothy's Grasmere journal. Did she reveal more of her heart? How much, indeed, is compressed into these simple nature scenes? Shamefully, even in the twenty-first century, we lack a complete edition of Dorothy Wordsworth's journals.[26]

Woolf did not make Henry Crabb Robinson's mistake—and that of more recent critics—of faulting Dorothy for attending too much to nature and too little to her brother's and Coleridge's talk.[27] Woolf saw that Dorothy's journals, written on a hill or beside a stream, on a boat or while William napped, were not written for *us*, but for them—for herself, William, and Coleridge—and for art.[28] Dorothy had no need to reproduce their endless talk on poetry. They knew their views. The views they required were views of nature, and these she amply supplied.

The picture Woolf draws in her 1929 essay perfectly captures a diarist's and a poet's union in pursuit of art, but it also captures *Woolf's* own diary's role in *her* public art, *her* prose poetry: "It was a strange love, profound, almost dumb, as if brother and sister had grown together and shared not the speech but the mood, so that they hardly knew which felt, which spoke, which saw the daffodils or the sleeping city; only Dorothy stored the mood in prose, and later William came and bathed in it and made it into poetry. But one could not act without the other" (*CR* 2: 153). Likewise, Woolf's public prose poetry cannot emerge without her diary.

2

The March of Headlines

Virginia Woolf's "curious props"—including her diary and other diaries—ably support her across 1931. She shows, in fact, such sure life command that she mocks the outer political scene in September 1931. Nevertheless, she adds newspaper headlines to her 1930–1931 diary—and her inner wars persist.

In 1931, the painter and writer Wyndham Lewis publishes a book in praise of Hitler. "I do not think that if Hitler had his way he would bring the fire and the sword across otherwise peaceful frontiers," Lewis blindly tells his readers. "He would, I am positive, remain peacefully at home, fully occupied with the internal problems of the *Dritte Reich*. And as regards, again, the vexed question of the 'antisemitic' policy of his party, in that also I believe Hitler himself—once he had obtained power—would show increasing moderation and tolerance" (47–48).

In 1931, Oswald Mosley recruits Vita Sackville-West's husband, Harold Nicolson, to edit the New Party's journal. England needs action, Mosley writes in this journal titled, imperatively, *Action*. The Nicolsons and the Woolfs are close friends; Vita's and Virginia's love for each other remains strong. Vita and Christopher Isherwood contribute to *Action*, the first issue selling 160,000 copies (Berman 212n16). In October 1931, Harold Nicolson uses fascist code phrases in his call in *Action* for "[a] State in which energy and efficiency are always rewarded, and in which the bungler and the sluggard must go to the wall" (Berman 120). After all, the Labour Party has resigned on August 24, 1931, forcing its leader, Ramsay MacDonald, to form an all-party National Government. In September, Japan has invaded Manchuria, making the League of Nations seem ineffectual. The same month, England abandons the gold standard.

Closer to home, Leonard Woolf is "caught up, from now on, in what he called 'the intelligent man's way to prevent war,'" Hermione Lee explains (608). Virginia, in turn, battles war in her own intelligent way in her semiprivate diary and through her public works. Other diaries aid her. In December 1930, she makes double use of *The Journal of a Somerset Rector*, with its tale of a country suicide. She finds James Woodforde's *Diary of a Country Parson* further proof of life deathless in a diary. In May 1931, *The Private Diaries of Princess Daisy of Pless*—Vita Sackville-West's distant relative—offer rich matter for future works: for *Flush*, for *The Years*, and for *Three Guineas*.

Virginia Woolf's 1930–1931 Diary

> "I thought, to give this book continuity, I would copy every day the headlines in the paper."
>
> (November 11, 1930; D 3: 332)

Newspaper headlines begin to march across Virginia Woolf's diary on Armistice Day 1930. Another journal experiment, they serve in the hard-wrought (but successful) struggle that plays out across this 1930–1931 diary. One hundred and two entries chronicle the 481 days from September 8, 1930, through January 1, 1932—an entry now every four or five days, instead of six as in her previous diary, sign of the diary's increasing role as Woolf battles to finish *The Waves*. This diary's beautiful gray marble cover and solid gray spine mask the subtle war waged within on many fronts as Woolf fights to free herself to catch the hovering spirit of *The Waves*.[1]

Visions of bondage and freedom mix with tropes of war in this diary. Woolf wants her ship to sail and her horse to leap its fences, but both can be tied, and she must (forever) fight free. She embraces a paradox: that the literary *freedom* she seeks can be won only through *control*. Diaries again assist her: she divides her *own* diary's sixteen months into four "laps" for her "horse"—each lap resolutely planned and each bolstered with other diaries.

Her diary opens to "signalise" her resurrection from another country collapse. "After coming out here I had the usual—oh how usual—headache; & lay, like a fibre of tired muscle on my bed in the sitting room, till yesterday," she admits on Monday, September 8, 1930, and then exhorts herself, "Now up again & on again.... I shall attack The Waves on Thursday" (*D* 3: 317). Morning diary-writing again helps her, allows her, to reprise voices: practice for *The Waves*' soliloquies. Eleven of this first lap's eighteen diary portraits are composed primarily of talk.

Voices, in truth, intrude on her country solitude. "Mary & Barbara [Hutchinson]'s little medicine bottle heads appeared at the window. How I scowled!" Woolf exclaims in her second entry, September 24 (*D* 3: 318). Tellingly, she longs to escape to Roger Fry in France—Fry always an uplifting spirit in her diary—or to escape to Northumberland, home of the Wordsworths (*D* 3: 323, 320). "I need solitude. I need space. I need air. I need the empty fields round me; & my legs pounding along roads," she cries from London in her fifth entry, October 15, but even in the country these vital elements can be breached (*D* 3: 323).

Diary portraits again mark the poles of the tension. Woolf's third entry renders a rich likeness of Leonard's mother, eighty-year-old Marie Woolf, who insists on bringing Harold and Bella Woolf and Bella's husband to see Rodmell. "But there I am pinned down, as firmly as Prometheus on his rock, to have my day, Friday 26th of September 1930, picked to pieces, & made cheap & ugly & commonplace," Woolf cries to her diary; "for the sting of it is that there is no possible escape" (*D* 3: 321). She has seen herself as Prometheus before: in her 1921 diary, when her longer summer collapse, as she wrote *Jacob's Room*, left her housebound at Rodmell and denied her country walks (*D* 2: 132). Prometheus' plight, the fire-giver chained and perpetually tortured, dominates this 1930–1931 diary. "[N]o escape," she continues, "that wont make old Mrs Woolf begin to dab her eyes & feel that she is not being welcomed—she who is so 'painfully sensitive' . . . so entirely without any interest in my feelings or friends; so vampire like & vast in her demand for my entire attention & sympathy. . . . Lord Lord! how many daughters have been murdered by women like this! What a net of falsity they spread over life" (*D* 3: 321).

Against this vision of imprisoning and predatory old age, Woolf poses liberating and fiery Ethel Smyth. "Would you like me to write something about you?" Woolf asks Smyth in late October and then records this exchange: "Oh yes; what fun! But I should try some experiments. Oh what fun! How I should enjoy it! But I should get it all wrong. Yes, of course; or tear them up. Do just as you like" (*D* 3: 325). Could there be greater encouragement—or freedom? Woolf doubts whether Smyth's "fiery years of desire are over. . . . [I]t is a fine spectacle, & a curious one, this old woman summing up her experience" (*D* 3: 326). A model, in fact, of Old Virginia penning her memoirs.[2]

Woolf draws similar contrasting diary portraits of elderly *men*: the writers

Arnold Bennett and William Butler Yeats. Woolf's work can not only be *interrupted*, her soul imprisoned and preyed upon, but it also can be *chilled*. An encounter with Bennett in early December 1930 freezes her pen. "No I cannot write that very difficult passage in The Waves this morning (how their lives hang lit up against the Palace) all because of Arnold Bennett," Woolf opens her December 2 entry, turning to her diary in the morning to probe the stall (*D* 3: 334). She paints Bennett's portrait and repeats his conversation, including this story he tells of Irish writer George Moore: "He told me that a young girl had come to see him. And he asked her, as she sat on the sofa, to undress. And he said, she took of[f] all her clothes & let him look at her" (*D* 3: 335). The evening, Woolf writes, "left me in a state where I can hardly drive my pen across the page" (*D* 3: 335).

Fortunately, the month before, she meets a more invigorating spirit, a poet, not a novelist: Yeats in late life. Clearly moved, she opens her November 8 entry: "I pressed his hand when we said goodbye with some emotion: thinking This is to press a famous hand. . . . he is now a man of 65—& I am 48: & thus he has a right to be so much more vital, supple, high charged & altogether seasoned & generous. I was very much impressed by all this in action" (*D* 3: 329). She then describes his look and his inner and outer ease:

> Yeats was off, with vehemence even, kindling & stumbling a little, on dreams; . . . And so on to dreaming states, & soul states; as others talk of [Lord] Beaverbrook & free trade—as if matters of common knowledge. So familiar was he, that I perceived that he had worked out a complete psychology, which I could only catch on to momentarily in my alarming ignorance. . . . And so to modern poetry. . . . Yeats said that "we," de la M[are]. & himself, wrote "thumbnail" poems only because we are at the end of an era. Here was another system of thought, of which I could only snatch fragments. . . . He & de la M. can only write small fireside poems. Most of emotion is outside their scope. All left to the novelists I said—but how crude & jaunty my own theories were beside his: indeed I got a tremendous sense of the intricacy of the art; also of its meanings, it seriousness, its importance, which wholly engrosses this large active minded immensely vitalised man. Wherever one cut him, with a little question, he poured, spurted fountains of ideas. . . . He seemed to live in the centre of an immensely intricate briar bush; from wh. he could issue at any moment; & then withdraw again. (*D* 3: 329–30)

Here, as with Ethel Smyth, she finds the "immensely vitalised" spirit (and old age) she admires. Here burns a Promethean liberating spirit that kindles rather than chills.

In this November entry, Woolf contrasts Yeats with "Poor Tom" Eliot, who may be "as good a poet" but is "all suspicion, hesitation & reserve" (*D* 3: 331). However, Eliot, she admits, suffers his own Promethean agonies, and she ends her portrait of Yeats spurting his "fountains of ideas" with one of the most precise views we have of Vivien, Eliot's first wife, in late 1930:

> Was there ever such a torture since life began!—to bear her on ones shoulders, biting, wriggling, raving, scratching, unwholesome, powdered, insane, yet sane to the point of insanity, reading his letters, thrusting herself on us, coming in wavering trembling—Does your dog do that to frighten me? Have you visitors? Yes we have moved again. Tell me, Mrs Woolf, why do we move so often? Is it accident? Thats what I want to know (all this suspiciously, cryptically, taking hidden meanings).... And so on, until worn out with half an hour of it, we gladly see them go.... This bag of ferrets is what Tom wears round his neck. (*D* 3: 331)

Again a vision of predatory bondage: another writer consumed. This mindset links to Woolf's drive to free herself of live-in servants. Describing the cook she hired to replace the ailing Nelly, Woolf asks herself in her October 22, 1930, entry: "And how am I to detach her seaweed clinging from my kitchen?" (*D* 3: 324). Four days after she contrasts kindling Yeats with bitten and constrained Eliot, Woolf records her interview with Nelly Boxall. "To be free of this inspection this frying in greasy pans, at all costs," Woolf tells her November 12 entry. Soon after, Woolf adds a new paragraph to this entry: "And then I let her come back, for 3 months, from Jan. 1st. How am I ever to apologise to myself sufficiently?"— words that recognize that the fight for freedom lies within (*D* 3: 334).

"To be free"—of live-in servants, predatory visitors, leering male writers, even of the Hogarth Press—becomes Woolf's cry across this 1930–1931 diary.[3] Her fifth entry, October 15, opens with one of her useful denials: "I say to myself 'But I cannot write another word.' I say 'I will cut adrift—I will go to Roger in France . . . I will take my mind out of its iron cage and let it swim'" (*D* 3: 323). She wants to swim, to sail in *The Waves*.

That she does so amid these many trials testifies both to her courage and to her ability to marshal diaries, poets, and other uplifting figures to aid her as she soldiers on. Just as she copied lines from Wordsworth's *Prelude* into her last (1929–1930) diary, on the page opposite her December 22, 1930, entry she copies these lines from Dante's *Inferno*:

> ... nor pious reverence for my aged father,
> nor ev'n the bounden love which should have cheered
> Penelope, could overcome within me
> the eagerness I had to gain experience
> both of the world, and of the vice and worth
> of men; but forth I put upon the deep
> and open sea with but a single ship
> and with that little company,
> by whom I had not been deserted. (297)

She ends her January 10, 1931, entry, "I think a little Dante is indicated—Canto XXVI," where the above passage appears (*D* 4: 6). Dante thus fortifies her lonely sail. Opposite her March 16, 1931, entry, Woolf copies this line from John Keats to historical painter Benjamin Robert Haydon, whose diaries she reviewed in 1926: "I should say I value more the privilege of seeing great things in loneliness than the fame of a Prophet."[4]

Calculations opposite her second entry, September 24, 1930, reveal she has written 29,160 words on her second draft of *The Waves*—"a 3rd done," she estimates (*D* 3: 318n6). At the end of October she reports, "I'm now grinding out Waves again" (*D* 3: 326), and by Armistice Day, November 11, she seems sure enough of her novel to look beyond it. She thinks she will next write a book of criticism; however, she then turns to her *diary* and considers *its* possibilities, for she declares her plan to "copy every day the headlines in the paper" to provide "continuity" to the book (*D* 3: 332). Four headlines then appear.

Newspaper headlines add further texture to this already richly various diary. On the surface, they appear to signal an outward turn from the inward concentration on *The Waves*. However, Woolf does not fulfill her plan to copy headlines "every day"—just as she cannot write a daily diary. The headlines become *periodic*, even within her periodic diary entries, and they fade at the end of January 1931 as she nears completion of *The Waves*. Nevertheless, they disclose the news that strikes Woolf in late 1930 and early 1931. She notes war, and imperialism, and death (including suicide). The day that ended World War I seems to spur her headline notion. "Armistice day celebrations" is one of the four headlines in her first headline group. Three of the six later groups offer headlines on the coming Spanish Civil War, while another headline alludes to the Soviet prison camps.

Four of the seven headline groups track the Empire: "Prince of Wales's next Expedition"; "Lord Willingdon appointed Viceroy of India"; "Indian Conference"; "Gandi set free" (*D* 3: 332, 338, 339; *D* 4: 8). Interspersed among these headlines of imperialism and war are ones announcing suicide, death by drowning, or simply death itself. "Suicide of Peter Warlock," Woolf copies December 18, marking the death of the London composer (*D* 3: 337). "W.H.D. Douglas drowned" appears two days later, and her next entry, December 22, also starts with the headline "Horror death of Douglas" (*D* 3: 338, 339). This famous English cricketeer drowned when a steamer sank, his watery death joining that of the flying German princess Woolf imagines so vividly in her 1927 diary and, of course, the 1899 diary's imagined "TERRIBLE TRAGEDY IN A DUCK POND." Although she preserves "Gandhi set free" in her January 26, 1931, entry, the other headlines she preserves are "Pavlova to be buried at Golders Green," "Ripper murder on Blackheath," and "Death of Lady St Helier" (*D* 4: 8).

Headlines give a turn to this diary. Shorter entries emerge in this first diary "lap," as if in rhythm with the cryptic captions. Some entries seem penned just to add something to follow the headlines. On December 18, under the four headlines "Spain strikes," "Illness of M. Poincaré," "Suicide of Peter Warlock," and "Dyestuff Bill," Woolf captures her conversation with Lytton Strachey, Clive Bell, and Lord David Cecil in the staccato style she has used for her talks with Lytton in earlier diaries: "Talk about the riddle of the universe (Jeans' book) whether it will be known; not by us; found out suddenly: about rhythm in prose; Lytton is bringing out a new book of essays; what shall it be called; on living abroad; Clive says we (L. & I) are provincial.... Blenheim discussed; Lytton against it; Clive in favour; I say no sense of human personality" (*D* 3: 337). Here are *subject* reminders—much like news headlines.

The next entry juxtaposes Ethel Smyth's voice (and Woolf's disciplining one) against the December 19 headlines: "Spanish Rising," "Prince of Wales' Chill," "Carnera beats M.":

> "Violet so delighted me," said Ethel, "by saying precisely what I wished her to say...." Now I dont like this: I dont like that Ethel should know that I like compliments; I dont like liking them; I dont like Mrs Woodhouse fabricating them on the telephone. (*D* 3: 338)

The next entry offers a mere two sentences to follow the three headlines "W.H.D. Douglas drowned: six English lost," "New motor regulation," "Lord Willingdon appointed Viceroy of India" (*D* 3: 338). The first sentence reports Kingsley Martin's gossip of a possible merger of the *Nation* with the *New Statesman* (and job for Leonard); the second sentence—as with the previous entry—provides Woolf's negative retort.

The effect is one of multiple (and conflicting) voices. Public and private voices are juxtaposed, national and individual, a cacophony of fields. Woolf experiments here.[5] She enlarges her diary with headlines—news items that might assist Old Virginia when she comes to write her memoirs—yet the headlines also interact with her current project with *The Waves*. Against the four December 22 headlines, "Horror death of Douglas," "Indian Conference," "Fog. Intermittent," "Weather to be colder," Woolf poses art:

> It occurred to me last night while listening to a Beethoven quartet that I would merge all the interjected passages into Bernard's final speech, & end with the words O solitude: thus making him absorb all those scenes, & having no further break. This is also to show that the theme effort, effort, dominates: not the waves: & personality: & defiance: but I am not sure of the effect artistically; because the proportions may need the intervention of the waves finally so as to make a conclusion. (*D* 3: 339)

She likely also is unsure of the "effect artistically" of news headlines in her diary, or of the proportions; however, as in her novel, she tries to make her *diary* "merge all the interjected passages," "absorb all those scenes." She has endorsed "human personality" to Lytton, Clive, and Lord Cecil and demonstrated "defiance" (of Ethel Smyth and Kingsley Martin) in her two previous entries. In fact, she poses "personality" and ceaseless "effort, effort" against both Nature (the "fog" and "weather to be colder") and imperial man ("Indian Conference"). Headlines started November 11, she uses her December 12 diary entry to plan: "I think I have got my breath again & must be off for 3 or perhaps 4 weeks more," she declares. "Then, as I think, I shall make one consecutive writing of the waves &c—the interludes—so as to work it into one—" (*D* 3: 336).

To work it into one. This is her goal. But she is not quite there. "O solitude" will not be the last words of *The Waves*—although solitude appears to be her desire across the 1930–1931 diary. As the ominous headlines parade, Woolf poses her own words as her stanchion. At Christmas, influenza downs her in the country, steals the "precious fortnight of exaltation & concentration" she had counted on for *The Waves* (*D* 3: 340). The first "lap" of the 1930–1931 diary closes in full-circle fashion with Woolf seeking to rise from her bed. *Two* diaries now aid her: her own and another's. On December 27, she "moon[s] torpidly through book after book" as she waits to resurrect once more (*D* 3: 340). What strikes her, however, what "emerges like a bloody sun in a fog. a book worth perhaps looking at again in a clearer mood," is the diary of "The parson—Skinner—who shot himself" (*D* 3: 340).

In her next entry, she summarizes Skinner's *Journal of a Somerset Rector* in her *own* diary to test her power to write. In her long summary, we glimpse why the parson gripped her. "He much preferred solitude to the most brilliant society," she notes in this December 29 entry (*D* 3: 341). His only enjoyment was writing, even though his own son tells him he is "making himself ridiculous by his writings, & was insane" (*D* 3: 342). Once more Woolf personifies a diary and hints at its worth: "The blank pages of his diary alone neither sneered, nor hawked in his face, nor mocked him behind his back, nor plotted his downfall, nor called him mad" (*D* 3: 342). Suggestive, too, is her view of Skinner's end. The parson possessed a sympathetic brother who copied his diary for posterity as he penned it and made a fair copy for the British Museum of the endless diaries scrawled in the pastor's "crabbed & illegible hand" (*D* 3: 342). But, like Thoby, this brother dies and can collaborate no more. "Perhaps," Woolf posits, "the knowledge that even this confidant had failed him finally decided him," and she limns his suicide (*D* 3: 342–43).

That a diary, and a diary of a suicide, "emerges like a bloody sun in a fog" in late December 1930 must arrest us. And once more Woolf *uses* the diary, turns Skinner's loss of brother and suffering and madness into her own challenge. "Now this little narrative being run off . . . I daresay in 3 days I shall be beginning to play gently with the waves," she writes at the close of this entry. "This little Skinner sketch is in the wrong order; but I dont fumble for words. Could let my mind fly, am not as I prove now, used up by an hour's exercise" (*D* 3: 343).

Her mind now flies. She will close 1930 and the first "lap" of her diary full circle the next day. In fact, she begins the entry as if in mid-thought (or conversation). "What it wants is presumably unity; but it is I think rather good (I am talking to myself over the fire about The Waves). Suppose I could run all these scenes together more?—by rhythm, chiefly.... a saturated, unchopped, completeness; changes of scene, of mood, of person, done without spilling a drop" (*D* 3: 343). She has been trying this out in her headline diary.

Effort becomes her mantra. Her trusty "whipped horse" metaphor—with its roots in her diary mother, Fanny Burney—comes to her aid. "Now up again & on again" Woolf exhorts herself in her first entry on September 8 (*D* 3: 317). By mid-December she dismisses *social* fences. "I will never dine out again," she declares of the "[f]orced, dry, sterile, infantile conversation" of Arnold Bennett (among others). "So the [social] fence is not only leapt, but fallen. Why jump?" she asks herself (*D* 3: 337). Lords, ladies, and prodigious writers dismissed, she can end 1930 in literary harness. "[H]aving got astride my saddle the whole world falls into shape," this first lap ends; "it is this writing that gives me my proportions" (*D* 3: 343).

The diary's second lap begins with New Year's vows: "Here are my resolutions for the next 3 months; the next lap of the year," Woolf writes on January 2, 1931. "First, to have none. Not to be tied [*sic*] Second, to be free & kindly with myself, not goading it to parties: to sit rather privately reading in the studio. To make a good job of The Waves" (*D* 4: 3). The paradox once more looms: to be untied and *free* for her novel requires careful *command*—requires resolutions to have no resolutions. In her next entry, she pictures herself cutting loose when she masters *The Waves*: "But I shall fling off, like a cutter leaning on its side, on some swifter, slighter adventure—another Orlando perhaps" (*D* 4: 4–5). This adventure, of course, will be *Flush*.

On January 20 comes a, by now, familiar diary scene: the spontaneous eruption of future books. Suggestively, the moment comes in the bath as she anticipates collaborating the next day with another diarist, Ethel Smyth, in their public talk on "Professions for Women." "I have this moment, while having my bath, conceived an entire new book—a sequel to [A] Room of Ones Own—about the sexual life of women: to be called Professions for Women perhaps—Lord how exciting!" she opens her diary in the morning to exclaim (*D* 4: 6). This book appears to be her 1938 *Three Guineas*; however, Woolf's margin note dated May 1934 suggests this vision leads to her next novel, *The Years* (1937), as well (*D* 4: 6n8). That this new work represents a separate stream—and a new life—appears in her next entry, January 23, which continues the theme: "Too much excited, alas, to get on with The Waves.... And now Open Door [an early title] is sucking at my brain too. Such accidents cant be avoided" (*D* 4: 6, 7). She has "conceived," and the child is now sucking.

But she must fight this pull. Her next entry, January 26, written the day after her birthday, opens: "Heaven be praised, I can truthfully say on this first day of being 49 that I have shaken off the obsession of Opening the Door, & have returned to Waves: & have this instant seen the entire book whole, & how I can finish it—say in under 3 weeks" (*D* 4: 7). But it requires a fight.[6] On February 2, she imagines the novel's failure but dismisses the thought: "never mind: it is a brave attempt, I think, [& marks] something struggled for. Oh & then the delight of skirmishing free again" (*D* 4: 8). Two days later, her tardy doctor keeps her from dealing "a formidable blow at The Waves" (*D* 4: 9), but on February 7 she fights free. "I wrote the words O Death fifteen minutes ago," she tells her diary. "What interests me in the last stage was the freedom & boldness with which my imagination picked up used & tossed aside all the images & symbols which I had prepared" (*D* 4: 10).

Yet she knows that work on *The Waves* remains. She takes a break for journalism, but the struggle between bondage and freedom persists. When Arnold Bennett unexpectedly dies, she expresses sorrow and even affection for him in her March 28 entry; however, she also judges him "impeded": "much at the mercy of life for all his competence" (*D* 4: 16). She sees him as balked rather than in command of life's reins. Aldous Huxley, in contrast, "takes life in hand," she admires in her February 17 entry (*D* 4: 12). The Huxleys' travels make Woolf feel "unsuccessful": "Here, by some invisible rope, we are bound," she declares and once more longs to break free (*D* 4: 11–12).

They do so in mid-April, take a fortnight's motor tour of western France, but not before a weekend stay with diarist Beatrice Webb, which produces *two* diaries for Woolf to read: the diary excerpts Woolf admires in Webb's *Our Partnership* manuscript[7] and an unpublished "Russian diary"—probably H. D. Harben's—that Woolf also finds "very interesting" (*L* #2344, 4: 306 and 306n1). Inspired, perhaps, by these diaries, Woolf closes her diary's second lap by penning her own French travel diary "so as to make each day last longer" (*D* 4: 17). She pastes it into her 1930–1931 diary book. Like her summary of Parson Skinner's journal, it becomes a diary within a diary.

The return from France opens the third diary lap. "I have a 3 months lap ahead of me: the 3 summer months. What shall I do?" Woolf asks herself on May 3, and then sets forth a careful plan (*D* 4: 24). She wants "to finish off The Waves in a dashing masterly manner," but she knows this requires great control (*D* 4: 24–25). Just as she conceived her "quick-change" turn in her diary as she finished *Jacob's Room* to counter any chill of dispraise, she now devises "the Black Hole" to manage social distress. She likely discussed her plight with Leonard as they motored about France, for in answer to her May 3 diary query, "What shall I do?" she replies: "We are going to regulate 'seeing' people. There is to be a weekly black hole; a seething mass of people all eating tea together. We shall thus have more evenings free. In those evenings I intend to walk; to read, Elizabethans; to be mistress of my soul" (*D* 4: 24). Once more she will free herself through control.

She will partition off her Hogarth Press work, as well. Responding perhaps to this diary's tropes, Olivier Bell observes in her editor's preface to the 1931 to 1935 diaries that Woolf increasingly found her Hogarth Press work "a millstone round her and Leonard's necks" (*D* 4: ix). On May 3, 1931, Woolf declares that "[t]wo days are to be set aside for reading MSS: & they are not to leak into other compartments. These two decisions—the Black Hole, & Hogarth Press MSS, will I think make for an orderly & satisfactory summer" (*D* 4: 25).

Her diary once more floats her as she starts intense final work on *The Waves*. She opens her next entry, May 13, to declare that "[u]nless I write a few sentences here from time to time I shall, as they say, forget the use of my pen" (*D* 4: 25). Her June 2 entry opens with the same refrain: "Yes, it is very important to write a few sentences [in her diary], or I shall forget how." And on July 7, she exalts: "O to seek relief from this incessant correction (I am doing the interludes) & write a few words carelessly" (*D* 4: 29, 34). By August, advanced now to page proofs, she even begs her diary's pardon: "I should really apologise to this book for using it as I am doing to write off my aimlessness; that is I am doing my proofs—the last chapter this morning—& find that I must stop after half an hour, & let my mind spread, after these moments of concentration" (*D* 4: 40). Again one wonders if the other work could go on without the diary.

Her "Black Hole & Hogarth Press MSS" regimen appears to succeed, for Woolf speaks often of her sense of quiet during this summer lap; in fact, she equates rest with vital water. On August 10, she fights with Leonard "about seeing his family" but then uses her diary to slip her sour mood. "And now for Waves," she then writes. "Now my brood mounts: I think 'I am taking my fences. . . . I am forging through the sea. . . . ' I will now write a little at Flush" (*D* 4: 38). On September 3, she remarks, "Odd how I drink up rest—how I become dry & parched like a withered grass—how then I become green & succulent" (*D* 4: 42).

Yet, as hinted above regarding Leonard, even within this third lap of rest and quiet refreshment she still must fight. Her obliging August pledge to sit for Vanessa and sculptor Stephen Tomlin becomes, in her telling, a Promethean agony. "Oh dear," Woolf cries to her diary on August 7, the phrase always a signal of heartfelt woe: "what a terrific hemp strong heather root obstinate fountain of furious individuality shoots in me—they tampered with it, Nessa & Tommy—pinning me there, from 2 to 4 on 6 afternoons, to be looked at.... I foamed with rage" (*D* 4: 36–37). Here is Prometheus bound once more. Revealingly, she uses the language of her Yeats portrait ten months before. Now *her* "fountain of furious individuality" shoots forth; however, it is "tampered with," recalling Arnold Bennett's paralyzing December tale of a naked woman being "looked at" that freezes her pen. In August 1931, "to be looked at" fills Woolf with rage. In September, she considers "fir[ing] off" a rejoinder to Desmond MacCarthy's torpedo of *Mrs. Dalloway*, and she now battles with Ethel Smyth, as well, that still-fiery "vital spirit" of her first diary lap (*D* 4: 42).

As noted before, contrasting diary portraits often mark the poles of Woolf's thought. In lap two, Woolf admires Vita Sackville-West's lack of writerly ego. Vita "says she gets more pain than pleasure from praise of her books, which I believe to be true. Never was there a more modest writer," Woolf notes in her January 23 entry (*D* 4: 7). On August 15, she again lauds "Old Vita . . . , writing another novel; but as careless about it all as ever" (*D* 4: 39).

"Old Vita" contrasts with old Ethel Smyth, who becomes, in Woolf's March 1931 diary portraits, a self-torturing Prometheus caught in her own "net of falsity" (*D* 3: 321). Smyth's fall in Woolf's esteem turns on the sensitive fulcrum (for Woolf) of praise. When critics pan Smyth's new cantata in March, Woolf treats Smyth's howl as self-consuming—in fact, as imprisoning. That the piece is titled *The Prison* only adds irony. In her March 9 entry, Woolf describes her own "Sense of drum & blare: of Ethel's remorseless fangs" (*D* 4: 12). Ten days later, she finds Smyth impeded (like Arnold Bennett)—her artistic "outlet . . . stopped up. . . . a tortured & baffled spirit."[8] Woolf sees Smyth as "uneasy about her own greatness, requiring assurance, & snatching it rather hastily from such vague remarks as I could make. . . . Hence her terrific egotism: her insatiable desire for praise" (*D* 4: 14, 15). Woolf battles this flaw. In July, she (wittily) employs vampire and safari tropes to convey the fight's intensity. "I'm glad to drive my stake in firmly & so avoid complete overwhelming. I shout obloquies at her like gun shots," Woolf writes on July 7. "She takes them on her solid old body with a thud like that on an elephant's hide" (*D* 4: 34). That Woolf seeks to battle—and to discipline—Smyth's "insatiable desire for praise" across this diary underscores the composer's role as an elder alter ego.

Vita supplants Smyth in this diary's second and third laps. In May, Woolf reads the diary of Princess Daisy of Pless, Vita's relative, and describes to Vita four days spent "speculating upon [Daisy's] real character and life.... for I cant help liking her" (*L* #2376, 4: 337). At summer's end, she turns from the completed *Waves* to John Donne and to Vita's edition of Lady Anne Clifford's *Diary*, for *this* relative of Vita's was Donne's patron.[9]

In her essay "Donne after Three Centuries," Woolf pays tribute to diarist Lady Clifford. On September 21, Woolf once more poses a diarist and a poet against the politics of the day. "Here am I writing about Donne, & we have 'gone off the Gold Standard' this morning," she begins the entry as the third lap comes to a close. "Yes; & what could I do better, if we are ruined, & if everybody had spent their time writing about Donne we should not have gone off the Gold Standard—thats my version of the greatest crisis &c &c &c—gabble gabble go the geese, who cant lay golden eggs" (*D* 4: 45).

This diary's final lap begins nine days later. "I must make up my mind about the autumn lap, & my bearing. And do some quiet work," Woolf tells her diary on September 30, 1931 (*D* 4: 46). This last lap sees her "effort, effort" crowned with the triumph of *The Waves*. On July 19, 1931, Leonard had fortified her by calling *The Waves* "a masterpiece" and the best of her works (*D* 4: 36). However, in mid-September, Woolf projects "complete failure" for the novel when she learns of novelist Hugh Walpole's disappointment with the book. Her response, however, is to fight. "I mean I am acutely depressed & already feeling rising the hard & horny back of my old friend Fight fight," she tells her September 15 entry. "Never mind. Here I need not disguise my tumult of feelings" (*D* 4: 43).

That "Prometheus Bound" still shapes her thought appears in the next day's entry that takes from Shelley's poem of that name an image of free and happy nature. "Oh but this morning I'm like a bee in the ivy bloom—cant write for pleasure," she opens her diary, for the poet John Lehmann loves *The Waves*, and this causes her to be "flushed & flooded & ... at once inspired to write a Letter to a Young Poet" (*D* 4: 44). *The Waves* is published in early October and surprises Woolf with its success. "Really, this unintelligible book is being better 'received' than any of them," she opens her October 9 entry—amazed (*D* 4: 47). Five days later she can report that *The Waves* "has beaten all my books: sold close on 5,000; we are reprinting" (*D* 4: 47–48).

Now safe, "many works hover over me," she exalts in her October 17 entry (*D* 4: 49). A month later, one of these works seems to be her diary, for she confesses, "I scribble a page of what is called, I think, Diary or Calendar every morning . . . in which I catch such reflections—& shall one day publish them in a square grey-papered covered volume, very thin: a kind of copy book, with a calendar of the month stamped upon it" (*D* 4: 54). She has tried a calendar-fronted diary once before—in 1924 (*D* 2: 284). She now thinks to publish a diary of reflections.

For a full year—since November 11, 1930—Woolf has sought to give more "continuity" to her diary. When she abandons the news headlines on January 26, 1931, she turns to conjunctions to link her entries: "And," "But," "Yes," and "No" now open many entries. But she writes no diary entries for thirty-seven days, from November 18 to December 24, 1931. Headache on top of headache creates this long gap. Her distress mounts on December 15 at news of Lytton Strachey ill. As she does the year before, she uses a late December diary entry to test her brain. "If successful [in the diary today] I shall go out to the Lodge tomorrow, light my electric fire, & potter about," she tells her diary. "My brain will be filling. . . . All is again released" (*D* 4: 56).

Woolf's 1930–1931 diary reveals her extraordinary use of a diary both to practice the "merging" she seeks in her novel *The Waves* and to calibrate the paradox of freedom and control. In her next-to-last entry and last record of 1931, she first questions and then reaffirms her diary. "Shall I ever 'write' again? And what is writing?" she asks. And answers: "The perpetual converse I keep up. I've stopped it these 5 or 6 weeks" (*D* 4: 57). "I will finish this [diary] book, & begin another for 1932," she affirms and begins to float free. "Books come gently surging round me, like icebergs," she writes (somewhat alarmingly) (*D* 4: 57). That her diary is her flagship appears in her closing entry. "Anyhow, I must sail over the 7 days left here as smoothly, vacantly, serenely as may be," she vows January 1, 1932. "And use this page to sail on" (*D* 4: 61).

John Skinner's *Journal of a Somerset Rector*

Of the many diaries Virginia Woolf reads, John Skinner's *Journal of a Somerset Rector* holds a special place. Not only does this diary of a country suicide emerge "like a bloody sun in a fog" during Woolf's late December 1930 illness, but it also becomes another instance—as with her ghostly 1905 Cornwall diary—where she turns a semiprivate diary entry into public prose (D 3: 340, PA 297–98).

Parson Skinner's *Journal* sounded at least two notes that absorbed Woolf at the close of 1930. She is consciously turning inward, toward lonely solitude, as she fights to finish *The Waves*. Skinner lived from 1772 to 1839, and *he* "much preferred solitude to the most brilliant society," Woolf notes in her lengthy December 29, 1930, diary entry that summarizes his diary (D 3: 341). At age fifty-six, the parson writes in his 1828 *Journal*: "I hope I shall soon settle again to business, as my Christmas holidays have been too extended. I am never so well as when in peace and quietness, with plain fare and regular hours" (128). Like Woolf, Skinner is "perfectly indifferent" to "wherewithal I am clothed," he writes in 1829. "The great secret of life, if we look for comfort (happiness I will put out of the question), is to be constantly occupied, indefessus agendo [unwearied by doing]" (217).

The 1930 edition of the *Journal of a Somerset Rector* offers Skinner's diary only from ages fifty to sixty (from 1822 to 1832). It closes with the agonizing loss of a well-loved brother, another topic rife in Woolf's mind as she strives to rock Thoby to rest in *The Waves*. Russell Skinner became a crucial collaborator in his brother's *Journal*. Howard Coombs and the Reverend Arthur N. Bax, the editors of the 1930 *Journal of a Somerset Rector*, reveal that the parson wrote his journals in an "almost illegible" hand, but Russell made a fair copy of the volumes as he wrote them, often transcribing twenty-five pages a day (vii). The parson meant these fair copies for posterity; he willed them to the British Museum "for my countrymen's benefit" (viii). Woolf read this 1830 entry that reveals Russell's vital role: "four volumes of my Journals . . . have just been bound, making ninety-seven, and one which my brother has in blank paper to insert my letters on antiquities will be numbered ninety-eight, so that the hundred will soon be completed" (234).

The text Woolf read ends with Russell's death, in late December 1832. The parson's grief verges on violence. He draws seven blank lines in his journal and then pens a poem that starts, "These lines are now a blank forever / . . . Here is indeed a blank: who will fill it up?"[10] Woolf views the brother's death as the cause of Skinner's suicide. "Perhaps the knowledge that even this confidant had failed him finally decided him," she speculates in *her* diary (D 3: 342–43). The "failed confidant" could also be the journal.

Beyond its loss of a brother and wish for solitude, the *Journal of a Somerset Rector* shows Skinner to be an advanced thinker on women, which also may have touched Woolf. She writes in her diary that Skinner's "conscience refused to let him shut his eyes upon the sufferings of the halfwitted Mrs Goold," and she expands this tragic story in her 1932 *Second Common Reader* essay "The Rev. John Skinner"—where she misremembers the name as Mrs. Gooch (*D* 3: 341; *CR* 2: 91). In March and again in April 1822, the parson intervenes to aid the abused wife of Joseph Goold. When these efforts fail, he seeks out the woman's father and begs him to protect his daughter. In early August, her clothes catch fire, but as her husband has locked her alone in the cottage, she can neither escape nor summon help. Consumed in flames, she dies. The letter Skinner writes to her father the next day (which he copies into his *Journal*) reveals both his passion and his vigorous prose. "When it was in your power to assist your daughter, whose sufferings I have so long witnessed, and whose calamity called upon even *strangers* to take an interest in her welfare," Skinner exhorts:

> when, at the expense of a few pounds, you might have placed her in fit hands, and seen her properly taken care of, *You! her Father, refused to stretch out even a finger to lift your miserable daughter from the dust*; you turned a deaf ear to all the applications I made to you in her behalf.... [S]he was dutiful and affectionate to yourself, and kind and attentive to her children. If her husband had offended, if he was not to be trusted with the charge of his wife, the more it behoved you *to take her from his hands*, and put her under proper people.... but these applications were all disregarded, and through absolute neglect your daughter has perished miserably. (31)

Skinner cares about his own daughter, Anna, as well as for Mrs. Goold's plight. He sees to Anna's learning as well as to his sons'. An 1823 entry lists his expenses for their education: Owen sixty-two pounds; Anna fifty-four pounds; Joseph forty-two pounds.[11]

And if he seeks fair treatment for women, he also favors art over war. The parson makes sketches that he then tints to illustrate his journals. When his sons disappoint him, fail to follow the path he has "chalked out" for them—despite his sending them to Warminster School, and Owen to Oxford and Joseph to Sandhurst—he must turn to military appointments (200). However, he sees little merit there. He laments in his 1830 journal that "Joseph has good natural talents for drawing, which he might cultivate with success if he chose; I would readily pay for his learning to paint in oils . . . but this profession of an artist is infra dig., and our gaily dressed ensigns and lieutenants look down on all as beneath their notice who have not the permission to be shot through the head as they have, which permission is to be purchased at an extravagant rate by their unfortunate fathers and relatives" (254).

The parson loves history—another value he shares with Woolf. An antiquarian and etymologist (as well as artist, poet, and diarist), he is not as successful as she in publishing his works. At age fifty-five, Skinner reports to his *Journal* a sad letter from Hammond, "who says the booksellers in Town whom I commissioned him to speak to respecting the Etymologies will not do anything respecting the printing unless I indemnify them, in other words, pay the whole expense, as I did for the Wellow Pavement, and then give them twenty-five per cent. for the sale. I must therefore relinquish the idea of becoming a publisher of my works" (115).

His journals now must be his answer, will be his vindication. He writes them whenever he can seize the time. He embellishes them with sketches, has them copied, bound, and placed in three iron chests to protect them from fire. Like Woolf, he rereads his diaries and, even more than she, shares them with others, including his brother Russell, his sister-in-law, and his daughter and son during the long last illnesses that claim their lives.

Like Woolf, Jonathan Swift, André Gide, and many other of the most compelling diarists, Skinner writes his journals because they serve him in many ways. He repeatedly describes them as "records of humanity" and as a "record of the times" (224, 111). "I record these things not out of enmity to Mr. Bampfylde," he insists in 1827, "but as a record of the times, and records that may be depended on; for I never would defile my pages with these observations unless I could substantiate the truth of them" (111). We see here the historian's bent. The next year, during the Irish crisis, he writes: "Should my papers survive, it will be manifest what was the state of society in the time I wrote" (181). Again, two years later: "These memoranda will shew what was the situation of a Clergyman in the midst of his parishioners in the year 1830" (249).

Like most diarists, Skinner writes so that "all traces will not perish with me."[12] But this hardly is all. The parson wields a private ax. He *does* feel enmity for Mr. Bampfylde. He needs, therefore, not only to *record* the times but also to *defend* his opposition to them. "Whatever the world may say to my disadvantage, these at least will remain to shew I have not misspent my time during my pilgrimage through life," he tells his journal in 1828 (188). On the eve of a local coal strike, he explains to his 1830 diary: "I was occupied in my study the whole evening in writing some lines on the state of the times. Should they be read fifty years hence, they will shew at least that I was fully aware of the storm which was coming."[13]

Like Woolf—but for vastly different reasons—Skinner needs his diary to "hold converse with [his] own heart" and "to disburthen ... [his] mind," for he feels sorely used (257, 311). Woolf's *diary* turn on the *Journal of a Somerset Rector* engages, for in these semiprivate pages she is more willing to analyze and judge the parson than in her public *Second Common Reader* essay. He was "bred to the Bar, but became, unfortunately, a clergyman," she tells her diary, "without any aptitude whatsoever for the souls of the living" (*D* 3: 341). When the rector sees misconduct great or small, he feels it his "duty" to rebuke it. In Camerton parish, seven miles from Wells Cathedral, he finds himself surrounded by Methodists and dissenters—not to mention the Roman Catholics. He seeks out his parishioners to ask if they "had forgotten the way to Camerton Church" and receives insults for his pains (205).

Even those who come to church annoy him by falling asleep or failing to stand during the Magnificat or, worse yet, laughing during weddings or "hawking" during the service "in the manner the audience at a theatre expresses disapproval of an actor on the stage" (Skinner 1971, 56, 42). He tries to stare down these offenders and even asks them to stop, but often to no avail. Away from the church service he finds himself cheated out of tithes by the "brutified vulgar" who try to drown his favorite Newfoundland dog, Mungo, or tie a tin pot to the dog's tail, and even go so far as to throw stones at him, their parson, when he goes out for a walk (171, 131, 248; Skinner 1971, 30–31). Even the peacocks at the Squiress' manor irritate him with their screeching, and when the rats behind the wainscoting keep him awake, his tells his journal: "I was obliged to let them have their own way; as I am obliged to let the two-legged vermin have their way in my Parish" (152–53; Skinner 1971, 489, 490).

Skinner's *Journal* resembles Barbellion's *Journal of a Disappointed Man* (which Woolf read in 1920),[14] for it becomes both a desperate bid for posthumous regard and revenge against the world that fails him. Skinner conveys his hostility in this exclamation in his 1824 journal: "[T]o use a vulgar simile, they had kept me confined like a cat in a sack, and every coward had kicked and pinched me without the least possibility of my making any defence; or indeed, properly seeing who were my adversaries: but when the mouth of the sack was opened, some of the personages had better look to themselves!" (Skinner 1971, 261–62). The open "mouth of the sack," of course, is his diary.

Beyond the need for a multiuse diary, Woolf shared one more biographical tie to the embattled Skinner. Like her, he suffers a cascade of family deaths, a fate that robs him of persons who might have helped ease his social friction. Long before the 1930 edition of the *Journal* opens, Skinner loses, not yet Russell, but his *older* brother, Fitz Owen, who dies in his arms in 1810 when the parson is only thirty-eight. His two sisters die the same year. In 1811, consumption kills Skinner's three-month-old daughter, Tertia; and the next year—worst of all—Anna, his "dear" wife of seven years, also succumbs (Skinner 1971, 71).

Editor Peter Coombs writes of Skinner's 1805 marriage: "For five years John Skinner found happiness, and then the shadows began to close in and never passed again" (3). As Anna slowly drowns in consumption like all the others, Skinner tells his 1812 journal: "[S]he declares that the only wish she has to live longer is that she may continue to console me, and when she thinks how desolate I shall be, if left alone amidst the ill-disposed people of Camerton, without any friends to whom I may confide my cares, or who may soothe my mind when too much irritated by their misconduct, she feels indeed most wretched, and hopes and begs she may be spared" (Skinner 1971, 72). But she is not spared, and in 1813 he tells his journal: "The mortality in my family has been great indeed, as I have lost my wife and child, two sisters and a brother, two great-uncles and my father-in-law" (Skinner 1971, 3–4).

For a time, he finds escape in his antiquarian research that leads to notable excavations of Roman ruins,[15] but in 1820, when his diary-keeping daughter, Laura, dies at age thirteen, rectory solace seems lost for good. "I know not how I shall support this last blow," he tells his journal. "I have borne up against the malice and injustice of mankind with fortitude, but on this point I am most vulnerable and weak. . . . I had looked forward to the comfort and consolation of her estimable society to smooth the remainder of my days" (Skinner 1971, 134). In 1826, when his remaining three children displease and defy him, he becomes a tortured Lear, fleeing his home and parsing his estate. He copies into his 1828 journal the letter he writes to his mother: "I am ready to make any arrangement I am empowered to do for the purchase of a commission for Joseph by the sale of part of my marriage settlement; I am ready to allow Owen the interest of the third part. . . . My own mind tells me I have done everything I ought to do for my *ungrateful children*" (182).

That he sees himself in literary terms only magnifies his anguish. He exclaims: "I lay awake thinking upon the situation in which I have been placed by the malice of my fellow creatures, and the base ingratitude of my children. . . . Lighten this darkness, O Lord!" (197–98). By 1829, he is so "unhinged" he cannot perform a funeral service: "The weather still continues stormy and uncongenial for the time of year; but what are external tempests to disquietude of mind? 'Blow, blow, thou winter wind. Thou are not so unkind as man's ingratitude'" (148, 220). When Owen calls him mad in 1831 and says a commission on lunacy should probe his conduct, Lear becomes Jesus. "Father, forgive them [his children], for they know not what they do," he tells his October journal (278).

He is on the path to suicide. The 1930 text Woolf read preserves the parson's unraveling. In 1828, he feels "an unusual depression of spirits" and thoughts of his death start (162). In August, when the "wind blew and the storm raged," he longs for the Bishop of Wells' serenity: "Oh! that I could attain to this composure; but I fear I never shall, and I much doubt will ever be calmed excepting *in the grave*" (192). On his fifty-eighth birthday, May 11, 1830, he writes, "I feel certain indications which warn me not to expect a long life, and I am sure I do not desire it," and two months later he envisions being "taken off by some act of violence!" (246, 249).

Ominously, we see Woolf's own (occasional) "hate my kind" sentiments in Skinner's December 4, 1832, entry twenty-six days before Russell's death: "I have learned to value all around me at a very small price—let them go, the moth hath eaten them and the soil hath corrupted them—let them pass away and let me pass away too. I have no pleasure in the things which others covet. . . . I begin to dislike the countenance of my fellows. I like not my own when I see it in the glass!" (Skinner 1971, 471). Two days later, he continues: "[T]he fogs of the atmosphere penetrate even my mind, rendering it heavy, and all natural objects seem dull and insipid—will it ever recover its energies? I seem to apprehend it will not, yet I have some hope: the fatigues of my body had so entirely weakened my mind on my return from France four years ago I almost despaired of recovery but I did rally again and may do so hereafter; but I have so thorough a distaste for all things I am become as it were a mere caput mortuum" (Skinner 1971, 471–72). Four days later, Skinner writes: "I feel little interest in anything now . . . this year I have already numbered 60 winters and that is perhaps space enough to complete my trials" (Skinner 1971, 473).

Skinner may have suffered from bipolar disorder. The 1984 edition of *The Journal of a Somerset Rector* offers as appendix 3, the "Paper given to the Bath

Field Club in 1872 by H. J. Hunter Esq. M.D." who knew Skinner and describes his mercurial temperament: "[B]ut there was from time to time frequent change in him as seen from any fixed point. The barometer of his spirits showed a wide range of exultant rise and moping fall, and to know him well required that he should be approached from different sides and also at different times" (503).

The *Journal of a Somerset Rector* may have stood out "like a bloody sun in a fog" for Woolf in late December 1930—not just for the issues she shared with the parson but also due to Skinner's clear, vigorous prose. Skinner brings himself and his neighbors to life through strong memory and precise scenes. Woolf likely knew she was in the presence of rich material, for Skinner enters many of the 150-plus houses in his Camerton parish and brushes up against coal miners and farmers as well as Lord Hoare and the kindly Bishop of Wells. Skinner himself recognizes in 1830 that "someone who peruses my Journals will read this as they would a novel" (258). Intriguingly, Woolf used a similar figure—"as bright as fire in the mist"—in her important January 26, 1920, diary entry that announces her discovery of "a new form for a new novel," her first modernist novel *Jacob's Room* (D 2: 13–14).

Woolf recognizes immediately in her 1930 diary that the *Journal of a Somerset Rector* offers her "a clear hard picture of one type of human life—the exasperated, unhappy, struggling, intolerably afflicted" (D 3: 340). As noted before, in her semiprivate diary pages Woolf allows herself to analyze Skinner more than she will do when she transforms the entry for her *Second Common Reader* essay "The Rev. John Skinner," which she joins to an essay on James Woodforde's *Diary of a Country Parson* under the umbrella title "Two Parsons." Skinner should have been a lawyer, not a parson, she tells her *diary*: he was "without any aptitude whatsoever for the souls of the living" (D 3: 341). In her diary, she doubts his endless slights. "That they [his parishioners] were always bad, seems strange," she jibes, but then acknowledges, "but was to him true" (D 3: 341).

In her *Common Reader* essay, she hints that religion itself is to blame, noting that Skinner's "sermons and denunciations" made difficult Camerton times "perhaps even worse" (CR 2: 92). Parson Skinner resembles the Reverend Herbert Oakes Fearnley-Whittingstall, whom Woolf took time to observe in 1909 and describe in her diary's essay-entry "Jews and Divorce Courts." Of this earlier reverend, who resists his wife's bid for divorce, she wrote: "He had taken care never to sin: at the same time, he had not any pliancy.... [H]is character as a clergyman of the Church of England was more to him; who had clearly suffered, and done right, so far as he could see it. One believed him; but he explained the other side as he spoke. He was a man without pity or imagination;

a formalist and, perhaps, a selfish man. Moreover, his religion absorbed him. Religion had had much to do with it, I thought" (*CH* 16, 17).

Woolf clearly rereads the *Journal of a Somerset Rector* and makes the parson's portrait more detailed when she transforms it from her diary entry to the essay for *Common Reader* eyes. She also steps back and views Skinner's *Journal* through a historical lens. By contrasting "Two Parsons" and two diaries—Skinner's *Journal of a Somerset Rector* and James Woodforde's even longer *Diary of a Country Parson*—she brings out the differences in the men and in their times (as she routinely likes to do).

Unlike irritable John Skinner, James Woodforde "was of an equable temper," she explains (*CR* 2: 84). "James Woodforde was nothing in particular. . . . He had no special gift; he had no oddity or infirmity. . . . [T]here was no fanaticism, no enthusiasm, no lyric impulse about James Woodforde. . . . For once man is content with his lot; harmony is achieved; his house fits him; a tree is a tree; a chair is a chair; each knows its office and fulfils it" (*CR* 2: 85, 87). But Parson Woodforde lives from 1740 to 1803—not, like Parson Skinner, from 1772 to 1839. Woolf treats the two as representative figures of their times—in fact, as emblems of the difference between the eighteenth and nineteenth centuries. In the *Common Reader* essay, Skinner "seems to embody, even before the age itself had come into existence, all the strife and unrest of our distracted times. . . . Tormented and querulous, at the same time conscientious and able, he stands at the parting of the ways, unwilling to yield an inch, unable to concede a point, harsh, peremptory, apprehensive, and without hope" (*CR* 2: 90). Parson Woodforde's eighteenth-century *Diary*, in contrast, is "stuffed with food" (*CR* 2: 86).

In this light, Skinner is lifted from his personal plight to serve as harbinger of nineteenth-century and modern despair. And Woolf refuses answers to this despair in her *Common Reader* essay, choosing to close instead with a series of questions:

> Yet what had [Parson Skinner] done to make everyone hate him? Why did the farmers call him mad? Why did Joseph say that no one would read what he wrote? Why did the villagers tie tin cans to the tail of his dog? Why did the peacocks shriek and the bells ring? Why was there no mercy shown to him and no respect and no love? With agonizing repetition the diary asks these questions; but there was no answer. At last, one morning in December 1839, the Rector took his gun, walked into the beech wood near his home, and shot himself dead. (*CR* 2: 96)

Woolf distances and elevates John Skinner in her *Common Reader* essay. However, both her diary and essay treatments of his *Journal* reveal her awareness of his quite personal family drama with its parallels to her own. Her sympathies here embrace the children as well as the gifted but gloomy father. In the very first paragraph of her diary summary of the parson's *Journal*, Woolf writes: "Unfortunately too his wife died, of consumption, leaving him with 3 children. Of these the only satisfactory one was Laura, who inherited her father's love of collecting & tabulating, but also her mother's consumption, so that before she had collected, in a very orderly way, many cabinets of shells, she died; & the other children were unsatisfactory" (*D* 3: 341).

Laura Skinner dies at age thirteen, Virginia's age at her mother's death, and Woolf ends her *diary* treatment with the fact that Skinner was buried "in the grave of his wife & Laura" (*D* 3: 343). In short, in this first reference Woolf depicts a father and daughter deeply intertwined. She might also be projecting as she describes the son's plight: "& yet how could the unfortunate Owen endure to have his father with him?—his egotistic, exacting, morose, but devoted father? He gave pain even by his affection" (*D* 3: 342). These words capture her own complex ambivalence toward *her* father.

Intriguingly, when she reprises the story for her public essay, she corrects the number of remaining children and adds the fact that Laura keeps a diary. "His wife had died young, leaving him with four small children," she explains, "and of these the best-loved, Laura, a child who shared his tastes and would have sweetened his life, for she already kept a diary and had arranged a cabinet of shells with the utmost neatness, died too."[16] When the children were young, Woolf adds in the essay, their father "sometimes walked with them in the fields, or amused himself by making them a boat"—actions of her own father as well—yet two pages later she must add that "the querulous, exacting father could not help, for all his concern, exasperating the children whom, in his own crabbed way, he yet genuinely loved" (*CR* 2: 93, 95).

The *Journal of a Somerset Rector* spoke powerfully to Woolf, I believe, in its drama of a diary-keeping daughter and her gifted but exasperating father.[17] Did she see it too as a tale of diary triumph? She includes in her *Common Reader* essay Owen's taunt that "[n]o one would read the nonsense" in the journals (*CR* 2: 95). In his 1831 journal, the parson records Joseph's hurtful words when his remark that Joseph drank too much cider turns into a fight: "I suppose you will put in your Journals what has taken place, and of course make it all your own way; but I don't care, I shall never read it, and whatever you may think of your great collection of MSS. books, everyone, as well as myself, only laughs at your folly in thinking the occurrences of your parish and family events worth reading" (276).

The sons, of course, were quite wrong. The *Journal* makes for a stirring read. The *Journal of a Somerset Rector* first appeared in 1930. In 1933—after Woolf's 1930 diary entries and 1932 *Common Reader* essay—the British Museum bought twenty-five more Skinner manuscripts from a London bookseller, twenty-one of them "autograph Journals" (Skinner 1971, v). In 1971, Kingsmead Press issued an expanded *Journal of a Somerset Rector, 1803–1834*, adding the earlier and the final diaries, and this edition was reprinted in 1984 by Oxford University Press.[18] And, heavenly days, this more complete version opens with Woolf's 1932 "The Rev. John Skinner," which the editors describe as "a brilliantly penetrating, yet sympathetic study of Skinner, [that] forms a fitting introduction to the new work" (Skinner 1971, vi). In late 1930, however, Parson Skinner showed Woolf an embattled diarist, one fighting without and within.

James Woodforde's *Diary of a Country Parson*

The diary of a second country parson becomes, in Virginia Woolf's hand, a further case of diary triumph (alongside Parson John Skinner's *Journal*)—or rather, a show of *nature's* triumph and of life deathless in a diary. James Woodforde's *Diary of a Country Parson* did not burst on Woolf suddenly, like Skinner's 1930 *Journal of a Somerset Rector*. Instead, she tracked each emerging volume in her reading notebooks, beginning in 1924 when she sandwiched one page of notes on volume 1 of Woodforde's *Diary* between notes on Stendhal's early *Journal* and on *The Diary of the Lady Anne Clifford* (RN 102–03).

In 1923, Woodforde's great-great-great nephew, Dr. R.E.H. Woodforde, showed historian John Beresford the sixty-eight booklets, with their "marbled board sides and decorous leather backs" that comprise his forebear's diary, and allowed Beresford to edit them and bring them into print (5: 37). The first volume appeared in 1924, and Woolf's first reading notes soon after. In 1927, she made eight more pages of notes on volumes 2 and 3 of Woodforde's *Diary* to prepare for her August 17, 1927, *New Republic* review of volume 3, a review titled "Life Itself." She later added two more pages of notes on volume 4 (published in 1929) and a page on volume 5 (published in 1931) (RN 90). Brenda Silver provisionally dates six more lines of notes on volume 4 in yet another reading notebook kept from November 16, 1931, through July 11, 1932, when Woolf revised her 1927 review for its 1932 *Second Common Reader* reincarnation as "James Woodforde" (RN 233).

Like Woolf, Woodforde came from a family of diarists. His great-great-grandfather, Robert Woodforde (1606–1654), kept a diary. His great-grandfather, the Reverend Samuel Woodforde (1636–1701), was Izaak Walton's friend and also a poet who railed against Milton's blank verse. *That* parson Woodforde and his wife kept diaries that Beresford also hoped to print. Then there was Nancy, Woodforde's own niece, who lived with him from 1776 to 1803 (the final half of his life) and kept a parsonage diary, as well.[19]

James Woodforde seems the mildest of men and his diary among the dullest of diaries. Disappointed in preferment and then in love, Woodforde may have tempered his spirit. Or did his mildness *occasion* his loss of place and love?

At age twenty-three Woodforde's Oxford studies end when he is ordained a Church of England minister in 1763. He returns to his home in Ansford, Somerset, where his father serves as rector, and for the next ten years leads a rather easy life, taking on a few curacies around Ansford but also spending many hours fishing and visiting about. He hopes to succeed his father. In March 1771, during his father's last illness, he writes to Mrs. Powel to apply for the livings of Cary and Ansford in case his father should die. She promises him the Cary living but says nothing of Ansford, his primary home. His father dies in May, and in September, James begins to mention a Miss Betsy White of nearby Shepton as "a sweet tempered girl" (1: 111). "I like her much, and I think [she] would make a good wife," he tells his diary. "I do not know but I shall make a bold stroke that way" (1: 111).

Bold would not be a word one would pair with the placid parson we come to know across five volumes of food. Unhappily, family and clerical jousting appear to upset his course. He gets on well enough for nearly two years from his father's death. In March 1772, he enters into an agreement to serve the curacy of Castle Cary for thirty pounds a year "in addition to surplice fees" (1: 114). In July, the Bishop of Wells arranges for him to remain Curate at Ansford. However, all changes a year later when Woodforde reports in a July 1773 entry that his cousin, "Mr. Frank Woodforde was this morning inducted into the Living of Ansford, and he immediately sent me a Line that he intends serving Ansford next Sunday himself, which notice of my leaving the Curacy is I think not only unkind but very ungentlemanlike" (1: 118). *Ungentlemanlike* is strong censure from this parson who now, at age thirty-three, immediately bridles himself: "I must be content. Far be it from me to expect any favour at all from that House. All their actions towards me are bad. . . . I intend to quit the Parsonage House when my year is up . . . and to take up my residence once more at New College," Oxford (1: 118).

Somerset seems closed to him at the age of thirty-three. In Oxford the next year, he hears of a living open in Norfolk, and by a vote of twenty-one to fifteen he beats out another candidate for the post. In 1776, he goes off to Weston Longeville, a village of 360 souls nine miles from Norwich. The village offers a beautiful, spacious church and a parsonage where Woodforde remains for the rest of his days. He dies on January 1, 1803, at age sixty-two.

When Woodforde departs Somerset, he seems to lose touch with Miss Betsy White. In May 1774, when he returns to Ansford to marry his sister Jane to Mr. Pouncett, he tells his diary that he "went home with Betsy White and had some talk with her concerning my making her mine when an opportunity offered and she was not averse to it at all" (1: 132). However, he must not have kept in close (not to mention ardent) touch with her, for when he returns to Somerset in September she is in Bristol with her father, and when he comes again in February 1775 he finds she is "in Devonshire at Mr. Troit's and is to remain there till Easter" (1: 145). Even in those days of slower mail, a passionate lover could alert his love to his travel plans. In any event, in August 1775, Woodforde learns that Betsy will marry "a Gentleman of Devonshire by name Webster, a man reported to have 500 Pd per annum, 10,000 Pd in the Stocks, beside expectations from his Father" (1: 167). Betsy White, in short, finds herself a better—not to mention *firmer*—offer.

Woolf views this loss as the merest ripple in the parson's languid life stream. His "love affair ... was nothing very tremendous," she writes in her 1927 review and repeats in her *Second Common Reader* essay: "[W]e cannot help suspecting that he was glad to consider the question of marriage shelved once and for all so that he might settle down with his niece Nancy at Weston Longueville [*sic*], and give himself simply and solely, every day and all day, to the great business of living. Again, what else to call it we do not know. For James Woodforde was nothing in particular. Life had it all her own way with him."[20]

Woodforde lacked all professional ambition, as Woolf also saw. "It is idle to pretend that he was a zealous priest," she declares (*CR* 2: 85). He does not "relish it," for instance, when the Bishop of Norwich asks him to preach a sermon for the Charity Schools there, and he often gets himself excused (2: 219). Every year or two, from 1776 through 1794, he takes off for three or four months to visit his relatives in Somerset, hiring another minister to do his parish work, and in his final eight years, he scarcely goes to church at all, so "fearful" is he of the cold and the damp. (He hires himself now a full-time substitute.) So tranquil, in fact, is *this* parson that when he learns of someone's death, his most frequent diary comment is "I hope it will prove a happy Change" (2: 42).

What, then, fills the time of this country parson? What is this "living" that must be preserved? Unlike Woolf, Woodforde was a daily diarist, and his entries, so rote, so commonplace, so without flash or fire, cause Woolf to wonder why he bothers to keep a diary at all.[21] "One could wish that the psychoanalysts would go into the question of diary-keeping" begins both her 1927 review and her *Second Common Reader* essay on Woodforde's *Diary*. "For often it is the one mysterious fact in a life otherwise as clear as the sky and as candid as the dawn. Parson Woodforde is a case in point—his diary is the only mystery about him" (*CR* 2: 83). She dismisses several motives for his diary-keeping. "He does not unburden his soul in his diary," she notes; "yet it is no mere record of engagements and expenses. As for literary fame, there is no sign that he ever thought of it" (*CR* 2: 83). Unlike his later fellow Somerset rector John Skinner, Parson Woodforde shows no interest in Somerset (or Norfolk) history or etymology. His interests are not in the least political—or intellectual.

Woolf's *Second Common Reader* essay "Two Parsons" showcases different temperaments and different times. Parson Woodforde, like the later embattled Parson Skinner, meets his share of parish problems. In 1769, he is at odds with the Cary Singers who *sing* the communion response instead of *speaking* it as he has asked, and in Norfolk he does not hesitate to upbraid Forster, a tenant, who acts insolently to him at his tithing Frolic. However, Parson Woodforde finds ways to resolve disagreeable moments and lay them to rest. Unlike Parson Skinner, Parson Woodforde seeks to *avoid* dissension. In 1768, when factions split the Cary church, he refuses to go with one side to the Bishop. "I shall not go ... nor interfere at all concerning it," he tells his diary, "but to live peaceably with all men" (1: 79). Nothing has changed twenty-six years later in Norfolk when a dispute between two parishioners "made [him] very uneasy. ... As not knowing scarce how to act, so as to steer clear of blame from every Quarter" (4: 159). Parson Skinner, in contrast, will not cease from placing blame.

Parson Woodforde's more generous temper extends to cash gifts to Weston's poor families each St. Thomas Day (December 21), coins to the parish children each Valentine's Day, and invitations to Christmas dinner to the parish's six or seven elderly poor men and women, capped with a shilling as a gift. We never hear of Parson Skinner offering such largesse. Furthermore, Parson Woodforde—unlike Parson Skinner—is on the most amiable terms with his squire and squiress. As editor Beresford remarks, "the large quantity of Game which found its way to Weston Parsonage from neighbours lay and clerical testifies to Parson Woodforde's and Nancy's popularity, while the succulence of these gifts excites our unfeigned envy and admiration" (5: x). He means here hares, eels, and braces and leashes of pigeons.

The Diary of a Country Parson inspires one of Woolf's zesty turns on food, for if his diary reveals his life concerns, what Woodforde cares for is meals and visits. He wishes to manage his acres well enough to yield turnips, barley, wheat, and corn to exchange for fish, smuggled gin, and other niceties for his daily fare and social "rotation." "When we think of the Woodfordes, uncle and niece, we think of them as often as not waiting with some impatience for their dinner," Woolf (drolly) explains:

> Gravely they watch the joint as it is set upon the table; swiftly they get their knives to work upon the succulent leg or loin; without much comment, unless a word is passed about the gravy or the stuffing, they go on eating. So they munch, day after day, year in year out, until between them they must have devoured herds of sheep and oxen, flocks of poultry, an odd dozen or so of swans and cygnets, bushels of apples and plums, while the pastries and the jellies crumble and squash beneath their spoons in mountains, in pyramids, in pagodas. Never was there a book so stuffed with food as this one is. To read the bill of fare respectfully and punctually set forth gives one a sense of repletion. (CR 2: 86)

Perhaps it affected Parson Woodforde so.[22] Beyond repletion, Woolf suggests that diary-keeping offered the well-fed parson an intimacy he required and could find nowhere else—not from Nancy, or from Squire Custance and his good wife, or from his game-sending neighbors.[23] "When James Woodforde opened one of his neat manuscript books he entered into conversation with a second James Woodforde, who was not quite the same as the reverend gentleman who visited the poor and preached in the church," Woolf declares, and might be speaking of herself:

> These two friends said much that all the world might hear; but they had a few secrets which they shared with each other only. It was a great comfort, for example, that Christmas when Nancy, Betsy, and Mr. Walker seemed to be in conspiracy against him, to exclaim in the diary, "The treatment I meet with for my Civility this Christmas is to me abominable." The second James Woodforde sympathised and agreed. . . . It is easy to under-

stand why, in the quiet life of a country parish, these two bachelor friends became in time inseparable. An essential part of him would have died had he been forbidden to keep his diary. When indeed he thought himself in the grip of death he still wrote on and on. And as we read—if reading is the word for it—we seem to be listening to someone who is murmuring over the events of the day to himself in the quiet space which precedes sleep. It is not writing, and, to speak of the truth, it is not reading. (CR 2: 83–84)

Woolf describes Woodforde's diary here in words she has used for her own diary: as talk, as intimacy, as "not writing" but something else. Parson Woodforde beckons to her as one of her obscure men and women. His diaries are perfect samples of Monday or Tuesday, as she writes in her *Second Common Reader* essay.[24] Furthermore, through them we see Nancy. By now we expect that the Woolf who brings out Mrs. Hardy in her diary portrait of Thomas Hardy, and Mrs. Wells in her encounter with H. G. Wells, and Stella and Vanessa when it comes to Swift, would not neglect patient Nancy Woodforde, who eased her uncle's life and days. In revising her 1927 review "Life Itself" for the *Second Common Reader*, Woolf does most with Nancy, letting her speak in 1932, entering, in fact, into conversation with her, letting her voice a different view of the eighteenth century:

True, Nancy of the younger generation is visited now and then by a flighty notion that she is missing something, that she wants something. One day she complained to her uncle that life was very dull: she complained "of the dismal situation of my house, nothing to be seen, and little or no visiting or being visited, &c," and made him very uneasy. We could read Nancy a little lecture upon the folly of wanting that "et cetera." Look what your "et cetera" has brought to pass, we might say; half the countries of Europe are bankrupt; there is a red line of villas on every green hillside; your Norfolk roads are black as tar; there is no end to "visiting or being visited." But Nancy has an answer to make us, to the effect that our past is her present. You, she says, think it is a great privilege to be born in the eighteenth century, because one called cowslips pagles and rode in a curricle instead of driving in a car. But you are utterly wrong, you fanatical lovers of memoirs, she goes on. I can assure you, my life was often intolerably dull. . . . Your delight in old times and old diaries is half impure.

You make up something that never had any existence. Our sober reality is only a dream to you—so Nancy grieves and complains living through the eighteenth century day by day, hour by hour. (CR 2: 88–89)

The eighteenth century, like the nineteenth, twentieth, et cetera, brought illness and suicide as well as its share of boredom. The fifth and final volume of *The Diary of a Country Parson* is a journal of six fretful years of illness. In fact, Parson Woodforde's first twinges come in volume 4, in late 1794, and he soon becomes a "poor Invalide" (5: 164). In the final eight years of his life, this parson, heretofore so content to set off fishing or coursing the hares, or to walk to Squire Custance's manor, or to drive his little cart to Norwich to spend his day paying his bills and his night attending the theater, now barely ventures from his house or garden. Parson Woodforde offered Woolf a dismal view of a "poor Invalide's" life. He writes of the "fear on me" in 1799 and often of being "very fearful & nervous" (5: 177, 197). His sister, Jane, has died in 1798 and his brother, John, in 1799. A "great weakness inwardly," the parson tells his diary in May 1799, "which I take proceeds from too great depression of Spirits from many divers Family Losses and the unpleasant Prospect of things on that Account" (5: 196).

Parson Woodforde's *Diary* also records six suicides, including the attempt of Sarah Spooner, servant maid to Stephen Andrews, that earns a diary rebuke from the parson, who calls it a "rash & hasty bad action.... Pray God! she may sincerely repent of the same and never be guilty of such an action again" (5: 375). In her 1927 review, Woolf took time to observe that John, the parson's brother, "had the impudence to defend suicide to his old father" (331), but she cuts these words in her *Second Common Reader* revision, indeed passes swiftly over the parson's final illness and all talk of suicide.

Instead, she is taken—as with diaries she often is taken—by the chance to imagine and dream and fill in the gaps. When she writes in her 1927 review that Woodforde's *Diary* "is not writing, and, to speak of the truth, it is not reading," she adds to it an image she will soon use in *A Room of One's Own*: "It is slipping through half a dozen pages and strolling to the window and looking out. It is going on thinking about the Woodfordes while we watch the people in the street below. It is taking a walk and making up the life and character of James Woodforde" (330; CR 2: 84).

Woodforde's first *Diary* volume (read in 1924) also offered Woolf this description of a 1774 dinner for Oxford University's male students: "The first course was, part of a large Cod, a Chine of Mutton, some Soup, a Chicken Pye,

Puddings and Roots etc. Second course, Pidgeons and Asparagus, a Fillet of Veal with Mushrooms and high Sauce with it, rosted Sweetbreads, hot Lobster, Apricot Tart and in the middle a Pyramid of Syllabubs and Jellies. We had a Desert [*sic*] of Fruit after Dinner, and Madeira, white Port and red to drink as Wine" (1: 128). Surely this passage underwrites the famous dinner in *A Room of One's Own*.

The Diary of a Country Parson lives on through Woolf's imagination,[25] and although she allows Nancy to rebuke her at the close of her *Second Common Reader* essay, for making a dream of "sober reality," she still insists on the dream. Woolf closes her essay with a hymn—not so much to "James Woodforde" himself as to nature and to life everlasting through a diary:

> It is we who change and perish. Parson Woodforde lives on. It is the kings and queens who lie in prison. It is the great towns that are ravaged with anarchy and confusion. But the river Wensum still flows; Mrs. Custance is brought to bed of yet another baby; there is the first swallow of the year. The spring comes, and summer with its hay and strawberries; then autumn, when the walnuts are exceptionally fine though the pears are poor; so we lapse into winter, which is indeed boisterous, but the house, thank God, withstands the storm; and then again there is the first swallow, and Parson Woodforde takes his greyhounds out a-coursing. (*CR* 2: 89)

The *Private Diary* of Princess Daisy of Pless

"I've wasted 4 days when I wanted to write," Virginia Woolf complains to Vita Sackville-West on May 24, 1931. "And I've spent them partly reading Princess Daisy of Pless, speculating upon her real character and life and longing for a full account from you—who appear in a footnote as a distinguished author" (*L* #2376, 4: 337). The tie to Vita may have drawn Woolf to *From My Private Diary*, published in 1931, for in it Woolf caught this glimpse of teenage Vita in 1909, visiting Princess Daisy, her distant relative, at the Castle Fürstenstein in Silesia. "The party included . . . Victoria Sackville-West and her daughter," Princess Daisy tells her *Private Diary*. "They brought a Hungarian band with them and we danced. Then I led them a follow-my-leader on horseback and hid from them in the woods; we had a glorious ride" (251). Such was the (prewar) life of aristocrats.

Mary-Theresa Olivia Cornwallis-West—who became Princess Daisy of Pless

—was born at Ruthin Castle in north Wales in 1873. Her great-grandfather had been Lord Chamberlain to Queen Victoria, and, as Princess Daisy puts it in the opening chapter that introduces her *Private Diary*, "The friendship of the British Royal Family for ours was almost an inheritance" (3). Daisy was a tall, blonde society beauty, and she includes in her *Diary* lively letters from King Edward VII and Queen Alexandra, as well as from King George V. Daisy regularly receives Christmas gifts from each monarch, and in 1909 she and her husband (Prince Hans) are King Edward's guests for Ascot Week. Daisy also plays bridge and croquet with King Edward and his mistress, Alice Keppel. Her many *Diary* references to "fascinating" Keppel likely enhanced Woolf's interest when she met Keppel herself in 1932 (98).

Princess Daisy is nothing if not fascinatingly connected. Her brother George marries Lady Randolph Churchill, Winston Churchill's mother, and when this marriage ends, he weds Mrs. Patrick Campbell, the famed actor. Daisy visits Baron Rothschild in 1896 and dines on the *North Star*, Cornelius Vanderbilt's yacht, in 1903 (39, 105–06). In 1905, elderly Count Metternich, the German ambassador to England, falls in love with her, "as far as he knows how" (if her *Private Diary* is to be believed), and two years earlier in Vienna, the Archduke Franz Ferdinand enters her box at the opera and remains "for some time"—unusual behavior for the archduke, which creates a "great effect" (164, 101).

But *My Private Diary* offered Woolf more than just views of the rich and the royal. It supplied material for works to come: for *Flush*, *Three Guineas*, and particularly for *The Years*. In 1891, Daisy is married off to Hans Heinrich XV, Prince of Pless, Count of Hochberg, Baron of Fürstenstein, one of the wealthiest heirs in the German Empire.[26] At eighteen she becomes in one stroke wife, princess, and hostess of Castle Fürstenstein in Silesia and, in 1907, when Hans' father dies, of Castle Pless, as well.

"I cant help liking her," Woolf writes to Vita (*L* #2376, 4: 337). Woolf recognized in Daisy, perhaps, several of her own traits. Daisy writes early of her "quenchless interest in human life," yet she also sought in nature escape from culture's chains, just as Woolf did (5). "When in doubt about anything I am accustomed to look to nature for help and guidance and nearly always receive it," Daisy declares in her book's opening pages (4). "But for real joy, for the complete realization of nature, give me space and distance; no enclosure, but freedom to let my thoughts wander into the beautiful gardens of my imagination" (10).

The contours of Daisy's chains emerge in this 1903 entry:

I got restless and sat on the balcony looking at the papers (*longing* to play the piano but afraid to make a noise).... After dinner I could resist no more my piano, so I hummed while playing with the soft pedal down. Hans, furious, said I... was drowning the conversation, so I really didn't know what to do, but felt inclined to cry. I looked at a great perfumed lily in a silver vase at the end of the piano, and wished I could be in a soft, sweet-scented, peaceful country where perhaps people grow and live freely—nothing forced or unnatural, tamed or "squeezed in." (111)

In later years, she offers a parallel portrait of her dog *Wolff* that Woolf may have recalled when she wrote the next-to-last chapter of *Flush*:

[W]e met Hansel and Lexel [her young sons] and Joseph (the valet) and Braga (my maid) all going after poor dear old *Wolff* who never comes home now (except when he is hungry), because he has found the dearest little brown lady friend. When he was tied up because he had killed a cat she used to come and sit and stare at him. But now he is free and has run away with her into the mountains—"the call of the wild" (the title of that book which I love). It is a call we all have felt at times but may not answer. To be free, quite quite free, to run wild for a bit! What a lot of good it would do us all. Anyway I stopped them going after *Wolff* with bamboo poles to try and catch him, and looked myself with longing eyes up to the sunny side of the hill and longed to be following in *Wolff's* footsteps. (271–72)

Here, as in *Flush*, woman and dog are one.

As is now more than clear, Princess Daisy's *Private Diary* offered Woolf a window on another Victorian family (beyond Elizabeth Barrett's and her own) and on Victorian, Edwardian, and Georgian life in the highest English and German circles. If in her bath on January 20, 1931, Woolf conceived a book on "the sexual life of women" (*D* 4: 6), in May she found that Princess Daisy addressed that very state. "I had thought of calling this book *Better Left Unsaid*, a title prophetically chosen for me by a Victorian relative, long since deceased," Daisy begins her *Private Diary*.[27]

He, because he was undoubtedly male, and in the very best Victorian tradition, believed absolutely in females being seen and not heard. Not that he liked overmuch of us to be seen.... [F]rom our birth onward until we "came out" at the age of seventeen or eighteen we were secluded in a nursery and, when we did happen to meet anyone from the outside world, were admonished to keep our (as yet unopened) eyes demurely fixed on the ground. At our marriage to a man with whose christian name we had just been permitted to become vaguely acquainted, but of whom we knew practically nothing else, we were modestly swathed in a massive sheath of white shiny satin, and our face, dyed a deep maidenly crimson, because of the fact that for the first time in our virginal lives we were actually touching the elbow of a man, and, also—of course for the first time—listening to words about love and marriage.... Our nice bringing-up, unaided, had made it quite impossible for us even to have heard, much less understood, the outspoken, not to say coarse manner in which the Anglican Prayer Book in good round English lays down the "first cause for which matrimony was ordained."... This, then, was the convention into which I was most inconsiderately tumbled, and into which I never perhaps quite succeeded in fitting myself. (1–2)

The Princess dares here to address the body.

As Woolf fights to free herself to revise *The Waves*, she sees Princess Daisy's struggle against restrictive forces, but also her crippling. Daisy's husband was twelve years older than she, and she writes that to him and his parents she "was only a girl well under twenty who should have been content to sing, dance (very occasionally), embroider, and *listen* to her seniors' talk, according them a continuous, almost fulsome silent admiration. Long before suffragettes were ever heard of I refused to accept the dogma that men were by nature so much wiser and better than women. Yet in the circle into which I married in Germany this was a part of the general creed" (21). Eleven years after her marriage, she tells her diary that Hans loves her "rather as one would a picture on a wall or a decorative piece of furniture in a room" (67).

She longs to be more than ornamental; however, she is not allowed even to arrange a room in her home. In 1904, when she visits Alice de Rothschild's lovely garden with its nasturtiums (Daisy's favorite flower) growing into the trees and over the walls, Daisy vows to "write and tell Hans of this, as he was so furious when I planted them in the rocks at Fürstenstein" (138). Two years later, while Hans is away, she tries to create her own space in the woods away from the castle: "[W]e cut down trees and started to make a homely little garden by the river in the *Schwarzengraben*; it will be delicious, little old paths and a wooden railing with flowers all up it, and hedges of sweet briar and lots of roses growing in the trees. I am building a little thatched cottage too, one big room and a kitchen. I have not dared tell Hans; he would get furious at once, although it is doing no harm and I shall pay for it myself" (196).

Hans even controls her religion. "Since I married all religious peace of mind has left me," she tells her diary in 1896. "Hans is miserable if I go to a Protestant church, and more so if I take the Communion—indeed he is almost brutal to me about it" (41). He controls her travel, as well. That same year she tells her diary that "anything I can achieve must be done by kindness and tact. . . . I am going to England about November the 10th; I want to be at Newlands a little while, as I have to spend Christmas at Pless, and oh, it was a hard fight till I got him to say I might go; he never can understand the love I have for my own people and my old home" (47, 48). Daisy's "oh" is like Woolf's diary "oh dear." Six years later, Daisy notes that her diary again "shows how disappointed I was that I was not allowed to accompany my husband when he went to Washington on an official mission" (18).

Daisy's role is tightly proscribed. "I feel somehow like a lady in a harem," she tells her *Diary* in 1903. "I must not drive in an open carriage nor walk alone, nor see a man alone for tea unless I have asked others to come."[28] Hans, she says, "is as nearly perfect as any husband could be, as long as I help him and dress well and smile at his guests and act the part of a Prince's wife" (96).

She yearns for a larger role, yet as we watch her struggle from our vantage point in the twenty-first century, we see her warped by the very conventions she fights. Even eleven years into her marriage, the princess pines romantically for a white knight. "Yesterday we walked to the *Riesengrab* and I talked to [Hans] of the hospitals and the poor people," she writes in 1902. "It was lovely standing there, all the woods clothed in glorious autumn tints: but it made me feel lonesome, and long for someone who would be a help to me; someone to lean upon. I turned to look at my husband and there he was digging in the ground to make a little ditch and let the water fall down over the rock; he was delighted, and I felt as if I had two babies to look after instead of one" (64).

Four years later, she appears to have given up on Hans, for she now seeks an "unknown protector": "I only wish I could get quieter and more satisfied. All day long my soul cries out within me to some unknown protector: 'I am lonely, understand me, take care of me, hold my hand, be my guide; I am so tired of standing alone, and I have had to pretend so long, so long; let me see sunshine; give me peace; take me to a country of fair flowers and fresh Springs, where in love and harmony men and women work their common way to a higher destiny; away from the world of lies, criticisms and forced smiles'" (176). Daisy yearns childishly for male rescue. She is like the perfumed lily in the silver vase: a hothouse idealist.

Beyond the crippling romanticism, wealth also taints her. Assessing her younger sister's marriage prospects, Daisy tells her diary five years into her own marriage (before some of her illusions are ripped from her eyes):

> The Ilchesters are quite anxious for [Shelagh] to marry their son and spoke to Patsy and Poppets about it; he is a charming boy and one of the best matches in England; he is too shy to propose, and Shelagh says he is too young and will not encourage him one bit; he is only twenty-two, but I think she is throwing away a good chance, as a woman is almost bound to fall in love with the man who gives her everything, houses, jewels, horses, every penny she has; and, later on, her children; in fact the one to whom she owes everything—just as Hans gives me everything and is so good and dear. (51)

So "good and dear"? The *Private Diary* discloses other instances of Daisy's wigwag and hypocrisy. In 1904, in one of her characteristic romantic apostrophes, she writes: "I like the people round here to forget I am Princess Henry of Pless, and talk to me as to a fellow-mortal; and the night was so beautiful, I longed to hold out my hands and say: 'Let me be amongst you, come to me, let me help you, be with me . . . don't send me back to the top of my hill again, give me some word of greeting'" (151–52). In the next paragraph, however, she writes—apparently seeing no contradiction: "To-night I shall go again for a drive in the moonlight, and have promised to take Copie (Hansel's nursery-governess), laying down as a condition, however, that she must not make conversation with me" (152). Similarly, although she tells us at the start that she has harbored "literary ambitions" for as long as she can remember, her published *Private Diary* makes no mention of her use of the Fürstenstein Castle library with its fifty thousand volumes—one of the finest private libraries in Germany (22).

Princess Daisy seems trapped between desire and realization. Barred from direct action herself, when she tries to enlarge her influence she seems a Lady Macbeth, plotting her husband's rise. Hans' failings, in fact, relate to women. "The other day in Berlin Hans was asked to be present at a very little dinner to meet Countess Bülow and Countess Redern," Daisy reports:

> His answer to the old gentleman who asked him was: "Invite two prettier women and I will come." To begin with the answer was rude, and then to refuse to dine with the wife of the Chancellor is ridiculous; and particularly so as Countess Bülow is Italian, very clever, knows the world and has seen a lot, is a delightful companion and conversationalist,[29] and has great influence with her husband; and how on earth does Hans expect to be asked to their house when he is in Berlin and treated well and to be given the post of Ambassador, or Governor, by a man whom he scarcely knows, and whose wife he does not take the trouble to be polite to! (146)

Daisy also must endure the double standard. In 1909, a mix-up occurs in household letters and she finds Hans deep in an affair. She omits the precise details but prints her diary declaration that "[i]f ever I were to find out he *really* wanted to *marry* someone else I would separate from him *at once* and never believe in anything again."[30] Three years before, she must cope with what today we call sexual harassment:

> Leopold X, a relative, led the ball; he has been married two years; his wife has a little money but is dull and frightful; he is very tall and good-looking, but I should think stupid. He started a violent flirtation with me in a common (I imagine, a German soldier's) way by pressing his leg against mine at supper and then suddenly trying to get his leg over mine; we sat rather cramped at round tables; I heard his chair creak and wished he would fall over and upset the table. I did not dare move, but talked all the time to my supper partner, Count Reischach, the new Master of the Horse to the Emperor. The "distant cousin" got paler and paler and tight round his nose, and afterwards kept on whispering over my shoulder as my back was generally turned to him: *Je suis fou de vous; ich bin wirklich ganz verückt.* I was mad with rage. (183)

To read Princess Daisy's *Private Diary* is to watch a crippled, flailing butterfly. Daisy claims strong role models in her grandmother and mother, yet she feels she fails their standard.[31] In her *Diary* we watch her both nurture and belittle herself. Of her maternal grandmother, Lady Olivia FitzPatrick, Daisy writes that "[i]n spite of the cramping traditions and conventions in which she must have grown up, Grannie Olivia had about her something extraordinarily human, vivid, free and independent. True, she was always a great lady; but she was better than that, she was a real, outspoken, great-hearted gentlewoman" (3). Daisy's mother, "Patsy," in turn:

> somehow seems to have escaped entirely the benumbing and inhibiting influence of the less admirable side of Victorianism. To the extraordinary beauty, wit, brains, charm and fortitude she united an audacity and freedom which, in the society into which she was born, aroused gossip and even criticism. She did not care. When in 1872 she married my father, Colonel Cornwallis-West, she became her own mistress at the age of seventeen, and from that day until the day of her death in 1920, her own mistress she remained. Looking back, I marvel at her matchless courage and her abiding resolve to live her own life. How I wish, now that it is too late, that I had been sufficiently brave to follow her example. (4)

But Daisy's friends call her a "baby" (70), and she often is beaten down. "I was so proud of the way I had arranged the red salon downstairs with lovely embroidered cushions, old brocade-covered sofas and chairs from upstairs, and some furniture out of my boudoir and dressing-room," Daisy confides to her diary in the second decade of her marriage:

> I made the change as it is now too cold to sit in the big salon, and my beautiful piano would have been ruined near one of the windows there. The red salon looked so nice, but when Hans saw it he insisted on the space in front of the doors being left bare so that two people could pass in and out together; so all the cosiness vanished; it seemed ridiculous and I was angry.... I nearly cried with disappointment. I know I behave like a child, and I am an idiot and everything you like—but I was so pleased; and then never to get credit for anything, and to be told "I make nothing but blunders." (135)

When she writes stories in 1896 that her mother urges her to publish, Daisy declares, "probably they are great rubbish and very badly written" (40). Three months later she again tells her *Diary*, "Now I am going to write my story; I ought to be ashamed of myself for all the time I spend in wasting ink and paper!" (48). Her diary, in turn, is "stupid," "worthless and badly written," "a waste of time" that "does no good to anyone and only shows what a fool I am" (252, 209, 160, 50). Nevertheless, she keeps it.

Despite her own self-reproaches, readers cannot help but see that Daisy possesses ambitions, ideals, considerable courage, and the will (finally) to act. In 1902, she tells her *Diary*:

It is now two years since I started to go about among the working people: before that I was always being told it was not "princely" to do so and that if I went it would only mean giving money and help of that sort.... But I want to get to the heart of the people and understand them and now, in sheer desperation, I have broken bounds. I order my carriage and go where I choose: alms-houses, hospitals, homes for old people, everywhere. In time, my personal interest in my poorer neighbours will be acceptable and, I hope, helpful. (61–62)

In 1905, she pressures the state to clean a polluted Silesian river, and by 1910 she has created a milk depot in Waldenburg "where the poor women will be able to buy properly sterilized milk for their babies; [and] the milk will be prepared for children of all ages" (260). The same year she starts a lace depot in Hirschberg "where all lace will be brought in, and bought by me—or rather by a committee, and then sold to the shops; the workers, therefore, making as much profit as possible; and later, to put my money to make a pension fund for the workers. I have had this lace depôt in my head for some time, and I never give in—unless a matter seems quite hopeless—I will therefore fight on and gain the day" (257).

For Princess Daisy, like Woolf, was a fighter, despite the fact that, as Woolf also wrote acerbically to Vita, she harbored "a housemaids sensibility and the sentimentality of a Surbiton cook."[32] In 1902, at age twenty-nine, Daisy writes: "I am perhaps not quite an ordinary woman because I still see the need of fighting and do fight, whereas so many seem to give up the battle and are satisfied to float along upon the tide of existence" (60). Pregnant and thirty-seven, she exhorts her 1910 diary: "[G]ive me strength to fight on, and help others, and forget myself and life's disappointments, imaginary or real!" (264). During the birth of her third son, she contracts septic poisoning and nearly dies. "I longed to go," she tells her diary on January 1, 1911. "Then I felt little Patsy [her mother] near me, close close to me, and I thought of my boys.... and they dropped me... back into this sad, struggling and cruel little world, always divided against itself; and now I am again one of the strugglers" (268). In June 1914, the last year of this published diary, she declares: "But it has always been a battle, won sometimes in a garden, and sometimes on very rough ground" (281).

Like Beatrice Webb, that other well-heeled Victorian diarist, Daisy calls her diary "*My dear Unknown, or Unseen*" (209). She writes her diary at night in bed, or in her private garden, on trains or ships—even between the courses of a meal (xi). A periodic diary like Woolf's, it amounts to more than 600,000 words—

Woolf's to some 770,000 words (viii). Daisy sees her diary as a way to leave behind "some memorial, however humble, that will outlast *the years* and still keep our memory green—perhaps even fragrant—when all who knew and loved us are no more" (14; italics mine). She offers here the phrase "the years"—and she also supplies them.

She values her diary as more reliable and truthful than memory, and surely Woolf understood her assertion in 1913 that "[t]ouching this book is like raising the blind of a closed window and looking out again on an old landscape" (35, 278). In her opening chapter, Daisy declares: "[T]here are heaps of people, especially women, daily making mistakes, choosing wrongly, meeting success or failure or unhappiness, who might perhaps be helped by my record of how I faced—and survived—all these things. One of the most profitable and most constant ways in which my diary has been of help to me is that by looking back through its pages, it has enabled me, to some extent at all events, to judge myself on my own record" (14).

Despite her frequent jibes at its "worthlessness," the princess' diary brought her aid and comfort in extraordinarily difficult times. From her earliest days, Daisy possessed a remarkable voice—another gift from her mother. When she was sixteen, her doting father moved the whole family to Florence at great expense, so she could study singing. Daisy's first ambition was to be a professional singer. Her dreams foundered when she contracted typhoid and lost her voice. "Probably my long convalescence, and my disappointment at having suddenly to leave Italy, was solaced by trying to write," Daisy reflects in her *Private Diary*'s opening pages. "If so, it foreshadowed days to come, because some of my saddest and darkest hours have been brightened, and some of my bitterest losses and disappointments made more bearable, by keeping my diary" (6–7).

We watch Daisy use her diary to validate and to fortify herself. In 1908, she writes as if the diary is Hans: "[Y]ou *know* I *do* think of other people, all the servants and agents, but it *is* only fair that I should be able to spend three or two months every year" in England (232). Even here, though, she starts to backtrack from three to two months.

From My Private Diary offers excerpts from Daisy's diaries from 1896 to 1914. Alongside all else, it sheds light on the buildup to the Great War from one who knew personally most of the major players. Signs of discord emerge as early as the second year of Daisy's *Diary* when she tries to raise funds from German women living in England for a Silver Jubilee gift for Queen Victoria. Her drive falls miserably flat. "[M]y subscription . . . is in England a failure," Daisy tells her diary on May 21, 1897; "the feeling now between Germany and England can really be called nothing less, I think, than hatred" (58). That "feeling" involved the German-Dutch Boers in South Africa and their conflicts with the British that would soon bring the Second Boer War.[33]

On a 1903 visit to England, Daisy bridles at the steady snipes at her husband's homeland (87), and on November 1, 1905, when she dines at the races with King Edward, Alice Keppel, and others, "They got on the subject of Russia and the brutality of the Russian Cossack soldiers; the King at once changed the subject because of me I suppose; it is horrid. It makes me feel like a foreigner here—as in Germany—when politics are discussed. The King did not mention Hans or Germany, and, for the first time in any place where I was present, he scarcely spoke to me; he must hate the Germans" (173). She immediately writes to both King Edward and to his nephew, the German Emperor, Kaiser Wilhelm, trying to spur better rapport; however, as the diplomatic reply she prints from German prime minister Count von Bülow admits, relations were strained (174–75).

On July 31, 1913, the British royals—now King George V and Queen Mary—receive an even worse snub at the Berlin races during a state visit to Germany. "I was in the Royal Box with the King and Queen of England," Daisy tells her *Diary*. "The [German] Crown Princess had been much annoyed because her husband was away from us most of the time. When the Royal Visitors had gone I said to him: 'I think, Sir, you ought to have remained in the Pavilion all the afternoon and talked to the King and Queen of England!'" (277). She reports then their lengthy talk, during which she reprimands him for failure to keep to etiquette and noblesse oblige.

Princess Daisy kept up on politics and her *Private Diary* often proves prophetic. In 1904, when Prince Gottfried tells her he feels sure the Russian Czar will "meet his fate at the *hands of a murderer*," she writes: "I made him promise not to drive anywhere with any Grand Dukes as I don't want him to be blown up" (164). Sitting next to Winston Churchill at a 1909 dinner, she feels "awfully sorry for him, he is like a race horse wanting to start at once—even on the wrong race track; he has so much impetuousness that he cannot hold himself back, and he is too clever and has too much personal magnetism. . . . He is not happy if he is not always before the public, and he may some day be Prime Minister—and why not, he has energy and brains" (247). Toward the close of 1911, Daisy tries to interest the German Emperor in an effort to create a peacekeeping European Council, an early version of the postwar League of Nations (xii–xiii). In September 1912, she writes: "It is strange how the feelings of nations are changing; a socialist feeling is growing in us all without our knowing it or wishing it—even in China" (277).

Nevertheless, the *Diary*'s final entry of 1913 rings today with bitter irony. "Well, diary, good-night," Daisy writes; "perhaps 1914 will be better and happier; any good spirits that are near me as I write please save and help me."[34] She will need every good spirit she can muster, for she is in London in August 1914 and must leave care of her Saville Row house to a good-spirited American, Nancy Leeds, when she flees England to join her children in Germany. But Castle Pless becomes the Great Headquarters of the German Armies in the East from 1914 to 1917. We learn all this in Daisy's final chapter, where she describes her life from 1914 to 1931. Displaced from both her English and her German homes, she is looked on as a spy by many of her Silesian neighbors, so she becomes a Sister in a Berlin War Hospital and nurses on the French, Austrian, and Serbian fronts. She also works for the British prisoners-of-war in Germany—an index of her divided stance.

But she cannot stop her oldest son, Hansel, from fighting against the country of her birth, and she herself is refused entry into England. In the final chapter of *From My Private Diary*, Daisy describes her frantic efforts to enter England, even in 1919 *after* the war, for her mother lies dying in the English countryside and calls for her eldest child. Even Daisy's high connections fail her. She includes a polite letter from English Foreign Secretary Arthur Balfour denying her entrance. Even former Queen Alexandra can do nothing for her. "[A]s a woman, I have no country. As a woman I want no country. As a woman my country is the whole world," Virginia Woolf will write in 1937 (*TG* 109). In 1931, *My Private Diary* showed Woolf the fate of a woman who "marries a foreigner," as she will write in *Three Guineas* (108).

Ironically, Daisy's losses in the Great War may have freed her to become a writer. German defeat and postwar hyperinflation greatly undermine Hans' wealth and high position. In June 1920, Daisy reports returning to Castle Fürstenstein, where she was:

> formally received by Hans with considerable pomp. I think this was meant to convey to the world of Silesia that I was really a quite harmless person. The night of my arrival there were great festivities and, for a time, both Hans and I hoped and believed that we could settle down together happily after the war. But it was not to be; too much, perhaps, had happened in our personal, our domestic, and our national life to make such a

hope realizable. Moreover, I knew only too well that I could never again feel at home in Prussia.³⁵

They divorce in December 1923. Her legs begin to fail her, and she offers her "invalid's" state as one reason for "publishing so much" about herself (5–6). She pens her memoirs in 1928, *Daisy Princess of Pless by Herself*, drawing upon her diary (as Beatrice Webb did in her 1926 *My Apprenticeship*) and directly quoting 111 diary entries. So popular were these insider "reminiscences" that the memoir saw five printings in four months. This success led Daisy to publish *From My Private Diary* in 1931 and also a second memoir, *What I Left Unsaid*, in 1936.

Daisy Cornwallis-West died in 1943, within a few months of Beatrice Webb. Like Barbellion in his *Journal of a Disappointed Man*, she never names the illness—multiple-sclerosis—that claims her. In 1950, a new volume, *The Private Diaries of Daisy, Princess of Pless, 1873–1914*, combined the diary portions of the 1928 memoir with those from the 1931 *From My Private Diary*. In 2002, W. John Koch, a Silesian who grew up hearing stories of Princess Daisy, published a biography, *Daisy Princess of Pless, 1873–1943: A Discovery*, that includes further diary entries and attests to continued interest in the diarist. Indeed, because the 1931 *From My Private Diary* was edited to "avoid seriously hurting anyone's feelings by prematurely publishing too much" (xv), the time is surely ripe for a complete, uncensored version of the diary of Daisy Cornwallis-West.

Meanwhile, however, in May 1931, Princess Daisy's *Private Diary* gave Virginia Woolf a portrait of a freedom-seeking dog named *Wolff*, a vision of dog and woman as one. Only a few months later, she will begin *Flush*. *From My Private Diary* also offered Woolf a panoramic view of Victorian, Edwardian, and Georgian family life from a woman who dared to address the body and "the years." It showed her firsthand the fate of an English woman who "marries a foreigner," both in and after war (*TG* 108). More than anything, however, *From My Private Diary* showed Woolf another woman in a war for freedom—and the many barriers to success.

3

Adept Sailing before the Storm

In her "Letter to a Young Poet," published in June 1932, Virginia Woolf explains that once a writer knows herself, the "difficult problem" is to find "the right relationship . . . between the self that you know and the world outside," in short, between the inner and the outer (*E* 5: 315). Her next two diary books, the 1932 diary and the 1933–34 diary, help her to navigate that difficult strait. She needs this diary support, for she faces loss of friends and inner artistic strains while, at the same time, the gathering outer storm forms.

In March 1932, Woolf lunches with Alice Keppel, the late King Edward VII's mistress, who is "going off to Berlin to hear Hitler speak" (*D* 4: 81). In May, the French president is assassinated by the (self-described) "chief of the Russian Fascists" (*D* 4: 98n3). Several 1932 diary moments seem prophetic tableaus. In Greece in April, Woolf finds Germans "claiming, we thought, more of the Acropolis than any other nation" (*D* 4: 91). In June, Prince Dmitry Petrovich Svyatopolk-Mirsky, a Russian literary historian and critic, comes to call, "despair [sic], suffering, very marked on his face," to tell her he must return to Russia. Woolf then foresees his death: "I thought as I watched his eye brighten & fade—soon there'll be a bullet through your head. Thats one of the results of war: this trapped cabin'd man" (*D* 4: 112). Olivier Bell reveals that the prince did return to Russia "and apparently perished in a labour camp" (*D* 4: 112n16). Earlier in the month, Woolf reports economist John Maynard Keynes' words to George Bernard Shaw's wife: "We may go over the edge." Keynes speaks "in the low tone of a doctor saying a man was dying in the next room; but didnt want to disturb the company. This referred to the state of Europe" (*D* 4: 107–08).

In January 1933, Hitler assumes power as German Chancellor, and the Nazis begin to institutionalize a campaign against women workers, whom they call "double earners" (Pawlowski, *Virginia Woolf and Fascism* 8). The Nazi Sterilisation Law also begins, and Dachau, the first concentration camp, is set up near Munich. "The removal of 'asocial' elements, from the very early days of the seizure of power in 1933 onwards, was also sanctioned," Petra Rau explains, "as a justified cosmetic measure for the benefit of tourists" (11). The guidebook Baedeker, in fact, begins informing these tourists that in Germany "the raising of the right arm, accompanied by the words 'Heil Hitler,' has since 1933 largely superseded the practice of hat-raising. The army, navy, and air force retain the military salute; but [the Heil Hitler salute] is compulsory for officials, and for everybody when the national anthems are played" (Rau 15).

On July 30, 1933, Woolf tells her diary the story of a local Rodmell woman's generosity regarding an inheritance: "These little tributes to human nature are deserved after Hitler & Mussolini," she declares, revealing her diary's role as fascist counter (*D* 4: 171). In late November 1933, she consciously turns from the troubling outer world to the dual-voiced diary of Katherine Bradley and Edith Cooper, the aunt and niece verse dramatists who published under the name Michael Field. She finds there lesbian playwrights and their trials—and the word "outsiders."

Virginia Woolf's 1932 Diary

> "I believe I want this more humane existence for my next . . . to feel the width & amusement of human life: not to strain to make a pattern just yet: to be made supple, & to let the juice of usual things, talk, character, seep through me, quietly, involuntarily before I say—Stop, & take out my pen."
>
> (September 16, 1932; *D* 4: 124)

Virginia Woolf makes herself supple across her 1932 diary. We watch her steep herself with "life" and refill her well. This diary, in fact, breaks tellingly in two. Through July, the diary serves as both a refresher from the strain that has not left her from *The Waves* and as a collecting pool for works to come. In August, in the country, in the flood of new creation, Woolf lays the diary aside.

Seventy-four entries mark the 336 days from January 13 to December 19, 1932—an entry every four or five days, as in her last (1930–1931) diary—or so we might think. However, that would be wrong. Sixty-one entries (more than 80 percent) come in the first seven months of the year: six entries in January, ten in February, nine in March, five in April (which included travel), eleven in May, ten in June, and ten in July. In contrast, from August to December, Woolf pens either two or three entries each month—as in the heyday of her spare modernist 1920s diaries. The *Flush*, the "torrent" of creation, does come in 1932 (*D* 4: 133). In fact, three of the diary's last four entries lack dates, as if Woolf's mind now flows unmoored. With its gray marble cover, the 1932 diary resembles the last 1930–1931 diary book, but its pages are now blue instead of white—a telling shade, for Woolf's diary self-irrigation occurs in the face of strain, exhaustion, and loss.[1]

The 1932 diary begins with one of Woolf's fruitful declarations of her inability to write. "Oh but this is . . . not the first day of the year. It is the thirteenth, & I am in one of those lassitudes & ebbs of life when I cannot heave another word on to the wall. My word, what a heaving The Waves was, that I still feel the strain!" (*D* 4: 62). But she is, of course, heaving words onto her *diary* wall. In fact, she still needs morning diary-writing as she shifts from fiction to nonfiction, to the *Second Common Reader* essays. In this first entry, she declares herself "slower, thicker, more intolerant of the fling & the rash" (*D* 4: 63). "Writing becomes harder & harder," she repeats in her sixth entry at the end of the month. "Things I dashed off I now compress & re-state. And for purposes which I need not go into here, I want to use these pages for dialogue for a time" (*D* 4: 66–67).

The 1932 diary now becomes a diary of talk. Each of the next nine entries (January 31 to February 16) delivers a "Conversation piece"—as Woolf labels her February 2 entry (*D* 4: 68). These "pieces" can be complex. In this February 2 entry, for instance, Woolf records Ethel Smyth recalling *other* conversations:

> [A] bold tap at the drawing room door. In comes Ethel Smyth in her spotted fur, like an unclipped & rather overgrown woodland wild beast, species indeterminate. She wears, as usual, her 3 cornered Frederick the Great hat, & one of her innumerable relay of tweed coats & skirts. . . . Before she has sat down she is talking. "Really I think that building of the kind you describe at Rodmell is worse than death. After all one may say of death its natural: but this is a wanton desecration. Why your downs? Oh I know L[eonard]. wouldn't agree; but theres my Rupert Gwynne. He said, he pounced like a wolf on the fold the other day when they were talking against landlords—We, & I hope all my family for ever, he said, refuse to sell our land." (*D* 4: 69)

The next day Woolf offers a play scene:

Here I saw Clive look at Lytton's picture. "Dont have it moved. Have it cleaned, by all means, but it looks very nice there. Its the best thing of Lytton. R[oger Fry then says]. And that horrid vulgar picture by Henry [Lamb] is the one people will know him by. . . . Vir[ginia]: But its far the most like. R.[:] I did a portrait of Lytton, writing E[minent]. Victorians at Durbins. Vir: I'm a little annoyed that he left all his old books to Senhouse. Clive.[:] And his will? I've heard nothing. (*D* 4: 70–71)

And much more.[2]

Fifty-eight conversations enliven the year's seventy-four entries. Woolf seems keen to preserve voices, to flood herself with life, for in this diary Vanessa speaks, as do Ethel Smyth, Dora Carrington, Margery Fry, Helen Anrep, Lady Ottoline Morrell, Mary Hutchinson, Mrs. Woolf, and Nelly Boxall. We hear the voices of Leonard, Roger, Duncan, Clive, Adrian, Bob Trevelyan, Oliver and James Strachey, and even George Bernard Shaw.

"These conversation pieces are artfully contrived to assuage me, about 11.30, after toiling at correcting Donne, who is to introduce the second volume of the Common Reader," Woolf tells her diary on February 3. "I cant go on squeezing my sentences dry of water; & so write here for 20 minutes" (*D* 4: 70). The diary soothes and lubricates. Through it we can also trace Woolf's progress on the *Second Common Reader*. On February 16, she finishes "Donne after Three Centuries," with its nod to diarist Lady Anne Clifford. In late March and April, she polishes "Dr. Burney's Evening Party," her salute to her diary mother, Fanny Burney. She finishes "The Novels of Thomas Hardy" on July 3 and says she "should now attack Ch[ristina]. Rossetti. But Lord, how tired one gets of one's own writing" (*D* 4: 113). She wearies of her own voice and wants the irrigation of others' talk.

She "artfully contrive[s]" to surround herself with "Otway conversation" in her *diary*—the atmosphere she seeks for her essays. In fact, the *Second Common Reader* should be seen as her salute to diaries, with its essays on Swift's diary, Fanny Burney's, Dorothy Wordsworth's, and the diaries of those obscure country parsons Skinner and Woodforde.

What does Woolf mean on January 31 by the veiled "for purposes which I need not go into here, I want to use these pages for dialogue for a time"? (*D* 4: 66–67). Beyond helpful "Otway conversation" for her *Common Reader* essays-in-progress, she seems to draw on familiar voices for comfort in the wake of Lytton Strachey's January death. By August she admits her wish to "belittle" death and to "be found as Montaigne said, laughing with girls & good fellows" (*D* 4: 121). So she shows herself in this diary.³

For death wends its way: Lytton's death on January 21; Dora Carrington's suicide on March 11; and then Goldsworthy Lowes Dickinson's death on August 3—dear old Goldie. Woolf turns to her pen, and to her diary, to salve the pain. "I cant think of any words for what I mean, & yet go on writing, numb, torpid as I am," she writes in her January 22 entry, the day after Lytton dies (*D* 4: 65). She also moves savvily, perhaps instinctively, toward Roger Fry, one of her models of vigorous old age, and plans a trip to Greece with him for April. "The result of Lytton's death—this desire to be with friends," she explains on April 11 (*D* 4: 88). She seeks now outer support.

The low mark comes on May 25, soon after their return. Horror at faces returns and self-hatred and a sense of barrenness—always alarming signs with Woolf. Misspellings, unusual for Woolf, also suggest something amiss:

> [N]ow, since we came back, I'm screwed up into a ball; cant get into step; cant make things dance; feel awefully [*sic*] detached; see youth; feel old; no, thats not quite it; wonder how a year or 20 perhaps is to be endured. . . . All is surface hard; myself only an organ that takes blows, one after another; the horror of the hard raddled faces in the flower show yesterday; the inane pointlessness of all this existence; hatred of my own brainlessness & indecision: the old treadmill feeling, of going on & on & on; for no reason: Lytton's death; Carrington's. . . . Rodmell spoilt; all England spoilt; terror at night of things generally wrong in the universe; . . . worst of all is this disjected [*sic*] barrenness. And my eyes hurt; & my hand trembles.
>
> A saying of Leonard's comes into my head in this season of complete inanity & boredom. "Things have gone wrong somehow." It was the night Carrington killed herself. . . . I saw all the violence & unreason crossing in the air: ourselves small; a tumult outside: something terrifying: unreason. Shall I make a book out of this? It would be a way of bringing order & speed again into my world. (*D* 4: 102–03)

The words "ourselves small; a tumult outside" call to mind Woolf's 1905 Cornwall diary entry that she transformed into the published essay "A Walk by Night." In that entry, "[n]ight was weighing heavily on this little village," and she felt "the vague immensity of the air" (*PA* 298). Nearly twenty-seven years later, she again seeks to "bring order" to this outside tumult, to this "terrifying: unreason," through the written word. And she remains resilient in 1932. She quickly rallies, for her next day's entry begins: "And now today suddenly the weight on my head is lifted. I can think, reason, keep to one thing, & concentrate. Perhaps this is the beginning of another spurt" (*D* 4: 103).

Her strength in 1932 reveals itself also in her (mostly) positive view of old age. Her opening diary entry reveals not only her usual ambivalence toward aging but also her optimism: "our lives. How long will they be? Can we count on another 20 years? I shall be fifty on 25th, Monday week that is; & sometimes feel that I have lived 250 years already, & sometimes that I am still the youngest person in the omnibus" (*D* 4: 63). Ethel Smyth, in her role as Old Virginia in the flesh, continues to share this ambiguity with Woolf. On June 3, Woolf declares her dislike of "old ladies who guzzle"—meaning Smyth—and on July 22 she teases and rails at Smyth's "unattractive old age" (*D* 4: 106, 119). However, in February, when Smyth repeatedly declares "I'm worn out," Woolf counters in parentheses, "(but she looks like a ruddy sea captain . . .)" (*D* 4: 69). Woolf, in fact, writes to Smyth in March: "I say, live, live, and let me fasten myself upon you" (*L* #2543, 5: 29).

George Bernard Shaw, too, like William Butler Yeats the year before, provides a model of vigorous old age. In her June 3 portrait, Woolf again whispers her view in parentheses amid *his* lively talk: "(he leapt up his knees & clasped them in agony—he is never still a moment—he clenches his fists—he flings himself this way & that; he sprang up to go, as if he were 22, not 74 as L. remarked. What life, what vitality! What immense nervous spring! That perhaps is his genius . . .)" (*D* 4: 107).

Woolf's June 29 portrait of old Katharine Furse reveals how hard she works to transform suffering old age into life more vigorous and free:

> Where had the handsome Katharine gone: she who strode; had firm red cheeks; & was decisive, masterly, controlled even in the great trench [?] of her unhappiness? Heavens, what an injury life inflicts! To have replaced that dashing youth with this almost intolerable look of suffering: a grudging look; a scraped bare look; the ugly poor woman look. By dint of arrangement, by looking through half closed eyes I could, as the evening wore on & the light faded[,] piece together something fine: her eyes; small but penetrating; her gestures—they are still free & bold. . . . What is fine is that she conceals nothing; has no shrinking left; has been wrung & mangled out of the softnesses & sensibilities. . . . To harden to blunt to coarsen that is the worst damage age—& I daresay she's only 8 years older

than I am—can inflict.... Then Leonard came in, in his grey suit & blue tie, sunburnt; & I felt that we are still vigorous & young. (*D* 4: 112–13)

In October, caught up now in *Flush* and with the start of another literary experiment, Woolf declares: "how possessed I am with the feeling that now, age 50, I'm just poised to shoot forth quite free straight & undeflected my bolts whatever they are.... I dont believe in ageing. I believe in forever altering one's aspect to the sun. Hence my optimism" (*D* 4: 125). And on November 10, she confesses that "I dont think we've ever been so happy.... And so intimate, & so completely entire, I mean L. & I. If it could only last like this another 50 years" (*D* 4: 130).

Leonard completes. Roger Fry inspires. Conversation comforts. And writing (including diary-writing) helps to order and restore. Woolf's resurgence comes, too, perhaps from the fact that from January through July, as she strains to reimagine her *Second Common Reader* essays, notions for other works begin to store in her mind. From the start, *Flush: A Biography* serves as a respite from more draining work. As she struggled to finish *The Waves* during the summer of 1931, Woolf immersed herself in eight volumes of Elizabeth Barrett Browning's letters. She starts her mock biography of Elizabeth's beloved cocker spaniel, Flush, when she finally completes her novel, for on September 16, 1931, she writes to ask for a photo of Vita's spaniel, Henry, telling Vita it relates to "a little escapade by means of wh. I hope to stem the ruin we shall suffer from the failure of The Waves" (*L* #2436, 4: 380).

The Waves, of course, succeeds beyond the Woolfs' grandest hopes, and perhaps on this momentum, she turns from escapade to serious literary criticism. Her own *Second Common Reader* portraits could stand beside Lytton's 1931 *Portraits in Miniature and Other Essays*—and also beside Desmond MacCarthy's 1931 *Portraits* and 1932 *Criticism*. But she keeps *Flush* in mind. On March 17, 1932, she writes to thank Vita for the spaniel photo and asks if she can keep it and possibly use it in her "story" (*L* #2556, 5: 35), and on her last night in Greece in early May she preserves in her diary the joyous freedom she will grant *Flush* in the fall—a vision that recalls Princess Daisy's dog, Wolff, from the year before. "I had the vision, in Aegina, of an uncivilized, hot new season to be brought into our lives," Woolf tells her diary, "—how yearly we shall come here, with a tent, escaping England, & sloughing the respectable skin; & all the tightness & formality of London; & fame, & wealth."[4]

On July 31, 1932, Woolf admits to John Lehmann that she "nibble[s] at Flush" but must correct her proofs of the *Second Common Reader* (*L* #2615, 5: 83).

When the *Reader* finally goes to the printer on August 29, she turns to *Flush* once more as respite, as tonic—as she did the year before. "A happy lively summer this—& I enjoy my freak of writing Flush," she ends her September 2 entry, "—& think it a good idea—this easy indolent writing once in a way—to let my brain cool" (*D* 4: 123). It cools well, for Woolf no longer needs morning diary-writing as she breezes through Flush's tale.

She writes only two diary entries in September, the first, the above, touting her joy in writing *Flush*; the second, September 16, when she *does* need her diary to cope with repugnant trespass. This entry opens: "I'm in such a tremor that I've botched the last—penultimate chapter of Flush . . . & can scarcely sit still, & must therefore scribble here, making myself form my letters" (*D* 4: 123). The cause? Wishart uses Leonard's photograph of her instead of Lenare's, and Leonard's photo shows her legs and makes her feel "my privacy is invaded . . . & I am revealed to the world (1,000 at most) as a plain dowdy old woman" (*D* 4: 124). Being looked at again stalls her. However, she writes through her distress in this entry, and in early October comes a powerful new flood of creation that turns her from *Flush* to something harder.

As noted above, she thinks occasionally of *Flush* from January to July. More often, however, her mind broods on (and stores) material for the book she calls a sequel to *A Room of One's Own*. The 1932 diary allows us to watch this work, called "A Tap [or Knock] on the Door," transform from a sequel essay to the experimental turn-and-turn-about "essay-novel," The Pargiters, by year's end. In her 1932 diary's first entry, "A Tap" is part of the "programme" Woolf sets forth. "And I want to write another 4 novels: Waves, I mean; & the Tap on the Door," she writes on January 13 (*D* 4: 63). On February 12, when she should be finishing her essay on Donne, she admits:

> My mind is set running upon A Knock on the Door (whats its name?) owing largely to reading "[H. G.] Wells on Woman"—how she must be ancillary & decorative in the world of the future, because she has been tried, in 10 years, & has not proved anything. So in this mood I record Mary's telling me last night how she loved cigars; but Jack refuses to let her smoke them—against his idea of what his wife should do—silly affectation—or to let her dress in a dress cut low at the back. Cant go out with you in that frock. Go & put on another. Its indecent—yet will praise Diana [Cooper] for wearing the same. "I threw everything out of the window once" she said. "He treats us—Barbara & me—as if we were tame

leopards—pets belonging to him." As indeed they do, since neither has a penny except of Jack's earning & giving. (*D* 4: 75)

Five days later, Woolf is "quivering & itching to write my—whats it to be called?—'Men are like that?'—no thats too patently feminist: the sequel then, for which I have collected enough powder to blow up St Pauls. It is to have 4 pictures" (*D* 4: 77). She presses herself, however, to "go on with the C. Reader—for one thing, by way of proving my credentials" (*D* 4: 77).

At the end of February, when Trinity College, Cambridge, invites her to follow in her father's footsteps (and Desmond MacCarthy's) and give the prestigious Clark Lectures, "A Tap on the Door" and women figure in her complex response. "But I shall refuse," she tells her February 29 entry, "because how could I write 6 lectures . . . without giving up a year to criticism; without becoming a functionary; without sealing my lips when it comes to tilting at Universities; without putting off my Knock at the Door" (*D* 4: 79). In her next entry, she longs "only for freedom" to write that book (*D* 4: 80). Revealingly, she views the Clark Lectures in sexual terms, as an undesired pregnancy: "I should be impregnated with the lecturing manner: its jocosity, its emphasis; then I should be jaded by the time I approached a tap" (*D* 4: 80).

The Greek terrain (so like Cornwall) proves more fertile than Cambridge.[5] Woolf whispers in parentheses in her May 2 entry "(I'm thinking of the book again)," after noting that "the male virtues are never for themselves, but to be paid for. This introduces another element into their psychology—to be paid for: what will pay. This can be sublimated but the alloy remains" (*D* 4: 95). And in her next entry, on her last night in Greece, she confesses, "Oh but I've thought too much, about my little book. . . . I'm subterraneously sunk in scenes . . . make up arguments, see pictures, keep dropping something new into the cauldron, which must bubble as richly as possible before its poured & stilled & hardened" (*D* 4: 96). In short, her well fills, her cauldron bubbles. On her return, "What to do about . . . women; my book on professions," is part of her May 25 despair (*D* 4: 102).

On September 16, as she takes control of the photo violation, she pens the words used in my epigraph that capture her year's journey to date: her need and wish "to be made supple, & to let the juice of usual things, talk, character, seep through me, quietly, involuntarily before I say—Stop, & take out my pen" (*D* 4: 124). Her diary has helped her to salve both exhaustion and loss. It has brought her "the juice of usual things, talk, character." On October 2, she prepares to stop (and to turn inward). "I want to shuffle off this loose living randomness: people; reviews; fame; all the glittering scales; & be withdrawn; & concentrated," she declares (*D* 4: 125).

Mitchell Leaska reports that on October 11, Woolf, "with an almost fresh manuscript volume before her, dipped her pen and wrote 'THE PARGITERS: An Essay based upon a paper read to the London/National Society for Women's Service'" (*The Pargiters* xvi). The *Second Common Reader* is published two days later, but Woolf tells her diary, "I havent give [*sic*] it a thought, being entirely absorbed in my Essay" (*D* 4: 128). By November 2, she has "entirely remodeled" her essay: "Its to be an Essay-Novel, called the Pargiters—& its to take in everything, sex, education, life &c; & come, with the most powerful & agile leaps, like a chamois across precipices from 1880 to here & now" (*D* 4: 129). Her high spirits here recall her 1924 diary, wherein she pictures herself and Leonard as Attic goats leaping over precipices—a far cry from the terrifying 1920 diary figure of life as "a little strip of pavement over an abyss" (*D* 2: 308–09, 72).

Creation now floods, as her continuing words reveal: "I have been in such a haze & dream & intoxication, declaiming phrases, seeing scenes, as I walk up Southampton Row that I can hardly say I have been alive at all, since the 10th Oct. Everything is running of its own accord into the stream, as with Orlando" (*D* 4: 129).

In late May, when Woolf analyzed her depression, she suggested her brain was "jaded with the conflict within of two types of thought, the critical, the creative" (*D* 4: 103). The Pargiters resolves the conflict by joining the modes, by alternating critical essay with illustrating novel: the essay-novel.[6] Woolf now presses her turn-and-turn-about tack into one whole, and she feels the move's merit. Her November 2 entry continues, "I must brood & chew & dream, & be entirely natural, feeling as I do for the first time that this book is important. Why do I feel this, & I never felt it in the least about the others?" (*D* 4: 130).

She opens her next entry, November 10, to report she has completed "the child scene—the man exposing himself," the second "chapter" of the novel portion of The Pargiters and one of this work's most memorable scenes. Woolf dares now to write the body. By December 17, in the diary's next-to-last entry, Woolf reveals that she has "almost written out my first fury—234 typewritten pages since Oct. 10th—& shall put my brain to rest for a few days at Monks House" (*D* 4: 132).

The downs "backed" this new volume, she tells her October 2 entry: "[W]hat a free life that is" (*D* 4: 125). In truth, the country nurtures her across the year. On February 8, she and Leonard walk "among those primeval downs, like a Heal bed, L. said, so comfortable" (*D* 4: 74). On March 24, nature moves her to reject

Carrington's end: "[T]omorrow is Good Friday & therefore we are at Rodmell on the loveliest spring day: soft: a blue veil in the air torn by birds voices. I am glad to be alive & sorry for the dead: cant think why Carrington killed herself & put an end to all this.... And the country is lovelier & lovelier... still with great empty spaces, where I want to walk, alone, & come to terms with my own head. Another book? What? Merciful to be free, entirely to think this out" (*D* 4: 85). On July 21, when Adrian's "suicidal face" haunts her dreams, "And my head aches; & my back; & I'm sapped; wilted. Never mind," she writes, her patented diary dismissal. "I shall lie in the cool at Monks House" (*D* 4: 118).

Woolf links *Flush* to country coolness. And why not, for she strips her dog of culture[7] and lets him run happily, nakedly free. In August, Woolf tells her diary, "[T]he downs this windy sunny day looked wild & remote; & I could rethink them into uncultivated land again" (*D* 4: 120). She closes her 1932 diary with the promise of country aid. "Yes, today, Dec. 19th, Monday, I have written myself to the verge of total extinction," she begins emphatically (even melodramatically), bringing this diary full circle to its January start, when she could not "heave another word on to the wall." However, she then continues: "Praised be I can stop & wallow in coolness & downs, & let the wheels of my mind—how I beg them to do this—cool & slow & stop altogether. I shall take up Flush again to cool myself" (*D* 4: 132).

What an easy, assured diarist Virginia Woolf is in 1932. "Oh but this is, as I always say," she casually starts this diary—as if smack in the midst of talk (*D* 4: 62). "Only the most hardened scribbler could attempt to write in the Orient Express," she crows on May 10 and then pastes her twenty-eight smaller white travel diary pages into her larger, blue-paged diary book (*D* 4: 99). She continues to *link* her entries with "And" (9 entries), "Oh" (4), "Now" (3), "So" (2), and "Yes" (4), and she closes her 1932 diary on perhaps the most euphoric note of all her diaries. She has reason to feel in high sail. *The Waves*, her most difficult book, has surpassed all her previous works in sales, and she has followed this novel with her much admired *Second Common Reader* essays.

Perhaps Woolf flies too high at the close of this diary. She begins the year with a poignant question and a forecast: "Can we count on another 20 years?... I want to write another 4 novels: Waves, I mean; & the Tap on the Door; & to go through English literature, like a string through cheese, or rather like some industrious insect, eating its way from book to book, from Chaucer to Lawrence. This is a programme" (*D* 4: 63). We know what she cannot know on January 13, 1932: that she does not have twenty years before her, but only nine, and that she will write just two more novels, not four. But she will complete *Flush*, "Tap on the Door" (in fiction and nonfiction), and a biography she does not yet conceive of, and her *Second Common Reader* will forward the march through English literature that *Between the Acts* and "Anon" will reprise. But she cannot know this on December 19, 1932. On that day, all seems afloat:

> By Heaven, I have written 60,320 words since Oct. 11th. I think this [The Pargiters] must be far the quickest going of any of my books: comes far ahead of Orlando or The Lighthouse. But then those 60 thousand will have to be sweated & dried into 30 or 40 thousand—a great grind to come. Never mind. I have secured the outline & fixed a shape for the rest. I feel, for the first time, No I mustn't take risks crossing the road, till the book is done. . . . to me it is so important. . . . I have never lived in such a race, such a dream, such a violent impulsion & compulsion—scarcely seeing anything but the Pargiters. (*D* 4: 132–33)

Virginia Woolf's 1933–1934 Diary

> "Being headachy after Pargiters & Goldsmith & ever so many people I have spent the whole morning reading old diaries, & am now (10 to 1) much refreshed. This is by way of justifying these many written books. . . . The diary amuses me."
>
> (July 7, 1933; *D* 4: 166–67)

"Never mind" could be the motto of Virginia Woolf's 1933–1934 diary. Little seems to daunt her, for as the many water tropes across this diary attest, she persists in high sail from October 1932. She rallies from the long strain of *The Waves* and *Second Common Reader* compression, and creative flood after flood propels her. Now "very wary, very adept," as she acknowledges in this diary's second entry, she summons her "cohorts" as she broaches the shoals of form (*D* 4: 135, 167). Nature—that great cohort—sustains her, and diary questions press her on. Talk, too, floats her as she plies her turn-and-turn-about tack. In January 1933, she even constructs her own "perfect writing board, with pen tray attached" so as never to see a "sudden sentence dissipate itself all for lack of a pen handy" (*D* 4: 141). Woolf takes on catches of books at the same time she seals her philosophy of anonymity. Should it surprise us that every two or three months she seeks out a diary—including twice her own—as she moves forward in *The Years*?

Woolf's public writing dominates this 1933–1934 diary, kept in a sturdy, large diary book, but now with a floral cover.[8] Ninety entries log the 503 days from December 23, 1932, through May 9, 1934—an entry, on average, every 5 or 6 days. When 1933 turns to 1934, pragmatic Woolf declares it "too wasteful" to begin another diary book "& leave all this blue paper blank" and sails on (*D* 4: 200), an act that parallels the continued flow of The Pargiters (*The Years*).

But first she must dispatch *Flush*. In fact, she opens her diary on December 23, 1932, in "dejected rambling misery," in one of her "grey welters,"[9] over the sad state of *Flush*. "[H]aving just read over the 30,000 words of Flush & come to the conclusion that they won't do," she turns to her diary (*D* 4: 133). She cannot see how to make "anything" of this mock biography: "its too slight & too serious" and would take a month's "hard work" to set right. "Never mind," she ends the entry—her habitual firm dismissal (*D* 4: 134). Eight days later, her second entry shows her deep in the "hard work": "I am so tired of polishing off Flush—such a pressure on the brain is caused by doing ten pages daily—that I am taking a morning off" (*D* 4: 134). Morning *diary*-writing will refresh her once more.

In this diary, visions of freedom again mix with the water tropes. On January 3, 1933, Woolf confesses she has tried to "re-write that abominable dog Flush in 13 days, so as to be free—oh heavenly freedom—to write The Pargiters" (*D* 4: 139). In her next entry, two days later, having rewritten *Flush*'s Whitechapel scene for the third time and needing, therefore, to "disport" herself on her "free blue [diary] page," she declares that recovery of her ability to *read* not only fuels her but also mediates the literary jealousy that plagued her in 1921. She believes envy at David (Bunny) Garnett's success will not:

> slink out its green paws.... if only because I'm in sublime reading fettle: seriously I believe that the strain of The Waves weakened my concentration for months—& then all that article compressing for the C[ommon].R[eader]. I am now at the height of my powers in that line, & have read, with close & powerful attention, some 12 or 15 books since I came here [to the country]. What a joy—what a sense as of a Rolls Royce engine once more purring its 70 miles an hour in my brain: so that if Bunny's book is a good one, there will be another stretch of road ahead of me for a few days.... I am also encouraged to read by the feeling that I am on the flood of creativeness in The Pargiters—what a liberation that gives one—as if everything added to that torrent—all books become fluid & swell the stream. (*D* 4: 142)

All books . . . swell the stream—including her diary and those of others.

On January 21, 1933, she remains hard at work on *Flush*. She opens her next entry, January 26, to exalt *Flush*'s close. "Nobody can say I dont take trouble with my little stories," she insists—that "Nobody" (shades of her diary mother, Fanny Burney) most notably herself (*D* 4: 145). She corrects the proof in late April 1933 and learns in May that the British Book Society will "probably take Flush" as a fall selection (*D* 4: 160). In August, the United States Book-of-the-Month Club follows (*D* 4: 175). On September 2, she treats *Flush* as a pot boiler and continues to see herself in full sail: "We have steadied the old ship & sail through blue days again. L. is having the new pond made, the old one re-grouted, & is going to pave the front garden. Flush, I think with some pleasure, has made these extravagances possible. We should net £2,000 from that six months dogged & dreary grind. What will people say of that little book I wonder, without great anxiety" (*D* 4: 176–77).

When *Flush* appears in October, she once more says, in effect, never mind: "Well now I must let this slip over me without paying it any attention. I must concentrate on The Pargiters" (*D* 4: 181).

That she views *Flush* as a mere "rill"—or small brook—aids her response (*D* 4: 181). In fact, she treats public response as mere "rain drops" (*D* 4: 186). In truth, she can hardly *feel* these raindrops, for her novel floods on. This work on "the sexual lives of women" pushes out all before it. In the weeks after its first appearance (in the bath) on January 20, 1931, it threatens to blot out *The Waves*. It overwhelms *Flush* in October 1932 and looks to do so again at the start of the 1933–1934 diary. "[M]y thoughts turn with excitement to The Pargiters, for I long to feel my sails blow out, & to be careering with Elvira,[10] Maggie & the rest over the whole of human life," Woolf confesses in her second diary entry (*D* 4: 134). In her next entry, January 3, 1933, the work overtakes the *diary* as well—as it will do several times. Describing her love of masks and the disorientation they give, Woolf whispers: "(here I lapsed for 5 minutes into Elvira's thoughts about civilization . . .)" (*D* 4: 139). At the end of March, she finds herself once more intertwined with Elvira Pargiter (*D* 4: 147–48).

For this morphing Pargiter work pulses forth. On January 5, 1933, Woolf is still "on the flood of creativeness" with this essay-novel (*D* 4: 142). June 13 finds her again in "full flood," as she is June 20 and July 20 (*D* 4: 162, 165, 168). Her first entry of 1934 shows her "divinely happy" during her country sojourn "& pressed with ideas—another full flood of Pargiters. . . . floating rather rapturously in the Raid scene."[11] In mid-March 1934, she is "on the crest of the Kitty

Eleanor scene" and feels "some magnificent chapters wait me" (*D* 4: 204). Five days later, when Tavistock Square repairs and fights with Nelly keep her from getting "into flood," she still records a "brilliant flash . . . how to compact the rather fluid Eleanor."[12] And through it all Woolf records her joy.

In truth, she controls this flood "very adeptly" with her turn-and-turn-about writing tack. She describes the method in her diary's third entry, January 3, 1933: "indeed, its a good discipline, this new one, of forcing one's brain the other way for a time—see how vigorously it spurts back" (*D* 4: 139). On February 2, she revises The Pargiter's first section (titled "1880") "rather more completely than usual" and decides to leave out the essays, "compacting them in the text" (*D* 4: 146). In early January, in contrast, she had pictured the book as "a series of great balloons, linked by straight narrow passages of narrative" (*D* 4: 142). She now compresses her essay-balloons.

By April 6, she has written herself out: "I've brought it down to Elvira in bed—the scene I've had in my mind ever so many months, but I cant write it now. Its the turn of the book. It needs a great shove to swing it round on its hinges" (*D* 4: 149). So she decides to abandon the sail for two months and write instead on Oliver Goldsmith, the essayist *and* novelist, poet *and* playwright. She may seek literary transfusion from him as well as rest. All books "swell the stream," as she suggests in January, and The Pargiters next takes a turn toward drama.

In late August, her Goldsmith essay done, Woolf decides to write an essay on *another* playwright and novelist, Ivan Turgenev, "for I intend to space the arduous sections of The P.s with serene criticism" (*D* 4: 174). Turgenev, she notes, kept a diary for Bazarov, the lead character in his novel *Fathers and Sons* (*D* 4: 173). A diary furthers *his* fiction as well as hers.

She finishes her Turgenev essay in late October, and on November 25, she plans to write on "literary painter" Walter Sickert, to her mind a great novelist, poet, and biographer in paint. She wishes to fill a "lull" in her novel: "I mean theyre sitting in Kensington Gds & I want a breath before I go on to Kitty's Party" (*D* 4: 190). And once more the novel suffuses the *diary*: "(I at once make her say I oughn't to have been doing this kind of thing & then I see Lord Lasswade. But stop.)" By December 17, she finishes chapter 4 of the novel ("1908"), and: "The question that now fronts me as a writer is the war chapter. That I shall leave for a few days to simmer. No doubt the brew will spout out suddenly at Rodmell" (*D* 4: 193). It does, and by January 16, 1934, she is "floating rather rapturously in the Raid scene" and notices that her *diary* entry "is rather the style of Here & Now" (*D* 4: 199).

As the above passages hint, questions of form seep through this diary as Woolf's careering work-in-progress moves from essay, to essay-novel, to novel. Questions propel this diary: 131 questions in the 90 entries, 53 of these on writing (20 directly on The Pargiters/The Years). Woolf seeks depth, breadth, and new combinations for this work. "Isnt it all too quick, too thin, too surface bright?" she asks herself on April 6, 1933 (*D* 4: 149). On April 25, she presses further: "I must be bold & adventurous. . . . I mean, The Waves going on simultaneously with Night & Day. Is this possible? . . . But I like these problems, & anyhow theres a wind & a vigour in this naturalness. . . . It should include satire, comedy, poetry, narrative, & what form is to hold them all together? Should I bring in a play, letters, poems?" (*D* 4: 151–52).

On August 16, "nibbling at The P.s & thinking Oh Lord how am I ever going to pull all that into shape!" Woolf again declares, "Never mind," and turns to Turgenev: "I want to discuss Form. . . . T. says one must find a new form for the old subject. . . . The essential thing in a scene is to be preserved. How do you know what this is?" (*D* 4: 172).

Woolf finds similar traits in the three artists she picks as recharge for her novel. Goldsmith, Turgenev, and Sickert all were cosmopolitan, she suggests, "Citizens of the World," as Goldsmith called himself. All kept themselves aloof from society and created art in several forms. Turgenev, whom she introduces in her published essay with words from the Goncourt brothers' diary, was one of the few writers who could "combine the fact and the vision"; he also suppressed the egotistical "I" in favor of the "I" who "sees as far as he can impartially and honestly, without wishing to plead a cause or to justify himself" (*E* 6: 11, 14). Sickert, she finds, "composes his picture . . . just as carefully as Turgenev, of whom he sometimes reminds me" (*E* 6: 42). In fact, she closes her "Walter Sickert: A Conversation" with a vision of Sickert in sail that mirrors her own present state—a view, too, of outer world and inner art and their ideal mesh:

> From [Sickert's] photograph you might take him for a highly distinguished lawyer with a nautical bent; the sort of man who settles a complicated case at the Law Courts, then changes into an old serge suit, pulls a yachting-cap with a green peak over his eyes and buffets about the North Sea with a volume of Aeschylus in his pocket. In the intervals of hauling up and down the mainsail he wipes the salt from his eyes, whips out a canvas and paints a divinely lovely picture of Dieppe, Harwich, or the Cliffs of Dover. That is the sort of man I take Walter Sickert to be. (*E* 6: 46)

But questions of form still press. By mid-April 1934, after seeing *Macbeth*, Woolf ponders Shakespeare and, once more, the outer and inner:

> [T]he play demands coming to the surface—hence insists upon a reality wh. the novel need not have, but perhaps should have. Contact with the surface. Coming to the top. This is working out my theory of the different levels in writing, & how to combine them: for I begin to think the combination necessary. This particular relation with the surface is imposed on the dramatist of necessity: how far did it influence Sh[akespea]re? Idea that one cd work out a theory of fiction &c on these lines: how many levels attempted. whether kept to or not (*D* 4: 207).

Woolf's water mindset so dominates this diary that she sees the country, the Hogarth Press, and even people through this lens. She opens her country holiday at Rodmell on July 30, 1933, to ask "how far places influence one's mood.... I am organising life here, & so far rather well. Reading & walking & swimming into lucid depths, powerfully—thats how I put it" (*D* 4: 170). Thirteen days later, she collapses in the country—as so often occurs: "I went to bed for 2 days & slept I daresay 7 hours, visiting the silent realms again.... am pulled under; now is this some odd effort; the sub-conscious pulling me down into her?" (*D* 4: 171–72).

The Hogarth Press changes guard once more in February 1933—Margaret West for Miss Scott Johnson—but never mind. However, on October 20, Leonard ill with flu, herself "spattered" with *Flush* response, Woolf tells her diary, "last night I came to the decision to stop the career of the Hogarth Press.... Here we stop & take a fresh course—We go to Rodmell tomorrow & I shall there broach the new scheme.... to me the Press has lost its spring & balance, & could regain it if it now made a constriction to the old ideals. We might start the magazine."[13] The Press, in short, needs overhaul and a change of course. Perhaps the Press should move to Monk's House, she thinks suggestively, for the country is always linked to nature and the subconscious.

Portraits subside in this diary as Woolf steers her novel. Only twenty-two likenesses of any length appear in the ninety entries. So focused, adept (and awash) now is Woolf that even George Bernard Shaw earns her offhand wave. When the Woolfs lunch with the Shaws on June 16, 1933, Virginia records: "Shaw's paddle actually out of the water. Cutting no ice.... Shaw ... very jaunty, upright—sea green eyes red face.... A man of perfect poise—spring—agility—never to me interesting—no poet, but what an efficient, adept, trained arch & darter! His wires, his spring, at 76 entirely astonishing.... he has the power to make the world his shape—to me not a beautiful shape—thats all" (D 4: 163–64). In short: never mind. She seeks her own shape, her own form.

In September, she shrugs off T. S. Eliot as well when he comes to Rodmell to report his triumph in America and his divorce from Vivien—although she does so with some regret: "He is tight & shiny as a wood louse (I am not writing for publication). But there is well water in him, cold & pure. . . . & if I had time, & if I could move the heavy stone of his self esteem an inch or two higher, I should like to talk out to Tom about writing. Only there's always the reservation—I cant talk about "my writing"; so that talk about his writing palls [?]" (D 4: 178). Alas: never mind.

However, when novelist Stella Benson dies unexpectedly in December at age forty-one, Woolf views her as a fellow sailor whose death, like Katherine Mansfield's, lessens her sail. "A dreary island, she lived on," Woolf notes of Benson's life in a war-torn arena, "talking to Colonels."[14]

If she turns to her essays on Goldsmith, Turgenev, and Sickert for "serenity" (and guidance) amid the tacks and turns of The Pargiters, her diary brings relief even from these essays. On July 7, 1933, "[b]eing headachy after Pargiters and Goldsmith & ever so many people," Woolf spends the entire morning reading her old diaries and finds herself "much refreshed"—and even amused (D 4: 166–67). In September, she reads a book on an important diarist to her, Beatrice Webb, and on November 14, she turns from an invited evening out with Ethel Smyth in favor of an evening in with the "Michael Field diaries" (D 4: 189).

The next month, she turns to her own diaries again, now for another sort of refreshment: "[t]o freshen my memory of the war" (D 4: 193). If her own diaries amused her in July, they now move her: "How close the tears come, again & again; as I read of L. & me at the Green: our quarrels; how he crept into my bed with a little purse, & so on: how we reckoned our income & I was given tea free for a treat. The sense of all that floating away for ever down the stream, unknown for ever" (D 4: 193). Her diary, of course, helps to stave this loss, preserves the years.[15]

In late January and early February 1934, during another headache and now a bad one, Woolf tries to read Arthur Young's travel diary in France in 1787, 1788, and 1789 but finds "too many revolutions on hand," what with her own Great War chapter afloat and the news of Russian and Spanish upheavals in the daily press. She declares, "I want turnips & peace & settlement" (D 4: 201). She seeks now a new biography of diarist Dorothy Wordsworth. On May 8, 1934, in this diary's next-to-last entry, we learn that Woolf tracks down Swift, Stella, and Vanessa during her Irish holiday. She wishes to see with her own eyes sites linked to Swift's *Journal to Stella* (which she celebrated in a 1925 essay and revised for the *Second Common Reader*).¹⁶

Almost all Woolf's "cohorts" are in place, the "props" that float her (including diarists and many diaries). However, a squall and a cloud loom on the horizon to cause a slight alert beyond that directed at the ongoing haze of her novel's form. On April 28, 1933, Ethel Smyth introduces the Woolfs to her friend, the German-Jewish conductor Bruno Walter. The next day, painting his diary portrait, Woolf observes that:

> he cant get "the poison" as he called it of Hitler out of him. "You must not think of the Jews" he kept on saying "You must think of this awful reign of intolerance. You must think of the whole state of the world. It is terrible—terrible. That this meanness, that this pettiness, should be possible! Our Germany—which I loved—with our tradition—our culture—We are now a disgrace." Then he told us how you cant talk above a whisper. There are spies everywhere.... We must refuse to meet any German. We must say that they are uncivilized. We will not trade with them or play with them—we must make them feel themselves outcasts—not by fighting them; by ignoring them. (*D* 4: 153)

An accurate historical summary—and thoughts for *Three Guineas* to come.

Should we worry, too, that Woolf continues to turn from Ethel Smyth across this diary? Smyth no longer serves for Woolf as a kind of "Old Virginia" in the flesh—that is, as a model of productive old age. Woolf's break with Smyth turns, as noted earlier, on that sensitive issue of praise. With *Flush*'s publication in October 1933, Woolf seems to shed her ego (just as Flush sheds his fur). On October 29, Woolf claims her "philosophy of anonymity" (*D* 4: 186). A month later, she makes in her diary "a footnote about the soul":

> I think I've got rid of vanity: of Virginia. Oh what a riddance. I've not read an article on me by a man called Peel in the Criterion. I feel this a great liberation. Then I need not be that self. Then I can be entirely private. I have cut the string that ties me to that quivering bag of nerves—all its gratifications & acute despair. Time I did. It is another great discovery. One sees people lunging & striking at a thing like a straw horse & its not me at all. I sit back in comfort & look round. I wonder if Nessa has always been like this? It is calming. It is dignified. One does not seek uneasily for opinions on oneself. How have I come to this? Will it last? How will it work? ... A rough note only which I meant to make some time ago. (*D* 4: 191)

Thus when Smyth arrives on March 14, 1934, "to deposit her horrid gnawed bone or sucked chocolate—C. St John's praise [of Ethel] to wit—at my feet," Woolf recoils (D 4: 204). "A very ruthless shoving woman in some ways," Woolf now declares, seeing Smyth no longer as an older self who might be teased or argued out of ego but now as a pathetic boasting bully. In "cut[ting] the string" to "vanity. . . . that self. . . . that quivering bag of nerves," Woolf also cuts the tie to Smyth, who now seems less an encouraging older spirit than a praise-obsessed ego to be left behind. Woolf yearns now to be "entirely private." "I will not be 'famous' 'great,'" she insists on October 29, 1933. "I will go on adventuring, changing, opening my mind & my eyes, refusing to be stamped & stereotyped. The thing is to free ones self; to let it find its dimensions, not be impeded" (D 4: 187). And Smyth now, sadly, impedes.[17]

"Old Virginia" now must become a projected spirit once more—rather like that of William Shakespeare. The diary that starts in the "grey welters," over the sad state of *Flush*, ends with Woolf's May 9, 1934, visit to Shakespeare's tomb—shades of *Night and Day*—where she finds all she seeks:

> All the flowers were out in Sh[akespea]re's garden. . . . I cannot without more labour than my roadrunning mind can compass describe the queer impression of sunny impersonality. Yes, everything seemed to say, this was Shakespeare's, had he sat & walked; but you wont find me not exactly in the flesh. He is serenely absent-present; both at once; radiating round one; yes; in the flowers, in the old hall, in the garden; but never to be pinned down. . . . Now I think Shre was very happy in this, that there was no impediment of fame, but his genius flowed out of him. (D 4: 219–20)

As Woolf's genius flows from her. As the outward war rises, the 1933–1934 diary surges forward, a diary of flood and liberation, as a "very wary" but "adept" Woolf cuts her ties to ego, to Ethel Smyth, and even (finally) to Nelly Boxall. Diaries and diarists replace them as Woolf tacks toward absence-presence, for this diary preserves the paradox: while she jettisons individual ego "all books . . . swell the stream."

Michael Field's *Works and Days*

In November 1933, Virginia Woolf refuses an invited evening out to hear Ethel Smyth's "March of Women" and Rebecca West speak on married women's right to earn in order to "sleep over the fire" and read T. S. Eliot's criticism "& Michael

Field diaries, alone thank God" (*D* 4: 189). The 1933 *Works and Days: From the Journal of Michael Field* held substantial allure. It offered another dual-voiced diary, like that of the Goncourt brothers that proved so suggestive to Woolf in 1917,[18] but now a dual-voiced *women's* diary and that of English women writers, as well.

Katherine[19] Bradley and Edith Cooper, aunt and niece, published poetry, a play, and verse drama under the pen name "Michael Field." In 1933, Woolf seeks to *combine* poetry, play, narrative, essay, and more in her own work-in-progress, *The Years*. The "Michael Field diaries" also offered a vivid description of Walter Sickert, the painter Woolf plans to sketch. Bradley and Cooper even relished (and recorded) tea with Roger Fry and Goldsworthy Lowes Dickinson before Woolf knew that joy. Aunt and niece seem to know everyone in British literary, theater, and art circles from 1875 to 1914—the period covered in *Works and Days*.[20] Even more to the point, their *Journal* revealed the trials and triumphs of English women writers and offered Woolf another lived version of "the years."

Katherine Bradley was born in Birmingham in 1846,[21] the daughter of a wealthy tobacco merchant who died of cancer before she was two years old. On Katherine's fourteenth birthday, in 1860, her older sister, Emma, married the Kenilworth merchant James Cooper, and in 1862, Emma gave birth to their first child, Edith. Mrs. Bradley and fifteen-year-old Katherine had moved in to assist the young family—aid needed even more when Emma Cooper became a permanent invalid after the birth of her second daughter in 1863.

Katherine must have seemed more like an older sister than an aunt to Edith Cooper. Katherine was "ardent for knowledge," according to painter Sturge Moore, the *Journal*'s coeditor (xv). Emma Donoghue reports that as a young girl Katherine was prey to "gloomy fits" and was "notorious for her deep blushes"—much like teenage Virginia Woolf (14–15). From her earliest days Katherine adored poetry, wrote letters in rhyme, and cherished Sir Walter Scott's "Lady of the Lake."

Mrs. Bradley dies in 1868, leaving Katherine an inheritance that she immediately uses to enroll in the Collège de France at Paris, where she falls in love with Alfred Gérente, a sculptor and stained-glass artist much older than she. He dies, leaving her heartbroken and marking his death in the diary. She returns to England and, in 1874, enrolls in the new Newnham College for women. However, sixteen years later, when Newnham invites her back in triumph as a published poet, Bradley tells the *Journal*: "The green scum of the ditches affects me as I drive to Newnham. Beholding it, I feel how vain it is to try to belong to Oxford" (127).

In late 1874, Katherine turns also for guidance and support to John Ruskin's utopian project, the Guild of St George. She is twenty-eight. Ruskin's letters from 1875 to 1880, included in *Works and Days*, showed Woolf the obstacles a Victorian woman poet faced in starting out. "I shall be very proud of you for a Companion; being especially pleased by what you say of the sorrow of independence and the comfort of obedience," Ruskin writes to Bradley on January 17, 1876. "I see from your sister's letter that you amuse—or exert—yourself in verse writing. Some of the best poetry of the modern times is by women (Mrs. Browning, Miss Ingelow and Miss Proctor)" (145–46). These last words hold promise and, in fact, Bradley has already sent him her first book of poems, the 1875 *New Minnesinger*, with its homage to Elizabeth Barrett Browning.

His next letter, January 20, 1876, establishes the condescending tone that will mark all his remaining letters. "Dear Miss Catherine," he writes, misspelling her name, "You would not laugh at my not having read your book if you knew—as I hope you will soon know—how much too serious my life is to be spent in reading poetry (unless prophetic.) But I did accidentally open the *Minnesinger* and liked a bit or two of it—and I don't think I threw it into the waste-paper basket—generally the receptacle without so much as opening, of all books of poetry sent me by the authors" (146–47).

When Katherine writes a sonnet to him in early 1877, he responds from Venice: "I can only answer your beautiful letter with questions. Chiefly is that lovely sonnet really your own" (151). But two months later he advises her "to give up dreaming, and writing verses as far as you possibly can. By way of soft fall from such a Paradise, could you not take up any poet whom you really delighted in, and consider what he has said for or against St. George's principles—and what other sound advice he has given touching human life" (154).

Matters erode from there, for Ruskin sinks to abuse when she writes him at Christmas 1877 that she has lost her faith in God and finds comfort in a dog. "I scarcely know how to deal with you. You are *too* stupid—saying I don't care for your grief—You double-feathered little goose!!" he rails from Oxford. "I have no time to-day to write more—and am really too scornful of you—and of the egotism and shallowness which can be consoled by the love of a dog and by an entirely lying jingle of a song about fairies, for the loss of a God! . . . Yet I love dogs fifty times better than you do—that's another of your stupid misunderstandings" (156–57). Two days later he continues: "I have at once to put you out of the St. George's Guild—which *primarily* refuses atheists—not because they are wicked but because they are fools.... You think YOURSELF abused indeed just now—but that is simply because you thought yourself very clever—and are astonished that I think nothing of your poetry—and less than nothing of your power of thought" (157–58).

In the end, Bradley writes "False" on her Ruskin letters; nevertheless, she keeps them. She might have known all would end badly as early as June 1876, when she came to the defense of the Irish feminist writer Frances Power Cobbe, whom Ruskin chastised. "It is not the wrongness of her views, but her insolence in proclaiming them—contrary to St. Paul's order. 'I suffer not a woman to teach,'" Ruskin writes to Bradley, and when she still defends Cobbe, he elaborates three months later: "You were quite right in much of the feeling you had towards Miss Cobbe; she is a very worthy and conscientious person, but has the unfortunate modern habit of talking violently of things she knows nothing whatever about. I only called her a clattering saucepan—a saucepan is a very good thing in its place; but not when it clatters" (148–49).

Bradley's niece, Edith Cooper, likely helped her deal with Ruskin's dismissal. Edith began to write at age ten (*Works and Days* 314). She is seventeen in 1879, in the midst of this high-handed correspondence. While making beds one day, niece and aunt decide to dedicate their lives to poetry:

> It was deep April, and the morn
> Shakespeare was born;
> The world was on us, pressing sore;
> My Love and I took hands and swore
> Against the world, to be
> Poets and lovers evermore

In 1881, they publish their first joint work, *Bellerophôn*.

George Meredith, the poet, novelist, and friend of Leslie Stephen, offered a more generous and complex form of literary "support" than Ruskin's, but one that, in the end, also will disappoint. In 1889, Bradley and Cooper send Meredith a copy of *Long Ago*, their new volume of poems inspired by the Greek poet Sappho. Meredith's June 12, 1889, reply offers substantial praise. "I have not recently or for years read verse that moved me so for the faultless flow in it and the classic concision," he writes from Box Hill. "It could have come only of the deep love of your poetess [Sappho], combined with genius to express it, such as she would have smiled on. The hedonic philosophy, informed by realist passion, is given in a manner to make it new, almost convincing, as if her blood were in your lines. . . . The volume will be treasured" (*Works and Days* 66–67).

The next year, they send him their new verse drama *The Tragic Mary*, on Mary, Queen of Scots. He offers further praise and commiserates with them as a fellow victim of harsh reviews:

> I have now read your *Tragic Mary*. I have also seen a Review of it, most unjust, to my thinking. Let me hope that such stuff has not wounded. I fancied I was the only one to receive that kind of measure from English Reviewers.—Your verse is abused. I should pronounce it a singularly dramatic, nervous line, credibly uttered to the ear by the speaker, as one reads. Your Mary, who feels "the hailstorm rushing through her blood," and who "never can grow holy among men," is the possible Mary, an arresting study. . . . Of course the book is bleak—and [a] final catastrophe is wanted to close it with reflective emotion following a tragic blow. But I read it with my proper thirst. I put it aside impressed, I retain the sense of poetical power in drama, rare at all times. Once more of the verse, it shows, to my judgment, a measured advance. (*Works and Days* 70–71)

In 1892, when Meredith sends Bradley an inscribed copy of *Modern Love*, she dares to ask whether they might call on him at Flint Cottage. "[W]e are not far away [at Reigate]," she explains. "We can almost hear the bleating of the same lamb" (*Works and Days* 73). Cooper, whose vivid journal descriptions dominate *Works and Days*,[22] provides a detailed portrait of Meredith's home and its owner during their 1892 call. Of their walk in the garden, she notes:

> He and I are side by side—what an opportunity! . . . I speak of the ideal retreat he has in the Chalet and of the fret with which home life wears away the brain-force of women. . . .
>
> He speaks of the hatred between men and women—he has known men who abhorred women, and women who abhorred men. The depth of this sex-enmity can be gauged by men's after-dinner talk. . . . To root out from man the sense of contempt toward woman is the great point to gain, and this can only be done by giving her knowledge of the world and an independent status. Therefore Meredith holds that the labour for the franchise is ill-advised—it exasperates the deep opposition of men;

whereas woman's best course would be quietly to enter the trades and professions, win their independence and then enfranchisement would come as the ripe fruit of their still growth, for which their sex would be ready....

He believes that women have intelligence, distinct from, but equal to, men's, and that there is far deeper likeness in physical strength than appears, owing to the false education and debilitating conditions that mould women. "I do not believe that Nature would choose for breeding a strong and a weak—she wants a strong and a strong." (*Works and Days* 83, 85)

Here is a primary source for Woolf's "On being despised" (*D* 4:271).

Meredith's frank views and kind encouragement surely mean much; however, when he starts to give advice (as well as praise) relations fray. On October 6, 1893, Meredith writes to Bradley rather charmingly of their play *A Question of Memory*: "[I]t is good: I think it should act well. But bear to hear this from me:—I do not find in your dramatic prose the complete ring that there is in the sound and volume of your blank verse lines. In the *Tragic Mary* and *Stephania*, for example. Only by having you beside me and reading to you, could I give the notion of the 'translated' tone of some parts of the dialogue.—I would offer to come to you, but am pressed to work all through the day. Will Michael Field dine with me?" (*Works and Days* 88).

Two years later, again he writes, again no doubt fired by the wish to help: "Now bear with me, I have little praise for the line or the characters of your *Attila*. If you had irony in *aim* you should not have made drama.... Will you come and hear more? I have not time to write a criticism. It seems to me that your present failure comes of the design to do too much. Your naturally splendid dramatic line sinks broken under the burden of satire and stage constrictions" (*Works and Days* 90–91).

Cooper delivers another rich diary entry on this visit: "George faces [Katherine], his eyes on her face nearly the whole two hours and a half. I have time to watch him and listen with a notebook open in my brain" (*Works and Days* 92). She captures his look—"His head is of Elgin marble perfection"—and his "brilliant talk" (92, 99). "You and I are outcasts," he tells them. "We are doing work that is not wanted. I am only alive because I *would live*" (98). Bradley thanks him "for letting us come and for scolding us," yet "One goes away chill," Cooper writes, a creative state Woolf also knew (99).

During an 1896 visit, when Meredith ignores them in favor of a woman critic "who makes three hundred a year 'in picking over *our* work,'" Bradley and Cooper withdraw (102). "With the absorption of age he hardly notices Michael's [Katherine's] hand with a touch," Cooper records; "—he says to me carelessly, 'You will excuse my rising,'—I am silent and bow like a snow-laden tree, while Michael's voice rings out as if a challenge were thrown down, 'Goodbye, Mr. Meredith,'—an alarmed, hurrying 'God bless you'—and we are in the cab with seething hearts" (108).

The breach does not heal, for Meredith writes them on July 26, 1898: "Let me hope that your mood may have softened since you wrote to me: and also that you did not write in such a tone to another" (108). He still tries to buoy them: "Be sure that readers appreciative of animated lines will be keenly sensible of the fact of an existence of hostility to Michael Field.... Refuse to be wounded by the comments: refer your mind to the public which values you, and continue to produce what you can issue with the knowledge that it is good.... If you are in the temper for taking advice, my simple words may be of service" (108–09). They make no comment on this letter.

Perhaps Bradley and Cooper recoil from Meredith because they have known—and continue to know in the 1890s—warmer support. In 1883, Cooper sends Robert Browning her signed review of his volume *Jocoseria*. "You have been very good and patient with my poetry and I thank you heartily," he replies on July 7, 1883, forging a bond that lasts beyond his death in 1889 (*Works and Days* 1). Edith Cooper is twenty-one and Browning seventy-one in 1883; Katherine Bradley is thirty-seven, near the age of Elizabeth Barrett—now dead more than twenty years—when Browning first met her. In homage to Barrett's *Aurora Leigh*, Bradley chose the pen name Arran Leigh for her 1875 *New Minnesinger*. She and Cooper publish their first joint book of poems, the 1881 *Bellerophôn*, under the names Arran and Isla Leigh.[23]

Editor Moore writes that to Browning, "in many unhoped-for ways," Bradley and Cooper must have seemed like "the past returning": "His own work was again studied and pored over by a most distinguished poetess. He was reading verse which he admired and behind which he discovered exceptional gifts of refinement and goodness" (*Works and Days* xxii). After they finally meet in June 1885, Cooper writes to him, "Your belief in us will go on, literally all our days through, goading us and yet keeping us patient in our labour.... If you should find any tricks of style, any individual mannerisms, that break the unity of our work, will you be a critic as stern as you have been disinterested? We love our work too earnestly to be hurt by any educating severity" (*Works and Days* 9–10).

But unlike Meredith, Browning is too wise—or too loving—to adopt the critic's role. He gives them love instead. In 1885, Cooper writes, "[H]e stood fondling our hands, with a touch that conveyed what he could not speak.... Ah! he was gracious and fatherly. As we parted he ... left us the benediction of his belief [in us]" (*Works and Days* 11). In May 1886, when they visit him at Warwick Crescent, he takes Cooper's hand as they depart and says: "'You are beginning where I am leaving off'" (*Works and Days* 16).

In May 1888, Bradley records Browning's talk of the Sapphics and interest in Tiresias, whom he once thought to treat: "When I remarked that I wished he had treated it, he said, 'No: it ought to be treated by a woman.' He said to Edith, that he liked the second series of poems even better than the first, and prophesied that they would make their mark. But he refuses to write a preface. We must remember we are Michael Field. Again he said, 'Wait fifty years'" (*Works and Days* 20).

Six years later, Cooper will tell their *Journal*, "In Browning an overplus of the Intellect was vitalized by the Heart. In Meredith the living Heart rarely kindles the over-plus of Intellect" (99–100). Fortunately, after Browning's death, Bradley and Cooper become part of the aesthetic movement of the 1890s and find support from George Moore and Oscar Wilde (as well as from Walter Pater). They meet Moore and Wilde at a gathering in July 1890. Bradley describes Moore as "a brother—one of the guild of letters. His admiration for *William Rufus* is unbounded.... He has even proposed it to the Théâtre Libre as one of the English plays to be acted" (*Works and Days* 134). Moore writes to them soon after and offers further aid: "If I like the new play I shall be glad to write an article about it in *The Hawk*, and an article in that paper will be of use to you because it goes among theatrical folk.... If you can arrange it I shall be very glad to come down and see you.... I did like *William Rufus* and the first plays whose names I have never been able to pronounce, much less to spell" (*Works and Days* 194–95). They agree to meet, but Moore warns them:

> I shall have a lot to say about play-writing, and my criticism though often incorrect is never vague.... I have received *Rufus*. I do not think it would be possible to arrange it for the stage. You must write something for the stage. If you like we'll go through an act of *Rufus* and I'll tell you why I think it could not be arranged for acting. Stage composition is something quite different. The intention is different.... perhaps I do not understand

the subject and there are numberless other perhaps—still we shall aestheticise agreeably. (*Works and Days* 197)

He thus charmingly disarms. Cooper's journal entry on the visit captures his look and her gratitude: "We talked much of the construction of plays for the stage: he made me realise the leading fault of our work—its want of rhythmical progression—the haphazard development of plot which has contented us. The firm yet pliant structure of a work is one of the requirements of style. And preparation for events and entrances is the true forethought that gives dramatic art integrity and musical movement" (198).

However, they lose sight of Moore. When they meet again by chance in Paris in 1897 and Cooper describes the "bare scenario" of their new verse drama *Anna Ruina*, she tells the *Journal*, "He holds that, as usual, with all our talent, we go irritatingly wrong at the end of Act Two. But we have to ask if the Creator Spiritus thinks with him. George tells us in confidence that he likes all we write—even when it is bad. He asks, 'Who does the love scenes?—they are so good. You get such words in them'" (201).

Oscar Wilde aids them more practically and across a longer time. Sporting a lilac shirt, heliotrope tie, and "great primrose pink," Wilde tells them during their first 1890 visit that their *Tragic Mary* and Rossetti's poems are "the two beautiful books (in appearance) in the century—but he was going to surpass us, and would send us an early copy of his *Tales*" (*Works and Days* 139). In 1893, when he learns one of their plays will be produced, he troubles to give them this counsel:

> Dear Michael Field, . . . Tell Grein to select only young actors—there are possibilities of poetry and passion in the young—and picturesqueness also, a quality so valuable on the stage. Shun the experienced actor—in poetic drama he is impossible. Choose graceful personalities—young actors and actresses who have charming voices—that is enough. The rest is in the hands of God and the poet.
>
> I look forward to listening to your lovely play recited on a rush-strewn platform, before a tapestry, by gracious things in antique robes, and, if you can manage it, in gilded masks.
>
> So, you see I have nothing to tell you, except that I am your sincere admirer. (*Works and Days* 141)

The next year, he points them to his agent:

Dear Michael Field, write to Miss Elizabeth Marbury. . . . She manages all my plays. I have written to her. I am a wretch not to have answered sooner—but I have no excuse; so you will forgive me.

Your third act [of *A Question of Memory*] was quite admirable—a really fine piece of work—with the touch of terror that our stage lacks so much—I think the theatre should belong to the furies—Caliban and Silenus, one educated and the other sober, seem now to dominate, in their fallen condition, our wretched English drama. (*Works and Days* 142)

Despite Wilde's and Browning's support, it should be clear by this point that criticism rained on Michael Field. Editor Moore writes that "[a]fter the first flush of acclamation [in 1883] their work was treated with ever-increasing coldness by the literary world" (*Works and Days* xvi). As early as 1884, Bradley begged Browning "to set the critics on a wrong track" regarding their dual authorship and gender. "The revelation [of dual authorship] would indeed be utter ruin to us; but the report of lady authorship will dwarf and enfeeble our work at every turn," she insists. "Like the poet Gray we shall never 'speak out.' And we have many things to say that the world will not tolerate from a woman's lips. We must be free as dramatists to work out in the open air of nature—exposed to her vicissitudes, witnessing her terrors: we cannot be stifled in drawing-room conventionalities" (*Works and Days* 6). In November 1933, Woolf also might have identified with Bradley's next words: "[W]e have made a desperate fight for the freedom of our privacy" (6).

Bradley rails more than Cooper at their critical blows. In the 1890s, when they hear of the triumphant return of writer Olive Schreiner, Bradley reflects in the *Journal* on her own narrow life:

Olive Schreiner home from the Cape, after years of brute, wild life in Africa. The ambassador pays his respects to her, Watts asks to paint her (he is refused), she goes the round of the great. Lovers from Africa come after her—to sink on their knees as soon as they land. . . . Meditating on all this I am filled with jealousy; this woman has been worshipped—she has known solitude—she has walked naked in the open air, she has handled politics, she has set up one and put down another.

I have lived at Durdans, neither breathing nor being breathed upon. (193–94)

Later in the decade, Bradley exclaims again to the *Journal*: "What good times men have, what pipes, what deep communings! And the best of our brains is given to conjecture of what is passing in these male heads. Yet if women seek to learn their art from life, instead of what the angels bring down to them in dishes, they simply get defamed" (202).

Less fiery than Bradley, Edith Cooper finds, early on, a more sanguine philosophy toward dispraise. In 1889, she tells Robert Browning: "I was nearly slain by a review in the *Athenaeum*, when I was but a child, after that I had never been hurt by any judgement; it had killed such sense of pain entirely" (*Works and Days* 31). In 1893, their prose play *A Question of Memory*, based on an incident in the 1848 Hungarian uprising, is produced at the Independent Theatre. *Works and Days* offers the authors' fascinating rehearsal diary. Oscar Wilde reserves a box on October 19, 1893, but Cooper reports waking after opening night

> to the surprise of finding every morning paper against us. . . . I am in helpless pain like a dumb animal at first. . . . The evening papers are worse than the morning. They are like a lot of unchained tigers. We are hated. . . . [B]ut though everything is against us, we are strong, thank Heaven and our race. . . . When I said to Addleshaw that I would go through the whole experience again, now I knew how it would end—he replied, "A man would not."—"But then, you see, I am a woman, and to bring out a play is experience of life—just what women feel so crushingly that they need. You men get it like breathing." (*Works and Days* 181–82, 184)

Hermione Lee suggests Ethel Smyth as the model for Miss La Trobe, the lesbian playwright of Woolf's last novel, *Between the Acts* (581). However, Woolf may also be saluting Michael Field—and offering a better reception.

Between 1884 and 1914, Bradley and Cooper published more than thirty-five works under the name Michael Field. Like the playful Stephen children, the two delighted in nicknames for themselves and for others. Edith was Henrich, Henry or Henny, Puss, Pussie, "my Persian," P., or "Field." Katherine was Sim (for Simiorg, a fabulous wise Eastern bird), the "old wise fowl," or "Michael," and painter Charles Ricketts was "lizard" and painter Rothenstein "The Heavenly Dog."[24] In 1897, after Edith's father dies in a tragic Alpine accident, aunt and niece move from Reigate to an eighteenth-century house in Richmond with balconies overlooking the Thames and a garden leading to the stone arch of Richmond Bridge.[25]

On February 6, 1911, forty-nine-year-old Cooper guesses she has fatal cancer. Her doctor concurs. In the *Journal*, Cooper calls the next two weeks "the greatest in experience of my life" (301). When the Indian poet Rabindranath Tagore comes to call in 1913, Cooper tells him she is happy to meet one who "esteems" pain as much as she does: "All my friends, even Mr. Sturge Moore, regret it for me—and it has been 'the holiest experience of my life.' . . . I have just been suffering pain. It is a great solitude. And I have been able to think of things with a quietness I would not have lost" (*Works and Days* 320).

From the Journal of Michael Field tells a love story, as well as a rich tale of art and death. In 1895, Bradley and Cooper pay a long visit to Robert Browning's sister and his painter son, Pen, in Asolo, Italy, seeking the "live force" of the dead poet (*Works and Days* 217). Pen tells them "how well it was" that Browning died "before age imprisoned him," before "the ailments of age would have been an humiliation to him—would have put him in a cage" (*Works and Days* 216, 17). Woolf may have recalled these words in 1941.

In the days before Edith Cooper's death, in 1913, she writes in one of her last *Journal* entries:

> I am moved to read Michael's [Katherine's] poems to me.—*Old Ivories*—*The Dear Temptation of Her Fate*—*Atthis, my darling* of *Long Ago*—the loveliest nocturne of love ever created, *Palimpsest*—to say by heart
>
> > "A girl
> > Her soul a deep wave pearl."
>
> I am moved to show him [Professor Francis Brookes, their cousin and intimate friend] triumph and joy in this lovely praise, and in showing him my so often guarded mood before my glory, I also let my Love understand what her poet's gift has been to me—her poet-lover's gift. Think of it! She has often read these lovely poems to me, she has not heard them tender but high-voiced from my lips. (323–24)

Bradley's entry follows:

> I find I am listening to Henry's voice—Hennie reading my love poems to her, aloud to Francis. Of course I have never listened to them before—she read the famous sonnet *A window full of ancient things*, also *Atthis* and others.
>
> For a little while I am in Paradise. It is infinitely soft between us. Warm buds open. I feel at least I have merited gems of passionate love.

And Francis, who has loved me so well, listens to the singing amid the boughs, that is not for him—listening as he would to a nightingale overhead. It is an intense moment. A moment not of memory—but of creation.[26]

As a final act of love, Bradley keeps her own cancer diagnosis from Cooper. She follows Cooper to the grave nine months later, naming the painter Sturge Moore their literary executor, with instructions to wait fifteen years, then open their journal at the end of 1929, read it, and publish "so much and whatever parts" he thought fit (*Works and Days* xv). He was to supplement the diary from the bundles of letters written by or to them at the time. According to Moore, their journal, which they titled *Works and Days*, consisted of twenty-six cream-colored vellum folios the size of office ledgers, one for each year from 1888 to 1914.

While Jules de Goncourt did all the writing in the Goncourt brothers' journals, taking dictation from his older brother, Edmond, while adding text of his own, *Works and Days* offers two distinct pens and voices and sometimes two entries per day. Since Bradley and Cooper used the same book, journal entries of one could be read, amended, and expanded by the other. Editor Moore and his son, who assisted in the transcription, could easily discern the script of aunt or niece, although they found the script "often baffling" and laborious to decipher.[27]

Works and Days offered Woolf another writers' diary. She found in Bradley and Cooper her own love for the visible world—"the touching poetry which clings to all material things" (ix). She found also their delight in talk. Rothenstein describes the women's "smiling gaiety" and Bradley as "stout, emphatic, splendid and adventurous in talk, rich in wit; [Cooper] wan and wistful, gentler in manner than [Bradley], but equally eminent in the quick give and take of ideas" (x, ix). Their *Journal* supplied Woolf with further views of the Brownings and of the lives of female "outsiders" who sought anonymity and privacy. "We have again been by the current of events and not in it . . . outsiders in a deep sense," Cooper writes during their 1895 Asolo days (*Works and Days* 217). In her own pivotal 1903 diary, twenty-one-year-old Virginia Woolf consciously chooses the outsider role; however, Michael Field's diaries reinforce the word "outsider," which will be central to Woolf's 1938 *Three Guineas*. In late 1939, Woolf will turn to the diaries of painter and designer Charles Ricketts, Michael Field's good friend.

Editor Moore notes that Bradley and Cooper included in their *Journal* drafts of their poetry and elaborate descriptions of paintings, as well as a record of their thoughts and days. Regrettably, to fulfill their instructions, Moore chose a thematic form for the journal excerpts. Rather than a chronological unfolding of *The Journal of Michael Field*, readers find instead twenty-seven topical chapters—separate chapters on "Robert Browning," "George Meredith," "Herbert Spencer," "John Ruskin," and "Oscar Wilde" as well as on "Victorians Great and Small," "The Nineties," "Death in the Mountains," and "Death Comes Home." In these chapters, Moore unites journal entries with the letters to and from the famous authors. Given Bradley's and Cooper's rich interplay with major artists across forty years, the resulting volume brims with lively firsthand sights and insights. A similar topically chaptered volume could be made by combining Woolf diary excerpts with her letters to and from T. S. Eliot, Lytton Strachey, Roger Fry, Katherine Mansfield, George Bernard Shaw, and others. What we miss, however, is the sense of an unfolding diary.

At the close of his introduction, Rothenstein admits that he longs "for more extended extracts" (*Works and Days* xiii). He hopes that readers will demand "further material from this rich quarry" (xiii). Editor Moore calls *Works and Days* a "first selection" and reveals that he judged Bradley's journal entries on Father Vincent MacNab, her Catholic confessor, "too personal for present use."[28] Sadly, a fuller Michael Field journal has not yet appeared in print, although the journals reside (helpfully indexed) in the British Library. A fuller print version of the journal may yet come, however, for 2004 saw the first Michael Field conference and 2006 the formation of a Michael Field society.[29]

The 1933 *Works and Days: From the Journal of Michael Field* delights us with colorful diary threads, but we miss the interwoven whole. Nevertheless, it offered Woolf in late 1933 the trials of English women writers across "the years" and testimony on women as "despised." It showed her lesbian playwrights wishing to "be free as dramatists to work out in the open air of nature"—a wish Woolf grants in *Between the Acts*—and it gives her the phrase "outsiders in a deep sense."

4

Warnings

"By the summer of 1934," Hermione Lee writes, Hitler's "ambitions and his methods were fully apparent" (644). The Nazis issue regulations to eliminate women doctors[1] and lawyers in Germany; in German universities, the quota for female students is reduced to 10 percent (Pawlowski 8 and n25). German birth control and sex counseling clinics are closed, and the antiabortion law is strictly enforced (Gättens 26n10).

Virginia Woolf's second 1934 diary starts in May. In June, Oswald Mosley, guarded by his cadre of Blackshirts, attracts fifteen thousand to London's Olympia Auditorium for a rally of his (now) British Union of Fascists. Most of those present agree that Mosley should be made Britain's dictator, its Hitler (Sonnenberg 91). By June 1934, David Bradshaw reports, anti-Semitism has "become a key component of Mosley's demogogy" ("Hayams Place" 179). On October 28, 1934, Mosley stages a vicious attack on Jews during another British Union of Fascist rally, now at the Royal Albert Hall. This is, "in effect, a declaration of war upon the Jewish community in Britain," one commentator notes (Bradshaw "Hayams Place," 183). Had Mosley won power, Bradshaw explains, the British Union of Fascists "would have forcibly expelled British Jews deemed to be enemies of the Fascist state, while those allowed to remain in Britain would have been deprived of their citizenship" (179).

British women, in some circles, however, were taking their own very different "action" in 1934. Ray Strachey, Lytton Strachey's sister, becomes head of the Women's Employment Federation, which fights for women's entry into the higher professions—and for their promotion once there. Virginia Woolf counters in her novel *The Years* Hitler's (and Mosley's) drive to erase women, and in 1934 she also reaches out to the London Society for Women's Service Marsham Street Library (now the Fawcett Library). Minutes from a library committee meeting state that Woolf "generously offered to buy books for the Library . . . and would also try to get for the Library from the secondhand booksellers any old books required, especially those needed to fill any gaps in the collection of classics written by women" (Green 214–15n5).

Beyond the above national and international threats, Woolf faces inner personal (and artistic) loss and outer public attack across this diary. She starts to speak of "warnings" in this journal. But André Gide's *Pages de Journal, 1929–32*, give her direction in August 1934. In September, Guy de Maupassant's travel diary *Sur l'eau* (*Afloat*) helps her to navigate through Roger Fry's unexpected death. She enters its words in her diary and also uses *Afloat* for a key moment in *The Years*. In October, Alice James' *Journal* helps Woolf calibrate British women's social and sexual lives in the first decades of *The Years* and shows her—as do Gide and Maupassant—a fierce fight, both within and without, between constraint and freedom.

Virginia Woolf's Second 1934 Diary

> "[H]ow we all fought with our brains loves & so on; & must be vanquished. Then the vanquisher, this outer force became so clear; the indifferent. & we so small fine delicate. A fear then came to me, of death."
>
> (September 19, 1934; D 4: 244)

A tremor passes through Virginia Woolf's second 1934 diary. To those who know her fate, this diary stirs feelings of trepidation and recognition that precipices lurk amid the fluid downs. "I broke off, after sticking my Irish papers into the old book, & felt I suppose a little shiver," Woolf begins this diary on May 18, 1934 (D 4: 220). The "shiver" likely stems from her on-setting flu; nevertheless, it presages the blows to come.

Woolf remains, nonetheless, in sail—albeit with a bit less vigor. With the success of *Flush*, she need not hurry, she tells herself in her second entry, May 22: "I've enough money to last a year. If this book [Here and Now which becomes *The Years*] comes out next June year its time enough" (D 4: 221). On July 2, she receives £300 from her American publisher Harcourt Brace, and by August 17 she sees that "even if H. & N. cant be published till Oct. year [1935], still I have £1000 or thereabouts saved" (D 4: 238). Leonard upgrades her writing tools. He gives her a traveling ink pot on October 2 "by way of congratulation" when she finishes the first draft of Here and Now (D 4: 246). A new writing board comes for Christmas. Best of all: her new writing lodge by the churchyard wall at Monk's House, which she enters at the end of the year. A *Flush* reward, it offers improved views of the downs.

Thus provisioned, Woolf attacks her fears. She takes French lessons twice a week from Janie Bussy—just as she studied Italian the year before. "This is a real solid triumph, to have made myself face that curious fear—about French—& have now, I think, routed it," she boasts in her July 17 entry (*D* 4: 226). Four days later she declares: "I am going to come down with both feet on this dress mania: this shyness; this tremendous susceptibility: & it is not so very difficult, once faced" (*D* 4: 229).

Sixty diary entries help her face life (and death) during the 239 days from May 18, 1934, to January 11, 1935—an entry, on average, every four days, an increase from the every five or six days of her last diary and a sign she needs the diary to aid her sail.[2] Questions there can propel her: eighty-seven questions across her sixty entries, forty-three (almost half) on writing (fifteen on *The Years*).[3]

She still proceeds adeptly, but with caution, with lulls between salvos on Here and Now, and with repeated advisories in her diary. "I make this note by way of warning," she writes in her second entry on May 22. "What is important now is to go very slowly; to stop in the middle of flood; never to press on; to lie back & let the soft subconscious world become populous; not to be urging foam from my lips.... I must... nurse my rather creaking head & dandle it with French & so on as cunningly as possible" (*D* 4: 221). She treats her head as if it were a baby. "A note, by way of advising other Virginias with other books that this is the way of the thing: up down, up down—" she tells her future selves on November 17.[4]

She shifts to other forms for the lulls—to her ongoing "Phases of Fiction" book of criticism, to articles, and even to *Freshwater*, her play—but the word "jaded" now starts to recur along with the notes of warning. "Is my brain dwindling?" she opens her July 19 entry. "I get so knotted & jaded; never mind" (*D* 4: 226). A month later, she repeats, "I am too jaded to write that horrid book, I mean [Phases of] Fiction, this morning" (*D* 4: 238). So she turns to her diary. To be "jaded" means to be worn out, as by overuse or overindulgence. It means to become world-weary, run-down, fatigued, or spiritless. A "jade," in fact, is a broken down or useless horse, a nag—an alarming shift for a writer who spurs herself to take her fences.

Nevertheless, she presses forward with Here and Now, helped by the fact that she still feels in creative flow. After a three-week layoff for flu, she finds herself on June 18 "[i]n flood with Here & Now, praise be. Yet—very wary; only just now I made up the scene with Renny & Maggie: a sign I am fertilising" (*D* 4: 222). July goes mostly to this fertilizing, this well filling. As so often before, she saves the novel for the country. On July 28 she crows: "I'm free to begin the last chapter; & by a merciful Providence the well is full, ideas are rising, & if I can keep at it widely freely powerfully I shall have 2 months of complete immersion. Odd how the creative power at once brings the whole universe to order.... I'm going to indulge in a series of quick sharp contrasts: breaking my bonds [?][5] as much as ever I like. Trying every kind of experiment. Now of course I cant write diary or letters or read because I am making up all the time" (*D* 4: 232). But she writes "diary" at this moment.

She then struggles to express her good fortune[6] to have "to some extent forced myself to break every mould & find a fresh form of being, that is of expression, for everything I feel & think. So that when it is working I get the sense of being fully energised—nothing stunted. But this needs constant effort, anxiety & risk. Here in H. & N. I am breaking the mould made by The Waves" (*D* 4: 233).

In light of such toil and daring, how could she *not* be fatigued? She tells her July 19 entry: "On the whole a well managed summer, if my head were more vigorous. Oh these long books, what a tremendous effort they are—to whole [hold?] the entire span on my shoulders" (*D* 4: 227). On August 21, she declares that the "lesson of Here & Now is that one can use all kinds of 'forms' in one book. Therefore the next might be poem, reality, comedy, play: narrative; psychology, all in one. Very short" (*D* 4: 238). These words describe her next novel, *Between the Acts*. On August 30, her current novel-in-progress intrudes on her diary once more, and three days later she exclaims, "I dont think I have ever been more excited over a book.... I am doing the scene where Peggy listens to them talking & bursts out. It was this outburst that excited me so. Too much perhaps" (*D* 4: 241).

But Roger Fry's unexpected death on September 9 not only freezes creation but also expands Woolf's vulnerability to other distress. Her first entry after his death reveals the void she now sees: "I feel dazed: very wooden.... And I'm too stupid to write anything. My head all stiff. I think the poverty of life now is what comes to me. a thin blackish veil over everything.... The substance gone out of everything. I dont think this is exaggerated. It'll come back I suppose. Indeed I feel a great wish, now & then, to live more all over the place, to see people, to create, only for the time one cant make the effort" (*D* 4: 242). Tellingly, at this crisis she turns to her diary—and to others' diaries—to probe the sorrow.

As with Lytton Strachey's death in 1932, she feels "a strong instinct to be with ones friends," but she also feels "[v]ery jaded; cant write; all my books seem a completed jerked [?] failure" (*D* 4: 243). On September 18, she reports Vanessa "infinitely mournful & struck, like a statue, something frozen about her.... This has gone out of the day—that laughter; that energy; & we were all thinned & stunted.... I feel... very jaded now" (*D* 4: 244).

But she rouses herself to finish her novel, for she opens her September 20 entry: "today... the other thing begins to work—the exalted sense of being above time & death which comes from being again in a writing mood. And this is not an illusion, so far as I can tell. Certainly I have a strong sense that Roger would be all on one's side in this excitement, & that whatever the invisible force does, we thus get outside it" (*D* 4: 245). This diary passage offers a powerful testament to art: *that whatever the invisible force does, we thus* [through art] *get outside it*. And ten days later she can close the morning with this diary boast: "The last words of the nameless book were written 10 minutes ago; quite calmly" (*D* 4: 245).

She thus rallies from Fry's death.

However, the novel's completion leaves a vacancy that, joined to the void of Fry's death, renders Woolf particularly exposed to Wyndham Lewis' untimely attack in *Men without Art*. "A brief note," she begins her October 11 entry, once more in warning mode. She retains her philosophy of anonymity, for she steers clear of Lewis' book. Nevertheless, she senses its thrust and battles those specters *praise* and *blame* once more. The fight rages in the press for more than three weeks, and her diary serves as one of her strongest aides. She writes fourteen diary entries in October—more entries than any other month in this diary, one almost every other day. "Now I know by reason & instinct that this is an attack," she tells her diary on October 11; "that I am publicly demolished: nothing is left of me in Oxford & Cambridge & places where the young read Wyndham Lewis" (*D* 4: 250). She turns savvily to Keats for aid:

> My instinct is, not to read it. And for this reason: well, I open Keats: & find: "Praise or blame has but a momentary effect on the man whose love of beauty in the abstract makes him a severe critic on his own works. My own domestic criticism has given me pain beyond what Blackwood

or Quarterly could possibly inflict. . . . This is a mere matter of the moment—I think I shall be among the English poets after my death. Even as a matter of present interest the attempt to crush me in the Quarterly has only brought me more into notice."

Well: do I think I shall be among the English novelists after my death? I hardly ever think about it. Why then do I shrink from reading W.L.? Why am I sensitive? I think vanity. I dislike the thought of being laughed at. of the glow of satisfaction that A B & C will get from hearing V.W. demolished: also it will strengthen further attacks. . . . Already I am feeling the calm that always comes to me with abuse: my back is against the wall: I am writing for the sake of writing: &c. & then there is the queer disreputable pleasure in being abused—in being a figure, in being a martyr. & so on. (D 4: 250–51)

Here is deep diary honesty, the report of "disreputable" masochistic thoughts.

The crisis of the second 1934 diary comes on October 17. As in 1921 (and many lesser times), Woolf "medicines" herself with her diary:

I am so sleepy. Is this age? I cant shake it off. And so gloomy. Thats the end of the book. I looked up past diaries—a reason for keeping them—& found the same misery after Waves. After Lighthouse I was I remember nearer suicide, seriously, than since 1913. It is after all natural. I've been galloping now for 3 months . . . well, cut that all off—after the first divine relief [of finishing], of course some terrible blankness must spread. There's nothing left of the people, of the ideas, of the strain, of the whole life in short that has been racing round my brain. . . . This time Roger makes it harder than usual. . . . Yes, his death is worse than Lytton's. Why I wonder? Such a blank wall. Such a silence. Such a poverty. How he reverberated! And I feel it through Nessa.

But selfishly, I cant throw it off as I did the first week after his death; when it became all the colours of the setting sun, in my excitement. Now theres the dulness, the cold to face & no protection. And so W.L. had the power to sting. No thats over. Only I cant get up any steam. I'm so ugly. So old. (D 4: 253)

We know those last five words—the heralds of trouble. However, as she notes, her past diaries aid her, give her a longer view. A week later she can report that Stephen Spender defends her in the *Spectator* (D 4: 254), and two days later "Old Yeats" adds his private praise. "What he said was, he had been writing about me. The Waves. That comes after Stendhal he said. I see what you're at" (*D* 4: 255). However, she is "too jaded ... to whip [her] brain," she tells her diary (*D* 4: 256–57). And on November 2, she opens the *Spectator* to find Lewis "on me again. An answer to Spender" (*D* 4: 259). She uses this diary entry to soothe herself and leave all praise and blame—at least momentarily—behind:

> Well L[eonard]. says I shd. be contemptible to mind. Yes: but I do mind for 10 minutes: I mind being in the light again, just as I was sinking into my populous obscurity. I must take a pull on myself. I dont think this attack will last more than 2 days. ... And about 2 in the morning I am possessed of a remarkable sense of driving ey[e]less strength. And I have L.: & there are his books; & our life together. And freedom, now, from money paring. ... if only for a time I could completely forget my self ... then I should be what I mostly am: very rapid, excited, amused: intense.[7]

She thus tolls her supports.

Perhaps, however, the strongest boost in this October war with Lewis comes at the point of greatest crisis—from news that Roger Fry's sister may ask her to write his life. Readers of Woolf's diary know the vital role Fry has served. In December 1918, in another spell of creative chill, he offered her a model of vigorous, productive old age, a model for the encouraging "elderly Virginia" she immediately creates as she moves toward her second diary stage and her mature diary style. Fry was "[d]ignified & honest & large," she reflects at his funeral, a "'large sweet soul'—something ripe & musical about him—& then the fun & the fact that he had lived with such variety & generosity & curiosity"—all traits, of course, she admired, and possessed (*D* 4: 243). Since Fry served for Woolf as an invigorating spirit, to write his biography would mean to resurrect this spirit, to renew this life. Yet she shrinks October 17 from the first mention: "I dont feel ready to. I dread the plunge into the past" (*D* 4: 253–54). Revealingly, as with Lytton's death, in 1932, she seeks the human voice. "I would like to write down more actual conversation; but its such hard work," she tells her diary a sentence later and then offers a small play scene of Vanessa and Duncan talking of Roger at tea (*D* 4: 254). Vanessa says: "[S]omeone will be certain to write about Roger—so it had better be by us" (*D* 4: 254).

With hope of Roger's "life" to come and her November 2 triumph over Lewis' attack, Woolf can turn again to her novel; however, she needs her diary as a test of her ability to write. She opens her November 14 entry: "Here

I am taking a morning off to breathe in [in her diary] before I tackle . . . that book [the novel]" (*D* 4: 261). On December 30 at Rodmell, she again needs her diary, but as she has left it behind in London, she improvises with loose sheets that she will paste in later. "It was stupid to come without a book, seeing that I end every morning with a head full of ideas about The Pargiters," she chastises herself (*D* 4: 266). She now thinks to call her novel Ordinary People. She vows to reduce the work to 150,000 words and finish retyping in May 1935. "And sometimes my brain threatens to split with all the meaning I think I could press into it," she admits. "The discovery of this book, it dawns upon me, is the combination of the external & the internal. I am using both, freely. And my eye has gathered in a good many externals in its time" (*D* 4: 274). She has united the outer and the inner.

In fact, she has faced—and overcome—much in the second half of 1934: Roger Fry's death and Wyndham Lewis' attack. This diary registers, too, tremors of the rising fascism. Woolf's July 2 entry opens with a phone call from Osbert Sitwell: "'And can't anything be done about this monstrous affair in Germany?'" he asks, and she then describes

> the sensation of sitting here & reading, like an act in a play, how Hitler flew to Munich & killed this that & the other man & woman in Germany yesterday. A fine hot summers day here & we took Philip [Woolf] Babs & 3 children to the Zoo. Meanwhile these brutal bullies go about in hoods & masks, like little boys dressed up, acting this idiotic, meaningless, brutal, bloody, pandemonium. In they come while Herr so & so is at lunch: iron boots, they say, grating on the parquet, kill him; & his wife who rushes to the door to prevent them. It is like watching the baboon at the Zoo; only he sucks a paper in which ice has been wrapped, & they fire with revolvers. And here we sit, Osbert & I &c., remarking this is inconceivable. . . . And for the first time I read articles with rage, to find him called a real leader. Worse far than Napoleon. (*D* 4: 223–24)

At the Hutchinsons on July 24, they discuss Hitler with T. S. Eliot[8] and Desmond MacCarthy, and on August 7 Woolf records Maynard Keynes' canny words: "They're doing something very queer with their money. I cant make out what. It may be the Jews are taking away their capital. Let me see, if 2000 Jews were each to take away £2,000—Anyhow they cant pay their Lancashire bill. Always the Germans have bought cotton from Egypt, had it spun in Lancashire: its a small bill, only ½ a million, but they cant pay. Yet theyre buying copper all the time. Whats it for? Armaments no doubt. . . . Theyre doing something foolish—no Treasury control of the soldiers" (*D* 4: 235–36).

On October 9, Woolf ends her entry in headline fashion, "The King of Jugoslavia & Bartou murdered this evening," and fifteen days later Yeats tells her it takes a country three hundred years to absorb a war (*D* 4: 250, 256). He insists there has not yet been time to create after 1914. A month later, Victoria Ocampo describes to Woolf her interview with Mussolini, who tells her that no great man needed women and cites as proof Caesar, Napoleon, and Bismarck (*D* 4: 263). Ocampo's words turn Woolf's thoughts to women. Even before, on August 21, Woolf thinks to write as her next work a play about the Parnells (the Irish freedom fighters), "or a biography of Mrs. P[arnell]" (*D* 4: 238). In late October, "by way of a rest," she pens an article on Queen Marie of Romania, a writer who, Woolf notes, "rides after her emotion fearlessly and takes her fences without caring for falls" (*D* 4: 254; *E* 6: 53).

On the first day of 1935, as Woolf reads of St. Paul, she tells her diary "I want to write On being despised" (*D* 4: 271). Her mind keeps "pumping up ideas" for that work, which will become *Three Guineas* and which she hopes to start in August 1935 (*D* 4: 271). In her next (and next-to-last) diary entry, January 6, 1935, she describes herself "sparring" with Princess Elizabeth Bibesco, the Asquiths' daughter, on the best way to fight Hitler: "[W]hen she asked me to join the Cttee of the anti-Fascist Ex[hibitio]n., I asked why the woman question was ignored" (*D* 4: 273). In her last diary entry, January 11, she decides to attend this meeting of the Cambridge Anti-War Council.

Woolf's second 1934 diary registers both triumph and tremor. In the wake of Roger Fry's death, Woolf completes the first draft of *The Years* and pens in her diary a moving testament to artistic creation: "that whatever the invisible force does, we thus get outside it" (*D* 4: 245). She maintains her philosophy of anonymity in the face of Wyndham Lewis' long outside attack; in fact, she moves toward her "populous obscurity." And she turns her mind increasingly to women and war. An impressive achievement this; Woolf's creative "flow" persists.

However, her second 1934 diary also emits subtle and overt warnings. Woolf feels jaded—world-weary and spiritless—even before Fry dies. Her artistic "effort, anxiety, and risk" cannot help but take a toll. The writing she turns to for respite ("Phases of Fiction," journalism, and her play, revealingly titled *Freshwater*) lacks the recharge of her previous "adept" forays into the works of Oliver Goldsmith, Ivan Turgenev, and Walter Sickert—all multigenre artists and

"Citizens of the World." Fry's death means loss for Woolf of another invigorating spirit, a model of her own vibrant old age. Fry's energy both stirred and shielded her. In its absence, as she tells her diary, she feels "the vainness of this perpetual fight, with our brains & loving each other against the other thing: if Roger could die."[9] The diary that opens with a shiver ends with words that parallel those near the close of Woolf's final (1941) diary. On January 11, 1935, Woolf writes:

> I cant read Dante of a morning after the struggle with fiction. I wish I could find some way of composing my mind—its absurd to let it be ravaged by scenes; when I may not have read all Dante before I—but why harp on death? On the contrary, it is better to pull on my galoshes & go through the gale to lunch off scrambled egg & sausages. Louie & L. will eat liver. Lambs liver is more tender than calfs, said Louie, thus filling up a blank in my knowledge of the world.[10]

André Gide's *Journals*

On a "triumphant" day in August 1934, a day of writing, walking, and reading in the country, Virginia Woolf opens André Gide's 1929 to 1932 *Journal* and finds it "full of startling recollection—things I cd have said myself" (*D* 4: 241). Roger Fry has urged Woolf to read the *Pages de Journal, 1929–1932*, which has just come out in France.[11]

In December 1926, Woolf had "read voraciously" Gide's frank autobiography, *If It Die . . .* (*Si le grain ne meurt . . .*). Therefore, in 1934 she may have recalled some of the stepping stones she shared with Gide. Both lost a parent at an early age: Gide, his father, when he was eleven; Woolf, her mother, at age thirteen. Like Woolf, Gide was "painfully shy" as a youth but found joy in summers at the sea at the family estate in Normandy (*Journals* 1: v). There, according to Justin O'Brien (his *Journals*' English translator), the boy spent his days "walking with his cousins . . . and voraciously reading" (1: v). Like Woolf, Gide read hungrily across his life, partly to redress his spotty education. Woolf read, for instance, his April 21, 1932, *Journal* entry, which confesses he has "got into the lazy habit of reading while walking, while eating, of not being able to go without reading" (*Journals* 3: 230).[12] His *Pages de Journal, 1929–1932*, may have propelled Woolf to Ernest Renan and his book *St. Paul* at the start of 1935, for Gide grapples with both in the *Pages* (81–83, 113).

Gide also evolved, like Woolf, his own country/city rhythm. Both diarists were born in their nation's capital; however, Gide's restless moves invite much deeper thought than Woolf's country/city, nature/culture, unconscious/conscious, female/male divide. Woolf read, for instance, this revealing July 14, 1930, Gide entry: "Never have I been able to settle in life. Always seated askew, as if on the arm of a chair; ready to get up, to leave" (*Journals* 3: 118). In his 1905 journal, which Woolf will read in 1939, Gide wrote: "Only in movement can I find my equilibrium" (1: 148). This is true of Woolf, too.

Born in 1869, Gide was a bit more than twelve years older than Woolf. In the early 1890s, he found his way—he was now in his early twenties—to poet Stéphane Mallarmé's Tuesday night Paris salons, an act mirrored a dozen years later in Woolf's London Thursday evenings. In 1909, Gide cofounded the monthly *Nouvelle Revue Francaise* (the *New French Review*) that soon launched a publishing house. Each entity gave Gide a voice in cultural affairs, just as the 1917 Hogarth Press would do for Woolf.[13] Like Woolf, Gide was a novelist, essayist, literary critic, and diarist; he was a playwright, poet, and translator, as well.

In the *Pages de Journal, 1929–1932*, Woolf saw how often her mind meshed with Gide's. In late August 1934, as antifascist groups seek *her* support, Woolf sees Europe's crisis absorb Gide's 1931 and 1932 journals. "The Spanish revolution, the struggle of the Vatican against Fascism, the German financial crisis, and, above all, Russia's extraordinary effort . . . all this distracts me frightfully from literature," he tells his *Journal* in July 1931 (3: 179). In December 1932, he refuses to join an antiwar organization. Gide copies into his *Journal* his letter to l'Association des Ecrivains et Artistes Révolutionnaires, a letter that may have stayed in Woolf's mind for her own *Three Guineas* (which she structures as letters): "Solicited by the A.E.A.R., which wants to count me among its recruits, I reply: No, dear comrades. . . . I believe that my co-operation . . . can be of more real advantage to your (to our) cause if I give it freely and am known *not* to be enrolled" (*Journals* 3: 250). Gide takes here the outsider's role.

Gide also talks of illness in his diary in words Woolf, in fact, has used. "In bed since Friday evening," he tells his *Journal* on October 28, 1929: "[H]aving broken off all connections with the outer world, or at least with society. . . . A very long and unbroken succession of hours, of undifferentiated hours. I hardly dare confess how delighted I am, for fear of seeming affected" (3: 74–75). Nine months later he adds: "I believe that illnesses are the keys that can open certain doors for us. I believe that there are certain doors that only illness can open. . . . Charles-Louis Philippe very prettily called illnesses the poor man's travels" (3: 119).

Woolf read in Gide's 1929 *Journal*: "Not a day goes by without my imagining my death ..." (3: 66). These words are one of the *Journal*'s refrains. Gide seems, in truth, more death-haunted than Woolf. He muses on January 17, 1929: "I wonder that there are not more people to jump into the river, and judge that humanity, all in all, shows remarkable guts" (*Journals* 3:38). Then, characteristically, he turns on his thought: "It is perhaps also because humanity lacks that little bit of courage that is necessary to end it all."[14] Woolf read his September 1929 vision of "[t]he ugliness, the vulgarity of the people in the métro"—a vision she had confided to her diary in 1915 (*Journals* 3: 62; *D* 1: 5). Nevertheless, both diarists possessed extraordinary resilience.

Beyond parallel thoughts on illness and war, Woolf and Gide also often shared the same literary taste. Both revered Montaigne and published essays on him. Woolf read Gide's praise of Thomas Hardy in his August 22, 1930, entry. Both diarists met Aldous Huxley and confided reservations to their diaries. Neither could abide Huxley's *Point Counter Point*; Gide, in fact, could not finish it.[15] Woolf saw Gide turn from novelist Rosamond Lehmann as well: "How easy it would have been for me to get the approval of the majority by writing *Les Faux-Monnayeurs* [*The Counterfeiters*] in the accepted fashion of novels, describing persons and places, analyzing emotions, explaining situations, spreading out on the surface everything I hide between the lines, and protecting the reader's sloth!"[16] Gide, too, sought to break the mold.[17] In his July 29, 1930, entry, he reveals his diary's role in this drive. "I cling to this notebook as if it were to console me for the slow growth of my *Oedipe*," he declares. "How much easier it is to work according to an accepted aesthetic and ethic! Writers who are submissive to a recognized religion advance sure of every step. I owe it to myself to invent everything. At times it is an immense groping toward an almost imperceptible light. And at times I ask myself: what is the good of it?" (3: 121).

Gide's diary served him in ways akin to Woolf's. He, too, must be counted among the world's great diarists. As with Woolf, Gide's journal flourishes because it serves him in myriad ways. He launched his journal at age eighteen or nineteen—about the age James Boswell began his. Like fourteen-year-old Virginia, Gide began his journal in tandem with—and likely as aid to—other literary work, in fact, according to translator O'Brien, "as an exercise in spontaneous rapid composition, since, disliking to write rapidly, he must force himself to do so here" (*Journals* 1: xv, 91, 98, 219; 2: 33, 410; 3: 398). Like Woolf, Gide kept a lifelong *periodic* diary. Like her, he penned titled *essay-entries* in his early diaries, reread his journals, corrected himself, and added later margin notes. "The feelings I noted down the last few days strike me as exaggerated to the very edge of insincerity," he upbraids himself in his October 15, 1929, entry (*Journals* 3: 69). The month before he notes: "Reread, before giving them to be typed, some notebooks of my prewar journal. What interests me most in them today is finding, over so long a period of time and so late, moral constraint and effort. How long I had to struggle!" (3: 62).

Like Jonathan Swift, Fanny Burney, Woolf, and others, Gide sought in his *Journals* a trusty confidant. "Entrust my thoughts to this notebook from day to day," he commands himself on February 1, 1931 (*Journals* 3: 146). The journal will "console" him as he writes his public works (3: 121). Touchingly, he writes on October 6, 1929: "Quickly a few lines before going to bed and solely in order not to let go" (3: 65). "I cling to these pages" becomes another *Journal* refrain, an answer to "Not a day goes by without my imagining my death." On February 7, 1916, Gide writes, "I cling desperately to this notebook; it is part of my patience; it helps keep me from going under."[18]

Like Woolf, Gide uses his diary both to shame himself and to talk himself through woes. "I set down here shamelessly and at length my lamentation, in order to blush for it, I think, a little later on, and in the hope of at least learning something from it," he declares in 1929—again a sentiment expressed by Woolf (*Journals* 3: 38). In September 1931, he writes: "This tiresome mood might change on the way. I begin this notebook in order to help it do so" (*Journals* 3: 185).

Gide's *Journals* do more, however, than just anchor his "inner life" and massage it (3: 160). Like Woolf's diary, his journals serve as needed reservoir for his teeming thoughts. "There remain too many things that I should have liked to say, and should have said, and have not said, and which clutter up my mind," he declares in his clear, parsing, self-critical way in a 1929 entry (*Journals* 3: 85). Here the journal serves as refuge for what he does not yet dare speak. In February 1931, again affirming his journals' use, he declares: "I also see myself too often checked by the too great abundance of over-ramified thoughts that form a tangle when I have gone too long without writing. So that in such cases my silence comes not from a lack of things to say, but from their tumultuous abundance" (*Journals* 3: 146). He must let these tangled thoughts loose. Like Woolf, Gide also pens his *Journals* to keep in writing trim. "But I no longer take any pleasure in chatting with this notebook," he complains on January 8, 1932, in his journal's forty-third year. "Now that, far from Paris, I am freer, I want to get back into the habit, for a time, of conversing a bit with it every day. If only in order not to let my pen grow too dull" (3: 210).

Thus multiply compelled, Gide writes his *Journals* in bed (like Swift and Princess Daisy of Pless), on trains, in cafés—even at the barber. While he and Woolf shared many of the same *motives* for journal-keeping, Gide's journals early on became much more public than hers. Woolf's diary exists for her not as "writing" but as some vital intermediary state. Gide, too, launched his journal with no thought of publication; however, he soon changed his mind. Essentially a moral philosopher, he found his journal reflections moved easily to published works. Tellingly, his first book, printed anonymously, bears the title *The Notebooks of André Walter*, which both telegraphs and masks (slightly) the link to himself. This 1891 volume employs the diary form and draws heavily on Gide's first journals (*Journals* 1: v).

Woolf read Gide's September 20, 1930, journal confession that his important 1897 paean to freedom, *The Fruits of the Earth* (*Les Nourritures terrestres*), which he judged his most spontaneous and sincere work, was "in great part made of extracts from journals and notebooks" (3: 192). Journals also loom large in Gide's fiction. His 1909 tale *Strait Is the Gate* (*La Porte étroite*), which Woolf will take up two months before her death, tells of Alissa who commits suicide but leaves an illuminating diary behind, just as the more famous Édouard pens a revealing journal in Gide's 1926 novel *The Counterfeiters*. Gide even published separately *The Counterfeiters' Day-book* (*Le Journal des Faux-Monnayerus*), the journal of the writing of *The Counterfeiters*. He published next two travel diaries: his 1927 *Voyage au Congo* and 1928 *Le Retour de Tchad*. In fact, after 1909, with the *Revue Nouvelle Francaise* seeking his work, he started to publish there extracts from his journals.

From early on, therefore, Gide pens his notebooks with one eye to public use. He allows his struggles with Christianity, which he traces in diary form in a separate green notebook, to be published in a small brochure titled after a passage in the gospel Matthew, *Numquid et tu . . . ?* (*Art thou also . . . [of Galilee]?*). In his 1929 diary, he refers to his newly published *An Unprejudiced Mind* (*Un Esprit non prévenu*), a work that offered thoughts on art, religion, and life, many taken from the *Journals*. In short, Gide's journals served as both seedbeds for, and also blooms in, his public works. His *Journals* show even more clearly than Woolf's the permeable membrane between semiprivate diary and public literary work. One also senses that for Gide, as for Woolf, the public texts could not exist without the journals.

Yet despite their similar diary motives and many sympathetic thoughts, Woolf's diary could never be taken for Gide's—nor Gide's for hers. In 1939, Gide's *Journal, 1889 to 1939,* appeared, and in July 1939 Woolf plunged into now fifty years of his diaries, a thick volume she continued to read for a year. "An interesting knotted book," she remarks in her own July 28, 1939, diary (*D* 5: 227). On November 5, 1939, she writes to Dorothy Bussy that "[a]ll the intelligentsia is reading" Gide's *Journal*, "and out of snobbery I followed, and found you there: and then reread Si Le Grain ne meurt with amazement at the frankness. Why, if he can say all that, cant I come out with the comparatively modest truth about Roger and his affairs? Yes, I find Gide very bracing and drastic, and a little stringent. So very French: and here we're so very plumpuddingy" (*L* #3564, 6: 368). Like Dorothy Wordsworth's diaries, Gide's *Journals* brace Woolf with their pungent severity. Gide told his journal in 1907: "I must never let up in my harshness toward myself, never move backward or recant, but rather plunge farther along my path, austerely and fiercely" (1: 200).

Woolf's diary certainly strikes one as more direct, garrulous, amused, and, well, "plumpuddingy" than Gide's "immense groping toward an imperceptible light"—although the pudding and mutton only make Woolf's flashes of insight stand out in higher relief, like a lightning storm seen through the windows of a lively country house.[19] Gide writes from such abundance one senses he could do even *more* with his journals—had he wished.[20] In fact, we know he *has* done more but ripped away pages that fail to meet his stringent standards (as he occasionally admits) (*Journals* 1: 28; 2: 5, 133, 142).

Unlike Woolf's diary, Gide's is not a journal of brilliant portraits, although it might have been. His portraits, when they appear, capture look and talk and subtle nuance. However, his most frequent likenesses, those of the poet Paul Valéry, focus on Gide as much as on the older poet he admired. In each sketch, we learn of Gide's "frightful feeling of insolvency" next to Valéry, of Gide's regret "quite selfishly, that Valéry has never made an effort to understand me better" (*Journals* 3: 58, 151). Gide also can retail a witty mot, but he does it not so much for joy as to correct others' misquoting and set the record straight. Similarly, he can evoke the natural world, as his priceless entries on his pet starling disclose;[21] however, here, too, his mind rarely stays.

At age twenty-four, Gide conveys the key to his journals at the close of his 1893 diary. "Imagination (in my case) rarely precedes the idea; it is the latter, and never the former, that excites me," he explains (*Journals* 1: 36). Ideas excited Gide—not people, or even nature. His *Journals,* as Woolf saw, collect his ever-widening reflections on freedom and constraint, truth and falsehood, and his related obsessions with the authentic and the sincere. "The only drama that really interests me and that I should always be willing to depict anew is the debate of the individual with whatever keeps him from being authentic, with whatever is opposed to his integrity, to his integration. Most often the obstacle is within him. And all the rest is merely accidental," Gide tells his *Journal* in 1930 (3: 116). Gide speaks here of the war within.

In August 1939, Woolf chooses to take ten minutes for her diary, rather than to compress her biography of Roger Fry. "I thought of several things to write about. Not exactly diary. Reflections," she begins. "Thats the fashionable dodge. Peter Lucas & Gide both at it."[22] On November 1, 1939, Gide's *Journals* remain in her mind. She exclaims: "Oh how gladly I reach for this free [diary] page for a 10 minutes scamper after copying & re-copying, digging in those old extract books for quotes all the morning! And how <compose> adapt oneself to the sense of freedom? How compete with the compression & lucidity & logic of Gide writing his Journal? Well, the plain truth is I cant. Yet ideas shoot into my head perpetually. Only as my head is always on the anvil—for I will finish [*Roger Fry*] this week—they skim away uncaught" (*D* 5: 244).

Gide's many notebooks helped him to net his evolving thoughts. His life state—an only child of independent wealth—assisted his contemplative life, his self-absorption. Gide's head was not "always on the anvil." Furthermore, Gide wrote in the tradition of Montaigne, La Rochefoucauld, Pascal, and Rousseau, all of whom he regularly reread. Like Woolf, he even savored the wry pensées of Jules Renard's *Journals*—a further extension of that line. Gide's *Journals* supply more than the intellectual, moral, and spiritual quest of a brave and painstaking mind; they provide striking aphorisms along the way, as well. "The conventional is the only thing that never looks like 'pose,'" Gide tells his *Journal*, and again "[t]he most beaten paths are certainly the surest; but do not hope to scare up much game on them" (3: 75, 105). "I am always inclined to look upon art itself as a game, and upon the Cosmos as God's game," he famously writes in 1930, and in 1912, "Catholicism is inadmissible. Protestantism is intolerable. And I feel profoundly Christian" (3: 89; 1: 319). "Great works do not so much teach us," Gide wrote, "as they plunge us into a sort of almost loving bewilderment"—a sentence that describes his *Journals* (3: 106).

On February 2, 1940, Woolf again admires Gide the diarist. "I wish I could conglobulate reflections like Gide," she tells her diary. "Half of his are daily jottings.

Then something solid forms," and she once more thinks of her own "fine covey" of thoughts "lost on Asheham down, & walking the river bank" (*D* 5: 263).

However, by July 24, 1940, the day before *Roger Fry* appears, Woolf tires of diaries—tires of Gide's diary and even of her own. The year before she saw Gide's and Peter Lucas' journals as a response to the brutal war atmosphere: "Neither [Gide nor Lucas] can settle to creative art (I think, sans Roger, I could). Its the comment—the daily interjection—that comes handy in times like these. I too feel it" (*D* 5: 229). However, in July 1940, now "sans Roger" and having thought regularly on Gide for a year, Woolf declares, "I make these notes, but am tired of notes—tire of Gide, tired of de Vigny notebooks. I want something sequacious now & robust. In the first days of the war I cd read notes only" (*D* 5: 304). She wants, in short, a more elaborated work of art—such as her next work, *Between the Acts*.

Was she surprised, and disappointed too, that in *Journals* from 1889 to 1939, Gide the ceaseless reader, the Gide who reads Aldous Huxley and Rosamond Lehmann and writes astutely of countless other writers, does not once address her work? How could Gide *not* know Woolf's novels and essays? He reads Lytton Strachey's "Cardinal Manning" in 1918, offers a rich response to Strachey's *Books and Characters: French and English*, and mourns Strachey's absence at the 1922 European discussion groups (*Journals* 2: 236, 309–10). Gide visits Chartres with Roger Fry in 1924 and esteems Jacques Raverat and Dorothy Bussy across the decades. How could Woolf's name and work escape him? Was the work, in fact, too close?[23]

Woolf saw that Gide enjoyed a long friendship with Arnold Bennett. Gide reads Bennett's *Journals* as well as twenty-one other diarists whom he mentions in his *Journals*—including Pepys, Swift, Tolstoy, Stendhal,[24] the Goncourt brothers,[25] Jules Renard,[26] and Eugène Delacroix—whom Woolf also read. Although he seems not to see *her*, Woolf admired Gide's bracing, lucid, freedom-seeking, ever-stretching *Journals*, diaries so "full of startling recollection," things she could have said herself (*D* 4: 241). In fact, she may have drawn her 1939 "Reading at Random" title from this 1936 Gide journal entry:

> When "it's not going right," I walk up and down in my room, then, somewhat through impatience, I seize almost at random a book from my shelf (not one of those books lying on my table which I am "in the course" of reading, but one of those old constant companions, which are always there, to which everything brings me back) and open it really at random.

This "random chance" would make me believe in the devil or in providence, for I fall at once, almost every time, on the page, on the sentence, on the words I just happen to need to start off again. (*Journals* 3: 335)

Peggy Pargiter does this in *The Years*. However in July 1940, Woolf tires of such "notes" and notebooks—perhaps an ominous sign. On January 20, 1941, she turns to Gide's fiction, to his story of female self-destruction, *Strait Is the Gate* (*Le Porte étroite*). She recently had finished her own parallel short story of a woman's suicide and the revealing diary she leaves behind: "The Legacy." But Gide's *fiction* brings no life. "[F]eeble, slaty, sentimental," Woolf records (*D* 5: 354).

However, in the summer of 1934, Gide's freedom-seeking, outsider's *Pages de Journal, 1929–1932*, show her both the distractions of war and a letter of one who refuses to join an antiwar society. In 1939, he gives her the "Reading at Random" title, and his "knotty" *Journals* brace her for more than a year.[27]

Guy de Maupassant's Travel Journal *Sur l'eau (Afloat)*

Afloat (*Sur l'eau*), Guy de Maupassant's slim, artful 1888 travel diary, proves useful for Virginia Woolf in 1934. On August 21, 1934, Woolf tells her diary that she read Maupassant's first novel, *Une Vie* (*A Woman's Life*), the night before and found it "rather marking time & watery" compared to the final chapter of her own novel, *The Years*, on which she works (*D* 4: 238). She then takes up Maupassant's travel journal, which she likes much more.

Leo Tolstoy, whose own diary Woolf will soon read, called *Sur l'eau* Maupassant's best work ("Introduction to the Works of Guy de Maupassant" 41). Not exactly a fictive diary like Anaïs Nin's or (in parts) Lady Charlotte Bury's *Diary of a Lady-in-Waiting* or Barbellion's *Journal of a Disappointed Man* (which Woolf read, respectively, in 1908 and 1920), *Sur l'eau* rather is a brilliant mosaic. Maupassant draws from several of his sea cruises along France's southern coast, as well as from more than thirty of his published pieces, for *Sur l'eau*, a diary covering one voyage of a mere eight days. In what has been called his most "intentionally personal" prose, the French writer, now famous at age thirty-seven, with four of his six novels and most of his three-hundred-some short stories imparted, intertwines light travel prose with his own deep reflections on solitude, society, war, and the writer's state (*Afloat* 9).

Maupassant's very title, *Afloat*, likely resonated with Woolf, who has linked herself with ships from at least age seventeen and her 1899 Warboys diary, when she likened her mind to "a restless steamer paddle urging the ship along, tho' the wind is fallen & the sea is as still as glass" (*PA* 138). In the 1888 *Afloat*, Maupassant marks his escape from culture to nature, anticipating Woolf's own. In his third entry, April 8, he confesses that "[t]he caress of the water on the sandy banks or on the granite of the rocks moves and softens me, and the joy that overwhelms me when I can feel myself pushed by the wind and carried by the waves, comes from my giving myself up to the brutal and natural forces of the world, my going back to a primitive life" (52).

For Maupassant, as for Woolf, water offered a rich trope for the dive into the unconscious. In the disarming (and deceptive) two paragraphs he places at his diary's start, Maupassant writes:

> This journal contains no interesting story or adventure. Having been, last spring, on a short cruise on the Mediterranean coast, I amused myself by writing down each day what I saw and what I thought.
>
> In short, I saw water, sun, clouds and rocks—there is nothing else to tell—and I thought simply, as you think when the waves rock you, make you languid, and carry you on.

On his fourth day, halfway through the voyage, when he reflects on the writer's state, Maupassant rises in the dark to fish in Agay Bay, the place he "love[s] best" (71). His two crewmen bait "the innumerable hooks hanging along the line," and in a passage that anticipates Woolf's own portrait of the writer as angler in her 1931 "Professions for Women," Maupassant writes: "Suddenly the line I was holding in my hand trembled, I jumped, then nothing, then a light tug tightened the cord rolled round my fingers, then another stronger one moved my hand and, heart beating, I began to pull the line, gently, eagerly, looking deeply into the blue and transparent water . . ." (70, 71). More successful at this moment than Woolf, whose line falters on the shoals of the body in "Professions for Women," Maupassant reels in "blue [fish], red ones, green and yellow ones, shining, silvery, striped, golden, with rainbow spots, patches, these pretty rock fish of the Mediterranean, so variegated, so brightly coloured, which seem to be painted as a feast for the eyes, then the *rascasses* with barbed spines, and Moray eels, those hideous monsters" (71). Surely each scene conveys its author's work.

Water quickens Maupassant's powers. "[M]y curiosity is awake," he declares on his first day, "that special curiosity of sea voyagers, which makes them see everything, observe everything, makes them excited about the slightest thing" (27). However, like Woolf, he knows, too, the sea's danger. "On this little sea-tossed boat, which a wave can fill and overturn," he writes on his second day, "I know and I can feel how the things we know about are as nothing, for the earth floating in a void is even more isolated, more lost than this barque on the waves. Their importance is the same, their destiny will come about. I am glad I comprehend the emptiness of belief and the vanity of the hopes that are engendered by our insect-like pride!" (42).

Maupassant proclaims the artlessness of *Afloat* at its start and at its close, and the diary *form* aids the illusion. These tacks conceal the extraordinary artfulness of the work. As he sails forth at the whim of the wind and the wave, both sights and sites become wayposts of his mind. In such a state, everything seems elemental and the voyage a record of the writer's solitude, sadness, and (even suicidal) despair.[28] When he sets sail from Antibes on day one, Maupassant personifies his eleven-meter cutter, the *Bel-Ami*, which feels "more alive. . . . on leaving the dead water of the port."[29] On this first day, Maupassant celebrates the great violinist Niccolò Paganini, that "gifted and macabre artist," whose good fortune (in Maupassant's eyes) was to be buried for a time in a nearby island in the Mediterranean Sea (29). "Wouldn't we have preferred the extraordinary violinist to have stayed on the spiny reef, where the waves sing in the strange gashes of the rock?" he asks (30). Gide, too, of course, is a "gifted and macabre artist."

After only a few hours, however, high winds halt Maupassant's sail, and he finds himself forced into Cannes for his second day, a place he sees as artificial, as "death's pleasant and scented antechamber" (36). Cannes is "a town of titles," of princes and celebrities (31). Maupassant rails at their worship, for Cannes is also "society's hospital and the European aristocracy's cemetery"—a truth the town tries to disguise (36). In fact, Maupassant feels "in the presence of Death" along "the length of this lovely coastline" (37), so he retreats to the water and his boat.

Later, he ventures out to inspect the fleet in the harbor from which he launches seamlessly a diatribe on the horrors of war. In 1870, when he was almost twenty, Maupassant dropped his law studies to volunteer for the Franco-Prussian War. Among the French soldiers in the December 1870 retreat from Rouen, he escaped the war in late 1871 when his father bought a man to replace him, the only rescue possible from his seven years' army time. In his long, passionate antiwar turn in *Afloat*, Maupassant argues against poets and career soldiers whose hearts quicken to the drums of war:

I heard the explosion of a fusillade from the shore. It was the Antibes regiment doing shooting exercises on the sand and among the pine trees. The smoke ascended in white wisps, like cotton clouds evaporating, and you could see the red trousers of the soldiers running along by the sea.

Then the naval officers, interested all of a sudden, turned their telescopes towards the land and their hearts lifted at this simulated war.

When I think of that word, war, I feel as appalled as if it were a question of witchcraft, of inquisition, of something far-off, ended, unspeakable, monstrous, against nature....

The little infantrymen running about over there are destined for death just like the flocks a butcher drives along the roads. They will go and fall on the plain, their head split by a sabre blow or with a ball in the chest, and these are young men who could have worked, produced, been useful....

War! Fighting! Butchery! The massacre of men! And we have today, in our time, with our civilization, with the breadth of knowledge and the degree of philosophy which we suppose the human mind to have attained, we have schools where they learn to kill, to kill from far away, perfectly, many people at the same time, to kill poor devils of innocent men, who have family responsibilities and no criminal records.

And the most astounding thing is that the people do not rise up against the government.... The most astounding thing is that the entire community does not rebel at the word "war." (45, 46)

If day two plunges Maupassant into the grief of death and war, he turns toward love on his third day as life's only aid. Fair weather comes and he launches forth once more at 3 a.m. "It seemed like leaving the world behind... that there will be no more shore" (50). At 1 p.m., when the wind drops, he has his crewmen use his small dinghy to tow the *Bel-Ami* into Agay. In town once more, he walks into the forest where he meets two lovers "in dreamlike rapture" (54). Maupassant feels "sadness" come into his heart: "Happiness had brushed past me, a happiness I was not familiar with and which I sensed to be the best of all" (54).

He sees the lovers again when he dines alone at the Agay Inn, and again on the beach, "gazing at the sea," as he starts to embark. "They were filling the bay, the night, the sky, such was the love they were emanating, spreading to the horizon, making them large and symbolic," he states (55). When, from his boat, he sees their profiles one last time in the inn window, he feels his solitude and in his heart "such a desire for love that I nearly cried with distress" (55). He then rhapsodizes on the moon as a symbol of "unrealizable hopes and inaccessible desires," and in this third entry's tour de force close, the slim moon sinks into the water as the lovers close their window (60). "Deep distress crushed me," Maupassant writes, "and I went down to my cabin" (60).

But he cannot sleep. Remorse grips him, and he gives over his fourth entry to thoughts on how artists differ from others. They live with the torture of "second vision," he writes, "which is at the same time the strength and the entire unhappiness of writers" (62). Maupassant possessed a photographic memory. He recalls scenes of human suffering that make him hate the world. At 3 a.m., he begins to fish from his dinghy and in seven hours nets his miraculous, colorful catch. Here is the triumph of art—but the effort brings a headache: a ten-hour migraine.

On his fifth day, April 11, Maupassant docks in Saint-Raphaël. Raphael is the patron saint of travelers; the name in Hebrew means "God heals." Once more Maupassant seems to seek love, but when he meets a wedding party at a church, he sees only human ugliness and the horror of crowds. In an artful turn, he rails at length at crowds, at the mob, only to join it at the end. To escape society's horror, he takes his dinghy up the Argens River and there identifies with the snakes he sees, "the viscous and repellant race of animals who have icy blood. I love these cold and shy creatures which are feared and avoided; to me they have something sacred about them" (80). Entry five ends in the marsh with "the confused revelation of an unknowable mystery, the original breath of primitive life, perhaps a bubble of gas which came out of a marsh as the day died" (80). Maupassant identifies with this cold, primitive, but foundational force.

If the diary's center days disclose the writer's tortured dual state—his triumphant catch, yet still the "unknowable mystery" of life—the final three entries complete the sad sail and bring Maupassant back to (dead) land. On day six, he leaves Saint-Raphaël for Saint-Tropez and sees "an artistic resort" on the way (84). He reflects on solitude over lunch, but the commercial travelers beside him lead him to turns on the French mind, on French women, and on French conversation and wit. He reprises, in order, the famous words of French kings.

On his seventh (and next-to-last) day, he turns inland (and inward) toward the abandoned Carthusian Monastery of La Verne, ruins he associates with "infinite solitude" and "unforgettable sadness" (98). At the monastery he "understood—there was nothing around us, nothing but death" (103), and, as if to drive the point home, he surrounds this moment with the story of a colonel's daughter (and her husband, who dwells nearby). In the first half of the story—before Maupassant reaches the abandoned monastery—he tells of the couple's inspiring love, a tale that recalls the two lovers at Agay. When the colonel refused to let his daughter marry the humble man she loved, she ran away and built a love-filled life with him in the countryside. However, on Maupassant's return from the sad monastery in ruins, he learns the end of the lovers' tale: "for thirty years the man, the old, deaf man, had had a mistress in the neighbouring village, and . . . his wife, having learned of it by chance from a carter who was passing and who chatted about it without knowing who she was, had run off desperate and shrieking up to the granary, then jumped out of the window. . . . jumped into the void" (104–05).

So much for true love. Maupassant retreats once more to his boat, and as he goes to bed, he receives a telegram from a friend: an invitation to meet in Monte Carlo. On day one, in the "rapture of being alone," Maupassant describes his "peace that nothing will disturb . . . no blue telegram. . . . They cannot call to me, invite me, take me anywhere, oppress me with smiles or harass me with courtesy. I am alone, really alone, really free" (26). But on day seven, shaken now by the abandoned monastery and the tale of suicide, he makes haste to see a friend.

In *Afloat*'s last entry, in an emblematic tableau, Maupassant now faces a titanic storm. In his zeal to meet his friend on land and in the folly of pride, he foolishly tells his crew not to put his small dinghy onto the cutter's deck. Instead, the tiny row boat is left trailing the *Bel-Ami* on a forty-meter line. As the storm rages, Maupassant again rejects the crewman's plea to seek shelter in Cannes. He presses on to Antibes. The "little sea-tossed boat, which a wave can fill and overturn" that he mentioned on day two, now meets its death:

> Bernard shouted to me, "The dinghy, sir."
> I turned round. A monstrous wave had filled it, rolled it, enveloped it in its foam as though it were devouring it and, breaking the painter that attached it to us, kept it, half sunk, drowned, a conquered, vanquished prey, which it was going to throw on the rocks on the far-off cape. (42, 108)

Maupassant has met death repeatedly along the coast of France—and now to his own small boat. But the larger cutter reaches Antibes, and Maupassant takes the four o'clock train to "have dinner with my friend in the Principality of Monaco" (109). Sadly, he finds there love further profaned. The rapt lovers from Agay (in entry three) now sit by the roulette wheel. Money now replaces nature's waves. Maupassant writes that "[t]he sound of money, continuous as the waves, a light, formidable, profound sound, filled the ears as you entered, then it filled the soul, moved the heart, disturbed the mind, maddened thought. It can be heard everywhere, this noise that sings, cries out, calls, tempts, and tears apart" (113). The diarist sees the young woman from Agay Bay, "her whole face contorted and ill humored . . . the beautiful one who was in love in the sunny woods and the gentle moonlight" (113). The lovers lose their gold Louis, and as they depart Maupassant feels "something terrible had come between them" (113).

Across this melancholy, hope-dashed, death-strewn diary, Maupassant plays with the poles of prison and freedom. The entire sea voyage, of course, is a drive to escape society's prison and the horrors of the land. Maupassant toys exquisitely with escape—escape to freedom, love, and art. On day one, he sails by the island of Sainte-Marguerite, "where Bazaine and the Man in the Iron Mask were imprisoned" (25), and on day two he describes at length the punished French General Bazaine's bold escape. For surrendering Metz during the Franco-Prussian War, Marshal Bazaine was first sentenced to death and then imprisoned for twenty years. But he escaped. Saint Marguerite herself was imprisoned and escaped from inside a dragon.

On day six in Saint-Tropez, Maupassant sees the clerks freed for lunch and offers a powerful turn on the slavery of clerks. The two old law clerks are "like two old beasts of burden unharnessed for a moment to eat their oats from the bottom of a sack. Oh freedom! Freedom—the only hope, the only dream, the only happiness!" (86). And on the diary's final day, Maupassant plays with the notion of a prisonless land. He finds it in Monaco but then tells the witty (yet finally horrifying) tale of a murderer whose crime frustrates the prisonless Monaco court. The man first is condemned to death; however, since Monaco has neither guillotine nor executioner—never before needing them—he is sent to a makeshift prison. However, when costs for his food and guard surpass the cost of renting a guillotine and executioner, the prince dismisses the guard and makes the murderer his own guard. The man gracefully accepts this state and politely walks each day to the castle for his meals. This so frustrates the prince that he has the murderer expelled from Monaco, at which the agreeable man sets up a house just over the border in France. Feeling wholly mocked, the prince, in the end, orders France to execute him, so the man meets his end in France. Another French death. And Maupassant ends *his* journal with the touch of a hand on his shoulder.

Afloat came to Virginia Woolf's aid in 1934. Solitude and art's lonely outpost increasingly drew Woolf as the 1930s unfurled. She knew, too, the pain of headaches; in fact, Maupassant's vision of the writer as a tortured Prometheus was her own since 1921. On his third night, after the lovers close the shutter and the hopeful moon sinks into the sea, Maupassant thinks on "everything towards which [his mind] had tried to soar, without being able to break the chain of ignorance that held it back" (62). Here is Prometheus, the fire-giver, chained. "Then why this distress at living, when most men only feel its satisfaction?" he asks. "Why this unknown torture gnawing at me? . . . It is because I have in me this second vision, which is at the same time the strength and the entire unhappiness of writers" (62).

In her first diary entry after Roger Fry's shocking death, September 9, 1934, Woolf copies lines from *Afloat* to explain her own distressed state:

Maupassant, on writers—(true I think).
"In [a writer], no simple feeling exists any more. Everything he sees, his joys, his pleasures, his pain, his despair instantly become subjects for observation. He analyses in spite of everything, in spite of himself, endlessly, hearts, faces, gestures, intonations." (D 4: 242; *Afloat* 63)

She then copies his diary declaration that a writer is "never to suffer, think, love, feel like everyone else does, kindly, truly, simply, without self-analysis after each joy and after each sob" (*Afloat* 63). It helps her, perhaps, to know that others share her painful dual state, for she even jots the page number of Maupassant's words in her diary margin. For future reference? For Old Virginia's memoirs?

Maupassant also writes in *Afloat* that when a writer "is writing, he cannot refrain from throwing into his books everything he has seen, everything he has understood" (64). (This line could pass as a gloss for *Afloat*.) In August 1934, Woolf finds Maupassant's novel *A Woman's Life* "marking time & watery" (D 4: 238). However, she salutes Maupassant the helpful, artful *diarist* in her own novel-in-progress, *The Years*. In that work's final chapter, on which she labors in August 1934, she endows her woman doctor, Peggy Pargiter, with Maupassant's view:

Peggy, marooned when the dance started, over by the bookcase, stood as close to it as she could. In order to cover her loneliness she took down a book. . . . He'll say what I'm thinking, she thought as she did so. Books opened at random always did.

> "The mediocrity of the universe astonishes and repels me," she read. That was it. Precisely. She read on. " . . . the pettiness of everything fills me with disgust . . ." She lifted her eyes. They were treading on her toes. " . . . the inadequacy of human beings overwhelms me." She shut the book and put it back on the shelf.
>
> Precisely, she said. (*TY* 383)

The book, of course, is *Sur l'eau*, and Woolf makes readers work to understand Maupassant's words by giving them in the original French. David Bradshaw, who first identified the source in 2002, notes the two sentences from *Afloat* that precede "[t]he mediocrity of the universe": "It is true that, on certain days, I feel the horror of what exists, to the point of wishing to be dead. I sense to the point of acute pain the unchanging monotony of the landscape, of faces and of thoughts" (*Afloat* 51). *Afloat* ends back on land, the woman's suicide left behind, and Woolf omits these lines in *The Years*.

Woolf possessed stronger love for her fellow creatures than "icy blooded" Maupassant—although she, too, has her moments of hate for her kind. She also did not share his total "emptiness of belief" (*Afloat* 42). However, she also was not burdened with the mental tortures of fatal syphilis which would lead to a suicide attempt and finally claim Maupassant in only five years. Woolf ends *her* novel's scene with Peggy placing Maupassant's book back on the shelf. "She went towards them [the family party]," the scene ends (*TY* 383).

Maupassant's brilliant travel diary, *Afloat*, clearly touched Woolf in 1934. It showed her an inner and outer fight for freedom. It offered her immediate aid at Roger Fry's death: insight into the artist's painful dual state. It supplied words for her diary and a key moment for her novel *The Years*—and antiwar fuel for *Three Guineas* to come.

Alice James' *Journal*

Henry James called his sister's diary "a new claim for the family renown" (Burr 85). Nevertheless, he suppressed it. Only through women's acts of remembrance did this diary survive and begin to reach readers more than forty years from its close at Alice's death in 1892. Virginia Woolf wrote "Alice James" in her own October 2, 1934, diary entry in the list of library books "read or . . . reading" (*D* 4: 248). The work was the 1934 *Alice James: Her Brothers—Her Journal*, edited (and expurgated) by Anna Robeson Burr.

James' *Journal*, of course, offered several pulls. Woolf might catch a sister's view of Henry James, who entered Woolf's own childhood as an old family friend.[30] At age fifteen, in fact, in her very first (1897) diary, Virginia parodied pertly his labyrinthine talk (*PA* 63). In autumn 1907, twenty-five-year-old Virginia took tea twice with Henry James during her holiday at Playden, near his Sussex home in Rye. She read then his 1907 *The American Scene* and her own "scene making" gift begins in her Playden diary (MOB 142). Was there a link?

Even more important, as Woolf turns to revise *The Years* in October 1934, Alice James' diary offers a further view of women's social and sexual lives. "[T]wo thousand years of Christianity, as interpreted by the pious of all nations, necessitates that, when a poor girl goes wrong, she should be ejected from all societies to which she belongs, instituted for the purpose of keeping her in the straight path," Alice jeers in an 1890 diary entry (Burr 135). The next year, she observes that "there is no need to make rules regulating the walking together of male and female students, for as all the latter would presumably be governesses or teachers, any man student would rather throw himself into the Cam than be guilty of the bad form of walking with any one of them, however pretty and attractive she might be and desirable as a companion outside of university recognition" (Burr 241).

The caustic strength (and clever strategy) of James' diary rests in her willingness to mock herself at the same time she questions her culture's codes. In the first year of her diary, James seems obsessed with propagation and regularly marks her disgust. Of a nearby English family, she records in June 1889: "This is No. 5.... I wonder if it is indelicate in a flaccid virgin to be so preoccupied with the multiplication of the species; but it fairly haunts me,—something irresistible and overwhelming, like the tides of the sea or the Connemaugh flood—a mighty horde to sweep over the face of the earth" (Burr 94).

The next year, "surprised and shocked" to hear that Ellie Emmet, whose heart (Alice thought) "was seared by sorrow," was thinking to marry again, James notes: "'Twould seem to the inexperienced that one happy 'go' at marriage would have given the full measure of connubial bliss, and all the chords of maternity been vibrated under the manipulation of six progeny; but man lives not to assimilate knowledge of the eternal essence of things, and only craves a renewal of sensation" (Burr 203–04). James thus drolly mocks the marriage and motherhood myths.

"[D]enied ... marriage by obtuse and imperceptive man," she cracks in the last year of her life, she notes the barriers women face who choose a different path (Burr 238). "I was greatly touched . . . with Constance Maud's talk about her music," James tells her diary. "She wants to devote herself to it seriously as a profession, but as she is a daughter and not a son, her tastes are set aside, and she has to do parish work! and that pretty badly, I fear. Her compositions are very good, they say, and original; isn't it too bad? She says she doesn't know how she would live without her music" (Burr 120).

Beyond such notes on human excess and constraint, James' diary helped Woolf date social change. Alice arrived in England in November 1884. In March 1891, she writes from Woolf's own Kensington that "[t]he change that has come, even since I have been here, is most extraordinary; young girls going to dances alone, and the mothers not even invited. Bessie Clarke, Mrs. Stanley Clarke's charming daughter of twenty, told K[atharine]. that she rode at 8 a.m. in the Park because she had no groom to go with her; and her mother would not allow her to ride alone at twelve, as so many of the girls did. She and Minnie Emmet seemed to be going about alone in omnibuses whenever they wanted to" (Burr 212). All this would be useful for Woolf's Pargiter tale, with its early references to "street love" and the fact that in 1880 London "Eleanor and Milly and Delia [Pargiter] could not possibly go for a walk alone—save in the streets round about Abercorn Terrace, and then only between the hours of eight-thirty and sunset.... For any of them to walk in the West End even by day was out of the question. Bond Street was as impassable, save with their mother, as any swamp alive with crocodiles" (*The Pargiters* 36, 37).

Sadly, editor Burr cut the following 1889 diary passage that anticipates Woolf's powerful *Three Guineas* turn on "unreal loyalties." James asks: "When will women begin to have the first glimmer that above all other loyalties is the loyalty to Truth, i.e., to yourself, that husband, children, friends and country are as nothing to that" (Edel 60). James' diary stands as a monument to truth to oneself—and to the role of a diary in achieving this truth. James was born in New York City in 1848, the youngest child and only daughter with four brothers, two extraordinarily gifted. Her adored brother Henry (the novelist) was five years her senior; her less sympathetic brother William (the philosopher), six. Like Ralph Waldo Emerson, whom she knew, Alice found her diary voice by first keeping a commonplace book.[31] In December 1886, at age thirty-eight, she begins to preserve poems, aphorisms, and passages from novels and other works—"the words of famous writers, and these seem to speak for Alice," notes James biographer Leon Edel, who published in 1964 a fuller edition of Alice's *Diary* (2).

By May 1889—at age forty—Alice is ready to speak for herself. She launches her own voice and diary. "I think that if I get into the habit of writing a bit about what happens, or rather doesn't happen, I may lose a little of the sense of loneliness and desolation which abides with me," she begins from Royal Leamington Spa in northwest England (Burr 87). Almost three years of periodic diary follow, 161 entries in which Alice preserves her final days and stakes her claim as an artist: sixty-eight entries the first year; sixty-three the second; and a mere thirty during the shortened but luminous last year when she succumbs to breast cancer at age forty-three.[32] James kept this important diary in two "ordinary English scribblers" smaller than Woolf's more spacious diary books.[33]

Edel notes James' "supreme need" to perpetuate herself—a trait of many great diarists (20). On the last day of 1890, when she can no longer lift a pen, she begins to dictate her diary to her "better half," Katharine Peabody Loring (Burr 184). She continues to dictate across her final fourteen months. In her last six weeks of life, she asks to have the diary typewritten. "[T]hough she never said so, I understand that she would like to have it published," Loring later declared (Edel v). In her final hours, James worries over a phrase in her last entry and cannot rest until she gets it right.

As her first diary entry lays bare, James thought a diary would serve her in several ways. She hopes diary-writing will relieve her loneliness and desolation. She also views the diary as a space to enlarge her voice. "My circumstances allowing of nothing but the ejaculation of one-syllabled reflections," she explains in her second line, "a written monologue by that most interesting being, myself, may have its yet to be discovered consolations" (Burr 87). This playful self-mockery recalls fifteen-year-old Fanny Burney's opening diary bow to "Nobody." In both centuries, the self-mockery forestalls criticism of female presumption and allows the diarist to proceed.

James then closes this entry with an artist's claim. "I shall, at least, have it all my own way," she declares, implying that elsewhere her will does not prevail, "and it may bring relief as an outlet to that geyser of emotions, sensations, speculations and reflections which ferments perpetually within my poor old carcass for its sins; so here goes,—my first journal!" (Burr 87). She anticipates here Woolf's and André Gide's diaries as relieving reservoirs—an "outlet" that clearly excites her.

Eleven months later, James sees her journal as a site for women's theories, just as twenty-one-year-old Woolf does in her own pivotal 1903 diary. "I remind myself all the time of a coral insect, building up my various reefs of theory by microscopic additions drawn from observation, or my inner consciousness, mostly," James writes (154). Like Burney, Gide, Woolf, and many other diarists, James also uses her diary as a confidante—and for talk. "Where do you suppose I went this morning?" she exclaims in June 1889, as if chatting with an "other": "Into a hayfield amid the hay-makers; it was divine!" (Burr 93). At the end of the first year, she declares that "scribbling my notes . . . in that they clarify the density, and shape the formless mass within" makes life "inconceivably rich" (Burr 157).

If Alice James could not be a famous writer like her brother Henry, she demands, at least *here*, control of her own life tale. Physical and social constraints shape her world and explain a great deal of the diary, which also seeks (and finds) escape from these restraints. Alice James knows that *her* place in the world is small and at the margins. She writes of her "narrow range"; her "microscopic field"; her "cramped" view (Burr 128, 103, 138). Her caustic humor allows her to distance herself from and cope with this life state, her "little destiny" (Burr 209). Her final Kensington diary opens with an ironist's exclamation: "How amusing it is to see the fixed mosaic of one's little destiny being filled out by tiny blocks of events,—the enchainment of minute consequences with the illusion of choice weathering it all!" (Burr 209).

She knows many barriers rise from without. Constance Maud's musical gifts "are set aside," just as pungent language lies outside her own reach. "One day when my shawls were falling off to the left, my cushions falling out to the right, and the duvet off my knees,—one of those crises of misery, in short, which are all in the day's work for an invalid," James writes in 1889 in her self-mocking, yet instructive, way, "K[atharine]. exclaimed, 'What an awful pity it is that you can't say damn.' I agreed with her from my heart; it is an immense loss to have all robust and sustaining expletives refined away from one" (Burr 119–20).

The British class system and its stuffy "refinements" strike James as even more restrictive than her own American culture; her protest explains the many article clippings that pepper her diary. "I find myself, as the months pass, more and more oppressed by the all-pervasive sense of pharisaism in the British constitution of things," she opens a February 1890 entry. "You don't feel it at first, and you can't put your finger upon it in your friends; but as the days go by you unfold it with your Standard in the morning, and it rises dense from the Pall Mall Gazette in the evening; it creeps through the cracks in the window frames like the fog, and envelopes you through the day" (Burr 137–38).

Alice's sympathies rest with other outsiders: with the Irish, the working class, and the poor. Nevertheless, she knows her privilege. "I saw, on Sunday in the River Walk, two workmen, about thirty, clean, intelligent, sober and serious and I did so long to stop and ask them what they thought of it all," she writes in August 1889, "but, ah! me, I'm hopelessly relegated among the smug and the comfortable" (Edel 55). Of formal religion, which she rejects, she writes in 1891: "But of all the repulsions, the greatest is that of a religion subscribed to in conformity to an outward standard of respectability,—not the spontaneous inspiration of the aspiring souls" (Burr 221).

James knows her culture limits her, yet she admits, too, that she restrains herself. Tensions ripple across James' diary between constraint and freedom (as in Gide's *Journals,* Maupassant's *Sur l'eau,* and Woolf's diary) and between passivity and action. In November 1890, James describes "a never ceasing belief in and longing for *action,* relentlessly denied; all safety valves shut in the way of the 'busy ineffectiveness of women'" (Burr 184). In her first dictated entry to Katharine Peabody Loring, she declares that her place "does violence to a primordial instinct and fills one with a constant sense of shame and weakness to turn one's back and not shape the accidents of nativity to one's purpose, and extract from whatever barrenness the fullest and richest measure of development" (Burr 192).

But James learned early on to stifle herself. In February 1890, in a paragraph preferring "this blessed moment of middle life" to youth, she writes: "Owing to muscular circumstances, my youth was not of the most ardent, but I had to peg away pretty hard between [ages] twelve and twenty-four, 'killing myself,' as some one calls it—absorbing into the bone that the better part is to clothe one's self in neutral tints, walk by still waters, and possess one's soul in silence" (Burr 144).

James speaks for the "passive hero" in her diary. "The active can't be much thrilled, of course, by the passive hero who is so little picturesque and reverberating as he lies hidden in reeking cellars and freezing attics, chained like a galley-slave to his oar of endurance for countless years," she writes in July 1889, clearly thinking of herself (Burr 99). Her diary offers her action *within* passivity—much like Woolf's country *within* London.

Illness moves one to life's sidelines—as both Woolf and Gide knew. Like the diaries of James' fellow cancer victims, Edith Cooper and Katherine Bradley (aka Michael Field), James' is a diary of illness—although it is much more. James' headaches, bouts with nerves, and disdain for doctors surely struck a sympathetic chord in Woolf.[34] A diary offered James space to tell her life story as she saw it. "I shall put down everything I can think of in this precious reservoir," she writes six months into her diary (Burr 115). In October 1890, she poses her lived experience against brother William's claim, in "The Hidden Self," that "the nervous victim 'abandons' certain portions of his consciousness" (Burr 181). Alice writes: "I have never unfortunately been able to abandon my consciousness and get five minutes rest" (Burr 181). She then explains her state:

> I see how it began in my childhood, although I wasn't conscious of the necessity until '[18]67 or '[18]68 [ages nineteen or twenty], when I broke down first, acutely, and had violent turns of hysteria. As I lay prostrate after the storm, with my mind luminous and active, and susceptible of the clearest, strongest impressions, I saw so distinctly that it was a fight simply between my body and my will—a battle in which the former was to be triumphant to the end. Owing to some physical weakness, excess of nervous susceptibility, the moral power *pauses*, as it were, for a moment, and refuses to maintain muscular sanity, worn out with the strain of its constabulary functions. As I used to sit immovable, reading in the library, with waves of violent inclination suddenly invading my muscles, taking some one of their varied forms, such as throwing myself out of the window or knocking off the head of the benignant Pater, as he sat, with his silver locks, writing at his table, it used to seem to me that the only difference between me and the insane was that I had only all the horrors and suffering of insanity, but the duties of doctor, nurse, and strait-jacket imposed upon me too. (Burr 181–82)

At age twenty-two, Woolf actually threw herself from a window. She knew, too, the "mind luminous and active, and susceptible of the clearest, strongest impressions," after a "storm" of nerves.

In the last month of her life, James describes a recurrence of nervous breakdown at age thirty: "The fact is, I have been dead so long, and it has been simply such a grim shoving of the hours behind me as I faced a ceaseless possible horror since that hideous summer of '[18]78 when I went down to the deep sea, and its dark waters closed over me ... now it's only the shrivelling of an empty pea-pod that has to be completed" (Burr 250). Woolf, too, knew breakdown at about age thirty.

Ten of James' 161 diary entries refer to suicide—her own or others'—a striking sum. In the fourth month of her diary, she writes: "They say that there is little doubt that Mr. Edmund Gurney committed suicide. What a pity to hide it; every educated person who kills himself does something toward lessening the superstition. It's bad that it's so untidy. There is no denying that, for one bespatters one's friends morally as well as physically, taking them so much more into one's secret than they want to be taken. But how heroic to be able to supress one's vanity to the extent of confessing that the game is too hard" (Burr 108).

James savors especially suicides that vex the church. "A man has committed suicide in St. Paul's, which I allow is inexcusably sloppy of him," she writes on October 4, 1890, putting herself in the tut-tutting clergy role; "[B]ut it has caused a delicious fuss and fluster among the shovel-hats. The Cathedral will have to be re-consecrated, they fear; but perhaps they may be able, with their highly developed muscles of evasion, to wash out the stain of blood by an 'Act of Reconciliation'!" (Burr 176).

James' diary may strike some as angry and bitter. It struck Leon Edel so (17–18). Alice insists on her "thistledown personality" and role as "unsentimental spinster" on the sofa (Burr 232, 162). Nevertheless, as she records her life trials—again and again she finds, in the concrete world and in the individual mind, escape from her physical and social chains. In the second month of her diary, James writes of the natural world: "How grateful I am that I actually see, to my own consciousness, the quarter of an inch that my eyes fall upon; truly the subject is all that counts!"[35] On August 13, 1890, she writes: "[H]ow darksome then the last stages, if we have not made our own . . . individual and inextinguishable radiance, to warm the memory and illuminate the mind" (Burr 168).

Like twenty-one-year-old Virginia Woolf, who wished to throw herself on the earth and absorb nature's breath, forty-one-year-old James starts her second diary year in May 1890 by "longing to see a shaft of sunshine shimmering through the pines, breathe in the resinous air, and throw my withered body upon my mother earth, bury my face in the coarse grass, worshipping all that the ugly, raw emptiness of the blessed land stands for,—the embodiment of a huge chance for hemmed-in humanity" (Burr 162).

Alice suffers a sudden illness in August 1890 that whips Henry home from Venice to move her from Leamington Spa to London and the South Kensington Hotel. The illness leads Alice to a series of entries in which she declares her philosophy. "There has come such a change in me," she opens her August 18, 1890, entry. "A congenital faith flows through me like a limpid stream, making the arid places green, a spontaneous irrigator, which the snags of doubt have never interrupted nor made turbid the easily flowing current; a faith which is my mental and moral respiration, which needs no revelation but experience and whose only ritual is daily conduct" (Burr 169). On October 10, 1890, she elaborates:

> How it fills one with wonder to see people old enough to have stored experience never apparently suspecting that of all the arts the art of living is the most exquisite and rewarding, and that it is not brought to perfection by wallowing in disabilities.... The paralytic on his couch can have, if he wants them, wider experiences than Stanley's slaughtering savages; ... and the peaceful cotton-spinner win victories beside which those of the reverberating general are dust and ashes. Let us not waste, then, the sacred fire, and wear away the tissues in the vulgar pursuit of what others have and we have not; admitting defeat isn't the way to conquer, and from every failure imperishable experience survives. (Burr 179)

Here, Woolf sees another battler.

In late May 1891, James learns of her breast cancer. She calls her doctor, Sir Andrew Clark, a "blessed being" for naming her other maladies as well (Burr 231). They include cardiac complications, nervous hyperesthesia, spinal neurosis that has impaired her legs for seven years, and rheumatic gout that has plagued her for twenty. The next day she explains herself more fully. She opens her June 1, 1891, entry as if addressing the public:

> To any one who has not been there, it will be hard to understand the enormous relief of Sir A. C.'s uncompromising verdict [of fatal breast cancer], lifting us out the formless vague and sitting us within the very heart of the sustaining concrete. One would naturally not choose such an ugly and gruesome method of progression down the dark valley of the shadow of death, and of course many of the moral sinews will snap by the way; but we shall bind up our loins and the blessed peace of the end will have no shadow cast upon it.
>
> Having it to look forward to for a while seems to double the value of the event, for one becomes suddenly picturesque to one's self and one's wavering little individuality stands out with a cameo effect.... The grief is all for K[atharine]. and H[enry]., who will *see* it all, whilst I shall only *feel* it, but they are taking it, of course, like archangels, and care for me with infinite tenderness and patience. Poor dear William, with his exaggerated sympathy for suffering, isn't to know anything about it until it is all over. (Burr 231–32)

In her final eight months of life, James gives eloquent voice to what, decades later, Elisabeth Kübler-Ross called the stages of death. In June, she laments future losses. "I see a new volume of Anatole France out, which will never be read by me!" she exclaims (Burr 233)—a line Woolf will echo in her January 11, 1935, diary: "I may not have read all Dante before I—but why harp on death?" (D 4: 274). Eight days later, James starts to let go of worldly ways. "Half a dozen times a day I find myself saying: 'I must ask K. about that,' or, 'I must find out about this,' with the idea that some day I may need the knowledge," she muses, "when suddenly I am stopped by the thought that the 'some days' are over for me,—a thought natural and simple and of a most desirable complexion. It seems more like the gentle dropping of natural things than the taking up of spiritual ones..." (Burr 237).

In July, she records "a delicious consciousness of wide spaces close at hand. ... Imagine the emancipation that it will be, after seven years of this stifling land, where 'form' is the god of gods!" (Burr 239). In September and October she declines all spiritual saps. "[H]ow little all assurances of one's own immortality seem to concern one, now.... References to those whom we shall meet again make me shiver" (Burr 242). Of the myth of penetrating evil at death, she writes on October 31: "[A]n impossible strain upon humanity is the asking that it should reflect any illumination other than the individual or personal one" (Edel 221). In December, she continues to shed her intellectual stays, and on February 2, 1892, she opens her diary to summarize her state:

> This long, slow dying is no doubt instructive, but it is disappointingly free from excitement, "naturalness" being carried to its supreme expression. One sloughs off the activities, one by one, and never knows that they're gone until one suddenly finds that the months have slipped away and the sofa will never more be laid upon, the morning paper read, or the loss of the new book regretted. One revolves with equal content within the narrowing circle until the vanishing point is reached, I suppose.
>
> Vanity, however, maintains its undisputed sway, and I take satisfaction in feeling as much myself as ever, perhaps simply a more concentrated essence in the curtailment. (Burr 250)

On February 28, 1892, James prays that when she dies William will not set his medium, "the dreadful Mrs. Piper ... loose upon my defenceless soul," and in her last two diary entries, she turns poetic (Edel 231). Six days before her death, she dictates: "Of what matter can it be whether pain or pleasure has shaped and stamped the pulp within, as one is absorbed in the supreme interest of watching the outline and the tracery as the lines broaden for eternity" (Edel 231–32).

In her diary's last entry, two days before her death, thoughts of suicide rise once more. "I am being ground slowly on the grim grindstone of physical pain, and on two nights I had almost asked for K's lethal dose; but one steps hesitatingly along such unaccustomed ways, and endures from second to second," she declares. "I feel sure that it can't be possible but that the bewildered little hammer that keeps me going will very shortly see the decency of ending his distracted career. However this may be, physical pain, however great, ends in itself and falls away like dry husks from the mind . . ." (Burr 252).

"The difficulty about all this dying is that you can't tell a fellow anything about it, so where does the fun come in?" James gamely quipped in her December 11, 1891, entry (Edel 223). But, of course, she *has* told us much about it—a great gift. She died on March 6, 1892, whispering to Henry that she couldn't, just *couldn't*, live another day (Edel 16). Loyal Katharine Loring proved loyal to the end. She carried James' diary back to her home in Beverly, Massachusetts, where, according to Edel, "she edited the manuscript by straightening its punctuation a little, altering an occasional word, deleting some passages, and introducing half-a-dozen footnotes" (v).

In 1894, Loring had four copies printed, one for each of the three surviving James brothers and one for herself. She tried first the two oldest brothers. William James, she later wrote, never thanked her for her copy or made any suggestion as to its publication (Edel v). Henry urged her to refrain. Alice never told him she kept a diary, he explained in a letter to William,[36] and he had gossiped to her freely. Loring should have "sunk a few names," Henry wrote, and used more initials. "When I see that *I* say that Augustine Birrell has a self-satisfied smirk after he speaks—and see that Katharine felt no prompting to exercise a discretion about the name, I feel very unhappy and wonder at the strangeness of destiny" (Edel vi). In a May 28, 1894, letter to William, Henry praised "the life, the power, the temper, the humour and beauty and expressiveness of the Diary in itself," its "wondrous vigour of judgment," its "heroic . . . individuality, its independence—its face-to-face with the universe for-and-by herself" (Edel 18–19). "What I should LIKE to do *en temps et lieu*," he writes his brother, "would be should no catastrophe meanwhile occur—or even if it should!—to edit the volume with a few eliminations of text and dissimulations of names, give it to the world and then carefully burn with fire our own four copies" (Edel 19). But he never fulfilled this wish; rather, he destroyed his copy.

In the early 1930s, long after the brothers' deaths, Loring presented Robertson James' daughter with her father's copy. Loring made this gesture, she said, from friendship and because Robertson's children were "the only grandchildren who have ever taken any interest in me, or have asked me about my relations with the James family" (Edel vi). Robertson's daughter, Mary James Vaux, saw merit in Alice's diary and, wishing remembrance of the two younger James brothers as well, commissioned the 1934 *Alice James: Her Brothers—Her Journal*—the text Woolf read.

According to Edel, Burr (the volume's editor), worked from Loring's printed version rather than from the original two "scribblers." Regrettably, Burr deleted Alice's passages in French—which Woolf likely would have savored—as well as Alice's clippings from the English papers "because they concern events long past, relating often to minor Parliamentary debates and English local politics, but also because they dilute the rich flow of her own observation and feeling" (i). Woolf thus missed James' full critique of British "forms." As Edel commented in 1964, when he restored the full text from photocopies of both the original manuscript and Loring's privately printed version, "Far from 'diluting' Alice's journal," the clippings and commentary are integral to it (viii).

What did Woolf think of Alice James' diary, with its "cold-blooded" observations and "mortuary inclinations" akin to Maupassant's (Burr 161, 251)? No record survives. Surely, she saw a spirit chafing at social restraints. She saw a Victorian woman fighting for freedom across "the years"—a fight she is waging herself at this moment, as are the Pargiter women (and men) in her novel. She also saw much on suicide. At minimum, she saw affirmed in a diary both "imperishable experience" and the "sustaining concrete" (Burr 179, 231).

5

Tightness & Struggle

"Leonard has turned on the wireless to listen to the news, and so I am flicked out of the world I like into the other," Virginia Woolf writes to Lady Ottoline Morrell in October 1935. "I wish one were allowed to live only in one world, but thats asking too much" (*L* #3066, 5: 429).

Total war—as a concept—appears in General Erich Ludendorff's 1935 volume *Die totale Krieg*. The general insists, Stuart N. Clarke explains, that "modern war" is "all encompassing and . . . no-one could or should necessarily be spared by the military"; "civilians were combatants and should be treated accordingly" (107). In May 1935, the Woolfs view Nazi Germany first hand. In the fall, Mussolini defies the League of Nations and invades Abyssinia (Ethiopia).

Woolf's 1935 diary reveals the three daunting challenges she now faces. It also showcases her great courage and effort, for she seeks to answer each trial, each blow, with a book. Her inner artistic battle involves a creeping tightness. She seeks to keep loose (and supple) as she tightens and tightens *The Years*. Is this possible? Her diary, as usual, helps her. She turns to other diaries, as well. In September, Woolf reads a country doctor's diary for the years 1849 to 1932 and then literary critic John Bailey's *Letters and Diaries, 1861–1931*. She reads, in short, male voices across "the years" chronicled in her novel. She enters into a dialogue with these diarists in her public fiction and nonfiction.

Virginia Woolf's 1935 Diary

> *"A curious sense of complete failure. . . . I cant write this morning. Cant get into the swing. . . . My head is all jangled. . . . I think no: merely go on. . . . And perhaps read a little Shakespeare. Yes, one of the last plays: I think I will do that, so as to loosen my muscles. But oh this anxiety, & the perpetual knocking of the cup out of my hand."*
>
> (July 16, 1935; *D* 4: 331)

Struggle quickens Virginia Woolf's 1935 diary, a contest between creeping tightness and Woolf's drive to remain loose and supple in her art. The diary itself thickens, for Woolf pens 121 entries across the 336 days from January 19 to December 20, 1935—an entry now, on average, every two to three days instead of four, as in her last diary. Three formidable challenges confront Woolf in 1935. She answers each with a book—a striking act in itself.

The first challenge is the loss of Roger Fry. His death triggers the tightness, the creative chill. "I feel dazed: very wooden," she writes on September 12, 1934, her first entry after Fry's unexpected death, on September 9. "And I'm too stupid to write anything. My head all stiff" (D 4: 242). If Woolf's lost mother haunts her 1905 Cornwall diary, Roger Fry haunts the diary of 1935. "Roger's ghost knocked at the door," Woolf reports in her first entry, January 19, 1935. "And the horrid winter lap begins; the pale unbecoming days, like an aging woman seen at 11 o'clock" (D 4: 275). When she dines February 8 with Vanessa, she exclaims "oh dear"—her diary phrase of heartfelt woe—"how the ghost of Roger haunted us! . . . An extraordinary sense of him: of wishing for him; of vacancy" (D 4: 279). On March 25, his shade reappears, again at dinner. "[A] great desire for Roger," she repeats. "Again the sense of him coming in with his great dark eyes, & his tie pin & his brown shoes & how, speaking in that very deep voice he would have discussed Max Eastman & Epstein. We only flick the surface—some means of communication—some other instrument needed to combine us all in harmony. . . . And all would have been deepened, & made suggestive" (D 4: 290). She then gives her patented diary waive: "But never mind. This is inevitable, & we must blow on the bellows" (D 4: 290). Now *she* must be the instrument: *she* must animate the wood.

However, her "flow," her "flood," seems checked in the first five months of 1935. Only in the first weeks of June, when Vanessa sends her Roger's letters, does Woolf again use the word "fluent" to describe her work. Fry once more seems to invigorate her.[1] Roger's sister and literary executor, Margery Fry, formally asks Woolf to write his biography on June 20, spurring Woolf to think of multiple books to come: "[I]t appeared that they are counting on me to write a life. . . . This morning theres a book (in the Lit. Sup.) complaining that women have dropped their sacred task. This floods me with my Professions book. . . . And here I am wedged—no, buoyant—in a floating storm of scenes at the end of [*The Years*]" (D 4: 323, 324). Roger's letters may have caused her renewed buoyancy. His "life" means his (and her) renewal.

On August 21, Woolf reports that Roger's papers will arrive in two days. In mid-September, awash now in Roger's ink, she decides to imbibe Roger's prose in small refreshing drops. On September 26, a visit to Rymans "to buy a case for [her] Roger notes" leads to a plan to make her *diary* more elastic. "In future," she writes, "I shall write in loose leaf books" (D 4: 344). She repeats this pledge on December 10. She has tried loose-leaf diaries before. Her first mention of such diaries (meant to "snare a greater number of loose thoughts") appears in late 1918 when she visits Fry, creates "Old Virginia" as a parallel invigorating spirit, and moves toward her mature diary style (D 1: 228). This is followed by actual use of loose-leaf diaries in 1927, 1928, and half of 1929. In fact, from late 1918 forward, Woolf links *Fry* with refreshment and diary expansion—as occurs again here.

"Drops" of Fry accompany a renewed flood of fiction in late September and October. On October 2, when war talk at the Labour Party Conference makes Woolf unable to write *The Years*, she tells her diary suggestively, "I will do some Roger," and her next entry, October 15, reveals her success: "I have been in such full flush, with Years all the morning, Roger between tea & dinner" (D 4: 346). She decides to write her "Next War" book in the spring of 1936, "while I go on accumulating Roger. This division is by the way perfect, & I wonder I never hit on it before—some book or work for a book thats quite the other side of the brain between times. Its the only way of stopping the wheels & making them turn the other way, to my great refreshment" (D 4: 347).

A week later, when her social life unsettles her mind for *The Years*, she again turns to Fry. "I have shut the book—Sal & Martin in Hyde Park—& spent the morning typing out Roger's memoirs. This is a most admirable sedative & refresher. I wish I always had it at hand" (D 4: 347). In short, Woolf taps Fry's animating spirit regularly in 1935. His "life" means renewal.

On March 11, before Roger's letters arrive in June to imbue her, Woolf speaks again of feeling empty. "[I]f my hands werent so cold," she writes, "I could here analyse my state of mind these past 4 months, & account for the human emptiness by the defection of Vita; Roger's death; & no-one springing up to take their place" (D 4: 287). In this vulnerable, "springless" state, she suffers her second blow: new literary attacks in March. She opens her March 16 entry to register these "swingeings" or thrashings: "I have had 3 severe swingeings lately: Wyndham Lewis [in October and November 1934], Mirsky; & now Swinnerton. Bloomsbury is ridiculed; & I am dismissed with it" (D 4: 287–88). She counters with poignant bravura: "I didnt read W.L.; & Swinnerton only affected me as [a] robin affects a rhinoceros—except in the depths of the night" (*D* 4: 288). As in October 1934, she turns to her diary to treat the pain. She writes four March entries before the March 16 attack and twelve in the sixteen days from March 16 to March 31. She pens eighteen more entries in April—the most of any month in 1935.

The new outer attacks clearly distress her, for they resurrect those old bothers: praise and blame. If she answers Fry's death with his life (his biography), *The Years* must be her reply to critical attack. She opens her March 18 entry to declare:

> The only thing worth doing in [*The Years*] is to stick it out: stick to the idea, & dont lower it an inch, in deference to anyone. . . . & Swinnerton's sneers, & Mirsky's—making me feel that I'm hated & despised & ridiculed—well, this is the only answer: to stick to my ideas. And I wish I need never read about myself, or think about myself, anyhow till its done, but look firmly at my object & think only of expressing it. Oh what a grind it is embodying all these ideas, & having perpetually to expose my mind, opened & intensified as it is by the heat of creation to the blasts of the outer world. (*D* 4: 289)

Once more the outer world threatens her inner art. Her March 21 entry begins, "Too jaded again to tackle that very difficult much too crowded raid chapter [in *The Years*]" (*D* 4: 289). The next day she notes her tightness. She is "knotted" once more. "I have resolved to leave that blasted Chapter here, & do nothing at Rodmell. . . . I cannot read; my mind is all tight like a ball of string" (*D* 4: 290).

Woolf writes her own plight into *The Years*. In the novel's important World War I raid scene, Eleanor Pargiter asks the "foreigner" Nicholas, "[H]ow can we improve ourselves . . . live more . . . live more naturally . . . better. . . ." He responds:

> "The soul—the whole being," . . . He hollowed his hand as if to enclose a circle. "It wishes to expand; to adventure; to form—new combinations?"
> "Yes, yes," [Eleanor] said, as if to assure him that his words were right.
> "Whereas now,"—he drew himself together; put his feet together; he looked like an old lady who is afraid of mice—"this is how we live, screwed up into one hard little, tight little—knot?"
> "Knot, knot—yes, that's right," she nodded. (*TY* 296)

Woolf's soul, too, wants "to expand; to adventure; to form—new combinations."

As with the Wyndham Lewis attack in 1934, others rise to Woolf's defense in the *Times* and the *Spectator*. But male voices still trespass. The country, like her diary (and like Roger Fry), remains a site for supple creation.[2] "I shall be glad when we can stretch a little at Monks House," Woolf tells her diary on April 15 (*D* 4: 300). However, Kingsley Martin's "chatter of egotism" on April 23 quashes this plan. Woolf's diary entry begins: "Kingsley coming at eleven of our first fine morning & staying till 6 has completely taken away any power I may have over the art of fiction" (*D* 4: 305). Her next entry, April 25, opens: "Whether it was Kingsley or not, the usual headache wings its way about me, rather like a fowl soaring & settling & giving me a peck in my back: clouding my mind. . . . I am not going to write a word of fiction until June 1st" (*D* 4: 306). She images here Leda's rape by the swan.

In total lock now, she tries to imagine the looseness she seeks. "All desire to practice the art of a writer has completely left me," she opens her next entry on April 27. "But after a months holiday I shall be as tough & springy as—say heather root; & the arches & the domes will spring into the air as firm as steel & light as cloud—but all these words miss the mark" (*D* 4: 306). She imagines here the "spring" she needs.

Woolf's tight-loose battle, as she tries both to tighten and to make supple *The Years*, stands at the heart of the 1935 diary. Seventy-four of her 121 entries refer to *The Years*—61 percent. She describes the novel as a "cup" perpetually knocked from her hand (*D* 4: 331). To spring back from Roger's death, from critical attack, and from further male trespass, she turns repeatedly to her diary—and to others' diaries, as well. In late March, as she medicines herself from Swinnerton's blows, she decides to make natural history notes in her diary for use in *The Years*. She reverts to nature, in short, for succor (as well as to her diary) and employs her staccato 1917–1918 Asheham House diary style: "Spring triumphant. Crocuses going over. Daffodils & hyacinths out. . . . I want to make vegetable notes for my book. How soft & springy & fresh the air was yesterday—like the sea!" (*D* 4: 292). She describes here once more the *spring* she needs.

Portraits and talk in this diary also serve *The Years*. The "talk" that enlivens the *diary* keeps Woolf supple for her novel's "character dialogue." She preserves talk at parties, at dinners, and in the park—practice for the dialogue during the parties, dinners, and park strolls that make up *The Years*. Woolf knows her "accursed love of talk," her "chatter parties" (*D* 4: 347), can tighten and jangle her for *The Years*; she nevertheless partakes—partly for her art. "Why does one do these things?" she asks herself on June 28. And answers: "Because this is life, after all. One has to" (*D* 4: 328). This question follows one related to her Fry biography: "Can one report talk?" (*D* 4: 328). Her diary proves that she can. On March 1, she notes of talk with Janet Vaughan, "This led to a fruitful discussion—fruitful for my book I mean" (*D* 4: 283). And so Woolf "froth[s][her]self into sparklets" (*D* 4: 348): she blows on the wood.

Woolf thus works directly and diaristically on *The Years* across 1935, despite its frequent knock from her hand. In mid-April, she learns that the book may be serialized in the United States and must be sent there in October; however, her £990 store chest buttresses her poise (*D* 4: 301). On July 17, she finishes her "first wild retyping" of the novel and finds it 740 typed pages or 148,000 words—leaner even than the 150,000 she planned in January (*D* 4: 332, 274). However, she sees now how further to shorten the book's close.

By mid-August a new tightening starts. Her diary now suffers. "I work without looking up till one: what it now is," she tells her August 16 entry, "& therefore I must go in, leaving a whole heap of things unsaid: so many people, so many scenes, & beauty, & a fox & sudden ideas."[3] On August 22, she thinks to call the novel *Other People's Houses*. Finally, she writes beside her September 4 entry: "And I think I will call the book 'The Years'" (*D* 4: 337). The next day, she "[c]ant pump up a word" for Sara in bed, but she will wait a day or two to refill her well. "It has to be damned deep this time—740 pages in it," she reflects and calls *The Years* psychologically "the oddest of my adventures": "Half my brain dries completely.... And, even today, when I'm desperate, almost in tears looking at the chapter, unable to add to it, I feel I've only got to fumble & find the end of the [tight] ball of string—some start off place, someone to look at Sara perhaps—no, I dont know—& my head would fill & the tiredness go" (*D* 4: 338). Again she makes up her novel as she writes her diary.

Woolf's next entry, September 6, hints at a link between *The Years* and Woolf's pivotal 1903 diary. Woolf feels a scene forming: "Why not make an easier transition: Maggie looking at the Serpentine say.... Isn't it odd that this was the scene I had almost a fit to prevent myself writing? This will be the most exciting thing I ever wrote, I kept saying. And now its the stumbling block. I wonder why? too personal, is that it? Out of key? But I wont think" (*D* 4: 338–39). Woolf's 1903 diary's final essay-entry, titled "The Serpentine," describes a young woman's suicide in the Serpentine, a woman with "No father, no mother, no work" (*PA* 212)—an added nuance to Maggie Pargiter, with Sara close by.[4]

In the published novel, Maggie's mother (soon to be dead) directs Maggie's attention to the Serpentine as Maggie's father (soon also to die) drones on. Father, mother, and daughter are off to a dance, "the eternal waltz . . . like a serpent that swallowed its own tail," Woolf writes, turning to Maggie's sister, Sara Pargiter, who is at home hearing dance music through her bedroom window (*TY* 129). Woolf now repeats the imagery from her 1903 diary's *first* entry, "A Dance in Queen's Gate," in which *she* takes in the destructive social dance from *her* bedroom window. In this entry, at age twenty-one, Woolf compared natural and artificial light and described the social dance as a serpent suffocating the dancers as it moves heedlessly on: "They are sucked in by the music. And how weary they look—pale men—fainting women—crumpled silks & trampled flowers. They are no longer masters of the dance—it has taken possession of them. And all the joy & life has left it, & it is diabolical, a twisting livid serpent, writhing in cold sweat & agony, & crushing the frail dancers in its contortions" (*PA* 166–67). Woolf's scene in *The Years* recalls this 1903 (double) serpentine/Serpentine death, and it also repeats her modernist aesthetic of changing, melding light. "There was the Serpentine, red in the setting sun," Woolf writes in *The Years*. "The lights—the sunlight and the artificial light—were strangely mixed" (131). Here is another instance of Woolf's persistent drive to probe (and merge) nature and culture.

On October 27, Woolf revises Kitty's party, and her November 21 entry reveals how the revision proceeds: "The thing is to take it quietly; go back; & rub out detail. . . . I want to keep the individual & the sense of things coming over & over again & yet changing. Thats what so difficult: to combine the two" (*D* 4: 353–54). Woolf gives this thought to Eleanor Pargiter at the end of *The Years*: "Does everything then come over again a little differently? . . . If so, is there a pattern; a theme, recurring, like music; half remembered, half foreseen? . . . a gigantic pattern, momentarily perceptible?" (369).

And six days later, Woolf reaches "the no man's land that I'm after; & can pass from outer to inner, & inhabit eternity. A queer very happy free feeling, such as I've not had at the finish of any other book. And this too is a prodigious long one. So what does it mean?" (*D* 4: 355). It means *she* now writes a "prodigious" novel—the word she uses in her 1921 diary for Joyce's *Ulysses*. She now compasses the outer and the inner.

If "drops" of Roger Fry's prose lubricate and refresh Woolf as she tightens and tightens *The Years,* she turns her third challenge to account as well through her "Next War" book: *Three Guineas*. In fact, *this* nonfiction book supplies the "flood" often checked in *The Years*. One wonders, however, whether the raging *Three Guineas* aids—or deters—Woolf in 1935? The outer war now threatens directly the inner (artistic) war.

Fully one-third of this diary's entries refer either to the mounting world crisis or to Woolf's *Three Guineas* response: 41 of the 121 entries. Over tea on February 5, Eliot and Leonard argue about A. A. Milne's January antiwar tract *Peace with Honour*. The next weeks embroil Woolf with Clive Bell over the Anti-Fascist Exhibition Committee. On February 26, she exclaims to her diary: "But Lord what a lot of work still to do [on *The Years*]! It wont be done before August. And here I am plagued by the sudden wish to write an Anti fascist Pamphlet. L. & I . . . had a long discussion about all the things I might put in my pamphlet. He was extremely reasonable & adorable, & told me I should have to take account of the economic question" (D 4: 282). Three days later, Janet Vaughan, Madge Vaughan's physician daughter, tells Woolf she has lost her position "because the Beit fellowship (?) decided that no woman can do research work. This led to a fruitful discussion—fruitful for my book I mean—of the jealousy of the medical male: vested interests; how its partly that they dislike competition; partly that they cling to the status quo" (D 4: 283).

From at least as early as 1927, when she begins cutting clippings for her later war scrapbooks, Woolf sees "the woman question" as central to any talk of fascism and war (D 4: 273). Tyranny in the private home—in Germany or England—links to tyranny in the public sphere. The war within and the war without are inextricably linked. Hierarchy became patriarchy, then patriotism, then fascism, and, finally, war. Janet Vaughan's dismissal is one tread in the fascist march.[5] On April 9, Woolf flies into a passion over an encounter with E. M. Forster on the London Library steps. She re-creates the scene in her diary—and imagines a response:

> "And Virginia, you know I'm on the Co[mmi]ttee here," said Morgan. "And we've been discussing whether to allow ladies [on the London Library Committee]—
> It came over me that they were going to put me on . . .
> " . . . But they were all quite determined. No no no, ladies are quite impossible. They wouldnt hear of it."
> See how my hand trembles. I was so angry. . . . And so I quieted down & said nothing & this morning in my bath I made up a phrase in my book

on Being Despised.... yes, these flares up are very good for my book: for they simmer & become transparent: & I see how I can transmute them into beautiful clear reasonable ironical prose. (*D* 4: 297, 298)

These last words echo Woolf's 1919 *diary* credo: her wish that her diary entries will coalesce into a mold "transparent enough to reflect the light of our life, & yet steady, tranquil composed with the aloofness of a work of art" (*D* 1: 266).

"On Being Despised" absorbs Woolf for most of the remaining April days. "I rather itch to be at that book," she tells her next entry, April 12 (*D* 4: 298). Two days later, she can no longer resist and makes "a rash attempt" at a draft of On Being Despised, "with the interesting discovery that one cant propagate at the same time as write fiction. And as this fiction [*The Years*] is dangerously near propaganda, I must keep my hands clear" (*D* 4: 300). But three days later, she again asks her diary: "How far could I let myself go in an anti fascist pamphlet? I think of dashing off my professions for women" (*D* 4: 302).

On April 20, she starts to record the "emphatic scares" from the "public world" (*D* 4: 303). The German exile Ernst Toller insists that war draws near: "Wants the allies to declare war on Hitler. Belgium keeps its aeroplanes at active service level, all ready to rise into the air. But as Germany could be on them before they rose this seems useless.... And—there are incessant conversations—Mussolini, Hitler, Macdonald [*sic*]. All these people incessantly arriving at Croydon, arriving at Berlin, Moscow, Rome; & flying off again—while Stephen [Spender] and I think how to improve the world" (*D* 4: 303).

Two days later, the Woolfs invite Ralph Wigram of the British Foreign Office to tea for counsel on their May motor trip through Germany. Once more we see Woolf's precise, even prescient, grasp of the world's state. She describes Wigram as "a nice rigid honest public school Englishman":

Started almost at once telling us about Hitler.... Hitler very impressive; very frightening.... Made speeches lasting 20 minutes with out a failure. Very able. Only one mistake on a complicated point. Very well coached. And all the time a tapping sound. Wigram thought An odd day to have the masons in. But it was the sentry marching up & down the passage. Everything came out. We want.... We have a parity in the air already. The Germans in fact have enough aeroplanes ready to start to keep us under. But if they do kill us all? Well they will have their Colonies. I want room to move about Hitler said. Must be equal, & so on. A complete reversal to pre-war days. No ideals except equality, superiority, force, possessions.... Talks of himself as the regenerator, the completely equipped & powerful machine.... Wigram & the rest frightened. Anything may happen at any moment. Here in England we havent even bought our gas masks. Nobody takes it seriously. But having seen this mad dog, the thin rigid Englishmen are really afraid. And if we have only nice public schoolboys like W. to guide us, there is some reason I suppose to expect that Oxford Street will be flooded with poison gas one of these days. And what then? Germany will get her colonies.[6]

Six days later, Woolf talks of war with her nephew, Julian Bell, and Alix Strachey. She asks them "whether one can give people a substitute for war" (*D* 4: 307). Julian says human beings "have the danger emotion: must climb mountains, fight bulls" (*D* 4: 307). He says, "[A]ll the young men are communists in order to gratify their desire to do things together & in order to have some danger" (*D* 4: 307). Woolf suggests that the danger rush "doesnt last more than a few months in case of war"; she argues that "many people have found life exciting without war and bull fighting" (*D* 4: 307). They ponder whether the lust for danger might be diverted onto some harmless object. Could some fantasy be supplied? Woolf asks them if war ever won any cause. Alix names England's civil war. This talk fuels *Three Guineas*' opening on the psychological motives for war.

On May 9, Woolf views German danger firsthand. As she waits outside German customs, she sees a car with a swastika pass, while Leonard hears a little boy cry Heil Hitler. Woolf notes that she and Leonard became "obsequious— delighted that is when the officers smile at Mitzi [Leonard's marmoset]—the first stoop in our back" (*D* 4: 311). Street banners proclaim "The Jew is our enemy" and "There is no place for Jews." And as they drive "out of range of the docile hysterical crowd. Our obsequiousness gradually turning to anger. Nerves rather frayed" (*D* 4: 311). With relief they reach Austria. On May 21 in Rome, Woolf again considers "dashing off my book on Professions," and back in London June 13, she wants to visit Rebecca West—"partly about fascism" (*D* 4: 314, 321). A week later, a new book's complaint that women "have dropped their sacred task.... floods" her again with her "Professions book" (*D* 4: 323).

In this light, one wonders how she can write *The Years* at all. However, it, too, offers a strong antiwar brief: a plea for *difference* and *change*, for *new combinatons*. World tensions mount in late August. "Abyssinia. Cabinet summoned.

Sitting today," Woolf records on August 21 and wonders: "Should I like to be old Baldwin?" (*D* 4: 335). While all talk of Mussolini at Abyssinia's door, Woolf learns of America's regard for *A Room of One's Own*; this wakes her "insensate obsession" to write its sequel, *Three Guineas* (*D* 4: 335). On September 4, the League of Nations meets in Geneva to try to avert the use of force. "The most critical day since Aug 4th 1914," Woolf quotes the newspapers to her diary, and the next day records her own "stew about war & patriotism" (*D* 4: 337, 338). Tellingly, she turns to a *diary* for aid. "Thank God, John Bailey's life is out," she writes, "I shall seek consolation there" (*D* 4: 338). The work is *John Bailey, 1864–1931, Letters and Diaries*.

Abyssinia mobilizes in late September, and, on October 2, Woolf attends the Labour Party Conference in Brighton, where she sees pacifist leader George Lansbury resign under furious attack. Woolf ponders, "[W]hat is my duty as a human being? . . . And how far does anybodies single mind or work matter? Ought we all to be engaged in altering the structure of society?" (*D* 4: 345, 346). She finds the women delegates "very thin voiced & insubstantial. On Monday one said, It is time we gave up washing up. A thin frail protest, but genuine. A little reed piping, but what chance against all this weight of roast beef & beer— which she must cook?" (*D* 4: 345). Woolf reports that her own sympathies rest with Dr. Alfred Salter, who calls for nonresistance: "He's quite right. That should be our view" (*D* 4: 345).[7] She has just read Dr. John Salter's diaries.

On October 15, Woolf invites writer Ruth Grüber to discuss "a book on women & fascism" and reports that the Brighton Labor Conference was "the breaking of that dam between me & the new book, so that I couldn't resist dashing off a chapter: stopped myself; but have all ready to develop—the form found I think—as soon as I get time" (*D* 4: 346–47). She tells her October 27 entry that at any moment this book "becomes absolutely wild, like being harnessed to a shark; & I dash off scene after scene" (*D* 4: 348). Reaching for a book three days later, she opens by mistake her first draft of The War (or The Next War), which she now thinks to call "What are we to do." She reads the first page and her "mind is once more flooded with the desire to be at that argument" (*D* 4: 348). She had gone to a Peace Conference the day before and found "[e]ven more than the usual shower of anti-Fascist leaflets" (*D* 4: 350).

Leonard's antifascist book *Quack, Quack!* had appeared in May, and on November 21 shouts of abuse (in German) beneath his window wake him in the middle of the night. Woolf anticipates abuse for *her* antiwar book, too. "After our dinner at Raymond's with Aldous [Huxley] & the subconscious hostility I always feel there, I'm facing the fact that my next book, Professions, The Next War, will need some courage," she admits. "2 million women all longing for men, Aldous said. Raymond insisted, with his little hard squeak, that men were now unfairly treated . . ." (*D* 4: 354).

In short, major challenges try Woolf in 1935. She must counter the death of Roger Fry (model of her vigorous old age) as well as critical attack and the beat of war. In November, Leonard tells her that earnings from the Hogarth Press will be thin, a fact that would change if she could only finish *The Years*. But she often feels "tight," "knotted," "wooden," "jangled," "jaded," and "too tired" as the days unfold (*D* 4: 290, 319, 276, 297, 330, 331, 289, 301, 288, 296, 332, 336, 338, 339, 346, 353, 359). And why wouldn't she feel so? *The Years* is her second longest and, in many ways, most ambitious novel: nearly half-again the length of her last novel, *The Waves*, with twenty portraits instead of six, and a span of fifty-seven years.[8] Her drive to merge fact and fiction in this work, cultural critique and art, often falters. Ideas "are sticky things: wont coalesce; hold up the creative, subconscious faculty," she writes on February 20 (*D* 4: 281). "[O]ne cant propagate at the same time as write fiction," she tells her diary on April 14 and again on November 1 (*D* 4: 300, 350). Yet she refuses to rush or to compromise her art.

And she continues to experiment. In her May travel diary, after she describes the sailing ships at Aix-en-Provence and "the sparkling fading red & yellow night lamps," she adds: "But that kind of perfection no longer makes me feel for my pen—Its too easy" (*D* 4: 314). In November she heralds "a further stage" in her "writers advance"—"a far richer grouping & proportion" of the inner and the outer and the "I" and the "not I"—and plans to apply the discovery in both biography and fiction (*D* 4: 353). Editors call for her work, an encouraging boost. In November, Bruce Richmond asks her to write more leading articles for the *Times Literary Supplement*, and J. R. Ackerley seeks her prose for the BBC journal the *Listener* (*D* 4: 353). And she continues to make diary notes for "Elderly Virginia's" memoirs—or for some other future public prose.

Sadly, Ethel Smyth remains a source of tightness—rather like Kingsley Martin. Nevertheless, Woolf offers one of her benevolent "mixed" sketches on March 22: "Ethel last night—dear old woman, so wise in her way; but her voice is like a needle stabbing stuff. And so I got more tight wound than ever. But still I felt, she is generous & ample—a note to make for her portrait" (*D* 4: 290). Woolf projects here again the state she needs.

Woolf's diary thus continues to serve her in many ways. Slotted in 1919 for her quiet half hours after tea, the diary becomes by 1935 a vital morning aid. It serves as a soothing pillow, a "bolster," when she is too tight (or tired) to revise *The Years*, as the diary's opening sentence reveals: "The play [*Freshwater*] came off last night, with the result that I am dry-brained this morning, & can only use this book as a pillow" (D 4: 274). She uses it often in 1935 to "dream" herself back into *The Years*. Like a cool pillow, her diary also helps temper her mind hot from creation. "I see I am becoming a regular diariser," she notices on March 27. "The reason is that I cannot make the transition from Pargiters to Dante without some bridge. And this [diarizing] cools my mind" (D 4: 291–92). Her diary thus serves as pillow and bridge—or pillow *as* bridge to her subconscious.

She makes "vegetable notes" in her diary for use in *The Years*, asks herself questions,[9] sketches "mixed" portraits and talk to keep life flowing and her pen supple, for it is now her *diary*—rather than her novel—that supplies fresh prose. "Since Oct. 16th [1934] I have not written one new sentence, but only copied & typed," she complains to her diary on March 11, 1935. "A typed sentence somehow differs; for one thing it is formed out of what is already there: it does not spring fresh from the mind" (D 4: 286).

And Woolf desperately needs spring. Among Woolf's novels, *The Years* most resembles a diary in form. Diaries offer the combination she seeks in *The Years*: "the individual & the sense of things coming over & over again & yet changing" (D 4: 353–54). Woolf turns to other diaries in the fall for "consolation," fuel, and spring. "But its odd how one longs to uncurl the spring in the brain—to let fly," she tells her diary (D 4: 316).

Dr. John Salter's *Diary*

Virginia Woolf resolves to wrap her brain "in green dock leaves" for a few days in early September 1935. She seeks leaves cool and astringent, like Dorothy Wordsworth's diary pages read in 1929. Among books selected for this 1935 anodyne is the diary of "an old dr. called Salter," she tells her September 6 diary entry (D 4: 339). Specifically, it was *Dr. Salter of Tolleshunt D'Arcy in the County of Essex: Medical Man, Freemason, Sportsman, Sporting-Dog Breeder and Horticulturalist: His Diary and Reminiscences for the year 1849 to the year 1932*. Salter's friend, J. O. Thompson, compiled the work, which was published in 1933. Woolf knows the diaries of several country *parsons*; she has published essays on them. Now she will meet a country doctor. Salter's *Diary* supplied, too, a male lens on the years 1880 to 1932—that is, for all but five of the fifty-seven years shown in Woolf's novel-in-progress, just named *The Years*. His diaries provide fuel for her antifascist "pamphlet," as well.

The 1933 edition of Salter's *Diary* begins in Sussex with eight-year-old John's sole stark entry for 1849: "Father died at Arundel" (3). Compiler Thompson trims the diary, which may have been daily, so precise and thorough is the diarist we come to know.[10] Woolf met much to identify with and to admire in John Salter, who also represented the "typical Englishman and sportsman" her novel and her antifascist book must persuade (190). Beyond his loss of a parent at an age even younger than Woolf, Salter describes his "very weak constitution" at age fifteen, yet a doctor's pledge that it could be strengthened with "great care" (6). Teenage John races boats and skates on the Serpentine, and he resembles Dr. Joseph Wright of "The Pargiters" in his loving reverence for his mother. In 1858, when Salter "enter[s] upon the world for the first time," at age seventeen, his mother gives him "a splendid Bible, hoping I might use it, and I will every night before going to bed, for her sake. No one ever had a better mother or sister than I" (12). Like the Woolfs', Salter's long marriage is childless; however, he finds sustenance in nature; in fact, he becomes a prize-winning dog breeder and horticulturist, as well as a doctor, diarist, and more.

In his youthful diary slang, Salter seems a model for P. G. Wodehouse's Bertie Wooster. He exclaims "By Jove," "by Jupiter," and "by gad" and describes "rattling good fellows" at cricket and "the jolliest girls" at dances (8, 12, 42, 76, 7). However, Salter's brain was that of Jeeves. Sent to Grix's School on the beach at Littlehampton at age nine, the precocious boy solemnly tells his diary that "[a] desire for excellence is highly commendable when sought after in a proper way" (3). By twelve he wins the school's top prize, setting the stage for a life of perpetual prizes ably won. "Nothing but the best would satisfy him," the Bishop of Chelmsford explained at Salter's funeral, following his death at age ninety (404). These words fit him to a *T*. As early as age sixteen Salter judges Laura Duke the belle of the ball and sets out to win her. "My best partner was Laura—she was the best there," he tells a February 1858 entry (7). Five days later, he walks with Laura in the lane, "having a jolly chat. She *is* a rattling girl, and no mistake! By Jove, she is!!" (8). Such drama as resides in Salter's *Diary* springs from his lengthy and nearly toppled courtship. On August 28, 1858, Laura shows the now seventeen-year-old John that she likes him and two days later returns a kiss. "I know she loves me now," he tells his diary. "By Jupiter, what a happy time!" (12). But the next day, "we were compelled to wish each other 'Goodbye' for a long time, for I am about to enter upon the world for the first time. She promised to write, etc., etc." (12).

Salter enters a five-year medical apprenticeship with his uncle, who runs a large country practice in Great Berkhampstead, northwest of London. "If the apprentice conducted himself well, and the master could spare him," Salter explains in the "Reminiscences" that follow his "Diary," "he might spend the last three years in a London hospital" (247). All this transpires, but it places a strain on the young lovers, Laura a year-and-a-half older than John. In May 1859, she ends their correspondence, judging his nature too cold. "Never shall I get over it," the seventeen-year-old writes in her melodramatic way. "There's nobody but Laurie to suit me. My life is now like a barren waste. But I will never despair. I shall do my best for the sake of the dear ones at home. Were I to put my mad designs into execution I should break their hearts" (13). Happily, he suffers only a summer. When he returns to Sussex in August, he convinces Laura of his warmth. She repledges her love and seals it with a ring he is to wear in Great Berkhampstead. Four months later he gives her a ring, "a very fine one indeed" (24).

The love endures and in 1864, Salter acts with his characteristic decisive dispatch. On September 26, the twenty-three-year-old signs a medical partnership with Dr. Walker at Tolleshunt D'Arcy, a country village in South Essex. The next day he takes possession of D'Arcy House there and the next buys a horse and trap, a cat "of the rough, brush-tailed Russian breed," a pug dog, and a Newfoundland (56). He also buys an "extraordinar[ily] thick" wedding ring for Laura Duke. They marry October 12, 1864, in Arundel, and honeymoon in Paris and Geneva; back in London on October 24, he is elected a Fellow in the Obstetrical Society. In the next sixty-eight years, he will deliver some seven thousand babies: that is, a baby every day for nineteen years (377). On October 29, the newlyweds are "[r]eceived with great cheering at the entrance to the village" (56).

Salter tells his diary at age nineteen, "Something has ever told me that I am appointed to some great thing, and I know I shall succeed. But how? I feel I was born for something higher than the life of a country doctor" (30–31). That "higher" role becomes that of a great English sportsman (as he says of Lord Derby): the role of one able both to judge and to breed "the best." Salter owns his first dog at age eighteen: a Russian boarhound. In Essex, in his time free from patients, he begins to course greyhounds, and this leads him to the roles of both dog judge and dog breeder. Compiler Thompson reports that Salter owned 2,696 dogs across his life—2,123 of which he bred himself (401). He breeds champions in six sporting breeds: greyhounds, pointers, retrievers, Gordon setters, Irish setters, and Sussex spaniels. An elected vice president of the English Kennel Club, he would have lifted an eyebrow at spaniel Flush.

So famous becomes Salter's own kennel that in 1875 he sends setters to the King of Sweden and, in 1876, pointers to the Shah of Persia and, in 1882, greyhounds to an Indian Rajah (74, 76, 83). In 1878, when Salter is thirty-six, Edward, the Prince of Wales, invites him to judge the dogs at the Paris International Exhibition. Salter's fame spreads to Russia, where he changes the style of dog judging. When he travels to Glasgow in 1893 to judge the sporting dogs for the Scottish Kennel Club, he learns his name is "a household word in Scotland as to dogs" (100). In his eighties, he is called one of the two or three best judges of sporting dogs in the world (188), and an American pointer book claims his pointers brought that breed to the front in the United States, superseding setters (217).

Salter moved easily from breeding dogs to breeding roses, blood-red alstroemeria, and other flora. According to Thompson, from 1888 to 1931, Salter won "no less than 1,400 prizes and awards for various exhibits from his garden and hothouse. Most of the awards were in the 1st Class" (403). From his first days, therefore, Salter builds a life of perennial prizes and growing fame as fillip to the daily reward of healing the sick and bringing new life into the world. His neighbors trust his judgment. They elect him justice of the peace when he is forty-six, a post he keeps to the end of his days, adding to it regular reelection to the Tollesbury County Council and requests that he run for parliament (137). He becomes a 32nd degree Mason, as well.

One finds little reflection or introspection in Salter's *Diary*—or even in his "Reminiscences," fifty-nine short, titled topics that follow and barely amplify the diary. John Salter was a man of action, of science and sport, not one who paused to "conglobulate thoughts" like André Gide—at least not in the entries Thompson prints. The doctor would rather record technological advance. He marks the telegraph wire into D'Arcy on November 2, 1872; Lister's antiseptic operations in 1878; the telephone line to Tollesbury in 1895; his tricycle (in 1896); car (1902); phonograph (1907); first aeroplane sighting (1913); and radio (1923). He records historical events as well in his clear, direct prose.

Through this rewarding outer progress we catch only brief glimpses of Salter's feelings, mostly in diary passages on his dogs, but they increase his appeal. "Poor little 'Spider' breathed her last in her own armchair to-day," Salter tells his 1914 diary. "No suffering, thank goodness. We are all cut up about it. I hope

I shall see my dogs again some day" (154). In 1915, we find him "in the greenhouse by my dear old dog Judy for an hour, thinking over the happy days gone by. She has been my constant companion for fifteen years—in the house, in the car, and in the field. How I shall miss her! I wonder whether she will go where I go hereafter? . . . Poor dear, how I love her! I couldn't help a good cry—rather stupid, but unavoidable" (157). In 1923, again comes: "My poor dear dog Thelma died in the night, quite peacefully. When I came home she got out of her basket under the dining-room table, and although both deaf and blind she knew I had come in, staggered towards me, found me out and kissed my hand—bless her! . . . Where she goes I shall be quite content to be" (197).

Like Woolf's own thrust of humans back into nature, Salter places his wife and himself with his dogs. Once won, Laura Duke Salter recedes in the diary as the judge, breeder, and prize-winner comes to the fore. Only in her final illness and death, in 1904, do we meet Salter's regard. "Christmas day—how I miss my partner of forty years!" he exclaims to his diary three months after her death (133). On September 29, 1913, he writes: "My poor dear died nine years ago to-day—bless her heart" (151). The next day he adds: "I feel very unsettled and lonely, but must keep my tail up to the end somehow" (151).

Salter's *Diary* thus offers Woolf one of her own complex, "mixed" portraits: the life of an able, hardworking, often sympathetic John Bull. *Diary* entries disclose the doctor's unceasing toil. "At work all the morning, dog-breaking in afternoon, confinements at night," he notes in 1875 at the age of thirty-three (75). "Brighton Dog Show—8 dogs, 12 prizes. Afterwards my night bell going all night. Oh, the pleasures of a county doctor's life!" runs a specimen day when he is forty-six (89). Four years later, he records a specimen *month*: "During this month I have driven 1,384 miles—i.e., 44 ⅔ miles per day. 857 patients on my visiting list. Longest days, 15, 15, 13 hours, longest days in harness (horse), 10 ¼, 10, 9 ½, 9 ½, 9. Pretty well, thank you, for an old man" (97). He now is fifty. At age seventy-six, he pens this 1918 entry: "A round of my patients, and then to Maldon for Attendance (education) Sub-Committee, then a district education meeting, followed by a Tribunal, and finally an Old Age Pension and State Pension Committee. Retracing my way homewards, saw some more patients, and then round the garden and premises" (171). In his eightieth year, he first tallies then asks of his diary: "Patients, Bench, patients, writing, gardening, bath, dinner, smoke, read, and bed. What could be better?" (185).

What might be better, Woolf might have replied, were Salter's views of "sport" and war. His diary reveals the complexity of these matters, good preparation for *Three Guineas*. Salter's lifelong—at times irrational and dangerous—zeal for prize-fighting often confounds. Perhaps he sought as a teenager to build his "weak constitution" (6). More fundamentally: what was his life if not a series of prizes won? He offers a further explanation in his "Reminiscences" essay titled "Prize-Fighting in the 'Sixties'": "There was a time when I liked to put the gloves on myself. I was the size and weight for it, I liked it, and my activity came just when prize-fighting was resuscitated by the match between Heenan and Sayers—America versus England. Although prize-fighting had got rather low and brutish up to then it took a fresh lease, and women as well as men became jubilant about the idea" (271). Although illegal, "[i]t was quite the fashion for young-men-about-town to box and to pretend they could box" (271).

At twenty, Salter enjoys boxing on Derby Day and takes pride in his black eyes and smashed nose (39). At age twenty-one, he organizes a Gymnastic Club at King's College School in London and becomes its captain. The club offers boxing, fencing, and single-stick. He continues eager to spar even when he loses an eye to the "sport"—behavior that seems at odds with common sense, not to mention his medical rationality. Surgery brings him an artificial eye at the age of twenty-five, yet he still spars four months later, coming away with a black eye and a swollen lip. When provoked across his days, Salter reverts to his fists. At fifty-four he tells his diary, "Some of the Magdalen Street roughs fell foul of me, and I had to give one chap something for himself" (103). When he is seventy-three, he exclaims: "I told the General Manager of Insurance Co. that if he or any of his staff of my age cared to try conclusions for twenty minutes with boxing gloves, I would demonstrate whether I had become less of a man than formerly, or not!" (154).

Fisticuffs and prize-fights are manly sport for Salter. At age fifteen at King's College School, he explains, "there was an A department, for boys going into the professions, and a B department for those intended for trade" and the *A*s looked down on the *B*s "and there was a good deal of antagonism, with fighting every day. Among the most redoubtable warriors, who fought almost as a band of brothers, were those known as the Hoi Sloiteroi—Ted Pollock, Jim Connor, and my humble self" (246). Manly sport, too, is Salter's beloved shooting. According to Thompson, Salter first took out a shooting license in 1860—age eighteen—and from 1865 to 1925 his "bag" totaled 62,504 head of 104 varieties of game, including eleven wolves.[11] Here too he adds to the sport, for he learns in 1877 that he is England's largest wild duck breeder (77).

A jarring June 1917 diary passage links hunting with war. "Doing my game accounts for last year, I discovered the killed amounted to 7,237," the doctor writes, "about as many as we took prisoners in the late Messines battle!" (164). It is this hunter and pugilist Woolf's antiwar book must persuade. Salter's *Diary* lays bare the strange contradictions of war. Salter often voices war's glories. Several of his entries support Julian Bell's April 28, 1935, insistence to Woolf that "the danger emotion" draws men to war (*D* 4: 307). "Sir Evelyn Wood told me he would have given his ears to go to the war," Salter records in 1899 at the start of the Second Boer War.[12] In a striking May 1900 entry, Salter first shows his distress at the Russian "sport" that pits fox terriers and dachshunds against badgers and foxes, calling it "uninteresting and cruel," and then continues:

> I left the business, and felt quite sick at it. In the evening a banquet was given to me by the Imperial Society. The many pleasant things said were translated to me. I replied, and after speaking of the show and their dogs—telling them in what they excelled and in what they were defective—I touched on the South African War, and I hope converted them a little when I said we considered it one of the most righteous wars we had ever been engaged in and that they had been misled. I roused them to enthusiasm when I said that if we were not agreed on every point, we were brothers in one thing—and that was Sport. (118)

On August 1, 1914, Sir Claude de Crespigny gives seventy-three-year-old Salter a 303 Government rifle and two hundred rounds of ammunition, "in case I want arms during the approaching state of war—which seems to be quite imminent," Salter explains. "It will be a big business while it lasts, but the German Emperor has been wanting it for some time.... We are calm, and confident, and mean to make any sacrifice to go through with it" (153–54). On August 4, he reports war "begun in earnest.... I changed and went for a walk—partly to get into training for shooting; partly in case I am wanted to go out and fight" (154). The next day, wounded from both sides flood into Harwich.

While Salter's *Diary* documents "the danger emotion," it also supports Woolf's view that the danger rush "doesnt last more than a few months in case of war" (*D* 4: 307). When zeppelins raid Ramsgate and Margate in May 1915, Salter tells his diary, "This war is awful" (156). From 1916 on, he contrasts war with nature, as Woolf regularly does in *her* diaries, and denounces it more forcefully. "A pair of nightingales have [*sic*] taken up their quarters in the garden and sing gloriously. What a sin that there should be war!" he exclaims in April 1916

(160). In March 1918, when Salter (like Woolf) can hear "Distant gun firing—telling of the work going on in France," he continues: "And a lovely summer's day—bright, warm, sunny, and still. A sin for men to be killing each other!" (172).

Salter's *Diary* corroborates many of Woolf's own diary entries during the Great War. Zeppelins fly over his Essex home, just as they do over Asheham House in Sussex (159). He offers two vivid descriptions of London air raids that authenticate her raid scene in *The Years*. Woolf may have drawn on this December 18, 1917, Salter entry:

> After the Bench to Freemasons' Hall to help to consecrate a new [Masonic] lodge, the Benfleet. Although I had had nothing to eat all day and felt rather jaded to start with, it is astonishing what a fillip *work* is. I pulled myself together and did the ceremony as well as I ever did in my life. There was a big air raid going on all over London the whole time. Relays of German aircraft kept coming for three hours, and the anti-aircraft guns going on all round made it distinctly lively. At 10.30, with the air raid still going on, I set out to walk to the City, which looked dead and deserted. Hardly a soul was to be seen, and it was nearly dark. A fire in Farringdon Street set going by a bomb enlivened matters in that direction, but as soon as the first bugle sounded, denoting "all clear," the whole place woke up. Omnibuses and taxis flew about—bugles sounded in all directions—people thronged the streets, and London was itself again. The people must have been in the dugouts, tubes, etc. I never saw such a resurrection. (169)

Compare this with Woolf's words in *The Years*: "The bugles blew again beneath the window. Then they heard them further down the street; then further away still down the next street. Almost directly the hooting of cars began again, and the rushing of wheels as if the traffic had been released and the usual night life of London had begun again" (295).

Salter's Armistice Day entry also corroborates Woolf's. "After work in Colchester I went by the 10.34 fast train to London," he tells his diary. "[T]he day began with excitement, and by night nearly everything was disorganised and chaos—especially London, which was a pandemonium! At 11 o'clock Peace began, and also the orgies attendant thereon" (174).

Salter's *Diary* supplied Woolf with evidence not only of the "danger" lure of war but also of the strange "uniform" disease she will decry in *Three Guineas*. Six months into the Great War, seventy-three-year-old Salter decides to raise a volunteer corps of locals—an action that reprises his "Volunteer Story" as a teenager following the Crimean War. In his "Reminiscences," he speaks of the volunteer movement in words that mirror his boxing fervor:

> After the Crimean War in 1854–55 a Volunteer movement was started in England. In September, 1860, when I was 19, I was made Ensign of the 7th Hertfordshire Rifles. . . . There was great enthusiasm, and we had a Company of about 80 in Berkhampstead. . . . For a boy of 19 I was very proud of my position and uniform, and I became very enthusiastic in my drill and looking after the men. We put on whatever embellishments our tailors dictated. With the richer men they crowded on gold and silver galore. There was no particular regulation about it, so on a field day some of the appearances were grotesque. Lord Essex appeared, for instance, in a cocked hat like an Admiral. . . .
>
> A cavalry officer named Col. Ibbetson, a tremendous martinet, came down to inspect us on our first field day. . . .
>
> . . . Looking at me, a simple Ensign, he exclaimed, "My gracious, man, you've got as much gold on your collar as I have!" . . . He then informed us that it was our duty to have this most important matter rectified, which I can tell you we were not slow in doing! (258–59)

Sixty years later, Salter tells a March 1920 entry: "Received a memo. from the Army Council, thanking me for my services during the Great War, and informing me that I may retain my rank and wear His Majesty's uniform on special occasions" (181).

How does one reach this able, industrious, conscientious man who can both revel in and be sickened by sport and war? Woolf writes in *Three Guineas*:

> As it is a fact that she cannot understand what instinct compels him, what glory, what interest, what manly satisfaction fighting provides for him—'without war there would be no outlet for the manly qualities which fighting develops'—as fighting thus is a sex characteristic which she cannot share, the counterpart some claim of the maternal instinct which he cannot share, so is it an instinct which she cannot judge. The outsider therefore must leave him free to deal with this instinct by himself, because liberty of opinion must be respected, especially when it is based upon an instinct which is as foreign to her as centuries of tradition and education can make it. (107)

An active Conservative across his days, Salter's November 9, 1928, diary entry amuses, for he disparages there his doppelganger, Dr. Alfred Salter, "The Socialist Member for a part of London . . . giving a lecture on temperance in Chelmsford this evening. . . . I hope they won't take me for him!" (222). This is the Dr. Alfred Salter whose call for "nonresistance" at the October 2, 1935, Brighton Labor Party Conference Woolf will strongly endorse (*D* 4: 345).

And contradictions persist, for diarist John Salter, the lifelong Conservative who dismisses "socialistic trash" in 1892, joins a Committee on Old Age Pensions in 1899, declaring them: "A good thing—ought to be done by the State" (98, 112). And at age eighty-three he calls for national health. As he draws up his bills in February 1925, Salter reveals his sensitivity: "Making out bills—a most unpleasant job, especially when they are due from *friends* and have been owing a long time. I find I have left some of my friends unreminded for ten years—some more than that—when I know they have been low in pocket and ill in health. We ought to be paid by the State! However, I did some useful work, though horribly unpleasant, for bill-making bothers me and upsets my nervous system. It even gave me a toothache and a very restless night" (200). However, Salter never reconciles his sick feelings with his political views.

Did Dr. Salter's *Diary* give Woolf the medicine she wished for in September 1935? Did his *Diary* cool and brace her, wrap her mind in "green dock leaves"? It certainly served both *The Years* (especially the raid scene) and *Three Guineas*. In a fascinating section of his "Reminiscences" that he titles "The Psychology of Men," Salter writes of a barrister friend who takes him to Newgate to view a woman's hanging. Salter describes vividly the drunk, rough crowd outside the prison:

> Behind [the parson] came a woman. Her hands were tied behind her back, but she walked firmly and steadily forward. At the sight of her a roaring shout went up. The crowd shook their fists and hurled maledictions at her, but she looked calmly, and almost as though she never heard. She was a fine woman and comely, and she stood up straight to the end, and died like a Trojan.
>
> I was horrified. The vulgar crowd—the utter absence of respect due to one about to pass beyond our ken, the hangman who went about the business as though he was hauling up a bundle of old clothes—and the burial service read before the Soul had passed. I clutched on to Hudson.

> For the first time in life I felt really ill and as though I should faint.
> ... "Do you mean to say that's all?" he cried. "Have we come all this way just to see this? Good Heavens! Salter, do you mean to tell me they don't wriggle or kick or do anything? This is an imposition. Why, they ought to place the coffin on her back and make her run round with it first—or do something. It's absolutely disgusting."
>
> I agreed with him that it was disgusting—but I did not mention that it did not strike me in the same way as it did him. I felt as if I would like to go and rescue her. The scene made me so sick that I couldn't bear it, and went away. . . .
>
> I was also impressed by the fact that no impression seemed to be made on my barrister friend. . . .
>
> There was a great difference between the psychology of two men. (250–51)

To some, Dr. Salter's *Diary* may read today as a tissue of cultural contradictions unrecognized. It can be read, too, as one of the most fortifying senior diaries extant. Like Woolf, Salter constantly uses his diary to spur himself on. On his seventy-ninth birthday, he writes, in 1920: "I have done a great deal of varied work right through my life. I don't think I have ever been idle many minutes! That probably is the secret of having kept fit and not aged much" (182). Salter's *Diary* serves as a testament to usefulness—and to the regenerative power of diaries. "Began reading my diary with a view to making extracts," Salter tells his diary at age eighty-eight. "It is very interesting to begin life again!" (227).

The 2002 *Annotated Bibliography of Diaries Printed in English* calls the 1933 Salter text "[a] fine diary and an extraordinary record of a strong and active life." Noting that editor Thompson omitted much detail of Salter's medical practice, the writer declares: "[I]f the manuscript exists an expanded edition would be welcome" (859). As in most cases with trimmed diaries, we miss what is withheld. Nevertheless, Dr. Salter's *Diary* offered Woolf rich fodder in September 1935—matter for *The Years* and for *Three Guineas*.

John Bailey's *Diaries*

As Mussolini menaces Abyssinia on September 5, 1935, Virginia Woolf, "in a stew about war & patriotism," exclaims to her diary: "Thank God, John Bailey's life is out, ... I shall seek consolation there" (*D* 4: 338). The work, *John Bailey, 1864–1931: Letters and Diaries*, arrived two days later. Diaries, in general, feed and console Woolf across her days; however, the special solace she seeks from literary critic John Bailey's *Diaries* likely rose from his ties to her old friend Violet Dickinson, who sheltered her and propelled her as a professional writer in 1904. Eighteen years older than Woolf, Bailey began *his* essays for the *Times Literary Supplement* in 1902, only three years before Woolf's own first *TSL* review. Woolf knows him, then, through his *Times* pieces, but also as one of Violet's circle; in fact, the *Diaries* disclose that Bailey met his wife, Sarah Lyttelton, at Dickinson's home (298n1).

Bailey's mother died when he was only nine. His wife, who edited the *Letters and Diaries* (and who came to tea with Virginia in 1906), reports that Bailey's health was "never robust" (15). As a boy, reading compensated for this physical limitation, and Bailey admired Woolf's diary father, Sir Walter Scott. Beyond this affirmation of shared literary taste, Woolf perhaps also sought consolation in Bailey because they broached literature in similar ways. On his twenty-fifth birthday, Bailey tells his 1889 diary: "I will go right through a course of English poetry. I have begun with Chaucer, and think I shall write here my impressions of each" (36). Bailey aimed always to "general culture, not specialism" (55), and in the first diary entry his wife chooses to print, he defends spontaneous poetry over poems that "show labour" (28)—a Walter Scott view.

With the large exception of "Oxford," Bailey lived the literary and intellectual life Woolf also enjoyed. At twenty-five, he writes to his close Oxford friend Arthur Hughes, son of Thomas Hughes, who wrote *Tom Brown's School Days*: "I have wished to live the life we both love but (generally) under the familiar conditions—England, Oxford, London, society, magazine articles, libraries—all the outward machinery of intellectual life.... However, I often doubt myself and dread the fussiness and publicity of London and fear lest its insincerity and its mean hopes and fears should creep in over me too" (35). At an earlier age than twenty-five, Woolf also harbored fears of London's cruel crush.

Although literature stood highest for Bailey—and particularly poetry—he savors art, as well. In 1887, after coming down from Oxford at age twenty-three, he takes rooms in the Temple and devotes the next nine years to reading and to gallery visits (10). He tells his 1889 diary that at the Grosvenor Gallery he feels "so intensely happy" he can hardly contain himself: "It made me feel that I could never be a lawyer and that somehow art and letters and an imaginative life of some kind must be *my* life" (36). Bailey relishes nature's beauty, as well. In the prefatory note that launches Bailey's *Letters and Diaries*, historian George Trevelyan, Woolf's friend, writes that "the defence of the vanishing beauty and peace of the English countryside" was Bailey's "secondary occupation" (7).

As Mussolini begins his march, Bailey's *Diaries* offer Woolf the refuge of a shared literary and intellectual stage whose players she knows well. However, he was nearly a generation older than she and of a higher and more leisured class. To read his *Letters and Diaries* was to meet her own friends (or friends from other diaries)—friends closer to Bailey, however, than to herself, and some whom she scorned. Bailey was serving as private secretary to the statesman George Wyndham in 1900 when he married Sarah Lyttelton. His *Letters and Diaries* offer frequent praise of Prime Minister Arthur Balfour (as well as of Wyndham), men Bailey meets regularly at the Literary Club. Bailey's March 1, 1920, diary entry refers to Wilfrid Scawen Blunt's *Diaries*, which Woolf read in 1918—and decried. (She will pick them up again in 1936.)[13] "Dined Literary," Bailey writes: "I sat between Arthur Balfour and Herbert Fisher [Woolf's cousin] and had very pleasant talk. . . . Our talk ranged over . . . George Wyndham, Wilfred [*sic*] Blunt, whose abuse of confidence [Balfour] thought scandalous—in revealing G.W. and Winston Churchill's private conversation [in his published diaries], all three being still alive" (205–6). The Bailey volume Woolf reads includes letters of mutual praise between Bailey and fellow critic Edmund Gosse, as well as from John Squire, for whom Bailey wrote and who calls Bailey's *Dr. Johnson and His Circle* "the best short book on the subject extant" (13).

Hoping for consolation from Bailey's *Letters and Diaries*, Woolf finds instead this male back-slapping club. "John Bailey's life, come today, makes me doubt . . .—what? Everything," Woolf tells her own diary on September 7, 1935. "Sounds like a mouse squeaking under a mattress. But I've only just glanced & got the smell of Lit. dinner, Lit. Sup, Lit this that & the other" (*D* 4: 339). As *The Years* and *Three Guineas* vie for her pen, Woolf also may have smelled too much Oxford devotion in Bailey's *Diaries*—along with the male "Lit. dinners." Bailey studied at New College, Oxford. When he departs, he tells his 1887 diary: "I came up with no definite bent or any way of life: I leave with a most definite bent towards literary and intellectual work, with perhaps some public work as well if it may be" (31)—a quite accurate forecast (as often occurs in diaries).

Forty-one years later, his reverence for the university remains. "To Oxford," he records in his 1928 diary. "Perfection.... looking more like the earthly Paradise than usual—and how the air of it is drenched with emotion to me as well as beauty" (10). A month later, he writes to Will Vaughan to thank him for his five-pound gift to the Oxford Preservation Society and declares: "You say Oxford is 'no national playground.' I say it is much more than a playground: it is a spiritual inheritance, perhaps the greatest work of art the nation has produced.... [O]ur generation can do few or no better services to those that come after than the preservation of a place whose beauty and dignity has been the best sort of education to so many of the best Englishmen" (288).

To his credit, Bailey sends his daughters to Lady Margaret Hall, Oxford's women's college. However, he sees no reason for women to vote—although his seven-year-old daughter disagrees. "I was talking about S's speech (on Woman Suffrage)," he notes in his 1909 diary, "and, arguing laughingly, said that women had best do first what their fathers and then what their husbands advise them. 'No,' said Jenny, 'they ought to be independent, like the United States of America!'" (116). Five years later, he describes a Felixstowe hotel fire—the hotel "burnt to a ruin by these crazy women [suffragettes]. The first time I have seen their folly with my own eyes—a terrible demonstration of how our social system exists by consent and is largely at the mercy of any fool or knave who will risk himself to destroy it" (146).

Bailey senses his privilege rests on unsteady ground. "To-night took up a horrid Socialist book which has made me very uncomfortable," he confesses at age thirty to his 1894 diary:

> Nothing else ever really depresses me but this hideous doubt which comes now and then, of whether one is justified in living on rents and interest at all? I shall not act on it, no doubt, and indeed I am generally convinced of its unreasonableness, but the awful inequality of our social conditions is enough to give one pause, and certainly is responsible, in my case, for more hours of discomfort and uneasiness than anything else. The solution to all such questions is, I hope, this: that it is better to accept the amazingly rapid improvement that is going on than to plunge into any Socialistic Medea's cauldron! (53)

He thus rationalizes his "rents and interest."

Woolf reads *John Bailey, 1864–1931: Letters and Diaries* at the same time she reads *Dr. Salter: His Diary and Reminiscences for the year 1849 to the year 1932*.

She thus taps a second *male* view of the decades showcased in her novel-in-progress, *The Years*. Bailey's vision of Oxford University life as an "earthly paradise" and "a spiritual inheritance, perhaps the greatest work of art the nation has produced" imbues the Oxford sections of *The Years*—in fact, undergirds the Edward Pargiter/Kitty Malone Lasswade conflict. It may fuel Woolf's re-vision of universities in *Three Guineas*, as well. "[H]ow strange it looks, this world of domes and spires, of lecture rooms and laboratories, from our vantage point!" Woolf exclaims in *Three Guineas*. "How different it looks to us from what it must look to you!" (23).

Bailey's *Diaries* offered more evidence, too, of what Julian Bell described to Woolf in April 1935 as the "danger" lure of war. Although Bailey tells his wife in 1917 that art and spring have their role in war—"in consolation, in restoring balance, and in giving one the feeling of how eternal art and the spring are, and how temporary and passing war is" (179)—he offers a more elitist, simplistic, and romantic view of war than the hunter-pugilist Dr. Salter. In her introduction to her husband's *Letters and Diaries*, Sarah Bailey writes that "[t]he War presented itself to [John Bailey] simply as a contest between right and wrong, between civilization and barbarism, and he never had any doubt either of the rightness of our cause or of its ultimate triumph" (16). When the Great War begins, Bailey launches his public lecture titled "Why we are at war" (153). He first takes a special constable post guarding a power station and then, when his health falters, offers his service to John Buchan in the Foreign Office, where he summarizes French and Spanish newspapers for the War Cabinet.

On June 12, 1916, Bailey preserves in his diary "the finest thing I have yet heard—the highest reach of the heroic spirit" (172). As an English ship raced to battle, soldiers onboard saw scores of drowning men from another English warship: "[A]s they rushed by, unable to stop for a moment to save anyone, these [drowning] men gave their last breath in a cheer. *Morituri salutant*, indeed—almost more than *morituri*" (172). And on March 27, 1919, again at "The Club": "Kipling told us he had been struck with the number of Colonial soldiers who felt that they had for the first time been in a world which was full of life, of incidents, of variety, of memories of art and history—and who felt that they would never again be able to stay content in Australia or Canada, with nothing great in them but space" (188). This view challenged Woolf's April 1935 counter to her nephew that "many people have found life exciting without war" (*D* 4: 307). And on Armistice Day, Bailey does not see the vulgar "orgies" both Woolf and Dr. Salter see. He exclaims instead to his diary: "The great day... The whole day has been a tumult of joy and of loyalty. I had great difficulty in making my way to the Foreign Office through the surging crowd of singing, dancing, shouting people. *Laus Deo!*" (187).

John Bailey's *Diaries* hardly console. They supply, instead, matter for Woolf to counter in *The Years* and in *Three Guineas*.[14] The volume also shows the hazards of the "Letters and Diaries" blend. Well-meaning Sarah Bailey fails to serve her husband well as a diarist. She admits in her introduction that her decision to include his *"journal intime"* was an afterthought. Diary entries, she felt, "would supplement his letters and help to give a picture of his daily life" (9). She succeeds partly here. Bailey's specimen day, December 8, 1894, offers a clear view of his life at age twenty-eight:

> "A typical day"! . . . Breakfast 9.20. *Times* and letters. Writing at Gibbon (article on), 11.15. 1.20 Lunch, Saintsbury Lyrics. Out 3–5 p.m. Tea with Watson's new volume of poems. Writing Gibbon till 7.15. Dinner at club. Back here 9 to read Lucretius with [Bruce] Richmond and [Campbell] Dodgson. Then at 11.15 went in to F. Smith and had long talk on marriage. Bed 12.30, an hour later than usual. (53)

Sarah Bailey expurgates her husband's diary in three ways. She selects a too-small portion of his entries and then not only edits *these* with ellipses but also substitutes blanks and initials for names she wishes to mask. From forty-six years of diary-keeping (and perhaps more), she offers only 264 diary entries; that is, only, on average, 5 or 6 entries per year. One can hardly pare a diary to such an extent and still have a meaningful diary.

Once more we wish for a full diary.[15] To mix "Letters and Diaries" is to distrust and to obscure the writer's power in each distinctive form. More diary—or just the diary—might make Bailey a fuller figure. Instead, he emerges as an ardent dabbler—a privileged dilettante.

Woolf long knew John Bailey's work. She begins a November 16, 1912, letter to Lytton Strachey, "Really, if you go on writing, you will vitiate John Bailey's stock phrase 'the art of letter writing is dying out—'" (*L* #653, 2: 12). She repeats this on December 6, 1936, when Violet Dickinson sends her typescript copies, bound in two volumes, of her own 350 youthful letters to Violet (*L* #3197, 6: 90). But from the first Woolf scoffs at Bailey. At age twenty-one, she mocks him as an arbiter in an October 2, 1903, letter to Dickinson: "I've written this letter without any effort to make it grammatical. John Bailey wouldn't approve" (*L* #105, 1: 98). A month later, in another letter to Dickinson, she again challenges

Bailey: "Madge [Vaughan] has been here from 5 to 8.... She doesn't think much of John Bailey either. Those words will jump out writ in scarlet in the Lyttelton atmosphere" (*L* #122, 1: 109).

Envy may fuel some of this youthful scorn, for in a letter written likely in mid-December 1904—the month Woolf's first published work appears in Mary Kathleen Lyttelton's *Guardian* pages—Virginia writes wittily to Madge Vaughan: "I wish I could write letters like John Baileys.... By the way, I am going to see Mrs Arthur Lyttelton tomorrow, my Editress. I hear that she thinks it an *honour* to publish John Baileys works. What then, must she feel it to publish mine, I ask you?" (*L* #202, 1:167).

John Bailey, in short, figures in that rich, anxious, envious time that saw Woolf's birth as a professional writer. Woolf, in fact, evokes Sarah Kathleen Lyttelton Bailey's name in the context of consolation in one of the (protectively deceiving) letters she writes to Dickinson in the days after Thoby Stephen's death. On December 8, 1906, Virginia writes to Violet: "Well, it rains outside, and the only comfort is a book and a fire; and these you can have too I hope, besides which you may think of your hall table with its flowers and its coronets; and of your husband, and of your Kathleen—I dont know what is missing in your Heaven; except a small animal that burrows with its snout" (*L* #317, 1: 258). The small animal, of course, is Woolf.

That Woolf leaves Bailey behind is clear from letters in 1920 and 1921. On June 24, 1920, Woolf writes to her sister, Vanessa: "Madge [Vaughan] is reviewed in the Times, by John Bailey I think, all lies, very polite, and as dull as ditchwater" (*L* #1132, 2: 434). The next year, she queries (again) of Violet Dickinson: "Who admires John Bailey? I dont; and I gather that Lytton Strachey feels quite safe against John's version of old Victoria. Still poor John is thin; he must be protected; you are his old friend and yet you laugh at him" (*L* #1206, 2: 496).

Bailey's world was not Bloomsbury. Bailey quotes Roger Fry admiringly in a 1910 letter, and Sarah Bailey includes a polite 1922 letter from Lytton Strachey to Bailey, who has thanked Lytton for helping him to think better of Racine (117, 217–18). However, in a 1925 diary entry, Bailey calls Matisse "the very god of the idolatry of the Clive Bell school of criticism" (255). Woolf might also have chafed at Bailey's 1914 diary allusion to her father, Leslie Stephen, as one of the "curious cases" who "developed a new ease and pleasantness directly they had not long to live" (151). Woolf most recoiled, however, from Bailey's 1927 diary record of a Literary Society chat with Desmond MacCarthy. In 1905, Bailey brought out the standard text of *The Poems of William Cowper*. In his April 4, 1927, diary entry, Bailey expresses surprise at Desmond's love of Cowper: "He had my edition. . . . said he had given Cowper lately to Virginia Woolf, of all people, and she had caught his enthusiasm" (270). To this, Woolf exclaims in her own 1935 diary: "[T]he one remark to the effect that Virginia Woolf of all people, has been given Cowper by Desmond, & likes it! I, who read Cowper when I was 15—d—d nonsense" (*D* 4: 339). Nevertheless, Bailey gave her an Oxford to counter in *The Years* and in *Three Guineas*.

6

Misguided General

Hitler takes his first prize, the Rhineland, unopposed in March 1936. Thomas Cook, nevertheless, issues a tourist brochure inviting a "Heil! Summer!" No irony intended. No dissonance seen. Petra Rau writes that "Cook did not just advertise the fact that holidaying in Nazi Germany was an unproblematic choice, but with these images naively contributed to the normalization of this new Germany and its fascist semiotics within the modern European political landscape" (16). In England, at the same time, the Archbishops' Commission was putting up "fierce resistance" to the notion of women Anglican priests (Pierson 218).

Virginia Woolf fights her own dramatic inner war across the year. Her 1936 diary reveals, more clearly than any other of her diary books, the diary's foundational role in Woolf's artistic renewal—a role she does not fully understand. We also see with great clarity in 1936 the role of *other* diaries in her renewals. In August 1936, amid dangerous illness, Woolf reads the diaries of Bertrand Russell's parents, Lord and Lady Amberley. She lives again in their world and takes direction for *Three Guineas*. In early November, she reads Ellen Weeton's *Journal of a Governess*, and, in December, the diaries of Stephen MacKenna, who translated the Greek philosopher Plotinus into melodious English. She makes use of these diaries in *Three Guineas*.

Virginia Woolf's 1936 Diary

> "A divine relief has possessed me these last days—
> at being quit of it [The Years]—good or bad. And,
> for the first time since February I shd. say my mind
> has sprung up like a tree shaking off a load."
> (December 30, 1936; D 5: 44)

Atlas unburdened. Sisyphus freed of the rock. Prometheus unchained. Virginia Woolf's 1936 diary even evokes a Christian resurrection: death to new life, the rock rolled away. Despite its two long alarming breaks, despite its brevity (for Woolf's *1930s* diaries at least), or perhaps *because* of its spareness, the 1936 diary offers a unity of drama unsurpassed in Woolf's thirty-eight diary books.[1]

A mere fifty-three entries mark the 368 days from December 28, 1935, to December 30, 1936, an entry, on average, every seven days (rather than the two or three days of the 1935 diary)—the change in itself a flag. However, even every seven days would give a false picture. More than half the year is lost in this diary: a two-month gap from April 10 to June 10, followed by three valiant entries, before silence again engulfs the diary for more than four months—from June 24 to October 29.

The diary lays bare the crisis—although Woolf only half sees. Her savvy habit of rereading her old diaries fails to keep her from repeating her mistake of 1921. Put simply: in 1936 Woolf overworks herself to the brink of destruction; she dams her (vital) refreshing streams with work. In 1921, the ambition (and jealousy) that spurred Woolf to substitute Russian lessons for her teatime diary-writing, so as to keep pace with Leonard, led to summer collapse and "all the horrors of the dark cupboard of illness" (*D* 2: 125). In 1936, Hogarth Press and political matters less in her command send her to the edge once more.

In November 1935, Leonard tells Virginia that Hogarth Press profits will be lean (*D* 4: 353). On January 3, 1936, the pressure tightens, just as she is to start the "final" revision of *The Years*. "This suddenly becomes a little urgent," Virginia tells her diary, "because for the first time for some years, L. says I have not made enough to pay my share of the house, & have to find £70 out of my hoard. This is now reduced to £700, & I must fill it up" (*D* 5: 3). *The Years'* American serialization would nicely fill the coffers, as would stateside publication of the novel; however, this means she *must* finish the book.

Woolf's diary and Roger Fry now serve as interchangeable—in fact, reinforcing—springs of refreshment. The relative absence of both Fry and diary in 1936 (compared to 1935) reveals Woolf's perilous state. Fry's ghost haunts the 1935 diary. Woolf draws on his invigorating spirit throughout that year. Because she now often uses *morning* diary-writing to cool (and refresh) her heated brain, in the final months of 1935 she begins to read Fry's prose "between tea & dinner [when she formerly wrote her diary].... to [her] great refreshment" (*D* 4: 346, 347). On October 22, 1935, she also types out Fry's own memoir in the morning and heralds it "a most admirable sedative & refresher. I wish I always had it at hand" (*D* 4: 347). Indeed.

A portent of the 1936 crisis comes in her first diary entry, December 28, 1935. Woolf feels so "congested," that is, so suffocated from the heavy slab that is *The Years*, that she "cant even copy out Roger" (*D* 4: 360). In her third entry, two days later, she again seeks to draw on Fry's spirit. She observes once more that "[r]eading Roger I become haunted by him" (*D* 4: 361), and on January 4, 1936, she commands herself, suggestively: "And now to do Roger; & then to relax. For, to tell the truth, my head is still all nerves; & one false move means racing despair, exaltation, & all the rest of that familiar misery: that long scale of unhappiness" (*D* 5: 4). On January 10, "[t]o show [her] state," she confesses that she turns to Fry again in the morning when unable to press on with *The Years*: "My head is so springless" (*D* 5: 5).

But the next day she stumbles. She makes the "one false move." Since she can work only for brief spurts on *The Years*, she tells her diary that she thinks of continuing *The Years*' revision after tea (*D* 5: 6). In short, she will substitute work on the novel for her diary and Fry refreshment.

Diary time now must be "stolen," if it occurs at all. A February 1936 entry opens: "It is now the 9th of Feb & I have three weeks in which to finish my book. Hence this stolen minute . . . is the first I have had in wh. to make even this elementary note. I work 3 hours in the morning: 2 often after tea. Then my head swells & I sleep" (*D* 5: 12). On February 25, she again opens her diary: "And this will show how hard I work. This is the first moment—this 5 minutes before lunch—that I've had to write here. I work all the morning: I work from 5 to 7 [p.m.] most days. Then I've had headaches. . . . I have sworn that the script shall be ready, typed & corrected, on the 10th March. L. will then read it. . . . So I'm quite unable either to write here, or to do Roger" (*D* 5: 13). Alarmingly, she then adds that she is "enjoying it" on the whole, sign she neither senses fatigue nor fully fathoms the creative lift that Fry and her diary bring.

She refers to Fry only four more times in the year, for her 1936 diary (like her first 1905 diary) focuses almost exclusively—even obsessively—on her professional prose at hand. Along with Fry and the diary itself, portraits and talk shrink in this diary until the final months of the year. Woolf also finds no boost in journalism. "I can no longer write for papers," she notes in her first entry in 1936. "I must write for my own book" (*D* 5: 3). Thirty-nine of her fifty-three diary entries speak of *The Years*—an even higher percentage than in 1935. Like a besieged (but misguided) general, Woolf cuts off her regular lines of replenishment to give her full force to *The Years*.

However, as in 1921, her subconscious—that intermediary state that is her diary—owns her plight. The first words of the 1936 diary confess: "Its all very well to write that date in a nice clear hand, because it begins this new book, but I cannot disguise the fact that I'm almost extinct" (*D* 4: 360). In fact, she feels suicidal. "And why should I lead the dance of the days with this tipsy little spin?" she asks, alarmingly (*D* 4: 360).

She can, however, mark progress. On January 5, she feels "[f]urther work must be merely to tidy & smooth out," and two days later she says she needs to "only use my craft not my creation" in the final sweep (*D* 5: 4). Shouldn't this ease the pressure? Hardly, for she now begins her frantic relay race to March 10. She retypes pages with her revisions to give to her typist, Mabel, who will send a formal typescript back to her for final hand edits by March 10.

American pressure plays a role in this frenzied spring race. Yet despite her Herculean efforts, on March 10 *The Years* remains unfinished. Woolf opens her March 11 entry, "Well yesterday I sent off 132 pages to Clark [their Scottish printer]. We have decided to take this unusual course—that is to print it in galleys before L. sees it & send it to America" (*D* 5: 15). She says "we" made the decision, and there is no reason to doubt her.

That she sends only some pages suggests that other pages still need her eye. The Woolfs seem ready at this point to sacrifice Leonard's verdict in order to speed the book toward galleys for America in May. From this distance, America's flattering wish for *The Years* seems the golden straw that crushes the camel. If America did not press, would Woolf have placed her head in such a narrow vise? Victoria Glendenning declares that Leonard imposed the deadline, thinking it would help Virginia finish *The Years* (289). If so, he soon saw his error. However, on March 11 Virginia tells her diary she feels "more at ease," and she throws herself into another month-long, now three-way, relay: from her typewriter to Mabel's and back again and then off to the printer.

She receives her first galley proofs on March 18, which pile up, for she is still sending pages to Mabel. "If I can do 25 pages daily I shall be done by Tuesday next," Woolf tells her diary on Wednesday April 1. "And then the proofs. How its to come out in May, God knows" (*D* 5: 22). Her next entry, April 9, opens: "Now will come the season of depression, after congestion suffocation. The last batch [of corrected typescript] was posted to Clark . . . yesterday. L. is in process of reading. . . . The horror is that tomorrow, after this one windy day of respite . . .

I must begin at the beginning & go through 600 pages of cold proof. Why oh why?" (*D* 5: 22).

Neither God nor Virginia knows why—or how—and *The Years* does not "come out" in May. Diary editor Olivier Bell reports that "news that her American publishers . . . were unable to publish the book until the autumn" gave Woolf welcome relief (*D* 5: 23). Did Leonard orchestrate this delay? Biographer Hermione Lee says he did (629). Whatever the source, relieved now of the immense pressure, Woolf allows herself to collapse.[2]

After a two-month diary lapse, her three June entries offer a portal on her stricken state. "I can only, after 2 months, make this brief note, to say at last after 2 months dismal & worse, almost catastrophic illness—never been so near the precipice to my own feeling since 1913—I'm again on top," begins her June 11 entry (*D* 5: 24). Yet her deep depression shows itself in her overwrought next words: "I have to re-write, I mean interpolate & rub out most of The Years in proof." She cannot mean this. Nevertheless, she uses her diary to spur herself on: "Now I am going to live like a cat stepping on eggs till my 600 pages are done. I think I can—I think I can—but must have immense courage & buoyancy to compass it. This, as I say, my first voluntary writing since April 9th. after wh. I pitched into bed" (*D* 5: 24). She now starts one last time to revise *The Years*.

Ten days later, her next entry reveals the ravaged Promethean life she lives in London: "After a week of intense suffering—indeed mornings of torture—& I'm not exaggerating—pain in my head—a feeling of complete despair & failure . . . here is a cool quiet morning again, a feeling of relief; respite: hope. Just done the Robsons: think it good. I am living so constrainedly; so repressedly: I cant make notes of life" (*D* 5: 24). Her third June entry telegraphs her precarious state: "A good day—a bad day—so it goes on," she begins on June 23. "Few people can be so tortured by writing as I am. . . . My brain is like a scale: one grain pulls it down. Yesterday it balanced: today dips" (*D* 5: 25). These are the ominous last diary words for more than four months.

In these months, however, Woolf engineers her resurrection. She retreats from London to the country—always a good sign, a chance to hear nature's voice.[3] Although not ready yet for her own diary, she starts to read *other* diaries in July. She dips once more into Wilfrid Scawen Blunt's *Diaries* and, better, in August, into the lively diaries of Bertrand Russell's parents, which the Woolfs agree to publish as the two-volume *Amberley Papers*. These diaries bring life and stir her mind.

As noted before, Woolf uses contrasting diary portraits to project her own conflicts. Nowhere does this appear more baldly than in her 1936 diary. On March 20, twenty days before her own collapse, Woolf preserves in her diary a haunting portrait of a woman who faints at her door. Like the suicidal young woman in the Serpentine in Woolf's 1903 diary, this "mere wisp—22—suffering," appears to have no mother, no father, no work (*D* 5: 19). The young woman, in fact, tells the Woolfs she is a "Jewess" (*D* 5: 19). "But my God—no one to help her," Woolf tells her diary, and this encounter seems emblematic, not only of Woolf's own threatened interior state but also of the outer plight of Europe's Jews (*D* 5: 19). "Some horror become visible," Woolf tells her diary (*D* 5: 19).

Yet on October 30, in the most affirming of choices for her first diary entry after more than four months' silence, Woolf counters the haunting vision of the woman in collapse with a portrait of a courageous elderly woman, Lady Sibyl Colefax, rising from her husband's death and her own sudden poverty. At this critical moment, Woolf chooses Sibyl as the diary test of her own writing life. The entry opens: "I do not wish for the moment to write out the story of the months since I made the last mark here. I do not wish, for reasons I cannot now develop, to analyse that extraordinary summer. It will be more helpful & healthy for me to write scenes; to take up my pen & describe actual events: good practice too for my stumbling & doubting pen. Can I still 'write'? That is the question, you see. And now I will try to prove if the gift is dead, or dormant" (*D* 5: 26).

Writing then the date "Tuesday [October] 27th," Woolf launches into a vivid portrait of Lady Colefax, her furniture up for auction at Argyll House—the most detailed scene and portrait in the 1936 diary. Lady Colefax, who first looks to Woolf like "a dried up bird," echoes Woolf's words at the start of the entry. She says to Woolf, "I cant let myself talk, or I should sink into such depths . . . I should never recover" (*D* 5: 27). Instead, Lady Sibyl starts to tell stories; in fact, tells Woolf she plans a book, an anthology of love poems. And Woolf ends the entry with the older woman risen, triumphant, and starting to work:

> She talked in a scattered nervous way, like a hen fluttering over the edge of an abyss. A brave hen. . . . I still felt something genuinely rising from the depths in her: a desire to fight her adversity, a momentary desire to break down; but then she was up again & off again. When the door opened & Fielding croaked out "The car, m'lady" she was glad of the call to action & we swept through the wind swept fluttering lighted streets, sitting together in the Rolls Royce while she told stories, adequately indeed rather

brilliantly, of George Moore & Wells, of Henry James & Carrie Balestier [Rudyard Kipling's wife]. The machine had got going again, after its momentary paralysis. (*D* 5: 28)

Animal tropes, as well as portraits, convey Woolf's resurrection. When Hitler invades the Rhineland unopposed, Woolf tells her March 13 entry: "This is the most feverish overworked political week we've yet had.... [H]ow near the guns have got to our private life again. I can quite distinctly see them & hear a roar, even though I go on, like a doomed mouse, nibbling at my daily page" (*D* 5: 17). Woolf is "almost extinct" in her first diary sentence and "a doomed mouse" in March. In June, after her two-month collapse, she is able to transform the doomed mouse into "a cat stepping on eggs," a more hopeful—though still cautious—trope (*D* 5: 24). On November 3, however, in the 1936 diary's final crisis, the cat, too, dies. Woolf writes:

> When I had read to the end of the first section [of revised proof] I was in despair: stony but convinced despair.... I must carry the proofs, like a dead cat, to L. & tell him to burn them unread. This I did. And a weight fell off my shoulders. That is true. I felt relieved of some great pack.... Now I was no longer Virginia, the genius, but only a perfectly insignificant yet content—shall I call it spirit? a body? And very tired. Very old. But at [the] same time content to go on these 100 years with Leonard. So we lunched, in a constraint: a grey acceptance.... How dead I felt—(*D* 5: 29)

Woolf seems to accept here the death of her genius: of her writing gift.

Leonard, one of her vital props (like nature, Roger Fry, poets, and diaries), now throws her the lifeline she needs. Woolf tells her diary on November 5: "The miracle is accomplished.... He says [*The Years*] is 'a most remarkable book—he *likes* it better than The Waves.' & has not a spark of doubt that it must be published" (*D* 5: 30). This assurance brings life. On November 24, Woolf portrays the moment as the resurrection it was: "But I've been on the whole vigorous & cheerful since the wonderful revelation of L.'s that night. How I woke from death—or non being—to life! What an incredible night—what a weight rolled off!... And I've touched ground. Whatever happens I dont think I can now be destroyed. Only work work is essential. Roger.... &c.... Up & off again, like the gull in the poem" (*D* 5: 35, 36).

The doomed mouse, the dead cat, is now off again like the gull in George Meredith's poem "Juggling Jerry," the gull who leaves death behind and is "off for new luck." Woolf repeats here the phrase she used twenty-six days before for Lady Sibyl, the "brave hen," "fluttering over the edge of an abyss," who then is "up again & off again" (*D* 5: 28). Woolf, though, is more than a brave hen: she is a soaring gull. She thus links herself once more to the soaring birds of her crucial 1905 Cornwall diary, where she describes ships as "silent voyagers . . . coming & going, alighting like some travelling birds for a moment & then shaking out their sails again & passing on to new waters" (*PA* 296).

To be "Promethean" means to be daringly creative and original. The brother of burdened Atlas, Prometheus' own torture, chained to the rock, becomes Woolf's state in 1936, as it did in 1921 and again in 1930 and 1931. In depicting *The Years* as a slab or stone throughout the year, Woolf also calls to mind the ordeal of Sisyphus, eternally rolling the rock uphill—a rock that in 1936 almost crushes her. Yet Woolf links herself to Antaeus in the above passage as well, Antaeus who cannot die while touching mother Earth. "And I've touched ground," she declares after nearly Herculean strangulation. "Whatever happens I dont think I can now be destroyed" (*D* 5: 35).

In one of the most dramatic sequences in Woolf's entire diary, she manages to resurrect herself as a writer once more. On November 10, Woolf tells her diary that "the old fountains only want this paving stone of a book off them to spring up" (*D* 5: 31). And they spring. She can write articles once more. She turns her Lady Colefax *diary* portrait into the close of her "Am I a Snob?" Memoir Club essay in late November,[4] and, in December, her article "Why Art To-day Follows Politics" appears in the *Daily Worker*. The essay describes how politics burden art.

And she rights herself from her January 11 misstep. The entry that follows Leonard's November 5 rescue begins with resolutions: "I must do my proofs & send them off. I *must* fix my mind on it all the morning. I think the only way is to do that, & then let myself do something else between tea & dinner. But immerse in The Years all the morning—nothing else. If the chapter is difficult, concentrate for a short time. Then write here" (*D* 5: 31). She preserves her post-teatime for renewal and resumes her own diary as aid.

And she takes on other diaries, as well. In early November, she reads governess Ellen Weeton's diary and wishes to write on it in a Hogarth Press broadsheet. Instead, she uses Weeton's diary in *Three Guineas*. In December, she reads Greek translator Stephen MacKenna's *Journal and Letters*, which influence *Three Guineas*, as well. At November's end she even starts to read Dante again—another fine prop.

Woolf's diary signals her return to "life" once more. In December, she turns with zest to the melodrama of the abdicating king—another (now national) crisis of work and commitment. In four riveting diary entries, Woolf captures both the facts and the shifting mood of the royal crisis when King Edward chooses his love, American divorcee Wallis Simpson, over country and crown. Once more we see the Woolfs' front row seat on world events. A week before the first newspaper reference to the scandal, Woolf tells her diary: "L. has a confidential story about the King & Mrs Simpson, told him in secret by K[ingsley]. Martin" (*D* 5: 38). Talk then bursts from her December 7 entry, for Woolf turns herself into a news conduit (and historian):

> It was on Wednesday 2nd Dec that the Bishop commented on the Kings lack of religion. On Thursday all the papers, The Times & D[aily] T[elegraph]. very discreetly, mentioned some, domestic difficulties; others Mrs Simpson. All London was gay & garrulous—not exactly gay, but excited. We cant have a woman Simpson for Queen, that was the sense of it. She's no more royal than you or me, was what the grocer's young woman said. But today, before the PM. [Prime Minister] makes his announcement to the House, we have developed a strong sense of human sympathy; we are saying Hang it all—the age of Victoria is over. Let him marry whom he likes. In the Beefsteak Club however only Lord Onslow & Clive take the democratic view. Harold [Nicolson] is glum as an undertaker, & so are the other nobs. They say Royalty is in Peril. The Empire is divided. In fact never has there been such a crisis. That I think is true. Spain, Germany, Russia—all are elbowed out. The marriage stretches from one end of the paper to another. Pictures of the D. of York & the Princesses fill every cranny. Mrs Simpson is snapped by lime light at midnight as she gets out of her car. Her luggage is also photographed. Parties are forming. The different interests are queueing up behind Baldwin, or Churchill. Mosley is taking advantage of the crisis for his ends. In fact we are all talking 19 to the dozen; & it looks as if this one little insignificant man had moved a pebble wh. dislodges an avalanche. Things—empires, hierarchies—moralities—will never be the same again. Yet today there is a certain feeling that the button has been pressed too hard: emotion is no longer so liberally forthcoming. And the King may keep us all waiting, while he sits, like a naughty boy in the nursery, trying to make up his mind. (*D* 5: 39–40)

Her next entries deliver a similar lively firsthand, many-voiced unfolding of this historic moment, including Woolf's December 10 sense that it "made us all feel slightly yet perceptibly humiliated. Its odd, but so I even feel it. . . . Rather an ignominious flight—I feel again" (*D* 5: 41).

The 1936 diary that opens with Woolf "almost extinct" and yearning to "stretch [her] cramped muscles" ends in the chatter of life, the King's farewell, and, in the final entry, Woolf's mind "sprung up like a tree shaking off a load" (*D* 4: 360; 5: 44). But she dangerously overworks herself in 1936 and—just as foolhardily, monomaniacally—abandons her props.

She does not, however, quite lose sight of her diary as a source for Old Virginia's memoirs, for she takes up her diary on January 19 to write: "I open this, forced by a sense of what is expected by the public, to remark that Kipling died yesterday; & that the King (George 5th) is probably dying today. The death of Kipling has set all the old war horses of the press padding round their stalls" (*D* 5: 8). And on November 30 she can confide to Old Virginia: "There is no need whatever in my opinion to be unhappy about The Years. It seems to me to come off at the end. . . . In fact I hand my compliment to that terribly depressed woman, myself, whose head ached so often: who was so entirely convinced a failure; for in spite of everything I think she brought it off, & is to be congratulated" (*D* 5: 38, 39).

The Diaries of Lord & Lady Amberley: *The Amberley Papers*

"Did you ever hear tell of the Amberleys—Bertie Russell's parents?" Virginia Woolf asks Vita Sackville-West on August 27, 1936, from the depths of her summer collapse. "She's a fascinating problem."[5] Bertrand Russell's courageous, freethinking parents died tragically at ages thirty-two and thirty-four, their promise unfulfilled. "Bertie" was only two when his mother died, in 1874, and just three at his father's death. He and his older brother, Frank, were raised by their grandparents, the Russells, their grandfather twice prime minister of England.[6]

In *The Amberley Papers: The Letters and Diaries of Bertrand Russell's Parents*, Russell resurrects his lost parents, the mother and father he barely knew. Their new life, through diaries, likely fortified Woolf, who was resurrecting herself at this time. On September 18, 1936, Woolf employs her "deep old desk, or capacious hold-all" trope from her 1919 diary credo to describe the *Amberley Papers* to Ethel Smyth (*D* 1: 266). "Bertie Russell has sent us, to publish . . . sweepings of old desks—2,000 pages: so fascinating and tragic, I live almost as much with the Amberleys in the 80ties as here and now" (*L* #3173, 6: 73). The "80ties," the first decade of Woolf's novel-in-progress *The Years* (earlier called *Here and Now*), is an intriguing slip, for the Amberleys' diaries and letters span 1854 to 1876. Today the Amberleys' saga would make a poignant, stirring art film, for their lives showcase the obstacles (family and social) faced by advanced religious and social thinkers of that time. *The Amberley Papers* give direction to Woolf's next work, *Three Guineas*—in fact, supply its structure—and may also have offered warning of the world's hostility to bold thought.

The Amberley Papers' two volumes offer 1,050 diary entries and just 611 letters. Bertrand Russell and his wife, Patricia, the volumes' editors, give excerpts from young John Russell's diaries and from his wife, Kate's; however, Kate's diary overshadows her husband's: 717 entries from Kate to 333 from John. No wonder Woolf called Kate Stanley Russell a "fascinating problem."

Virginia Woolf lived in the Amberleys' world and called it all "absorbing" because their *Diaries* resurrected those she knew. Kate mentions Woolf's father, Leslie Stephen, seven times in her diary and almost always as an impediment to female friendship or sisters' love. On December 17, 1866, Kate tells her diary: "We heard fr. Minnie Thackeray that she was engaged to be married to Mr. Leslie Stephens [*sic*] and that was the reason of her putting us off the last time" (1: 538). On March 27, 1867, Kate tells her diary that Annie Thackeray "was in a doleful state of mind at the prospect of her sister marrying and not feeling well herself she had taken a little cottage at Wimbledon to establish herself there for a little time independently" (2: 23). (Shades of 1908 Virginia alone in Manorbier, Wales.)

Beyond glimpses of her father, Woolf saw anew through Kate's diary the whole Freshwater scene. She learned from Kate's diary more of the artistic trials her great-aunt, the pioneer photographer Julia Margaret Cameron, faced—hardships William Allingham's diaries had touched on in 1907.[7] Kate records an 1866 visit to Mrs. Henry Taylor where she saw "some exquisite photos done by Mrs. Cameron, who is going to give it up for 2 years as she nearly ruined herself" (1: 463). Four months later, Kate visits G. F. Watts in his studio and talks to him for an hour, for he is painting her sister, Blanche. Kate describes among his sketches an allegory of "death (as a woman) and time (as a young man) walking hand in hand and judgement behind them bearing the sword waiting"—an allegory that seems, in retrospect, poignantly prophetic (1: 481–82).

The Amberleys meet Woolf's godfather, James Russell Lowell, during their

1867 American tour, and they know Lytton Strachey's parents. Lady Strachey, in fact, becomes one of Kate's strong supports on women's suffrage. Woolf also may have quickened to Kate's admiration for both Thomas and Jane Carlyle. Kate's 1859 diary record of her visit to their Chelsea home displays her virtues as a diarist—even at age seventeen. We see Kate's memory for talk and her eye for detail, her thoughtful intuition, and her bent to compose a scene:

> [W]e stayed till 11 listening to [Carlyle] talk. I enjoyed it excessively for he held forth to us on all subjects, abusing every thing & every one. He said he did not know one good man in all England & that he thought we were going down into a state of destruction very rapidly. Also he said he never read a newspaper but trusted to others for the news. He was a sad spectacle of a philosopher pent up quite alone with his own thoughts. . . . Mrs. Carlyle sat patiently by & when asked if it was always the same she said "Always" with a sigh. Nero, her little dog, also sat there listening. It was language quite out of the common way, sad, but a great deal of truth in it—(1: 56, 57)

Six months later, Carlyle visits Kate's family at Alderley Park, and once more the seventeen-year-old diarist absorbs the scene:

> He talked a great deal in the evening, abused Mill's book on Liberty & said we did not want liberty & it was all nonsense . . . & he talked about running people through with a red hot poker and then laughed very much at the idea.
> . . . At luncheon he said he thought all novels stupid & he did not know any good ones written by women, he abused every one in turn which was mentioned—& he said . . . he thought women had better not meddle with those things but be quiet with darning stockings, a very different idea from Mrs. Mill's in her Enfranchisement of Women; he talked of her & said she was a silly woman, at least not so clever, but that Mill admired her because she was kind to him. . . .
> I enjoyed his visit here very much & I always like to listen to him one always learns something—(1: 62–63)

We see here Kate's great receptivity.

The Amberley diaries thus revive the England of 1854 to 1876. They also introduce *other* diaries and reunite Woolf with diarists she likes. Kate's imperious Aunt Louisa Stanley sends her (for political instruction) extracts from her 1819 journal during the Peterloo Massacre. Young John Russell, like Woolf herself, takes Walter Scott as his diary lodestar. John starts at least three of his diary volumes with Scott's "Time rolls his ceaseless course," and he favors Scott to read to the several young ladies he courts.

But the surprise gift from *The Amberley Papers* is the touching view of diarist Thomas Sanderson before he becomes a diarist, before he becomes Cobden-Sanderson and the artist of *The Book Beautiful*. (Woolf praised Cobden-Sanderson's *Journals* and his pursuit of his mystic *Credo* in a 1926 review.) In 1860, former prime minister John Russell sends young John, his eldest son and namesake, to his own school, the University of Edinburgh, for "nothing was to be learned in the English universities" (1: 216). John stays but a year. He moves to Trinity College, Cambridge, for the 1861–62 years, but it also does not suit him, and he comes down in February 1863. Amberley's chief Cambridge gain appears to be the friendship of an older student, Thomas Sanderson, whose integrity and courage young John admires.

If friendships reveal character, the deep ties between Amberley and Sanderson suggest Amberley's intellectual depth and moral worth. Did it cross Woolf's mind that her father, Sanderson, and Amberley all lived at Trinity College in 1861–62, and all lost their religious faith? When Sanderson comes to lunch on November 20, 1863, twenty-year-old Amberley records their "most interesting conversation," as well as the social perils of unbelief. Sanderson "avows openly that he has entirely given up his belief in revealed religion, & is much of the same opinion as I am on all questions of this nature. He declares to his friends (with greater candour than I have yet reached) that he is no longer a Christian. I hope I may be able to make the avowal, should my views not alter, but I dread the effect, as I should be thought dangerous, & I know not what else" (1: 278). Though neither knows it in 1863, Sanderson is on his way to his mystic *Credo* and Amberley to his *Analysis of Religious Belief*. Sanderson wrote perceptively to Kate thirteen months into her marriage: "You are a remarkable person, & all the more remarkable having so reserved a husband & so serious-minded a friend" (1: 422).

Katharine Stanley Russell *was* a remarkable person, as both her diary and her brief lifework attest. A charmingly bad speller who ran her sentences together—flaws of her faulty education—Kate ever possessed a searching mind.[8] *The Amberley Papers* show Kate's eagerness to read as a teenager. In her first diary entry included, she is reading Horace Walpole's *Castle of Otranto* at age fourteen. On view, too, is her early pliant nature, one willing to conform to others' views. At seventeen, Kate writes to her mother of a Quaker woman's autobiography, "Maude has finished the 1st Vol of Shimelpenik [Schimmelpenninck] & has *allowed* me to read what you told me I might read so I am going to read the 4 first Chapters" (1: 64). Later chapters, Bertrand Russell explains, recorded religious doubts. "Papa says I may read the two first vols of the Mill on the Floss & stop there," Kate writes her beloved brother, Lyulph, in 1860, when she is eighteen. "Mama has not finished it yet but says I may not read it. I am so sorry. At Holmwood [sic] they call it an odious book & advise me not to read it" (1: 77).

We see the blinders placed on English upper-class girls in 1860. Bertrand Russell notes that Kate's father "forbade his daughters to read Thackeray, on the ground that the picture of London society in his novels was too accurate to be good for young girls" (1: 14). In 1861, Kate confides to Lyulph that "Aunt Ally very much objects to all the new books which say that people ought to have a work to do in the world & that women ought to 'better themselves'; she thinks that everyone's duty is to be as quiet & retiring & unobtrusive as possible & contented" (1: 137). Two-and-a-half years later, in rather a panic, twenty-one-year-old Kate writes to Amberley's step-sister during their courtship, as if to assure the Russells: "I fully agree with you about home being first of all & before all. I hope you did not think I minded Mama not allowing me to read or do certain things for I do not; also she is wonderfully lax in her restrictions & I would not like ever to read what is not meant for me" (1: 280).

Fortunately, the intellectual gates lift when she weds Amberley. As Bertrand Russell notes in 1937, Amberley's "thinking was remarkably honest, and he invariably acted upon the conclusions to which it led him" (1: 144). This, naturally, brought him (and Kate) no end of trouble, for he continued the Russell family progression from Whig aristocrat (his grandfather) to Liberal aristocrat (his father) to become himself (like Colonel Strachey) "a 'rad'[ical] of the first water." At about eighteen, Kate wheedles permission to read John Stuart Mill's *On Liberty* and—despite Carlyle's abuse—likes it very much. She reads it again a year later and writes her brother that she "delight[s] in it how clear the arguments are & so simple I can quite understand it. I wonder it has not made more stir in the world & made people think more.... I should have thought it would have prepared the way for Essays & Reviews."[9] The 1860 *Essays and Reviews* caused Kate, Amberley, Sanderson, Leslie Stephen, and others to question their religious faith.

In March 1864, during the six-month separation from Kate that the Russells force on John to test his love, he meets Mill in person: a key moment. Ironically, they meet at Chesham Place, the Russell's London home—ironic, for from this time forth, Mill becomes Amberley's moral and intellectual father, replacing Lord Russell, whom young John will try less and less to please.[10] John's diary shows the intellectual partnership already launched with Kate before their delayed (and begrudged) marriage. "In C[hesham]. P[lace]," he notes, "I found a most kind note from Lady S[tanley]. enclosing photographs of Kate. I sent over for Kate's reading several books, which I hope she may study while I am away.... At dinner I met J. S. Mill, in whom I was of course greatly interested. He speaks in a very gentle voice, and is not in appearance like a great man" (1: 297). Three months later, Amberley visits Mill in Avignon.

In February 1865, three months after her marriage, Kate herself meets Mill and his step-daughter, Helen Taylor, at a weekend at the Grotes. From there, with Mill's and Taylor's full blessing, the twenty-two-year-old Amberleys launch their religious study and social activism. Kate and John return to Rodborough, their home in western England, and begin to teach classes for working men and women. "You have an interesting and useful subject of study in your factory girls," Helen Taylor writes to Kate in June 1865. "The whole question of women's working, at least as regards married women, is a difficult one.... *Education is certainly the first and most pressing* [*question*]" (1: 435–36; italics mine). In November 1865, Jane Carlyle writes to tell Kate that she has sought out and taken on as a "protegee" a young female "genius" who lives over a tailor's shop (1: 428).

On January 20, 1866, Kate's diary records her own crossroads. Benjamin Jowett, the Oxford University Greek professor who contributed the essay on "The Interpretation of Scripture" to *Essays and Reviews*, visits the Amberleys. "At the Railway station we talked of not going against the world & doing as every one did," Kate tells her diary, "and he strongly urged it [*not* going against the world] in every thing that was not positively wrong, & said for instance a woman shd. never have the character of an esprit fort. I did so disagree with him—It was worldly wisdom without doubt, but then is that to be the rule of our actions—I may change but now I feel a strong inclination to go against the world" (1: 464). She is twenty-three.

In March 1866, she attends a lecture on physiology by Dr. Elizabeth Garrett, the first woman to qualify as a physician in England, and in June meets her in person at Mill's Blackheath home. Garrett describes to Kate the many barriers she had to overcome to achieve her goal. This leads to the 1867 plan to create a school for women doctors, and, in 1869, to Kate's funding a fifty-pound scholarship for a female medical student (2: 275). Women's education—the destination of Virginia Woolf's first *Guinea*—occupies both Amberleys' schedules during their five-month American tour in the fall of 1867. Kate hides her pregnancy from the Russells, for she knows they will press her to stay behind. Amberley visits Chicago high schools in October 1867 and writes back to Kate in Philadelphia of his surprise to find mixed classes of boys and girls. In fact, the girls learning Greek and Latin outnumber the boys. The Latin teacher, he tells Kate:

> also informed me that they [the girls] usually made the best pupils. They do not sit on the same benches as the boys, but they do precisely the same work.... Boys & girls mix in the grammar schools also. They tell me that the system is found to answer perfectly well & that no inconvenience of any sort arises from it.... One thing seems evident, that the mixture of the sexes has a tendency to raise the education of women as they then learn the same subjects as men, which they are less likely to do otherwise. (2: 59, 60)

Emily Dickinson's "preceptor," Colonel Thomas Wentworth Higginson, penned a portrait of Kate in an 1868 *Atlantic Monthly* article. He found her "as frank and simple as any American girl"—although she was a viscountess:

> and with much more active interest in real things than was to be found in most of the Newport dowagers who shook their heads over her heretical opinions.... She talked with the greatest frankness about everything, being particularly interested in Vassar College, then the only example of its class; and she persistently asked all the young girls why they did not go there, until she was bluntly met at last by a young married woman as frank in speech as herself though less enlightened, who assured her that no society girl would think of going to college, and that nobody went there except the daughters of "mechanics and ministers." (2: 111–12)

The Amberleys bring back to England in 1868 word of many education advances. In 1869, as Virginia Woolf knew, Kate's mother, Lady Stanley, becomes one of the five founders and benefactors of Girton College, England's first residential college for women.[11]

The step from women's education to women's suffrage and other rights is hardly a step at all but rather the larger plateau. In December 1866, Dr. Garrett sends Kate correspondence to read on the women's vote. On May 27, 1867, Mill does his part. He moves for nonsexist language in the new Reform Bill. As

Kate watches from the Ladies' Gallery in the House of Commons, he moves his amendment: "[T]hat the word person shd. be inserted instead of the word man. The house was very thin but he was listened to with the utmost attention and respect.... [T]he numbers were with Mr. Mill 73 against 196. There was a good deal of laughing in the division lobby A[mberly] said at their being so many for women and there was laughing when the question was put— Mill was much pleased and everyone was surprised at the number for him; he wrote and told me he wd. have had 100 if all had voted who promised him" (2: 36, 37). In 1869, Kate and Amberley work for the Married Women's Property Bill, which gave married women control of their own property. Kate tells an April 1869 entry: "I walked all about Littleworth to get signatures at the cottages [for the Bill]. A[mberley] went with me. I had 235 signatures—chiefly women" (2: 266).

That fall Kate writes her first article, which she titles "Claims of Women." She sends it to Helen Taylor, who persuades her to give it first as a public lecture—another bold move. On May 20, 1870, Kate stands up before her Stroud neighbors and the press to declare the "Claims of Women." "I was not in the least nervous & felt my voice cd be heard," she tells her diary that night. "There was hardly any applause & it seemed to fall very flat.... I gave my MS to the reporter" (2: 330).

She is now twenty-eight and has come all this way in the face of formidable social and family discouragement. In May 1867, for instance, she must tell her diary that Liberal leaders John Bright and John Blackie both object to women's suffrage, "Bright saying that women wd. lose much by it and Blackie saying men were trees and women flowers and flowers might as well wish to become trees etc." (2: 34). Three days later, Thomas Huxley tells her, "The fact is we are still in the harem stage though in the last stage of it and those men who like to keep women in the doll state are not out of it." But all the same, she adds, "Huxley does not think that women will ever be equal to men in power or capacity" (2: 35).

The London *Times* first praises her lecture, but only to dismiss her:

> Lady Amberley has the merit of resting the Women's Rights question on plain, intelligible grounds. Of all the many speakers on the subject—male and female—she has told us in the clearest terms what she wants, why she wants it, and how she hopes to obtain it.
>
> ... That the means and the privileges of education should be accorded to girls as well as boys, that married women should have rights over their

own property, and that widows should be recognized as proper guardians of their own children—all these are certainly rational propositions, admitting here and there of debate, but representing neither impossible nor unreasonable demands. Very different, however, is the claim that "all professions should be open to women," and still more the stipulation that "public opinion should sanction what are now thought unfeminine occupations"; nor do we exactly see how or why legislation is to secure "the same wages for the same work."

... If the women of this country were fairly polled upon the question, not merely two out of every three, but ninety-nine out of every hundred, would unhesitatingly reject the character which these noisy agitators would fain thrust upon them. (2: 331–34)

Virginia Woolf's second *Guinea* will go to help all qualified *persons* earn their livings in the professions. The Stroud *Journal* prints a letter signed "A He-Critter," which asks: "What man would care to make a business contract, called marriage, with a case-hardened, slang-talking female clerk, traveller, or attorney, who owed no 'subordination,' and whom the law made mistress of his purse in the most unlimited sense? Is there a man courageous enough to be the husband of a female physician, or a member of Parliament, or a Lady Chief Justice?" (2: 337).

Public rebuke may sting, but family censure can cut deeper. Kate could hardly expect support from her brother Algernon, who became Monsignor Stanley in 1868. "We had several discussions together, on Popul[atio]n. & Women's Rights," Kate tells her diary in December of that year. "Algernon & I differed on everything nearly but we were glad to meet" (2: 157). Less gladsome are letters from Aunt Louisa Stanley, who writes at the beginning of 1868, "Another point I entirely differ from you both is in the Emancipation of Women" (2: 100). Furthermore, at the Ladies Conference in October 1869, when Kate is asked to take the chair at the meeting on the Married Women's Property Bill, she feels she must consult Maggie Eliot, John's second cousin once removed, who has accompanied her. Maggie says she had better not as she still wears mourning for her father's June death (2: 291).

The Russells, in short, prove even more disabling than the Stanleys, for the Amberleys faced correspondence like this from Amberley's cousin, Arthur Russell, a member of Parliament, and his French wife, Laura. In 1868, Laura writes to Kate: "Arthur has received a letter from Miss Lydia Becker, asking him whether, if he is returned to Parliament, he will there advocate female suffrage,

& vote in favour of it. Arthur answers her that he will not support female suffrage (with my positive sanction)" (2: 450).

Before Kate's 1870 "Claims of Women" speech, Arthur Russell seeks to pass the buck in a letter to Amberley: "I have no desire to oppose factiously the Women Suffrage Bill, but these are questions in which one must vote as one's wife bids one" (2: 451). This is the Mrs. Arthur Russell who, even in 1926, evokes fear in Virginia Woolf. In her May 25, 1926, diary entry, Woolf writes: "The heat has come, bringing with it the inexplicably disagreeable memories of parties, & George Duckworth; a fear haunts me even now, as I drive past Park Lane on top of a bus, & think of Lady Arthur Russell & so on."[12] In "22 Hyde Park Gate," Woolf's 1920 Memoir Club talk, she described Lady Arthur Russell as "a rude, tyrannical old woman, with a bloodstained complexion and the manners of a turkey cock" (*MOB* 171).

At the end of the year, Amberley patiently inquires of his cousin:

> Do you, as I infer from your speech, think paving, lighting, & girls schools the sole public questions which women ought to be interested in? If not, how can you defend their voting in municipal elections & sitting on schoolboards & oppose having the parliamentary suffrage? And if education is a proper subject for them to vote about why may they influence the election of schoolboards which control particular schools & not that of M.P.'s who have the whole subject to consider & legislate about? Or is there some radical distinction between this & the other questions that come before Parliament, so that this is fit for women, the others not? (2: 458)

That his own distinguished Liberal father will not support women's suffrage is perhaps hardest for Amberley and Kate to bear. In 1867, Earl Russell votes against Mill and the vote for women. He writes to Amberley in America that he plans "to move on education, & have learnt much from yours & Kate's letters. But as to girls I think we must keep them at home, & not send them to school!" (2: 96). In December 1870 he writes to his son, "I am much pleased at Miss Garrett's success. She ought to have a vote for Westminster, but not to sit in Parliament. It would make too much confusion" (2: 386).

Lady Russell's mind-numbing letters no doubt equally mortified, for she manages to belittle beneath her surface support. To her credit, she ever offers to keep the Amberleys' children—and ends up, in fact, raising Bertrand and

Frank. However, her letter to Amberley before Kate's 1870 public lecture shows her tack of cloaking her disapproval: "With regard to K's portly figure filling the chair at the Stroud meetg yr father & I feel just alike that we had rather she didn't—However I try to think we are old & prejudiced—... but hitherto without success" (2: 327). In such a climate, the Amberleys hardly unburden their souls to the Russells, so when Lady Russell reads of Kate's lecture in the *Times*, she writes miffed to her son:

> I had been telling I don't know how many people that I was sure the rumour that she was going to lecture was false—they must either think me very untruthful or her very secret—I agree with (I think) 9 of her 10 points & shd agree in the 10th if it cd. be a point at all—i.e. "that public opinion [should sanction what are now thought unfeminine occupations]" &c—It's quite impossible to be more earnestly anxious than I am that emplymts & professions shd be as open to women as men—tho' I don't a bit wish for them in the H[ouse]. of C[ommons].... Best love to my oratorical D[aughter].I[n].L[aw]., & tell her I understand perfectly why she didn't tell us she was going to lecture—she was afraid my speech might come in the way... You dear old Boy, I'm sure you were very proud of yr wife that night & so shd I have been. (2: 341)

But was she really? To Kate herself, Lady Russell does not hesitate to suggest that she raises up "some imaginary giants for the purpose of fighting them—the biggest is the natural inferiority of women wch as far as I know nobody maintains" (2: 342). To this, Kate forthrightly replies in an unsent letter: "I do not at all agree with the rest of yr letter about old truths or about putting up an imaginary giant. If you had read as much of the stupid literature on the subject as I have for & against you wd see that women are considered *inferior*" (2: 343).

And then blunt Aunt Louisa must weigh in: "I have been terribly ashamed of my Goddaughter & think it is a great pity she was not born an American without either noble name or rank, a simple Kitty Hopkins—I wonder you do not go & settle in America their ways wd suit you far better, I do not suppose you find many English women who will help you in crying out for their rights" (2: 350). In 1872, when Kate becomes president of the Bristol and West of England Women's Suffrage Society, Lady Russell cannot restrain her pen. The Russells' reading of Shakespeare's *Henry V* is interrupted, she writes Kate, by the newspaper report of Kate's:

chairwomanship & the speeches of you both—We had been surprised by the announcement in Johnny's letter—we did not even know that you were anything so long & great as P.W.B.W.S.S.! . . . We have now read the whole & I congratulate you on getting so well thro' what must no doubt have made you somewhat nervous—& also on the contrast of yr speech with the flippant & absurd one of Miss Sturge—I am not in the least disposed to make fun of you—I am strongly for the cause, you feel that speaking for it in public is yr vocation & if so it's all right you shd do so—*One* of yr vocations, I prefer to say—neither the greatest, highest, nor most difficult—but let it by all means have its place in yr life if it takes the form of duty to yr mind—If you never do anything naughtier than presiding & speaking at public meetings, we may well be proud of you—if you never do anything better we may well be ashamed of you! The greater part of Johnny's speech is very good—. . . Were I to speak on the subject, I shd take him as my model—& have out all the much vexed & irrelevant arguments founded on woman's character, wch always repel me . . . (2: 484–85)

Does this not both rebuke and make fun of Kate?

Six months later, Queen Mary's grandmother, the Duchess of Cambridge, cuts Kate in public. "I know you," she declares, "you are the daughter in law but now I hear you only like dirty people & dirty Americans. All London is full of it; all the clubs are talking of it. I must look at yr petticoats to see if they are dirty" (2: 499). "She *served you right*," the relentless Aunt Louisa then writes, "& you deserve it for you have a strange turn for all sorts of queer company and since your exhibition at that very low place at Bristol where you stood up and harangued about Women's rights I shd wonder at *nothing* odd you may do."[13]

Fortunately, the Amberleys had each other, and Lady Stanley, John Stuart Mill, and Helen Taylor—and those dirty Americans. In November 1867, Kate finds that Dr. Oliver Wendell Holmes favors women doctors, and in Boston she visits Dr. Lucy Sewell's female hospitals and lying-in wards and likes Sewell "very much" (2: 71). Nine days later, the Amberleys hear Lucretia Mott preach "an hour extempore." "[W]e both enjoyed it very much," Kate tells her diary, "and I agreed with every word of it. She brought in a few words about women's rights and said they shd. not be content with only being the poetry of life" (2: 74). The Amberleys name their daughter—carried during the trip—Rachel Lucretia in honor of Mott.

The next day, when they stay in Hartford with Harriet Beecher Stowe, the author of *Uncle Tom's Cabin* confides to Kate that she "had found people dreadfully decorous and proper in England, and that sometimes it made her long to scream" (2: 74). In December 1867, the Amberleys meet Elizabeth Cady Stanton in New York, "a lady who lectures and speaks on women's suffrage and prostitution," Kate notes in her diary. "[S]he has just been stumping in Kansas for 3 months; old now and grey curls; she began at 12 years old to wish for this and brought about the first woman's Convention at Albany 20 years ago, whh. made Mrs. Mill write her article" (2: 78).

Helen Taylor writes to Kate in February 1868: "[Y]ou gave me immense pleasure by letting me know your favourable impression of the [American] women's rights women. Magna est veritas! you must be with us on this, the greatest question of politics, since the battle against negro slavery is won. There is no other misery left in the world equal to the misery of wretched women, and to fight against it is the greatest work in our generation" (2: 102).

In 1870, Harriet Beecher Stowe's letter to Kate differs seismically from Lady Russell's. "I must seize a moment to thank you for sending me your admirable address before the Stroud Institute," Stowe's June 23 letter begins:

> It is one of the best and most complete presentations of the whole subject I ever saw & we in America must thank you for it. It is a noble *deed* for you to speak because *you* are in no sense in need of the rights or a sufferer from the wrongs you speak of—
>
> ... Go on my dear, you are sure to conquer & you fight charmingly & your victory must precede ours. You preceded us in negro emancipation & you will in this—you handle your weapons beautifully. There is some sense in rank & all that sort of thing, sometimes, when the right sort of person makes it a fort for fighting the battle of humanity & there are weak fashionables here in America who will hear a Viscountess or Duchess when they wd scoff at Miss Stanton and Susan Anthony. *That* you see, amuses me—for I don't like you one whit the more for your rank & station—tho I do like you more for the *use* you are making of it.
>
> I like you for being a whole hearted large souled generous woman brave & courageous—gallant & chivalrous & bless God that you *happen* in this day of ours to be in the *nobility*. Lord Amberley's utterances please me no less. ... We hope to see him one day Premier of England. (2: 353, 354)

Lord Amberley never becomes prime minister. He labors across his life under even more pressure than Kate. His burden: to be the eldest son of "a great man" with all the expectations that brings. John's diaries, even at age eleven, show him a most serious, formal boy. "But Lo!" he exclaims:

> Mr. Gibbs, tutor to the Prince of Wales and Prince Alfred had sent an invitation for me to come to the Palace, and play with the two aforesaid Princes from four till six. . . . We went into the Garden; saw the Gymnastics; played at football; and went to a pond where the Princes gave every person a bag of food with which to feed the ducks.
>
> We then beheld the Queen walking; she came to us. We took off our hats, as she approached; when quite near bowed. Mr. Gibbs told her who I was; she asked me how Papa and Mama were; how old I was; &c. &c. We fed the ducks. The Queen came back again with Prince Albert. . . . I liked my Royal Visit very much indeed. (1: 145, 146)

John knows he is the son of "a great statesman," as he writes in his Harrow diary at age sixteen, for he loses election to the Harrow Debating Society when some members say they could not talk freely in front of him. "I am glad the Monitors had no personal feeling against me, but I am very sorry to have the doors of the Debating Society thus closed against me, because I am the son of a great statesman," Amberley tells his diary, but then reckons, "But my being his son was probably the only reason in favour of my being elected at all" (1: 178). Shortly after, his classmates reconsider, and we see that the Harrow Debating Society serves as the practice court for parliament.

But a theme starts in Amberley's adolescent diaries: his longing for love and sympathy. It begins at sixteen as a typical boy's-school crush on his schoolmate, Arthur O'Neill (1: 176–77, 180–81, 187–88, 189–90, 193, 196–98, 201–03). At seventeen, however, when he visits the O'Neills' Irish castle, he shifts to their visitor, Jane Grey. "She spoke to me freely of my reserve, & said that some one had said it was partly shyness, partly pride; that great readers were never great talkers, &c., all of which was very good for me," he tells his diary in 1860 (1: 211). Two days later, he reads her Tennyson's *Locksley Hall* and tells his diary: "It was most delightful to find that she so thoroughly sympathized with me in my admiration of it. Then we talked till luncheon-time, & she asked me several questions about what I wished to be, meant to be, etc, expressing an opinion that she should hear of me as a great man some day" (1: 213). The next day he confides: "It was a most painful moment . . . leaving Miss Grey just as I was growing interested in her & fond of her" (1: 214).

Amberley's next two diary books are missing—as are his first four diaries before age eleven. Did Amberley (or his parents) destroy them? On July 11, 1863, he meets Kate Stanley and tells his diary: "[S]he is wonderfully intellectual" (1: 255). In October, he and Kate carve his name on an Alderley Park tree, a Stanley tradition, and on February 2, 1864, he writes: "Tea with the Stanley's today to be continued weekly" (1: 288). But Lady Russell intervenes. Amberley's life dilemma sounds in his February 17 diary entry:

> This evening Mama spoke to me about KS. which of course I did not at all like. It seems I am to be "prudent" not to get "involved" &c. I am so "very young" that I cannot be trusted to judge for myself. Ah me! I feel myself oppressed & crushed by the great monster "conventionality" against whose fearful weight it sometimes appears to be my lot to struggle forever—& in vain! . . . when shall I find one in whom my soul can repose in peace? . . . [I] almost wished that I could die at once rather than be condemned to this awful blank of not having a single friend who can give me that sympathy for which my whole nature is ever yearning. (1: 290)

On her part, Kate sounds terrified in her March 22, 1864, letter to her mother at the start of the Russells' six-month imposed separation. "I hope the correspondence between you & Chesham Place has not continued; they might not like it if they knew, & I should be so sorry to vex them in any way as I have hopes that they may still like me some day" (1: 296).

Lord Russell finally accedes to the marriage in September 1864, but only as a side point in a letter whose first subject is Amberley's "com[ing] into parliament soon" (1: 318). From the start, Amberley's brief engagement and November 8, 1864, marriage are intertwined with his father's search for a parliamentary seat for him. "But I know that we both put Duty above everything else," Amberley warns Kate before they marry, sounding most Victorian (1: 340). To Kate, dear Aunt Louisa crows two months after the wedding, "you are a delightful help Mate for a future Statesman & one already primed for Liberalism by Lyulph" (1: 353).

In *The Amberley Papers*, election dramas unfold on the heels of the courtship drama. Amberley chooses first to represent working men in Leeds; however, he loses. But fortune's wheel turns. The prime minister, Lord Palmerston, dies unexpectedly in October 1865, and the nation turns to its foreign secretary, Lord Russell. He becomes prime minister once more, and when Amberley himself wins a seat from Nottingham in May 1866, the Russells offer their son and daughter-in-law 10 Downing Street as their pied-à-terre.

Amberley hires the actor Horace Wigans for speaking lessons—unlike Kate, he was never physically robust—and he prizes the chance to serve with Mill in the House of Commons. He is only twenty-three. In January 1866, Jowett tells Kate that few men Amberley's age have his power of speaking and writing; however, Jowett also advises Amberley to retire from the world for five years to prepare himself for public life. Instead, when the Liberal government falls, Lord Russell supports a five-month American tour for John in the fall of 1867, where he meets with President Andrew Johnson, Secretary of State William Seward, and America's other leading lights—and thus gains foreign contacts and seasoning.

Kate's July 7, 1868, diary entry back in England reveals Amberley's plight: "There have been several seats talked of and offered to Amberley. South Devon is very anxious to have him but the great expense and being a county makes him hold back. He nearly settled on Cambridge but found a personal canvass was requisite and objected on that ground, whh. I quite approve. Cheltenham and Tewksbury both wd. have had him but are too corrupt. . . . In fact letters come every day fr. some place or other" (2: 119).

Lord Russell's fifty-seven letters to his son in *The Amberley Papers* are models of tact, delicacy, and direct political talk. That he does not *directly* pressure his son likely made him harder to resist. In 1860, Lord Russell wants his son to attend Edinburgh, *his* university, and in 1868 he wants Amberley to repeat his great South Devon election victories of 1832 and 1835. John bows to his father's wishes and agrees to face two Conservative candidates for the November 1868 South Devon election, one the incumbent.[14]

But Amberley is not his father and 1868 is not 1832. Though expected and willing to serve in parliament, Amberley enjoyed an advantage over many other candidates aged twenty-five, or even older. His economic independence allowed him to speak his mind and not to compromise if it meant hedging truth. His nomination speech in August 1868, included in *The Amberley Papers*, offers a clear, honest, and eloquent statement of his precise views. One cannot imagine a better voice for these views.

His loss of his Christian faith in the early 1860s made him question in parliament (in 1866 and after) Christian privileges of all sorts, including Sunday restrictions and faith-based scholarships. Dissenters found Amberley broadminded and just; however, many South Devon ministers felt him a great foe. Misfortune then struck in the guise of the smallest prenomination private query. Amberley belonged to the Elliptical Club, a group of men and women who met to discuss challenging social topics. Unluckily, he happened to be in the chair at the July 1868 meeting focused on overpopulation, insufficient food, and family size. A club that admitted women and, beyond that, accorded them equal speaking rights with men was in itself radical in 1868. Today, Amberley's comment and query seem innocuous, even astute. He observed that he believed "women would naturally have a stronger feeling against large families [than men], had they any say in the matter, and if their opinions were more heard" (2: 170). (He likely had suffrage in mind.)

He then suggested that the issue called for medical solutions and asked the doctors and other scientists present, "[H]ow could married persons limit the number of their offspring without injuring their health?" (2: 172). The meeting was a private one, as was the club; however, someone present reported the entire meeting to the press, which led to published protests across the British Isles from the *British Medical Journal* and the *Medical Times and Gazette*. Amberley's South Devonshire opponents made political hay from his rational query, and Amberley found himself forced to explain at every campaign stop that he did not advocate abortion—that low American practice—but rather that he sought only to explore answers to a complex problem (one that still exists).

Political dirty tricks throve in 1868 as well as today. Amberley met cartoons, fliers, and angry voters wherever he went. He became ill in early November but soldiered out on Polling Day to see his overwhelming defeat. He never ran for office again. Instead, he retreated even farther west and began the program of quiet study both Mill and Carlyle approved. As Kate early suspected, he was not cut out to be a great statesman like his father. Rather, he was a writer on social and philosophical questions, like John Stuart Mill.[15]

The 1870 Franco-Prussian War causes Amberley to interrupt his religious studies and erupt into ink. On the last day of 1870, Kate sounds one of Woolf's signature diary phrases when she tells her diary: "The great public event has been this awful war in France which has filled one's mind almost to the exclusion of all else" (2: 388). In America three years before, Elizabeth Colt took the Amberleys on a tour of her Hartford gun factory. "We . . . saw a horrible new gun, called 'the Gattling gun' which fires 400 shots a minute," Kate tells her diary. "[W]e saw it go off; it turns quite easily by a handle, a horrid sight to see" (2: 75). When on December 24, 1870, Lord Russell writes to tell John that his younger brother, Willy, will enter the army, Kate tells her diary: "I don't at all approve as I hate war, the army, & the military tone" (2: 388).

At that moment, John is penning his article "Can War Be Avoided?"—an essay that calls for a federation of nations (analogous to the later League of Nations and United Nations) with a governing body called the Federal Council to which each nation would send six members. In printing passages of Amberley's lucid forward-looking article, Bertrand Russell writes in 1937 that the essay "is so much concerned with issues that are to the fore at the present day, and deals with them in so able a manner, that its leading passages deserve to be reprinted" (2: 428). The excerpts reveal Amberley's idealism, precise mind, and graceful prose: "There is plainly visible a growing detestation of the odious massacres which, from time to time, disgrace the world, & a growing desire to find some honourable means of doing without them," he writes (2: 436). Virginia Woolf will give her third and last *Guinea* to the male treasurer of an antiwar society.

Kate Russell confesses in a November 1870 diary entry that she "rather vexed" Amberley by saying she liked "Can War Be Avoided?" better than anything he had ever written (2: 380). He tells her he "does not know if it is worth anything & does not wish to publish it certainly not with his name" (1: 380). In January 1871, he sends drafts first to Mill and Helen Taylor and then to his father and mother. Mill praises the piece, sends notes, and urges publication. Lord Russell is "cautious" (as Bertrand puts it) (2: 428).

Cousin Arthur Russell, M.P., writes to Amberley on February 12, 1871: "Since I am to give you an opinion about your MS. I think you ought not to publish it with your name, because I hope you will do much good in this country as a political writer—and this would injure the authority of your judgment in political matters. As far as I know your plan is Garibaldi's, Victor Hugo's and Mazzini's—to me it seems quite impractical of execution and fanciful—in politics I think you should always write for the present state of the world, if you wish to do good" (2: 461–62). And so it goes. Amberley, of course, heeds Mill and Helen Taylor. His signed essay appears in the May 1871 *Fortnightly*.

Lord Russell's decision to sell Rodborough in 1870, the Gloucester estate Amberley thought would be his, may partly have been a scheme to bring Amberley closer to the Russell fold. If so, he failed. The Amberleys look in Wales and set up their final home even farther away than Gloucester: at Ravenscroft, near Tintern Abbey.

Sadly, John Stuart Mill dies unexpectedly in May 1873. Kate writes to her mother: "We are both very miserable at the loss to us of the warmest & truest friend we have known & one who will make a great blank in our lives. Amberley is very unhappy about it—He was so particularly kind & affectionate to Amberley approving of him in every way so much that Amberley will miss his strong moral support much & his warmth of interest & tenderness. We had been looking forward to seeing him here in July" (2: 541).

A month later, Amberley suffers an unexplained epileptic seizure and is told to curtail his work. They seek out the warmer clime of Italy in the winter to restore thirty-one-year-old Amberley to health. But eight-year-old Frank, their eldest child, contracts diphtheria in May 1874 on their return, and Kate nurses him in London. When he recovers and is thought to be no longer infectious, all five Amberleys (Kate, Amberley, Frank, Rachel Lucretia, and two-year-old Bertrand) return to Wales. "But in those days," Bertrand explains, "it was not realized that the diphtheria bacillus often lingers in the air passages long after the illness is past" (2: 566). In June, six-year-old Rachel Lucretia comes down with diphtheria, and Kate, who nursed her, soon follows.

Nine days before Frank's birth, in 1865, Kate confided to her diary the realistic fears women then faced:[16] "There is nothing about the baby I could wish to say to [Amberley] if I died. He would be sure I feel to do everything with it that I could wish—If I should die I should like him to have it much with him & make a great companion of it & then call it Kätchen [his pet name for her] but a more perfect guide & father for one's child no woman could have" (1: 401). Kate succumbs to diphtheria on June 28, 1874, and Rachel Lucretia five days later. "I thought the cup of misery had been full enough, but it seems not," Amberley writes to his mother on July 3. "The child too had to go, and I have lost for ever the sweet caressing ways and the affectionate heart that might if anything could have been some consolation. And now I feel that the desolation is indeed complete. Yet I think I must be almost dead to feeling" (2: 571).

Few records remain, the editors report, of the nineteen months between Kate's death, in June 1874, and John's from bronchitis in January 1876. Just before Kate's and Rachel Lucretia's deaths, Willy Russell, Amberley's soldier brother, "became insane," and, "[f]rom this time onwards," Bertrand writes, "the material becomes scanty; a great deal was destroyed by the Russells after Amberley's death in order to preserve secrecy in certain respects" (2: 533). Secrecy regarding what? Willy's mental illness? Amberley's views, or his decline? Did the Russells—or the long-lived Lady Russell—destroy Amberley's first four diaries and the two diary books spanning ages seventeen to nineteen, or did he destroy them himself, or merely lose them?

And why does Kate's diary stop on January 1, 1872—she a faithful diarist? Bertrand Russell reports that two pages are torn from Kate's 1866 diary, which, he suggests, likely gave her side of a row with Lady Russell (1: 524n1). Did Kate tear these pages out—or did one of the Russells?

Kate Stanley Russell's gift as a diarist rests in her ability to report in clear, precise, and quite complete fashion the persons, talk, and events of her days and then add to it a fillip of profound thought. The Gatling gun fires 400 shots a minute and "turns quite easily by a handle." Nero, the dog, sits by and listens to the blustering Thomas Carlyle, "a sad spectacle of a philosopher pent up quite alone with his own thoughts." Kate's open-hearted embrace of life—so attractive—sounds through her habitual diary refrain that she "likes very much" this new person, or that lecture, or yet another new book. *The Amberley Papers* supply enough excerpts from Kate's diary to make us want it all.

So, too, with John Russell's even more writerly diaries. Amberley wrote most of his diary in shorthand, like Samuel Pepys. He adapted an obsolete eighteenth-century shorthand system, which Adrian Stephen, Virginia Woolf's brother, helped Bertrand and Patricia Russell verify. Was the young Russell merely aping the famous Pepys, or did he feel the need to mask his private thoughts?

Like Woolf, young John reread his early diaries and critiqued them. At age seventeen, he complains in his fifth diary: "It makes me laugh to look back to all the useless little entries I made then; as, for instance, 'The present arrangement is:' & then a list of lessons & lesson hours; or 'Staid in bed for breakfast;' &c. &c. . . . Shall I ever laugh or wonder at what I am writing now? I hope not; yet who can tell?" (1: 182, 183). Like Woolf, young Amberley feels out possible terrains for his diary. The Harrow diaries, Bertrand Russell reports, are "almost entirely composed of religious and moral reflections" (1: 175).

Gradually, the diary becomes John's confidant for emotional vent as well as for intellectual and spiritual search. His December 13, 1863, entry confesses that his temperament is "more lonely & unsocial (I fear I shd add unamiable)" than his family's. He "long[s] for some one friend to whom I could confide the plan of my life, & explain that the petty interruptions caused by visits to country houses, the petty inconvenience caused by being expected to comply altogether with the ways of others, or to make my hours altogether suit theirs, are things which I cannot treat as entirely trivial & unworthy to give me a moment's vexation" (1: 282–83).

Regrettably for diary lovers, with his marriage eleven months later, John becomes a less faithful diarist. "Since my engagement I have not been able to write my journal & I now give it up as a regular practice," he writes on November 8, 1864 (1: 342). Kate, perhaps, now fills the role of confidant: the "one friend to whom I could confide the plan of my life" and the not-so-petty vexations. The new demands of married life and preparing himself for parliament, not to mention his private writerly agenda, likely absorb Amberley's days. He cedes regular diary-writing to Kate and records now in his diary (Bertrand Russell tells and shows us) only "salient events" (1: 143). After Kate's death, in June 1874, Amberley records in his diary what he reads and what he writes, but nothing else, his son reports (2: 573). He spends most of the nineteen months in Wales and manages to finish his huge book, *Analysis of Religious Beliefs*.

Not the least of the charms of *The Amberley Papers* is Bertrand Russell's blunt assessment of his parents. Of the Amberley's inadequate medical care, Bertrand writes: "Mr. Audland was not a very wise or learned physician, and Kate and Amberley were themselves very foolish about medical matters. Knowledge and care would have prevented their early deaths" (2: 384n1). Amberley's book dedication to Kate reveals his great love for her, the vital role she served for him, and his honest, discriminating mind:

> With all reverence and all affection, to the memory of the ever-lamented wife whose hearty interest in this book was, during many years of preparatory toil, my best support; whose judgment as to its merits or its faults would have been my most trusted guide; whose sympathy my truest encouragement; whose joyous welcome of the completed work I had long looked forward to as my one great reward: whose nature, combining in rare union scientific clearness with spiritual depth, may in some slight degree have left its impress on the page, though far too faintly to convey an adequate conception of one whose religious zeal in the cause of truth was rivalled only by the ardour of her humanity and the abundance of her love. Ravenscroft November 1875 (2: 573)

In 1937, Bertrand Russell calls his father's book "flat and dull" (2: 573). He finds, too, in the book's last pages words that hint that Amberley foresaw his coming death. Amberley writes:

> Were we thus permitted to find in our fellow-creatures that sympathy which so many mourners, so many sufferers, so many lonely hearts, have been compelled to find only in the idea of their heavenly Father, I hesitate not to say that the consolations of the new religion would far surpass in their strength and their perfection all those that were offered by

the old. . . . Meantime, while we are still far from the promised land, the adherents of the universal religion are not without a happiness of their own. . . . No man can truly oppose their religion, for he who seems to be hostile to it is himself but one of the notes struck by the Unknowable Cause, which so plays upon the vast instrument of humanity as to bring harmony out of jangling sounds, and to produce the universal chords of truth from the individual discords of error. . . . Even though torn away when, in their own judgment, they have still much to do, they will not repine at the necessity of leaving it undone, even though they are well aware that their names, which might have been illustrious in the annals of our race, will now be buried in oblivion. (2: 574–75)

Virginia Woolf wished in her 1908 diary to bring harmony from jangling discord through her art (*PA* 392–93). In her 1939–1940 memoir, "A Sketch of the Past," she will declare, with John Russell, all humans part of the world's "pattern," its work of art (*MOB* 72).

Lord and Lady Amberley are not lost in oblivion. They live again through their diaries (and letters). Bertrand Russell's resurrection of his mother and father in 1936 aided Woolf's own resurrection that fall. In her next book, *Three Guineas*, she will follow the line of thought that extends from both Amberleys. She will give her first guinea for women's education, her second guinea to assist all persons in the professions, and her third to the male treasurer of an antiwar society.

Journal of a Governess: Ellen Weeton

Protest pours from deprived diarist Ellen Weeton, who speaks in Virginia Woolf's *Three Guineas*. In late October or early November 1936, J. R. Ackerley, literary editor of the *Listener*, invited Woolf to review a new book: *Miss Weeton: Journal of a Governess, 1807–1811*. Woolf read the *Journal* in the throes of her own literary crisis, when she thought to burn *The Years* after her Promethean labors and to accept the death of her literary "genius" (*D* 5: 29). She opens her November 11, 1936, diary entry with her complex response to Ackerley's request:

Armistice Day—completely forgotten by us. I'm going along quietly, rather ashamed of my extreme deliberation [on the proof of *The Years* rescued by Leonard's praise]. Cant review Miss Weeton either. Joe will only allow me 800 words of unsigned [review]; 1500 of signed. An amusing illustration of the virtues of capitalism. Its the advertisement, not the article, they want. And its the advertisement I dont want. But anyhow the book is bad mostly; & to compress Miss W. into 800 words would not be worth doing in the eyes of eternal truth, or any other. . . . Again I am confirmed in my project of some private sheet. (*D* 5:32)

Woolf edges toward anonymity here. She does not want to advertise her name but rather to do justice to Ellen Weeton "in the eyes of eternal truth" in her own private broadsheet—as she wished to do with her diary father, Sir Walter Scott. In a few months she will use Weeton's words in *Three Guineas*. In fact, Ellen Weeton's stunted, but unsilenced, life served as a moving illustration of female sacrifice for "Arthur's education fund," which Woolf will decry in *Three Guineas*. It offered shocking instance, too, of male tyranny.

Like diarist Dorothy Wordsworth, Ellen Weeton was born on Christmas Day into a loving and well-heeled family in northwest England—but in 1776, five years after Dorothy. Gender difference rose with her very name, as Ellen writes at age thirty-two in the "Retrospect" editor Edward Hall places before her journal and journal-letters. Ellen's father was a richly rewarded slave-ship captain and privateer. "[K]nowing that the ship *Nelly* in which he was sailing, was a great favourite of his," Ellen explains in her 1809 "Retrospect":

> [my mother] thought to win his affection for me by naming me after it, as she had heard him say that he could wish his children to be all boys. When he returned, and she told him this, he expressed himself as very sorry that she should have been hurt by what he said; declaring that he loved me as much as Edward (who was only 11 months older than I); but, he said, unless a father can provide independent fortunes for his daughters, they must either be made mop squeezers, or mantua makers, whereas sons can easily make their way in the world. (6–7)

Precocious Ellen basks briefly as her father's pet. "I was . . . a great favourite with my father," she continues. "He, like all other fond parents, thought me a prodigy of wit and beauty. I have heard my mother say that she and my father taught me the Alphabet one Sunday afternoon, and that I entirely learned it when I was little more than two years" (7). But like Woolf and Dorothy Wordsworth, Ellen loses her parents early on. Her father dies at sea when she is only five, propelling the formerly prosperous Lancaster family toward poverty when his £12,000 in captured prize money is denied. After two years, Ellen's mother moves Ellen and her three-year-old brother Tom—Edward has died—to Upholland, a small village, where she hopes to live more cheaply. Four years later, unable to support her children on her small income, Mrs. Weeton opens a village school with eleven-year-old Ellen as her assistant at both school and home.

Here "Arthur's education fund"—or, in Ellen's case, "Tom's education fund"—comes into play. Seven-year-old Tom is sent to Mr. Braithwaite's School, "a most excellent one for boys, where he continued as a day scholar until his education was completed," Ellen explains in her "Retrospect." "My mother had no servant, and her life as well as mine was from this time a life of slavery" (13). Ellen's various prose—her journal, her journal-letters, her "Retrospect" at age thirty-two, her "Occasional Recollections" at age forty-one, and second "History" at forty-seven—invite study as products of deprivation.

Like Woolf and Dorothy Wordsworth, Ellen Weeton harbored deep love for a sibling, a love, in her case, unreturned. At Upholland, three-year-old Tom became Ellen's sole playmate and companion. She writes that Tom was "the promoter of mirth and frolic; the stimulator of my studies. . . . I revered and loved my mother, but I loved my brother a great deal better. I used to console myself with the idea that when he was established in business, I should, as we had from almost infancy promised each other, again live with him" (19). Mrs. Weeton intends Tom for the law and their financial rescue; therefore, she apprentices him at age fourteen to a Preston attorney.

But the brilliant child is Ellen, not Tom. Like Virginia, Ellen adores books from her earliest years. At four, when she sits for a portrait for her doting father to take to sea, she rejects the little dog or toy the painter begs her to cradle and asks to hold a book instead. However, she gives up buying books the next year when her father dies: "I saved, and gave to my mother all the half pence I received; and the praises she bestowed upon me almost compensated me for the mortification I endured; for such was my excessive fondness for books, that I used to spend all my money that way" (9).

Beyond fondness for books, Ellen loved to scribble (like Woolf and Fanny Burney). "When my brother was away [at school], and my mother too busy to attend to me, I had no resources but reading and scribbling," she explains in her "Retrospect"; "for I was a scribbler (in chalk or even with a pen) before I was taught to write" (15). In her thirties, Ellen turns from her private review of Madame de Staël's novel, *Corinna*, to offer a long discourse on her own failed promise. "Whether I should have made any figure in literature or no, is not for me to decide; but surely no one's ardour was ever more damped than mine," she begins:

My mother and my brother shewed the strongest disapprobation of every little production I shewed them, yet notwithstanding the little encouragement I met with, I could not forbear composing sometimes. At eleven years old, I wrote a play. As this was my first production, except a letter now and then and an immense heap of prose Enigmas, my mother had not reflected on the consequences that might possibly follow a little encouragement or approbation, and permitted me to dedicate three whole weeks to the writing of my play. How busy was I! how delighted! ... From that time my mother continually checked any propensity I shewed to writing or composing; representing to me what a useless being I should prove if I were allowed to give up my time to writing or reading, when domestic duties were likely to have so frequent a call upon me. ... This kind of conversation ... was too frequently repeated to allow a possibility of my forgetting it; and too many living instances were pointed out to my notice, to permit me to be blind to the injurious consequences of females dedicating their time to the increase of literary knowledge. Yet that impression had little apparent influence; for what I before did openly because my mother seemed pleased with it, I now practiced by stealth, till she found it necessary positively to prohibit the use of pen and ink, or slate pencil, except whilst receiving instruction from her or the writing master. ... He was not so watchful, and I could finish more than my expected share of arithmetical or grammatical exercises, and have some time to spare; but alas! I was obliged to rub off my slate, almost as soon as written ... lest my mother should come to examine when the writing master was gone. If I had really no true genius, the check I so early met with was of infinite service to me—(172–74)

When Ellen is twenty, her mother dies of exhaustion. Four years remain in sixteen-year-old Tom's legal apprenticeship. Ellen holds his fate and her own in her hands. Their mother's income "was much too small to support both my brother and myself," Ellen explains; "therefore, according to her dying request, I continued the school for my own support, whilst the income of an estate at Sunderland was appropriated to my brother's use until he was of age, and for two years after" (25).

From ages twenty to twenty-seven, therefore, Ellen continues to sacrifice for Tom. "O Brother!" she exclaims in an 1810 journal entry, "sometime thou wilt know perhaps the deprivations I have undergone for thy sake, and that thy attentions have not been such as to compensate them. For thy sake I have wanted food and fire, and have gone about in rags; have spent the flower of my youth in obscurity, deserted, and neglected."[17]

Ellen makes her huge sacrifice in the mistaken hope that, when Tom becomes a lawyer, he will offer his home to her for the rest of their days; in short, that their early camaraderie will resume. But Tom Weeton is no William Wordsworth. He comes of age in 1802, completes his legal clerkship, and departs Preston for London. Even then the selfless (and deluded) Ellen turns down a marriage offer. She refuses a proposal "from a young man of great abilities and most excellent character," she records. "It will be a disappointment to my brother, thought I, if I marry. It will quite unsettle him. So too, my aunt said. He was in London at that time" (37). Tom fails there within three months and retreats to Wigan, near Upholland, where, in 1803, he hastily marries the daughter of a Wigan factory owner, "neither of them being able to command a farthing," Ellen explains (34–35). She offers to share her Upholland home with the young couple, for she still cherishes the reunion dream. However, the factory owner intervenes. Wishing to hide Tom's ties to a lowly school mistress, he whisks the newlyweds to Leigh. Of the dashing of her own and her mother's plans, Ellen writes at age thirty-two:

> [My mother] thought my brother would repay us when old enough for all these deprivations. But it was a vain expectation, for like all his sex, when he was grown up, he considered what had been done for him was his right; that he owed no gratitude to us, for we were but *female* relatives, and had only done our duty. And obligations which were too great to be forgotten, he has had the ingratitude to deny. Strange that so tender-hearted a boy should become so selfish a man. . . . My mother did not live to discover it. (23)

As the betrayal sets in, lonely Ellen turns to her pen. Like Woolf, Ellen quickened to society but was shy as a girl and far from a social success. However, she loves to talk with those she values and who show her some regard. She keeps a slate beside her, in fact, to record thoughts to share with her brother or in her other written works. "A propensity to converse, is, I think, so natural to the human species without distinction of sex," she writes her brother in 1809, "that where there is little, or no opportunity of talking, most of those who are capable of it are apt to transcribe their thoughts, whether they are worth the trouble or not; and this, I think, must have been the reason that I have always had such an itch for scribbling—the being almost unavoidably so much alone" (195–96).

In 1804, in her late twenties, Ellen begins the first of what will be eight quarto volumes carefully composed with a quill pen. Only five of the eight books have surfaced to date, but they offer a poignant twist of the "journal-letter" intermixed with a private periodic diary. Ellen did more than just write letters to her few friends; she felt the need to *copy* these letters into her journal books—a process that took five hours on average and often several days, since she reveled in long letters (xiii).

Woolf calls *Journal of a Governess, 1807–1811,* a bad book "mostly" in her own 1936 diary. This view might have sprung from several of the book's traits. Editor Hall, a painstaking historian and sympathetic editor, nevertheless miscasts Weeton and her prose through his title—a fact Woolf could hardly fail to see. With four of the eight volumes in his hand in 1936, spanning the years 1807 to 1825, Hall knows Weeton served as a governess only twice, and each time for fewer than two years. In point of fact, she was more a "school mistress" than family "governess," but Hall is caught in the romance of Ellen as an earlier Jane Eyre or Charlotte Brontë—and thinks (rightly, perhaps) the title *Journal of a Governess* will attract.

This 1936 volume offers ninety-nine copied letters and only sixteen journal entries. Hall thus also strains a bit to justify his *Journal* title (as he does with *Governess*). He claims in his introduction that Ellen's "own admission that she preserved copies of her Letters to serve as a Journal for future reference, justifies the title of this book. And an expressed wish is being realized, in the publication of her Journal" (vii).

In Hall's care in 1936 were Weeton's volumes 2 and 3 (covering October 1807 to February 1811), volume 7 (recording July 1822 through June 1825), and an extra volume that offered "a form of religious Diary under the title of 'Occasional Reflections' for the year 1818 and a fragment entitled 'The History of the Life of N. Stock, 1824'" (xii). "N. Stock" was Nelly's married name, for she married disastrously in 1814, a fact only touched on in the volume Woolf read.

Lacking volume 1, we cannot know whether Ellen began with a journal entry or with a copied letter. The ninety-nine copied letters Woolf read in *Journal of a Governess, 1807–1811,* were performances for specific readers, as most letters are. Perhaps Weeton wished to save them as products of her literary skill. "Any ridicule I may thoughtlessly scatter, is not meant to wound, but only to amuse—perhaps tinged with a latent desire to excite a little admiration at my talents," she writes her brother in 1810 (306). Having to erase her slate scribbles as a girl, perhaps she could not bear to let her words disappear. "I am often at a loss when I begin a letter," she writes to a Mrs. Whitehead in 1808, "but before

I have written the first page, Ideas come floating in like full fraught vessels in a fine sea-port in serene weather" (66).

Conscientious editor Hall reports that Ellen's letters averaged 1,700 words (xiii). She knew their strength lay in their length and detail, furnished by her strong memory. Toward the close of her third volume, she writes a friend, "My only reasons for undertaking such a piece of work is, that it has been a great amusement during many a solitary hour when I had no other employ, when I should only have been engaged in some fine, tedious piece of needlework or other" (xiii). "Were I to abridge my words, my dear friend," she continues, "'that I might have more room' as you flatteringly request . . . those letters would lose half the merit they possess. Permit me to say, without being suspected of an indirect method of seeking a compliment. . . . like Samson, I know where my strength lies" (xiii–iv). In a later letter Woolf may not have read, Weeton writes in 1812 to an Isle of Man friend:

> You will sometimes find that I relate little events in my letters, with extreme minuteness. I will tell you why I do so. . . . Great events seldom occur in common life; and where an epistolary correspondence is frequent, trifles must compose the greater part of it; and if those trifles are not accurately delineated, they sink to nothing. To me, the everyday pleasures and anxieties in the domestic life of my friends, have an interest at all times; and I relate my own little affairs, in hopes to draw forth a similar communication from them. (2: 60)

That she hopes to draw forth praise—her little compliment—seems clear as well and may be the reason Woolf calls this a bad book "mostly." Like Jonathan Swift and Woolf herself, Weeton uses her journal and "journal-letters" as sites for self-praise—a fact likely to vex Woolf, who has fought ego in her own diary since 1920 (and in Ethel Smyth as well).[18] Ellen gamely addresses herself in an 1808 letter to Mrs. Whitehead: "Upon my word, Miss Weeton, but you are complimenting yourself very highly! Well! it is only to save others the trouble. I often do it, whilst I declaim against Flattery!" (66). To her brother, she chides in 1810: "Hm-m-m, I tell thee what, Tom, thou never praisest me now; or if thou dost, it is bestowed so delicately, that my craving, gross capacity, does not discover it. (If this strong bait will not do, I do not know what will—aside). I shall be obliged to tell thee wherein my excellencies consist" (306).

Like the Reverend John Skinner's querulous *Journal of a Somerset Rector*, the *Journal of a Governess* records ill-treatment and offers defense. Ellen found she needed a journal as well as her copied "journal-letters," for in the journal she could more freely vent her distress. In an 1810 journal entry, she explains that with her letters, "Prudence sometimes suggested that it would be improper to discover all the truth to the friend or acquaintance I addressed" (276). The sixteen actual journal entries may have annoyed Woolf, for they voice grievance after grievance. The second of the sixteen complains of Miss Chorley, Ellen's Liverpool landlady, and her rudeness to Ellen; the third, in December 1808, describes the scene where Miss Chorley insists on reading Ellen's journal, even tries to seize the book, causing Ellen to flee the room with the journal and lock it up. "And very careful have I been ever since to keep my box locked," she adds (133). Five long journal entries follow, each complaining of ill treatment, especially from Miss Chorley, who now scorns her.

By August 1809, Ellen has moved from Miss Chorley's Liverpool home to a cottage with the Smiths outside the city. Her ninth journal entry complains of Mrs. Smith's temper; her tenth, of the endless harangue she receives from her brother's wife for her "ridiculous behaviour" since her residence in Liverpool in talking of the narrowness of her income (186–87). Her twelfth entry complains of her brother's ill-usage; the next of Mr. Pedder's "tyranny," whose house she has entered as a governess in early 1810 (258), and her sixteenth and last journal entry in the volume decries Pedder's 1811 tyranny, as well. Her 1818 "Occasional Reflections" starts out as a diary of her religious state of mind but subsides into the "agitation, anguish, and despair" that "have driven all thoughts of religion away" (2: 159). Hall should have called his volume Journal of a Disappointed Woman. He does call her journal books "an amazing gesture for posthumous justice—and even, may it so happen, literary fame"[19] (2: 192).

Ellen Weeton's relentless self-absorption is the making of her journal books, as Woolf saw better with the Reverend Skinner. Ellen knows she has been ill-used, and she *must* mark it down. She carries her journal books with her wherever she moves, books that Hall calls her "justifications" of her life (2: 170). Despite her few opportunities, she refuses to be squelched. To read her today is to be overcome with the hardships she suffered and to admire her spirit, which seeks ever to improve.

When she starts the first of her journal books in 1804, she has begun to see that Tom will neither bring her into his home nor repay her for her seventeen years as assistant or head school mistress on his behalf. She begins to explore with this selfish brother, and with her equally selfish Aunt Barton, ways to leave the school and Upholland. By 1808 she succeeds. On July 11 she quits the school and takes up temporary residence with her brother at Leigh. "I have been almost wild with joy to think that I had broken loose, and commenced eternal holiday; and I hope to continue in the same wild state, and never know what it is to be tame again," she writes in August 1808 to her friend Miss Bolton. "I am intoxicated with large draughts of liberty, and would rather be deprived of food than of such a beverage" (103, 104). Early in the letter she exclaims that she has "for twenty years ... been imprisoned in a school, and has but just been let loose!" (103).

Miss Chorley befriends her in Leigh and invites her to stay in her Liverpool home. However, her attempted trespass of Ellen's journal spurs Ellen to flee. She lodges with the Smiths on the banks of the Mersey, where she is happy for awhile. Here she invests in cottage properties and astutely betters her lot. However, the Smiths argue violently and even physically, which unnerves the genteel Ellen. She moves back into Liverpool to stay with the kinder Winkleys; however, she cannot rest content to read and write and play her flageolet and enjoy her hard-won freedom (and leisure).

She must seek to increase her wealth—and to help her undeserving brother. Still cradling dreams of her brother's early love, in December 1809 Ellen answers an ad for a governess at Dove's Nest at the head of Windermere Lake. She boldly asks for thirty guineas a year, a high salary for that time—much higher, Hall tells us, than Charlotte Brontë earned years later (202 and 202n1). Ellen's demand shows her sense of her worth. Thirty-four-year-old Edward Pedder agrees to the wage. He comes from an important Preston banking family and has an eleven-year-old epileptic daughter from his first marriage. That wife died, however, and he has married his pretty seventeen-year-old dairy maid who wants instruction, as well. In her journal entry, Ellen confesses that her true motive in taking the governess/companion post is to seek a powerful connection for her brother (204).

Ellen warms to the Lake Country. She cannot resist boasting to her cruel Aunt Barton in January 1810:

> I have hitherto had great reason to rejoice that I left Holland, for I have since [1808] made my income more than twice what it was; first, by selling advantageously out of the funds, and next, by a fortunate purchase, for which I can at any time receive more than I gave. In addition to which, I am now kept, and receiving a handsome salary, without undergoing half the slavery I used to do. If I can but give satisfaction here, I may, in a few years, save sufficient to purchase a tolerable estate; and by the time I am no longer wanted here, may have an income to support me handsomely. (228–29)

In the flush of her success, she immediately offers to pay for one year of schooling for her cousin, Richard Latham, on the condition that his older brother, Henry, continues to attend school—a further sign of her too-kind heart.

However, within two months of her arrival, her eleven-year-old charge dies in a self-caused fire. (Shades of the Brontës!) The young wife begs Ellen to stay on as her companion and friend, for she sorely needs one, as Ellen's journal and journal-letters disclose. On February 4, 1811, Ellen writes to Miss Winkley back in Liverpool: "[T]he unhappy temper of the master of this house, the continual quarrels in which he involves himself with his domestics and acquaintances, his brutal conduct towards his poor suffering wife, and his tyrannical treatment of me, have had such an effect on my health and spirits, that if I have any value for my life, I must endure it no longer, and am quitting Mr. P's house about the middle of next month" (321–22).

Miss Weeton: Journal of a Governess, 1807–1811, ends with this copied letter. Editor Hall, with more of Weeton's volumes still in hand, hopes this first volume "will justify" publication of a second (323). He can boast already of America's call for a special edition. When volume 5 surfaces unexpectedly on the Isle of Man, Hall finds himself with even more of Weeton's prose to unfold. *Miss Weeton: Journal of a Governess, 1811–1825*, appears in 1939, but I cannot prove Woolf read it. If she did not see it, she missed Ellen's increased turn to her journal, much like Woolf's own in the 1930s. *Journal of a Governess, 1811–1825* offers 196 journal entries and just 88 copied letters.

After escaping at age forty-five a brutal seven-year marriage that usurps her property and allows her, when she leaves, only three visits a year with her beloved six-year-old daughter, Mary, Ellen revives sufficiently to become a fine travel diarist. She records vividly her solitary sojourns in London and Wales. Woolf might have relished Weeton's journal records of her visit to Fitzroy Square in 1824, her walks through Kensington Gardens and St. James's Park, and her steam packet trip to Richmond, where she dines in Richmond Park "in the hollow of an old oak tree" (2: 296). On July 12, 1824, Ellen waits for two hours with the crowd on George Street to see Lord Byron's funeral. The next year, she climbs Mount Snowdon in Wales.

Woolf does not forget Ellen Weeton. In *Three Guineas*, she turns to Weeton as one of few examples of nineteenth-century women with professional lives. "Happily old boxes are beginning to give up their old secrets," Woolf reports:

> Out the other day crept one such document written about the year 1811. There was, it appears, an obscure Miss Weeton, who used to scribble

down her thoughts upon professional life among other things when her pupils were in bed. Here is one such thought. "Oh! how I have burned to learn Latin, French, the Arts, the Sciences, anything rather than the dog trot way of sewing, teaching, writing copies, and washing dishes every day.... Why are not females permitted to study physics, divinity, astronomy, etc., etc., with their attendants, chemistry, botany, logic, mathematics, &c?" (*TG* 75–76)

"That comment upon the lives of governesses ... reaches us from the darkness," Woolf declares (*TG* 76). Woolf lets Ellen Weeton speak and to emerge from the darkness of her stark and narrow life.

In her "Retrospect," Ellen warns her daughter to "never indulge any foolish family pride" (10)—one of the "unreal loyalties" Woolf will decry in *Three Guineas*. Furthermore, across her work Ellen shows a marked dislike of war. Regarding her beloved father's death in a sea battle, she writes in 1809: "'He that liveth by the sword shall die by the sword.' The warrior is not in the sight of God a man of honour and glory, whatever his fellow men may think. It is a dreadful life, a dreadful death" (11). In her 1824 London journal, she turns into St. James's Park to see the Panorama of the Battle of Waterloo. "I liked it very well, but I am not very fond of anything relating to Battles, and that was the reason why I had deferred this visit so long," she tells her journal. "I had once intended not to see it at all" (2: 306).

Editor Hall believes Weeton stopped her journal at age forty-eight with her travel journal to Wales. He senses weariness that may be just a pause. In point of fact, at the start of this vigorous travel, Ellen defines a new audience and purpose for her journal, just as Katherine Mansfield does at the start of her important 1916 diary and Woolf does in 1919. "As we were proceeding along, amidst the noise of steam, and steam-engine paddles, and double drum, clarionet, fiddle, and French-horn, I leaned over the side of the vessel, much interested with the gliding scenery, and considering whether I should any longer continue this Journal; for I always feel my own littleness in the world, and can assign no reason why I have continued it so long," Ellen writes in May 1825, "but—the thought of my darling Mary shot into my mind—I will continue it for thy sake, my little one; those expressive eyes of thine will one day perhaps read a mother's thoughts with eagerness; thy warm and tender heart will enter into all a mother's feelings; and to delight my child, I will continue it. Bless thee, my love" (2: 362). Ellen now writes for her daughter, as Mansfield will write for her dead brother and Woolf for "elderly Virginia." These projected readers allow the diarist to write on.

The blank page-and-a-half that Hall finds at the end of Ellen's volume 7 leads him to think she stopped the journal. However, she might have started anew in a fresh journal book, a book yet to be found. Would such a dedicated, needy scribbler stop her words? Two months before she inquires of Miss Hawarden: "Have the Literati of Wigan commenced a Newspaper yet? . . . Perhaps if they knew—the learned ones of Wigan—that so able a pen as mine might be engaged in their service, they would proceed; tell 'em, will you?" (2: 335).

Editor Hall turns over every church and town record to trace Ellen's fate. Before she leaves for Wales, Ellen launches a new strategy to gain more time with her now ten-year-old daughter. Friends sign a petition on her behalf to present to her bitter ex-husband, Aaron Stock. Perhaps he succumbs to this social pressure, for Hall finds that in 1827 Stock departs Wigan for Ashton-in-Makerfield, and Ellen, who has moved back to Wigan, is admitted to Hope Chapel there. In 1829, Mary is received into Hope Chapel, a fact that causes Hall to believe Mary may have chosen her mother over her father. Indeed, the house Stock leaves behind in Wigan becomes the property first of Mary and then of Ellen.

Sadly, with her 1825 journal the lights flicker out on Ellen Weeton. Hall thinks she might have died in 1844 at age sixty-seven, or even as late as 1851. However she lived out her final decades, she left a record of a sister's sacrifice for a brother's education and career—and an eloquent cry to be more than her narrow world allowed. "My chief delight is to learn, and to be with those who know how to teach," she writes her brother in 1809:

> I often feel as if I were not in my proper sphere, as if I possessed talents that only want awakening—that are ready to bud, did they find the least encouragement, and—that will wither for want of it. I could, Tom, I think I could have been something greater, something better than I am, had not my natural genius been repressed, and—like the blighting winds to the rosebud—been shrivelled almost to nothing. Thou will smile at this as an effusion of vanity—I cannot help it—thou knowest not the ardour, the enthusiasm that often glows within me, almost beyond my power to conceal it. (196–97)

Three Guineas provides Woolf's remedy to Weeton's blighted state.

Stephen MacKenna's *Journal*

Greek translator Stephen MacKenna wrote a crossroads diary: a journal to mark (and to assist) a turning point in life. "I did read MacKenna," Virginia Woolf writes to Lady Ottoline Morrell on December 26, 1936, "and wondered what sort of man he was. I think a very queer mix: I liked him, . . . I liked his life" (*L* #3204, 6: 96). She read the *Journal and Letters of Stephen MacKenna*, published in 1936, two years after MacKenna's death, at age sixty-two. This legendary talker and self-made scholar gave to English readers not only six volumes of Plotinus, the neo-Platonic philosopher, but also a translation that "for beauty . . . will certainly never be surpassed" (Sleeman 316).

Woolf could find much to identify with and to "like" in MacKenna's life, besides their shared love for the Greeks. Born in Liverpool in 1872, ten years before her, MacKenna also lost a parent at an early age. His namesake writer father, Captain Stephen MacKenna, died of malaria when Stephen was only eleven. The captain fought for Garibaldi and kept a "singularly candid diary which startled his family after his death," according to classical scholar E. R. Dodds, who edits the son's *Journal and Letters* and launches them with a lengthy memoir (4). In life, the captain's deeds so shocked his own mother that she first cut his allowance and then severed him from her will, an act that drove him to journalism for his livelihood and to pen romantic soldier-of-fortune tales for the young. At his death, in 1883, Captain MacKenna's ten children were dispersed, young Stephen and his brother, Robert, sent to two maiden aunts in Ramsgate.

Like teenage Virginia, young Stephen was frail—"too delicate," as he wrote near the end of his life (5). To compensate, Dodds reports, he developed "a precocious interest in literature and politics" (5). His aunts send him to Ratcliffe College, a small Catholic boarding school in Leicestershire, where he starts a debating society and argues passionately "that the complete independence of Ireland must and would be brought to pass within his lifetime" (5)—one of the two themes of his life (the other Plotinus). MacKenna shines in English, and John Squire would later call him "one of the greatest prose writers of our time" (6), yet he fails his admission tests to London University, where he hopes to earn a classical degree. He refuses to retake the exam and so, like Woolf, forges his way in the literary and intellectual world without university training, a particular hardship for an aspiring Greek scholar.

University gates closed, the aunts turn to the church. Stephen enters now a Catholic religious order but departs after a few months, appalled by the ritual of self-flagellation. "It was the damn 'discipline' did it," he writes a friend: "we had to take the beastly thing every morning: I couldn't stand it. It wasn't the pain.... It was the absurdity of the thing, the coddology of the thing—whacking oneself as if one were a lazy old donkey!" (7). A clerkship is found for him in a Dublin bank—donkey work MacKenna follows for five or six years. "When I was a child, a boy, a young man adolescent, I felt at no time that I had any right or place in the world," he told his journal at age thirty-five (104).

But he lives now at least in Dublin, and he possesses, in rash excess and noble flourishes, the Irish gift for talk. Woolf may have been drawn to MacKenna's *Journal* to glimpse what she had hoped to do for burbling Desmond MacCarthy in 1919, when she wished to publish *his* diary—or at least the sweepings of his desk (*D* 1: 241–42). Dodds reports that most who knew MacKenna swore he talked better than he wrote, and he wrote sublimely well. Images tumbled from MacKenna's lips—just as they do from Woolf's in her diary. Writer Padraic Colum, who offers the short preface to the *Journal and Letters*, reports that MacKenna's speech "was apt, original and witty; his mind was like a violin string, his voice vivacious and many-cadenced, often taking on the mounting enunciation of the Gaelic speaker" (xi). Dodds adds that "[w]hen he was moved by anger or awe or pity, MacKenna's speech had such dignity and imaginative splendour as was achieved by no Irishman of his time save W. B. Yeats" (41).

In 1896, at age twenty-four, MacKenna abandons the bank for the journalistic pen, his father's work and that of an older brother. In Paris as the correspondent for an English Catholic journal, he meets the Irish playwright J. M. Synge, who writes him in 1904, "I miss my talks with you."[20] In *Ulysses*, James Joyce has the real-life librarian Richard Best declare: "Mallarmé, don't you know ... has written those wonderful prose poems Stephen MacKenna used to read to me in Paris" (187). In Paris in 1902, thirty-year-old MacKenna meets Mary Bray, an American pianist, whom he marries in 1903 and calls "the gayest, chatteringest thing that ever walked" (183).

Society operated as a powerful stimulant on MacKenna, as it did on Woolf. As he immerses himself more and more in his lifework, he begins to shun society as Woolf began to do in the 1930s, for he said it made him "talk too much and too recklessly" (41). He turns, like Woolf, to Beethoven's symphonies. He would play one each morning at breakfast as he savored his tea and plumy cake—and, like her, he uses Wordsworth's *Prelude* as further prop. In a 1926 letter to Liam O'Rinn, he recommends the *Prelude* as a warm-up to fine style.

"Perhaps even better than Ruskin. . . . would be a good page or two of Wordsworth, the Sonnets (sublime) or chunks from the *Prelude*—intoned; aloud," he suggests; "or rather softly voiced: that's a superb style, nearly all utterly simple and utterly grand" (233).

The turning point in MacKenna's career comes in 1907. He begins a journal that he pens for three years but then saves across countless moves and the remainder of his days. He faces a crisis of wealth and vocation. In Paris, with his beautiful brown burning eyes, wild shock of black hair, and melodious talk, he charms more than Synge, Auguste Rodin, Maud Gonne, and Mary Bray. Gordon Bennett, editor of the *New York Herald Tribune*, begins to hire MacKenna to do interviews for his paper. In this role, MacKenna meets J. D. Rockefeller, who buys him a walking stick. Joseph Pulitzer admires MacKenna's work and hires him away for his competing *New York World*. MacKenna serves first as a special correspondent, but Pulitzer soon promotes him to continental bureau chief with a staff of assistants, a central office in Paris, and a princely salary.

Dodds writes that "[b]etween 1903 and 1907 MacKenna had his first and last taste of what is called success" (23). In 1903 he is in Berlin, and in 1904 in London. The winter of 1904–1905 finds him in Russia for the aborted revolution, where he visits Tolstoy in his humble cottage. In the autumn of 1905, MacKenna is sent to Stockholm and then to Budapest and back to Paris, but when politics flag Pulitzer expects him to report society scandal. "I cannot go on with this work. I am a journalist, not a muck-raker," MacKenna confides to his cousin, Ambrose Kelly, about 1906 (29). The next year, he tells his journal: "It is certain that to handle the daily fact for the daily press is neither work to my heart nor freedom to any man: it is for those who have stifled the innermost self—for the unhappy, then, or for the fallen" (30).

In 1896, at age twenty-four, MacKenna had published (anonymously) his first translation: an English version of Thomas à Kempis' *Imitation of Christ*. In Russia in 1905, he sees an edition of Plotinus' *Enneads,* and by the beginning of 1907 he ponders the huge task of translating the whole of Plotinus for the first time into English. On his birthday, January 15, 1907, MacKenna feels "a great moral upheaval—35 and nothing done, and almost certainly nothing ever to be done" (30). The periodic diary he then starts records what can only be called his life calling. On March 29, 1907, he muses to his journal:

> There is something high fantastical in the thought that if every day of my life I had a good hot piece of gossip, about some millionaire fool or some

powerful business man at play, to cable to New York, I should be well off and considered from New Year to Christmas; but if I put comely English about Plotinus and give him for the first time—and perhaps for all time—entire and clear and pleasantly readable to America and Australia and England, I shall certainly go about in old clothes and shrink from facing a post-office clerk. (104–05)

MacKenna breaks with Pulitzer soon after, the manner a newspaper legend. Pulitzer arrives in Paris and treats his bureau chief as an errand boy. MacKenna responds with a wire: "Refuse to deliver to you six chickens and six ducks: this is my resignation" (32). He turns over his duties and his handsome flat overlooking the Luxembourg Gardens to his friend, Colonel Arthur Lynch, and retires to a cottage at nearby Clamart to reflect. In July 1907, he moves to London, and in the summer of 1908 to Dublin, where he remains, with one interval, for the next sixteen years.

MacKenna began a commonplace book at age twenty-five. This 1897 notebook, Dodds reports, consists of extracts from MacKenna's reading, almost all related to two topics: "the problem of style and the problem of conducting one's life" (20). Here MacKenna writes, too: "That Christianity instead of Platonism became the religion of the later ages is the eternal proof of the imbecility of man" (21).

Regrettably, Dodds chooses to print only one-third of MacKenna's 1907–1909 crossroads diary, a shame, for it is a writer's diary supreme. Dodds believes MacKenna composed this journal with no thought of publication; however, he reread the single manuscript book in 1915, made a few stylistic corrections, and then penciled (but later struck out) this first page note: "I think there is much printable in this book" (92). His calculations on the journal's last page led Dodds to believe MacKenna thought to "print" about one-third of the journal (92). Following this lead, Dodds offers only seventy-one journal entries: forty-nine entries for 1907; eighteen for 1908; and four for 1909. They show that the journal served MacKenna in several vital ways. In the first January 1907 entry that Dodds chooses to print, MacKenna muses on life purpose: "One of the very most surprising things in life is the contented aimlessness with which it is so often, almost always, lived. Few live for joy in life, fewer still for something to be done with their life" (93).

Even before he owns his *own* life purpose, he begins to prepare for it in the *Journal*. On January 30, 1907, he ponders language and style. "I find that everything I write either is full of gross faults against the logic of expression or else is muddy and clogged—in either case is unreadable, even to myself," he complains.

> I am inclined to put the change down to three main causes, cable-journalism, the use of the typewriter, and a failure-bred distaste for all writing. The sense of the [cable] tariff checks the picture-making faculty, hinders the easy play of fancy: the typewriting seems to lead towards the lapidary and away from the fluid: journalism, especially of a low and impersonal kind, long pursued, necessarily rusts the imaginative faculty, for it creates the dread of any statement that is not warranted by some outer evidence and of any phrase that is not stamped in the vulgarest mould. (94, 95)

On February 6, he compares the virtues of Anglo-Saxon words to Latinate forms and throughout the month studies, in turn, Milton's *Areopagitica*, Coleridge's *Biographia Literaria*, and De Quincey's essays. He begins to build a personal thesaurus of classical English word usage. Found with his journal at his death, it contains many thousands of words. Dodds reports that he later made himself similar, though less complete, thesauri for Greek and Irish.

On May 4, 1907, the day he leaves Pulitzer and the *World* behind, MacKenna declares his goals: "Henceforth it is to be first Ireland and second politics, supported by journalism (or literature, if the gods were good), and then—third but very dear—Greek and Plotinus. And I like to set down for my own later memory this true word: that though my thoughts of making a career in politics are due, unquestionably, to my breach with the *N.Y. World*, yet I act in entire honesty, believing that I may serve some good end and make my life in every spiritual and 'teleological' way better, as being vowed to a noble cause which has always had all my love and hope" (107).

MacKenna uses his journal to weigh his competing passions and, like Woolf, to plan. "Now begins the task," he writes on May 20, 1907:

> to make money by writing, to learn Irish and master the problems and politics and personalities of Ireland, to keep Greek bright and Plotinus simmering, to watch modern French literature and not to let modern Greek slip out of my mind. I am to read much English literature, especially the rich older writers, but with the greatest care to save myself from the snare of "specialising": my one end, ever clearly in view, must be, after enjoying in all simplicity their beauty, to pluck their mystery

from them, to learn in my degree their art and to harvest me their words, their rich strength: they are to be to me not a "subject" but for delight and for use. (107)

By December 1907, however, Plotinus seems to choose *him*—and to overtake Irish independence. MacKenna tells his journal on December 5: "Whenever I look again into Plotinus I feel always all the old trembling fevered longing: it seems to me that I must be born for him, and that somehow someday I must have nobly translated him: my heart, untravelled, still to Plotinus turns and drags at each remove a lengthening chain. It seems to me that him alone of authors I understand by inborn sight" (114). Six days later, he records: "Found myself, surprised myself, with a prayer on my lips, a prayer to Plotinus that I might translate him" (116).

On his next birthday, January 15, 1908, he rebukes himself for starts unfinished. "36 to-day, and nothing done," he begins, echoing his last year's entry. "I am interested in Plotinus: to translate him into beautiful English and then to interpret him and press him into the use of this century seems to me, has always seemed to me, really worth a life" (117). In October 1908, he confides: "I feel a great need of having on the work-table some piece of writing, serious and linked, which every day I might bring nearer to an end firmly set for some gravely formed purpose" (31).

For the next twenty-two years, Plotinus will salve that need. In late 1908, MacKenna's translation of Plotinus' essay on beauty (*Ennead* I.vi) appears in a limited edition of three hundred. It sells out and is twice reprinted but earns MacKenna only four or five pounds (36). But he is launched—with his journal's aid. Dodds omits or abbreviates, he tells us, four types of journal entries: ones "still in the rough, and therefore failed of concentration or clarity.... some which lacked personal quality, being purely exercises in style; some which gave alternative expression to thoughts already set down; and a very few which appeared too private for publication" (92). Of course rough entries, repeated thoughts, and exercises in style are of signal interest in a writer's diary. Intimate words illuminate, too.

Nevertheless, in the 71 printed journal entries—and the 102 letters as well—Woolf saw a writer who shared her painstaking (and often painful) devotion to art. MacKenna voices despair in his 1908 journal but then spurs himself on: "The more I read—in every language I trifle with, English, French, Latin, Greek, even the rather lush Gaelic—the more I see that I really have yet no skill at all in writing.... All I have, after all these years with their practice if not their effort, is a great enjoyment of the skill of others, with a quickening sense of the materials that lie to the prose-writer's hand. Perhaps, too, I have a large, ready stock of words. But the store is not the main thing: it is the use that counts" (126, 127). In August 1908 he sounds quite like Woolf: "A day of nothingness, of prehumous death: pains and laze and brainlessness" (129).

The *Enneads* slowly emerge, the first tall volume in 1917. "If it were not for two things, I could have printed a year ago," MacKenna writes to his English patron, E. R. Debenham, in early 1916: "[T]hey are perfect clearness and expressive cadence: perfect clearness to those, bien entendu, who will take the trouble to understand the terms and what the whole is about; cadence that shall help to clearness, and that shall further be a satisfaction in itself.... I like pebbles in my brooks and little bends in my roads and raggedy edges to my clouds" (147). As he toils on volume 2, he repeats to Debenham in February 1918: "It is only now a question of intensity of the clarifying and 'beautifying' power; but unfortunately this is the uncontrollable thing; it requires all my energy, a quickness of mind and feeling amounting to almost what we call inspiration in the poets. And I can't bear to think of putting any Plotinus forth that is not quite as noble, as lucid, as generally readable as the best mind in me can, under its best inspiration, produce."[21]

Near the close of her own ordeal with *The Years*, it likely fortified Woolf to see another's high standards and pains. "[O]ut of four workless, unwork-able, days there bees [*sic*] perhaps one on which I can work: to lose that were sin and shame," MacKenna writes to Dodds, whom he consults on the most difficult passages: "[T]he four by the way don't represent won't-work days but no-can-produce days: I sit with splitting head agonising to tears and either I understand nothing or can reproduce nothing: after from 1 to 2 hours session I curse God and rise and play the guitar or clarinet or mandola or mandoline or mandocello or domra or squeejee and recover my native sweetness of universal love: so to bed, and next day and next may be the same: then comes *the* day and Plotinus pegs on an inch and is almighty pleased with himself" (254).

MacKenna suffered the agonies of typescripts and proof Woolf has just traversed. "At every possible moment I tinker with the typescript, and find it slowly getting better," he writes his patron in the midst of volume 2; "a second typing (to embody the improvements) ought to see things right before too long" (158). But then, in 1923, again to Debenham: "I should have understood that what looked very nice and 'all but ready' in MS. and in typescript would look appallingly unfinished, crude, 'failured,' when one was about to publish" (186). As he writes his brother, Robert, in 1923 as he readies volume 3: "[W]hat I have done with Plotinus is a miracle, the miracle of persistent resteadying of a mind that dips and tosses and disappears like a cork on the waves of your Bay of Islands" (187).

Dodds does MacKenna an injustice to equate him with H. F. Amiel, the Swiss scholar whose famous diary records his paralyzing introspection and inability to pen public work.[22] Across twenty-two years, MacKenna produced six volumes of Plotinus that Yeats called "worthy at its best to take its place among the masterpieces of English prose." Dodds calls MacKenna's Plotinus "one of the very few great translations of our day," a feat particularly remarkable given the vast difficulties Plotinus poses in text, language, and thought (81). Others have called MacKenna's Plotinus "the finest English translation of any Greek classic."[23] In his 1931 review of the final volume, J. H. Sleeman declared that "[i]n working through Mr. MacKenna's translation side by side with the original[,] one is again and again struck by the extraordinary beauty and felicity of the rendering. Mr. MacKenna is always an artist in words, and Plotinus emphatically is not" (315).

Irish freedom, MacKenna's second passion, impeded his great Plotinus, as did other wars. While Woolf might have taken heart from MacKenna's writerly struggles and final success, she also saw in his character's "queer mix" quixotic views of war and nation, alongside recoil from war. As *Three Guineas* steeps in her mind, she must compass MacKenna's honest words as well as the views of that hardworking English "sportsman" and diarist Dr. John Salter.

MacKenna's namesake father, as earlier noted, fought for Garibaldi and Italian independence as one of the Kinnegad Slashers. In early 1897, war erupted between Greece and Turkey. Twenty-five-year-old Stephen learned that Garibaldi's son had raised a new legion of Redshirts to fight for the Greeks. Stephen "knew that he must do as his father had done," Dodds reports (13). On Greek soil in an international volunteer brigade, MacKenna (happily) sees no real battle, for he has never held a gun. On sentry duty his first night, he has to be taught how to salute, challenge, and hold his rifle. "I do not understand, monsieur, the etiquette of this situation," he politely tells his astonished Greek officer (15). Likewise, although he stands on Dublin's O'Connell Street on Easter Monday 1916 and hears the Irish Republic proclaimed, and on Tuesday or Wednesday offers to join the doomed men at the Post Office, Patrick Pearse saw the "uselessness of the sacrifice," Dodds declares, "for [MacKenna] was unarmed and untrained, even had he been physically fit to handle a weapon" (52). Pearse kindly refuses MacKenna's suicide.

Two years before, the Great War unhinges MacKenna's already sensitive nerves. In late 1913, the MacKennas travel to London for treatment of Stephen's neurasthenia. In early 1914, while Woolf recovers in the Twickenham sanatorium, MacKenna enters a sanatorium for nervous cases in Kent. In December 1914, he writes from Hove to his friend Thomas Bodkin: "I'm heartbroken over the war that has enabled his Most Reverence and Eminence of Armagh to declare with undeniable truth that Ireland will always leap into the breach in loyal devotion to the British Empire" (143). To his English patron, he writes:

> [M]yself I sicken at all the blood, the mowing down of the youth of Europe, the stop, dead, of all we have thought of as civilisation, the multiform, wide as the world almost, agony and desolation. Plotinus mocks at all such emotions . . . and this tho' Plotinus had been a soldier and seen, ce qu'on appelle vu, on no small scale too, the horrors which his "Sage" . . . declares a trivial ragged fringe on his beautiful inner peace. For my part I find this war, with all that it entails to the world and to my own poor little land, setting me blaspheming. (145–46)

MacKenna blames the Great War for his wife's poor health. "I suspect war food as the cause of the primal internal trouble, and war-grief as nerve-wracking her so that she does not cure as naturally as—would seem natural," he writes a friend. "She really does grieve over the carnage, the hold-up of civilisation, the nasty silly passion of victory keeping the big men from lifting the finger that would save the world's young things from death and dismemberment" (150). To Debenham, he writes in February 1918: "I can't think why you Magnates do not end the appalling business. . . . I have myself a brother in this war. . . . He is the father of a young family in Australia—he will probably die in the 'Great Onset'—for what? He has written to me from the Front *asking me to tell him* why he left his profession, his wife, his intellectual and mystic life, his 'kids'" (152).

Violence does not end for the MacKennas with the 1918 Armistice, for many Irish still wish to be free. British shootings in 1920 and the 1921 "campaign of terror" bring daily fear and danger to the couple, for MacKenna writes for the *Freeman's Journal*, then the leading Irish nationalist daily. Dodds writes that "[t]hroughout 1921 MacKenna, like a great number of other people in Ireland, lived in nightly expectation of being raided and arrested" (59). MacKenna tells his patron: "I'm the sole Non-Military Anti-Britonist in my country: the mad military mind has us in tongs" (179). Through it all he manages to bring out volume 2 of Plotinus in 1921. "The civil war of 1922 filled him with shame and grief," Dodds continues. "There was no place for such a man in the Ireland of the gunmen" (62). When the Irish sign the treaty, MacKenna leaves Ireland for good. His beloved wife dies on July 4, 1923, leaving MacKenna to carry on alone.

MacKenna knows his fierce nationalism cannot be rationalized. "I am lost in wonder at the mystery of Patriotism," he tells his journal in December 1907. "Why should I care what Ireland is now when I do not live in it, or what Ireland may become when I am dead? Yet I do, with a passion of love and pity and rage" (116). In the next-to-last journal entry Dodds includes, MacKenna writes in April 1909:

> I notice, with curiosity, that the longer I live, though many hopes fail and fall away and at last are almost forgotten, two stay firmly with me and grow. Neither is held by my reason; both have to do with the heart and are for the impossible, as reason says coldly. I hope for the freedom of Ireland, soul and body freedom, Gaelicism and a flag: and I hope even yet to be able some day to write well—in English! . . . The first hope I cannot account for: "this bird has built its nest with me." It can be only a reachback to the dead sons of Enna through centuries of Gaelic life. (132–33)

After her famous *Three Guineas* decree, "as a woman, I have no country. As a woman I want no country. As a woman my country is the whole world," Woolf adds: "And if, when reason has said its say, still some obstinate emotion remains, some love of England dropped into a child's ears by the cawing of rooks in an elm tree, by the splash of waves on a beach, or by English voices murmuring nursery rhymes, this drop of pure, if irrational, emotion she will make serve her to give to England first what she desires of peace and freedom for the whole world" (109).

MacKenna's diary passage then continues: "The other hope [to write well in English] seems to have a moral foundation. It is hard at best to find any meaning in life at all; impossible, unless by way of some action, something by which one especially lives, bringing out some singular quality, and something by which one adds to the sum of life, shaping by some personal means the larger form of the world" (133).

Stephen MacKenna adds to the sum of life and shapes the world with his art. In his final years, he turns to nature and ends his days on the Cornwall moors—just north of St. Ives. He writes his patron in October 1923 that "[m]usic, with one finger, and the calm beauty of fields and trees and the simplicity of children, these are the only things that keep me from the burst brain that at times seems to threaten—a sort of boiling in the brain pan with most singularly no sense of ill health, generally even no physical lassitude" (190). To Dodds he writes from Cornwall fifteen months before his death: "Man's world such a putrid horror set against such a non-human loveliness—slums and sordor against the rising and the setting of the sun and moon and spring and autumn—not forgetting the sadder but delicate beauty of the winter" (300).

Like Woolf, MacKenna rejects most honors. In 1924, when Yeats announces that the Royal Irish Academy "crowned" MacKenna's work and awarded him a gold medal, MacKenna explains to the press that he can accept no honor "from a Society whose title seems to imply any connection between Ireland and the English throne" (82). Invited to join the academy in later years, he writes to A. E. that "all my life long I have hated publicity and all distinction: I'd not have signed Plotty had I had my way. . . . I bless the Academy; mildly wish it well—simply can't be of it" (301, 302). He is an outsider, too.

Toward the close of his "Memoir," Dodds poses a question he refuses to answer: "Whether in fact MacKenna's Plotinus is worth the enormous price that was paid for it—not only in effort and suffering, but in the sacrifice of the other potentialities that lay in his rich natural endowment—" (81). Dodds notes both the irony and the achievement, calling the Plotinus "a noble monument to an Irishman's courage, an Englishman's generosity, and the idealism of both" and "an astonishing performance for a journalist who had never crossed the threshold of a university."[24] Had not the Plotinus so absorbed MacKenna's mind, he might have penned a glorious, chatty, richly various *life diary* as well as a crossroads journal. Instead, he showcases how diaries can both herald and aid change. The turn in the life path made, the need for the diary ends.

Dodds could not know in 1936 that MacKenna's *Journal* might fortify another writer in need of support. It showed, too, war and patriotism as beyond reason's ken and led, I believe, to an important reply in *Three Guineas*.

7

Storm-Tossed & Exposed

The Spanish Civil War begins in 1936 and, in February 1937, Virginia Woolf's nephew, Julian Bell, says he will enlist to fight the fascists. In July 1937, war also erupts between China and Japan.

Blindness, however, persists in many quarters. Ethel Sands, Woolf's friend, tells her in February 1937 that *her* nephew, Parliamentary Liberal Party leader Sir Archibald Sinclair, "see[s] no danger ahead for England" (*D* 5: 58 and 58n10). Two days later, Christopher Isherwood and Sally Graves say they "now think things are going well in England, & that Madrid wont fall" (*D* 5: 59). Clive Bell and Leonard Woolf seek to minimize Julian's danger for Vanessa and Virginia. "Clive & L. said that there was no more risk in going to Spain than in driving up & down to Charleston," Virginia records. "Clive said that only one man had been hurt by a bomb"; in fact, he says it is "spirited of [Julian] to go" (Quentin Bell 2: 256). Julian Bell himself tells his younger brother of his wish to organize "an alternative army, police, & administration . . . on the Hitlerian model" (Lee 685).

English broadsheets shared this myopia, Petra Rau reports. These broadsheets, "[f]rom 1937 onwards . . . although alert to Nazi showmanship and persecution of the Jews, tended to focus on Hitler's 'undoubted accomplishments': 'the virtual ending of unemployment, the fine new buildings and roads, and its seeming spiritual and physical regeneration of the German people'" (8–9). A 1937 report on the British Health Services suggested that Great Britain was "less fit" than some European nations, notably Germany, and "the most effective solution" might be military conscription (Rau 10).

These outer storms—now reaching Woolf's own family circle—darken her own (deserved) high sail. America's *Time* magazine features Woolf on its cover, sign of international literary fame. The Hogarth Press, in 1937, reaps unprecedented profits: £2,442, due mostly to the success of *The Years* (Staveley 298). Yet so tossed is Woolf by the outer crises—and exposed—that she cannot savor her success. In February 1937, she sees her own anguish in the final diaries of Leo Tolstoy and his wife. She reads *The Final Struggle: Being Countess Tolstoy's Diary for 1910, with Extracts from Leo Tolstoy's Diary of the same period*. She finds there inner and outer wars (recorded in many diaries)—and a war fought over diaries, as well.

Virginia Woolf's 1937 Diary

> "Meanwhile, suffer me now & again to write out my horror, the sudden cold madness, here.... Also my own psychology interests me. I intend to keep full notes of my ups & downs, for my private information. And thus objectified, the pain & shame become at once much less. And I have proved to my own conviction that I can write with fury, with rapture, with absorption still."

(March 2, 1937; *D* 5: 64)

Upheavals, inner and outer, unsettle Virginia Woolf's 1937 year. She draws, in fact, literal diary graphs of her ups and downs. Deaths near—and steadily nearer—deflate the public success and private joy that exalt her at times to heights. However, she harnesses herself in her first diary entry and ably rides out the year.

She introduces death immediately in her opening diary entry, only to counter it with a woman doctor and her own vow to "canter"—always a bow to her diary mother, Fanny Burney. Sculptor Tommy Tomlin "is dead & buried," Woolf begins her diary's second sentence on January 10, 1937 (*D* 5: 47). She treats the loss as the death of ego, that nemesis she ever seeks to banish (and a rife presence in *this* diary). "We said on the whole perhaps it was a good thing," she tells her diary, "because for the past 3 or 4 years ... he seemed ravaged by his own misery; couldn't work, had been a failure; tore everyone & everything to bits in a kind of egotistic rage" (*D* 5: 47). *She* will do better. She records her visit to physician Octavia Wilberforce and closes by medicining herself: "Oh but I'm going to think of Cleopatra's Needle when I get on to my old nightmare: & so canter past it. I think I can too.... Work, work, work—thats my final prescription" (*D* 5: 50). Cleopatra's Needle survived a watery death in the Bay of Biscay on its way to London in 1878 when the ship transporting it capsized. Furthermore, Cleopatra herself, though a suicide, never ceased to be courageous and bold.[1]

If Woolf cut herself off from journalism in 1936, one of her many refreshing streams, she returns savvily in 1937 to carefully chosen articles, as she did with such success in 1934 with her Goldsmith, Turgenev, and Sickert tributes. She resumes her turn-and-turn-about tack: articles as both respite from and refreshment for her yearlong work on *Three Guineas*. Woolf dallies with a piece on Edward Gibbon across the first four months of the year. In June, she chooses to write on William Congreve. With an historian (Gibbon) and a playwright (Congreve), she begins to move toward her own historical pageant, *Between the Acts*. She calls Gibbon and Congreve "immortal," proof that art survives death (*E* 6: 89, 114).

Woolf's refreshed spirit in 1937 stems in part from sheer relief from the burden of *The Years*. She can expand now in new directions, including in her diary. She takes now a large two-ring loose-leaf notebook—another push, as in 1927 to 1929, to snare more stray or loose thoughts. However, the gloomy black stationer's cover will not do. She troubles to cover the black with printed paper. The new diary cover looks like flowers floating on tiny waves.[2]

Woolf uses this loose-leaf diary as a lifeboat through the March publication of *The Years*. Although she writes seventy-seven diary entries across the 343 days from January 10 to December 18, 1937, an entry, on average, every four or five days, she pens ten entries in February and seventeen in March—proof of the diary as vital prop. "I hope to float over the horrid March 15. . . . I must plate myself against that sinking in mud," she tells her diary on January 28, already anticipating *The Years*' publication day.[3] On February 15 she seems "plated," for when the *Observer* offers "2 little mildly appreciative notes" on the novel, she observes "with pleasure, that all praise & blame & talk about that book seems like tickling a rhinoceros with a feather" (*D* 5: 55). She credits her armor partly to her "1932 philosophic revelation: one doesnt matter" and also to her immersion in *Three Guineas* (*D* 5: 55).

However, three days later she learns that America's *Saturday Review* dismisses her as a mere "maker of films & laces; a sitter in shaded drawing rooms." She seizes her diary to "lay this demon" to rest, for, as in her earliest days, these chilling words freeze her pen (*D* 5: 56). "This kind of sneer has an inhibiting effect for the moment," she tells her diary on February 18. "But I must be quit of the need even of defending myself. I want to forge ahead, on my own lines" (*D* 5: 56).

Once more she links London with trespass: "But in London where I am exposed[4] all day & every day to criticism some plating of resolution is absolutely needed. And I think I've got it by the tip of the tail—a new kind of indifference.... how little the goodness or badness of my books affects the world. And there is the world—represented by picture galleries, the Caledonian Market, Gibbon, Nessa, going to MH. [Monk's House], walking, planning new arrangements of the room, & always throwing my mind 2 or 3 miles ahead" (*D* 5: 56).

Two days later, she plates herself through her usual tack of projecting failure for her book. "I think I anticipate considerable lukewarmness among the friendly reviewers," she tells her diary, "—respectful tepidity; & a whoop of red Indian delight from the Grigs who will joyfully & loudly announce that this is the long drawn twaddle of a prim prudish bourgeois mind, & say that now no one can take Mrs W. seriously again.... And since we shant get away till June I must expect a very full exposure to this damp firework atmosphere" (*D* 5: 58). Again she feels "exposed"; yet to picture failure is to tame it for Woolf. "Well, now that I've written that down I feel that even so I can exist in that shadow," she adds (*D* 5: 58).

But despite these protective shields, the "old nightmare" strikes on March 1. It takes its familiar form: coldness, dryness, cruel laughter, and her wish to walk it all away. "I wish I could write out my sensations at this moment. They are so peculiar & so unpleasant," she begins, and wonders if this is menopause:

> A physical feeling as if I were drumming slightly in the veins: very cold: impotent: & terrified. As if I were exposed on a high ledge in full light. Very lonely. L. out to lunch. Nessa has Quentin & dont want me. Very useless. No atmosphere round me. No words. Very apprehensive. As if something cold & horrible—a roar of laughter at my expense were about to happen. And I am powerless to ward it off: I have no protection. And this anxiety & nothingness surround me with a vacuum.... Then a great restlessness seizes me. I think I could walk it off—walk & walk till I am asleep.... And I cannot unfurl my mind & apply it calmly & unconsciously to a book. And my own little scraps look dried up & derelict. And I know that I must go on doing this dance on hot bricks till I die.... [T]he exposed moments are terrifying. I looked at my eyes in the glass once & saw them positively terrified. (*D* 5: 63)

This alarming entry anticipates entries in 1940 and 1941. In 1937, however, diary pen strokes once more soothe Woolf. She ends the entry with the whispered (parenthetical) word *confidence* and a line graph showing "normal," then a drop, and then a rise to March 2 (*D* 5: 64).

But that entry, too, starts in terror: "I'm going to be beaten, I'm going to be laughed at, I'm going to be held up to scorn & ridicule—I found myself saying those words just now," she begins, but again seeks to "medicine" herself with her diary: "[S]uffer me now & again to write out my horror, the sudden cold madness, here" (*D* 5: 64). She then probes possible merits of her plight: she may get *some* praise for *The Years*; in any case, she can take pride in facing the music; and they have sold 5,000 copies before publication, so she is adding to the coffers and doing her share "& not merely subsiding into terrified silence" (*D* 5: 64). Also her own psychology interests her. Days later, she draws another line graph that starts at "normal" March 2 and charts a rise in her "spiritual temperature" to a high plateau March 3 through 6, when it drops back toward "normal" (*D* 5: 65).

Her next entry, March 7, continues to project and reassure. "Now I have broached the fatal week & must expect a sudden drop," she declares: "Its going to be pretty bad, I'm certain; but at the same time I am convinced that the drop needn't be fatal. . . . In short either way I'm safe, & look forward, after the unavoidable tosses & tumbles of the next ten days, to a slow, dark, fruitful spring, summer & autumn" (*D* 5: 65). We can understand her nerves. *The Years* will be her first book in four years—since the 1933 *Flush*—her longest silence since the gap between her first novel, *The Voyage Out* (1915), and second, *Night and Day* (1919).

Happily, as in the past, all her fears prove wrong. On March 12, the *Times Literary Supplement* praises *The Years*, and *Time and Tide* calls her a first-rate novelist and great lyrical poet (*D* 5: 67). When Basil de Sélincourt recognizes *The Years* as a creative and constructive book in two columns of praise in the *Observer*, her relief overflows: "money is assured: L. shall have his new car; we will be floated again; & my last lap—if I've only 10 years of life more—should be fruitful. Work—work. But at the moment, the relief is so great . . . that I feel myself rocking up & down" (*D* 5: 68).

To her shock, *The Years* becomes an American best seller. On June 1, Woolf sees the novel top the *New York Herald Tribune*'s "Bestsellers List" (*D* 5: 90). By September 26, she reports American sales between forty and fifty thousand (*D* 5: 111).

As Woolf soars or falls with every boost or blow, she tries at the same time to fight ego. Here is an inner war—as the outer war storm grows. She transforms

Tomlin's death into the (positive) death of ego in her first entry, and her diary portraits across the year often highlight vanity. On February 18, for instance, she notes that Stephen Spender has "a child's vanity about himself. Interesting to me at the moment, as I'm working out the psychology of vanity" (*D* 5: 57). She confesses on August 17 to "musing on the nature of Auden's egotism," (*D* 5: 107), and on September 26 she sees in T. S. Eliot her own furtive tango with self. Will she ever conquer "I"?

Her diary helps her—she can record ego and analyze it there—and so does *Three Guineas*, which brings back her old creative flood. In no other of her diary books do private and public events—the wars within and the wars without—so entwine and imbue her literary art, her cultural critique. Throughout the year she stores in her diary matter for her antiwar book. In her first entry, January 10, she notes that even Dr. Octavia Wilberforce had to fight for an education, had to fight for a profession. Her family "coerced her . . . to stay at home. Only through a great struggle did she break off & become a doctor" (*D* 5: 49). Wilberforce's battle mirrors that of Dr. Elizabeth Garrett, England's first licensed doctor, conveyed in Kate Amberley's diary.

On January 28, Woolf formally begins *Three Guineas* "& cant stop thinking it" (*D* 5: 52). She finds herself "[s]unk once more in the happy tumultuous dream" (*D* 5: 52). But in February, she must face war directly in worrisome Julian Bell, Vanessa's son, who declares his aim to fight in the Spanish Civil War. "Cornford's son was killed there last week," Woolf tells her diary on February 12 (*D* 5: 54). Vanessa reacts with "submerged" despair, but Virginia will fight against the "danger lure" of war. "[T]hats my instinct," she writes: to fight. "I feel like the man who had to keep dancing on hot bricks. Cant let myself stop. Hence I suppose I write here; wh. explains why Tolstoy & his wife kept diaries" (*D* 5: 54, 55). Diaries, as has been shown, can be vital aides in life's fight.

By February 18, she has completed thirty-eight pages of *Three Guineas*. But now Stephen Spender comes to call, *his* young life, like Julian's, upended by the war. Spender marries Inez Pearn, causing his longtime companion, Tony Hyndman, to join the International Brigade. Spender, too, means to go to Spain, and Woolf probes it all in her diary:

> Now [Spender] is torn two ways: so Inez sits there [in Paris], in order, should he be killed in Spain—but he's only broadcasting—she may have her job to fall back on. A curious interpretation of marriage, dictated by the guns. I like him: told him not to fight. He said it was the easiest thing

to do. I said give up speaking [for the war]—he said But it brought in money. He argued that we cannot let the Fascists overrun Spain: then it'll be France; then us. We must fight. L. said he thought things had now gone so far it did not matter. Fighting did no good. S. said the C.P. [Communist Party] which he had that day joined, wanted him to be killed, in order that there might be another Byron. (*D* 5: 56–57)

On February 24, she is "off again" on *Three Guineas*—using her Sibyl Colefax/George Meredith resurrection phrase. She achieves "a little canter" she thinks will flash her past *The Years*' reviews (*D* 5: 61). Four days later, she finds herself (again) composing a public work while she pens her diary. "I'm so entirely imbued in 3 Guineas that I can hardly jerk myself away to write here," she begins her February 28 entry. "([H]ere in fact I again dropped my pen to think about my next paragraph—universities—how will that lead to professions & so on). Its a bad habit" (*D* 5: 62). Yet a productive one.[5] Two days later, she feels that her absorption in *Three Guineas*' university section will be her "great defence against the cold madness that overcame [her] last night" (*D* 5: 64). In fact her "spiritual temperature" rises "with a rush" the next four days, which she attributes to her "good gallop at 3 Guineas" (*D* 5: 65). On March 12, she harnesses herself to *Three Guineas* to carry her through her reviews. "I have once more loaded myself with the strain of 3 Gs. at which I have been writing hard & laboriously," she writes, somewhat masochistically (*D* 5: 67). When reviewers call *The Years* a masterpiece of fiction and poetry, she sees the success as an aid to *Three Guineas*: "[T]his means that 3 Gs. will strike very sharp & clear on a hot iron" and will be debated (*D* 5: 68).

April 15 brings another "long close political argument" with Julian, Spender, and Kingsley Martin. The questions are these: "What is our duty? What is the responsible man like KM to do?" (*D* 5: 79). Woolf tells her diary that she "sat there splitting off my own position from theirs, testing what they said, convincing myself of my own integrity & justice" (*D* 5: 79). She finds Julian "peppery & pithy.... Obstinately set on going to Spain—wont argue; tight; hard fisted—has amusing phrases 'joining for duration of the quarrel'" (*D* 5: 79–80). They discuss hand grenades, bombs, and tanks, "as if we were military gents in the war again. And I felt flame up in me 3 Gs. wh. has been submerged by Gibbon & BBC" (*D* 5: 80).

When Julian comes again on May 4 with Richard Chilver and his wife, Sally Graves, Julian complains bitterly of *his* education, *his* lack of professional preparation. Woolf also sees Chilver's plight through her second guinea (on the professions). Chilver would like to leave the Air Ministry "& become a carpenter—make good chairs—but of course wont & cant, though Sally urges. Another aspect of the professional question. Air Ministry long hours, hard work; but regular and safe" (*D* 5: 86). Woolf ponders here male professional burdens as well as female.

Julian's stubborn drive toward war shadows the Woolfs' May holiday in France. "If it weren't for Julian going to Spain I should be wholly content on our French journey," Woolf tells her diary on April 30 (*D* 5: 83). But she uses the trip for her book. She tells her diary that she "would like to talk to innumerable people in hotels about their jobs" (*D* 5: 90).

Back in England on June 1, she recopies—and rewrites—her first guinea on women's education, for Lady Simon sends her a private report of a recent meeting at Newnham College for women to discuss "the great question if gowns should be worn" (*D* 5: 92). Gowns figure in the broader wish: should they ask for equal admission once more?[6] Julian leaves for Spain on June 7, and on June 11, Woolf hears that writer Rosamond Lehmann's husband lies wounded there, the man beside him dead. But she presses on. On June 16 she finishes *Three Guineas*' first chapter on education, "much re-arranged." On June 23, a long trail of Basque refugees crossing Tavistock Square brings tears to Woolf's eyes. "Children trudging along . . . impelled by machine guns in Spanish fields to trudge through Tavistock Sqre" (*D* 5: 97). This leads her to Albert Hall on June 24, where she and Leonard share the stage with African American actor and singer Paul Robeson at a meeting of the National Joint Committee for Spanish Relief.

After taking a breath with Congreve, Woolf starts her second guinea on June 28, "that very difficult chapter" on the professions, but she is "heartened by reading some of the first [chapter]: saw it as 3 Chapters suddenly" (*D* 5: 100). The next day, when Isherwood calls to beg her to send a message to the International Writers Congress meeting in Madrid, she is in "full flush" on guinea two (*D* 5: 101). A gap of eleven days then opens in the diary. "A gap: not in life, but in comment," Woolf begins her July 11 entry. "I have been in full flood every morning with 3 Gs. . . . I am in the middle of my magic bubble. . . . Then I think of Julian near Madrid" (*D* 5: 101). The next day she opens her diary to *stop* herself from thinking of *Three Guineas*. However, once more the war tempers her fluid writing sail. Alone with Vanessa the night before, Woolf feels "the immeasurable despair just on tother side of the grass plot on wh. we walk—on wh. I'm walking with such energy & delight at the moment" (*D* 5: 102).

Eight days later, on July 20, she learns of Julian's death on July 18 in Spain. A gulf of seventeen days now opens in the diary as Woolf nurses Vanessa. However, she takes up her diary on August 6 to resume life's fight. "Well but one must make a beginning," she starts:

> Its odd that I can hardly bring myself, with all my verbosity—the expression mania which is inborn in me—to say anything about Julian's death.... But one must get into the current again. That was a complete break; almost a blank; like a blow on the head: a shriveling up.... Thats one of the specific qualities of this death—how it brings close the immense vacancy, & our short little run into inanity. Now this is what I intend to combat. How? how make good what I protest, that I will not yield an inch or a fraction of an inch to nothingness, so long as something remains? (*D* 5: 104, 105)

She is in combat. Eleven days later, she admits that she often argues with dead Julian on her walks, "abuse his selfishness in going [to war] but mostly feel floored by the complete muddle & waste. Cant share the heroic raptures of the Medical Aid, who are holding a meeting next week to commemorate the six who were killed. 'Gave their lives' as they call it" (*D* 5: 108). Her next (undated) entry (which Olivier Bell dates August 25) reports the eyewitness accounts of Julian's death. "Why do I set this down?" she then asks her diary. "It belongs to what is unreal now. What is left that is real?" (*D* 5: 109).

Her *Three Guineas* is real. So focused now is Woolf on this antiwar volume that she writes only three diary entries in September. She finishes her first draft on October 12, and on November 1 refuses to join the deputation to Prime Minister Neville Chamberlain that bears a petition asking for "[a]n international enquiry into the fundamental causes of rivalry and unrest among nations" (*D* 5: 118n6). *Three Guineas* gives *her* answer.

A twenty-six-day diary gap in November comes from a further *Guineas* flood. Woolf's November 30 entry opens with one of her assuring, connecting "Yeses": "Yes, its actually the last day of November; & theyve passed like a streak of hounds after a fox because I've been re-writing 3 Guineas with such intentness, indeed absorption, that several times 5 minutes past one has shown on the clock & I still at it. So I've never even looked at this stout volume" (*D* 5: 119). With *Three Guineas* she reverts to her pre-*Waves* days, for she no longer needs her diary as a morning prop.

Woolf's 1937 diary records a return of her creative flood. Although she faces increasingly more painful deaths as the year unfolds—Tommy Tomlin's in early

January; Margaret West's, the Hogarth Press' valued manager, at January's end; then her beloved Greek teacher, Janet Case, July 15; followed swiftly by Julian's shattering death in war—so buoyant, nevertheless, is Woolf that she transforms each loss to gain. Tomlin at last wins release from his ego. West's death brings the chance for the Hogarth Press to "lapse or change," to "get fresh scope for experiment & freedom" (*D* 5: 82, 113). In October, they think of a "Co-operative Press" (*D* 5: 118). Janet Case becomes immortal in both semiprivate and public prose: in Woolf's diary, in Woolf's published obituary tribute, and in Woolf's final novel. Three months before Case's death, Woolf tells her diary of Janet's belief "in some sort of life in common" after death, "not as individuals. Some mystic survival" (*D* 5: 76). Lucy Swithen, in *Between the Acts*, embodies this view. And, of course, *Three Guineas* will be Woolf's passionate counter to Julian's unnatural death.

Overall, Woolf exudes her own formidable diary spirit in 1937, despite her roller-coaster dips into terror, her plunges and peaks. She can release at last the flood that is *Three Guineas* and can extend her mind toward other forms: throw her mind, as she says, "2 or 3 miles ahead" (*D* 5: 56). Her new loose-leaf diary is part of this motion; it serves her in the old ways—and in new ways, as well. She poses writing questions in her diary and explores their solutions.[7] She uses this diary skillfully to manage her work. To "ease" herself into correcting her Gibbon article on April 14, she takes "10 minutes rapid writing" in her diary (*D* 5: 79). A week later, she turns to her diary to "uncramp" *after* compressing her BBC talk (*D* 5: 80). The diary helps her to stay fluid.

She also uses her diary for avoidance in 1937, that is, to divert her mind or slow it down. Her July 12 entry opens, "To stop myself from thinking about 3 Gs. I will chatter here" (*D* 5: 102). A week later, she confesses, "I am scribbling to avoid my Congreve: to avoid deciding whether to finish *that* off this last 10 days [of July], or storm the last section of 3 Gs. Cant make up my mind" (*D* 5: 103). In her first entry after Julian's death, August 6, Woolf takes up her diary to begin life again but also "to escape from the thought" of Vanessa, as she does again August 17 (*D* 5: 106).

In 1937, Woolf uses her diary to mark her happiness as well as her terror—her highs as well as her lows. She still finds joy in the country. On a cold, bright Easter morning, as she scribbles in her diary over the Monk's House fire, she looks up and then writes: "As for the beauty, as I always say when I walk the terrace after breakfast, too much for one pair of eyes. Enough to float a whole population in happiness, if only they wd. look."[8] With *The Years'* triumph secured, she quotes Wordsworth in her April 9 entry: "Such happiness wherever it is known is to be pitied for tis surely blind," only to counter: "Yes, but my happiness isn't blind. That is the achievement, I was thinking between 3 & 4 this morning, of my 55 years. I lay awake so calm, so content, as if I'd stepped off the whirling world into a deep blue quiet space, & there open eyed existed, beyond harm; armed against all that can happen" (*D* 5: 78).

But the war and the deaths unsettle the inner "deep blue quiet space." On September 26, Woolf writes, "If Julian had not died—still an incredible sentence to write—our happiness might have been profound. 'Our'—L.'s & mine . . . now that we are floated financially, & perhaps to shift the Press & take a new house, & privately as happy & rounded off as can be—but his death—that extraordinary extinction—drains it of substance" (*D* 5: 111). On October 12, she repeats: "We have the materials for happiness, but no happiness. All this summer, I find myself saying that verse, Lowell's, about those whose coming steps we listen for: the verse about the nephew killed in the war" (*D* 5: 113).

At the end of the year, when Leonard falls ill, Woolf summarizes her rollercoaster year in her final entry and brings her diary to a full-circle close with words on death and work. "Oh this cursed year 1937—it will never let us out of its claws," she begins:

> Now its L.'s kidneys: Rau says he may have a chill, or it may be something wrong with the kidneys; possibly the prostate gland—that perennial horror. . . . And once more my only refuge is work. . . . The great cat is playing with us once more.
>
> How much do I mind death? I wondered last night . . . & concluded that there is a sense in which the end could be accepted calmly. That's odd, considering that few people are more immensely interested by life: & happy. (*D* 5: 121)

But she has felt intimations of a "vacuum," "a vacancy," a "nothingness." She has felt "exposed." And the outer great cat of war will not stop its play.

The Late Diaries of Leo & Countess Tolstoy

A titanic battle—captured in a fleet of diaries—crosses Virginia Woolf's sail in February 1937. *The Final Struggle: Being Countess Tolstoy's Diary for 1910, With Extracts from Leo Tolstoy's Diary of the same period* appeared in English in 1936.

Woolf's diary reveals that she identifies with the anguished Tolstoys—and with their need for their diaries.

Woolf long admired Tolstoy's prose.[9] In 1917, reviewing Tolstoy's early work, *The Cossacks,* she praised his powers of observation and thought; his "extraordinary union of extreme simplicity . . . with the utmost subtlety"; his "profound psychology and superb sincerity" (*E:* 2: 79). A later, December 1917, review posed a question that stayed with her across her days: what is the secret, she asked, of Tolstoy's searing realism?[10]

Woolf knew Tolstoy's work well in 1937, and she also knew his life. She knew of the marital strife that closed with Tolstoy's famous flight and death at a railroad junction in 1910. The Woolfs, perhaps, first heard details from David ("Bunny") Garnett, whose mother, Constance Garnett, translated Tolstoy's work and visited the Tolstoys in Russia. Woolf's early sympathy with each partner can be seen in her December 1917 review of *Rebels and Reformers: Biographies for Young People,* by diarist Arthur Ponsonby and his wife, Dorothea, for she closes her review by contrasting the Tolstoys' worldviews:

> But the struggle still continues; we find the rebel flame burning at its purest in the cry of little Ivan Tolstoy [the Tolstoys' son], who, when his mother told him that Yásnaya was his property, stamped his foot and cried, "Don't say that Yásnaya Polyána is mine! Everything is everyone else's." No less true and persistent is the other cry which comes to us from the mouth of Countess Tolstoy. Her husband, she knows, goes ahead of the crowd, pointing the way. "But I am the crowd [. . .] I live in its current, and see the light of the lamp which every leader, and Leo of course, carries, and I acknowledge it to be the light. But I cannot go faster; I am held by the crowd and by my surroundings and habits." (*E* 2: 197–98)

In 1922, the Hogarth Press published Leonard's and Samuel Koteliansky's translation of the *Autobiography of Countess Sophie Tolstoi*—where she gives her side of the final conflict. The next year, the press published Virginia's translations with Koteliansky of *Tolstoi's Love Letters* and A. B. Goldenweiser's *Talks with Tolstoi.* A Russian composer and pianist, Goldenweiser was one of the diarists taking daily notes in 1910 as the Tolstoy marriage capsized.

In 1926, Woolf even goes to hear a London lecture by another diarist on the scene, one who played a more prominent role in the drama than Goldenweiser: Tatiána, the Tolstoys' oldest daughter. "Countess Tatiána spoke, and I hated us all, for being prosperous and comfortable; and wished to be a working woman, and wished to be able to excuse my life to Tolstoi," Woolf writes to Vita Sackville-West on January 31, 1926. "Not that it was a good lecture. It was quite dull. But seeing his daughter, a shabby little black old woman, a perfect lady, with his little eyes, excited me; and made the whole world inside my head spin round, and the tears come to my eyes—but this is what always happens to me when the disgusting and foetid story of the Tolstois married life is told me and by their daughter too" (L #1617, 3: 236).

Leo Tolstoy started his diary at age eighteen, during his abbreviated university days. In 1854, he pens a diary self-portrait that lays bare both the facts of his life and his habit of self-rebuke. "What am I?" he asks his diary:

> One of four sons of a retired lieutenant-colonel, left orphan at seven years of age in the care of women and strangers,[11] having neither a social nor a scientific education, and becoming my own master at seventeen years of age; without any large fortune, without any social position, and chiefly without principles: a man who has mismanaged his affairs to the last degree, who has spent the best years of his life aimlessly and without pleasure, and who finally banished himself to the Caucasus to escape from his debts and above all from his habits . . . but with enormous self-esteem. (*The Private Diary of Leo Tolstoy, 1853–1857*, 81–82)

He is twenty-five.

In these early notebooks Tolstoy starts the diary habits that persist through his days. Unlike Woolf, he is a (mostly) daily diarist. "[S]o that thoughts that occur to me may not be forgotten, note them down systematically in a book under the following headings: (1) Rules, (2) Information, (3) Observations," he tells his diary in October 1853 (*The Private Diary* 25; hereafter *TPD*). Three months later, he tries a "Franklin-like journal"; that is, a journal of self-perfection, only he reverses Benjamin Franklin by naming the vices to resist rather than the virtues to attain, a subtle (but telling) shift (*TPD* 72). By August 1854, he is telling his diary: "irritability, lack of character, and idleness. The most important thing in life for me is to amend these faults. From to-day onward I will complete my Diary every day with that phrase" (*TPD* 96). He (drearily) does so for a while, beats himself with these flaws. When he lapses from his incantation, he "re-start[s] the Franklin Journal" on May 31, 1855, and adds three more defects to overcome: Thoughtlessness, Vanity, and Disorder (*TPD* 120–21).

Like Woolf, Tolstoy rereads his diaries and, even more than she, draws on them for his published work. (In this respect, he resembles André Gide.)[12] By the end of his life, he has streamlined his lists of "Rules, Information, Observations" to the single "to be noted" in his 1910 diary, followed by a numbered list of his thoughts. His youngest daughter, Sásha, copies these out for his further use.[13] From at least Maxim Gorky's 1920 *Reminiscences* of Tolstoy on, Woolf knew Tolstoy lived in a freer diary climate than her own. He shares his diary from the start: with an 1856 love; with his wife-to-be in 1862; with his children; with Gorky[14] and others equally. This largesse will come back to haunt him in 1910.

Tolstoy's wife, Sófya Andréevna Behrs, launched her own diary at age eleven. However, sadly (like Fanny Burney), she burned her early diaries before her marriage at eighteen to the thirty-four-year-old Tolstoy. Her August 1882 entry sets the stage for the tragedy to come:

> Twenty years ago, happy and young, I began to write this book, the story of my love for Liovochka. There is hardly anything in it except love. And now, twenty years later, I am sitting up alone in the night, reading it and weeping over my love. For the first time in our life, Liovochka left me and went to sleep in his study. We quarreled about a trifle. . . . I pray God for death; it is dreadful to live without his love, and I felt clearly that his love had left me. . . . He is penetrated with Christianity and thoughts of perfection. I am jealous of him . . . (*Leo Tolstoy: Last Diaries* 22, 23)

Those who write of the Tolstoys' final Strindbergian fight-to-the-death always nod to the rift's complexity. However, no one disputes that the pair's incompatibility reached far back and came to the fore in the late 1870s with Tolstoy's religious crisis. He repudiated formal religions and advocated instead a spirit of universal love based on a literal reading of the Sermon on the Mount. This view led him to renounce his title and estates and don the simple dress of the Russian peasants. He became a vegetarian, gave up liquor and tobacco, wrote against war and capital punishment, and, most of all, wished to stop *selling* his works but rather issue them for free. The countess, however, was "held by . . . [her] surroundings and habits," as Woolf wrote in 1917. She had no wish to lose her title or to change her life. She liked being a countess and the wife of Russia's most popular writer. Had she not with her own hand transcribed *War and Peace* (1869) and *Anna Karenina* (1876) for him? No small task that.[15] Furthermore, she had been pregnant sixteen times, had three miscarriages, and raised nine children past infancy. In clinging to Tolstoy's estates, title, and copyrights, she felt she fought for her children's status as well as her own.

The pair's maneuvers, their forays and retreats, up to the final 1910 crisis, can be seen in key dates. In 1883, Tolstoy turns over to the countess full power of attorney to manage his property. He also verbally gives her control of all his writings through 1880. The next year, he tries to leave his birthplace—his estate 120 miles south of Moscow called Yásnaya Polyána (Clear Meadow)—but he returns. Near this time, the countess refuses to copy his work when she disapproves of his *Criticism of Dogmatic Theology* (1885). Their daughters take up the task: Tatiána (until she marries), then Másha (until her death in 1906), and finally Sásha. In 1891, Tolstoy announces to the press that all his work *after* 1880 is free to anyone to publish, and in 1892, he legally transfers his estates to Countess Tolstoy and his nine surviving children. In a March 27, 1895, diary entry, he asks his heirs to renounce copyright to *all* his works, even those before 1880, but he does not demand it. "The fact that my works have been sold these last ten years has been the most painful thing in my life," he tells his diary (*The Final Struggle* 30; hereafter *TFS*). Sergius Leovich, his oldest son, who edits *The Final Struggle*, reports that three copies of this diary entry were made at the time: one for himself as oldest son, one for copyist Másha, and the last for V. G. Chertkóv, Tolstoy's editor and publisher. In 1897, Tolstoy again tries to leave Yásnaya Polyána—and again returns. In 1905, Countess Tolstoy starts her memoirs, drawing on (and quoting from) both her own and Tolstoy's diaries.

The year 1910 opens on this long-standing uneasy truce. Tolstoy is eighty-one; Countess Tolstoy sixty-five. The Day Book the countess keeps shows the vigorous lives they both lead. All the while the final tragedy unfolds, the countess is editing a new (twelfth) edition of Tolstoy's collected works that she plans to sell,[16] penning her own autobiography, sitting for a bust sculpted by her devoted son, Leo Lvóvich, and managing the Yásnaya Polyána estate.[17] Tolstoy, on his part, is revising endlessly his last important work, *The Way of Life*, as well as his *For Every Day* and *A Cycle of Reading: Thoughts of Many Writers on the Truth of Life and Conduct*. In the richest of ironies, he writes an article on insanity.

During the first five months of 1910, Tolstoy hardly mentions his wife in his diary. His mind rests instead on his daily correspondence (with its pleas for his help) and on his spiritual thoughts and works. Like Woolf in March 1937, he regularly takes his spiritual temperature—"I feel well in my soul" a frequent diary phrase (*Last Diaries* 53, 69, 94, 100, 106, 109, 114, 129, 142, 158, 161, 167, 168, hereafter *LD*).

His thoughts also hover on life and death. He often ends a diary entry with the initials "i. I. l." (if I live) and then writes the next day's date. Like Woolf, he often replies to his ending phrase, in his case by beginning the next entry with the word "Alive" (*LD* 55, 56, 57, 82, 83, 85, 86, 88, 89, 97, 103, 108, 118, 121, 129, 133, 135, 140, 144, 146, 150, 162, 167, 168, 175, 178, 188, 209, 218). However, as the year unfolds, he often qualifies that word: "I am alive, but it's hard" (July 15, 1910); "Alive, but in bad shape" (August 1); "Alive, but not entirely" (October 30) amid his flight and eight days before his death.

The inciting action for the tragedy that unfurls is, I believe, the return of Vladimir Chertkóv, Tolstoy's spiritual associate and publisher. Tolstoy likely saw in Chertkóv a younger version of himself. The son of a wealthy family, nobles closely tied to the St. Petersburg court, Chertkóv was a gifted, twenty-six-year-old officer of the guard in 1880 when he resigned his commission and retired to his family estate to better his peasants' lives. His ideals thus rose independently of Tolstoy. Soon after they meet in 1883, however, Chertkóv becomes a devoted Tolstoyan—in fact, the leading Tolstoyan. He founds with Tolstoy The Intermediary, a publishing house that offers edifying and didactic works in cheap editions for the masses, including many by Tolstoy.

Chertkóv's moment of greatest courage comes in 1896. He leads a campaign to support the Doukhobor sect, whose members, practicing Tolstoyan non-violent resistance, refuse to serve in the tsar's army and suffer cruel persecution for their stand. The government exiles Chertkóv for nine years. He settles in England and publishes Tolstoy works forbidden by the Russian censor. Finally, in 1905, he is allowed to return. He builds a home in Telyatinki, some three miles from Yásnaya Polyána; however, the Tsarist government intervenes. It forbids him to live in the same province as Tolstoy. Skirting this ban, in May 1910, Tolstoy manages to meet Chertkóv just over the province border. In June, the government eases its surveillance to allow Chertkóv to stay at his home in Telyatinki while his mother lives there.

A banished Chertkóv was one thing; a Chertkóv on the scene competing for her husband's time (and manuscripts) was both irritant and threat to Countess Tolstoy. Her June 20, 1910, Day Book records the odd moment that starts it all. Forced to be at Yásnaya Polyána to handle her business affairs, she either misreads or willfully disregards Tolstoy's letter from Meshchérskoe, where he is visiting Chertkóv. "Leo Nikoláevich makes no reference to his return," she writes in her Day Book. "I have become unnecessary to him. He puts the Chertkóvs first. I must create *my own* personal life, or my own *personal death*" (*TFS* 99).

In *The Final Struggle*, Sergius Tolstoy appends Tolstoy's full letter. He writes: "We have decided to leave on the 25th. It is good to be on a visit, but better at home" (100n2). So clearly Tolstoy made "reference to his return." However, on June 22 the countess has Varvára Mikháylovna, her own copyist, send this telegram to Tolstoy: "Countess Tolstoy has serious nervous upset, insomnia, tears, pulse hundred, asked me to telegraph. Varia" (*LD* 246n2). Tolstoy responds: "More convenient to come tomorrow afternoon, send telegram, if absolutely necessary shall come tonight" (*LD* 247n1). The words *More convenient* enrage the countess, and she attributes these words to Chertkóv. She replies immediately in her own hand: "Think absolutely necessary," but signs it Varia (*LD* 247n1).

Is her mind unsettled, or is this a test of power? Or both? On this day she starts a second diary—as if her Day Book will not suffice. Through Tolstoy's death in November she will write *two* diaries, the second expanding the shorter Day Book notes. She appears to add this diary to reinforce her anxiety (and jealousy), even to enlarge them—the very thorns that torment her. Here is a diary to *foment* rather than to soothe.

On June 23, as she awaits Tolstoy's return, she introduces thoughts of suicide in a diary entry she titles *Memorandum before death*. She will use suicide as a threat again and again in the coming days—a tack that may have caused Woolf's disgust. "All the methods of suicide passed through my mind, and the best of them all seemed to be to sink beneath the waves of the sea," the countess writes in her *Memorandum*. "I did not like the idea of throwing myself on the rails before a train, though I thought of going to Stolbovóy and lying down there under the train in which Leo Nikoláevich would be traveling *more conveniently*" (*TFS* 103).

The countess' June 25 Day Book entry offers a scene that could serve as tableau for the entire last half of the Tolstoy marriage. With him back under her roof, she writes: "He drove with me to Ovsyánnikovo at my request though contrary to his own wish. . . . Leo Nikoláevich kept trying to get out of the carriage and leave me. I cried. I don't know whether he noticed it, but he did not leave me and we drove up together" (*TFS* 107).

The next day, with him secured, the countess turns her mind to his *diaries*. Her own lengthy diary entries on this day suggest that the power struggle afoot is for more than control of Tolstoy's person, but for control of the historical record, as well. The countess opens her June 26 diary entry as if she addresses history: "Leo Nikoláevich, my husband, has handed over all his diaries from 1900 onwards to V. G. Chertkóv" (*TFS* 108). She hardly needs to tell herself he is her husband:

He began to write in a new note-book while a guest at the Chertkóvs', where he went on June 12th. In that diary, which he has let me read, he says among other things: "I want to resist Sófya Andréevna by kindness and love." Resist! What has he to resist, when I love him so much and so ardently, and when my one thought and care is that things should be well with him? But he feels he must represent himself to Chertkóv and to future generations who will read his diaries as an unhappy and magnanimous man struggling against some kind of imaginary evil....

My children, and you people who worship Leo Nikoláevich! Know all of you that he *killed* me, has killed me spiritually and will kill me physically. (*TFS* 108–09, 111)

However, in a further entry that evening, the death will be *his*. The countess recreates the day's scene for her diary: "When I first asked Leo Nikoláevich where his diaries from 1900 onwards were, he replied quickly that he had them. But when I asked him to show them to me, he hesitated, and confessed that they were at Chertkóv's.... I need them as material for my own memoirs.... It is all a conspiracy against me. It has been going on for a long time, and will only end with the death of the unfortunate old man..." (*TFS* 113).

Like the lost handkerchief in *Othello*, Tolstoy's diaries become a totem for the countess: a visible symbol of her lost love. She calls his diaries "the holy of holies of my husband's soul" (*TFS* 152n2). Yet in this real-life tragedy, it is as if Othello would demand the lost handkerchief be returned not to Desdemona but to himself, to do with as he pleased: guard it, alter it, or even destroy it. In a letter to Chertkóv on July 1, the countess exclaims: "give me back Leo Nikoláevich's diaries! It is his *thoughts* that are dear to you, and not the paper on which they are written! Give the diaries back to me to copy—I am ready to copy them all out for you myself. But give me back the actual *note-books* in the handwriting that is so dear to me! You know that all his former note-books are in my keeping, and I have constantly used them for my work. Why do you deprive me of the pleasure of reading them over?" (*TFS* 378).

The next day, she tells her diary:

As for the stolen diaries, I obtained a note from Chertkóv pledging himself to return them to Leo Nikoláevich when his work on them is finished, which he will make haste to do. And Leo Nikoláevich has verbally promised to pass them on to me....

But I know that all these pledges and promises are only a deception....

Chertkóv knows very well that Leo Nikoláevich has not long to live, and he will keep on dragging out and delaying the work he has devised on the diaries, and will not hand them over to anyone.

This is the true story of my grief during the last years of my life. I will now write up my diary every day. (*TFS* 125–26)

The countess turns the three weeks from Tolstoy's June 23 return into a new showdown, but now for his diaries. On July 13, she tells her diary: "Leo Nikoláevich rode on horseback with Sukhotín [Tatiána's husband] and Goldenweiser. I searched for his last diary but did not find it. He knows that I had devised a way of getting it and reading it, and has hidden it somewhere. But I shall find it—if it is not with Chertkóv, Sásha, or the doctor. Where can he have hidden it from me? We are like two silent and cunning enemies, spying on and suspecting one another!" (*TFS* 149). That evening, she notes again in the diary written to the world:

> Let it be granted that I am deranged, and that I have an *idée fixe* that Leo Nikoláevich should get back his diaries from Chertkóv and not let them remain in his hands....
>
> What is necessary for everyone to be happy again and to do away with all my sufferings?
>
> *To take from Chertkóv the diaries—those few black leather-cloth notebooks—and to put them back on the table, letting him have one at a time to take extracts. That is all!*
>
> If my cowardice passes, and I finally decide on suicide, what a simple request this will appear to everybody to have been.... They will explain my death by everything on earth except the real reason—by hysteria, nervousness, or innate badness—and no one *will dare*, when looking at the corpse killed by my husband, to say that I could have been *saved* in so simple a way, by their *returning to my husband's writing table four or five leather-cloth note-books*. (*TFS* 150)

On July 14, Tolstoy follows his usual tack. He compromises once more. He writes a letter to the countess listing five points:

1. I will not give my present private diary to anyone. I will keep it myself.
2. I will take back from Chertkóv the diaries of previous years, and will keep them myself, probably in the bank.
3. If you are anxious lest certain pages in my diaries, written under a mo-

mentary impression and where our conflicts and disagreements are mentioned, should be made use of by future biographers ill-disposed towards you, I want first of all to point out that such expressions of transitory feelings, in my diaries or in your own, can certainly not give a correct idea of our true relations. But if you fear it, I will gladly take an opportunity of mentioning in my diary, or simply in a letter, how I understand and appreciate your life. . . .

4. If my relations with Chertkóv now distress you I am ready to give up seeing him, though I must remark that I should find this trying. . . .

5. If you do not accept these conditions of mine for a peaceful and kindly life, I shall take back my promise not to leave you and shall go away. But I shall certainly not go to Chertkóv. I will even make it an absolute condition that he should not come to live near me. But I shall certainly go away, for to go on living as we are now doing is impossible.[18]

The frenzy that surrounds the diaries' transfer shows the distrust poisoning the air. Tolstoy's private secretary, V. F. Bulgákov, also kept a diary and offers a vivid record of the day. Tolstoy sends his daughter Sásha to Telyátinki

> to fetch back the diaries, and she stayed there a very long time. As I afterwards learnt from Varvára Mikháylovna [the countess' copyist], Chertkóv's most intimate friends had a sudden reunion. . . . And they all set to work in great haste to extract and copy out passages in the diaries which compromised Sófya Andréevna, and which she might suppress.[19] Then the diaries were wrapped up. . . .
>
> And at Yásnaya Polyána they were awaited with equal agitation and impatience by Sófya Andréevna.
>
> Goldenweiser relates how [Sásha] tried to hide her arrival with the diaries from Sófya Andréevna. . . . She intended to seal them up and hide them in a cupboard, but suddenly Sófya Andréevna ran in, seized the diaries, and began to turn over the pages and read them. [Tatiána] stopped her and reminded her that she had promised not to read them. . . . Sófya Andréevna checked the dates and the number of the diaries, which were afterwards wrapped in paper, sealed, and put away in a locked cupboard. Next day Mikhaíl Sergéevich put them in the bank at Túla in Leo Nikoláevich's name. (*TFS* 156–57n1)

As *Othello* so poignantly reveals, doubt (and jealousy) once ignited can rarely be quelled. "But my soul has grown sore, and still grieves about something," the countess tells her Day Book this "happy day" she wrests the diaries from Chertkóv (*TFS* 156). She cannot relinquish her wish to control. Varia, her copyist, also kept a diary and preserved this unnerving July 15 scene. Tolstoy goes to the countess' room to try to calm her and comes out:

> greatly upset, and said: "I can't! I can't! This [the diaries] is my last sacrifice." Sófya Andréevna fell on her knees in the corridor before Leo Nikoláevich's bedroom and seized hold of his legs and screamed: "This is my last request! Give me the key [to the bank lockbox] and let me have an authorization to take the diaries. I don't believe that you won't return them to Chertkóv." "Get up. Please get up! For God's sake stop this and leave me alone!" cried Leo Nikoláevich in a trembling voice. Sófya Andréevna jumped up, ran to her room, and then cried out: "I have drunk the whole phial. I have poisoned myself!" Leo Nikoláevich rushed to her, but she said in a calm voice: "I said that on purpose to deceive you. I didn't drink it." (*TFS* 158n3)

The doctors are "called in," she tells her July 19 entry. The second doctor, a neuropathologist, recommends that the couple separate to ease the torment. Tatiána invites Tolstoy to her estate. "The Vorónka [River] is very low—like my life—and at present it would be difficult to drown in it," the countess tells her diary. "I went there chiefly to try whether it is at all possible to sink in the water" (*TFS* 170). She suspects Tolstoy keeps secrets from her, intuition, in fact, correct. The diary clash spurs him to work in secret on a final will. In it, he gives the rights to *all* his work to his youngest daughter, Sásha, who shares his philosophy, with an accompanying note placing the editing and first publication in the hands of Chertkóv, who is to open publication for general use.

Getting wind of this will, the countess tells her July 24 diary: "We shall see which of us conquers if he begins war on me! My weapon is death. That will be my revenge, and the shame will be his and Chertkóv's, who have killed me. They will say *she was mad*. But who drove me mad?" (*TFS* 178). In a letter that night, she writes that "[t]he doctors advised me to go away" (*TFS* 185). However, she refuses. She follows Tolstoy to Tatiána's estate.

Four days later, Tolstoy starts his *own* second diary. "I no longer have a diary that is frank and simple," he tells his diary on July 28, a hint at two roles his diary serves. "I must start one for myself alone" (*TFS* 192). From the next day on, like his wife, he now keeps *two* diaries: his long-standing diary for Sásha to copy and for others to read and his new, entirely private, "Diary for Myself Alone" (as he writes at its start).

The countess, however, remains fixed on his diary as totem. If she cannot control his love, she can at least hold and control his diaries. In a cruel and desperate move on August 3, she uses his November 29, 1851, diary entry to try to convince him that his regard for Chertkóv reveals his lifelong homosexuality. "Yesterday I proposed to Leo Nikoláevich that if he wanted to understand my jealousy of Chertkóv he should read his old diary of 1851 concerning his love for men. He became terribly angry at this, and cried 'Go away!' and ran up and down the room like a wild beast" (*TFS* 201).

The countess cannot tear her mind from Tolstoy's diaries—as if they hold the answer to her grief. She opens her August 16 diary entry: "Is happiness and joy of life possible when Leo Nikoláevich, and Sásha at his instruction, constantly and intensively hide something from me in Leo Nikoláevich's diaries; and I just as intensively and cunningly try to find and read what is hidden from me, and what is told to Chertkóv about me—and through him to the whole world? I did not sleep all night, my heart overflowed, and I devised all possible means to read what Leo Nikoláevich so painstakingly hides from me" (*TFS* 227–28). The next day, in a reprise of the opening June gambit, she presses Tolstoy to name the day he will leave Tatiána's estate and return to Yásnaya Polyána, but he resists. "But I won't go away on any account," she tells her diary. "I will throw everything up and let it all be lost. Who will master whom?" (*TFS* 231).

The next day, she learns of the government's new decree that Chertkóv can live at Telyátinki without restriction. To quiet her anguish, Tolstoy confirms his promises to her: "(1) Not to see Chertkóv at all. (2) Not to give his diaries to anyone, and (3) Not to let either Chertkóv or Tapsel take photographs of him" (*TFS* 234). Once more the countess has expanded her demands. Those who view her 1910 acts as bold moves to shape the Tolstoy story find support in her press at this time to increase the number of images of herself with Tolstoy and to eliminate photos of Chertkóv.

The countess returns to Yásnaya Polyána ten days before her husband, and in his absence, she rearranges his study. She moves two large photographs he had hung over his writing table: one of himself with Sásha; the other of Chertkóv. She moves the first photo to his bedroom; Chertkóv's image she hides behind a curtain. In their places she hangs a photo of Tolstoy's father and one of herself. Tolstoy returns for their wedding anniversary, September 23, and on this day the countess preserves a poignant scene that seems another emblematic tableau: "I wanted to go to my husband, but on opening the door I heard him dictating something to Bulgákov, so I went out to wander about in Yásnaya Polyána, recalling the happy times (not very many) of my forty-eight years of married life. Afterwards I asked Leo Nikoláevich to let us be photographed together. He agreed, but the photograph came out badly" (*TFS* 278).[20]

Three days later, passing Tolstoy's study again, the countess sees he has restored the vanquished photos. Her diary takes up the tale:

> Not seeing [Chertkóv] himself, he could not part with his portrait! I took it down, tore it into little bits, and threw them into the earth-closet. Of course Leo Nikoláevich was angry, justly reproaching me with depriving him of freedom (he is quite mad on that subject now) which he had never troubled himself about or thought of before. What does he want *freedom* for, when we have loved one another all our lives and have tried to make everything pleasant and joyful for one another? Again I was seized by a mad despair, again a most bitter jealousy of Chertkóv arose within me, and again I wept to exhaustion and gave myself a headache. I thought of suicide.... I went to my room, got out a toy pistol and started practising, thinking to procure a real pistol later on. When Leo Nikoláevitch had returned from his ride I fired another couple of shots, but he did not hear them. (*TFS* 284)

He heard them, but he ignored them.

Tolstoy's "Diary for Myself Alone" becomes the sacrifice he, in the end, cannot make. In late August, he begins to lock up in a portfolio his "Diary for Myself Alone." The countess, in turn, must stalk it. "He has procured a key now to lock up his diary," she tells her diary on August 21 (*TFS* 237). Five days later, she repeats: "Leo Nikoláevich ... carefully locks his diary away from me, but the diary is at home and it may fall into my hands all the same" (*TFS* 245). On October 3, Tolstoy suffers five convulsions. Countess Tolstoy gives herself to his care; however, Bulgákov, Tolstoy's secretary, makes this diary note:

> But things did not pass off without a regrettable incident. Despite her agitation Sófya Andréevna managed to take from Leo Nikoláevich's writing-table a portfolio containing papers, and to hide it. The children noticed this....
> ... At night, taking advantage of the fact that her husband had fallen asleep and all the others had dispersed, Sófya Andréevna took from her

little cupboard ... the small portfolio she had abstracted from Leo Nikoláevich's study, and carried it to her own room. Tatiána Lvóvna met her.

"Why have you taken that portfolio, Mamma?"

"So that Chertkóv shouldn't have it."

But she gave up the portfolio on Tatiána Lvóvna's demand. (*TFS* 296–97n)

Sergius includes his own note: "When we had undressed my father and put him in bed, my sister Tatiána ... handed me the small diary which she found in his blouse pocket for me to return it to him next day. Next morning my father awoke after a deep sleep, recognized Sásha and asked her where his little diary was. She replied: 'Sergéy has it,' and called me. I gave him the diary and said: 'I have not read it.' I was glad to hear him reply: 'It would have been all right if you had.' It was a continuation of his 'Diary for Myself Alone.'" (*TFS* 297–98n)

On October 12, the countess confronts Tolstoy with her knowledge of his will. She tells her Day Book: "Decided to-day to tell Leo Nikoláevich that I know of his will, made with Chertkóv, leaving his rights as author for the benefit of the public, and that that is a bad action. He was silent all the time" (*TFS* 310). To her diary, she adds:

> I told him that what he was doing was not right, that he was preparing evil and discord, and that our children would not yield up their rights without a struggle....
>
> I am hurrying to get out the edition before Leo Nikoláevich takes any extreme step, which may be expected of him in his present uncompromising mood....
>
> In the evening I showed Leo Nikoláevich his diary of 1862 (which I copied out long ago). It was written when he fell in love with me and proposed. He seemed to be surprised by it, and afterwards remarked: "How distressing!" But I have retained one consolation—my past![21] (*TFS* 311, 312)

On October 16, the countess tells her diary, "I could not sleep, and thought continually of how to rescue Leo Nikoláevich's diaries from the State Bank in Túla" (*TFS* 322). The next day the same, and on October 19:

> Yesterday evening I was much disturbed by the disappearance of Leo Nikoláevich's diary from the table where it always lies in a locked portfolio. And when Leo Nikoláevich woke up at night I went to his room

and asked whether he had given the diary to Chertkóv. "Sásha has it," he said, and I was somewhat pacified, though it offends me that she should have it and not I. Sásha copies *thoughts* out of the diary, evidently for that hateful Chertkóv who cannot have clean and good thoughts *of his own*. (*TFS* 329)

On October 25, Tolstoy tells his Diary for Myself Alone: "Always the same oppression. Suspicion and spying, and on my side a sinful wish that she should give me occasion to go away. How weak I am! I think about going away. Then I think of her position and am sorry for her and cannot" (*TFS* 339). The "occasion" (the climax) falls on October 28—and, not surprisingly, turns on his diary. The night before, the countess asks Tolstoy to leave his study doors open. He wakes up and, through a crack in his bedroom door, sees her comb through his papers. She leaves, and he decides to flee. He summons his doctor and Sásha, and the two men leave before dawn. He tells his diary:

> Both day and night my every word and movement must be known to her and under her control. . . .
> I could lie there no longer, and suddenly took the final decision to go away. . . . At last we took our places in the railway carriage and started, and my fear passed off and pity for her rose in my heart—but no doubt that I had done what I had to do. Perhaps I am mistaken and am merely justifying my action, but it seems to me that I have saved myself—not Leo Nikoláevich but that something of which there is sometimes a spark in me. (*TFS* 347)

The next morning, the countess reads part of Tolstoy's note to her, telling her not to seek him, and then throws herself into the pond—only to be rescued by Sásha, Bulgákov, and another. She writes Tolstoy on October 29 the only letter he receives from her before his death, on November 7. In it she cries out: "Lëvochka, my dear one, my darling, return home! Save me from a second suicide, Lëvochka, my life-long friend. I will do everything, everything that you wish! I will cast aside all luxury, your friends shall be mine, I will undergo a cure, and will be mild, tender, and kind. . . . We will simplify everything amicably, we will go away wherever you like and live as you like" (*TFS* 394).

Her next day's letter continues to supplicate and explain. "Is it possible that one stupid gesture of mine will destroy my whole life? You told Sásha to say that my having rummaged suspiciously among your papers was the last straw that caused you to leave home.... I really don't know what made me go into your study and touch your diary to convince myself that it was in its place. I used to do that always but had never done so recently" (*TFS* 395). Her last letter, November 2, illuminates her psychology: "Every day I made up my mind to say to you that I wanted you to see Chertkóv, but somehow I always felt ashamed to *allow* you anything" (*TFS* 398).

The sad last year of the Tolstoy's long marriage is one of the most fully documented marriage years extant. That almost every player kept at least one diary allows those on the outside to view the tragedy almost like a film, shifting from one viewpoint to another. Along with Tolstoy's private secretary, Countess Tolstoy's copyist, and the pianist Goldenweiser, Tatiána and Sásha also kept diaries, as did Tolstoy's doctor. *The Final Struggle* can hardly be surpassed as a richly layered text.

His mother dead in 1919, Sergius Tolstoy seeks an objective stance in his twenty-three-page preface to his parents' 1910 diaries. At the end, however, he hints at his motive for bringing forth the diaries. "After Sófya Andréevna's death Chertkóv published a book, *The Last Days of Tolstóy* (London, 1922), which is a one-sided diatribe against her," Sergius notes. "The appendix in which he says that he does not condemn her is not at all convincing, for the whole book is a continuous condemnation of her. I hope that the publication of the Diaries of my father and mother, together with the commentaries, will be sufficient to show the erroneousness of V. G. Chertkóv's judgments" (45).

English translator Aylmer Maude then trumps Sergius with his own thirteen-page introduction before the preface. Here Maude weighs in with his own views as both Tolstoy biographer and translator. The countess often distorted facts and was "mentally-unbalanced," Maude asserts, while Chertkóv, too, posed many difficulties, being "domineering, quarrelsome, and vindictive" (20, 19). Maude correctly notes an irony of the whole battle royale: that the countess' drive to hold the diaries actually played into Chertkóv's hand, for it helped convince Tolstoy he needed legally to deed his writing away from her control. And despite her son's hope that the diary record will counter Chertkóv's harsh condemnations, for many readers *The Final Struggle* shows the countess falling victim to the very fate she feared: that her husband would appear magnanimous and oppressed and she the tormented tormentor.[22]

Had she been a better student of the early Tolstoy diaries she held, Countess Tolstoy might have seen his final spiritual journey presaged early on. Like diarist Stephen MacKenna, Tolstoy recorded his calling in his diary. At age twenty-six, he tells an 1855 entry: "Yesterday a conversation about Divinity and Faith suggested to me a great, a stupendous, idea to the realisation of which I feel capable of devoting my life. That idea is the founding of a new religion corresponding to the present development of mankind: the religion of Christ but purged of dogmas and mysticism—a practical religion, not promising future bliss but giving bliss on earth.... *Deliberately* to contribute to the union of man by religion, is the basic thought which I hope will dominate me" (*TPD* 114). Surely Tolstoy, too, bears some blame for the prolonged marital misery through his half measures and indecision.

Anna Karenina's opening words float over the Tolstoys' 1910 diaries: "All happy families are alike; every unhappy family is unhappy in its own way." *The Final Struggle* can be read as a tragedy of a marriage gone wrong; as a case study in jealousy; as a power struggle pure and simple over substantial assets;[23] and as a fight to control the Tolstoy narrative (and legacy). Virginia Woolf could identify with many aspects of Tolstoy's life. Like him, she was fiercely observant and impressionable. He anticipated, furthermore, some of her own intellectual moves. He embraced the cooperative movement before she did, and his antiwar views must have engaged her in 1937 as she worked on her own *Three Guineas*. He wrote, Maude explains, of "the patriotic hynotization of the nations" (*TFS* 16). In *Three Guineas,* she will call national patriotism one of the "unreal loyalties" (78, 113). His diaries, like hers, also show his ongoing war with ego.

However, Woolf likely saw herself in the embattled countess too: an older woman penning her memoirs, struggling with nerves and doctors and charges of insanity. In February 1937—as in her 1917 review—Woolf takes no side in the Tolstoy conflict. Instead, she views the Tolstoys through her own nervous days. "Why should I write here?" she opens her diary on February 12. "Only that I am devilishly anxious. L[eonard]. is going to a Harley St specialist at 4 today to get a report: whether the sugar means diabetes or prostate gland or nothing serious. And I must face facts: how to keep cool, how to control myself, if it is a bad report" (*D* 5: 54). She then shifts to her fears for Julian Bell bent on war and ends her entry: "I feel like the man who had to keep dancing on hot bricks. Cant let myself stop. Hence I suppose I write here; wh. explains why Tolstoy & his wife kept diaries" (*D* 5: 55). Eighteen days later, she uses the same figure for her recurring terror: "And I know that I must go on doing this dance on hot bricks till I die" (*D* 5: 63).

The Tolstoys kept their diaries for many reasons—as did Virginia Woolf.

Tolstoy used his diary as a tool in his ceaseless drive for philosophical insight and self-perfection. He used it to take his spiritual temperature; as a repository for rules, information, and observations; as the chalice that brewed his scorching realism from something "simple and fresh." In the end, he felt it held the "spark" of his genius: "not Leo Nikoláevich but that something of which there is sometimes a spark in me."

The countess used her *Day Book* to record her days and her second diary to reinforce, even amplify, her fears and to share her suffering with the world. In a February 14, 1937, letter to diarist Eddy Sackville-West, Woolf regresses before the towering Tolstoys to the refrain of her first diary at age fourteen. "I'm reading the Countess Tolstoy's diaries, and his diaries, and both their public diaries and their private: and wonder what the diary instinct is—since it caused them both infinite anguish," she writes to Eddy. "But how the Russians always triumph over us when they take up the pen! No room for more" (*L* #3218, 6: 107). Her own diary, as we have seen, helps her soothe her (now) growing anguish as well: her dance on hot bricks.

8

Hitler Darkens the Waters

By 1938, Hitler "had taken over and was dictating the narrative of European history," Natania Rosenfeld notes (122). Virginia Woolf's books—including her diary—offer a counter narrative. In March, Hitler moves on Austria as Woolf finishes *Three Guineas*. Through her acute sensitivity, she captures in a haunting diary image the precise world state: Hitler and Stalin are "like drops of dirty water mixing" (*D* 5: 129). Her challenge, from 1938 onward, becomes how to keep *moving*—how to escape being drawn into the mud.

When longtime friend Lady Ottoline Morrell dies in April, Woolf imbues her *Times* tribute to this art patron with the attributes she seeks herself: "It was that inner freedom, that artist's vision, that led her past the decorated drawing-room with all its trappings to the actual workshop where the painter had his canvas, and the writer his manuscript." But Woolf also adds that, at the end, when deafness grew and Lady Ottoline "was often ill," she "made no more efforts to gather the many coloured reins into her own hands; to drive her team with reckless courage through a world that, she felt, was destroying all she cherished" (*E* 6: 126).

In May, Woolf watches her niece, Angelica Bell, dance to scenes based on Goya's *Disasters of War*. In August, while the world waits, suspended, as Hitler pauses at Czechoslovakia's door, she takes heart from the newly found diary of the Reverend Francis Kilvert, the Victorian vicar (and poet) from the Welsh river Wye. His diary's "gipsy beauty" lives again in the character Mrs. Manresa in Woolf's final novel, *Between the Acts*—as do his amusing cows. Kilvert offers Woolf a lush natural human voice amid the welter of war.

Virginia Woolf's 1938 Diary

> "The only doubt is whether what we say reaches [Hitler's] own much cumbered long ears. (I'm thinking of Roger [Fry] not Hitler—how I bless Roger, & wish I could tell him so, for giving me himself to think of—what a help he remains—in this welter of unreality.)"
>
> (September 10, 1938; D 5: 167)

Diary covers matter to Virginia Woolf. "I chose a gay cover to counteract what I suspected—," she tells her December 11, 1938, entry, looking back to the diary's start (*D* 5: 191). As with her previous 1937 diary, she has covered a staid black, two-ring loose-leaf notebook with a floral print: now teal flowers and diamonds patterned on a beige background.[1] Despite this handsome nature cloak, tensions cut through this diary. War and *Three Guineas* seem locked in a race. When lull follows delay on the European stage, Woolf tries to "keep moving" (*D* 5: 139). She returns to first sources across the year; she gathers her props and pushes for freedom.

She launches her 1938 diary with both affirmation and curse: "Yes, I will force myself to begin this cursed year" (*D* 5: 125). These words echo her first diary entry after Julian Bell's death in July 1937: "Well but one must make a beginning" (*D* 5: 104). Clearly, she rereads at least her *last* diary entry of 1937 before starting the new diary book, for that last entry opens "Oh this cursed year 1937—it will never let us out of its claws" (*D* 5: 121). She thus links her 1937 and 1938 diary books—but her years now are cursed. "How am I to describe 'anxiety'?" she asks herself on January 9 in this first 1938 entry (*D* 5: 125).

Remove the outer storms—Leonard's troubling illness, Julian's death, and the rising guns of war—and Woolf's own ship rides high. *The Years* brings continued unprecedented wealth. On January 5, 1938, Woolf acknowledges receipt of $5,160 from Harcourt Brace for the American edition of *The Years,* followed by another $1,000 in April; in March comes a further £4,000 (*L* #3347, 6: 202; *D* 5: 138, 130). They plan a library for Monk's House "in spite of Hitler" (*D* 5: 130).

Woolf can also tell her March 12 entry that "our last Leonard & Virginia [Hogarth Press] season is perhaps our most brilliant" (*D* 5: 130). Beyond *The Years*, they have published Vita Sackville-West's *Pepita*, and Christopher Isherwood, and more. This success leads them—finally—to ease their press load. On February 23, they sell Virginia's half of the Hogarth Press to John Lehmann for £3,000. Lehmann becomes Leonard's partner and manager; *he* will direct their seven clerks. "[B]ut now we have a partner I dont intend to be fixed in London any more," Woolf crows to Ethel Smyth in October, highlighting the *movement* and freedom she seeks (*L* #3456, 6: 289).

New editions of her *Common Reader* and *To the Lighthouse* appear in 1938, and editors by turns annoy her and amuse her in their press for her work. Even age—that former bogey—now bears no sting. "L. says we are old," Woolf tells her June diary as they journey to Skye. "I say we are middle aged" (*D* 5: 149). Creation flows; it does not cease. "[F]ree for fresh adventures—at the age of 56," she exalts to her April 12 entry as she reads her *Three Guineas* proof. "Last night I began making up again: Summers night: a complete whole: that's my idea" (*D* 5: 133).

Two weeks later, the further setting of her final novel, *Between the Acts* (first called Poyntzet Hall, later Poyntz Hall), unfurls. "[H]ere am I sketching out a new book," she marvels to her diary on April 26, but then uses her diary to bargain with her muse: "only dont please impose that huge burden on me again, I implore. Let it be random & tentative; something I can blow of a morning, to relieve myself of Roger: dont, I implore, lay down a scheme; call in all the cosmic immensities; & force my tired & diffident brain to embrace another whole—all parts contributing—not yet awhile" (*D* 5: 135). This "random" book to relieve her mornings sounds a bit like her *diary*. "But to amuse myself, let me note," she continues: "why not Poyntzet Hall: a centre: all lit[erature]. discussed in connection with real little incongruous living humour; & anything that comes into my head . . . a rambling capricious but somehow unified whole—the present state of my mind?" (*D* 5: 135). Again this last sounds like her 1919 *diary* credo.

The novel lifts her across the year. "I've written quietly at Poyntz Hall," she remarks, pleased, to her diary on the June day *Three Guineas* appears. "And now I can be off again, as indeed I long to be," she adds, invoking the "off again" Sibyl Colefax/George Meredith resurrection refrain (*D* 5: 148). Poyntz Hall lets Woolf "frisk" and "gallop" in 1938 and serves as her turn-and-turn-about counter to her (now plodding, but vital) biography of Roger Fry, as well as to the threatening war. "I'm taking a gallop in fiction, after bringing Roger to his marriage," she writes in her August 4 entry (*D* 5: 159). At the end of August, "strung into a ball with Roger—got him, very stiffly to the verge of America," Woolf tells her diary, "I shall take a dive into fiction; then compose the [Roger] chapter" (*D* 5: 164). In the diary's final entry, she sums up rather fully the remarkable Pointz Hall: "I've written too 120 pages of Pointz Hall. . . . I rush to it for relief after a long pressure of Fry facts. . . . To be written for pleasure" (*D* 5: 193).

Three Guineas burst forth not for pleasure but from compulsion. Like a deep, seething volcano it erupted, magma to clear away (and transform) tyranny, injustice, and war. This work, and the looming war, dominate Woolf's 1938 diary. More than half her entries—fifty-one of eighty-eight—refer directly to *Three Guineas* and its reception. The book is the "spine" that holds Woolf erect after Julian's death in war (as she notes in a March 1938 entry). Earlier, in her first entry, January 9, she confesses that she "battened... down" her anxiety with her *Three Guineas* work (*D* 5: 125). On February 1, she shows the book to Leonard. She thinks it may have more practical worth than her novels. On February 3, she "spurt[s]" to Judith Stephen ideas for a new women's society at Newnham College. "This is putting flesh & blood on the ideas in 3 Gs," she tells her diary (*D* 5: 127). Four days later, as she walks over the downs, she thinks of launching an illustrated sheet called The Outsider—further application of the work (*D* 5: 128).

Her March 12 entry that opens "Hitler has invaded Austria: that is at 10 last night his army crossed the frontier, unresisted" leads to her declaration that *Three Guineas* "remains, morally, a spine: the thing I wished to say, though futile" (*D* 5: 129, 130). Ten days later, the outer war and Woolf's inner (artistic) struggle again conjoin: "The public world very notably invaded the private at MH. [Monk's House] last week end. Almost war: almost expected to hear it announced. And England, as they say, humiliated. And the man in uniform exalted. Suicides" (*D* 5: 131). Yet she ends with hope: a bookseller finds the *Three Guineas* proofs "exciting."

As with her last (1937) diary, Woolf summons her diary to float her through her publication straits. She writes eighty-eight diary entries in the 345 days from January 9 through December 19, 1938, an entry, on average, every three or four days rather than every four or five, as in 1937—a sign of increasing need.[2] However, save for one day's break, she writes entries each day from May 24 through 31 before *Three Guineas*' June 2 debut. Greeted with great praise, angry blame (particularly from Q. D. Leavis in *Scrutiny*), and unconscionable silence from many of her male Bloomsbury friends, *Three Guineas* is understood today as "not only powerful proof of a political Woolf, but [as] material for... feminist reconstructions of culture" (Low 92). As Erin G. Carlston explains, Woolf sought "to mobilize a revolutionary—though certainly rational and free-willed—subject who will understand that the fight against tyranny demands a radical transformation of the world, *including* the individual and the private sphere" (154–55). At the end of the year, Woolf tells her diary that a "suspended judgment upon that work then seems fittest."[3]

In truth, the world seems suspended. Hitler, Mussolini, and Stalin darken the 1938 waters, cloud the mind. As Hitler invades Austria, Woolf tells her March 12 entry that his *trespass* combines with the Russian *spy* trials "like drops of dirty water mixing" (*D* 5: 129). In September, when Hitler pauses to time his pounce on Czechoslovakia and the start of World War II, Woolf turns again to her diary to help her navigate. She writes fourteen diary entries in September, the most of any month that year, and she turns to questions to light the way. She asks 156 questions across her 88 diary entries, but now only 67 on writing and 26 (one-sixth) on the coming war. "What would war mean?" she asks her September 5 entry. "Darkness, strain: I suppose conceivably death" (*D* 5: 166). She writes on September 10 of this "welter of unreality," a *welter* a wallow or toss in the mud or high seas (*D* 5: 167).

Again the outer war and the inner artistic war join. "Headachy, partly screw of Roger: partly this gloom [of pending war]," she confesses on September 14. "And whats the private position? So black I cant gather together. . . . So we're committed, for the rest of our lives, to public misery. This will be slashed with private too. . . . But all wallows & wavers in complete chaos. . . . All slipping consciously into a pit" (*D* 5: 170).

As she did with the abdication crisis in 1936, Woolf turns herself into a reporter in September 1938 to capture the shifting currents of thought. Does she do this to balance herself? Or for her memoirs? "The public fluctuates," she tells her diary on September 22: "Chamberlain flying today to Gotesberg (?). A strong opposition has risen. Eden, Churchill & the L[abour]P[arty] all denounce serving C.S.[Czechoslovakia] on the altar & bidding it commit suicide. CS. very dignified & tragic. . . . The prospect of another glissade after a minor stop into abyss. All Europe in Hitler's keeping. What'll he gobble next? Thats the summary of us in Sussex" (*D* 5: 173).

She notes the vast mobilization and evacuation plans that spring up as Britain readies the gas masks and sandbags and moves its children from the towns. And when September 30 comes:

> terms are being made at Munich. . . . it means peace. That was the upshot of the stop press in The Times this morning. They are agreeing to let some Germans into [Czechoslovakia] today: then English Italian & French are to enter & guarantee: then a 3 months pause. Three months in which to settle the question, instead of bombs on London & Paris today! . . . Such a reversal was never known: save that there was always a huger nightmare unreality that clouded all distinct feeling.

> ... It would have meant our last 15 years of life spent in battling for a thread of liberty; keeping the Press going among the deaths of the young. (*D* 5: 176, 177)

The year becomes, in short, an "Oh dear" ordeal. Woolf's exclamation of heartfelt woe sounds four times in this diary, more than in any other diary book. "Sunday evening alone with Nessa: oh dear—That signifies my desperation," is a typical entry: "Julian not there, I mean. The wound bleeding; & nothing to be said. So I will buy a chair this wet day, in order to keep moving" (*D* 5: 139).

Besides moving forward, Woolf also turns to the past, to first sources, for support. She thinks back to her mentor, Sir Walter Scott. "I'm in a dazed state," she tells her diary on April 29, "hovering between 2 worlds like a spiders web with nothing to attach the string to. Why not write about Scott's diaries, so bring in the immortal novels?" (*D* 5: 138). That was her own early path: Scott's diaries and then *her* novels. She seems to prime her *own* work here (as well as to recall Scott's).

"Off we can go to Scotland for a holiday that I dont really need," she tells her diary on June 11, yet adds, "but still a freshener before Roger wont come amiss" (*D* 5: 149). She visits Scott's tomb at Dryburgh Abbey and finds it apt yet imperiled. "[T]here's something fitting in it," she notes. "For the Abbey is impressive and the river running at the bottom of the field, and all the old Scots ruins standing round him. . . . An airy place but Scott is much pressed together. . . . there's Haig's [tomb] stuck about with dark red poppies" (*D* 5: 152). Field-Marshal Earl Haig, commander-in-chief of the British Expeditionary Force in World War I, served as president of the British Legion. It sold red poppies as remembrance of war. War thus encroaches even upon Scott, but Woolf will read John Buchan's biography, *Walter Scott*, when she returns.

If she recalls her diary father in 1938 and picks a flower at his tomb, she rallies herself with her diary mother, Fanny Burney, through her "frisk" and "gallop" on Pointz Hall. She even nods to Pepys three times across the year, the last rather ominously: "Mr Perkins brought gas masks about 10.30. & so at last we went to bed" (*D* 5: 175). As the world darkens, Woolf looks to the lodestars of her early diary years—including her own early diaries. On August 17, she tries to preserve an "amazing" sunset and, as with her Warboys diary at age seventeen, she feels unsatisfied (*D* 5: 161).

She even resurrects from that Warboys diary her vital "churning paddle-wheel" trope. Late in 1938, her churning brain will save her from the mud once more. "But I open this, to note, at the foot of the last pessimistic page . . . the fact that pessimism can be routed by getting into the flow: creative writing," she writes on November 25. "A passage in ["The Art of Biography"] came right. After an incredible empty churning & grinding. Cold tears standing behind my eyes. It came right & I'm floated" (*D* 5: 189). Her next entry opens: "More brain churning to add a passage to L[appin] & L[apinova]. & all my courage needed" (*D* 5: 189).

Earlier, in August, as tanks with gun carriages cross her downs, she turns to *other* diaries—to new "lives." She reads the diary of Francis Kilvert, the Victorian Vicar of Bredwardine, and then Lady Frederick Cavendish's diaries edited by John Bailey, whose own diaries she knew. In September, she returns to Wilfrid Scawen Blunt's diary to pluck his scorn for the French Impressionists for use in *Roger Fry*. Following the Munich accord, Harold Nicolson allows the Woolfs to read his diaries to glimpse the behind-the-scenes fray. "This was very interesting," Woolf writes to Vanessa on October 3. "They had all been convinced that war was inevitable. The cabinet had tried to control Chamb[erlain]—the younger members that is. They were certain he was going to sell us" (*L* #3449, 6: 279). Nicolson's diary likely reinforced Woolf's sense of a diary's use for memoirs. She affirms this goal in her August 17 entry in one of her characteristic multiquestion probes. She forgets whether she preserved her niece, Angelica, acting at Pulborough, "so casual am I in what I say or dont say: & have half a mind one of these days to explain what my intention is in writing these continual diaries. Not publication. Revision? a memoir of my own life? Perhaps."[4]

Woolf turns to both old diarists and new as the war clouds form. Like André Gide, she clings to her diary in the face of death; however, unlike Gide, she clings to *other* diaries, too. She turns also to Roger Fry, that vital force, that model for her diary's "Old Virginia." Fry's life (and art) become, in 1938, Woolf's retort to war—after her first, more direct, thrust in *Three Guineas*. For Fry, too, was a battler. She wrote to him of his 1931 retrospective show: "What . . . moved me to deep admiration was the perpetual adventure of your mind. . . . How you have managed to carry on this warfare, always striding ahead, never giving up or lying down and becoming inert and torpid and commonplace like other people" (*L* #2331, 4: 295).

In her diary, we can track the Fry biography with ease. Fry means life to Woolf across this year: her answer to death and war. In her August 17 entry, Woolf records the death of an old woman who lived at Mount Misery, a woman who drowns herself in the River Ouse:

> The body was found near Piddinghoe—my usual walk. . . . She used to moon over the downs with a dog. Once she came to the shop late on Sunday to beg 2d of paraffin—she was alone in the dark. They threatened to turn her out—farm wanted. She had killed her dog. So at last off she goes, on Monday perhaps when the tide was high in the afternoon, & jumps in. Louie says her brother found a drowned woman the other day at Barcombe Mills—a horrid sight. So I order dinner hastily & come out here to brew more Roger. (*D* 5: 161–62)

Roger here will counter death. Her September 5 entry opens, "Its odd to be sitting here, looking up little facts about Roger & the M[etropolitan] M[useum]. in New York . . . when it may be the 3rd Aug 1914"—that is, the day before war (*D* 5: 166). "I dont feel that the crisis is real—" she opens her next entry, September 10, "not so real as Roger in 1910 at Gordon Square, about which I've just been writing" (*D* 5: 167).

On September 14, she declares, "If it is war, then every country joins in: chaos. To oppose this with Roger my only private position. Well thats an absurd little match to strike" (*D* 5: 170). Nevertheless it is light—and life preserved and renewed. Her dreams reveal the interior struggle that wages between outer death and inner artistic life. "Dreamt of Julian one night: how he came back: I implored him not to go to Spain. He promised. Then I saw his wounds," she tells her September 17 entry, but then adds: "Dreamt of Roger last night. How he had not died. I praised Cezanne. And told him how I admired his writing. Exactly the old relationship" (*D* 5: 172). Her dreams (and diary) lay bare her wish: Julian alive, though wounded; Fry alive, their old relationship restored—Fry as a vibrant model. That day Woolf writes revealingly to Ethel Smyth that she is "chained to my RF, who is, in himself, magnificent" (*L* #3443, 6: 272).

With war imminent on September 28, Woolf takes herself to the National Gallery, "being warned by a sober loud speaker to get my gas mask as I walked down Pall Mall." She looks at Renoirs and Cezannes and tries "to see through Roger's eyes: tried to get some solidity into my mind" (*D* 5: 174–75). In her diary's final entry, she can boast of taking Fry's life to 1919—that is, through World War I. As Hitler's "savage howl" sounds, as he dirties the waters, Woolf whispers in parentheses in her September 10 entry: "[H]ow I bless Roger, & wish I could tell him so, for giving me himself to think of—what a help he remains—in this welter of unreality" (*D* 5: 169, 167).

The *Diary* of the Reverend Francis Kilvert

Mystery and heartbreak haunt the diary of the Reverend Francis Kilvert, the kindly poet/vicar on the River Wye. "I've been enjoying Kilvert greatly," Virginia Woolf writes to William Plomer, her friend and Hogarth Press author, on August 18, 1938 (*L* #3433, 6: 266). Plomer edited what came to be three volumes of *Kilvert's Diary* published in 1938, 1939, and 1940.

Kilvert lived only to age thirty-eight and died in 1879. In 1937, Plomer came across twenty-two old notebooks "variously shaped and bound.... closely written in a sloping, angular hand" (1: 9). With two maddening gaps and a third at the end, the notebooks render Kilvert's life from January 1870 to March 13, 1879—six months before his death. Plomer found the diaries "so interesting" that he skimmed "the cream" from the first eight notebooks and published it in 1938 as a trial offering (1: 9). This first volume delivers, he explains, roughly one-third of Kilvert's diary, from January 1, 1870, to August 19, 1871.

Kilvert becomes Woolf's fourth country parson diarist.[5] At first glance he most recalls mild, food-loving Parson Woodforde, who lived a century before him. Like Woodforde, Kilvert studies at Oxford University; he is ordained a priest in 1864 at age twenty-three. Like Woodforde, he returns to his home (in his case, near Chippenham in Wiltshire) to serve as curate to his father, the rector of Langley Burrell. Again like Woodforde, he shows no itch for professional rise—although for nobler cause: Kilvert wants to aid his aging parents. Furthermore, he seems loath to tamper with Providence's plan. Fortunately, after two years as his father's curate, he accepts the curacy in Clyro, which brings him to Wales and the Wye Valley—terrain he comes to love. He stays there for seven years, during the period of volume 1 of his published *Diary*, but then returns to aid his dear, but increasingly deaf, father at Langley Burrell in 1872.

Kilvert's humility manifests itself in 1875 when the Bishop of St. David's invites him to become rector of St. Harmon's back in Wales. "I hope I have not acted selfishly in leaving [my father]," Kilvert tells his June 1875 diary. "I have not sought this or any other preferment. Indeed I have rather shrunk from it. And as it has so come to me without my wish or seeking of my own it seems as if the Finger of God were in it and as if I were but following the calling of His Voice and the beckoning, guiding and leading of His Hand" (3: 327–28). He moves to St. Harmon's and after a year is promoted to Vicar of Bredwardine, back near Clyro, the Wye River, and the Black Mountains he adores. There his days end—just as love smiles.

Kilvert's mind often burned with love. It rarely dwelled on philosophy, and it absolutely recoiled from theological dispute—again like Parson Woodforde. Virginia Woolf also read volume 2 of *Kilvert's Diary*, which came out in 1939. He complains there that he and friends "sat up till 1 o'clock disputing about the Athanasian Creed, Bonley taking the High Church ground and Westhorp and I the liberal view. Of course we left off exactly where we began, and no one was convinced. I hate arguing" (2: 186). Kilvert prefers daffodils to dogma. He likes the poor and hates the "Swansea snobs." "In the afternoon I had the happiness to have all the poor people to myself," he tells his March 1872 diary. "None of the grand people were at Church by reason of the snow. So of course I could speak much better and more freely" (2: 157).

He spoke in dulcet tones, if we can believe his father. In March 1876, his father tells him that as he was preaching "there came back upon my ear an echo of the tones of the sweetest human voice I ever heard, the voice of John Henry Newman. No voice but yours ever reminded me of him" (3: 244). The voice came from a tall, dark-skinned, round-faced young man who insisted, despite his barber's counsel, on wearing a square-cut beard.

Kilvert's eyes, though, remain the mystery—both his gift and his curse—and may explain his life. In a September 1871 entry, he speaks of his "poor disfigured eyes" (2: 37). Were they scarred? Misshaped? Crossed? Mutilated? Plomer wonders in his introduction to volume 1 whether this defect "sharpened his powers of vision, for such is often the case" (1: 13). Whatever the outer flaw, Kilvert possessed the keenest eye for the visible world, a Wordsworthian eye—Dorothy's as well as William's. *Kilvert's Diary* swims in sensory prose. Drawn to natural beauty of every sort, he would fall in love with faces—often of the children he taught—and so often lost his heart.

Kilvert teaches children in the parish school and plays with them on his pastoral calls. At his Clyro school his eyes are ravished by "Gipsy Lizzie," a shy beauty, but he also visits his "dear little lover" Mary Tavener, the deaf and half dumb child. "When I opened the door of the poor old crazy cottage . . . the girl uttered a passionate inarticulate cry of joy and running to me she flung her arms round my neck and covered me with kisses," he writes in June 1875. "Well. I have lived and I have been loved, and no one can take this from me" (3: 197). He yearns for children of his own to love. On a July 1875 holiday to the Isle of Wight, he preserves this scene:

> The tide was going out, a number of children were paddling in the shallow water left by the white retreating surges, and it was a fair sight to watch

the merry girls with their pretty white feet and bare limbs wading through the little rippling waves or walking on the wet and shining sand. Oh, as I watched them there came over me such a longing.... Oh that I too had a child to love and to love me, a daughter with such fair limbs and blue eyes archly dancing, and bright clustering curls blown wild and golden in the sunshine and sea air. It came over me like a storm and I turned away hungry at heart and half envying the parents as they sat upon the sand watching their children at play. (3: 206)

He is thirty-four and a bachelor but (like Woolf) can picture it all.

What his eye could see, his heart could love. *Kilvert's Diary* tantalizes from start to end with mysteries of one lost love after another. In November 1870, Kilvert records his long confidential talk with kind Mrs. Venables, his vicar's wife in Wales. "She said she hoped to see me some day with a number of children about me, my own children," he confides. "Never, I said, adding I did not believe that I should ever marry. Then came out by degrees my attachment to C. She was very much surprised when she guessed the right name after trying Mary Bevan, Fanny Higginson, Flora Ross, Lily Thomas. 'She'll never marry,' she said gravely. 'I know it,' I said" (1: 263). We are as surprised as Mrs. Venables—and who is mysterious C?

Ten months later, Daisy Thomas replaces the unobtainable C. "Perhaps this may be a memorable day in my life," Kilvert tells his September 8, 1871, entry (2: 27). "To-day I fell in love" (2: 29). Unlike Parson Woodforde, who promises "bold strokes" but then falters, Kilvert takes prompt and bold steps to win his love. On September 11, he seeks Mrs. Venables' counsel, and two days later he asks Daisy's father for her hand. How unworldly he seems for a thirty-year-old—even in 1871 Wales. Mr. Thomas, he records, said "a great many complimentary things about my 'honourable high-minded conduct,' asked what my prospects were and shook his head over them. He could not allow an engagement under the circumstances, he said, and I must not destroy his daughter's peace of mind by speaking to her or showing her in any way that I was attached to her" (2: 32). Daisy is nineteen. But Kilvert quotes Shakespeare on the course of true love and declares that "[w]hat has happened only makes me long for her more and cling more closely to her, and feel more determined to win her. On this day when I proposed for the girl who will I trust one day be my wife I had only one sovereign in the world, and I owed that" (2: 33). The next day he writes his father "to tell him of my attachment and ask what my prospects were as far as he knew" (2: 34). Both his parents write him "very kind letters" September 17 stating that "if they had inherited their natural share of the Worcester money they might have retired from Langley in my favour, but now that is impossible. They cannot afford it" (2: 35–36).

Jane Austen redux. Kilvert needs a living. The next day, good Vicar Venables promises to write the Bishop to request the needed post. Kilvert, in turn, wonders what Daisy thinks of his "poor disfigured eyes, whether she loves me better or worse for that. She must know. She must see. Yet it does not seem to make any difference against me with her. Perhaps she is sorry for me. And they say pity is akin to love" (2: 37). But all is lost five days later when Mr. Thomas writes to Kilvert, "bidding me give up all thoughts and hopes of Daisy. It was a great and sudden blow and I felt very sad" (2: 43). Six months later, Mrs. Venables urges him to speak to Daisy's father once more before he leaves Clyro to resume the curacy at Langley Burrell. "But my position is no better now than it was 6 months ago and I cannot humiliate myself before him again for nothing," Kilvert wisely tells his diary (2: 176).

But Daisy stays in his heart. Two years later, when he visits his old parish, he asks his March 1874 diary: "My poor, poor Daisy. When we parted the tears came into her eyes. She turned her face away. I saw the anguish of her soul. What could I do?" (2: 430). In July, he confesses that he thinks continually of Daisy and recalls her in the romantic—even erotic—terms that characterize his prose: "I see even now her beautiful white bosom heaving under the lace edging of her dress, and the loose open sleeve falling back from her round white arm as she leaned her flushed cheek upon her hand looking anxiously at me as I coughed.... Sweet loving Daisy, sweet loving patient faithful Daisy" (3: 48).

However, patient Daisy is not to be. In fact, a month later Kilvert reprises himself when he serves as groomsman at a wedding. "This may be one of the happiest and most important days in my life, for to-day I fell in love at first sight with sweet Kathleen Mavourneen," he tells his August 1874 diary (3: 63). Again he moves swiftly. After the wedding, he writes the bride, his friend Adelaide, "telling her of my love for Kathleen" (3: 68). But Kathleen, too, eludes him. As they correspond and the months unfold, she seems his spiritual superior. "Her sweet pure thoughts came to me at a time when I sorely needed them and they have done me much good," he tells an October 1874 entry. "But they show me only still more clearly what I have often felt before, how much nobler and holier her thoughts are than mine, and how much higher she has climbed up the hill than I have done. Yet I am trying to follow, and I thank God that I ever knew her and (I hope I may say) won her friendship" (3: 94). As the bells ring in 1875, Kilvert both thanks and supplicates his God: "He gave me a friend and a true, true love, and the New Year, please God, shall *not* take her away" (3: 131).

But Kathleen Mavourneen, the "sweetest noblest kindest bravest-hearted girl in England," never comes near (3: 66). Is it his eye? Is it his still dismal prospects as his father's curate, for Kilvert still lacks a living of his own? He is the least material of men. Welsh Daisy denied; English Kathleen afar and above, he falls in love in September 1875 with Ettie Meredith Brown, "a true gipsy beauty" (3: 229). Here the first diary gap occurs: a six-month gulf. Every sign points to Kilvert's most overt physical moves. When his diary resumes in March 1876, we find that Ettie has made him a "beautiful sermon-case" and he has sent her a poem commemorating "The Ridge." However, now he recalls "the happy days of last summer before all our trouble came and our separation," for Ettie now is "far away beneath the pines that sigh beside the southern sea" (3: 238, 243–44). Three days later, he recalls "[a]ll the Bournemouth memories of last December . . . and those wild sad sweet trysts in the snow and under the pine trees, among the sand hills on the East Cliffe and in Boscombe Chine" (3: 246). In April, Kilvert sends Ettie a long letter and a manuscript book of his poems. That evening, she sends him "two such sad sweet little verses, beginning 'When shall we meet again'" (3: 256).

But they never meet again. Soon after, Kilvert receives "a long sad sweet loving letter from my darling Ettie, a tender beautiful letter of farewell, the last she will ever be able to write to me" (3: 260). Enclosed is a "kind friendly little note" from Ettie's mother saying "she is afraid Ettie and I must hold no further communication by letter or poetry or any other way. . . . She says she knows I care for Ettie too much to wish to cause her needless unhappiness. It is true" (3: 260).

In June 1876, Kilvert finally takes the St. Harmon's living that will bring him between £300 and £400 a year. However, in January 1878 he tells his diary that he is "glad to hear that Ettie Meredith Brown is to be married . . . to Mr. Wright, the brother of her brother-in-law" (3: 361). In September, he learns his "gipsy beauty" will sail for India on October 5 to be married there (3: 423). Was it his face? His fortune? What stands in the way?

A mystery of another kind looms in *Kilvert's Diary* volume 3. The diarist, now thirty-seven, lies ill in his Bredwardine vicarage in January 1878 when he hears his "gipsy" Ettie will wed. In April 1878, he again reports: "Indoors all day with a bad cough, having caught cold yesterday. I feel the air too keen amongst the mountains" (3: 389).

In June, his friend Palmer offers him (via Canon Walsham How) a new position as permanent chaplain at Cannes. "He thought it might perhaps be desirable to accept it on account of my health," Kilvert tells his diary (3: 397). Once more he moves swiftly. He writes his father, Mr. Venables (his surrogate father), and Canon How regarding the post. The next day he calls on a Miss Cornewall who just returned from Cannes to ask about the place. "She said she thought the Chaplaincy must be a very delightful position," he tells his diary (3: 398). When Dr. Giles makes a house call to one of Kilvert's servants, Kilvert asks his doctor "if I ought to go to Cannes on account of my health" (3: 398). Dr. Giles says, "Go by all means. It is the very place. It may prolong your life for some years" (3: 398). Two days later, Kilvert records: "Corresponding and thinking with some perplexity about the offer of the Cannes Chaplaincy" (3: 398). Frustratingly, he writes but one sentence more on Cannes in the published *Diary*. One week after the offer, and having recorded only sensible happy urgings, Kilvert tells his June 27, 1878, entry: "Wrote to Palmer and Walsham How to decline the Cannes Chaplaincy" (3: 399). Fourteen months later, he is dead.

Why does he decline Cannes without even the visit he gave to St. Harmon's before he took that post? What did his father say? And Mr. Venables? What swayed him from his doctor's counsel and the kind care of those about him? Virginia Woolf loved such mysteries. Vacant diary space invited her mind. Editor Plomer, on his part, deeply regrets Kilvert's refusal, "for the South of France might have given him a new lease of life and us a wonderful extension of the Diary" (3: 9). Perhaps by now Kilvert loved the Wye Valley too much ever to depart. Perhaps he could not bear to leave his parents and nearby sisters. In any case, he travels at least as far as Paris after saying no to warm climes in June, and there he meets the diary's final mystery: his wife.

We read nothing of Elizabeth Anne Roland, for Kilvert's diary stops abruptly on March 13, 1879. They marry August 20, 1879, in Oxfordshire, return to Bredwardine, and just over a month later Kilvert suffers peritonitis and dies. His diary notebooks pass to his wife. Plomer believes she "did away" with "those parts she thought too intimate," removed the pages (or destroyed whole notebooks) that recorded, perhaps too frankly, the six-month "gipsy Ettie" affair (1: 6). However, why does the second and longer gap occur, the almost eighteen-month gap between Kilvert's June 27, 1876, visit to Canterbury and December

31, 1877, when the diary resumes? We lose here Kilvert's whole tenure at St. Harmon's. Did he fall in love again? Kilvert's overly discreet wife seems also to have removed the last six months of his diary and, with it, all reference to herself.

She needn't have bothered to shield him. Despite his insatiable eye for female beauty young and old, Kilvert's truest love may have been poetry. In 1870, the first year of his published diary, he has one hundred cards printed with his poem "Honest Work" to give out to his friends and neighbors. He wants to write songs "which shall be sung by the girls of Hay and Glasbury, and at village concerts and about the hills" (1: 135). He reveres Robert Burns, the Scottish poet, and yearns to be a similar poet-troubador. He collects Wiltshire and Welsh folklore, old stories, songs, and sayings that enliven his diary and show his deeper side, one akin to Parson Skinner's and the Reverend Cole's antiquary pursuits.

Kilvert becomes a local poet who celebrates place but also mourns in verse the deaths of children. In 1876, Mr. Hill tells him that "[t]he girls have got your poetry which came out in the *Hereford Times*. 'The Rocks of Aberedw' and 'Clyro Water.' . . . The rhymes all come in so beautiful" (3: 279). Kilvert longs to be more than a local poet and troubadour, but like Parson Skinner before him, he meets both family and public chill. On May 1, 1874, he walks the terrace with his father, telling him of the poet William Barnes "and discussing with him the advisability of publishing a book of my own poems. I wish to do so. He rather discourages the idea" (2: 444). Ignoring his father's caution, in March 1878 he writes to the publisher C. T. Longman "to ask him if and on what terms he would publish a small book of poems for me" (3: 380). Four days later, he receives a letter from Longman, "very courteous but not encouraging the idea of my publishing a book of poems" (3: 380).

So he must self-publish for his friends and loved ones and be content with the *Hereford Times*. In truth, as Plomer hints, his real gift was for the prose poetry of his diary. There he tosses off at random sonorous sentences like this: "We came back down Monnington Walk and under the solemn and melancholy soughing of the firs that sounded like the surges of the sea" (3: 164). Such lines spurred some reviewers to link Kilvert to Gerard Manley Hopkins.

As the war drums sound, Virginia Woolf greatly enjoys at least the first two volumes of *Kilvert's Diary*. And why wouldn't she? He evokes her childhood. Kilvert is devoted to his brother, Edward (as Woolf is to her sister, Vanessa). In July 1870, he holidays in Cornwall, resurrects it with his lush language, and anticipates the sentiments Woolf pens in her own haunting 1905 Cornwall diary. Kilvert first visits the Vicar of St. Ives, who tells him that the smell of fish about

Godrevy "is sometimes so terrific as to stop the church clock" (1: 189). Five days later, he records a regatta and prepares for "the grand expedition" to Land's End the next day (1: 192, 193). Three days later at Gurnard's Head, he "wandered round the cliffs to the broken rocks at the furthest point of the Head, and sat alone . . . listening to the booming and breaking of the waves below" (1: 200).

The day before his August 6 departure, "crossing the moor we caught sight of the top of Godrevy Lighthouse . . . and heard the roaring of the sea" (1: 204). In his last Cornwall entry, he declares:

> All the bright memories and names of the places (now so dear) together visited crowding up. The wild restless longing, the hopeless yearning, the gnawing hunger of regret. . . . I seemed to see again the buried church, the ancient British church in Gwythian Sands, the white lighthouse, the spray on the rocks, the heaving bay . . . and the name kept on coming up, Godrevy, Godrevy. With a mournful cadence, Godrevy, farewell. Unknown till yesterday. But now how dear, a possession for ever, a memory for ever. And now a thing of the past, drifting hourly further away. (1: 207–08)

This sensitive diarist, with his keen eyes and strong visual imagination, adores Cornwall but recoils from sportsmen's cruelty—and from the brutalities of war. In May 1871, when his hosts invite him to watch a hunt, he confesses later to his diary:

> I went but I did not like it and soon came away. Most of them were shooting with rifles. Trevellyn shot the best. He is a capital shot. He shot a rabbit with his beautiful little rook-rifle like a long saloon pistol. The old rooks were all scared away, sailing round at an immense height in the blue sky, and it was pitiable to see the young rooks bewildered, wheeling and fluttering helplessly from tree to tree, and perching, only to be tumbled bleeding with a dull thud into the deep nettle beds below, by the ceaseless and relentless crack crack of the beautiful cruel little rifles, or to see them stagger after the shot, hold on as long as possible and then, weak from loss of blood, stumble from their perch, and flutter down, catching at every bough, and perhaps run along the ground terrified and bewildered, in the agonies of a broken wing. It may not be cruel, but I don't think I could ever be a sportsman. It seemed dreadful to bring death and misery into such a sunny lovely scene, among the helpless innocent unsuspecting birds, when everything else was glad and rejoicing, merely for the sake of sport. (1: 335)

Ernest Hemingway could not register a hunt better.

The rooks' slaughter Kilvert saw with his own sharp eyes. With his mind's eye, he saw again the 1873 Indian mutiny recounted by his friend Gough:

> He landed at Calcutta and his regiment marched through Cawnpore 48 hours after the Massacre. He said the scene was horrible, so horrible, shocking and disgusting that it could not be explained or described. Women's breasts had been chopped and sliced off and were still lying about with their other parts which had been cut out.... A child's head had been cut off and was lying on the ground with the lips placed by a devilish jest as if sucking the breast of a woman which had also been chopped off. Numbers of the poor women had jumped down the great well with their children to avoid the horrors which were being perpetrated on the bodies of women all over the place.... The scene of shameful horror was indescribable. Gough saw 500 mutineers executed at once, the rank and file shot by musketry, the ringleaders blown from guns.... Those who were blown from guns were tied with their arms fastened tightly to the wheels and their chests pressing against the muzzles of the cannon. A small square piece of wood was hung round their necks and came between the chest of the men and the muzzle of the gun. At the discharge the man was blown all to fragments but his arms remained tied to the wheels of the gun. (2: 310–11)

Kilvert escapes both war and hunt for most of his days—and even London, too. "How delicious to get into the country again, the sweet damp air and the scent of the beanfields," he tells a May 1872 entry. "I do loathe London. I walked up by Cocklebury through the cool fresh damp lane, green and fragrant."[6] Like diarist Dorothy Wordsworth before him and Woolf soon to come, Kilvert battened on country rambles. Melancholy like Woolf, he too preferred lonely, untraversed ground. "I like wandering about these lonely, waste and ruined places," he writes of Wales in 1871. "There dwells among them a spirit of quiet and gentle melancholy more congenial and akin to my own spirit than full life and gaiety and noise" (1: 307). Despite his love of children and the poor, he tells his April 1870 diary that he has "a peculiar dislike to meeting people, and a peculiar liking for a deserted road" (1: 83). In 1872, when he travels third class "out of politeness" with another rector, although he has paid for a second-class ticket, he writes that he "had much rather have gone alone for I hate talking while travelling by railway" (2: 188–89). He wants his undisturbed gaze.

Kilvert is a sojourner, like Woolf. At age thirty-one he makes up a family motto: Peregrinamus. "It hath a solemn, lovely, melancholy sound," he tells an October 1872 entry. "'We are pilgrims,' it saith. 'We are on pilgrimage.' . . . 'We are strangers.' 'We are foreigners.' 'We are sojourners.' Only sojourners for a little while" (2: 280).

Kilvert's country days may shield him from war, if not from rook slaughter, but, like Woolf's other country parsons, he cannot escape suicide. In March 1871, he must attend an inquest "on the body of the barmaid of the Blue Boar who a day or two ago went out at night . . . up the Wye to Glasbury and threw herself into the river. . . . She was enceinte" (1: 50). Three months later, a woman cannot bear to come to Clyro church "because her sister who committed suicide . . . by drowning herself in the Wye below Boatside is buried opposite the Church door" (1: 156). The next March, Anne Phillips "ran down from Clyro Court, threw herself into the river and was drowned" (1: 308), and in October, Kilvert hears the "tragic story" of Mary Meredith. Mary goes with Bill Price, who gets her with child, but her brother, John, will not give her her own money from the bank so Bill will marry her. "Moreover he and his father were very angry with Mary for being with child and disgracing them. Whereupon poor Mary seeing no hope of marriage became melancholy mad. . . . The woman . . . ran down to the river as hard as she could go and plunged headlong in" (2: 46–48).

Despite such sober scenes, the first volume of *Kilvert's Diary* was "very warmly welcomed," Plomer notes in his 1939 introduction to volume 2 (9). The second volume offers the cream of the next eight notebooks, August 23, 1871, to May 13, 1874. That Woolf read this second volume can be inferred from several letters. "And what about Kilvert? Vol. 3?" she writes to Plomer on December 28, 1939 (*L* #3576: 6: 377). And nine months later, "But I want Kilvert," she writes him on September 15, 1940. She writes here of Kilvert as she does of Roger Fry: "I take the unfashionable view that Kilvert . . . [is] more real than war. Why do people think whats unpleasant is therefore real?" (*L* #3645, 6: 432).

Kilvert's Diary struck a chord with readers. Volume 3 appeared in late 1940.[7] A one-volume abridged version of the whole came out in 1944 and was reprinted in 1947, 1950, and 1956. In 1960, Plomer brought out a "new and corrected" edition of the original three volumes, with a few small factual changes and a new preface. Looking back, he suggested that the *Diary*'s appearance "in troubled times" caused it to be "cherished by many readers who found it an escape-route from public alarms and private anxieties into a world already lost but still within living memory" (1: 5). "Perhaps more than any other writer," Plomer declared, "Kilvert can give us the illusion of participating in English country life in the eighteen-seventies" (1: 5).

Woolf, I think, would have challenged Plomer's view of *Kilvert's Diary* as "illusion" and "escape." Kilvert and his diary were real; Hitler, the unreality. Kilvert endures, and his diaries (like Dorothy Wordsworth's) also brace. In his 1940 introduction to volume 3, Plomer reported that fond reviewers compared Kilvert's prose to that of Hopkins, Marcel Proust, D. H. Lawrence, and diarists Samuel Pepys and Henri-Frédéric Amiel (13). In truth, *Kilvert's Diary* skews so far from ambitious Pepys, that quintessential diarist of the metropolis, that we can only connect them through the fine words Plomer offers in 1960 regarding the difficulty of the diary form: that it calls for "a special blend of honesty and appetite for life which gives the power to record everyday happenings while magically freeing them from banality and triviality" (1: 5).

Reviewers who saw in *Kilvert's Diary* a kinship with Dorothy Wordsworth's journals came closest to the mark. Kilvert himself felt affinity with the Wordsworths. His Welsh borderlands harbored Wordsworth haunts. Wordsworth and Burns were Kilvert's lodestars. He pens his own poem "Tintern Abbey" after his 1875 pilgrimage there. Nevertheless, he speaks more of Dorothy Wordsworth in the published *Diary* than of her brother. In March 1871, Kilvert receives an invitation to meet Miss Hutchinson, William's niece and Dorothy's god-daughter. Kilvert turns himself into Boswell to record her talk:

> Miss Hutchinson said that once, when she was staying at the Wordsworths', the poet was much affected by reading in the newspaper the death of Hogg the Ettrick Shepherd. Half an hour afterwards he came into the room where the ladies were sitting and asked Miss Hutchinson to write down some lines which he had just composed. She did so, and these lines were the beautiful poem called the Graves of the Poets. He was very desultory and disinclined to write. His ladies were always urging him to do so however. And he would have written little if it had not been for his wife and sister. He could not bear the act of writing and he wrote so impatiently and impetuously that his writing was rarely legible. (1: 318)

In July 1871, Kilvert receives from Miss Hutchinson "a relic very precious to me, a little poem of her aunt Dorothy Wordsworth in her own handwriting" (1: 377). Has this poem survived? For his thirty-fourth birthday in 1875, Kilvert's mother gives him Dorothy's *Recollections of a Tour Made in Scotland*, her diary of her 1803 travel with her brother and Coleridge to pay tribute to Burns and Scott. Although more romantic than Dorothy's astringent journals, Kilvert's diaries mirror some of her journals' traits. Like Dorothy, Kilvert loved to ramble and to use his eyes. His diary is remarkably shorn of ego, a fact that might have impressed Virginia Woolf in 1938 and 1939. "He was certainly not a man wrapped up in himself," Plomer stresses in his introduction to volume 1 (11). "His great virtue," Humphrey House observed, "is the power of conveying the physical quality of everything he describes" (2: 11).

Kilvert's June 1876 diary record of Canterbury Cathedral eerily echoes Dorothy Wordsworth's own Scottish diary words at Castle Rose—words that describe Woolf's modernist prose. In 1803 Dorothy wrote that they "stood some minutes watching the swallows that flew about restlessly, and flung their shadows upon the sunbright walls of the old building; the shadows glanced and twinkled, interchanged and crossed each other, expanded and shrunk up, appeared and disappeared every instant; as I observed to William and Coleridge, seeming more like living things than the birds themselves" (Knight 1: 164). Kilvert writes: "I watched the jackdaws disturbed from their usually quiet haunts and sailing round and round the central tower at a great height in the cloudless sky, and I marked their shadows upon the grey rich sunny Tower, how they crossed and recrossed, shrunk and grew, disappeared and appeared again, flitting softly and silently to and fro like the dim ghosts of birds who had inhabited that same tower centuries before" (3: 339). Kilvert also shows Dorothy's ear for village talk.

Kilvert twice records the Wordsworth family view that Dorothy's walks caused her decline (1: 234, 319). He himself marvels in an April 1871 entry that when Dorothy "was middle aged and growing elderly she thought nothing of walking from Brinsop into Hereford, six miles and back, if she wanted a thimble" (1: 319). Kilvert's final diary entry pays homage to Dorothy Wordsworth. He himself now walks to Brinsop on March 13, 1879:

> We met a fine old lady walking with a tall staff as high as her shoulder. . . . A fine sunset gleam lit up the grand old manor house. . . . On the lawn grew the cedar planted by William Wordsworth the poet. Young Mr. Edwards . . . was carpentering in the greenhouse. He courteously took us into a noble sitting room . . . nicely furnished with a fine painting of the poet over the chimney-piece. And here dear Dorothy Wordsworth spent much of her time. (3: 456)

In 1939, Plomer called *Kilvert's Diary* "a minor classic" (2: 11). In 1960, he placed Kilvert among the best of English diarists (1: 5). Kilvert wrote a (mostly) daily diary, penning it in the mornings or at night—whenever he found time—and like Woolf, he reread his diaries. He kept his diary for one of the reasons Woolf kept hers: to mark the wondrous world. "In the afternoon as I was sitting under the shade of the acacia on the lawn enjoying the still warm sunshine of the holy autumn day it was a positive luxury to be alive," he tells his September 1873 diary (2: 375). Fourteen months later, he asks a question Woolf will ask of *her* 1938 and 1939 diaries: "Why do I keep this voluminous journal?" He answers: "I can hardly tell. Partly because life appears to me such a curious and wonderful thing that it almost seems a pity that even such a humble and uneventful life as mine should pass altogether away without some such record as this, and partly too because I think the record may amuse and interest some who come after me" (3: 107).

Plomer declares in both 1939 and 1960 that he brought forth the most vivid parts of Kilvert's diary. He says, in fact, in 1939 that "[o]ur picture of Kilvert, his life and times, will . . . be [with volume 3] as complete as it can possibly be made without printing the Diary in its entirety, an enterprise that is perhaps unlikely ever to be undertaken" (2: 12). But by 1960, he found that a Kilvert Society had sprung up, with Hereford as its hub. The Welsh border region Kilvert loved now often was called "Kilvert country." In 1976, a John Betjeman documentary on Kilvert, *Vicar of This Parish*, was broadcast on BBC television, and in 1989, Richard Maber and Angela Tregoning brought out *Kilvert's Cornish Diary*, an illustrated book offering a fuller version of the 1870 Cornwall journal.

Plomer admits in his 1940 introduction to volume 3 that the "necessary abbreviation" of this last volume "has prevented a just impression . . . of [Kilvert's] constant devotion to parochial duties" (8). Anthony Powell, in his 1989 *Times Literary Supplement* review of the new *Kilvert's Cornish Diary*, notes that "the additions and corrections presented . . . were well worth making and give an idea of Plomer's limitations" (716). Powell calls Plomer's editing "at times arch and rather condescending" (716). He laments Plomer's suppressions of Kilvert's puns: "Plomer (as befitted a young man looked well on by Bloomsbury) removed these" (716).

Fortunately, selections different from Plomer's were published in 1960 under the title *Journal of a Country Curate: Selections from the Diary of Francis Kilvert*, and in 1992 with the title *Kilvert, the Victorian: A New Selection from Kilvert's Diaries*. Stark proof of the fragility of diaries arises in the sad fate of the original diaries. Relatives destroyed almost all the original twenty-two diary books—only three survive—and Plomer's own transcription was destroyed in the Blitz, a tragic illustration of art lost to war.

Kilvert's diary, despite this sad fate, possesses the accruing grace of diaries. As we hear yappingales call in the dingle, or the winter ice crack loud on the river, or see the Wye Valley "blotted out in a drive of white rain" (1: 47), characters slowly emerge. We see kindly Mrs. Venables put her feet up on the grate to settle in for a bit of gossip; and Kilvert's deaf but noble father; and John Morgan, Clyro's old Peninsular veteran; and Priscilla Price, who remembers Queen Caroline and King George IV. Kilvert mails his first postcards in October 1870 ("A happy invention") and describes the new lawn tennis and the first fireworks seen in Clyro (1: 236; 2: 203).

Kilvert does not overrate himself and so allows us to see him in most endearing scenes. In September 1871, for instance, when he preaches on the Good Samaritan extempore at Bettws, "A red cow with a foolish white face came up to the window by the desk and stared in while I was preaching" (2: 26). A month later at Newchurch, he finds himself in more distress as he preaches "the old harvest sermon on Ruth and Boaz": "[A]lthough the Vicar had assured me the pulpit would be almost up to my chin it was scarcely above my waist and in order to see to read my sermon I was obliged to crouch down in it and lie on one side on the ledge and stick one leg out behind" (2: 53). Such are the joys of a country parson.

But the whole world meets with these charming mishaps. In February 1870, when they miss their train, dear Miss Child and her sister find themselves stranded in London Bridge Hotel with an owl in a basket, an owl that persists in hooting all through the night despite their putting it "up the chimney, before the looking glass, under the bedclothes, and in a circle of lighted candles which they hoped it would mistake for the sun" (1: 32).

Between the Acts' "gipsy beauty," Mrs. Manresa, may be Woolf's nod to *Kilvert's Diary*—as well as to Vita Sackville-West's grandmother, Pepita (as more frequently claimed). Woolf also transports Kilvert's amusing cows, who look in as the (human) drama unfolds. Woolf was "galloping" on *Between the Acts* in August 1938 and later. Jed Esty points out that "when the audience begins to lose interest in the pageant" in *Between the Acts*, "the lowing of the cows draws them back into the dramatic circle" (250n73). In the novel, Woolf writes that the cows "annihilated the gap; bridged the distance; filled the emptiness and continued the emotion" (140–41).

Kilvert muses in his 1872 diary, "I wonder who will one day long hence read and smile over these records of hopes and fears and thoughts and desires, when the fire has gone out and the ashes grown cold" (2: 176). His gravestone proclaims the simple truth of diaries: *"He being dead, yet speaketh"* (2: 13). Virginia Woolf greatly enjoyed Kilvert's diary and clearly wanted more. It gave her engaging details for *Between the Acts*. It gave her a natural (even lush) human voice. It showed her life immortal: solid life to cling to amid the "unreal" welter of war.

9

War Shades Life & Work

"The sense of apprehension," writes Hermione Lee, "which filled [Virginia Woolf's] writings from 1939 onwards, applied to Europe, but also to herself" (714). The year 1939 should be seen as a series of outer, literal *trespasses*—of conscious attacks. On January 24, General Franco stands "at the gate of Barcelona," Woolf tells her diary (*D* 5: 201). In five days, the city falls. On March 22, Madrid "surrender[s]" (*D* 5: 211). The week before, Hitler marches into Prague and proclaims that "Czecko-Slovakia has ceased to exist" (*D* 5: 208n9).

"Alive at last to the dangers of Hitler's military and territorial ambitions in Eastern Europe," diary editor Olivier Bell explains, "a disillusioned Mr Chamberlain announced on 31 March that Britain and France would guarantee support to Poland should her independence be threatened (which it was); . . . [A]fter the invasion and annexation of Albania by Mussolini's troops on Good Friday (7 April)—this guarantee was extended to Greece and Roumania" (*D* 5: 213 n1). Undeterred, on July 11, Hitler militarized the Free City of Danzig, Poland.[1]

This outer war begins to touch England directly in late August 1939. Woolf now sees soldiers in Rodmell village. On September 1, Germany moves further on Poland, which evokes England's formal declaration of war. Mothers and children are evacuated from London to Rodmell, and the blackouts start. On September 17, England's HMS *Courageous* is torpedoed and sunk in the Bristol Channel, more than five hundred lost.

If the dictators darkened the waters in 1938, in 1939 the war edges closer: it shades, unavoidably, Woolf's life and work. Although her fluency is affected, she remains bold. In January, she dons the mask of Cleopatra (perhaps ominously) for her brother Adrian's costume party. She starts her memoirs (at last) in April—using the diary form. And she continues her inner artistic struggle to resurrect *Roger Fry*. As Rhonda Sonnenberg notes, "Woolf's voice resonated in [this] work, as though by drumming Fry's wisdom into herself she might better endure this latest war" (104).

Across the year, Woolf also seeks life enduring through her own diary and in many other diaries as well. Some diarists aid her—like her diary father, Sir Walter Scott. However, in July, she finds in F. L. Lucas' *Journal under the Terror, 1938*, an invitation to noble suicide. In the *Journals of Charles Ricketts, R. A.*, the brilliant outsider and friend of Michael Field (which Woolf reads in late December), she meets a diary stopped by war.

Virginia Woolf's 1939 Diary

> *"Over all hangs war of course. A kind of perceptible but anonymous friction. Dantzig. [sic] The Poles vibrating in my room."*
>
> (July 11, 1939; D 5: 225)

Virginia Woolf describes her mind as "in a torn state" in December 1939 (D 5: 249). Torn, in fact, today is her physical diary itself—victim to Hitler's bombs. The red cover to this loose-leaf notebook has not survived. Woolf likely once more chose a bright cover "to counteract what [she] suspected"—as she did in 1938 (D 5: 191). Her May travel diary of her Brittany motor tour also does not survive. All that remains are sheets of ivory paper, a few blue ones in the middle. But they reveal much.

As often occurs in Woolf's diaries, tension stirs between constraint and freedom, restriction and expansion—and the diary helps her fight to be free. Alarms, however, sound as this diary's pages unfold, for missing along with its cover—or reduced—are many of her previous diaries' vital signs. Woolf's creative flow, her fluidity, slackens, and she must work to replenish it this year. January flows somewhat well. On January 18, Woolf finds herself "in full flood" with her novel Pointz Hall (*Between the Acts*)—perhaps, she admits, due to *Harper's* praise of her short story "Lappin and Lapinova" (D 5: 200). Inez Spender commends her as a "poet-novelist" on March 3, causing her "jadedness" to "thaw" enough to write more of Pointz Hall (D 5: 207). Woolf seems to lean on praise more in 1939 than in 1938, a worrisome sign.

By May 1, however, she is "dried up about Roger," a particularly troubling fact, for he has always been her refresher (D 5: 217). In mid-May, she hopes two weeks' "rambling" in Brittany will fill her "dry cistern of a head" (*D* 5: 218). The missing pages imply the trip's failure. London pressures then drain her in June and July, for in entries on July 30 and 31 she quotes T. S. Eliot's "Human voices wake us & we drown" to signal her wish to escape from London to the country. "Such an expansion after the London pressure," she exclaims July 30 at Monk's House. "I take my brain out, & fill it with books, as a sponge with water" (*D* 5: 228).

But the war once more trespasses, prevents the refill she craves. Book publishing suffers in wartime, forcing the Woolfs to "turn journalist" again. In the last four months of 1939, war distractions keep Woolf on the surface. The outer keeps her from the inner—not at all her creative plan. "So distracted I've scudded over the surface of the days," she confesses on September 23 to explain an eleven-day diary gap (*D* 5: 237). On October 7, she writes more alarmingly: "Cha[m]brun now demands a dog story. . . . In short I'm more on the buzz than when I was contemplating books only. And it keeps me feverishly skating over the thin ice" (*D* 5: 241). In the diary's final entry, December 17, she complains she never reaches "the depths" in her diary; "I'm too surface blown" (*D* 5: 251). However, she ends still trying to fill her well.

Water metaphors, in short, no longer surge through Woolf's diary, as they did in the 1938 and earlier diaries: from May onward, she is no longer in "flood." Her valiant horse figures that so often reinforce her diary's water tropes also falter in 1939. The word "jaded" reappears, as it did across her 1934–1935 diary as she labored over *The Years*, a "jade" a broken-down horse. "I'm too jaded to write," Woolf ends her second entry on January 9, 1939 (*D* 5: 198). On April 15, she notes that Leonard is "galloping through *his* book," *Barbarians at the Gate* (*D* 5: 215; emphasis mine); then adds: "I should like a holiday." Her May 1 entry that opens, "A bad morning, because I'm dried up about Roger," continues: "I'm determined tho' to plod through & make a good job, not a work of art. . . . My hand, as I see, wont write" (*D* 5: 217).

Woolf plods in 1939; she does not leap her fences. On August 28, she lingers in her writing lodge "on this possibly last night of peace," and asks: "Will the 9 o'clock [radio] bulletin end it all?—our lives, oh yes, & everything for the next 50 years? . . . Of course I have my old spurs & my old flanks. No I cant get at it. . . . How difficult, unexpectedly to write" (*D* 5: 231, 232). On September 3, and "certainly the last hour of peace," she again ends her entry, "& certainly I cant write" (*D* 5: 233, 234). Three days later, hearing their first air raid siren, "my brain stops. . . . all creative power is cut off" (*D* 5: 234, 235).

The outer war impinges on, often checks, her inner artistic steed. Her diary conveys her plight. Her November 30 entry opens: "Very jaded & tired & depressed & cross, & so take the liberty of expressing my feelings here" (*D* 5: 248). Yet she never stops plodding. Journalism's distractions offer her, at least, several "ponies"—if not full-grown horses. "I'm driving so many horses in my team," she tells her December 9 entry and lists them: "So, these are the little wild ponies that tug me so many ways at once" (*D* 5: 250).

As noted often before, Woolf's horse figure links always to her diary mother, Fanny Burney, who begged her father to let her leap her fences and vault to other pastures beyond fiction (in fact, to a comic play). In her previous diary book, the 1938 diary, Woolf repeatedly evokes the horse trope for her "frisks" on her final novel, *Between the Acts* (with *its* comic play). In 1938, "galloping" and "frisking" on that novel offers turn-and-turn-about relief from the factual grind of *Roger Fry*. But in the 1939 diary, all reference to the novel stops on July 31.

Instead, Woolf plods on with *Roger Fry*. The 1939 diary's opening sentence refers to the Fry biography in progress. Woolf, in fact, escapes from Fry to "inaugurate this important volume" (her diary)—escape that recurs often across the year. Once more she declares "the dominant theme" for the year will be "work: Roger" (*D* 5: 197). True to her word, forty-six of the diary's seventy-three entries refer to the biography—63 percent. *Roger Fry: A Biography* reflects the constraint/freedom paradox Woolf must compass this year. For Fry to spring to life, he must be anchored, tethered by countless facts. Woolf cannot soar free. She opens her second entry to complain that Roger is "all too detailed, too tied down—I must expand, first on this irresponsible page [her diary]" and then in fiction (*D* 5: 197).

Sadly, like Ethel Smyth, Fry now rarely brings life. On March 11, Woolf finishes the first draft, "the first sketch of Roger," and sees a "terrible grind to come: & innumerable doubts, of myself as biographer: of the possibility of doing it at all." Nevertheless, she allows herself "one moments mild gratification" at completing the work. "There may be a flick of life in it—or is it all dust & ashes?" she asks (*D* 5: 207, 208).

Concern for Woolf's creative force mounts, however, when we see her repeat in 1939 the dangerous path of *The Years*. The writer who so accurately gauged her production in the 1920s—and even through *Flush* in 1933—now once more overestimates her ability to revise. On April 26, in her second month of revision, Woolf offers one of her habitual diary plans. "I've done a ¼—100 pages of Roger," she begins. "I ought to have finished it by the end of July—only we may go away. Say August. And have it all typed in September.... Well—then it will be out this time next year [late April 1940]. And I shall be free in August—What a grind it is" (*D* 5: 215–16). On September 3, as she waits the announcement of war, she boldly calls the war "bosh & stuffing compared with the reality of ... writing, & re-writing one sentence of Roger" (*D* 5: 233).

However, something unforeseen occurs in September and October—perhaps the formal declaration of war. Woolf finishes the second draft of *Roger Fry*, but she does not send it to the typist as she planned in April; instead she repeats the pattern of *The Years* and embarks on *another* revision. "Needless to say, its still to be revised, compacted, vitalised," she tells her diary on October 6. "And can I ever do it? The distractions are so incessant" (*D* 5: 240).

Roger Fry, that previously invigorating spirit, has now become a "grind." "Oh how gladly I reach for this free page for a 10 minutes scamper after copying & re-copying, digging in those old extract books for quotes all the morning!" Woolf opens her diary on November 1 (*D* 5: 244). Her next entry, November 9, begins the same: "How glad I am to escape to my free page.... The worst of journalism is that it distracts. Like a shower on the top of the sea" (*D* 5: 245). At the end of November, she sends the first chapters of *Roger Fry* to the typist, but on December 16 she still "[c]ant get the marriage chapter right. Proportion all wrong" (*D* 5: 250). She claims she does not "fuss" quite so much as she did over *The Years*, that she "learned a lesson ... I shall never forget. Always I say to myself Remember the horror of that" (*D* 5: 250). But her last diary entry, December 17, shows her still "titivating Roger" (*D* 5: 252).

She may cling now to Fry as a lifeboat in the mad storm of war.[2] The war now nears, distracts, and numbs the mind. Why wouldn't Woolf's creation slow? More than half her 1939 entries mention the encroaching war: thirty-seven of seventy-three. On January 22, a "battered couple," the Spiras, Jews exiled from Austria, seek the Woolfs' help. "[W]ar is coming close again, just as in September [1938]," Woolf tells her diary (*D* 5: 201). A week later they visit the dying Freud, exiled too in London. Freud tells them it will take a generation to work out Hitler's poison. On March 16, as noted, Hitler marches into Prague.

From March 1939 forward, the war shades, more than ever before, Woolf's life and work. On April 11, as she makes plans to revise *Roger Fry*, she must factor in this horror: "Then there's the war," she notes: "The finest Easter possible has this purple background. We wait like obedient children to hear what we shall be told when Parliament meets on Thursday.... Maynard, even Maynard, cant find much that's hopeful now that Italy has nipped off Albania. . . . I should, if it weren't for the war—glide my way up & up in to that exciting layer so rarely lived in: where my mind works so quick it seems asleep; like the aeroplane propellers" (*D* 5: 213–14).

Four days later, she observes the "odd . . . severance that war seems to bring: everything becomes meaningless: cant plan" (*D* 5: 215). In this atmosphere she must spur herself, as she does on July 11: "Over all hangs war of course. A kind of perceptible but anonymous friction. . . . Everything uncertain. . . . Work, work, I tell myself" (*D* 5: 225). When Britain's "Crisis" comes at last at the end of August, when Germany and Russia shock the world with their Non-Aggression Pact, Woolf turns herself into a reporter once more, perhaps for her memoirs. "Search light on Rodmell Hill," she tells her August 25 entry. "Order double supplies & some coal. . . . Difficult to work. . . . I add one little straw to another, waiting to go in, palsied with writing. . . . Underneath of course wells of pessimism. Young men torn to bits: mothers like Nessa 2 years ago" (*D* 5: 231). To the end of the year, Woolf envisions young men torn, people "battered" like the Spiras—and her mind "torn," as well. On August 28, she employs the simile she used for the 1926 General Strike. "[T]heres a vast calm cold gloom. And the strain," she writes as she waits for the 9 p.m. radio bulletin. "Like waiting a doctors verdict. And the young—young men smashed up. But the point is one is too numbed to think" (*D* 5: 231).

War strains the Woolfs' happiness—inevitably. "We privately are so content," Woolf tells her August 28 entry. "Bliss day after day. So happy cooking dinner, reading, playing bowls. No feeling of patriotism. How to go on, through war?—thats the question" (*D* 5: 231). Sadly, the war takes over the diary in the final third of the year. On September 6, Woolf calls the war "the worst of all my life's experiences" (*D* 5: 234). She asks 136 questions across this diary's 73 entries, 34 (one-fourth) on the war. Half her questions from August 25 on relate to the fray.[3] She offers a vivid image and question in her September 6 entry. The war, she repeats, "seems entirely meaningless—a perfunctory slaughter, like taking a jar in one hand, a hammer in the other. Why must this be smashed? Nobody knows" (*D* 5: 235).

"Am I a coward?" she wonders on this September day (*D* 5: 234). The war turns Woolf's mind to age and death once more, a further change, for in June 1938, she blithely rejected Leonard's insistence that they were old (*D* 5: 149). Across her 1939 diary, Woolf seeks to transform old age and death. In her fourth entry, January 18, she admits that now she often comes "face to face, after tea, at odd moments, with the idea of death & age." But she counters: "Why not change the idea of death into an exciting experience?—as one did marriage in youth? Age is baffled today by my creative gift—still a bubble" (*D* 5: 200). In January, art can still "baffle" death. Six days later, Virginia and Leonard plan the books they will write "if we could live another 30 years"—a life-affirming act (*D* 5: 202).

As noted before, Woolf often paints portraits in her diaries that project her own conflicts. The 1939 diary further troubles, for Woolf offers only brief positive views of old age to counter lengthy portraits of its horrors. In January, she shows Freud "shrunk" but "alert," "an old fire now flickering" (*D* 5: 202). In December, she starts to read his work "to enlarge" her brain's "circumference. to give [her] brain a wider scope: to make it objective; to get outside. Thus defeat the shrinkage of age." She then adds: "Always take on new things. Break the rhythm &c. Use this [diary] page, now & then, for notes" (*D* 5: 248). She seeks here outside aid for her inner fight. But Freud sends her into a whirlpool instead. Revealingly, she immediately takes up John Stuart Mill's *On Liberty*, so admired by diarist Kate Amberley (Bertrand Russell's mother) and her diarist husband.

Despite this courageous year-end drive for "liberty" and to "defeat the shrinkage of age," Woolf's fullest diary portraits in 1939 depict old women in decline. Maurice Llewelyn Davies dies in April, causing Woolf to reflect on his seventy-eight-year-old sister, Margaret's, approach to age. Woolf feels Margaret "lives too carefully.... Why drag on, always measuring & testing one's little bit of strength & setting it easy tasks so as to accumulate years?" she asks (*D* 5: 214). Instead, Woolf plans to write "quick, intense, short books, & never be tied down. This is the way to keep off the settling down & refrigeration of old age. And to flout all preconceived theories" (*D* 5: 214).

In five entries from April to July, Woolf studies Leonard's mother, eighty-eight-year-old Marie Woolf. A "dismal tea" on April 28 spurs Woolf to call Mrs. Woolf "completely lifeless—like an old weed on a rock" (*D* 5: 216). In 1937, Woolf used a similar trope for *herself*. In August 1937, she had gone to Roger Fry's house at Highgate to "somehow freshen up if I am to write, to live, to go through the next lap with zest, not like old sea weed" (*D* 5: 115). In 1939, Woolf finds that Mrs. Woolf "still clings hard to life & cant be removed" (*D* 5: 216).

But Marie Woolf falls on June 28 and breaks two ribs. Woolf's view does not soften: "She will not die, so I assume. There is a terrible passive resistance to death in these old women. They have the immortality of the vampire. Poor Flora will be sucked drop by drop for years to come. This is I suppose a cruel remark to make. But honestly, everyone would be relieved if she could make an end of it" (*D* 5: 222). She does so four days later, and Woolf notes in her July 3 entry that "its been jading & somehow very depressing—watching her die" (*D* 5: 223). Woolf's compassion—as well as her honesty—then stirs: "I . . . have a regret for that spirited old lady, whom it was such a bore to visit. Still she was somebody . . ." (*D* 5: 223). After the July 5 funeral, Woolf tries to preserve Marie Woolf in her diary—perhaps for her memoirs: "The truth was, age had taken everything away that was real" (*D* 5: 225).

At year's end, Woolf finds Ethel Smyth in decline, as well. Woolf is annoyed at having to meet Smyth in March, and at the end of April prefers to stay home with Leonard rather than to see *The Wreckers*, Smyth's opera, with Smyth (*D* 5: 216). Woolf's December 8 portrait particularly alarms, for Smyth (like Roger Fry) first served as an in-the-flesh "Old Virginia" for Woolf: a model of productive old age. "[S]he has gone downhill," Woolf reports to her diary: "She is now shut up quite alone in her old age—talks to herself, about herself. I felt this pathetic: also somehow ugly; humiliating; watching the old baby sucking its corals; compliments; the old story of her genius & its non-recognition. How hideous to be reduced to that kind of feeblemindedness—at 84. Something pitiable, unvenerable; not imbecile, but near it. . . . And the old charm in abeyance" (*D* 5: 249). Loss of "the old charm" matters for Woolf, for she has written Smyth on May 14: "I rather count upon your presence on the earth—your effluence"—*effluence* an "outward flow" (L #3513, 6: 332).

But "effluence" ebbs this year. In its place are troubling hate-my-kind signs. "Why am I so old, so ugly, so—& cant write," Woolf asks her diary on March 11—always a troubling sign (*D* 5: 208). Four months later, she walks the London streets at night and sees those she passes as she does in 1915 before illness stops the diary. "[T]he crowds of deformed & stunted & vicious & sweating & ugly hooligans & harridans in the Tott[enham]. C[our]t. Road," she writes on July 12, "—the sticky heat—all this brooded, till I was saying, step out, on, on, in my usual desperate way" (*D* 5: 225). On July 28, Peter Lucas' "exhibition" of his mentally ill wife, Prudence, in his *Journal under the Terror, 1938*, leads Woolf to this diary question: "Shd. people show their naked skins?" (*D* 5: 227). She declares that diarist Eddy Sackville-West "shows his death mask," and she then recalls her "shudder" at Helen Anrep's son, Igor. Olivier Bell omits some of Woolf's cruel words in the published version of Woolf's diary; however, she includes Woolf's "dislike of Igor's great fleshy mouth" (*D* 5: 227).

Virginia Woolf struggles, in short, this year. Her courage, however, does not falter. In August, she once more seeks to turn age and death to more positive states: "To treat age as an experience that is different from the others; & to detect every one of the gradual stages toward death which is a tremendous experience, & not as unconscious at least in its approaches, as birth is" (*D* 5: 230). At the September 3 declaration of war, she pledges to "[k]eep the Press going" and to "take on some writing for some society" as her work against the war (*D* 5: 234).

She also seeks out diaries in 1939 as streams of life renewed. She touches base with the diarists that have braced her from the start. She winks wittily to Pepys as she closes her first entry ("So to lunch"), tracks down his church on January 31, and finishes out the day with his signature "& so to bed" (*D* 5: 197, 204). When the poet C. Day Lewis calls in May, Woolf wishes she "could repeat more words" (*D* 5: 218). Noting that "Boswell did it," she asks: "Could I turn B. at my age?" (*D* 5: 218). She then tries to capture Lewis' talk and later tries again to be "Boswell at Sissinghurst" (*D* 5: 218).

In August, she reads the first volume of a new edition of *Sir Walter Scott's Journal* and draws life from Scott's diary once more. In her lively essay "Gas at Abbotsford," she calls diaries "stepping-stones" and twice pictures Scott infusing life (*E* 6: 217). "Then, suddenly, the whole scene changes," Woolf writes in "Gas at Abbotsford": "Scott began in a low mournful voice to recite the ballad of Sir Patrick Spens.... So it happens, too, in the novels—the lifeless English turns to living Scots" (*E* 6: 215). Did she think of herself here: the lifeless English revived, even immortalized like Patrick Spens, the drowned sailor? Does she think of her own *Between the Acts* in progress when she asks in her essay: "Or was [Scott] the last of the playwright novelists, who, when the pressure of emotion is strong enough behind them can leap the bounds of prose and make real thoughts and real emotions issue in real words from living lips?" (*E* 6: 217). Here in "leap[ing] the bounds" Scott and Burney merge.

Woolf seeks life from *new* diarists as well as from the old. In January she reads the *Journal de Eugène Delacroix* and thinks she could write on his diary (*D* 5: 199). On February 6, she urges young Elaine Robson to keep at her diary. "I like your journal very much indeed. It tells me all sorts of interesting things," Woolf writes to the seven- or eight-year-old Robson. "I hope you write it every day and will let me read it when you have done enough. Please put in some poems" (*L* #3487, 6: 316).

In late July, she seeks to lubricate her dry mind with the diaries of the Reverend Francis Kilvert from the River Wye (volume 2), Gide (full diaries 1889–1939), and Peter Lucas' *Journal under the Terror, 1938*. "Its queer that diaries now pullulate," she tells her July 28 entry. "No one can settle to a work of art.

Comment only" (*D* 5: 227). Ten days later, thinking of Gide's and Lucas' diaries once more, she explains that "[i]ts the comment—the daily interjection—that comes handy in times like these. I too feel it" (*D* 5: 229).

As the outer war advances and the 1939 diary comes to a close, Woolf continues to draw on new diaries to feed her flow. She wishes to be less "surface blown," so she can write her thoughts on being an outsider. She reads now *Self-Portrait, Taken from the Letters & Journals of Charles Ricketts, R.A.*, the great friend of Katherine Bradley and Edith Cooper ("Michael Field"), those lesbian verse dramatists who called themselves "outsiders in a deep sense" (*Works and Days* 217). Woolf closes her 1939 diary affirmatively as she tries to bank the flow: "I'm reading Ricketts diary—all about the war the last war; & the Herbert diaries & . . . notes overflow into my 2 books" (*D* 5: 252).

Woolf reads at least seven new diaries in 1939. She seeks—perhaps desperately—to refresh herself, to refill her well. She also turns her mind more and more to her *own* diary, which remains a vital prop. On July 28, she composes herself after a fight with Leonard by reading through the year's diary. "Thats a use for it then. It composes," she observes. "I think shows one a stretch, when one's grubbing in an inch" (*D* 5: 227). She uses her diary to sum up her thoughts as they move the Hogarth Press and themselves from Tavistock Square to Mecklenburgh Square in London in late August and also uses it to take notes to "[b]reak the rhythm" in her professional prose (*D* 5: 248).

In 1939, a year of war distraction, trespass, and tears, only 52 of Woolf's 136 diary questions relate to her own writing. Surprisingly, nineteen of the fifty-two concern her diary. "But what are the interesting things?" she asks herself in late April. "I'm thinking of what I should like to read here in 10 years time. And I'm all at sea. Perhaps literal facts. The annal, not the novel" (*D* 5: 216–17). She wonders on June 29 why she escapes to her diary from revising *Roger Fry* and asks if she ever will read her diary again (*D* 5: 222). She opens her final entry to ponder again why she keeps her diary. "Once more, as so often, I hunt for my dear old red-covered book, with what an instinct I'm not quite sure," she writes, showing affection for her diary as she has done from the start. "For what the point of making these notes is I dont know; save that it becomes a necessity to uncramp, & some of it may interest me later. But what?" (*D* 5: 251).

Woolf particularly uses her diary for freedom and expansion in 1939—"to uncramp." She needs to expand "on this irresponsible page" on January 9 and to "reel" off her mind six months later (*D* 5: 197, 222). Diaries—her own and others'—help her expand in a year fraught with constraints. She wants Roger to fly free, but he is tied by myriad facts, the sentinel eyes of his sisters, and Woolf's own wish to guard Vanessa from wagging tongues. Readers of *Roger Fry: A Biography* learn nothing of Fry's early homosexual experiments and would never guess that passionate love for Vanessa colored a good share of his days. Cramped now (ironically) by *Roger Fry* and stalled July 31 on her novel, Woolf turns to her diary for the freedom she seeks.[4]

In 1939, Woolf looks to her own diary—and to the diary *form*—both as counter to war and as potential public art. "I'm thinking of a critical book," she tells her March 16 entry: "Suppose I used the diary form? Would this make one free to go from book to book—or wd it be too personal?" (*D* 5: 210). In April, as noted, she finally begins her memoirs (in diary form). On September 6, when the first air raid siren cuts off "all creative power," Woolf finds new life in nature and in her diary. "This book will serve to accumulate notes," she tells her diary after a walk. "And for the 100th time I repeat—any idea is more real than any amount of war misery. And what one's made for. And the only contribution one can make—This little pitter patter of ideas is my whiff of shot in the cause of freedom" (*D* 5: 235). In fact, "walking in the sun baked marsh" she thinks of making an article out of her "15 odd diaries" (*D* 5: 235).

F. L. Lucas' *Journal under the Terror, 1938*

Virginia Woolf recoils from F. L. Lucas' *Journal under the Terror, 1938*, when she reads it in July 1939. Her own floral-covered 1938 diary stands on her shelf—*her* record of that year as contrast or complement. She understands Lucas' and André Gide's need for their diaries as the dictators march. "No one can settle to a work of art. Comment only," she tells her July 28, 1939, entry (*D* 5: 227). Nevertheless, ten days later she separates herself from Gide and Lucas. "Neither can settle to creative art," she repeats and then whispers in parentheses "(I think, sans Roger, I could)" (*D* 5: 229). In August 1939 and again in July 1940 Woolf feels she can write not only her diary but more.

Woolf first met Frank Laurence ("Peter") Lucas, the young literary critic, poet, novelist, and playwright, in 1922 through their new Hogarth Press manager George "Dadie" Rylands. Across the next eighteen years, her diary portraits of this prolific Cambridge don reveal the consistency of her views. They show, too, her struggle with this charming Cambridge Apostle and her increasing recoil from his work.

Born in 1894 (and thus twelve years younger than Woolf), Lucas moves in Rylands' Cambridge crowd. A nineteen-year-old undergraduate at Trinity College when World War I begins, Lucas serves ably through that horror, although he is gassed and wounded—and wonders why he survived. After the war, he completes his undergraduate work in 1920 and earns a Classics Fellowship at King's College—the haunt of Leonard Woolf, Lytton Strachey, Roger Fry, John Maynard Keynes, and E. M. Forster. He expands beyond the classics and, in 1926, becomes a university lecturer in English Literature, as well.

Woolf registers her first impressions of Lucas in her opening diary entry of 1922. "He is a romantic: an innocent; a resolute boy" with a "scholar's unworldliness," she notes (D 2: 156). She senses she might talk intimately with him, "save that he is so young, so fresh: & not, after all, a born writer" (D 2: 156). He is twenty-seven; she, thirty-nine. But they share a love of the Greeks, and he can field any question she poses on the Romans or Greeks. He leaves, however, one of his plays, about which Woolf writes to Forster on January 21, 1922: "Lucas dined here... and brought a play; and I peep between the edges, and see it won't do" (L #1210, 2: 499).

Four years later, Woolf calls Lucas "a charming bony pink cheeked Don" in a 1926 letter to Vita Sackville-West (L #1622, 3: 244), but she tells her diary more: "He is a bony rosy little austere priest; so whole, & sane, & simple throughout one can't help respecting him, though when it comes to books we disagree" (D 3: 65). Lucas has launched his scathing attacks on T. S. Eliot and modernist poetry. "But Peter is, to my mind, too entire in his judgments; founded on book learning & prettiness into the bargain," she tells her March 3, 1926, diary. "He has no ascendancy of brain: he is not, & now never will be, a personage: which is the one thing needful in criticism, or writing of any sort, I think; for we're all as wrong as wrong can be. But character is the thing" (D 3: 65). More than three years later, she records the same response (D 3: 256–57).

Woolf discloses the roots of her Lucas unease in an April 1930 letter to Ethel Smyth: "The Lucases. I've struggled and rebelled against them all my life, but their integrity always makes me their slave. Much though I hate Cambridge, and bitterly though I've suffered from it, I still respect it" (L #2162, 4: 155). In October 1931, she repeats to her diary: "a visit from Peter Lucas t'other night. No, he had not read The W[aves]. But he has written an Epic. He is working as usual like a miner—bright red all over—egotistic—nice, charming, boyish, hard, imperceptive, not a writer I mean, though set on writing, & indeed has a play being acted" (D 4: 50).

Woolf brings this long history of respectful disregard when she opens the *Journal under the Terror, 1938*. Lucas shares, she may have noticed, several of her views. Like her, he seeks out untouched nature. "The healthy mind needs constant contact with Nature undefiled—not the Nature of public gardens, but Nature unfettered, as here in the Alps," he declares in his second *Journal* entry (31). At the end of January he tells his *Journal*, "I should not care much to be assured that the British Empire will exist in a thousand years: but I should die a little happier if I knew that the British countryside would even then be still unspoiled" (76).

He voices, in fact, Woolf's own hate/love for London. "I cannot love London, though brought up a Londoner," he tells his February 26 entry. "A theatre on a first night is an amusing place; but one is less oneself there, one's state of mind is cheaper, than in the wintry stillness of the woods to-day."[5] Lucas even tires of Cambridge. As a classical scholar, he tilts toward the pagan rather than toward Christianity. Extolling unfettered nature in that second *Journal* entry, he adds, "Perhaps it is because I have no religious feeling that I so value this awe of solitude.... If I had any god, it would be Pan" (31).

Even more than Woolf, Lucas writes his *Journal* to comfort himself as war drums sound once more. He means to aid others, too, and in this respect his melodramatically titled *Journal under the Terror, 1938*, differs greatly from Woolf's more private diary. Lucas writes his *Journal under the Terror* as a public work. That he dedicates the *Journal* "[t]o the curious (if men still read then) of a hundred years hence" as well as to Desmond MacCarthy, "Wisest of readers today," suggests he writes both for posterity and for a contemporary male coterie he later calls "*les âmes amies*" (67).

He launches the *Journal* at 11:30 p.m. on December 31, 1937, with a fourteen-page setting of the stage: "New Year's Eve, day sacred to resolutions. (One needs resolution, in these days, to face a New Year at all.) Mine is—to keep a journal for the year to come" (11). He admits to keeping journals before—"or fail[ing] to keep them"—and later suffering "unexpected regret for their untimely deaths" (11). He finds a lesson here: "How much they could tell us that has now slipped irretrievably away! We forget how much we forget":

> But this journal, if it can be kept alive, is not meant merely for my own private remembrance of the past. I dare to hope that parts of it may amuse the future also—supposing there is any future—supposing that future feels any curiosity about to-day. This is a message in a bottle, thrown overboard at a venture from this vast ship of ours that drifts fog-blinded,

with music and laughter, murder and battle, on board, towards breakers sounding ever louder in our ears.

It is an attempt to give one answer, however inadequate, however fragmentary, to the question that will surely be asked one day by some of the unborn—with the bewilderment, one hopes, of a happier age: "What *can* it have felt like to live in that strange, tormented and demented world? . . .

So I prepare my empty bottle for launching, not knowing what folly the unborn months may make of these pages; because it amuses and distracts me; and because I dearly wish some Roman of the crumbling Empire of Honorius or Valentinian had done as much for me, while he too watched the tides of barbarism lap higher and higher against the dykes of the civilized world. It would not replace Gibbon; but how it would supplement him! (12–13)

Lucas believes that historical insight can calm the current terror. He starts his *Journal* with three epigraphs. "And there were never heard of such troublesome and distracted times as these five years have been, *but especially for constables*," he quotes wittily from *The Journal of a Constable in the English Civil War*. He then offers Lord Chesterfield's warning that extravagant acts in the past—the Roman Emperor Caligula naming his horse his counselor, for instance—seemed less aberrant at the time to citizens "prepared for it by an insensible gradation of extravagancies from the same quarter." The link to Hitler, Mussolini, and Stalin seems clear. He closes with Prosper Mérimée's preference for anecdotal history.

Humanity, in short, has suffered terror before. The strength of Lucas' *Journal* lies in the support he draws from history and literature again and again across the year. His March 12 entry records Hitler's annexation of Austria—just as Woolf's diary does. Lucas fortifies himself, however, by quoting Hector's speech to Andromache in Homer's *Iliad*, "For holy Troy, I know it, the day of doom draws near," and then adds:

And with the beauty of that perfect poetry . . . comes a little of the calm that poetry can bring. . . . Here is something timeless and eternal, that not even the Dictators shall destroy. Those first two lines were spoken with tears, seven centuries after Homer, by Scipio in his turn as he watched the smoke wreathe up from blazing Carthage and thought of the like doom in store one day for Rome.

So generations utterly remote and different are linked in kinship, for a moment, by . . . golden lines. That bond at least endures. Or will even this poetry, that no Barbarian Invasions nor Dark Ages could destroy, perish also in the new barbarism of Dictators whose only Art is degraded to propaganda and whose only Science is prostituted to fill their arsenals with death? (113–14)

Shaken further on October 1 by the Munich "accord," Lucas returns to Homer and offers the most moving lines in the *Journal*:

Never writer felt more deeply than this war-poet [Homer] the tragedy of war. And the quality of mercy. . . . But when Hector leaves Andromache, knowing that he goes to a lost battle, he knows already that even glory is a pitiful consolation. Little is left in the end but the courage that meets its doom without disgrace; and brings us safely to the quiet of the heedless tomb. . . .

A world of doom; yet a world of loyalty and courage, beauty and pity; a world where hope is dim, but endurance and compassion are strong— that is what Homer has bequeathed. (284, 286)

Were this all, *Journal under the Terror, 1938*, although gloomy, might be the beacon in the darkness Lucas aims it to be. He stocks his *Journal*, too, with historical tidbits later readers might value, particularly on the worsening plight of the Jews. In April, appalled, he quotes from Ernst Hiemer's *The Poison-Fungus*, a child's book of seventeen stories that teach children to hate the Jews (144–45). In May, he hears of a Jewish professor in Germany not only fired but forbidden to use the public library. "Not even the ferocity of the Nazi mind is more horrible than its petty, meticulous malignity," he comments. "At St. Polten, near Vienna, the same spiteful ingenuity has devised a glass cabinet for the public exhibition of photographs of inhabitants snapped coming out of Jewish shops" (174, 175). In November, he documents the high price of escape: "A Jewish textile manufacturer is offered 900,000 marks for his business. The authorities prevent the purchaser paying him more than 400,000. Of this the unfortunate proprietor has to give half to the Labour Front. Wishing to emigrate, he further pays a flight-tax of 25 per cent. of his capital. The discount-bank then allows him to take abroad 8 per cent. of the residue. In the end he leaves Germany with 1,200 marks, having been swindled by the German State out of 98 ⅔ per cent. of his property" (332).

And when the pogroms start in late November, Lucas preserves for posterity these chilling words of *Das Schwarze Korps*:

The Jews must be driven into special streets, marked with a special badge, and deprived of the right to own land or houses. Then, being debarred from profitable occupations and forced to devour their own capital, *they will become criminals in accordance with their hereditary instincts*. When this stage had arrived, we should be faced with the *hard necessity* of exterminating the Jewish underworld by those methods we always use against criminals—fire and sword.

The result would be the final end of Jewry in Germany—its total annihilation. (342)

Lucas' November 24 entry reveals that in late 1938, Lucas and others thought the pogroms prearranged: "Several large new concentration-camps are said to have been prepared: Buchenwald, for example, was enlarged in October to welcome 25,000 instead of 6000 guests" (343).

Like Woolf in *Three Guineas*, Lucas links sport and war. He asks in his March 14 entry, "Is it wholly coincidence that General Goering is a mighty hunter before the Lord; and that Civil War is producing its most unspeakable cruelties in the land of bull-fights? In this vicious circle of our Inferno callous men make other things suffer, and by that suffering grow more callous still" (116).

Despite its valuable historical notes, the bulk of *Journal under the Terror, 1938*, settles for caustic "comment," for indignant "interjection"—as Woolf saw (*D* 5: 227, 229). Lucas' views come through clearly in the *Journal*. He calls for immediate air parity with Germany and for those nations that want peace to band together into "a real League [of Nations] to resist any attack on any of them" (71). "But to-day the honest men seem unable to band together," he laments; "it is the knaves that are thick as thieves" (72). He strongly opposes appeasement and particularly rails at its cant. His September 30 entry opens:

Hitler, Mussolini, Chamberlain, Deladier have met at Munich. . . . We shall have sold the Czechs for six months' grace and a disgrace that will last as long as history.

. . . In front of the radio one felt physically sick. . . . How can it be "peace with honour" to surrender a fellow-member of the League, a small nation that relied on us, betrayed now to its deadliest enemy? The surrender *might* have been necessary: the cant was not. . . . And any statesman with a sense of honour would at least have stilled that hysterical cheering of Cockney cads and said: "My friends, for the present, we are out of danger. But remember that others, who trusted in us, are not.

This is a day for relief, perhaps; but for sorrow also; for shame, not for revelling." (275–76, 277)

To his credit, Lucas offers more than warning words. When Britain declares war at last in September 1939, Lucas is one of the first academics tapped by the Foreign Office. His skill with languages and his infantry and intelligence corps experience from 1914–1918 make him an obvious choice for Bletchley Park's Hut 3, where he takes a valued role in the Enigma decode.

Despite his noble work in the war, Lucas' *Journal under the Terror, 1938* comes across today as self-righteous protest, as a flailing bid to exert influence, or at least, like the Reverend John Skinner in *his* diary, to say "I told you so." Lucas adds an opening "Note," for instance, when he publishes the *Journal* in May 1939: "I must ask the reader to believe that I have here antedated no prophecies or judgments in an easy effort to look wise after the event. Alas, it has not been hard, unless one was a Cabinet Minister, to foresee what was coming" (8). Ironically, Lucas senses the dangers of rant. "One grows terribly tired of righteous indignation," he tells his August 13 entry. "All rage is tiring. And this kind leads so easily to priggery" (232).

What strikes one most, however, is that for one so pitched on the present and coming terror, Lucas never mentions Woolf's antiwar work *Three Guineas*, published June 3, 1938. And she his early publisher. And she his friend and Monk's House host. Surely, he knew of *Three Guineas*. He boasts of reading six newspapers every day (250). Certainly Woolf's book offered apt matter for a *Journal under the Terror, 1938*. Lucas' failure even to acknowledge Woolf's outsider's views further undercuts his *Journal*'s ethos as a text on the coming war—and offers more proof of how blind her time was to her farsighted critique.

Woolf says nothing of this snub in her two 1939 diary references to Lucas' *Journal*. She does, however, decry his "exhibition" of his artist wife, Prudence, who suffered a mental breakdown in November 1938 (*D* 5: 227). Lucas hardly mentions Prudence until November. She skis with him in the opening Alps holiday and tramps beside him in Ireland and elsewhere. "And I, who am so happily married, must still lie sweating through the small hours about Herr Hitler and this menace against which no love can protect," he tells his diary on Valentines Day (93). On September 1, he declares, "My own life is so happy; war would wreck everything; and the shadow of war is deeply depressing" (247)—words echoed in Woolf's 1939 diary (*D* 5: 231). But Prudence Lucas, a potter and sculptor, falls ill in November, and Lucas "exhibits" her tragedy in thirteen entries in November and December. His November 10 entry opens:

> The Crisis seems to have filled the world with nervous break-downs. Or perhaps the Crisis itself was only one more nervous break-down of a world driven by the killing pace of modern life and competition into ever acuter neurasthenia.
>
> Now it has happened at my own hearth. Nothing ghastlier than to see the person one has known best in the world for seven years turn into an unknown who no longer knows herself—
>
> "Divided from herself and her fair judgment." (333–34)

After this link to Hamlet's Ophelia, Lucas turns to Sir Walter Scott's *Journal* for Scott's words at his wife's death.

A few days later Prudence turns against him, as Woolf turned against Leonard on occasion during *her* illness in 1913 and 1914. Lucas opens his November 14 entry: "The horror of nervous break-downs is the way in which the person dearest hitherto becomes the most hateful to this new personality, this changeling, this sick usurper that has become dictator in the stricken brain" (338). As always, he turns to literature for comfort, now to the medieval ballad of Sir Orfeo, whose Heurodis is reft away. "I can hardly work, let alone create," he then cries: "but, though at such times I could never write poetry, the poetry of others still keeps a momentary power to calm. One realizes how deep a part of human destiny unhappiness has always been—and yet what beauty the compassion and understanding of the human heart has made of it! And at least work is better than thinking, where neither thought nor deed can help" (338–39).

In the next weeks, he thinks of Prudence as a ghost and sees himself as "trapped" (341, 347, 346). On December 18, he confesses to being put out of his house for the weekend: "A pathetic scrawl: 'Mind you are gone before I come home . . .'" (356). He then exhorts himself with Chaucer's "God lene us for to take it for the beste!" (356). He departs alone for Roger Fry's St. Rémy-de-Provence on December 22, and on Christmas Eve says (with Woolf) "work is the only anaesthetic" (358).

Lucas cares unquestionably for Prudence. He worries December 12 that "if there's a war, it'll wreck her treatment" (353), and he delights to find in St. Rémy a book by Austrian psychologist Wilhelm Stekel, who seems "to understand such cases more intelligently" than others. "Thanks to Herr Hitler he may be a refugee in England now," Lucas muses (366).

Prudence Lucas' illness gives a dramatic—and ironic—turn to the *Journal under the Terror, 1938*. Lucas draws his title from the German cultural historian Arthur Moeller van den Bruck. In Lucas' long August 30 entry on Aurel Kolnai's "astonishing work" *The War Against the West*, he quotes this passage: "The Germans must exude 'Unheimlichkeit': they 'crave terror,' says Moeller-Bruck" (239, 241). Unexpectedly—and in ways that undercut his indignant thrusts at Chamberlain and the dictators—home terror proves more terrible than foreign war, the inner more disabling than the outer. "The Crisis of last September was nothing to this," Lucas tells his December 12 entry. "*That* did not break my gaiety: whereas this last month . . . And one has still to teach and lecture. No wonder the Roman church insists on celibacy" (353–54). In his last journal entry, coming full circle on the Dijon-Paris train, Lucas repeats the confession: "for ten months of this year I was strangely happy, even under the shadow of imminent war. Then suddenly my own world burst like a bubble, for reasons neither king nor dictator could cause or cure" (366–67).

But he has started his cure already. The medicine: literature and his historical turn of mind. "After seven years of very great happiness," he reflects on Christmas Eve, "once again, as twice before, I am suddenly uprooted.[6] Luckily human beings are better able than trees to replant themselves. And perhaps transplantation, however it tears our roots with anguish, may make us more fruitful in the end. . . . The present has grown for me a ghastly nightmare. But I have been through other nightmares. Some day I shall come also out of this. Tunnels end" (359, 360).

Happy, spry mind.

Like Virginia Woolf, Peter Lucas ably calls up supports to meet life's terrors. Like her, he turns to a diary and to other diarists, as well. He praises Samuel Pepys as "a very engaging philosopher" and a "quite audacious thinker on politics" (292, 293). "To read Pepys is in itself a 'return to Nature,'" he suggests (293). In contrast, he rejects Jonathan Swift for holding "a Reign of Terror" in literature with his "perpetual peevishness" (183, 184). "If one sees the world like that, would it not be more dignified to hop over a cliff and have done?" Lucas smugly inquires (184).[7]

On the one hand, Lucas' gift for lifting himself with words from the past might be thought a model for mental health. On the other hand, Woolf's 1929 diary words also ring true: "Incessant similes, perpetual quotation; he sees life with great ardour through books" (*D* 3: 257). And as a men's club—a Cambridge coterie—as well. Lucas ignores Woolf and her *Three Guineas* in his *Journal under the Terror, 1938*, but he dedicates his *Journal* to Desmond MacCarthy,

"Wisest of Readers To-day," and wraps himself in the robes of Lytton Strachey, Goldsworthy Lowes Dickinson, and Roger Fry across the year. In January, Lucas visits Rousseau's home in Chambéry and compares it to Strachey's house "under the Berkshire Downs, before tragedy knocked at its door" (27). The next day, he exclaims: "How books are improved by the right surroundings! Lytton Strachey once suggested that one should read Sir Thomas Browne sitting between the paws of the Sphinx" (33). In September, he writes: "As Lytton Strachey says, Bacon lacked poetry" (261).

In his first *Journal* entry, Lucas calls Goldsworthy Lowes Dickinson the one saint he has known: "But, of the two sides of him, I prefer to remember, not the tortured humanitarian, sleepless and haggard over the War, and the Peace, and all the pitiful madness of mankind, but the wise old sage, like an ivory-yellow mandarin in his black-silk Chinese cap, whose despair would suddenly relieve itself in a smiling headshake, a little crackling laugh, and a wave of his hands at the diabolical irony of things" (13–14). As such a mandarin Lucas also hopes to be seen. In March, Lucas identifies with Roger Fry, "the only person I ever knew who shared my impatience at passive grief" (129). Fry felt intensely, Lucas explains, "[b]ut if a mistress died, or failed him, he rose bleeding and marched away" (129). Et tu Prudence.

Woolf finds Lucas' "exhibition" of Prudence inexcusable in July 1939, and she further distances herself from him in August. But he drew a picture of a wife in breakdown and of a husband trapped. His warning of coming doom across the *Journal* and his call for a courageous march to the heedless tomb bear a romantic, moribund scent even today. No wonder Woolf recoiled. The *Journal under the Terror, 1938*, can be read as a call for honorable suicide. In October, Lucas declares:

> I believe that it should be a part of education to instil into children a truer sense of Nietzsche's "When you can no longer live proudly, die proudly." The Ancients, without growing morbid about suicide like the Japanese, were wiser in this than we. . . .
>
> Seneca himself at least lived (or died) up to his own precept, in the end. And Heaven knows modern Europe is no place to live in without a safety-exit. I often think it not the least of the virtues of a car that the fumes of its exhaust will convey one so smoothly down to the shores of Styx. None knows in these days when he may not need to be carried out of the world, as well as through it.

Morbid? But that *is* what a good many of us were thinking in 1938. (301, 303)

On December 21, Lucas quotes poet and scholar A. E. Housman on the safety of death: "Men run about always on the edge of the precipice, and when they are safely dead we can breathe again: if we have cared for them" (357). Virginia Woolf abjures Lucas' *Journal under the Terror* in July 1939, and in August she whispers that, sans Roger, she could settle to creative art, a sentiment she repeats as late as July 1940. But Lucas rears again in September 1940 and sucks the life from Woolf's work. "Yesterday in the Pub. Library I took down a book of Peter Lucas's criticism. This turned me against writing my book [Anon]," Woolf tells her September 17, 1940, diary entry:

> Turned me against all lit crit; these so clever, so airless, so fleshless ingenuities & attempts to prove—that T. S. Eliot, for example is a worse critic than F.L.L[ucas]. Is all lit. crit. that kind of exhausted air?—book dust, London Library, air. Or is it only that F.L.L. is a second hand, frozen fingered, university specialist, don trying to be creative, don all stuffed with books, writer? Would one say the same of the Common Reader? I dipped for 5 minutes & put the book back depressed. The man asked What do you want Mrs Woolf? I said a history of English literature. But was so sickened, I cdn't look. There were so many. Nor cd I remember the name of Stopford Brooke. (*D* 5: 321–22)

That Woolf could not replace mordant diarist and literary critic Peter Lucas with lively, boundary-crossing diarist and literary critic Stopford Brooke signals her failing state.

Charles Ricketts' *Journals*

"Outsiders" and war filled Virginia Woolf's mind in mid-December 1939. "I often think," she declares in her final 1939 diary entry. "And think the very thought I could write here. About being an outsider" (*D* 5: 251). She is reading, she reports, "Ricketts diary—all about the war the last war," Ricketts himself a quintessential outsider.

William Butler Yeats called Charles Ricketts "the magician," while George Bernard Shaw insisted that Ricketts possessed "a genius infinitely more fascinating than my own" (Fletcher 6; *Self-Portrait* 307). Woolf was reading the 1939 *Self-Portrait: Taken from the Letters & Journals of Charles Ricketts, R. A.*, collected by the artist T. Sturge Moore (G. E. Moore's brother) and edited by another Ricketts friend, the writer Cecil Lewis. The brilliant, multigifted Ricketts began as a wood engraver at age fifteen but soon became a book illustrator, book designer and publisher (most notably of Oscar Wilde and Michael Field), and then a painter in oils, sculptor in bronze, and theater designer to boot (Yeats' "magician").

In the sentence before she mentions Ricketts' diary, Woolf notes that she has been "titivating Roger," that is, sprucing up her biography of Roger Fry. I cannot prove that Woolf knew Ricketts personally or his lifelong companion, the painter Charles Hazelwood Shannon. She certainly knew him, however, through Fry's letters and reviews read for her Fry biography, if not also from a quarter-century of tales from Fry's own lips. Ricketts and Fry jostled each other in the art world, for both were discerning art historians and critics who parted paths when it came to Impressionism, Post-Impressionism, and Modern Art. They were friendly—sometimes not-so-friendly—rivals: for Oxford University's Slade Art Professorship in 1909, for the directorship of the National Gallery in 1915 (positions neither attained), and even to design sets for R. C. Trevelyan's 1929 opera *The Bride of Dionysus*.

Fry treated Ricketts with affectionate respect. In his review of Ricketts' 1903 book *The Prado and Its Masterpieces*, Fry praises Ricketts for aiming for "the most profound understanding of great imaginative creations" (Sutton 1: 12). Writing in 1904 to his *Burlington Magazine* coeditor, Charles Holmes, Fry lauds Ricketts' "extraordinary gifts" (Sutton 1: 221). When Ricketts designs the sets and costumes in 1906 for Wilde's play *Salome*, Fry writes to painter and writer A. F. Jaccaci that Ricketts' "superbly mounted" production offered "ideas of colour that surpassed belief. I've never seen anything so beautiful on the stage" (Sutton 1: 267).

In *his* corner, however, Ricketts took disagreements on art as attacks on his very identity and worldview and so often placed Fry among his "enemies." A window on the conflict comes through a 1902 Fry letter to Ricketts' protégé, Sturge Moore, regarding an article on Rembrandt by French painter Edouard Bréal:

> when I mentioned [Bréal] and [the article] to Ricketts there followed an explosion of contempt.... I went in the most amicable spirit, but Ricketts took pains to be insulting. Within five minutes I put up with far more than I care to reflect upon for the cause of peace and because unfortunately I

think so highly of them that I want to be on friendly terms. But there are limits to the vermicility of even a peaceful person like myself. However, I'm not going to try again—but let *us* have a wrangle before long: I enjoy that because you are a person with whom one not only *must* but *can* differ, which is a great thing. (Sutton 1: 190)

Ricketts served on the *Burlington Magazine* Consulting Committee during the years Fry shared the editorship with Holmes, another close Ricketts friend; in fact, Ricketts contributed eleven articles to the *Burlington* up to 1909. However, when Fry becomes sole editor that year, Ricketts resigns. Each man's words in private letters reveal his temperament. "Ricketts has resigned from the *Burlington* Consulting Committee because I am editor!" Fry exclaims to Trevelyan. "Isn't he funny? I hope I may persuade him to relent; not that he's important but I have a foolish liking for him" (Sutton 1: 309). Ricketts, in turn, writes to Sydney Cockerell, director of the Fitzwilliam Museum in Cambridge, that he left the *Burlington* "owing to the Cézanne preface by Fry. This was the last straw after several equivocal articles tending toward the praise of the tragic followers of Neo Impressionism. So if Fry's friends speak of my brutality you will understand. There are frigid forms of mental prostitution which no lover of the old masters and fine moderns ought to abide" (Delaney 246).

Ricketts loved the old masters. He embraced the Romantic and the heroic and particularly the symbolism of Puvis de Chavannes and Gustave Moreau, themselves great exponents of classical art. "Ricketts considered Post-Impressionism a disease that attacked all that was finest in the European tradition of art since the Renaissance," his biographer, J.G.P. Delaney, explains (247). Ricketts could not fathom Fry's Impressionists. Landscape painting bored Ricketts. He and Shannon preferred to paint in the studio rather than outdoors. "[I]n painting in glazes rather than by direct application," Delaney observed in 1990, "they were at variance with everything that was then, and still is, regarded as most progressive in the art of the time" (36).

Woolf may have turned to Ricketts' *Journals* to deepen her portrait of Fry. She may also have hoped for further glimpses of "Michael Field," Katherine Bradley and Edith Cooper, whose joint-diary she read in 1933. Once more Woolf's diary worlds meet and intertwine.[8]

At the 1890 Arts and Crafts Exhibition, Ricketts and Shannon saw a copy of Michael Field's verse drama on Mary, Queen of Scots, *The Tragic Mary*, with its stunning Selwyn Image cover. So taken were they that they bought the book and sent a letter of praise, along with a complimentary copy of *their* new journal, *The Dial*. In January 1894, by Michael Field's "express entreaty," the painter William Rothenstein took the women to The Vale, Ricketts' and Shannon's studio home in Chelsea (Delaney 87). At that point the women artists were far better known than Shannon and Ricketts, having published more than ten works; however, according to Delaney, "they soon fell completely under Ricketts' spell" (87). He was just over five feet tall with a pointed Vandyke goatee and "very talkative hands" (*Self-Portrait* vii; hereafter S-P). Ambidextrous, in fact, he painted with one hand while penning aphorisms with the other, including the Wilde-like gem "Superior people are never bored" (*S-P* x).

Woolf read Ricketts' 1900 diary record of Wilde's death: "I feel too upset to write about it. I know that I have not really felt the fact of his death, I am merely wretched, tearful, stupid, vaguely conscious that something has happened that stirs up old resentment and the old sense that one is not sufficiently reconciled to life and death. [Sturge] Moore had hardly finished giving us the news when a loud ringing was heard and Michael Field arrived, sobbing loudly in the hall" (*S-P* 49–50). In 1897, Ricketts had convinced Bradley and Cooper to move from Reigate to a home on the Thames in Richmond near his and Shannon's new abode. Ricketts designed jewelry along with books, sets, costumes, and his and Shannon's matchless homes and gardens; more than half his jewels were for the Fields, including the famous locket containing the miniature Cooper profile, one of only two portraits he made.[9] In 1908, Ricketts gifted Cooper and Bradley his bronze, *The Tragic Actor*, with only one condition: that they place it in the room where they wrote their tragedies. More importantly, he designed and published many of the Fields' books. Ricketts was the last friend to see Edith Cooper alive and recorded her poignant last words in his journal: "Not yet, not yet!" (*S-P* 244).

Cooper, Ricketts, and Shannon were close to the same age; Bradley more than a decade older. Ricketts quarreled more than once with Bradley. Nevertheless, she wrote him on the morning of her death, in 1914, and made him the chief beneficiary of her will. In gratitude and love, Ricketts presented Rossetti's watercolor *Lucrezia Borgia* to the National Gallery in the Fields' memory—to link forever their work *Borgia* (for which he had designed emblems) with Rossetti's. In 1926, he designed and installed a graveside monument to the writers. After their deaths he declared, "When we all come into our own, 'Michael Field' will be remembered, when the Thompsons, Addington Symons, etc. are forgotten"—a 1917 prophecy now coming true (Delaney 276).

Ricketts' *Journals*, in short, offered many lures for Virginia Woolf in late December 1939. She learned in the opening that Ricketts, too, lost his mother at age thirteen. He was born October 2, 1866, in Geneva, Switzerland, where his father was studying painting with the help of a paternal allowance. Ricketts' father, however, gave *his* son little aid. Delaney writes that "[b]y not going in for athletics and field sports [young Charles] disappointed his father, who sometimes used crushingly to address his only son as 'Mademoiselle'" (12).

Luckily, sympathy flowed from the boy's French-Italian mother. "He was her confidant," Delaney explains, "and shared with her not only a passion for music but also that animation and quickness of mind that seem peculiarly French" (12). Concern for her health, however, darkened his childhood as parallel concern would cloud Woolf's. When his mother died unexpectedly in 1880, Ricketts recalled, "I felt old as the earth" (*S-P* 7). Delaney sees the mother's death as the key to Ricketts' character: "Paradoxically, underneath his friendship with Shannon and his great vitality lay a loneliness, a tragic childhood, a deep pessimism about life.... The worst ... had already happened to him with his mother's death; happiness and security were ever after to seem precarious" (3, 14). (This also could be said of Woolf.)

From his mother's death—if not earlier—Ricketts' outsider days begin. His father brings him back to England, where he speaks English with a French accent. Like young Virginia, the fourteen-year-old is thought "too delicate" for school (Delaney 14). For the next two years he visits museums and reads day and night—whatever he wishes. When he needs his father most, his father first withdraws and then rejects him. This father, ill himself, apprentices him at fifteen to a wood engraver and enrolls him in the Lambeth City and Guilds Technical Art School, where, fortunately, he meets Shannon, a fellow apprentice. Ricketts senior then withdraws to the Isle of Bute in Scotland to pursue marine painting. He soon dies, leaving young Charles not just an orphan at age sixteen but cruelly slapped in his will. Delaney found that the father's personal estate, "amounting to only just over £133, was held in trust for Blanche [Ricketts' younger sister], who is mysteriously described as the 'only next of kin'" (17).

Fortunately, the sixteen-year-old could turn, and did turn, to his kindly paternal grandfather, Edward Ricketts, who had been chief clerk to His Majesty's Treasury. Young Charles shared with this grandfather a love of beautiful books, the grandfather "a connoisseur of fine editions" (Delaney 8). On an Italian tour, the grandfather began also to collect art—another passion the grandson will pursue. When Edward Ricketts dies in 1895, he leaves each of his eight grandchildren an eighth of his estate. Ricketts uses his £235 legacy to found the Vale Press, named for their studio-home.[10] He and Shannon now begin to publish beautiful books. The two have also begun to collect art. Amazingly, on an income that rarely exceeded £1,000 a year, they "amassed a superb collection which, particularly in drawings, rivalled those of contemporary millionaires" (Delaney 2).

To find a parallel for Ricketts and Shannon, Delaney notes, one must turn to the Goncourt brothers in France, who also gave their lives to art and to collecting (26). One difference: the Goncourt brothers wrote a collaborative diary (one more like Michael Field's).[11] Ricketts and Shannon kept separate diaries, although Shannon's stopped early on, in 1906. In 1939, Moore and Lewis offered to Woolf and the world only a portion of Ricketts' lively diary. *Self-Portrait taken from the Letters & Journals of Charles Ricketts, R.A.* offers 458 diary entries and 244 letters.

Like Woolf, Ricketts kept a periodic diary. Fascinatingly, he seems able to write *his* diary only when deep in other artistic work. Creating helps to focus his mind for the pen. At age thirty-three, he tells his 1900 journal: "When I am not working I find it impossible to record what has occurred to me: the stress of impressions is too great and varied, the field for musing too wide.... Away from work one's thoughts drift into an imagined contact with a world of opposition. I often hold converse with an imaginary public, and confess myself to myself. During work, the audience is the world of art, and the sole enemy one's own lack of power" (*S-P* 36–37).

Like Woolf, Ricketts rereads his diary and adds later notes. In despair during the Great War, he confesses to the Dutch artist R.N.R. Holst: "I have, however, managed to keep a diary, and glancing at it yesterday, I found myself deeply absorbed, as if it were the work of someone else. It is possibly too introspective, critical, and egoistical to interest others, but of this I am not sure" (*S-P* 252–53). He needn't have worried. The diary brims with interest: with incisive portraits of famous artists, flashes of humor, and touching remarks. It offers stories of Edward Burne-Jones' love for William Morris—and of Morris' cold heart (81–82); insights on Gilbert and Sullivan, whose works Ricketts staged;[12] and fascinating comparisons of Sarah Bernhardt, Eleonora Duse, and Gabrielle Réjane as actors (59–60).

As a travel diarist Ricketts also can please. Complaining of the need to tip incessantly in Venice, he sighs in an April 1899 entry: "One starts in the morning with enough coppers to sink a gondola, and in the evening one lacks the penny to buy an orange" (*S-P* 23). In 1901, he reveals his own approach to art—and his scorn for a certain type of critic. "There is something unaccountable to me in the habit of some eminent men of going to see things they despise merely for the pleasure of running them down," he writes. "With me, art is a function like eating. I choose the dishes I like best; it never occurs to me to taste dishes I dislike, that I may say funny things about them" (*S-P* 68). The same year, he poignantly declares: "It would seem that the excellent things of this world have only survived owing to a series of lucky chances"—further sign he sees life as both fragile and threatened (*S-P* 52).

Mysteries still surround Ricketts' diary—and Shannon's, as well. Editor Lewis does not tell Woolf and other readers of the 1939 *Journals* that Ricketts' defensive, secretive bent extended to his diary. We learn this only from Delaney's 1990 biography. Delaney studied the original journals, housed today in the British Museum, and reports that Ricketts "vigorously censored" his diary, "deleting passages, tearing out sections and pages, and even destroying volumes covering whole years" (3). The artist, he explains, "rigorously expurgated his diary of the more personal revelations" (24). Furthermore, like Samuel Pepys, whose private diary language both camouflaged and spotlighted intimate confessions, Ricketts shifted to Italian when emotions ran high. Delaney believes that "[e]xpressing his emotions in a foreign tongue somehow made them more impersonal, so that they could be faced up to and considered" (158).

Ricketts shifts to Italian in 1902 when Charles Holmes plans to wed—a sign (Delaney suggests) that Ricketts had been in love with the young Holmes, who looked like Ricketts' father (178). Shannon's diary stops in 1906, and editor Lewis omits from the 1939 *Journals* these words from Ricketts' September 7, 1906, entry: "I have . . . been frightened by the question, 'What should I do if Shannon got married?'" (Delaney 219). He then shifts to Italian to voice his fears. Ricketts may have destroyed all his own diaries from 1907 through 1913, for the 1939 *Journals* give no diary entries for these years, despite the fact that Ricketts refers to his 1911 travel diaries. In 1921, he tells Holst that he kept his journal "for about twenty years," that is, from 1898 through 1918 (*S-P* 335). Did Shannon also write diaries after 1906 that he (or Ricketts) destroyed?

Editor Lewis and Sturge Moore thus carefully fashion in 1939 the *Self-Portrait* they unveil through Ricketts' journals.[13] Lewis acknowledges that they have "curtailed" the many descriptions and critiques of art that lace the journals as too technical for the general reader (*S-P* 24n1). Delaney reports that the diary "abounds" with descriptions of Ricketts' *own* painting problems as well as of others' work (146). These, too, Lewis curtails. He also withholds some of Ricketts' most pointed accusations, for instance these February 9, 1916, diary words on Oscar Wilde's trial:

> I believe the crash of his scandal affected his contemporaries to a degree unknown to younger people. Not only did eminent men, his seniors, do nothing, but several friends behaved badly, Sarah Bernhardt, for instance, Degas, Gosse, and I believe Burne-Jones. Meredith was brutal and Morris indifferent. To the young of today, there is no kind of moral prejudice, it is only with men of my age, whose career was actually affected by the crash, that the story shows itself as a tragic event, in which the fiber of the nation seemed of poor quality. (Delaney 96)

Beyond the absent diary pieces, another mystery also lingers: why Ricketts stops his diary in 1918. He explores the matter in a 1921 letter to Holst: "Wishing to take a decision as to whether I should keep or throw away my diaries—which I have kept for about twenty years—I started reading them, they end with the war, and their lecture has saddened me for days . . . [O]ne seems to have been always preparing for something which never happens. The pages during the war quite upset me, I had forgotten how tragic those times really were" (S-P 335).

Ricketts, however, valued diaries. In 1920, he writes to twenty-two-year-old Lewis, who was then living in China: "I hope you keep a diary of impressions of Chinese life, etc. Even the daily aspect of the Forbidden City would interest you and others in years to come. Never think the present less interesting than the future. We waste our lives in preparing for something more interesting, which never comes" (S-P 329).

But the war upsets Ricketts and saddens him. His diary stops in 1918, and in his remaining twelve years of life he repeatedly says, "I died during the War: I have been dead for years."[14] The diary embodies a crucial part of Ricketts that dies in the Great War. Delaney writes that "[t]he effects of the war on Ricketts's character were never to be effaced. . . . He saw the war, as he had seen the Wilde trial, as an attack on art itself" (305, 278).

During the tense buildup to the Great War, Ricketts already sees its horrors. He marvels in his July 31, 1914, entry that "no one, be he intelligent or not, quite realizes the misery of war, let alone its serious and tragic aspects" (S-P 209). Throughout the war, he trembles for the world's art treasures, and he regularly petitions the British government for greater vigilance over works in the National Gallery, British Museum, and Westminster Abbey. On September 1, 1914, when reports reach him of the destruction of Rubens' *Miraculous Draught of Fishes*, he tells his diary of his "anxiety over the Puvis decorations at Amiens and the Cathedral.... A shell falling among the Puvis walls might blot out one-half of his life-work for ever" (*S-P* 215).

Ricketts' diary words anticipate Woolf's own diary entries in 1939 and 1940. He writes in May 1915: "We may have to mourn Verona, Padua, and Venice in ruins. A shell in the Arena Chapel would deprive the world of the second jewel in the great crown of Italian painting. After the Sistina, this series is the most important in Italian art.... I have been brainless and effortless for days" (*S-P* 239). Twelve days later, he notes: "One certain result of the war upon my character is a total blunting of perception.... I do not know if something has snapped in my mental mechanism, if I am merely tired out" (*S-P* 241). In July he writes, "The war is a daily strain upon the nerves, its possible duration and results are again a strain" (*S-P* 244). By the end of 1916, he is declaring "a feeling of unreality topmost on my thoughts" (*S-P* 274).

Armistice Day diary entries—in my research, at least—prove priceless mirrors of the soul. Ricketts' November 11, 1918, entry, so charmingly redolent of his outsider's[15] role, telegraphs his embattled, yet frontier-crossing, state. "First hooters announcing Armistice—I am crying like a pig," he begins. "Madame Rose asks us for a flag, we are without one. I go downstairs, bring up the Jeanne d'Arc banner painted months ago; this, embellished with a tuft of Arbutus, is put on the balcony."[16] Sadly Ricketts, with his powerful visual memory, impeccable taste, and passionate love of beauty in both nature[17] and art, ends his diary with the war. As with Wilde's trial, he feels not just *British* betrayal in the war but civilization's betrayal, as well.

"I'm reading Ricketts diary—all about the war the last war," Woolf tells her own diary on December 17, 1939 (*D* 5: 252). If she read Lewis' preface to *Self-Portrait*, she knew, too, that, like Peter Lucas, Ricketts came to live with a ghost near the end of his days: with a victim of brain trauma. In 1929, Shannon fell from a ladder while hanging a painting and suffered a concussion and strokes. "To live in the same house with a lifelong friend, to have that friend still moving in the house, apparently healthy and normal and yet quite gone, a fine painter sunk to a gentle imbecile," Lewis writes; "[Ricketts'] affectionate and sensitive nature was torn to shreds by it. Perhaps most of all, the fact that his friend did not recognize him, or if he sometimes did, viewed him with hostility, numbed him like a mortal wound. Yet there was nothing to be done" (*S-P* xii).

Despite this great blow, Ricketts (like Woolf) was resilient and placed his faith in art. "Art is the evidence of man's opposition to mere necessity and chance and the nearest approximation to a sense of immortality," became his oft-said credo (Delaney 26). "Shall we live to see ourselves secure and respected?" he asks his diary in 1914 (S-P 193). "After all, our work may mean something to someone else," he hopes at the close of his 1915 journal (S-P 251).

Regard for Ricketts' wide-flung, dazzling gifts has gathered in the past thirty-nine years—even more quickly than that for Michael Field. Stephen Calloway set the tone with his 1979 book *Charles Ricketts: Subtle and Fantastic Decorator*, with a foreword by Kenneth Clark. Joseph Darracott followed in 1980 with *The World of Charles Ricketts*, while in 1985 Eric Binnie focused on *The Theatrical Designs of Charles Ricketts*. Then came Delaney's full-scale biography in which he calls Ricketts a "superb writer" along with his other gifts (2). Sturge Moore first planned to publish Ricketts' complete journals and letters. Surely today the world would savor the full prickly and precise diary (at least the full diary Ricketts allowed to remain) and—as with Woolf—*separate* volumes of letters.

In 2003, Canadian playwright Michael Lewis MacLennan made Ricketts' diary the fulcrum of his award-winning play called *Last Romantics*.[18] "I was ... intrigued by how completely we could forget such brilliant and significant artists," MacLennan explains in the notes for this play, which resurrects Michael Field as well as Ricketts and Shannon. MacLennan calls Ricketts and Shannon "arguably the most intelligent and passionate proponents of the aesthetic movement."[19] *Last Romantics* opens with "Two or three journals ... piled somewhere" (5). In scene 6, Shannon pulls a letter from Ricketts' journal and reads it: a 1915 letter offering Ricketts the directorship of the National Gallery. In act 2, Shannon pulls a clipping from Ricketts' journal and later drops the journal and the clipping and returns to his painting (95, 96). In the next scene, Ricketts asks Edith Cooper, "How do you comfort yourself?" Cooper replies: "Memories. I read, the books we [she and Katherine Bradley] wrote together [including their diary]. Her voice is in there, mingled with mine." Ricketts then responds: "I have my journals. You think Shannon might one day read them?" (104).

In late December 1939, Virginia Woolf read them. She learned there more of Roger Fry for her biography-in-progress. She saw resurrected, too, those "outsiders" Katherine Bradley and Edith Cooper, along with Ricketts and Shannon. She also saw, alarmingly, a diarist stopped by war.

10

Encircled by War

Territorial attack intensifies in the years covered in Virginia Woolf's two final diary books: the 109-entry 1940 diary and the 10-entry 1941 diary. In April 1940, Germany invades Norway and Denmark. In May, with no pretext or warning, massive German air and land forces attack neutral Holland, Belgium, and Luxembourg. The Dutch government and Queen Wilhelmina flee to London. At this, British prime minister Neville Chamberlain resigns, and Winston Churchill is called on to lead a national coalition.

Leonard Woolf begins Fire Watch and Air Raid Precaution duties in Rodmell and finishes his book *The War for Peace*. Leonard writes in his autobiography of the philosopher G. E. Moore's visit: "There we sat in May 1940, Moore, Desmond [MacCarthy], Virginia, and I in the house and under a hot sun and brilliant sky in the garden, in a cocoon of friendship and nostalgic memories. At the same time the whole weekend was dominated by a consciousness that our little private world was menaced by destruction" (*Journey Not Arrival* 49).

France next succumbs in June 1940: Hitler's storm troopers parade up Paris' Champs-Élysées. Only England now remains. On July 19, Hitler asks England to surrender. In August, he orders a total blockade of Great Britain and begins a nighttime bombing assault. The German flying corridor to London is just east of Rodmell village. On her September walks on the South Downs, Virginia sees the hospital trains carrying British wounded home from defeated France (Oldfield 124). Rodmell also is just three miles from Newhaven, where the expected German invasion would land. Hermione Lee writes that "[a]lmost everyone [Woolf] knew, apart from Ethel Smyth . . . was fairly sure that [England was] about to be invaded and defeated. This may not have been the national mood, but it was certainly the mood of her circle" (717).

Nevertheless, as these last two diaries movingly show, Virginia Woolf fights on—in her public works and in her diary. Surrounded now and cut off, she holds on until she can fight no more.

Virginia Woolf's 1940 Diary

> "A perfect day—a red admiral feasting on an apple day.... The light is now fading. Soon the Siren; then the twang of plucked strings... But its almost forgettable still; the nightly operation on the tortured London.... A mist is rising; a long fleece of white on the marshes. I must black out. I had so much to say."
>
> (October 17, 1940; *D* 5: 330)

Virginia Woolf aims for a weightier diary in 1940, poignantly an *evening* diary for "Old Virginia." This will be her last complete diary year. In April 1939, she had begun her long-envisioned memoirs and now, war-harried, she seeks greater diary depth. "This very large sheet... begins a new year, on a new system," she gamely begins another loose-leaf diary on January 3, 1940. "Evening over the fire writing, instead of end of the morning scrambling. Thus I hope to write a better hand.... For unless I can put a little weight into this book, it'll have no interest, even for an old woman, turning the pages" (*D* 5: 255). The diary grows stout as Woolf herself grows lean: 109 entries preserve the 361 days from January 3 to December 29, an entry now every three or four days, a quickened pace from the every four or five days of her 1939 diary.

Once more the diarist stretches and expands. On February 2, she reminds herself to take "extracts from the papers" for her diary, and five days later she copies the following contrasting headlines: "Towards a Settlement with Japan. The next phase in India; Red rout in Finland. 5,000 killed" (*D* 5: 263, 264). She gathers bits to serve her later. "A curious letter from Hugh [Walpole] this afternoon, part of which I will copy, for I like reading old letters," she opens her March 26 entry (*D* 5: 274). A month later, she ends an entry by copying three advertisements. She closes this diary book with a list of war encroachments and friends' deaths—the outer and the inner—headed "1940," presumably reminders for her memoirs. "Is there a difference of temperature between the morning mind & the evening?" she asks herself in December (*D* 5: 345).

Faced with war and death, Woolf ratchets her production. She writes ten articles and two short stories to fill the coffers; achieves critical and (some) financial success with *Roger Fry: A Biography*; finishes the first draft of her final novel, *Between the Acts*, in November; adds weight to her diary; and creeps forward with her memoirs. All the while, she eyes "a new critical method—something swifter & lighter & more colloquial & yet intense: more to the point & less composed; more fluid & following the flight [of her mind], than [her Common Reader] essays" (*D* 5: 298). This last—the unfinished work "Anon"—sounds much like her diary style.

World War II forces Woolf to "turn journalist" again. "The worst year we've ever had in the Press, I gather," Woolf confides to her May 6 entry (*D* 5: 283). On July 5, she notes, "I must make money," and she can report, pleased, October 17 that she has spent "I dont know how much brain nerve earning £30 gs. with 3 little articles" (*D* 5: 300, 329). However, in her next-to-last entry, "Christmas Eve," she admits: "We are very poor; & my hoard is 450: but must not be tapped again. So I must write. Yes, our old age is not going to be sunny orchard drowse" (*D* 5: 346).

Across 1940, Woolf's diary and *Roger Fry* once more serve as interchangeable forces of renewal. In late January, in fact, Woolf tries to write "Transformations," her Fry biography's last chapter, in her *diary*. Her words depict her *own* last years as well as Fry's: "They were... years not of repose & stagnation... but of perpetual experiment"; "Physically, the strain was very great. His health had suffered" (*D* 5: 261). But diary composition fails. "No I cannot reel it off," she admits and stops (*D* 5: 261). But she keeps at the Fry re-vision, and when she finishes in March, she feels joy "to have given Nessa back her Roger, lost since Julian died" (*D* 5: 272). She has brought life. "Now for me begins the twilight hour," Woolf then tells her diary on March 21 (*D* 5: 272–73). *Roger Fry* gives her the joys of birth but also postpartum despair.

And now the war starts to encircle her work. Her May 13 entry opens with "some content[ment]" at posting her proofs of *Roger Fry* and the "peace that comes with it... because we're in the 3rd day of 'the greatest battle in history'" (*D* 5: 283–84). She refers to the German surprise attack on Luxembourg, Belgium, and Holland. *Roger Fry* has been, and will be, her answer. She notes the challenge: "So intense are my feelings (about Roger): yet the circumference (the war) seems to make a hoop round them" (*D* 5: 284). Fry's life is published on July 25 and, despite the war—or, perhaps, *because* of the war—does well. In August, Leonard orders a second and then a third edition.[1] Virginia tells her diary that she feels now "really & truly immune, &... that I could go on to the next thing—to many next things" (*D* 5: 310). She asks her diary: "Is it an illusion that I'm freer & stronger, as a writer, than ever?" (*D* 5: 310).

The 1940 diary touches deeply, for it reveals how hard Woolf fights not only the doldrums but also the harsh and isolating war. Her "weightier" diary represents just one battle front. "The war slowly enacts itself on a great scene: round our little scene," she tells her diary on December 8—another image of surround (*D* 5: 343). She tries to compass the war in her diary. She records troop advances and retreats. She quotes official and common-folk talk. "I should like to be able to take scientific notes of reactions," she tells her diary on July 26 (*D* 5: 306). On December 19, she writes, "It wd be interesting if I could take today, Thursday, & say exactly how the war changes it" (*D* 5: 344). She then does so vividly. The war overtakes her life diary: her *writer's* diary becomes now a *war* diary. Ninety-five of her 109 entries refer to the war.

Across 1940, Woolf treats her life as a sacrifice in a barbaric rite, nature helpless to assist. "Here I stop to insert a remark often occurring," she tells her February 8 entry, sensing the "unopened Spring": "how we're being led to the altar this spring."[2] "Yes, we are being led up garlanded to the altar," she opens her May 14 entry after Hitler's assault on the neutral Netherlands (*D* 5: 284). When France falls in June, the knives come closer. "[T]he war," she tells an undated entry that Olivier Bell dates June 27, "our waiting while the knives sharpen for the operation.... I mean, there is no 'autumn' no winter" (*D* 5: 299). In August she shifts her trope only slightly: "Its like the raising of the gallows tree, for an execution now expected in a week or fortnight" (*D* 5: 310). Then the bombs fall. "[T]he nightly operation on the tortured London," she personifies the city in October, a vision of repeated trespass. "I must black out," she then states. "I had so much to say" (*D* 5: 330).

Across the year she resists the blackout, the suffocation, the sacrifice. "But why waste even this half inch [of diary space] upon these blaring & boring politics?" she asks her March 20 entry (*D* 5: 272). "No, I dont want the garage to see the end of me. I've a wish for 10 years more" she declares on May 15, having noted two days before that Leonard has stored petroleum in the garage "for suicide shd. Hitler win" (*D* 5: 285, 284). On June 9 she repeats: "I dont want to go to bed at midday: this refers to the garage" (*D* 5: 293). Her October 2 entry evokes Thomas Gray's "Elegy Written in a Country Churchyard" to show nature profaned by war. "And all the air a solemn stillness holds," she quotes Gray's famous lines. It holds, she then adds, "till 8.30 when the cadaverous twanging in the sky begins; the planes going to London. Well its an hour still to that.... Should I think of death? Last night a great heavy plunge of bomb under the window. So near we both started. A plane had passed dropping this fruit.... I said to L.: I dont want to die yet" (*D* 5: 326).

She draws on her "props"—with only partial success. She summons her horse, but now it rarely leaps its fences. She wants to "kick [her] heels" March 26. On May 31, her imaginative faculty "springs up" and she invents the whole end of her final novel, *Between the Acts*. "And to me its the voice of the scent again," she declares happily (*D* 5: 291). Her Pegasus, her winged Fanny Burney steed, is off—at least momentarily. In June, she declares she must put her head "to the gallop" to fill the gap until *Roger Fry* appears, and on October 2 she is able to have a nice morning gallop "with Coleridge"—Samuel Taylor Coleridge's brilliant daughter, Sara, that is (*D* 5: 294, 326).

However, for most of the year, Woolf's eyes seem more on *others'* steeds, gauging the effort to ride. She reads G. K. Chesterton's *St. Thomas Aquinas* in late May and feels that "[h]is skittish over ingenious mind makes one shy (like a horse)" (*D* 5: 289). Ann Stephen, Adrian's daughter, visits in August and Woolf finds her skittish, too: "A great deal of force & spirit & yet always at the leap something balks her" (*D* 5: 312). Vita Sackville-West's friend Hilda Matheson keeps her hands too heavy on the reins and then dies in late October (*D* 5: 302). Only Vita remains able to place her hands "loosely upon so many reins" (*D* 5: 328). However, while bombs drop all around her on August 31, Vita tells Woolf of Cynthia North, "so lovely like a young colt . . . killed by a bomb she trod on" (*D* 5: 314). This makes Woolf feel "too jaded" to record her thoughts, *jadedness* also noted May 6, July 20, August 2, October 23, and November 17 (*D* 5: 314). The Germans "seem youthful, fresh, inventive," Woolf tells her May 25 entry. "We plod behind" (*D* 5: 287). Poignantly, she declares on June 22: "I feel, if this is my last lap, oughtn't I to read Shakespeare? But cant" (*D* 5: 298). On December 16 comes the ominous: "Its rather a hard lap: the winter lap" (*D* 5: 343).

Her related bird tropes show a similar distressed state. They enact one of the major tensions in Woolf's diary: that between constraint and freedom, constriction and expansion, the tight and the loose. In her fifth entry, January 26, Woolf gives herself "travellers notes," should she be lost: "I began one night, absolutely submerged, throttled, held in a vice with my nose rubbed against Roger—no way out—all hard as iron—to read Julian. And off winged my mind along those wild uplands. A hint for the future. Always relieve pressure by a flight" (*D* 5: 260). She then tries to write the last chapter of *Roger Fry* in her diary. Fry, she writes tellingly, had "freedom" and "vigour . . . with which he extended & enlarged his view" (*D* 5: 261). His last years were "full . . . of change" (*D* 5: 260).

On March 20, she longs to be quit of her final Fry corrections, to be "free" and "winging off on small articles & stories" (*D* 5: 272). Eleven days later, still tied, she offers this revealing fantasy: "I would like to tell myself a nice little wild improbable story to spread my wings after this cramped ant-like morning—which I will not detail—for details are the death of me. Thank God, this time next week I shall be free—free of entering M[argery Fry']s corrections & my own into margins. The story?—oh about the life of a bird, its cheep cheep. . . . A story dont come. . . . At the back of my head the string is still wound tight" (*D* 5: 276–77).

A week later, however, when she gives Leonard her corrected *Roger Fry*, she feels "wings" on her shoulders (*D* 5: 278). On August 10, she repeats the lament of her April 1939 diary, that the war clips her wings: "[I]f I had solitude—no men driving stakes digging fresh gun emplacements & no neighbours, doubtless I cd. expand & soar—into PH. [her novel *Between the Acts*] into Coleridge" (*D* 5: 310). If only . . .

Like her bird and horse figures, her water imagery takes a similar tempered turn. Creative flow returns with Pointz Hall (*Between the Acts*), Woolf's final novel. In her third entry, January 19, she records that she "made up a little of P.H. at 37 [Mecklenburgh Square], & think I've tapped something perhaps—a new combination of the raw & the lyrical; how to slide over. I think 2 years at Roger may have filled the cistern" (*D* 5: 259). On May 31, as often in the past, the novel spills over into the diary. "Scraps, orts & fragments, as I said in PH. which is now bubbling—" she opens her entry. "I'm playing with words; & think I owe some dexterity to finger exercises here" (*D* 5: 290). Tramping the downs, she has fully imagined her novel's end. "How amazing that I can tap that old river again; & how satisfying. But will it last?" she asks (*D* 5: 291). In October she crows: "I am filling my mind slowly with E[lizabe]thans" (*D* 5: 330).

She finishes *Between the Acts* on November 23, and immediately her thoughts "well up, to write the first chapter of the next book," which she names "Anon" (*D* 5: 340). Her creative force also shows itself five days before when she pictures male writers' works as small sandcastles that her powerful wave destroys. She has been reading Herbert Read's 1940 autobiography, *Annals of Innocence and Experience,* and describes Read, T. S. Eliot, H. G. Wells, and philosopher George Santayana as "[l]ittle boys making sand castles. . . . Each is weathertight, & gives shelter to the occupant. . . . But I am the sea which demolishes these castles" (*D* 5: 340).

Were these the only water tropes in the 1940 diary, we might relish Woolf's force and deep wellspring. We might second her August 6 sense that she is "freer & stronger, as a writer, than ever" (*D* 5: 310). However, a new water figure also enters this diary: Woolf's "ship" marooned in Shelley's "deep wide sea of misery." The tableau comes July 28—three days after *Roger Fry* appears. Woolf makes up a phrase at Monk's House: "a Season of calm weather" (*D* 5: 307). The June "doldrums" thus persist. "Yes for a moment I believe that I can compass a season of calm weather," Woolf tells her diary. "Yet 'they' say the invasion is fixed for Aug. 16th. A season of calm weather is the crown for which I'm always pushing & shoving, swimming like the hedgehog who cuts his throat with his paws Nessa said yesterday at C[harlesto]n, if he swims.... Thus our island will be invaded—my season of calm weather. Many <an island> a green isle—why cant I remember poetry?" (*D* 5: 307). She tries to recall here Shelley's "Lines Written among the Euganean Hills": "Many a green isle needs must be / In the deep wide sea of misery."

She sees herself as a green island or as a ship ringed by troubled seas—another image of surround. She has pictured herself as a ship since her second diary at age seventeen. She tries hard now to make the best of her threatened state. On June 12, proofs of *Roger Fry* dispatched, she cheerily projects herself as shipshape: "I feel decks cleared & scrubbed, & can set to, in a jiffy" (*D* 5: 295). However, waiting for reviews on August 2, she opens her diary to conflate *Roger Fry* with a ship in war: "Complete silence surrounds that book. It might have sailed into the blue & been lost. 'One of our books did not return' as the BBC puts it" (*D* 5: 308). On August 31, she wants once more to "swim into quiet water": that is, to write her novel-in-progress or an essay on Coleridge (*D* 5: 314).

But the German bombers rattle their Sussex windows in August, destroy their London homes in September and October, and hinder their London access. However, Woolf still seeks a positive side. She will lose her London servant, Mabel. "A great relief. I like being alone in our little boat," she tells her diary on September 14. "I like provisioning & seeing alls shipshape & not having dependants" (*D* 5: 320). Two days later, she starts her entry: "Well, we're alone in our ship" (*D* 5: 321). However, the next day, when diarist Peter Lucas' criticism sucks the life from "Anon," her island no longer seems green. "Our island is a desert island," she tells her diary. "So we, L. & I, are almost cut off" (*D* 5: 322).

"[H]ack an outlet," she has counseled herself in her January 26 "travellers notes": "Always relieve pressure by a flight" (*D* 5: 260). From almost her first diary days, Virginia's country/London rhythm resounds. While across her life she turns repeatedly from London constriction to the untrammeled countryside, she needs, in truth, the *movement*, the change, and the blend: the country-in-London (as she wrote in her pivotal 1903 diary). As with her ship figure, Woolf stresses now the virtues of her increasingly forced isolation in the country due to the encircling war. "[T]he break in our lives from London to country is a far more complete one than any change of house," she intuits as early as February 2. "Yes, but I havent got the hang of it altogether" (*D* 5: 263). She tells herself that "London, in nips, is cramped & creased"; nevertheless, its absence brings fondness: "Odd how often I think with what is love I suppose of the City: of the walk to the Tower: that is my England" (*D* 5: 263). She declares she cannot now "even imagine London in peace," but this denial frees her to do just that: "the lit nights, the buses roaring past Tavistock Square, the telephone ringing, & I scooping together with the utmost difficulty one night or afternoon alone" (*D* 5: 263).

She uses her next entry, February 7, to challenge herself. Since she no longer is "in the movement"—a crucial state for her—"& remote in this water sogged country, now's the time to see if the art, or life, creed, the belief in something existing independently of myself, will <weather the/stand the> hold good.... Well, if it dont stand like a flagstaff, then its been a washout" (*D* 5: 263–64). Two days later, reveling in a novel, she evokes Shakespeare's lines in *Coriolanus*:

Despising,
For you, the city, thus I turn my back:
There is a world elsewhere. (*D* 5: 266)

Gratifyingly, her next entry reports her invention of "pages & pages" of her lecture "The Leaning Tower" on her country walk up to Telscombe. She means it "to be full & fertile."[3]

Across the year she continues to stress the blessings of her isolated country days. On February 16, the blackened London windows depress her. The city seems "so much more cheerless than the country evening," she writes (*D* 5: 267). On March 29, she asks: "Is it age, or what that makes life here alone, no London no visitors seem a long trance of pleasure . . ." (*D* 5: 276). Yet she needs London too, for she opens this entry with the question: "What shall I think of that[s] liberating & freshening?" and then, tellingly, gives London as the answer in a vision that links London with her pen: "The river [is liberating and freshening]. Say the Thames at London bridge; & buying a notebook; & then walking along the Strand & letting each face give me a buffet; & each shop; & perhaps a Penguin. For we're up in London on Monday. Then I think

I'll read an Elizabethan—like swinging from bough to bough. Then back here I'll saunter" (*D* 5: 276). She imagines here the country/city rhythm—and the *movement*—she needs.

On July 5, she evokes London walks again—this walk with Elizabeth Bowen: "We walked from 37 through Temple, along river, up Thames Street, to the Tower, talking talking. . . . On top of bus, we talked again—a good idea; talking in many changing scenes: it changes topics & moods" (*D* 5: 301). London can still cause "extreme jadedness" and the need to "cool & expand on the marsh" (*D* 5: 302); however, on September 11, when she quotes Prime Minister Winston Churchill's "clear, measured, robust speech" on the threatened invasion, she once more exalts her birthplace. "Our majestic city," she quotes him, "which touches me, for I feel London majestic" (*D* 5: 317).

Valiantly, she offers specimen *country* days across her diary as counter to war; however, another aspect reappears: a sense of emptiness, of vacancy. It starts as early as her fourth entry, January 20:

> Then L. went & skated & I walked on the bank & home over the marsh. The beauty was etherial, unreal, empty. . . . All silent, as if offered from another world. No birds, no carts, men shooting. This specimen against the war. This heartless & perfect beauty. . . . But some emptiness in me—in my life—because L. said the rent [at Mecklenburgh Square] was so high. And then the silence, the pure disembodied silence, in which the perfect specimen was presented; seemed to correspond to my own vacancy . . . (*D* 5: 259)

On February 2, when she tries to imagine London in peace, she reminds herself to use "the present astonishing space" of country isolation "for Burke &c. . . . Yes, but I havent got the hang of it altogether. The immense space suddenly becomes vacant; then illuminated" (*D* 5: 263). Again on May 13, her "little moment of peace comes in a yawning hollow"—a surrounded vacant space once more (*D* 5: 284). On May 30, she notes that she can be happy in individual moments, "only theres no support in the fabric . . . theres no healthy tissue round the moment. It's blown out" (*D* 5: 290).

She wants in the country not the "circumference" of *war* but the "protecting & reflecting walls" of readers (*D* 5: 304). On publication eve of *Roger Fry*, July 24, she wonders in her diary whether the publication will allow her to "feel once more round me the wall [of response] I've missed—or vacancy? or chill?" (*D* 5: 304). When bombs shake their windows on August 16, she confesses she thinks "of nothingness" (*D* 5: 311). On September 29, her London home gutted, she again contrasts country and London days and tries to find sustenance enough in Sussex. This entry provides a clear view of her 1940 days. "I was thinking: (among other things) that this is a lazy life," she begins her country portrait:

> Breakfast in bed. Read in bed. Bath. Order dinner. Out to Lodge. After rearranging my room (turning table to get the sun: Church on right; window left; a new very lovely view) tune up, with cigarette: write till 12; stop; visit L.: look at papers; return; type till 1. Listen in [to the radio]. Lunch. Sore jaw. Cant bite. Read papers. Walk to Southease. Back 3. Gather & arrange apples. Tea. Write a letter. Bowls. Type again. Read Michelet & write here. Cook dinner. Music. Embroidery. 9.30 read (or sleep) till 11.30. Bed. Compare with the old London day. Three afternoons someone coming. One night, dinner party.... Telephone ringing. L. to meetings. KM. [Kingsley Martin] or [William] Robson bothering—that was an average week; with Friday to Monday here. (*D* 5: 325)

Yet she seems to feel something missing, for she adds: "I think, now we're marooned, I ought to cram in a little more reading. Yet why? A happy, a very free, & disengaged—a life that rings from one simple melody to another. Yes; why not enjoy this after all those years of the other?" (*D* 5: 325). She cannot enjoy it because she is "disengaged." Thirteen days later, she opens her diary with a similar resolution:

> I would like to pack my day rather fuller.... If it were not treasonable to say so, a day like this is almost too—I wont say happy: but amenable. The tune varies, from one nice melody to another.... But I was thinking I must intensify.... Partly I'm terrified of passive acquiescence.[4] I live in intensity. In London, now, or 2 years ago, I'd be owling through the streets. More pack & thrill than here. So I must supply that—how? I think book <making> inventing. And there's always the chance of a rough wave: no, I wont once more turn my magnifying glass on that.
> ... Queer the contraction of life to the village radius.... And we on our lovely free autumn island. (*D* 5: 328–29)

The war "circumference" surrounds; the village radius is too small. "[T]ime goes so heavy & slow," she notes on November 12, "that nothing marks the days" (*D* 5: 338).

She needs change. She needs a wider radius. But she is "marooned." On

May 6, she links her emptiness to her water figure when she learns of her niece Angelica Bell's love for the much older David Garnett. "Pray god she may tire of that rusty surly slow old dog with his amorous ways & his primitive mind," Woolf beseeches her diary. "It makes one feel oddly old: even to me comes the emptiness that Nessa feels, as I can guess. . . . So the land recedes from my ship which draws out into the sea of old age. The land with its children" (*D* 5: 282, 283).

She fights old age losses, just as she battles the war and the creeping sense of vacancy. She writes her 1940 diary for the "old woman" (herself), after all, and across the year "the old woman" becomes her emblem for life (*D* 5: 255). Thinking of her love for London on February 2, she writes: "I mean, if a bomb destroyed . . . the old woman reading I should feel—well, what the patriots feel" (*D* 5: 263). On May 15, calling war "all bombast," she adds, "One old lady pinning on her cap has more reality" (*D* 5: 285). And when the blitzkrieg starts, she writes on September 10: "The people I think of now are the very grimy lodging house keepers, say in Heathcote Street; with another night to face: old wretched women standing at their doors; dirty, miserable. Well—as Nessa said on the phone, its coming very near" (*D* 5: 317). Here are wretched old women in the sea of misery.

Lady Sibyl Colefax persists in Woolf's 1940 diary as the model of bold, fluid old age. In her third entry, January 19, Woolf reports being "touched" by Lady Sibyl's visit, particularly by the older woman's revelation that she had never liked George Duckworth, Woolf's abusive half-brother (*D* 5: 259). Five months later, Woolf praises Lady Sibyl's "heroism" and contrasts her "fluid worldliness" with that of T. S. Eliot, whom Woolf finds "ossifying" into "writers egotism" (*D* 5: 287).

Although Woolf's model in 1940 is the fluid "reading old woman," less attractive images of elderly women enter her diary, as well. Shopping for clothes on February 16, Woolf declares, "Of course I looked a shaggy dowdy old woman," and in September, as the air raid sounds and she decides "whatever happens" to "settle & sun on the moment," she then thinks of her age and offers diary words like those of the Reverend John Skinner, whose diary (and suicide) struck her profoundly in 1930: "58—not so many more. This is quite possible, in any condition. I sometimes think about violent death" (*D* 5: 269, 320). On December 19, noting Lord Beaverbrook's warning that the invasion will come in early February 1941, she writes alarmingly: "A certain old age feeling sometimes makes me think I cant spend force as I used" (*D* 5: 345). In her next-to-last entry, December 24, she foresees that "our old age is not going to be sunny orchard drowse," and in her final entry, December 29, she decries again "the hardness" of old age. "I feel it," she writes. "I rasp. I'm tart."[5] She then quotes Matthew Arnold's poem "Thyrsis," noting she even sought out his book to copy the lines:

> The foot less prompt to meet the morning dew,
> The heart less bounding at emotion new,
> And hope, once crush'd, less quick to spring again.

Woolf's marooned ship "draws out into the sea of old age" (*D* 5: 283). And the hate-my-kind revulsion begins. On February 8, Woolf discusses with Dr. Rita Hinden why nice ordinary people are "so repulsive in the mass" (*D* 5: 265). After *Roger Fry* appears, Woolf starts the term "leeches." In late July, to open her mail is "like putting my hand in a jar of leeches" (*D* 5: 306). All want to suck her blood. On November 29, she confesses: "I was thinking about vampires. Leeches. Anyone with 500 a year & education, is at once sucked by the leeches. Put L. & me into Rodmell pool & we are sucked—sucked—sucked" (*D* 5: 342). On December 16, she notes that her "old dislike of the village bites at me. . . . So petty so teasing are the claims of Gardners & Chavasses. I dont like—but here I stop" (*D* 5: 344).

Woolf desperately needs to "hack an outlet." But a refreshing path she cannot find. "One taps any source of comfort," she writes on June 9, when the Battle of France "wipes out London pretty quick" and she feels vacancy once more: "the writing 'I,' has vanished. No audience. No echo. Thats part of one's death" (*D* 5: 292–93). Sadly, *other* diaries rarely bring comfort or refreshment this year—or even appear. Her resuscitative reimagining of Walter Scott's diary, "Gas at Abbotsford," appears January 26, but (alarmingly) with Fry in her nest, she feels it a "dead pigeon" (*D* 5: 260). She thinks enviously of Andrè Gide's diary a week later and wishes she could "conglobulate reflections like Gide. Half of his are daily jottings. Then something solid forms" (*D* 5: 263). However, on July 24— the eve of *Roger Fry*'s appearance—she declares that she is tired of diary notes: "tire of Gide, tired of de Vigny notebooks.[6] I want something sequacious now & robust. In the first days of the war I cd read notes only" (*D* 5: 304). She now longs for a more elaborated work of art.

Sadly, Woolf never writes again on Lady Hester Stanhope, although she appears to welcome the assignment on March 20. It would have returned her to physician Charles Meryon's vibrant Boswellian diaries that she still recalls well: "[T]he book I read that Christmas at [Cornwall, 1909], & finished too soon, & put Lytton on the scent of" (*D* 5: 272). That Woolf finds little life from *others'* diaries this year is a harsh turn of fortune. That she seeks outlets through *other* books (as well as through diaries) can be seen in her May 29 words on Chesterton's *St. Thomas Aquinas*: "I want to send out parachutes into these remote places" (*D* 5: 289).

Her *own* diary now must be her parachute, her "life," her raft, her outlet. Woolf's diary now moves subtly toward public form. On November 12, she calls her diary words "semi public utterances" (*D* 5: 338), and throughout the year she expresses the need for greater privacy for her diary-writing than in earlier years and for greater discretion within it.

Virginia Woolf's 1940 diary moves and inspires with its persistent fight against the "circumscribing" war. Woolf tries to give greater "weight" to her diary as counter to war. In fact, she presses forward across the year on *all* literary fronts: the life-giving biography of *Roger Fry*; the "I-less" antiwar novel *Between the Acts*; new short stories; swifter, more fluid literary criticism—and her rich unfinished memoirs in diary form.

Despite the surrounding war, future promise glows from this evening diary. Woolf seeks a new outlet in the spring: the friendship of another woman writer. In Elizabeth Bowen, Woolf reaches out to the younger generation, as well. Her six-entry June stew over Bowen's imagined snub reprises the anxious-yet-rewarding Katherine Mansfield days, that "public of two" (*D* 1: 222). Woolf's stretching, curious mind hardly falters. She propels her mind (and diary) with an astonishing 221 questions across the year: 70 on her own writing; 45 on the war. Her creative wellspring remains, and she sees herself in November as the powerful sea demolishing male sandcastles. She writes, in fact, for the fluid, bold "old reading woman" she equates with England.[7]

When bombs destroy her London home, her response is to seek and preserve her diaries: "24 vols of diary salved; a great mass for my memoirs" (*D* 5: 332). That she still sees her diary as vital refreshment is clear from her action on December 6 when a van arrives at Monk's House with "old papers, letters, notebooks" from the London rubble. "I'm going to bind the survivors tonight," she tells her diary; "& in coloured paper they may refresh my eye" (*D* 5: 342).

Woolf strives valiantly to color and intensify her life in 1940. "But I want to look back on these war years as years of positive something or other," she tells her diary rather flailingly on October 12.[8] That the war clips her wings, surrounds her, and cuts off vital outlets is shown throughout the year and in the year's last entries. To create, she seeks "no whirlpools. . . . Nothing turbulent" in late December, but she has noted in October that "there's always the chance of a rough wave"—a fact she does not wish to analyze (*D* 5: 345, 329). The 1940 diary's last entries show the war penetrate her days and her fight to oppose it. In "Christmas Eve," her next-to-last entry, Woolf depicts "[t]he downs breaking their wave" and "the beauty of the country, now scraped, but with old colours showing" (*D* 5: 346). Referring to the Monk's House elms they have named "Leonard" and "Virginia," she writes, "I didnt like to pull the curtains[,] so black were Leonard & Virginia against the sky" (*D* 5: 346).

However, her final entry, December 29, opens alarmingly: "There are moments when the sail flaps" (*D* 5: 346). She again seeks nature's aid but cannot escape the war. She rides her bicycle "across the downs" to the cliffs but finds a "roll of barbed wired" hooped on the edge (*D* 5: 347). She rubs her mind "brisk" along the Newhaven road but finds bombed Newhaven "gashed"—the "City of the Dead" as she called it in her October 29 diary entry (*D* 5: 347, 334). "All desire to write diary here has flagged," she then admits and asks: "What is the right antidote?" (*D* 5: 347).

Happily, once more she finds it in art. She seeks out Arnold's poem "Thyrsis" to copy out lines on the ravages of age, and, miraculously, that *move*—and poetry—and her *diary*—renew her: "While doing so, the idea came to me that why I dislike, & like, so many things idiosyncratically now, is because of my growing detachment from the hierarchy, the patriarchy. When Desmond praises [T. S. Eliot's] East Coker, & I am jealous, I walk over the marsh saying, I am I; & must follow that furrow, not copy another. That is the only justification for my writing & living" (*D* 5: 347).

And she closes her "weightier" 1940 diary by "mak[ing] up imaginary meals" (5: 347).

Virginia Woolf's 1941 Diary

> "I did not mean to describe, once more, the downs in snow; but it came. And I cant help even now turning to look at Asheham down, red, purple, dove blue grey, with the cross so melodramatically against it. What is the phrase I always remember—or forget. Look your last on all things lovely."
>
> (January 9, 1941; *D* 5: 351)

Bitter cold seizes south Sussex as 1941 begins—bitter cold and snow. "This first day of the new year has a slice of a wind—like a circular saw," Virginia Woolf tells her first diary entry, ominously (*D* 5: 351). Her second entry opens nine days later: "A blank. All frost. Still frost"—but she tries to save (and savor) the scene (*D* 5: 351). Cold and war surround Woolf and isolate her, but she fights on. Her diary, begun promptly on January 1 in a stationer's loose-leaf notebook, offers one of several signs that life, though harried, proceeds as in the past. Woolf pens ten diary entries in the eighty-three days from January 1 to March 24—her last entry four days before her suicide and a subtle farewell. She writes five entries in January, a somewhat healthy number that would have yielded sixty entries had she persisted at this pace through the year. She writes three entries in February but only two in March as the illness that finally claims her works its way.

Her public prose continues, as well. On January 9, she reports revising her novel *Between the Acts*, and on January 26, she follows her turn-and-turn-about tack and gives herself two days of memoir-writing as a break from the novel. A month later, she can report *Between the Acts* done. Throughout this time she reads for her *next* book, which, on January 1, she retitles "Turning a Page." On that day she reports "a handful of Elizabethans" to read from their London flat debris (*D* 5: 351). By January 15, she has visited the London Library to collect "specimens" of English literature (*D* 5: 353). Five days later, she tells her diary, "I am reading—oh all lit. for my book" (*D* 5: 354). On February 7, when she ends her entry, "The Italians are flying. The 3rd week in March is fixed for invasion," she counters with her pen: "I must tune up for my Elizabethans" (*D* 5: 356).

She completes one book, reads for and starts the next, and weathers journalistic setback. In early January, *Harper's Bazaar* returns a short story it commissioned in October and also an article on Ellen Terry. On January 26, Woolf tells her diary she has "routed" her "depression" by sending the Terry essay to the *New Statesman and Nation* and by switching to her memoirs. "Ellen Terry" appears on February 8, and the day before Woolf tells her diary that she has been "writing with some glow" her review of a biography of Hester Thrale, the diarist and friend of Dr. Johnson and Fanny Burney (*D* 5: 355).

Across these days, Woolf turns her mind to her own diary, as well. She continues to reread her older diaries, and she reads her previous diary entry before adding more. Entries in this last diary book converse with each other, as her entries have done since 1915. On January 9, Woolf refers to her 1929 diary. Does she reread it for consolation? For refreshment? For her memoirs? Her wish for privacy for diary-writing also persists. She ends her first entry: "A psychologist would see that the above was written with someone, & a dog, in the room" (*D* 5: 351).

She raises nineteen questions in her ten diary entries—six on her writing, five of these six, surprisingly, on her *diary*, the sixth question how she might "englobe" her doctor, Octavia Wilberforce's story, perhaps first in her diary. In her first entry, Woolf asks "what does it matter" if she writes many diary pages, and in her next she raises questions she has asked her diary before: "Are these the things that are interesting? that recall; that say Stop you are so fair?" (D 5: 352). In this second entry, January 9, she also wonders if she "dare to say bowel" to describe the smoke "rolling ... convoluted" within the evening beauty (D 5: 352). These questions show concern for both the diary's *content* and its *style*. In her next entry, she questions her diary rereading. "Parsimony may be the end of this book," she reflects regarding their reduced income. "Also shame at my own verbosity, which comes over me when I see the 20 it is—books shuffled together in my room. Who am I ashamed of? Myself reading them" (D 5: 352).

In March, Woolf makes plans for April—for future visits to record. She invites T. S. Eliot to Rodmell and herself to Woking, intriguingly, to visit Ethel Smyth. However, her diary also signals uneasiness—and her acts to redress it. For those who know Woolf's diary, alarm grows from what is *absent* in the 1941 diary, as well as from what unfolds. Absent is Roger Fry, despite his successful resurrection in print the year before. That Woolf does not evoke his refreshing spirit suggests her hampered state. Nor does she mention *Between the Acts* in her diary after the mere note of its finish on February 26. She gives neither her own sense of the completed novel nor Leonard's—opinions she usually preserves.

Another prop, the Hogarth Press, figures only once in the diary and then as a museum relic of her past. Woolf's February 16 entry reports their visit to Letchworth, where the Press was moved in September 1940 when its London site was bombed. Woolf treats the print methods now in use as far from the hand-gluing and folding that once braced her days: "the slaves chained to their typewriters, & their drawn set faces, & the machines—the incessant more & more competent machines, folding, pressing, glueing & issuing perfect books. They can stamp cloth to imitate leather. Our Press is up in a glass case" (D 5: 356).

No horse rises in this diary to leap its fences. No bird flies free—no gull "up again & off again" for new adventures, no Lady Sibyl Colefax linked to this gull. The five entries with water tropes image dark seas—not the fluid well stream. Woolf's fifth entry, January 26, opens: "A battle against depression. . . . This trough of despair shall not, I swear, engulf me.... What I need is the old spurt" (*D* 5: 354–55). On February 7, when she has been "writing with some glow" of diarist Hester Thrale, she notes that "Mrs Thrale is to be done before we go to Cambridge. A week of broken water impends" (*D* 5: 355). Travel and company now seem interruptions to her flow; however, Cambridge has always been problematic. Her next entry, February 16, finds her "[i]n the wild grey water after last weeks turmoil" (*D* 5: 356). She declares on March 8, in her next-to-last entry, that she will "go down with [her] colours flying," and her final entry, March 24, offers an unsettling scene of her talk with a Rodmell woman who has lost two sons in the war: "Sitting there I tried to coin a few compliments. But they perished in the icy sea between us. And then there was nothing. A curious sea side feeling in the air today.... Everyone leaning against the wind, nipped & silenced" (*D* 5: 358, 359).

The war nips and silences Virginia Woolf in 1941. Eight of her ten 1941 entries refer to the war. Diary editor Olivier Bell writes that in 1941, "Virginia felt harassed by the straits and exigencies of wartime and generally dejected" (*AML* 499). The diary opens with Woolf linking London, now aflame, to the great London fire of 1665: "On Sunday night, as I was reading about the great fire, in a very accurate detailed book, London was burning. 8 of my city churches destroyed, & the Guildhall" (*D* 5: 351). The very diary she writes in, she notes, is a victim of the war: the ringed notebook "salvaged" from 37 Mecklenburgh Square, their bombed London home (*D* 5: 351).[9]

The war proper does not kill Virginia Woolf; rather, it is the isolation it brings. Perhaps only readers of Woolf's diary can sense the vital roles that change, movement,[10] and London play in her restless searching life—a unique case. From as early as age seventeen and her 1899 Warboys diary, Virginia finds herself sensitized in the country, which comes to represent for her untrammeled nature, the unconscious, the mother. Across her life, Woolf turns from London to the country again and again, yet London's role as the conscious outer world looms equally large: always it must be the country-*in*-London, the inner *and* the outer, the two making the whole, the movement back and forth required.

But London is burning in Woolf's opening diary words: her Guildhall. Her London flats are destroyed. Woolf explains London's role in a January 12, 1941, letter to Ethel Smyth:

> How odd it is being a countrywoman after all these years of being Cockney! For almost the first time in my life I've not a bed in London. D'you

know what I'm doing tomorrow? Going up to London Bridge. Then I shall walk, all along the Thames, in and out where I used to haunt, so through the Temple, up the Strand and out into Oxford Street, where I shall buy maccaroni and lunch. No. You never shared my passion for that great city. Yet its what, in some odd corner of my dreaming mind, represents Chaucer, Shakespeare, Dickens. Its my only patriotism . . . (L #3678, 6: 460)

Woolf needs London: the literary tradition she extends.

But London is "ravished" by the war:

I went to London Bridge. I looked at the river; very misty; some tufts of smoke, perhaps from burning houses. There was another fire on Saturday. Then I saw a cliff of wall, eaten out, at one corner; a great corner all smashed. . . . A complete jam of traffic; for streets were being blown up. So by tube to the Temple; & there wandered in the desolate ruins of my old squares: gashed; dismantled; the old red bricks all white powder, something like a builders yard. Grey dirt & broken windows; sightseers; all that completeness ravished & demolished. (D 5: 353)

All that completeness ravished. On February 7, she must tell her diary of another London bomb. Her busy "London streets are very empty—Oxford Street a wide grey ribbon" (D 5: 355). A month later, in her next-to-last entry, March 8, she arranges April visits "to make up for the sight of Oxford Street and Piccadilly which haunt me" (D 5: 358). She then writes, "Oh dear yes, I shall conquer this mood"—"Oh dear" always her diary words of deep concern (D 5: 358).

Woolf recognizes—as she does in her 1940 diary—that the country-*without*-London means more than geographical change. She writes in her January 9, 1941, entry: "The great change isnt [economizing] but the change to the country. Miss Gardner instead of Elizabeth Bowen. Small beer" (D 5: 352). Woolf wants refreshment: intellectual and sensory stimulus. Even so, as in her 1940 diary, she tries to find merit in her plight. "But, space, silence; & time," she answers. "I can sit down to a book. This I havent done since 1924, I suppose when we went to 52 [Tavistock Square in London]: & the scrimmage began" (D 5: 352). Poignantly, in this second entry she pays last tribute to the downs: "I did not mean to describe, once more, the downs in snow; but it came. . . . Look your last on all things lovely." The allusion, Olivier Bell notes, is to Walter de la Mare's

Fare Well (*D* 5: 351n2). On this same day, Woolf writes to her doctor, Octavia Wilberforce, of "this bitter and barren moment" (*L* #3676, 6: 458). On January 26, routing her depression, swearing "[t]his trough of despair shall not . . . engulf me," she then limns her state: "The solitude is great. Rodmell life is very small beer. The house is damp. The house is untidy. But there is no alternative" (*D* 5: 354–55).

If only she could go abroad—but where in Europe could she go? And would non-London answer? She then gives herself a "prescription," as she has done so often before with good effect: "Sleep & slackness; musing; reading; cooking; cycling; oh & a good hard rather rocky book" (*D* 5: 355). Six days later, her February 1 letter to Ethel Smyth both touches and alarms: "I read and read like a donkey going round and round a well; pray to God, some idea will flash. I leave it to nature. I can no longer control my brain" (*L* #3685, 6: 467).

As the 1941 days unfold, past props—such as reading—no longer lift (or fill the well). On January 9, Desmond MacCarthy's new book, *Drama*, strikes her as "small beer" (*D* 5: 352). Six days later, James Joyce's death spurs her to recall that he was only "about a fortnight" younger than she (*D* 5: 352–53). His books, she notes, will now "take their place in the long procession" (*D* 5: 253). She turns then to André Gide, whose diaries she admires. Regrettably, she reads on January 20 not his bracing, reflection-filled journals but his short novel of a woman's self-destruction, *Strait Is the Gate* (*La Porte Etroite*) (*D* 5: 354).

In February, travel also fails to lift. When she journeys to Cambridge and Letchworth, she complains oddly, "No country to look at" (*D* 5: 356). One might think this *change*, this *movement*, in itself would energize. It does not. Nor does Elizabeth Bowen in Rodmell (London-in-the-country)—nor even Vita at Rodmell—turn small beer to large. In February 1941, people (like travel and books) fail to boost—an alarming sign.

Hate-my-kind revulsion then enters Woolf's February 26 entry. In her first paragraph, Woolf writes: "Flora & Molly have just gone; leaving me to ask this bitter bright spring day, why they came?" (*D* 5: 356). She then switches to a conversation heard the day before in the ladies' bathroom at Brighton's Sussex Grill. She captures it and then writes: "They were powdering & painting, these common little tarts, while I sat, behind a thin door, p—ing as quietly as I could. Then at Fuller's. A fat, smart woman, in red hunting cap, pearls, check skirt, consuming rich cakes. Her shabby dependant [*sic*] also stuffing. . . . The fat woman had a louche large white muffin face. T'other was slightly grilled. They ate & ate" (*D* 5: 357). Woolf then repeats their talk and concludes: "Something scented, shoddy, parasitic about them. . . . Where does the money come to feed these fat white slugs? Brighton a love corner for slugs" (*D* 5: 357).

Alarmingly, she writes toward the close of this hate-my-kind entry, "No walks for ever so long. People daily" (*D* 5: 357). She needs to walk, of course; she needs *movement*. This entry ends with recognition of her country isolation:

> No walks for ever so long. People daily. And rather a churn in my mind. And some blank spaces. Food becomes an obsession. I grudge giving away a spice bun. Curious—age, or the war? Never mind. Adventure. Make solid. But shall I ever write again one of those sentences that give me intense pleasure? There is no echo in Rodmell—only waste air. I spent the afternoon at the school, marbling paper. Mrs D. discontented. & said, Theres no life in these children, comparing them with Londoners, thus repeating my own comment upon that long languid meeting at Chavasses. No life: & so they cling to us. This is my conclusion. We pay the penalty for our rung in society by infernal boredom. (*D* 5: 357)

A feeling of "blankness," of "vacancy" entered Woolf's diary in January 1940 as her country isolation began: the war her circumference, her Rodmell radius too small. This sense continues in 1941. With her hate-my-kind revulsion on February 26 comes "some blank spaces" in her mind (*D* 5: 357). She tells herself to "Adventure. Make solid," but then she states, "There is no echo in Rodmell—only waste air. . . . No life" (*D* 5: 357). In her last entry, she writes: "Everyone leaning against the wind, nipped & silenced. All pulp removed" (*D* 5: 359).

A bitterly cold winter paralyzed England in January and February 1915 and, perhaps, played a role in the end of Woolf's six-week-old 1915 diary before her long illness that year and the next. "I am sure however many years I keep this diary, I shall never find a winter to beat this," she wrote that year. "It seems to have lost all self control" (*D* 1: 33). In that diary she also said next to nothing of her soon-to-be published first novel *The Voyage Out*. She also expressed hate for her kind.

History now repeats.

In 1941, Woolf battles against the blankness, the echoless vacancy, the poisoning waste as the above passages reveal. Her diary aids her battle—one of her strongest props—through March 24. One understands why Leonard Woolf chose to end his first gift of Woolf's diary, the 1953 abridged *A Writer's Diary*, with the first two of three paragraphs of her next-to-last entry, March 8—for it illustrates her fight and her courage. "A pretty hat in a teashop," Woolf writes there of Brighton, "—how fashion revives the eye!"—a sign of her eye's need (*D* 5: 357). The second paragraph then begins:

> No: I intend no introspection. I mark Henry James's sentence: Observe perpetually. Observe the oncome of age. Observe greed. Observe my own despondency. By that means it becomes serviceable. Or so I hope. I insist upon spending this time to the best advantage. I will go down with my colours flying. This I see verges on introspection; but doesn't quite fall in. Suppose, I bought a ticket at the Museum; biked in daily & read history. Suppose I selected one dominant figure in every age & wrote round & about. Occupation is essential. And now with some pleasure I find that its seven; & must cook dinner. Haddock & sausage meat. I think it is true that one gains a certain hold on sausage & haddock by writing them down. (*D* 5: 357–58)

We see her here making rescue plans.

However, Woolf's courage and her powerful mind and pen illumine her more diffuse and subtle *last* entry, too. In this entry's first paragraph, Woolf finds nothing to say to the English mother who has lost two sons to the war. (She has had her say in her 1938 *Three Guineas* and in her works that follow.) She then thinks of Vanessa in Brighton and her mind begins to reach. "I am imagining how it wd be if we could infuse souls," she writes. Then she turns to her precious art: "Octavia's story. Could I englobe it somehow? English youth in 1900."

The restless mind has not ceased.

As World War II entered its second year, Woolf tried to imagine her death by a bomb in her October 2, 1940, diary entry. She wrote:

> I've got it fairly vivid—the sensation: but cant see anything but suffocating nonentity following after. I shall think—oh I wanted another 10 years—not this—& shant, for once, be able to describe it. It—I mean death; no, the scrunching & scrambling, the crushing of my bone shade in on my very active eye & brain: the process of putting out the light,—painful? Yes. Terrifying. I suppose so—Then a swoon; a drum; two or three gulps attempting consciousness—& then, dot dot dot. (*D* 5: 326–27)

Woolf ends her forty-four-year diary with no words for the war but with the wish to infuse minds, to englobe life. And with flowers. Her last diary words: "L. is doing the rhododendrons . ."

Dot, dot.

Is this not her hesitant farewell?

It is an intriguing, perhaps hasty, even perhaps artful close—not Katherine Mansfield's *three* ellipsis dots, not her own ellipses in *Three Guineas* that stand for what cannot be said—but *two* dots, hinting at both the silencing and the possibility of more.[11]

Epilogue

Joseph Goebbels, Hitler's propaganda minister, dictated each day "at great length" an account of what transpired the day before. He then had this diary typed on "especially heavy watermarked paper [in] large German-Gothic script of a sort one seldom finds on typewriters," Louis P. Lochner, the diary's English translator, reports. "There was triple spacing between the lines, and the margins were wide. No ordinary mortal in those days could have commanded such paper or permitted himself the luxury of such large type and generous spacing" (12). Virginia Woolf, in contrast, worried that the "parsimony" caused by the war would end her diary-writing at the very time she wished for a "weightier" diary (*D* 5: 352, 255).

Nevertheless, in her last dozen years, Woolf's handwritten diary served as a vital tool in her fight against fascism: its tyranny and wars. To understand this is to probe what Melba Cuddy-Keane calls "the political implications of genre" (273). From her teenage years, Virginia Woolf saw life as a struggle—as a battle. At age fifteen, she closes her first surviving diary by depicting herself with her "hand in the sword hilt—& an unuttered fervent vow!" (*PA* 134). In her third and final diary stage, from 1929 to 1941, she more than doubles her number of diary entries (from her second, lean modernist diary stage of the 1920s) as she faces the ever-nearing—and ultimately surrounding—outer war.

Judy Suh argues persuasively that a diary's very "ordinariness" works to counter fascism's false, hysterical melodrama (56). Theater director Peter Brook's description of the rise of melodrama *on the stage* captures uncannily Hitler's appropriated fascist script: an "incessant struggle against enemies, without and within, branded as villains, suborners of morality, who must be confronted and expunged, over and over, to assure the triumph of virtue" (15). A diary's commonplace moments, its "prosaic discontinuities," both deflate and defuse—and thus counter—the dictators' pumped-up play (Suh 56). In her 1932 diary, Woolf wants to "be entirely natural" (*D* 4: 130). She wishes "to let the juice of usual things, talk, character, seep through" her (*D* 4: 124).

Her complex *diary portraits* further challenge the fascist fantasy of villains and heroes. They offer an alternative view of humankind. Although Woolf will, in key moments, make contrasting portraits in her diary to probe her own struggles, even these figures—like all her other diary personages—are not only multifaceted but capable of change. In fact, Woolf recoils from frozen and rigid states across her days. Her diary helps her to keep fluid.

In her own diary (and in others' diaries) Woolf could hear the *natural*— and *individual*—*human voice*. This stood as vital counter to fascism's shrill hysterics in its radio broadcasts and publications. On October 25, 1939, Woolf asked Edward Sackville-West if his diary had taken shape: "I wish it would. I want some fragmentary but natural voice to break into the artificial bray to which we're condemned" (*L* #3562, 6: 366). Throughout the 1930s, Woolf seeks often for what is *real*. The Reverend Francis Kilvert's diary words are real—and his life endures, Woolf writes in 1940 (*L* #3645, 6: 432). Hitler is the unreality.

Michele Pridmore-Brown suggests that Woolf "hoped to change the rhythm and the rhyme underwriting patriarchy and fascism" (419). A diary preserves a different, always individual, rhythm. It offers life traces, ever-renewing fragments of life. Fragments work against any single, dominating narrative. Woolf's diary assisted her modernist prose, for it allowed her to experiment semiprivately with the fragment, to search beyond accepted patterns of order and significance. In the 1930s, this worked powerfully against the fascist march, as well. A diary's gaps invite the imagination of both the diary writer and the diary reader. For the diary *writer*, each new blank page (or entry) can offer something new. Together, entries offer "new combinations," the trait both Woolf and *The Years*' Eleanor Pargiter seek.

The diary *reader*, in turn, cannot help but imagine a range of alternative scenarios when diary gaps occur. Writing of the fragments in Woolf's final novel, *Between the Acts*, Cuddy-Keane suggests that "fragmentation permits a new and fluid sense of community" (274). Writer and reader join in pursuit of alternative views and forms. In this respect, fragmentation is "revisionary, and in a fully political sense" (Cuddy-Keane 283).

Comparing a diary entry to a snapshot, Suh notes that each captures a moment that can be returned to and examined—often profitably. In 1939, the

Woolfs' Hogarth Press publishes Christopher Isherwood's novel *Goodbye to Berlin*, which opens and closes with diary entries and offers photographic snapshots within. The "efficacy of the diary and camera," Suh explains, "lies in the capture of the otherwise fleeting moments . . . that might be revisited to detect patterns visible with the passage of time" (58). Woolf intuits this when she asks her 1935 diary: "Is there any 'use' in [diary] notes? Perhaps when the editing of the mind has gone further one can see & select better" (*D* 4: 312). A diary helps Woolf (and later readers) to see threads and patterns unrecognized at the time. When England finally enters World War II in September 1939, Woolf says of her *diary*: "This little pitter patter of ideas is my whiff of shot in the cause of freedom" (*D* 5: 235).

Virginia Woolf's diary is her last major work to reach the public. Its thirty-eight extant volumes provide unmatched access to the life of one of the world's most gifted writers and thinkers—and to the creative process itself. In three volumes I have sought to reveal the *foundational role* this semiprivate diary served for Woolf's public works and for her artistic renewal. Indeed, I believe that, as with Leo Tolstoy and André Gide, the published fiction and nonfiction would not exist without the diary.

In treating each of Woolf's thirty-eight diary volumes as a distinctive aesthetic unit, yet as part of a growing whole, I have tried to follow Woolf's lead in each separate book. I note the subjects she focuses upon and each diary's form, her repeated tropes, use of portraits and questions, habitual diary gestures—and even what is *not* said. My hope is that my readings of each diary will serve as springboards for *other* readings of each book. One is, after all, teasing out patterns in what is essentially (and attractively) a multivarious work. I have tried to keep before me Woolf's declaration that historians will try to make the story "much more definite than it is" and Eugène Delacroix's diary warning that "one must not be too absolute" (*D* 2: 92; Pach 536).

Those writing of Woolf's diary must ever resist a diary's tempting snares. Foremost, as Lili Hsieh warns, is the tendency to privilege Woolf's diary as the "authentic" place where the "real" Woolf can be found (29 & n19). When we write of Woolf's diary, we write of her "diaristic self." But what a fascinating "diaristic self" it is! I hope my work will encourage others to write on Woolf's diaries, for as Alexandra Harris writes, "[T]here will be no finished picture of Virginia Woolf" (164). The two ellipsis dots that end Woolf's diary telegraph as much.

When we write of diaries, we do well also to recall Lejeune's warning that there is "no such thing as a typical diarist" (154). Woolf's ever-stretching diary expands the boundaries of diary form. As a result, her diary helps illuminate the vast terra incognita of the diary and journal. (In her last years, she was experimenting—again—with the rare loose-leaf diary and was seeking to give her journal even more "weight.")

Woolf's semiprivate diary occupies the territory between her unconscious and her published prose. It was not "writing," she insisted, but something else (D 1: 325, D 2: 179). Situated so, it serves as a good indicator of Woolf's condition as her years unfold. Since she is acutely sensitive to her inner world, as well as to the outer world state, her diary serves as a particularly good barometer of both. I believe Woolf never fully understands how vital her diary is—and how revealing.

Part of her genius, nevertheless, lay in her ability to find the props she needed to further her art. A diary was attractive to Woolf, not only as terra incognita but also because it could serve her in many ways. Diary pen strokes soothed her. In her diary she could write away her "fidgets" and medicine her jealousy and despair. The diary served as her confidante, in fact, as a reservoir for her overflowing thoughts. It also was a compost heap for creation. From the diary's "heaps of nonassorted facts," art (with its new combinations) grew (D 3: 189). Woolf came to use her diary as her planner. Always it served as a practice ground for her public works.

In Woolf's final diary stage, we see most clearly (and poignantly) her use of her diary to create the "state" she needs. She needs "spring"—both the season and the movement—and she projects it in her diary. She needs to fly free, so she tries to tell herself in 1940 a "story" of "the life of a bird, its cheep cheep" (D 5: 276, 277). She resurrects herself as a writer with a diary portrait of Lady Sibyl Colefax, "up again & off again," rising from the ashes (D 5: 28). Woolf's final diaries allow us to see the crucial role Lady Colefax serves for Woolf in 1936 and after, a woman usually dismissed as an annoying society hostess. The final diaries allow greater nuance to our sense of Ethel Smyth, who plays an equally important role for Woolf as a fellow female battler. Woolf's thirty-eight diary volumes reveal—more clearly than any other work—the ways she continually drew on women for support.

Others' diaries—men's as well as women's—also supported and propelled Woolf throughout her life, and in her final diary stage she turns to others' diaries more and more. I hope this book adds to the understanding of both

Woolf and her intertextuality. Few lives are as fully documented as Woolf's. We know from her diaries, letters, reading notebooks, and published reviews and essays much of what she read and when she read it. We see that others' diaries prove both suggestive and challenging for Woolf and that she always works through these influences to respond in her own voice and style. John Bailey's diary effusions regarding Oxford, which Woolf read in 1935, give us richer appreciation of—in fact, underwrite—the Edward Pargiter/ Kitty Malone conflict in *The Years*, then in progress, as well as this exclamation in the 1938 *Three Guineas*: "How different it looks to us from what it must look to you!" (23). Stephen MacKenna's diary confession that his passionate Irish nationalism had no basis in reason—rather, simply, that "this bird has built its nest with [him]" (133)—leads, I believe, to Woolf's transforming reply in one of the most famous passages in *Three Guineas*: "And if, when reason has said its say, still some obstinate emotion remains, some love of England dropped into a child's ears by the cawing of rooks in an elm tree, by the splash of waves on a beach, or by English voices murmuring nursery rhymes, this drop of pure, if irrational, emotion she will make serve her to give to England first what she desires of peace and freedom for the whole world" (109). Woolf confessed to her diary that "reading Yeats turns my sentences one way: reading Sterne turns them another" (*D* 3: 119).

Among voracious readers, Woolf may be unique in her appreciation of the treasure hidden in diaries. That treasure may also involve a mother. Woolf lost her beloved mother when she was only thirteen. I am struck by how many of the diarists Woolf read shared a similar early parental loss.[1] A diary becomes, perhaps, a surrogate nurturer. Woolf speaks in her diary of a pen as her "baby's coral." In creating "Elderly Virginia" in 1919 at the start of her second, spare diary stage, Woolf begins to mother herself directly in her (now mature) diary. The diary-as-substitute-mother, in itself, may explain Woolf's pursuit of diaries across her days.

Woolf sought in others' diaries the natural human voice and also life traces beyond her own that she could transform into art. Diaries enlarged Woolf's circumference. She called diaries "stepping-stones" (*E* 6: 217). More than anything, Woolf used others' diaries "to refresh and exercise [her] own creative powers," as she wrote in "How Should One Read a Book?" using an excerpt from Fanny Burney's diary as illustration (*CR* 2: 239). Woolf used her *own* diary for similar exercise and refreshment. Her creative use of others' diaries may be unique to her; however, we may learn from her use a process employed by other writers—but not as easily known. Woolf's faith in diaries also reveals her faith in the common creative consciousness, the creative community, of folk.

Virginia Woolf's third and final diary stage records the ever-nearing wars *without* that assailed her (and finally surrounded her) and her (artistic) wars *within* as she sought to address constructively and creatively the outer world state. In the end, a diary becomes a perfect image for Virginia Woolf: fragile yet resilient; always subject to movement; rich in renewal; inevitably subject to death, yet deathless, as well.

Appendix
The Diaries Virginia Woolf Read

Listed below are the seventy-six traceable diaries Virginia Woolf read across her life and the year in which she first read the diary. In each case I have given the source that refers to the specific diary.

Before 1897 (and age 15)
Sir Walter Scott's journals. (*PA* 40)
Fanny Burney's diaries. (*MOB* 105)

1897
Samuel Pepys' diaries. (*PA* 62, 65–67, 69)
William Cory's journals. (*PA* 126)

1903
James Boswell's *Journal of a Tour to the Hebrides with Samuel Johnson, LL.D.* (*PA* 206)

1905
Journal of Rear-Admiral Bartholomew James. (Steele 180)
Mrs. St. George (pseudonym of Melesina Trench). *Journal Kept During a Visit to Germany.* (Steele 180)

1906
William Allingham's Diary. (*E* 1: 154–56)

1908
Leaves from the Note-Books of Lady Dorothy Nevill. (*E* 1: 178–83)
The Diary of a Lady-in-Waiting by Charlotte Bury. (*E* 1: 195–200)
The Journal of Elizabeth Lady Holland. (*E* 1: 230–39)

1909

Diaries of Dr. Charles Meryon, physician to Lady Hester Stanhope. (*E* 1: 325–30)

1910

Ralph Waldo Emerson's early *Journals*. (*E* 1: 335–40; *RN* 147)
Mary Coleridge diary extracts, *Gathered Leaves from the Prose of Mary E. Coleridge*. (*L* #525, 1: 426)

1913

The Diary of Frances Lady Shelley, 1818–1873. (*E* 6: 375–79)

1916

Mary Berry's *Journals*. (*L* #745, 2: 82; see also *L* #605, 1: 491)

1917

The *Journals* of Edmond and Jules de Goncourt. (Holroyd 415)
Stopford Brooke's diary. (*E* 2: 183–88)

1918

Henry Crabb Robinson's *Diary*. (*RN* 153–54, 194)

1919

Wilfrid Scawen Blunt's *Diaries, 1888–1914*. (*L* #1081, 2: 389; *L* #1082, 2: 390; *RN* 249, 292)

1920

W.N.P. Barbellion (pseudonym of Bruce Frederick Cummings), *Journal of a Disappointed Man*. (*D* 1: 267)
The Diary of John Evelyn. (*E* 3: 259–68; *CR*1 78–85)
Catherine Wilmot's travel diary, *An Irish Peer on the Continent (1801–1803): Being a Narrative of the Tour of Stephen, 2nd Earl Mount Cashell, Through France, Italy, Etc., as Related by Catherine Wilmot*. (*D* 2: 57)

1921

Anton Chekhov's diary and notebooks. (Hogarth Press publication; source of the title of Woolf's 1921 short story collection *Monday or Tuesday*)

1922

Tant' Alie of Transvall: Her Diary, 1880–1902. (L #1276, 2: 549; D 2: 216)

1923

James Boswell's *Journal of a Tour to Corsica; & Memoirs of Pascal Paoli.* (D 2: 256)

1924

Letters and Journals of Anne Chalmers. (E 3: 398–99)
Stendhal's early journals. (E 3: 416–18; RN 96, 100–03)
James Woodforde's *Diary of a Country Parson*, volume 1. (RN 103)
The Diary of the Lady Anne Clifford. (RN 100, 102–03)

1925

Jonathan Swift's *Journal to Stella.* (D 3: 33; E 4: 291–301; CR2 58–67; RN 50–52)

1926

Diary extracts in Beatrice Webb's *My Apprenticeship.* (D 3: 62, 74)
The Journals of Thomas James Cobden-Sanderson. (D 3: 109; E 4: 369–73; RN 127, 136)
Benjamin Robert Haydon's *Journals.* (E 4: 406–12; L #1676, 3: 295)

1927

Journal of Katherine Mansfield. (E 4: 446–49)
James Woodforde's *Diary of a Country Parson*, volumes 2 and 3. (E 4: 441–46; RN 89–90)

1928

The Diaries of Mary, Countess of Meath, Edited by Her Husband. (E 4: 552–53)

1929

Dorothy Wordsworth's *Journals.* (E 5: 113–21; CR2: 148–55; L #2057, 4: 79–80)
Jules Renard's *Journal.* (D 3: 264)

1930

Sarah Stoddart's (Mrs. William Hazlitt) "Journal of My Trip to Scotland." (RN 119)

1931

The Reverend John Skinner's *Journal of a Somerset Rector*. (D 3: 340–43; E 5: 423–30; CR2: 90–96)

H. D. Harben's "very interesting" Russian diary. (L #2344, 4: 306)

Princess Daisy of Pless' *From My Private Diary*. (L #2376, 4: 337)

1932

James Woodforde's *Diary of a Country Parson*, volumes 4 and 5. (E 5: 417–23, 428–29; CR2 83–89; RN 89–90)

The Blecheley Diary of the Rev. William Cole, M.A. F.S.A., 1765–67 and Cole's *A Journal of My Journey to Paris in the Year 1765*. (E 5: 289–94; RN 63)

1933

Thomas Creevey's diary extracts in *The Creevy Papers*. (D 4: 157)

Works and Days: From the Journal of Michael Field. (D 4: 189)

1934

Arthur Young's *Travels in France during the Years 1787, 1788, and 1789* [in diary form]. (D 4: 200, 201)

André Gide's *Pages de Journal, 1929–32*. (D 4: 241; Lee 645)

Guy de Maupassant's travel journal *Sur l'eau (Afloat)*. (D 4: 242; RN 213)

Alice James: Her Brothers—Her Journal. (D 4: 248)

1935

Dr. Salter: His Diary and Reminiscences from the Year 1849 to the Year 1932. (D 4: 339)

John Bailey: 1864–1931, Letters and Diaries. (D 4: 339)

1936

The diaries of Lord & Lady Amberley: *The Amberley Papers*. (L #3166, 6: 69; L #3172, 6: 72; L #3173, 6: 73)

Ellen Weeton's *Journal of a Governess, 1807–1811*. (D 5: 32; TG 75–76; RN 162, 287)

The *Journal and Letters of Stephen MacKenna*. (L #3204, 6: 96)

1937

The Final Struggle: Being Countess Tolstoy's Diary for 1910 with Extracts from Leo Tolstoy's Diary of the Same Period. (D 5: 55; L #3218, 6: 107)

1938

The Reverend Francis Kilvert's *Diary*, volume 1. (D 5: 228; L #3433, 6: 266)
The Diary of Lady Frederick Cavendish. (L #3435, 6: 267)

1939

Eugène Delacroix's journal. (D 5: 199)
André Gide's *Journal, 1889–1939*. (D 5: 227, 228, 229, 244)
F. L. Lucas' *Journal under the Terror, 1938*. (D 5: 227, 229)
The Reverend Francis Kilvert's *Diary*, volume 2. (L #3576, 6: 377; L #3645, 6: 432)
New edition of Sir Walter Scott's *Journal, 1825–1826*. (D 5: 237n)
Self-Portrait, Taken from the Letters & Journals of Charles Ricketts, R.A. (D 5: 252)
Henry, Elizabeth and George: Letters and Diaries of Henry, Tenth Earl of Pembroke and his Circle, 1734–80. (D 5: 252)

1940–1941

André Gide's *Journal, 1889–1939*. (D 5: 263, 304)
Henry Williamson's diary, *Goodbye West Country*. (D 5: 320, 321)
Florence Sitwell's teenage diary. (E 6: 255–59)
George Bagshawe Harrison's *An Elizabethan Journal: Being a Record of Those Things Most Talked About During the Years 1591–1594*. (RN 186)

Notes

Introduction

1. Lee 6. As it transpired, twenty-four diary volumes were in London, but another fourteen diary books were elsewhere. To date, Woolf's diary consists of thirty-eight handwritten volumes.

2. See my *Becoming Virginia Woolf: Her Early Diaries and the Diaries She Read* (Gainesville: University Press of Florida, 2014).

3. See my *Virginia Woolf's Modernist Path: Her Middle Diaries and the Diaries She Read* (Gainesville: University Press of Florida, 2016).

4. Diary historian Harriet Blodgett asserts that women "are more inclined" than men to read others' diaries (*Centuries* 266–67n42).

5. Aristotle, in his *Poetics*, said that "the tyrant is inclined constantly to foment wars" (Oldfield 148). Woolf first read the *Poetics* in 1905. Mark Hussey's 1991 volume *Virginia Woolf and War* greatly aided this interpretive trend.

6. Jed Esty, for example, reminds us that "thirties modernism . . . always entails aesthetic experimentation" (52).

Chapter 1. The War Within

1. This diary book is 8 ⅜ inches wide and 10 ¾ inches long, about the size of her other 1919 to 1929 diaries. As before, Woolf rules in blue ink a vertical margin for herself, now two inches from the left-hand edge, and places her entry's *dates* to the left of the line. She writes her entries most often in her favorite purple ink.

2. Woolf read Pepys' diary at age fifteen. I treat his diary in *Becoming Virginia Woolf: Her Early Diaries and the Diaries She Read*.

3. Several critics have noted the war imagery in *The Waves*; my goal here is to show the diary's parallel (and assisting) use. Jessica Berman argues, furthermore, that *The Waves* "may be seen as a novel about the possibility of community not only without charismatic leaders but also without any totalizing structure like that of state or nation. . . . Rather, in the positive interconnection of her community of characters

[Woolf] constructs an alternative model of social organization, that . . . is directly targeted at those in search of political answers to the British crisis" (115).

4. She will use almost the same words eighteen months later in her April 11, 1931, entry: "[M]y early mornings are terrible battles—Fight fight" (*D* 4: 17). On August 21, 1934, she writes: "& woke with all my back in hackles, like a cats, & the old cry Fight" (*D* 4: 238).

5. Woolf applies her horse trope to Shakespeare in her April 13, 1930, entry, and (as in her 1926 diary) declares he far surpasses her: "I never yet knew how amazing his stretch & speed & word coining power is, until I felt it utterly outpace & outrace my own, seeming to start equal & then I see him draw ahead & do things I could not in my wildest tumult & utmost press of mind imagine. . . . Indeed, I could say that Shre surpasses literature altogether, if I knew what I meant" (*D* 3: 300–301).

6. *D* 3: 288. See Anne E. Fernald's lengthier discussion of the whole entry (and of Byron's importance to Woolf) in *Virginia Woolf: Feminism and the Reader*. Of greatest note to my own project is Fernald's reminder that Byron's life exemplified both "poetic retreat and revolutionary action" (119). Furthermore, though crippled, Byron was a fine horseman; Woolf depicts him in her 1918 diary as "flogging his flanks," his method in *Don Juan* a "springy random haphazard galloping," which she seeks for both her diary and public prose (*D* 1: 181).

7. I treat the diaries of Walter Scott, Fanny Burney, James Boswell, and Samuel Pepys in *Becoming Virginia Woolf: Her Early Diaries and the Diaries She Read*.

8. Signs of much rereading appear in this diary, just as in the three 1918 diaries that precede Woolf's 1919 diary credo and her second (lean, mature, and modernist) diary stage.

9. Writing at breakneck speed, Woolf often left out apostrophes. All quotations from her diaries and letters will reproduce her text.

10. *D* 3: 264. *The Edwardians*' sales near 20,000—although "it is not a very good book" Virginia tells her diary (*D* 3: 306).

11. *D* 3: 312–13. Nine months earlier, she makes a similar observation in yet another of her vamping denials of her ability to write. "No I am too tired to write," she declares on December 14, 1929; "have been rushed, . . . have had toothache: & so sit passive, hoping that some drops will form in my mind" (*D* 3: 272).

12. On July 22, 1820, Dorothy wrote from Coblentz to her good friend Catherine Clarkson: "Journals we shall have in abundance; for all, except my brother [William] and Mrs. Monkhouse, keep a journal. Mine is nothing but notes, unintelligible to any one but myself. I look forward, however, to many a pleasant hour's employment at Rydal Mount in filling up the chasms" (Knight 1: xiii). William Wordsworth commemorated the tour with a series of poems titled "Memorials of a Tour on the Continent, 1820."

13. The Wordsworths lived in Dove Cottage from 1799 to 1808. I treat Woolf's reading of Cobden-Sanderson's diary in *Virginia Woolf's Modernist Path: Her Middle Diaries and the Diaries She Read*.

14. Woolf long admired Wordsworth's "Prelude." On April 13, 1911, she wrote to Saxon Sydney-Turner: "I am reading the Prelude. Dont you think it one of the greatest works ever written? Some of it, anyhow, is sublime" (L #565, 1: 460). Twenty-five years later, she again praises the poem in a September 18, 1936, letter to Ethel Smyth. "The Prelude. Have you read it lately?" she inquires. "Do you know, its so good, so succulent, so suggestive, that I have to hoard it, as a child keeps a crumb of cake? And then people say he's dull! Why have we no great poet? You know thats what would keep us straight: but for our sins we only have a few pipers on hedges like Yeats and Tom Eliot, de la Mare—exquisite frail twittering voices one has to hollow one's hand to hear, whereas old Wth fills the room" (L #3173, 6: 73).

15. For a brief time at Penrith she was given a French and arithmetic tutor. Later, when her uncle, a former Windsor canon, rescued her from her grandparents, she was encouraged to read and write after breakfast and to study French.

16. Darbishire, xiii; Gunn 21. Thomas De Quincey, who confirmed "the glancing quickness of her motions," wrote that Dorothy's eyes were "wild and startling and hurried in their motion . . . she was the very wildest (in the sense of the most natural) person that I have ever known; and also the truest, most inevitable" (Gunn 3; Darbishire xii). The three words, "thy wild eyes," that Woolf copied into her 1921 reading notebook came from William's famous poem on "Tintern Abbey" where he tells Dorothy he can "read / My former pleasures in the shooting lights / Of thy wild eyes."

17. Knight 1: 112. In a passage that William Knight (alas) omitted from his 1897 edition of Dorothy's journals, the edition Woolf read, Dorothy wrote on her 1820 continental tour: "It was a pleasing thought, after looking in vain to espy that road, that we were enclosed among the natural solitudes of the Alps unmastered by the equalizing contrivances of men" (Sélincourt 2: 263).

18. Knight 1: 164. Dorothy is drawn to swallows across her journals. One thinks of Woolf's "sister swallow" in her final novel *Between the Acts*, with its very different sister and brother (115–16).

19. Darbishire xii. Maria Jane Jewsbury wrote to Dorothy's niece, Dora, of one of Dorothy's visits: "I think you would smile if you knew all she did and saw. . . . Churches—Museums—Factories—Shopping—Institutions—Company—at home and abroad . . . and that she won all hearts before and around her. She is the very genius of Popularity—an embodied spell. I should be jealous of her for a continuance. I should be dethroned even on my own sofa—amidst my own circle" (Levin 73). In their biography, *Dorothy Wordsworth*, Robert Gittings and Jo Manton report that "many simple people . . . fell in love with Dorothy at first sight" (97).

20. CR 2: 154, 152. During their 1820 continental tour, Mary Wordsworth wrote to a friend that Dorothy "never hesitates—going in to the kitchens, talks to everybody there—and in the villages, on the roads . . . makes friends . . . gains information . . . jabbers [French and] German everywhere. She astonishes us all" (Gunn 227).

21. Susan Levin asserts that Dorothy focuses more on the women she encounters in her travels than on the men (81).

22. Levin observes that Dorothy's journals "provided raw material for at least thirty-five of William Wordsworth's poems" (172). Coleridge's three most famous poems, "The Rime of the Ancient Mariner," "Christabel," and "Kubla Khan," also draw on Dorothy's journals.

23. Kitty Malone Lasswade, in Woolf's 1937 novel *The Years*, chooses the country (and northern England) over Oxford and London. She is called "The Grenadier" (257). In the British Army, a grenadier was a member of the first regiment of household infantry. Grenadiers were specially selected foot soldiers in elite units who threw grenades. Woolf thus links Kitty to both her own diary father, Sir Walter Scott, and to female household battle.

24. Wordsworth wrote to eighteen-year-old Dorothy during his 1790 tour with Robert Jones: "I have thought of you perpetually, and never have my eyes burst upon a scene of peculiar loveliness but I have almost instantly wished that you could . . . be transported to . . . where I stood" (Gunn 34).

25. Woolf wrote in her January 26, 1920, diary entry of *Jacob's Room*: "I suppose the danger is the damned egotistical self; which ruins Joyce & [Dorothy] Richardson to my mind: is one pliant & rich enough to provide a wall for the book from oneself without its becoming, as in Joyce & Richardson, narrowing & restricting?" (D 2: 14).

26. As noted, William Wordsworth incorporated Dorothy's 1805 "Journal of a Ramble" into his 1810 *A Description of the Scenery of the Lakes in the North of England*. In this popular work's expanded fourth edition, titled now *Guide to the Lakes* (1823), he included a much-altered version of her "Journal" as a kind of appendix. In 1851, following William's death, his nephew, the Bishop of Lincoln, included a few extracts from Dorothy's Grasmere journal in his *Memoirs of William Wordsworth*. Finally, in 1874, her *Recollections of a Tour Made in Scotland* saw print in a full edition from Principal Shairp. It evoked poems from delighted readers and required a third printing by 1894. In 1889, William Knight printed much of Dorothy's Alfoxden and Grasmere journals in his *Life of William Wordsworth*, along with extracts from some of her other diaries. "None of these, however, were given in their entirety," he explains in his prefatory note to his 1897 *Journals of Dorothy Wordsworth*, the volumes Woolf read, but even here he adds, "nor is it desirable now to print them *in extenso*, except in the case of the *Recollections of a Tour Made in Scotland* in 1803" (1: vii). In 1941, Ernest de Sélincourt published an expanded edition of the *Journals of Dorothy Wordsworth*; however, he left out some passages found in Knight's edition and trimmed nearly one-fourth of the 1820 continental diary (1: xviii). In 1971, Mary Moorman published a new edition of the Alfoxden and Grasmere journals, as did Pamela Woof later. In 1997 a new edition of *Recollections of a Tour Made in Scotland*, with photographs, appeared. However, still to see print is Dorothy's complete 1820 Continental diary and her final diaries from 1824 to 1840. Gunn, who calls the Continental diary "a masterpiece, inexplicably

neglected," suggests the neglect comes because "the voice is not the voice of the rain falling in Grasmere, but one that takes us along at a rattling pace. Or perhaps because what has tended to be extracted from this is Dorothy on William's Pedestrian Tour, to the detriment of her own *Tour*" (226).

27. Robinson wails in his June 28, 1833, diary entry, "She travelled with her brother and Coleridge. Had she but filled her volume with their conversation, rather than minute description!" (2: 185). As late as 1986, Bruce Bawer also mistakes her diary motive. "[O]ne longs for a respite from [nature] descriptions," he writes. "One finds oneself, at such times, wishing that Dorothy had been a bit less interested in nature and rather more interested in *human* nature, in the eighteenth-century sense of the term; one wishes she had been more attentive to Pope's exhortation that 'The proper study of mankind is man'" (32).

28. The opening of Dorothy's September 16, 1803, entry describing their first days in Edinburgh, for instance, unfolds, "The sky the evening before, as you may remember the ostler told us . . ."—the "you," of course, is William (Knight 2: 124).

Chapter 2. The March of Headlines

1. This cover harkens back to the gray-blue marble covers of Woolf's first two 1918 diaries. Woolf continues to rule her blank pages with a blue vertical line two inches from the left edge; she rules, in fact, more pages than she fills.

2. Smyth, in fact, is writing her memoirs at this moment.

3. In late October 1931, Virginia and Leonard decide to give up the Hogarth Press despite its financial success, "& thus slip another shackle from our shoulders," she tells her diary, for "what's money if you sell freedom?" (D 3: 327). However, instead, further moves to reorder occur.

4. D 4: 14n5. I treat Haydon's *Journals* in *Virginia Woolf's Modernist Path: Her Middle Diaries and the Diaries She Read*.

5. "I like my experimental temper," she confesses in her Valentine's Day 1931 entry regarding her decision to curl her hair (D 4: 11).

6. Woolf's first thoughts of her lecture also take shape as fight. Early passages in "Professions for Women" underscore Woolf's vision of Smyth and herself as battlers. "I feel rather like an idle and frivolous pleasure boat lolloping along in the wake of an ironclad," Woolf says of Smyth but cancels these next words: "[S]he is one of the ice breakers, the gun runners, the window smashers. The armoured tanks, who climbed the rough ground, drew the enemies fire, and left behind her a pathway" (*Partgiters* xxvii).

7. The diary excerpts in Webb's previous memoir, *My Apprenticeship*, "tap . . . a great stream of thought," Woolf writes in her 1926 diary (D 3: 74). I treat the strong influence of Webb's diary in *Virginia Woolf's Modernist Path: Her Middle Diaries and the Diaries She Read*.

8. *D 4: 15*. In her October 15, 1931, entry, Woolf admires parts of Smyth's earlier work *The Wreckers*, but she also suggests its effect is "as if some song in her had tried to issue & been choked [?]" *(D 4: 49)*.

9. I treat Vita's edition of *The Diary of the Lady Anne Clifford* in *Virginia Woolf's Modernist Path: Her Middle Diaries and the Diaries She Read*.

10. 312. Editors Coombs and Bax end the 1930 edition there; however, the poem is followed by "Memoranda respecting my severe trials in 1832, which may well be called AGONIA" (Skinner 1971, 464). Skinner then writes the following odd, self-absorbed words that suggest he thinks of Russell only as he furthers the journal, "The contents of this volume are Journals from November 13, 1832 to February 24, 1833—covering the death of my brother Russell, when the power I had before enjoyed of transcribing my Journals by another hand ceased" (464).

11. 48. Regrettably, unpublished in 1930 were Skinner's earlier journals, which show him defending a raped servant (Skinner 1971, 21) and insisting on equal treatment for Queen Caroline during her 1820 trial.

12. Skinner 1971, 140. Skinner's favorite motto was "Nulla dies sine Linea," his editors tell us, and he wrote this poem that expresses several of his diary motives:

> Since life so soon must close, would we retain
> The hope of living to our friends again?
> Let each succeeding day which speeds so fast
> Afford some leisure to record the past—
> To note with pencil, or describe with pen,
> The works of Nature or the ways of men,
> So that, when summoned from this changeful scene,
> These records may declare we once have been,
> Nor purblind loitered on the arduous road
> Which leads, through Nature's works, to Nature's God. (vii)

13. 246. In his will, Skinner gives the journals to the British Museum "on the terms of making no extracts for fifty years after the time of my decease" (211).

14. I treat the *Journal of a Disappointed Man* in *Virginia Woolf's Modernist Path: Her Middle Diaries and the Diaries She Read*.

15. Skinner discovered and protected the "chambered tumulus" at Stoney Littleton, a mile and a half from Wellow (Skinner 1971, 82).

16. *CR 2: 91*. Woolf did not see Skinner's 1820 journal. It reveals even more fully the ties binding daughter, father, and diary. "Laura died at seven o'clock this evening," Skinner tells his journal on May 24, 1820. "I desired her books, which she daily read to be carried into my room, and I shall retain them as my constant companions" (Skinner 1971, 134–35). A week later he finds her journals: "The Journals she kept from the time she was educated at home; and it will be a lasting memorial of her capacity and intelligence; since she was able to learn so many different lessons, in Latin, Italian, and

French with perfect ease to herself; and continue her work and drawing as amusements. That part of the Journal relative to the keeping of her birthday, so affected me, I put down the book; but shall request my brother to transcribe the whole" (Skinner 1971, 136).

17. Walter Scott also plays a fascinating role in Skinner's *Journal*. During Laura's final days, Skinner tries to distract himself with Scott's "Monastery" but finds it no good (Skinner 1971, 133). In November 1820 he disparages *Guy Mannering* (Skinner 1971, 145). As a parson, he does not in general approve of novels. However, later in life, he turns to Scott again and again in the midst of his family strife. On February 5, 1830, he reports reading *Rob Roy*, and on February 10 "one of Sir Walter Scott's works" again, and on February 17 he finishes *Black Dwarf* (232, 234, 236). During Joseph's final illness, the parson tells his diary in October 1832: "[A]s soon as it was light I went downstairs and got Sir Walter Scott's 'Lay of the last Minstrel' from the bookcase, with which I was fully occupied till breakfast time" (297–98). In an 1828 letter to a fellow clergyman's wife, Skinner writes, "I would as a matter of conscience, even if left alone, continue to sing out lustily the Lay of the Last Rector, and even if it did no more service to survivors than the death-song of the expiring Indian" (175).

18. Woolf read the 665 entries from 1822 to 1832 printed in the 1930 *Journal of a Somerset Rector*. The 1971 edition offers 957 entries from 1803 to 1834; however, much material in Skinner's journals remains unpublished. Howard Coombs and Peter Coombs, his 1971 editors, describe their editorial principles when they report that the journals "are largely filled with sketches and records of tours, mostly of little general interest, for if he visited the British Museum he would begin to catalogue its contents, and his notes on the places through which he passed are mainly of the guidebook description. Hundreds of pages are filled with archaeological detail and theory, mostly dead stuff, but the Parochial Journal, where it exists, throws much light on the life of a Somerset village at the beginning of the nineteenth century" (vi). This last is what the *Journal of a Somerset Rector* provides.

19. Fourteen of Nancy Woodforde's annual pocket diaries survive and for the year 1792 an expanded diary, as well.

20. CR 2: 84, 85. In her 1927 review, Woolf wrote the wittier "we cannot help suspecting that he was glad to consider the question of 'bold strokes' and marriage shelved" (330).

21. A reproduced diary page confirms editor Beresford's report that Woodforde wrote "as clear as print" and neatly ruled off each day's entry (2: 62; 1: vii; 5: 37). He moves, in fact, swiftly through the day, packing in facts with such handy formula as "We gave them for dinner a fine . . ."

22. Editor Beresford reports that after thirty-three years of daily diary-writing, on May 1, 1791, Woodforde begins to make "a brief note of the daily dinner at the Parsonage. Hitherto he has simply set down the more succulent dinners provided for guests" (3: 270). Citing Louis XVI's fatal two-hour stop for dinner as he fled the French mob,

Beresford observes that the French King shared with Woodforde "that inordinate regard for dinner which marks the eighteenth century" (3: 281n).

23. When his visiting nephew, William, contemplates going to sea, Woodforde tells a 1778 entry: "When Bill goes away I shall have no one to converse with—quite without a Friend" (1: 231).

24. *CR* 2: 83. Editor Beresford underscores this virtue in his introduction to volume 2 when he reminds us that in 1780 two-thirds to three-fourths of the population of England and Wales lived in the country: "A diary, therefore, which illuminates that country life which was the life of the majority of the nation must clearly be of notable interest. The great ones of the earth—the statesmen, the generals, the practical men of genius—tend to monopolize, for obvious reasons, the page of history. It is a mistake. However eminent, important, and attractive such persons are, they compose but a small part of the picture of life. . . . It requires Parson Woodforde to describe daily things as they actually were" (viii).

25. The *Diary* also lives on through the Parson Woodforde Society, founded in 1968, which publishes a journal and a newsletter. In 2008, the society published *Walks around James Woodforde's Norwich*. The society has also published the full text of Woodforde's diary in seventeen volumes.

26. Daisy's own descent could be traced from Henry III (*Daisy Princess of Pless by Herself* 10).

27. The 1931 American edition is titled *Better Left Unsaid*.

28. 88. She finds Germany even more restrictive than England. She exclaims in a 1905 entry of her restaurant lunch with Oscar Herren, "not an extraordinary thing to do in England, but in Berlin—to lunch alone with a man!" (172). Two years later following Hans' father's death, she sneaks into a German theater so as not to be seen. She justifies herself to her diary by noting that in England "a daughter-in-law would not be prevented from going to the theatre after two months; but then German mourning, like everything else, is taken in extremely large doses" (218).

29. Like Fanny Burney more than a hundred years before, Princess Daisy also complains of society talk. "[T]here is no conversation," Daisy tells her 1903 diary, "one is obliged to sit tête-à-tête with a man (never three or four together), so there can be no arguments or discussions; you sit with your man, *c'est bien*; if he is the ordinary man his conversation is about friendship, and then love, to discuss which is, I think, always an opening to flirtation: if he is an old friend, he will ask, how do you get on in Germany, how many men are in love with you, what do they think of you there (he might be discussing a savage country), and similar inanities. Or another sort of man will tell you all about his hunting, polo ponies, golf or shooting. You will seldom find anyone to sit down with you and have a sensible conversation about current topics, the politics of different countries, what they tend to, socialism, even religion" (99).

30. 252. Despite her political flirtations, Daisy reveals her own standards to her diary the year before: "I have always refused to accept even playful admiration from

a married man! And I think a woman who flirts in earnest with a married man is a fiend!" (231). Describing the German emperor in her book's final chapter, Daisy writes that Kaiser Wilhelm was a "typical German ... a good family man who, when he can afford it, marries early, begets lots of children, never beats his wife and—forgets all about her" (283). Of the emperor's fate, she continues: "I am not quite sure that any apprenticeship, any friend or adviser, however faithful and disinterested, could have saved the Emperor from himself. Certainly no woman could have done so. In his secret heart he thought little of us women: he almost despised us" (288). Here is one source for Woolf's "On Being Despised."

31. Major Desmond Chapman-Huston, who edited *From My Private Diary*, writes perceptively of this insecurity in his introduction: "Whilst she appeared to the onlooker to have everything in the way of beauty, charm, position and wealth that life can offer, there was ever present the gnawing inner sense of failure which follows like their shadow all those who fail to come to terms with an uncongenial background from which they cannot escape. We are often annoyed at the spectacle of so much splendid energy frustrated" (xiv).

32. L #2376, 4: 337. "Could Bloomsbury be grafted on to Mayfair," Woolf then wittily asks: "[B]ut no: we're too ugly and they're too stupid."

33. Sybil Oldfield reminds us that "the Boer War constituted a devastating reverse to the international peace movement, erupting as it did only a few months after the first Hague Peace Conference of 1899" (24). This war "stimulated widespread (and lasting) righteous hatred of Britain as an imperialist bully—especially in Germany," Oldfield notes (24). Ethel Smyth, who was in Berlin during the war, reported that "English people were spat upon in the streets" (*Female Pipings in Eden* 39).

34. 279. Even more ironic is editor Chapman-Huston's nod to Daisy's 1918 diary hopes for future accord between England and Germany as a further instance of her "unusual political intuition," followed by his assertion in 1931 that her belief "is, we hope, being slowly but surely fulfilled" (xii, xiii).

35. 307. Ironically, she dies there.

Chapter 3. Adept Sailing before the Storm

1. This diary is the same large size as the 1919 to 1931 diaries: 8 ¼ inches wide and 11 inches long. While the 1930–1931 diary book boasts a plain gray spine, the gray marbleized design of the 1932 diary (gray membranes with black and white bubbles within) carries over to the spine, too. A red vertical line—perhaps printed—provides a left-hand margin 1 ⅝ inches from the left edge. All the blue pages are thus ruled—even the few not used—and Woolf writes most entries in black ink.

2. On this night, Woolf seeks to dismiss war, specifically the Sino-Japanese conflict over Manchuria that threatened foreign interests in Shanghai. She tells her diary that Leonard "gave his views on the subject of war with China & Japan. We said that war

is the dullest of all things. Not naval war, said Duncan.... That was exciting. Only for ten minutes, I said" (*D* 4: 71).

3. On January 29, 1932, Woolf writes to Ethel Smyth that she tries to "crack jokes" when she has the Stracheys to dinner: "What am I to joke about tonight?" (*L* #2515, 5: 10).

4. *D* 4: 97. On her return to England, Woolf sounds rather dog-like when she writes to Ethel Smyth on May 19, 1932, that she is in a vile mood: "[T]he transition from freedom and Greece to endless conversation in London makes me itch all over" (*L* #2586 5: 64).

5. In her March 17 entry, Woolf blames Cambridge-educated Lytton Strachey for Carrington's suicide: "He absorbed her[,] made her kill herself" (*D*: 4: 83).

6. In her 1931 essay "Aurora Leigh," Woolf praised Elizabeth Barrett Browning's pioneering "novel-poem" of that name and suggested this hybrid held promise. This train of thought may have led to the "essay-novel."

7. Susan Squier points out that "women have always had a problematic relationship to culture itself" (*Women Writers and the City* 4).

8. Rows of small teal, yellow, and burgundy urns with flowers color a beige background, each urn framed by a border of teal leaves alternating with cherries. This diary book is the same size as Woolf's 1919–1932 diaries—8 ½ inches wide by 11 inches long—and penned mostly in black ink.

9. *D* 4: 133, 134. One meaning of "welter" is to wallow, roll, or toss about, as in mud or high seas.

10. Elvira will become Sara (Sally) Pargiter in the published *The Years* (1937).

11. *D* 4: 199. Woolf writes to Hugh Walpole during this time frame: "Are you spouting ink like a whale? I am: too profusely. But they cant say of Hugh and Virginia that they're Mrs Ward's miscarriages: we are our own begetters anyhow" (*L* #2839, 5: 264). Mitchell Leaska, who studied The Pargiter manuscripts (written on blue paper, like Woolf's diary), describes them as "among the most heavily corrected manuscripts in the entire Woolf archive" (*The Pargiters* xx). Ideas and impressions, he says, "flood the page" (xix).

12. *D* 4: 205. Nelly's interference with The Pargiters may be the straw that leads to her dismissal.

13. *D* 4: 185. The nautical meaning of *broach* is "to veer or cause to veer broadside to the wind and waves."

14. *D* 4: 192. In her July 16, 1932, diary entry, Woolf described Benson's life as the wife of an English customs officer in China: "There's always fighting. Chinese planes come over very low down. Shoot with revolvers. She sits in her kitchen. All the inhabitants crowd round, thinking the English safe—pretend they're selling eggs. Chinese generals come to dine & stand rifles on each side of their chairs: send soldiers into the kitchen to see that the food isn't poisoned. She goes back for another two years" (*D* 4: 118).

15. Five margin notes attest to Woolf's rereading of this diary and also to the diary's continued role as a source for her memoirs and other public prose. She writes "Dostoevsky" in the margin of her August 16, 1933, entry, to clarify for any later self the "D." contrasted with Turgenev in the entry (*D* 4: 172). In the margin of the October 29, 1933, entry that speaks of her letter calling for "protection of privacy," she writes at some later time: "A man wrote to say that my letter is to be the basis of a new guild for the P. of. P. See January number of something or other" (*D* 4: 186). She thus seeks to direct a future Virginia—or reader. She also continues to link her entries with coordinating or conversational words. Five entries start with "Yes," while five others counter with "No." "And" opens five entries; "Oh," two; and the two consecutive entries that record Nelly Boxall's final days begin, revealingly, "I cannot."

16. I treat Swift's *Journal to Stella* in *Virginia Woolf's Modernist Path: Her Middle Diaries and the Diaries She Read*.

17. Woolf calls Smyth's February 17, 1933, visit, in fact, a "dry brittle hour" (*D* 4: 147). Her letters to Smyth across this time elaborate the break. On June 6, 1933, for just one example, Woolf writes bluntly to Smyth that she hates her autobiography: "I hate any writer to talk about himself; anonymity I adore. . . . my whole bent is away and away and ever so far away from Ethel Smyth, Lilian Bayliss, Virginia Woolf. I hate personal snippets more and more" (*L* #2743, 5: 191, 193). See also *L* #2686, #2809, #2811, #2846, #2859, #2867, #2871, #2875, #2877.

18. I treat the Goncourts' journal in *Becoming Virginia Woolf: Her Early Diaries and the Diaries She Read*.

19. Ivor C. Treby reports that both Bradley's and Cooper's wills spell Bradley's name "Katharine," as do certain letters (*Music and Silence* 17); however, I will follow the spelling Woolf read in *Works and Days*.

20. The volume offers vivid views of writers Herbert Spencer, Robert Browning, George Meredith, Paul Verlaine, William Butler Yeats, Arthur Symonds, George Moore, Edmund Gosse, and Max Beerbohm; theater artists George Bernard Shaw, Oscar Wilde, Gabrielle D'Annunzio, Eleonora Duse, Sarah Bernhardt, Elizabeth Robins, and Ellen Terry, with her "abnormal need of caresses" from her husband, painter G. F. Watts (82); and art critics and painters John Ruskin, Bernhard Berenson, Sickert, Fry, Pen Browning, Charles Ricketts, Charles Shannon, and William Rothenstein.

21. Sturge Moore, the coeditor of *Works and Days*, gives the erroneous date of 1848 (xv).

22. Donaghue calls Cooper "franker" in the journal than Bradley (30).

23. Treby suggests that Bradley might also have chosen "Leigh" in homage to Leigh woods (*Michael Field Catalogue* 29).

24. Bradley's 1876 Christmas greeting to her fourteen-year-old niece began "From Fowl to Fowlet" (*Michael Field Catalog* 29).

25. Today it is the Bingham Hotel.

26. 324–25. After an 1886 visit to Robert Browning during which Browning tells

them that he and Elizabeth "never knew anything of each other's work till it was finished," Bradley writes in the *Journal*: "I give thanks for my Persian [Edith]: those two poets, man and wife, wrote alone; each wrote, but did not bless or quicken one another at their work; *we are closer married*" (15, 16). Francis Brookes was a former suitor of Katherine Bradley.

27. xxi. Donoghue, who has studied the journals, reports that Bradley and Cooper often took turns writing in the journal every few days, often from their joint notes, a method, she suggests, that "allowed them to shape petty details into a grand narrative" (47).

28. xv, 310. In 1998, Donoghue called the published *Works and Days* "excerpts from the milder parts of their diary" (8)

29. The online Victorian Lives and Letters Consortium: A Collection of Digital Archives and Editions allows readers to see page scans of all thirty diaries. Adam Matthew Publications offers for purchase microfilm facsimile copies (in thirteen reels) of the thirty volumes of diary and eight bound volumes of correspondence between Michael Field and others held in the British Library.

Chapter 4. Warnings

1. Peggy Pargiter, the young doctor in *The Years*, should be read as Woolf's direct counter to this German move.

2. This sturdy diary book is the same large size as her 1919 to 1933–1934 diary books: 8 ¼ inches wide and 10 ⅞ inches long. The cover features paisley droplets with pink, black, and white spots within, on a background of diagonal gray stripes. The diary pages once more are blue with a red vertical line printed two inches from the left edge; the paper reverses after a few pages (leaving the red line on the back), so Woolf rules a margin for herself in blue ink. Entries are penned usually in black ink.

3. In a November 27, 1934, letter to Victoria Ocampo, Woolf apologizes for asking so many questions: "It is a bad habit, sprung of terror and delight" (*L* #2955, 5: 349).

4. *D* 4: 262. This diary offers other signs that she writes for future readers, including herself. She corrects for accuracy in her July 21, 1934, entry: "Duncan ill with very bad piles—operated on last night, or, since that sounds alarming, lanced" (*D* 4: 228–29). Next to the moving passage from Guy de Maupassant's diary that she quotes at Roger Fry's death, she gives the source and page number in the margin: "*Sur l'eau* 116" (*D* 4: 242).

5. The question mark in brackets signals editorial uncertainty regarding the word "bonds."

6. In this July 28, 1934, entry, she refers to R. C. Trevelyan's poem "To V.W.," which states: And among all most fortunate must you be, / Whose chosen art has left your spirit free / To range through all experience, in quest / Of such spoil as may please your fancy best. (*D* 4: 233n26)

7. *D* 4: 259–60. Throughout this diary she rebukes praise-seeking in others as well as in herself. On July 17, 1934, she deplores Osbert Sitwell's "childish vanity always striking the two notes: rank & genius: so easily touched by praise, so eager" (*D* 4: 225). On October 9, she records Rose Macaulay's "authors' vanity" and remarks: "She is a ravaged sensitive old hack—as I should be, no doubt, save for L." (*D* 4: 249, 250). Five days later, in the midst of her ego struggle, she recoils from Edward Sackville-West's book *The Sun in Capricorn*, which she calls a "ridiculous rhodomontade," *rhodomontade* being a pretentious boasting or bragging (*D* 4: 252). On November 26, she bothers to record Victoria Ocampo's news of French poet Comtesse Mathieu de Noailles "dying of extinguished vanity in a small flat. . . . demanded worship; was not old, but had outlived her fame" (*D* 4: 264). In a telling July 29, 1934, letter to Ethel Smyth, Woolf stresses reading as an antidote to "I": "[T]he state of reading consists in the complete elimination of the *ego*; and its the ego that erects itself like another part of the body I dont dare to name" (*L* #2915, 5: 319). On January 8, 1935, Woolf refuses to write an introduction to Gladys Ellen Killen's autobiography *Middle Age 1885–1932*, writing to her that "if a book is worth publishing, it is much better that it should stand on its own feet. . . . I'm sure your book doesnt want anyone to praise it" (*L* #2974, 5: 363).

8. Woolf still sees Eliot as "constricted" (rather than free) when he dines with them on November 19. Yet she notes with some assurance: "I cant be frozen off with this divine authority any longer" (*D* 4: 263).

9. *D* 4: 244. Woolf writes to Ethel Smyth on January 8, 1935: "I feel like a dead blue sea after all these deaths—cant feel any more" (*L* #2973, 5: 362). Significantly, she tells her November 12, 1934, diary entry that her resurrection of Fry will hinge on freedom: "If I could be free, then here's the chance of trying biography: a splendid, difficult chance . . . that is, if I *am* free" (*D* 4: 260).

10. *D* 4: 274. Woolf's next-to-last diary entry in March 1941 affirms: "I think it is true that one gains a certain hold on sausage & haddock by writing them down" (*D* 5: 358).

11. Hermione Lee writes that Fry made this recommendation in "one of his lively, energetic letters . . . saying how attractive he found the candour of Gide's journal" (645).

12. In the *Journal, 1889 to 1939*, which Woolf will read in 1939, Gide writes at age twenty-one that while "written pages are resting, you must read relentlessly, voraciously . . . for it is essential to know everything. Ideas will again begin to stir; you must let them have their way; one of them will soon dominate; then you can return to writing" (1: 6–7). Three years later, he tells his *Journal* that the "yearning to educate myself is the greatest temptation for me. I have twenty books before me, every one of them begun" (1: 35).

13. O'Brien notes that for thirty years the *Nouvelle Revue Francaise* "occupied the forefront of modern literature" and served as a model for literary reviews in England, Germany, and the United States (*Journals* 1: vii).

14. 3: 38. Gide mentions suicide several times in the *Journals*. "Yesterday, abominable relapse, which leaves my body and mind in a state bordering on despair, on suicide, on madness," he tells his journal on October 15, 1916 (2: 156), and in 1921 he sounds Woolf's hate-my-kind dis-ease. "All humanity seems to me desperately ugly and soiled," he writes. "What bestiality, what egotism in the expression of all these faces!" (2: 274).

15. In his March 18, 1931, *Journal*, Gide describes his third or fourth attempt to read Huxley's novel and final halt at page 115 (3: 154). Editor O'Brien points to the irony, for *Point Counter Point* "was deeply influenced by, not to say modeled upon, Gide's *Faux Monnayeurs* [*The Counterfeiters*]" (3: 154n20).

16. 3: 65. In his 1931 *Journal*, he calls to mind the Goncourt brothers' *Journals* (which both he and Woolf read) when he repeats, "I scrupulously ruled out of my *Faux-Monnayeurs* everything that another might just as well have written. . . . What is easier than to write a novel like others! I am loath to do so, that's all" (3: 181).

17. "[T]o assert himself an artist is always obliged to break things," Gide tells his 1891 journal (1: 13).

18. 2: 126. Gide tells his 1905 journal: "I cling to these pages as to something fixed among so many fugitive things" (1: 133). At his wife's death in 1938, he declares: "I was, I still am, like someone sinking into a stinking morass, looking all around him for anything whatever that is fixed and solid of which to catch hold, but dragging with him and pulling into that muddy inferno everything he clutches. What is the good of speaking of that? Unless, perhaps, so that someone else, desperate like me, will feel less alone in his distress when he reads me; I should like to hold out a helping hand to him [through his diary]. Shall I get out of this quagmire? . . . What does life still hold in store for me? I cling to this notebook, as I have often done: as a system" (3: 394).

19. Gide copied into his 1918 journal these sentences from his letter to Lady Rothermere, who also translated his work: "The chief difficulty comes from the fact that my sentence constantly suggests rather than affirms, and proceeds by insinuations—for which the English language, more direct than the French, feels rather a repugnance" (2: 222).

20. Gide published more than eighty works across his eighty-one years and won the Nobel Prize in Literature in 1947.

21. A further instance from the 1930 *Journal*: "Fish die belly-upward and rise to the surface; it is their way of falling" (3: 106).

22. *D* 5: 229. Lucas' book was titled *Journal under the Terror, 1938*. See page 282–92.

23. After Woolf's death, Gide writes from Algiers in his May 27, 1941, journal entry: "At the Heurgons' I yield to the intoxication of a new library, reading one after another a little Leopardi, then a little Dante, then a little Stendhal, then a little Virginia Woolf: wandering at random in a garden" (4: 218). He says no more.

24. André Malraux said that Gide's obsession with his journals drew him from art to life, away from Racine toward Stendhal (*Journals* 1: xiv).

25. "What vulnerable natures!" Gide exclaimed of the Goncourts in his 1902 journal (1: 98).

26. "Renard's *Journal*: it is not a river; it is a distillery," Gide tells his own journal in August 1926 (2: 383). A week later: "He produces the right note, but always as a pizzicato" (2: 383); and two days later: "Jules Renard's garden could do with a little watering" (2: 384).

27. In a 1999 *New Yorker* appreciation, Anthony Lane declares that Gide's *Journals* contain "the core of [his] creative burrowings" (77). "We like to think that diaries are written in the wings—in the half-dark, away from the action and the spotlight," Lane observes. "Since his death, however, Gide's journals have moved to center stage" (78).

28. Maupassant's deceptively simple language furthers the elemental spell. "[E]very epithet a paying piece," wrote Henry James, who knew Maupassant from Flaubert's Sunday afternoon salons (*Afloat* 8). Joseph Conrad wrote that Maupassant "thinks sufficiently to concrete his fearless conclusions in illuminative instances. He renders them with that exact knowledge of the means and that absolute devotion to the aim of creating a true effect—which is art" (*Afloat* 14).

29. *Afloat* 22. Maupassant named this boat after his second novel, *Bel-Ami*, which has been translated "The Ladies Man."

30. "He loomed up in my young days almost to the obstruction of his works," Woolf wrote to Stephen Spender on May 12, 1935 (*L* #3018, 5:392).

31. I discuss Woolf's 1910 review of Emerson's early journals in *Becoming Virginia Woolf: Her Early Diaries and the Diaries She Read*.

32. Woolf read excerpts from 146 entries in the 1934 *Alice James: Her Brothers—Her Journal*.

33. Edel ix. The first was 4 ½ by 7 inches; the second, 6 ¼ by 7 ¾ inches (ix). James followed a practice Woolf also, on occasion, would use: writing to the book's end and then turning it upside down and continuing on the remaining blank pages.

34. In her September 27, 1890, diary entry, James writes: "I suppose one has a greater sense of intellectual degradation after an interview with a doctor than from any other human experience" (Burr 175–76). In November she rails against "the ignorant asininity of the medical profession in its treatment of nervous disorders," and in an April 1891 entry she describes Katharine's twenty-four hours spent "in the afternoon with Doctor Hack Tuke to Bedlam, in the evening to a 'smart' dinner, and the next morning... at Clapton lifting up her voice in prayer as she knelt among Salvation lassies. It would be curious to know which of the three was the chief centre of lunacy" (Burr 183, 215–16).

35. Burr 90. Changing light attracted James just as it did Woolf. James writes in the second month of her diary that "[t]he infinite gradations of light and shade simply intoxicate one" (Burr 93). Nine months later, she writes of the "exquisite thirty seconds every day" after lunch when she "drink[s] in... the gradation of the light in transition" (Burr 151).

36. That Alice James fiercely guarded her diary project can be seen further in her recoil from George Eliot's journal and refusal to read the diaries of Maria Bashkertseff (later often compared to hers), or of Henri-Frédéric Amiel. Alice reads the third volume of George Eliot's *Letters and Journals* during the second month of her own diary. "What a lifeless, diseased, self-conscious being she must have been!" Alice exclaims. "Not one burst of joy, not one ray of humour, not one living breath in one of her letters or journals; the commonplace and platitudes of these last. . . . makes the impression, morally and physically, of mildew or some morbid growth. . . . What an abject coward she seems to have been about physical pain, as if it weren't degrading enough to have headaches, without jotting them down in a row to stare at one for all time, thereby defeating the beneficent law which provides that pain is forgotten. If she related her diseases and her 'depressions' and told for the good of others what armour she had forged against them, it would be conceivable, but they seem simply cherished as the vehicle for a moan. Where was the creature's vanity? And when you think of what she had in life to lift her out of futile whining!" (Burr 97–98). A year later, James opens her June 16, 1890, entry: "What sense of superiority it gives one to escape reading some book which every one else is reading. I never would read *Amiel*, and so far I have not succumbed to Marie Bashkircheff's [sic] *Journal*. I imagine her the perverse of the perverse. . . ." (Burr 165).

Chapter 5. Tightness & Struggle

1. Woolf wrote to Fry in 1927: "[Y]ou have I think kept me on the right path, so far as writing goes, more than anyone—if the right path it is" (*L* #1764, 3: 385).

2. The diary's cover offers a nature print of tiny gray and black flowers (or raying suns) on a light beige background. This sturdy book is the same large size as Woolf's 1919 to 1934 diaries: 8 ¼ inches wide and 10 ¾ inches long. Its (now) white pages are ruled with a red vertical line 2 ¼ inches from the left-hand edge, and Woolf pens most entries in black ink. She stitches in the thirty-two smaller pages of her ten-entry May travel diary to Holland, Germany, Italy, and France.

3. *D* 4: 334. In the margin of her October 15, 1935, entry she simply lists people and places "Seen" and works "Read" (including all Fry's early letters), as she lacks time to say more (*D* 4: 346).

4. Two days before, Woolf ends her September 4, 1935, entry: "Cant write today. . . . I dreamt of men committing suicide & cd. see the body shooting through the water" (*D* 4: 338). However, she tells her September 15 entry: "I never think, seriously, of dying" (*D* 4: 342).

5. Woolf's June 25, 1935, diary entry records and analyzes Leonard's home tyranny over the servants. In a year she battles her own creeping tightness, she decries his "extreme rigidity of mind": "L. is very hard on people; especially on the servant class. No sympathy with them; exacting; despotic. So I told him yesterday when he'd com-

plained about the coffee.... His extreme rigidity of mind surprises me; I mean in its relation to others: his severity: not to myself but then I get up & curse him. What does it come from? Not being a gentleman partly: uneasiness in the presence of the lower classes: always suspects them, is never genial with them. Philip & Edgar [Woolf] are the same. His desire, I suppose, to dominate. Love of power. And then he writes against it. All this I shall tell him again, for it doesnt matter, to me; in our relationship; & yet I hate people noticing it: Nessa; Dadie; even Kingsley Martin—who all admire & respect him. An interesting study. It goes with great justice, in some ways; & simplicity too; & doing good things: but it is in private a very difficult characteristic" (*D* 4: 326). Jed Esty praises Woolf's "grim perspicacity" in *Three Guineas* in showing "the mutually reinforcing links joining patriarchy to patriotism to imperialism to capitalism to war" (176)

6. *D* 4: 304. Compare this with Woolf's March 27, 1935, description of their visit to the Tower of London: "Yesterday we went to the Tower, which is an impressive murderous bloody grey raven haunted military barrack prison dungeon place.... And we watched the Scots Guards drill; & an officer doing a kind of tiger pace up & down.... The sergeant major barked & swore. All in a hoarse bark: the men stamped & wheeled like—machines: then the officer also barked: all precise inhuman, showing off—a degrading, a stupefying sight..." (*D* 4: 292).

7. Dr. Alfred Salter also opposed the use of economic sanctions against Italy. Instead, he urged Britain to acknowledge the evils of imperialism and shift her tropical colonies into the hands of an international body as an example for Mussolini (*D* 4: 345n2)

8. Biographer Hermione Lee notes that *The Years* "rewrote" all Woolf's earlier books (627).

9. Woolf pens 160 questions in her 122 diary entries, more than half once more on writing (88 of 160): nineteen on *The Years*, seventeen on *Three Guineas*, and eight on *Roger Fry*.

10. On November 17, 1929, for instance, eighty-eight-year-old Salter writes: "Got to the end of a job that has been engaging me mentally and bodily for years—that of posting up all the various enterprises of my life, with what they individually cost me. It was a most satisfactory clearance. I can estimate the cost of everything I have done throughout my life. That and a complete inventory of everything that belongs to me are now done" (229).

11. 402. In May 1932, His Royal Highness Prince George opened the Salter Collection, the shot and preserved animals and birds Salter bequeathed to the Museum of Oaklands in Chelmsford.

12. 114–15. In his "Reminiscences," Salter devotes a section to "Archer Musgrave," whose father was an officer for the Duke of Wellington. Archer himself fought for Garibaldi when only a boy and later says to Salter: "I think there's going to be a bit of a row in the East, and if so I want to be in it" (264).

13. I treat Blunt's diaries in *Virginia Woolf's Modernist Path: Her Middle Diaries and the Diaries She Read*.

14. Woolf might have found Bailey's March 27, 1915, diary entry particularly alarming in 1935: "Lunched with H[erbert]. Fisher, who had lately seen Kitchener (still maintaining his view of the long war). Grey told him that the last time he ever saw the Kaiser, at a luncheon-party, [the Kaiser] began abusing the Jews to him, and when Grey tried to calm him down and said we managed very well with our Jews in England, he replied, hissing with hatred: 'I tell you, Sir Edward, what ought to be done with the German Jews; they ought to be *killed, killed, killed!*'" (163).

15. In a 1929 letter to Will Vaughan, Bailey writes: "Not being fit for much else these last days I have been looking over old diaries and papers to save executors trouble, and I am surprised to find how much oftener I was ill in 1885–1890 than I am now. I seem to have had continual bad headaches" (295). Headaches and illness appear nowhere in the fifteen 1886–1890 published diary entries—and might have interested Woolf.

Chapter 6. Misguided General

1. This sturdy diary also boasts one of her most beautiful covers: a marbleized design of beige, gray, and black swirls with a little pink and a dab of white thrown in. The book must have seen use first for *The Waves*, for Woolf crosses out "The Waves 2nd Draft" in the cover oval and writes "Diary" instead. This diary is the same large size as the 1919 to 1935 diaries: 8 ⅜ inches wide by 10 ⅝ inches long. Woolf rules the book's blue pages with a red vertical line two inches from the left-hand edge and writes most entries in black ink.

2. Woolf writes to Ethel Smyth on April 14, 1936: "[N]ow hear from America they cant possibly produce before October. Thank God!" (*L* #3118, 6: 26). On April 20 she again writes to Smyth: "[W]e have had to put off The Years anyhow till the autumn; the Americans asked us to" (*L* #3119, 6: 27).

3. Woolf writes of the country at the close of her January 7, 1936, entry: "I've had one or two sublime quiet evenings here—evenings of immunity, using that word in its highest sense" (*D* 5: 5).

4. In "Am I a Snob?" Woolf equates herself more explicitly with Lady Colefax. "We were like two survivors clinging to a raft," Woolf writes (*MOB* 217). "I've got to go on," Lady Sibyl tells Woolf (*MOB* 218).

5. *L* #3166, 6: 69. Vita could, in fact, claim distant ties to Lord Amberley (young John Russell), for in 1844 Lady Elizabeth Sackville-West married Amberley's cousin, the ninth Duke of Bedford.

6. Earl Russell died at the age of eighty-six in 1878, two years after his son, so the boys were mostly raised by their grandmother, Lady Russell.

7. I treat Allingham's diary in *Becoming Virginia Woolf: Her Early Diaries and the Diaries She Read*.

8. At age twenty-two, Kate tells her diary that Mrs. Grote said George Sand "was a bad woman, was the death of Schoppin" (1: 375). She meant Chopin. Run-on sentences "ran" in the Stanley family. Her mother and her Aunt Louisa also pell-mell their thoughts with few stops.

9. I: 119. Lady Strachey shared Kate's experience. She wrote: "At nineteen I read John Stuart Mill's work on 'Liberty,' and was ever afterwards a fervent disciple of his" (Chaudhuri 64).

10. Bertrand Russell points out that Amberley's writing style resembles Mill's (1: 36).

11. Bertrand Russell reports that his grandmother, Lady Stanley, used to say: "I have left my brain to the Royal College of Surgeons because it will be so interesting for them to have a clever woman's brain to cut up" (1: 18). Lady Strachey was another founder, as was Emily Davies, whom Kate also knew.

12. *D* 3: 87. Laura Russell, who lived at 2 Audley Square, just behind Park Lane, died in 1910. She was sister-in-law to Virginia's mother's cousin Adeline, Duchess of Bedford, and "a hostess of considerable consequence" in George Duckworth's eyes, according to Olivier Bell (*D* 3: 87n32); in fact, he was briefly engaged to her daughter, Flora.

13. 2: 526–27. Officious Aunt Louisa also lectured Kate regarding diaries. Responding to one of Kate's letters from America, she writes: "[Y]our acct of the School was a very good one—I think it was much better for you to have written letters than kept a Journal [Kate did both]—so much more lively & agreeable. In a Journal you lose that very much, & keep to mere facts and become didactic" (2: 99). The first letter from Aunt Louisa included in *The Amberley Papers* offers Louisa's rebuke of sixteen-year-old Kate for not liking Jane Austen. "To me her personages are old & intimate acquaintances," Aunt Louisa boasts (1: 54). Does she not herself recall Lady Catherine de Bourgh?

14. Kate tells her diary on July 30, 1868: "A[mberley]. will not be in a hurry and has no ardent wish for any seat but will not say so for his father's sake" (2: 121).

15. As early as his Nottingham success, Kate tells her May 12, 1866, diary: "Selfishly I am heartily sorry to lose my summer in the country and the company of my old darling all to myself. I hate going to London. . . . I fear he will never shine in Politics, he wants readiness, and adaptability to people and circumstances; but his character will always inspire admiration and confidence in him" (1: 502).

16. Diary scholar Harriet Blodgett notes that the British medical establishment delayed chloroform for childbirth for thirty years (*Centuries* 174–75).

17. 224. Hall reports that Ellen earned six shillings a quarter for each of her fourteen students (vii). She thus lived on 336 shillings a year.

18. Hall calls "egotism" the "dominant and acknowledged feature" of Ellen's letters (x).

19. Diary historian and anthologist Harriet Blodgett considers Weeton a "very tal-

ented" writer and notes that "her style of attack is rare" in nineteenth-century English women's diaries (*Centuries* 229, 141).

20. Saddlemeyer 283. Among Synge's papers was a copy of Edward Fitzgerald's translation of the *Rubaiyat of Omar Khayyam* with the inscription: "To the Loyal and Sympathetic camarade J. M. Synge—this minusculous gifteen in memory of delightful talks and walks and of gladnesses and sorrows, minusculous too, shared in unclouded friendliness in the Quartier Latin 1899–1900. Stephen MacKenna" (Saddlemeyer 295).

21. 151–52. As he finishes volume 3 in 1924, he writes again to Debenham that "clearness is my Rachel, if that was the lady some Biblical gentleman toiled seventy years for and I think I remember didn't get in the end.... clarity—the first jewel of literature to the likes of me. I veritably believe this translation to be unique in its clarification of the most unclear writer that ever wrote. I'd be happy in death if they put on my tombstone: 'He toiled for clarity and by gum he got it.'" (200).

22. The Woolfs owned an edition of Amiel's diary, but I cannot prove she read it.

23. "Stephen MacKenna," Answers.com, September 27, 2008.

24. 81. Sir Ernest Debenham so admired MacKenna's 1908 translation of Plotinus' essay on beauty that he personally subsidized the handsome tall volumes and (surreptitiously) arranged a "publisher's advance" that helped to free proud MacKenna to pursue his work.

Chapter 7. Storm-Tossed & Exposed

1. In an early draft of *The Years'* "1910" section later excised, Sara and Maggie discuss Cleopatra's Needle. Susan Squier suggests that in this context the needle becomes "a domestic transformation of the phallas" and "a symbol of the feminist civilization to come"—a suggestive gloss on this 1937 diary passage (*Virginia Woolf and London* 151, 142).

2. The print's background is black, but on it flows a diagonal pattern of tiny pink flowers on leaves of teal. These small flowers and buds alternate with tiny circles of pink surrounded by white resting on small leaves (almost waves) of teal.

3. *D* 5: 52. As it happens, *The Years* will come out March 11 rather than March 15.

4. In her June 20 diary entry, Woolf continues to suggest a sexual nuance to her "exposed" London distress: "I'm rather cross, since I had hoped to have one unravished day [in London]" (*D* 5: 94).

5. "Now I'm making up my Broadcast," Woolf writes in her April 2 diary entry, and the next day makes it more explicit: "It will go like this: cant be a craft of words" (*D* 5: 76, 77).

6. Women at Cambridge University did not receive full and equal membership until 1947.

7. She asks 131 questions in the diary's 77 entries, and 97 (almost 75 percent) relate to writing, her own or others'.

8. *D* 5: 72. In her June 28 diary entry, Woolf again calls herself "much refreshed" at Monk's House (*D* 5: 99).

9. In 1908, as she penned her own continental travel diary, Woolf began a review of two travel books with this suggestive note on diaries: "Every one who writes at all writes a diary of impressions when he travels abroad. The scene is so new, so original, and so charmingly arranged as though on purpose to be looked at and written about, that the fingers curve round a visionary pen, and the lips form words instinctively. It would be pleasant to think that this habit is not altogether vain" (*E* 1: 200). She ends her review with a bow to Tolstoy and a jibe at his sleepy English counterparts: "While Tolstoy, Ibsen, and Nietzsche sent waves of fresh thought across the Continent, the English slept undisturbed or did not raise their eyes from their own affairs" (*E* 1: 203). One wonders if she was thinking of herself in a 1916 review that argued that prose (rather than poetry) "has been the chosen medium of the greatest writers of our time—of Dostoesvky, of Carlyle, of Tolstoy" (*E* 2: 70)?

10. *E* 2: 194. In the final year of her life, Woolf told her March 21, 1940, diary: "I read Tolstoy at Breakfast—Goldenweiser, that I translated with Kot in 1923 & have almost forgotten. Always the same reality—like touching an exposed electric wire. Even so imperfectly conveyed—his rugged short cut mind—to me the most, not sympathetic, but inspiring, rousing; genius in the raw" (*D* 5: 273).

11. His mother died when he was one and his father when he was seven.

12. Tolstoy exhorts himself in his January 2, 1854, entry: "Set down in my Diary only thoughts, information, or notes relating to work I am undertaking. On beginning each fresh piece of work look through this Diary and copy out in a separate notebook all that relates to the work" (*TPD* 61.) Three days later he tells himself to park "good, or well expressed" thoughts in his diary for later use (*TPD* 64).

13. Translator Aylmer Maude reports that Tolstoy did not intend his full diaries for publication: "When I was staying at Yásnaya Polyána in October 1910 he said that only some selected thoughts from them were worth publishing. He subsequently authorized Chertkóv to use his own discretion as to what should, or should not, be published after his death, and Chertkóv decided to publish everything" (*TFS* 109 n1).

14. In his *Reminiscences of Tolstoy, Chekhov and Andreev*, published by the Hogarth Press in 1920, Gorky writes: "In his diary which he gave me to read, I was struck by a strange aphorism: 'God is my desire'" (11).

15. Leah Bendavid-Val notes that the countess copied *War and Peace* "approximately seven times" (82).

16. In 1885, the countess had set up a publishing office and warehouse in a shed on their Moscow property.

17. The countess' granddaughter, Annochka, daughter of the Tolstoys' third child, Ilya, wrote in her memoirs: "In the morning she would record expenses, put things in order, try on her dresses, which were constantly sewn and made over. Having drunk plenty of coffee, she would begin playing piano scales, or run—it's impossible to say

about her that she walked—with oil paints to sketch a pond, a garden path, mushrooms, herbs, flowerets, a house. Then she would write something—she made entries in her diary almost daily" (Bendavid-Val 129).

18. *TFS* 152–55. The countess tells her July 14 diary: "Leo Nikoláevich came to my room, and I told him in terrible agitation that on the one side the return of the diaries and on the other my own life were in the balance. He must choose between them. And he chose—for which I thank him—" (*TFS* 157).

19. Sergius Tolstoy and translator Maude both note that earlier, Tolstoy yielded to the countess' request to erase certain entries in his 1888 to 1895 diaries that she thought unfair to her (*TFS* 344). Alexandra Popoff argues in her 2014 *Tolstoy's False Disciple* that Chertkóv also deleted passages in Tolstoy's diaries (35, 109–11, 200).

20. 278. In *Song without Words: The Photographs & Diaries of Countess Sophia Tolstoy*, Leah Bendavid-Val describes "the annual wedding anniversary photography sessions" after 1887 (10). The countess "brought out her fine clothes and got dressed up. Whenever she could she celebrated the occasion with a photograph" (210). Tolstoy, in contrast, "hated the experience and was against being treated like a celebrity" (70). Bendavid-Val believes the countess "made many of her photographs of him and their life together with posterity in mind" (9).

21. The countess rereads—and recopies—her own diaries as well as Tolstoy's, crossing out words and adding sentences.

22. Recently, Alexandra Popoff has tried to bolster Countess Tolstoy's case in two books: *Sophia Tolstoy: A Biography* (2010) and *Tolstoy's False Disciple* (2014). In a 2010 review of *The Diaries of Sofia Tolstoy* and three other books on Tolstoy, James Meek suggests that the countess "went out of her mind in 1910 not because she had lost her mind but because she thought she was losing her husband's" ("Some Wild Creature," *London Review of Books*, July 22, 2010, 5).

23. On September 10, 1910, a publisher approached the countess with an offer of one million rubles for Tolstoy's works (*TFS* 272n1).

Chapter 8. Hitler Darkens the Waters

1. She uses mostly black ink on white and blue paper and rules her pages in her usual fashion: a red vertical line two inches from the left-hand edge.

2. She also returns to morning diary-writing.

3. *D* 5: 193. In her April 12 diary entry, Woolf declares that she thinks *Three Guineas* has more substance than *A Room of One's Own*, "which, on rereading, seems to me a little egotistic, flaunting, sketchy: but has its brilliance—its speed" (*D* 5: 134).

4. *D* 5: 162. Woolf opens her September 28, 1938, entry, "This may be the last day of peace; so why not record it," and in October, when she loans Helen Anrep £150 and then frets, she tells herself: "I daresay this will make interesting reading to me one of these days, should I write a true memoir" (*D* 5: 174, 181).

5. Beyond John Skinner's *Journal of a Somerset Rector* and James Woodforde's *Diary of a Country Parson*, treated in this volume, Woolf reviewed *The Blecheley Diary of the Rev. William Cole 1765–1767* and Cole's *Journal of my Journey to Paris in the Year 1765* in the February 6, 1932, *New Statesman and Nation*. In a 1938 essay, she returned again to diarist Cole in her essay, "The Two Antiquaries: Walpole and Cole."

6. 2: 202. Compare this passage with Virginia's August 22, 1907, Playden diary words: "I think especially of walking up at night, from Rye, all the vague scents & coolnesses of a country evening washing over one's body" (*PA* 368–69).

7. I cannot prove that Woolf read it. She asks Plomer for volume three on December 28, 1939, and reiterates "But I want Kilvert" on September 15, 1940, six months before her death. If she read the third volume in her final months, she saw that Kilvert visited Salisbury Cathedral and its Close but also marveled at Stonehenge as "holy ground and the very Acre of God"—steps she followed in her pivotal 1903 diary (3: 223). More than anything, she saw he shared her ecstatic moments, what she called in 1939 her "moments of being." "As I came down from the hill into the valley across the golden meadows and along the flower-scented hedges a great wave of emotion and happiness stirred and rose up within me," he tells his May 1875 diary. "I know not why I was so happy, nor what I was expecting, but I was in a delirium of joy, it was one of the supreme few moments of existence, a deep delicious draught from the strong sweet cup of life. It came unsought, unbidden, at the meadow stile, it was one of the flowers of happiness scattered for us and found unexpectedly by the wayside of life" (3: 190–91).

Chapter 9. War Shades Life & Work

1. On November 30, Russia attacked Finland.

2. On October 25, 1939, Woolf writes to diarist Eddy Sackville-West, who has praised *The Waves*: "And a word of praise from a reader like you almost persuades me that I could get back to that world in spite of the war. As it is, I cling to Roger Fry and facts" (*L* #3562, 6: 366).

3. In 1937, more than 75 percent of Woolf's diary questions concerned writing, Woolf's own or others'. War siphons the percentage to less than 50 percent in 1939.

4. Alarmingly, however, Woolf tells her September 25, 1939, entry: "Roger seems hopeless. Yet if one cant write, as Duncan said yesterday, one may as well kill oneself. Such despair comes over me—waking early" (*D* 5: 239). Woolf's identification with Fry and his role as vigorous "life" for her show in her mid-July hate-my-kind struggle. "A bad morning," she opens her July 13 entry as she contemplates the move from Tavistock to Mecklenburgh Square. "A grim thought struck me: wh. of these rooms shall I die in? Which is going to be the scene of some—oh no, I wont write out the tragedy that has to be acted there. A free man thinks of nothing &c" (*D* 5: 226). Spinoza's famous declaration that "[a] free man thinks of death least of all things; and his wisdom

is a meditation not of death but of life," was read at Fry's funeral in 1934. Woolf calls *Roger Fry*'s final chapter "Transformations," and uses Spinoza's words both for herself here in her diary and as the closing words of *Roger Fry*.

5. However, he then qualifies his country paean with this dig at William Wordsworth: "Only one must remember Wordsworth's fate. Too much Grasmere; and then . . ." (99–100).

6. His first marriage, to E.B.C. ("Topsy") Jones, faltered in 1929 over her "flirtatious ways," according to Woolf's diary (*D* 3: 225); his subsequent love affair with married Sheelah Clutton-Brock foundered in 1931 after a bedroom-door row with her husband (also limned in Woolf's diary and letters).

7. Lucas evokes Dr. Johnson, "Bozzy," and the *Journal of a Tour to the Hebrides* during his own April journey to Scotland with Prudence (139–40). He refers to Regency diarist-gossip Thomas Creevey; quotes in French from Jules Renard's *Journal*; and twice links his own fate with the Goncourts. "And the Goncourts, if I remember, bristled with horror and indignation at the suggestion that they might be forgotten after a paltry two thousand years or so," he remarks wryly in January, while in September he finds himself once more in the French diarists' plight, for his novel comes out only to be trumped by the Munich crisis (64, 255).

8. Ricketts followed diarist (and bookbinder) Thomas Cobden-Sanderson's practice of binding extra endpapers in his books, and he offered designs for the rebinding of diarist Wilfrid Scawen Blunt's *The Love Lyrics and Songs of Proteus* (Watry 58, 59). Woolf reviewed Cobden-Sanderson's *Journals* in 1926 and read Blunt's diaries in 1918. I treat both diarists in *Virginia Woolf's Modernist Path: Her Middle Diaries and the Diaries She Read*.

9. Delaney 140. The other was of Cecil Lewis.

10. Sturge Moore says £500 in the 1939 *Self-Portrait* (105n1), but Delaney corrects him (95).

11. Woolf read the Goncourt brothers' *Journals* in the second half of 1917. They influenced her own diary portraits. See my *Becoming Virginia Woolf: Her Early Diaries and the Diaries She Read*.

12. S-P 73. Ricketts' costumes for *The Mikado* were so successful that they were used until the D'Oyly Carte Company closed in the 1980s and fetched the highest prices when the Carte wardrobe was sold (Delaney 352).

13. They omit, for instance, Ricketts' entire February 1, 1903, entry in which he worries, "My friend wants to spend Sunday evening with a model called H.D. I hope it is not the beginning of the end of our life together" (Delaney 159).

14. S-P x. Alice James also calls herself dead long before her literal death. She reveals this in her diary, which Woolf read in 1934. See page 132.

15. S-P 241. Ricketts long felt himself an outsider. In 1914, insulted at proposed treatment of his work in *The Art of the Book*, he copies his reply into his diary: "[Y]our suggestion that I should be represented by two pages satisfied me even less than a full

exhibition of my work as a designer of founts, pages, woodcut decorations, illustrations, paper, cloth and leather binding, etc. . . . I should like to be different, but I have had to stand outside any fair or intelligent estimate of my work for so many years that I have taken a taste to the situation and am contented with it" (*S-P* 191, 192). Three days later, he tells his diary that "[t]o stand outside common currents and popular aims is in itself a sign of character and originality" (*S-P* 192). When finally elected to the Royal Academy (late in life like Delacroix), Ricketts works on behalf of outsiders. He writes a friend in 1929: "My direct action in the R.A. hanging has been the creation of the larger Black-and-White Room whereby some 900 more works have been hung, and the salving of some 50 pieces of sculpture placed about the gallery, which would have been crowded out otherwise. I believe also that my securing important places on the line, Room N. 3, for outsiders is without precedent in the history of the R.A." (*S-P* 417–18). Like Woolf, Ricketts rejected honors. Offered an honorary degree from Cambridge in 1924, he writes Sydney Cockerell: "It is most kind of you to wish me to become a Doctor, it is sweet of you, but, please, don't think me ungracious, never think of it again; my imagination quails before any British honour; none were given to Rossetti; the little red French rosette is the only thing which might give me pleasure—or else, of course, the Garter with a tremengeous diamint star and a St George the size of a saucepan—but this is improbable. Again don't think me ungracious: both Shannon and I fear and hate all ceremonies and banquets" (*S-P* 348).

16. *S-P* 305. Delaney calls George Bernard Shaw's 1924 *St. Joan* "probably the production for which Ricketts is best remembered" (344).

17. Ricketts shared Woolf's passion for flowers; one year he spends more than £500 on blooms. "The house was often like a show," Sturge Moore writes in *Self-Portrait*, "for he appreciated blossom in mass and profusion as well as the separate perfection, which he knew how to set off by its unexpected disposition in vase or dish. He loved the oddities as well as the splendours of Nature's invention, and would laughingly say, 'That is the work of a very minor—perhaps of a fallen angel,' or 'The Almighty would not trust even an Archangel with this, and designed it Himself. His hand was even luckier than when He made Eve'" (134n1). Ricketts wrote Gordon Bottomley in 1918: "I am not sure there is not a human need for sermons at times, and I used to threaten the Michaels with a series of them on lilies, camellias, violets, tulips, etc." (*S-P* 297).

18. In 2004, Maureen Watry published *The Vale Press: Charles Ricketts, a Publisher in Earnest*.

19. MacLennan also dramatizes in *Last Romantics* the Ricketts/Fry enmity. In the scene depicting Ricketts' and Shannon's meeting, MacLennan has Ricketts say: "You should move in. I've got a large bed." Shannon: "I'm already lodging with Roger Fry." Ricketts: "That talentless scribbler? A young fresh pimple. You'll never develop your genius with him" (111). When Ricketts and Fry vie later for the National Gallery post, MacLennan has Ricketts say: "Fry? As director? That little ferret is blind to beauty. He'd fill galleries with that Impressionist bilge the Continent calls art" (55).

Chapter 10. Encircled by War

1. D 5: 311. In May, Woolf's American publisher, Harcourt Brace, gives her a £250 advance on Roger Fry as well (D 5: 289).

2. D 5: 265. Woolf first uses this image in her September 22, 1938, diary entry before the Munich accord: "Eden, Churchill & the L[abour]P[arty] all denounce serving C.S.[Czechoslovakia] on the altar & bidding it commit suicide. CS. very dignified & tragic" (D 5: 173).

3. D 5: 266. Similarly, on September 12 she reports that while "blackberrying" she "conceived, or remoulded, an idea for a Common History book—to read from one end of lit. including biog; & range at will, consecutively" (D5 318). This is "Anon."

4. Woolf uses the word *acquiescence* earlier (on February 16) in her envy of Margery Fry's old age mobility: "She is off to France, & pricked my apathy by suggesting that I should come—& made me deplore my spineless acquiescence; she so mobile" (D 5: 267).

5. D 5: 347. On July 24, Woolf describes Ray Strachey, dead at age fifty-three, as "tart" in her last days: "as if these petals had withered & she cd. no longer be confident" (D 5: 304).

6. Excerpts from Alfred de Vigny's notebooks, given the title *Journal d'un poète* when published posthumously in 1867, consist of pensées rather than journal entries.

7. Jean Moorcroft Wilson suggests that Woolf personifies London—rather than England—as "a battered but indomitable old woman" (119). In *Virginia Woolf: Life and London*, Wilson notes, too, that "[i]t was the contrast she needed.... What in many people would have seemed superficial was vital to Virginia's delicate balance" (115, 121).

8. D 5: 329. Portentously, she copies Seneca's bolstering words into her April 25 diary entry, "There is nothing in the world so much admired as a man who knows how to bear unhappiness with courage" (D 5: 282). Seneca was forced to commit suicide by the tyrant Nero.

9. Susan M. Squier notes that "[t]he impact of the London bombings upon Woolf's imagination cannot be overestimated" (*Virginia Woolf and London: The Sexual Politics of the City* 188).

10. Anne E. Fernald vividly tallies the importance of movement to Woolf in *Virginia Woolf: Feminism and the Reader*. She reminds us that the mark in Woolf's early experimental short story "The Mark on the Wall" turns out to be a snail, so "it will move" (69). Elizabeth Dalloway's bus ride across London—her movement—liberates her thoughts of vocation, just as Woolf's own "Street Haunting" walks free her artistic imagination (72, 73). Woolf's essential embrace of movement was undergirded, Fernald argues persuasively, from her early reading of Hakluyt's miscellaneous (diary-like) compendium of Elizabethan voyages.

11. I have stared long and hard at this final diary book in the Berg Collection at the

New York Public Library. A Berg archivist confirms the two dots. For a fine discussion of Woolf's use of ellipses across her works, see Rachel Bowlby's "The Dotted Line" in her *Feminist Destinations and Further Essays on Virginia Woolf* (Edinburgh: Edinburgh University Press, 1997), 137–45.

Epilogue

1. They include her diary mother, Fanny Burney; John Evelyn; Jonathan Swift; Stendhal; Dorothy Wordsworth; Ellen Weeton; Mary (Seton) Berry; Eugene Delacroix; Leo Tolstoy; Lady Frederick Cavendish; William Allingham; Wilfrid Scawen Blunt; Dr. John Salter; John Bailey; Katherine Bradley and Edith Cooper ("Michael Field"); Charles Ricketts; Stephen MacKenna; André Gide; and Alie Badenhorst.

Works Consulted

Primary Sources

Alice James: Her Brothers—Her Journal. Ed. and Intro. Anna Robeson Burr. Tortola, British Virgin Islands: Longwood Press, 1977. [An unabridged republication of the edition of 1934]. Print.

Alighieri, Dante. *The Divine Comedy of Dante Alighieri.* Italian text with English blank verse by Courtney Langdon. Vol. 1 *Inferno.* Cambridge: Harvard University Press, 1918. Print.

Arthur Young's Travels in France During the Years 1787, 1788, 1789. Ed. and Intro. Miss Betham-Edwards. London: George Bell & Sons, 1892. Print.

The Autobiography and Memoirs of Benjamin Robert Haydon (1786–1846). Edited from His Journals by Tom Taylor. Intro. Aldous Huxley. 2 vols. London: Peter Davies, 1926. Print.

Barbellion, W.N.P. *The Journal of a Disappointed Man & A Last Diary.* Intro. H. G. Wells. London: Chatto and Windus, 1919. Print.

Beatrice Webb's Diaries, 1912–1924. Ed. Margaret I. Cole. Intro. Rt. Hon. Lord Beveridge. London: Longmans, Green, 1952. Print.

Beatrice Webb's Diaries, 1924–1932. Ed. Margaret I. Cole. London: Longmans, Green, 1956. Print.

The Blecheley Diary of the Rev. William Cole. Ed. Francis Griffin Stokes. Intro. Helen Waddell. London: Constable, 1931. Print.

Blunt, Wilfrid Scawen. *My Diaries: Being a Personal Narrative of Events 1888 to 1914.* Foreword Lady Gregory. 2 vols. New York: Knopf, 1921. Print.

Boswell, James. *The Journal of a Tour to Corsica; & Memoirs of Pascal Paoli.* Ed. and Intro. S. C. Roberts. Cambridge: Cambridge University Press, 1923. Print.

———. *The Journal of a Tour to the Hebrides with Samuel Johnson, LL.D.* Ed. Robert Carruthers. London: Office of the National Illustrated Library, 1852. Print.

Boswell's Journal of A Tour to the Hebrides with Samuel Johnson, LL.D. Pub. from the original ms. Ed. Frederick A. Pottle and Charles H. Bennett. New York: Viking, 1936. Print.

Cole, Rev. William. *A Journal of my Journey to Paris in the Year 1765*. Ed. Francis Griffin Stokes. Intro. Helen Waddell. New York: Richard R. Smith, 1931. Print.

Creevey's Life and Times: A Further Selection from the Correspondence of Thomas Creevey Born 1768—Died 1838. Ed. John Gore. London: John Murray, 1934. Print.

The Creevey Papers: A Selection from the Correspondence & Diaries of the Late Thomas Creevey, M.P. Born 1768—Died 1838. Third ed. Ed. Sir Herbert Maxwell. New York: E. P. Dutton, 1923. Print.

The Creevey Papers. Revised ed. Ed. John Gore. New York: Macmillan, 1963. Print.

Daisy Princess of Pless by Herself. Ed. and Intro. Major Desmond Chapman-Huston. London: John Murray, 1928. Print.

Daisy Princess of Pless. *From My Private Diary*. Ed. and Intro. Major Desmond Chapman-Huston. London: John Murray, 1931. Print.

———. *What I Left Unsaid*. Ed. and Intro. Major Desmond Chapman-Huston. New York: E. P. Dutton, 1936. Print.

Dante, *see* Alighieri, Dante.

The Diaries of Leo Tolstóy. Trans. C. J. Hogarth and A. Sirnis. Preface by C. Hagberg Wright LL.D. New York: E. P. Dutton, 1917. Print.

The Diary and Letters of Madame D'Arblay (Frances Burney). With notes by W. C. Ward and essay by Lord Macaulay. 3 vols. London: Frederick Warne, 1892. Print.

The Diary of a Country Parson: The Reverend James Woodford. Ed. John Beresford. 5 vols. London: Oxford University Press, 1924–1931. Print.

The Diary of a Lady-in-Waiting by Charlotte Bury: Being the Diary Illustrative of the Times of George the Fourth interspersed with Original Letters from the Late Queen Caroline and from other Distinguished Persons. Ed. and Intro. A. Francis Steuart. London: John Lane, 1908. Print.

The Diary of Alice James. Ed. and Intro. Leon Edel. New York: Dodd, Mead, 1964. Print.

The Diary of Beatrice Webb. Ed. Norman and Jeanne MacKenzie. 4 vols. Cambridge: Belknap Press of Harvard University Press, 1982–85. Print.

The Diary of Benjamin Robert Haydon. Ed. Willard Bissell Pope. 5 vols. Cambridge: Harvard University Press, 1960, 1963. Print.

The Diary of John Evelyn. Ed. William Bray. Intro. Richard Garnett. 2 vols. London: M. Walter Dunne, 1901. Print.

The Diary of Lady Frederick Cavendish. Ed. John Bailey. 2 vols. New York: Frederick A. Stokes, 1927. Print.

The Diary of Samuel Pepys. Ed. Robert Latham and William Matthews. 11 vols. Berkeley: University of California Press, 1970. Print.

The Diary of Samuel Pepys. Ed. Henry B. Wheatley. 8 vols. London: G. Bell, 1962. First published in 10 vols., 1893–1899. Print.

The Diary of the Lady Anne Clifford. Intro. Vita Sackville-West. New York: George H. Doran, 1923. Print.

The Diary of the Lady Anne Clifford, 1616 to 1619: A Critical Edition. Ed. Katherine O. Acheson. New York: Garland, 1995. Print.

Diary, Reminiscences, and Correspondence of Henry Crabb Robinson, Barrister-at-Law, F.S.A. Ed. Thomas Sadler. 2 vols. Boston: Houghton, Mifflin, 1898. Print.

Dr. Salter of Tolleshunt D'Arcy in the County of Essex: Medical Man, Freemason, Sportsman, Sporting-Dog Breeder and Horticulturalist: His Diary and Reminiscences from the year 1849 to the year 1932. Comp. J. O. Thompson. London: J. Lane, 1933. Print.

The Early Diary of Frances Burney, 1768–1778. Ed. Annie Raine Ellis. 2 vols. Freeport, New York: Books for Libraries Press, 1971 (first published 1889). Print.

Extracts of the Journals and Correspondence of Miss Berry from the Year 1783 to 1852. Ed. Lady Theresa Lewis. 3 vols. London: Longmans, Green, 1865. Print.

The Famous Miss Burney: The Diaries and Letters of Fanny Burney. Ed. Barbara G. Schrank and David J. Supino. New York: John Day, 1976. Print.

The Final Struggle: Being Countess Tolstoy's Diary for 1910 with Extracts from Leo Tolstoy's Diary of the Same Period. Preface S. L. Tolstoy. Trans. and Intro. Aylmer Maude. New York: Oxford University Press, 1936. Print.

Gide, André. *The Fruits of the Earth.* Trans. Dorothy Bussy. New York: Knopf, 1949. Print.

———. *If It Die . . . An Autobiography.* Trans. Dorothy Bussy. New York: Random House, 1935. Print.

———. *Journal, 1889–1939.* Paris: Gallimard, 1939. Print.

———. *The Journals of André Gide.* 4 vols. Trans. Justin O'Brien. New York: Knopf, 1947, 1948, 1949, 1951. Print.

———. *The Notebooks of André Walter.* Trans. and Intro. Wade Baskin. New York: Philosophical Library, 1968. Print.

———. *Pages de Journal, 1929–32.* Paris: Gallimard, 1934. Print.

———. *Strait Is the Gate.* Trans. Dorothy Bussy. New York: Knopf, 1924. Print.

The Goebbels Diaries. Ed. and Trans. Louis P. Lochner. Afterword Brigadier General Telford Taylor. New York: Award Books, 1971. Print.

The Goncourt Journals, 1851–1870. Ed. and Trans. Lewis Galantière. Garden City, New York: Doubleday, Doran, 1937. Print.

Henry, Elizabeth and George (1734–80): Letters and Diaries of Henry, Tenth Earl of Pembroke and His Circle. Ed. Lord Herbert. London: Jonathan Cape, 1939. Print.

Jacks, Lawrence Pearsall. *Life and Letters of Stopford Brooke.* 2 vols. New York: Charles Scribner's, 1917. Print.

John Bailey, 1865–1931: Letters and Diaries. Ed. Sarah Bailey. Preface G. M. Trevelyan. London: John Murray, 1935. Print.

Journal and Letters of Stephen MacKenna. Ed. with a Memoir by E. R. Dodds. Preface Padraic Colum. London: Constable, 1936. Print.

The Journal of Elizabeth Lady Holland (1791–1811). Ed. Earl of Ilchester. 2 vols. London: Longmans, Green, 1908. Print.

The Journal of Eugene Delacroix. Trans. Walter Pach. Illustrated with Reproductions of the Paintings and Drawings of the Artist. New York: Covici, Friede, 1937. Print.

The Journal of Eugène Delacroix. Selected and edited with an Introduction by Hubert Wellington. Trans. Lucy Norton. London: Phaidon, 1951. Print.

The Journal of Jules Renard. Ed. and Trans. Louise Bogan and Elizabeth Roget. New York: George Braziller, 1964. Print.

Journal of Katherine Mansfield. Ed. J. Middleton Murry. New York: Alfred A. Knopf, 1927. Print.

The Journal of Sir Walter Scott. Ed. W.E.K. Anderson. Oxford: Clarendon, 1972. Print.

The Journal of Sir Walter Scott, 1825–32. Ed. David Douglas. Edinburgh: Douglas & Foulis, printed from the stereotype plates made for the edition of 1891, with a few inaccuracies corrected. Print.

The Journal of Sir Walter Scott, 1825–26. Ed. J. G. Tait. Edinburgh: Oliver and Boyd, 1939. Print.

The Journal of Sir Walter Scott, 1827–28. Ed. J. G. Tait. Edinburgh: Oliver and Boyd, 1941. Print.

The Journal of Sir Walter Scott, 1829–32. Ed. J. G. Trait and W. M. Parker. Edinburgh: Oliver and Boyd, 1946. Print.

The Journals and Letters of Fanny Burney (Madame D'Arblay). Ed. Joyce Hemlow with Curtis D. Cecil and Althea Douglas. 12 vols. Oxford: Clarendon, 1972. Print.

Journals of Dorothy Wordsworth: The Alfoxden Journal 1798; The Grasmere Journals, 1800–1803. Ed. Mary Moorman. Intro. Helen Darbishire. London: Oxford University Press, 1971. Print.

Journals of Dorothy Wordsworth. Ed. William Knight. 2 vols. London: Macmillan, 1897. Print.

Journals of Dorothy Wordsworth. Ed. E. de Sélincourt. 2 vols. New York: Macmillan, 1941. Print.

Journals of Ralph Waldo Emerson [1820–1824]. Ed. Edward Waldo Emerson and Waldo Emerson Forbes. Boston: Houghton Mifflin, 1909. Print.

Journals of Ralph Waldo Emerson [1824–1832]. Ed. Edward Waldo Emerson and Waldo Emerson Forbes. Boston: Houghton Mifflin, 1909. Print.

The Journals of Thomas James Cobden-Sanderson. 2 vols. New York: Macmillan, 1926. Print.

The Katherine Mansfield Notebooks. Ed. Margaret Scott. 2 vols. Minneapolis: University of Minnesota Press, 2002. Print.

Kilvert's Cornish Diary. Ed. Richard Maber and Angela Tregoning. Cornwall: Alison Hodge, 1989. Print.

Kilvert's Diary: Selections from the Diary of the Rev. Francis Kilvert. Ed. William Plomer. 3 vols. London: Jonathan Cape, 1960. Print.

Leo Tolstoy: Last Diaries. Trans. Lydia Weston-Kesich. Ed. and Intro. Leon Stilman. New York: G. P. Putnam's Sons, 1960. Print.

Lockhart, John G. *Memoirs of the Life of Sir Walter Scott.* 7 vols. Edinburgh: Robert Cadell, 1837-38. Print.

Lucas, F. L. *Journal under the Terror, 1938.* London: Cassell, 1939. Print.

MacLennan, Michael Lewis. *Last Romantics.* Toronto: Playwrights Canada Press, 2003. Print.

Maupassant, Guy de. *Afloat.* Trans. and Intro. Marlo Johnston. Drawings E. Riou. London: Peter Owen, 1995. Print.

———. *Sur l'eau.* Illus. de Lanos. Gravées sur bois par G. Lemoine. Paris: Librairie Paul Ollendorff, n.d. Print.

Meryon, Charles. *Memoirs of the Lady Hester Stanhope, As Related By Herself in Conversations with Her Physician.* 3 vols. London: Henry Colburn, 1845. Print.

———. *Travels of Lady Hester Stanhope: Forming the Completion of Her Memoirs Narrated by Her Physician.* 3 vols. London: Henry Colburn, 1846. Print.

Miss Weeton: Journal of a Governess, 1807–1811. Ed. Edward Hall. London: Oxford University Press, 1936. Print.

Miss Weeton: Journal of a Governess, 1811–1825. Ed. Edward Hall. London: Oxford University Press, 1939. Print.

Moore, Thomas. *The Life, Letters and Journals of Lord Byron.* London: John Murray, 1866. Print.

Partridge, Frances. *A Pacifist's War* [diaries 1939 to 1945]. New York: Universe Books, 1978. Print.

Pembroke Papers (1780–1794): Letters and Diaries of Henry, Tenth Earl of Pembroke and His Circle. Ed. Lord Herbert. London: Jonathan Cape, 1950. Print.

The Private Diaries of Daisy Princess of Pless, 1783–1914. Ed. D. Chapman-Huston. London: John Murray, 1950. Print.

The Private Diaries of Stendhal (Marie-Henri Beyle). Ed. and Trans. Robert Sage. New York: Doubleday, 1954. Print.

The Private Diary of Leo Tolstóy, 1853–1857. Ed. Aylmer Maude. Trans. Louise and Aylmer Maude. London: William Heinemann, 1927. Print.

Russell, Bertrand, and Patricia Russell. *The Amberley Papers: The Letters and Diaries of Bertrand Russell's Parents.* 2 vols. New York: Norton, 1937. Print.

The Scrapbook of Katherine Mansfield. Ed. J. Middleton Murry. New York: Alfred A. Knopf, 1940. Print.

Self-Portrait: Taken from the Letters & Journals of Charles Ricketts, R.A. Comp. T. Sturge Moore. Ed. Cecil Lewis. London: Peter Davies, 1939. Print.

Silver, Brenda. *Virginia Woolf's Reading Notebooks.* Princeton: Princeton University Press, 1983. Print.

Skinner, John. *Journal of a Somerset Rector.* Ed. Howard Coombs and Rev. Arthur N. Bax. London: John Murray, 1930. Print.

———. *Journal of a Somerset Rector, 1808–1834.* Ed. Howard Coombs and Peter Coombs. Bath, England: Kingsmead, 1971. Reprinted Oxford: Oxford University Press, 1984. Print.

Smyth, Ethel. *Female Pipings in Eden*. London: Peter Davies, 1934. Print.

Song without Words: The Photographs & Diaries of Countess Sophia Tolstoy. Ed. Leah Bendavid-Val. Washington, D.C.: National Geographic, 2007. Print.

Stead, C. K. *The Letters and Journals of Katherine Mansfield: A Selection*. London: Allen Lane, 1977. Print.

Swift, Jonathan. *The Journal to Stella*. Vol. 2 of *The Prose Works of Jonathan Swift, D.D.* Ed. Frederick Ryland. London: George Bell and Sons, 1900. Print.

———. *The Journal to Stella*. Vols. 2 & 3 of *The Works of Jonathan Swift*. Ed. Sir Walter Scott. Edinburgh: Constable, 1814. Print.

———. *Journal to Stella*. Ed. Harold Williams. 2 vols. Oxford: Clarendon, 1948. Print.

Thomas Creevey's Papers. Selected and ed. John Gore. Harmondsworth, England: Penguin, 1948. Print.

Webb, Beatrice. *My Apprenticeship*. New York: Longmans, Green, 1926. Print.

William Allingham's Diary. Ed. & Intro. Geoffrey Grigson. Carbondale: Southern Illinois University Press, 1967 [reissue of 1907 edition ed. Helen Allingham and Dollie Radford]. Print.

Woolf, Leonard. *Downhill All the Way: An Autobiography of the Years, 1919–1939*. London: Hogarth, 1968. Print.

———. *The Journey Not the Arrival Matters: An Autobiography of the Years 1939 to 1969*. New York: Harcourt Brace Jovanovich, 1969. Print.

Woolf, Virginia. *Between the Acts*. New York: Harcourt Brace Jovanovich, 1941. Print.

———. *Carlyle's House and Other Sketches*. Ed. David Bradshaw. Foreword Doris Lessing. London: Hesperus, 2003. Print.

———. *The Common Reader*. New York: Harcourt Brace Jovanovich, 1925. Print.

———. *The Complete Shorter Fiction of Virginia Woolf*. Ed. Susan Dick. New York: Harcourt Brace Jovanovich, 1985. Print.

———. *The Diary of Virginia Woolf*. Ed. Anne Olivier Bell. 5 vols. New York: Harcourt Brace, 1977–84. Print.

———. *The Essays of Virginia Woolf*. Ed. Andrew McNeillie and Stuart N. Clarke. 6 vols. New York: Harcourt Brace, 1986–2011. Print.

———. *The Letters of Virginia Woolf*. Ed. Nigel Nicolson and Joanne Trautmann. 6 vols. New York: Harcourt Brace, 1975–80. Print.

———. *A Moment's Liberty: The Shorter Diary, Virginia Woolf*. Abridged and ed. Anne Olivier Bell. Intro. Quentin Bell. New York: Harcourt Brace, 1990. Print.

———. *Moments of Being*. Ed. and Intro. Jeanne Schulkind. 2nd ed. New York: Harcourt Brace, 1985. Print.

———. *The Pargiters by Virginia Woolf: The Novel-Essay Portion of The Years*. Ed. and Intro. Mitchell A. Leaska. New York: Harcourt Brace, 1977. Print.

———. *A Passionate Apprentice: The Early Journals, 1897–1909*. Ed. and Intro. Mitchell A. Leaska. New York: Harcourt Brace Jovanovich, 1990. Print.

———. *Roger Fry: A Biography*. New York: Harcourt Brace, 1940. Print.
———. *A Room of One's Own*. New York: Harcourt Brace, 1929. Print.
———. *The Second Common Reader*. New York: Harcourt Brace Jovanovich, 1932. Print.
———. *Three Guineas*. New York: Harcourt Brace Jovanovich, 1938. Print.
———. *A Writer's Diary: Being Extracts from the Diary of Virginia Woolf*. Ed. Leonard Woolf. Afterword Louise Bogan and Josephine Schaefer. New York: New American Library, 1968. Print.
———. *The Years*. New York: Harcourt Brace Jovanovich, 1937. Print.
Wordsworth, Dorothy. *Recollections of a Tour Made in Scotland A.D. 1803*. Ed. J. C. Shairp. Edinburgh: James Thin, Mercat, 1974. A 500-copy facsimile of the text of the 1894 edition, published by David Douglas. Print.
———. *Recollections of a Tour Made in Scotland*. Intro., notes, and photographs Caro Kyros Walker. New Haven: Yale University Press, 1997. Print.
Works and Days: From the Journal of Michael Field. Ed. T. and D. C. Sturge Moore. Intro. Sir William Rothenstein. London: John Murray, 1933. Print.
Young, Arthur. *The Farmer's Tour through the East of England*. 4 vols. London: W. Strahan, 1771. Print.
———. *Travels in France during the Years 1787, 1788 & 1789*. Ed. Constantia Maxwell. Cambridge: Cambridge University Press, 1950 (reprint of 1929). Print.

Secondary Sources

The Autobiography of Countess Sophie Tolstoi. Trans. S. S. Koteliansky and Leonard Woolf. New York: B. W. Huebsch, 1922. Print.
Bawer, Bruce. "'My dear, dear Sister': The Life of Dorothy Wordsworth." *New Criterion* 4.5 (January 1986): 26–34. Print.
Bell, Anne Olivier. *Editing Virginia Woolf's Diary*. London: Bloomsbury Workshop, 1990. Print.
Bell, Quentin. *Virginia Woolf: A Biography*. 2 vols. New York: Harcourt, Brace, Jovanovich, 1972. Print.
Berman, Jessica. "Of Oceans and Opposition: *The Waves*, Oswald Mosley, and the New Party." *Virginia Woolf and Fascism: Resisting the Dictators' Seduction*. Ed. Merry M. Pawlowski. New York: Palgrave, 2001. 105–21. Print.
Binnie, Eric. *The Theatrical Designs of Charles Ricketts*. Ann Arbor: University Microfilms International, 1985. Print.
Blodgett, Harriet. *"Capacious Hold-All": An Anthology of Englishwomen's Diary Writings*. Charlottesville: University Press of Virginia, 1991. Print.
———. *Centuries of Female Days: English Women's Private Diaries*. New Brunswick, N.J.: Rutgers University Press, 1988. Print.
———. "A Woman Writer's Diary: Virginia Woolf Revisited." *Prose Studies: History, Theory, Criticism* 12.1 (May 1989): 57–71. Print.

Bowlby, Rachel. "Walking, Women and Writing: Virginia Woolf as *Flâneuse*." *New Feminist Discourses: Critical Essays on Theories and Texts*. Ed. Isobel Armstrong. London: Routledge, 1992. 26–47. Print.

Boyd, M. J. Review of *Journal and Letters of Stephen MacKenna*. Edited with a memoir by E. R. Dodds, *Classical Review* 51.2 (May 1937): 85–86. Print.

Bradshaw, David. "Hyams Place: *The Years*, the Jews and the British Union of Fascists." In *Women Writers of the 1930s: Gender, Politics and History*, ed. and intro. Maroula Joannou, 179–91. Edinburgh: Edinburgh University Press, 1999. Print.

———. "Virginia Woolf, Maupassant's *Sur l'eau*, and *The Years*." *Notes and Queries* 247 (n.s. 49).1 (March 2002): 88–91. Print.

Brook, Peter. *The Melodramatic Imagination: Balzac, Henry James, Melodrama, and the Mode of Excess*. New Haven: Yale University Press, 1976. Print.

Bunkers, Suzanne L., and Cynthia A. Huff, eds. *Inscribing the Daily: Critical Essays on Women's Diaries*. Amherst: University of Massachusetts Press, 1996. Print.

Calloway, Stephen. *Charles Ricketts: Subtle and Fantastic Decorator*. Foreword Kenneth Clark. London: Thames and Hudson, 1979. Print.

Carlston, Erin G. *Thinking Fascism: Sapphic Modernism and Fascist Modernity*. Stanford: Stanford University Press, 1998. Print.

Chambers, Leland H. "Gide's Fictional Journals." *Criticism* 10 (1968): 300–12. Print.

Chaudhuri, Nupur. "Bloomsbury Ancestry: Jane Maria Strachey, Feminism, and Younger Strachey Women." In *Women in the Milieu of Leonard and Virginia Woolf: Peace, Politics, and Education*, ed. Wayne K. Chapman and Janet M. Manson, 58–75. New York: Pace University Press, 1998. Print.

Clark, Lorna. "The Diarist as Novelist: Narrative Strategies in the Journals and Letters of Frances Burney." *English Studies in Canada* 27 (2001): 283–302. Print.

Clarke, Stuart N. "Virginia Woolf in the Age of Aerial Bombardment." In *The Theme of Peace and War in Virginia Woolf's War Writings: Essays on Her Political Philosophy*, ed. Jane M. Wood, intro. Karen Levenback, 101–18. Lewiston, N.Y.: Edwin Mellen Press, 2010. Print.

Clifford, James L. *Hester Lynch Piozzi (Mrs. Thrale)*. Oxford: Clarendon Press, 1941. Print.

Cottam, Rachel. "Secret Scratching: The Diary and Its Writing." Diss. University of Sussex, 1966.

Cuddy-Keane, Melba. "The Politics of Comic Modes in Virginia Woolf's *Between the Acts*." *PMLA* 105.2 (Mar. 1990): 273–85. Print.

Darbishire, Helen. "Introduction." *Journals of Dorothy Wordsworth: The Alfoxden Journal 1798; The Grasmere Journals 1800–1803*. Ed. Mary Moorman. London: Oxford University Press, 1971: xi–xx. Print.

Delaney, J.G.P. *Charles Ricketts: A Biography*. New York: Oxford University Press, 1990. Print.

Derracott, Joseph. *The World of Charles Ricketts*. New York: Methuen, 1980. Print.

DeSalvo, Louise A. "1897: Virginia Woolf at Fifteen." In *Virginia Woolf: A Feminist Slant*, ed. Jane Marcus, 78–108. Lincoln: University of Nebraska Press, 1983. Print.

———. *Virginia Woolf: The Impact of Childhood Sexual Abuse on Her Life and Work*. New York: Ballantine, 1989. Print.

Donaghue, Emma. *We Are Michael Field*. Bath, England: Absolute, 1998. Print.

The Early Life and Education of John Evelyn. With a commentary by H. Maynard Smith. Volume 11 Oxford Historical and Literary Studies. Oxford: Clarendon, 1920. Print.

Esty, Jed. *A Shrinking Island: Modernism & National Culture in England*. Princeton: Princeton University Press, 2004. Print.

Fernald, Anne E. *Virginia Woolf: Feminism and the Reader*. New York: Palgrave Macmillan, 2006. Print.

Fletcher, Ifan Kyrle. "Charles Ricketts and the Theatre." *Theatre Notebook* 22.1 (Autumn 1967): 6–23. Print.

Gättens, Marie-Luise. "*Three Guineas*, Fascism, and the Construction of Gender." In *Virginia Woolf and Fascism: Resisting the Dictators' Seduction*, ed. Merry M. Pawlowski, 21–38. New York: Palgrave, 2001. Print.

Gittings, Robert, and Jo Manton. *Dorothy Wordsworth*. Oxford: Clarendon, 1985. Print.

Glendinning, Victoria. *Leonard Woolf: A Biography*. New York: Free Press, 2006. Print.

Gorky, Maxim. *Reminiscences of Leo Nikolaevitch Tolstoy*. Trans. S. S. Koteliansky and Leonard Woolf. New York: B. W. Huebsch, 1920. Print.

———. *Reminiscences of Tolstoy, Chekhov and Andreev*. Trans. Katherine Mansfield, S. S. Koteliansky, and Leonard Woolf. London: Hogarth, 1934. Print.

Green, Barbara. *Spectacular Confessions: Autobiography, Performative Activism, and the Sites of Suffrage, 1905–1938*. New York: St. Martin's, 1997. Print.

Gristwood, Sarah. *Recording Angels: The Secret World of Women's Diaries*. London: HARRAP, 1988. Print.

Gunn, Elizabeth. *A Passion for the Particular: Dorothy Wordsworth; A Portrait*. London: Victor Gollancz, 1981. Print.

Handley, C. S. *An Annotated Bibliography of Diaries Printed in English*. 3rd ed. Aldeburgh: Hanover, 2002. Print.

Hannoosh, Michele. *Painting and the Journal of Eugène Delacroix*. Princeton: Princeton University Press, 1995. Print.

Harris, Alexandra. *Virginia Woolf*. New York: Thames & Hudson, 2011. Print.

Hemlow, Joyce. "Letters and Journals of Fanny Burney: Establishing the Text." In *Editing Eighteenth-Century Texts. Papers given at the Editorial Conference, University of Toronto, October 1967*, 25–43. Toronto: University of Toronto Press, 1968. Print.

Hewitt, David, ed. *Scott on Himself: A Selection of the Autobiographical Writings of Sir Walter Scott*. Edinburgh: Scottish Academic Press, 1981. Print.

Holroyd, Michael. *Lytton Strachey: The New Biography*. New York: Farrar, Straus and Giroux, 1994. Print.

Hsieh, Lili. "The Other Side of the Picture: The Politics of Affect in Virginia Woolf's *Three Guineas*." *Journal of Narrative Theory* 36.1 (Winter 2006): 20–52. Print.

Humm, Maggie, ed. *The Edinburgh Companion to Virginia Woolf and the Arts*. Edinburgh: Edinburgh University Press, 2010. Print.

Hussey, Mark, ed. and intro. *Virginia Woolf and War: Fiction, Reality, and Myth*. Syracuse: Syracuse University Press, 1991. Print.

Jackson, Anna. *Diary Poetics: Form and Style in Writers' Diaries, 1915-1962*. New York: Routledge, 2010. Print.

Joannou, Maroula, ed. and intro. *Women Writers of the 1930s: Gender, Politics and History*. Edinburgh: Edinburgh University Press. 1999. Print.

Joyce, James. *Ulysses*. Foreword Morris L. Ernst. New York: Vintage, 1961. Print.

Kazin, Alfred. "The Journal Keeper [André Gide]." In *The Inmost Leaf: A Selection of Essays*, 149–54. Westport, CT: Greenwood, 1974. Print.

Keynes, Geoffrey. *John Evelyn: A Study in Bibliophily with a Bibliography of His Writings*. Oxford: Clarendon, 1968. Print.

Koch, W. John. *Daisy Princess of Pless, 1873–1943: A Discovery*. Edmonton, Canada: W. John Koch Publishing, 2002. Print.

Lane, Anthony. "The Man in the Mirror: The Enduring Confessions and Unmatched Hedonism of André Gide." *New Yorker*, 9 August 1999, 72–78. Print.

Lee, Hermione. *Virginia Woolf*. New York: Knopf, 1997. Print.

Lejeune, Philippe. *On Diary*. Ed. Jeremy D. Popkin and Julie Rak. Trans. Katherine Durnin. Honolulu: University of Hawai'i Press, 2009. Print.

Letters of Leonard Woolf. Ed. Frederic Spotts. London: Bloomsbury, 1992. Print.

Letters of Roger Fry. 2 vols. Ed. and intro. Denys Sutton. New York: Random House, 1972. Print.

Levenback, Karen L. *Virginia Woolf and the Great War*. Syracuse: Syracuse University Press, 1999. Print.

Levin, Susan M. *Dorothy Wordsworth & Romanticism*. New Brunswick, NJ: Rutgers State University Press, 1987. Print.

Lewis, Wyndham. *Hitler*. London: Chatto & Windus, 1931. Print.

Lounsberry, Barbara. *Becoming Virginia Woolf: Her Early Diaries and the Diaries She Read*. Gainesville: University Press of Florida, 2014. Print.

———. *Virginia Woolf's Modernist Path: Her Middle Diaries and the Diaries She Read*. Gainesville: University Press of Florida, 2016. Print.

Low, Lisa. "'Thou Canst Not Touch the Freedom of My Mind': Fascism and Disruptive Female Consciousness in *Mrs. Dalloway*." In *Virginia Woolf and Fascism: Resisting the Dictators' Seduction*, ed. Merry M. Pawlowski, 92–104. New York: Palgrave, 2001. Print.

Mallon, Thomas. *A Book of One's Own*. New York: Ticknor & Fields, 1984. Print.

Marburg, Clara. *Mr. Pepys and Mr. Evelyn*. Philadelphia: University of Pennsylvania Press, 1935. Print.

Marginal Voices, Marginal Forms: Diaries in European Literature and History. Ed. Rachael Langford and Russell West. Amsterdam: Rodopi, 1999. Print.

Martinson, Deborah. *In the Presence of Audience: The Self in Diaries and Fiction.* Columbus: Ohio State University Press, 2003. Print.

Matthiessen, F. O. *The James Family: Including Selections from the Writings of Henry James, Senior, William, Henry, & Alice James.* New York: Knopf, 1947. Print.

Oldfield, Sybil. *Alternatives to Militarism, 1900–1989: Women Against the Iron Fist.* Lewiston, N.Y.: Edwin Mellon Press, 2000. Print.

Patten, John A. *Sir Walter Scott: A Character Study.* London: James Clarke, 1932. Print.

Pawlowski, Merry M., ed. *Virginia Woolf and Fascism: Resisting the Dictators' Seduction.* New York: Palgrave, 2001. Print.

———. "Virginia Woolf and Scrapbooking." In *The Edinburgh Companion To Virginia Woolf and the Arts*, ed. Maggie Humm, 298–313. Edinburgh: Edinburgh University Press, 2010. Print.

Pierson, Ruth Roach. "'Did Your Mother Wear Army Boots?': Feminist Theory and Women's Relation to War, Peace and Revolution." In *Images of Women in Peace and War: Cross-Cultural and Historical Perspectives*, ed. Sharon Macdonald, Pat Holden, and Shirley Ardener, 205–27. Madison: University of Wisconsin Press, 1987. Print.

Podnieks, Elizabeth. *Daily Modernism: The Literary Diaries of Virginia Woolf, Antonia White, Elizabeth Smart, and Anaïs Nin.* Montreal: McGill-Queens University Press, 2000. Print.

Ponsonby, Arthur. *Samuel Pepys.* New York: Macmillan, 1928. Print.

Powell, Anthony. Review of *Kilvert's Cornish Diary*. *Times Literary Supplement*, 30 June 1989, 716. Print.

Pridmore-Brown, Michele. "1939–40: Of Virginia Woolf, Gramophones, and Fascism." *PMLA* 113.3 (May 1998): 408–21. Print.

Rau, Petra. "The Fascist Body Beautiful and the Imperial Crisis in 1930s British Writing." *Journal of European Studies* 39.1 (2009): 5–35. Print.

Raymond, Jean Paul, and Charles Ricketts. *Oscar Wilde: Recollections.* Bloomsbury: Nonesuch, 1932. Print.

Ricketts, Charles. *Michael Field.* Ed. Paul Delaney. Edinburgh: Tragara, 1976. Print.

Rosenfeld, Natania. "Monstrous Conjugations: Images of Dictatorship in the Anti-Fascist Writings of Virginia and Leonard Woolf." In *Virginia Woolf and Fascism: Resisting the Dictators' Seduction*, ed. Merry M. Pawlowski, 122–36. New York: Palgrave, 2001. Print.

Rosenwald, Lawrence. *Emerson and the Art of the Diary.* New York: Oxford University Press, 1988. Print.

Saddlemyer, Ann, ed. *The Collected Letters of John Millington Synge*, Vol. 2, 1907–1909. Oxford: Clarendon, 1984. Print.

Selected Letters of Vanessa Bell. Ed. Regina Marler. New York: Pantheon, 1993. Print.

Sellers, Susan. "Virginia Woolf's Diaries and Letters." In *The Cambridge Companion* to *Virginia Woolf*, ed. Sue Roe and Susan Sellers, 109–26. Cambridge: Cambridge University Press, 2000. Print.

Shannon, Drew Patrick. "The Deep Old Desk: The Diary of Virginia Woolf." Diss. University of Cincinnati, 2007. Online source.

Simons, Judy. *Diaries and Journals of Literary Women from Fanny Burney to Virginia Woolf.* Iowa City: University of Iowa Press, 1990. Print.

Skidelsky, Robert. *Politicians and the Slump: The Labour Government of 1929–1931.* London: Macmillan, 1967. Print.

Sleeman, John H. Review of *Plotinus, On the One and Good, being the treatises of the Sixth Ennead.* Trans. Stephen MacKenna and B. S. Page. *The Journal of Hellenic Studies* 51 (1931): 311–16. Print.

Sonnenberg, Rhonda. *Still We Danced Forward: World War II and the Writer's Life.* London: Brassey's, 1998. Print.

Spater, George. "The Monks House Library." *Virginia Woolf Quarterly* 1.3 (Spring 1973): 60–65. Print.

Squier, Susan M. *Virginia Woolf and London: The Sexual Politics of the City.* Chapel Hill: University of North Carolina Press, 1985. Print.

———, ed. *Women Writers and the City: Essays in Feminist Literary Criticism.* Knoxville: University of Tennessee Press, 1984. Print.

Staveley, Alice. "Marketing Virginia Woolf: Women, War, and Public Relations in *Three Guineas*." *Book History* 12 (2009): 295–339. Print.

Steele, Elizabeth. *Virginia Woolf's Rediscovered Essays: Sources and Allusions.* New York: Garland, 1987. Print.

"Stephen MacKenna: Life, Works, Criticism, Notes." 29 May 2011, http://www.pgileir data/org/html/pgil_datasets/authors/Mac/ . . . S/life.htm. Internet.

Sturgeon, Mary. *Michael Field.* New York: Arno, 1975 (reprint 1922). Print.

Suh, Judy. "Christopher Isherwood and Virginia Woolf: Diaries and Fleeting Impressions of Fascism." *Modern Language Studies* 38.1 (2008): 44–61. Print

Tait, J. G. *The Missing Tenth of Sir Walter Scott's Journal.* Edinburgh: Oliver and Boyd, 1936. Print.

Tanner, J. R. *Mr Pepys: An Introduction to the Diary together with a Sketch of his Later Life.* New York: Harcourt Brace, 1925. Print.

Thain, Marion. *"Michael Field": Poetry, Aestheticism and the Fin de Siècle.* Cambridge: Cambridge University Press, 2007. Print.

Tidwell, Joanne Campbell. *Politics and Aesthetics in The Diary of Virginia Woolf.* New York: Routledge, 2008. Print.

Tolstoy, Leo. "Introduction to The Works of Guy de Maupassant." In *What Is Art? And Essays on Art*, trans. Aylmer Maude, 20–45. London: Oxford University Press, 1930. Print.

Treby, Ivor C. *The Michael Field Catalogue: A Book of Lists.* Bury St. Edmunds, England: De Blackland, 1998. Print.

———. *Music and Silence: The Gamut of Michael Field*. Bury St. Edmunds. England: De Blackland, 2000. Print.

Warner, Alan. *William Allingham*. Lewisburg, PA: Bucknell University Press, 1975. Print.

Watry, Maureen. *The Vale Press: Charles Ricketts, a Publisher in Earnest*. New Castle, Delaware: Oak Knoll, 2004. Print.

Williams, Harold. "Introduction." In *Jonathan Swift: Journal to Stella*, vol. I, ix–lix. Oxford: Clarendon, 1948. Print.

Willy, Margaret. *English Diarists: Evelyn & Pepys*. London: Longmans, Green, 1963. Print.

———. *Three Women Diarists* [Celia Fiennes, Dorothy Wordsworth, Katherine Mansfield]. London: Longmans, Green, 1964. Print.

Wilson, Jean Moorcoft. *Virginia Woolf: Life & London, A Biography of Place*. London: Cecil Woolf, 1987. Print.

Wood, Jane M., ed. *The Theme of Peace and War in Virginia Woolf's War Writings: Essays on Her Political Philosophy*. Intro. Karen Levenbeck. Lewiston, N.Y.: Edwin Mellen, 2010. Print.

Woof, Pamela. "Dorothy Wordsworth's Journals and the Engendering of Poetry." *Wordsworth in Context*. Ed. Pauline Fletcher and John Murphy, 122–55. Lewisburg: Bucknell University Press, 1992. Print.

Index

Ackerley, J. R., 149, 198
Adeline, Duchess of Bedford, 355n12
A.E. (George William Russell), 220
Aeschylus, 83
Alexandra, Queen. *See* Queen Alexandra
Allingham, William, 178, 331, 354n7, 363n1
Amberley, Lady. *See* Russell, Kate Stanley
Amberley, Lord. *See* Russell, John
Amiel, Henri-Frédéric, 217, 267, 352n36, 356n22
Anrep, Helen, 71, 358n4
Anrep, Igor, 279
Antaeus, 174, 175
Anthony, Susan B., 189
Anti-Fascist Exhibition, 109, 145
Archduke Franz Ferdinand. *See* Ferdinand, Archduke Franz
Aristotle, 337n5
Arnold, Matthew, 313, 315
Atlas, 169, 174, 175
Auden, W. H., 226
Austen, Jane, 260, 355n12

Bacon, Francis, 291
Badenhorst, Alie, 333, 363n1
Bailey, Jenny, 163
Bailey, John, 363n1; diaries of, 138, 148, 160–67, 255, 328, 334, 354nn14–15; edits Lady Frederick Cavendish's diaries, 255; and *Three Guineas*, 164, 165, 167, 328; and war, 164–65; and *The Years*, 164, 165, 167, 328
Bailey, Sarah Kathleen Lyttelton, 161, 162, 164, 165, 166

Baldwin, Stanley, 148, 176
Balfour, Lord Arthur, 66, 162
Barbellion, W.N.P (Bruce Frederick Cummings), 67; *Journal of a Disappointed Man*, 42, 118, 332
Barnes, William, 263
Barthou, Jean Louis, French foreign minister, 108
Barton, Aunt, 202, 205, 206. *See also* Weeton, Ellen
Bashkirtseff, Marie, 352n36
Bawer, Bruce, 341n27
Bayliss, Lilian, 347n17
Bazaine, Marshal Francois, 124
Beaverbrook, Lord (Max Aitken), 27, 312
Becker, Lydia, 185–86
Beefsteak Club, 176
Beerbohm, Max, 347n20
Beethoven, Ludwig van, 31, 211
Bell, Angelica, 249, 255, 312
Bell, Anne Olivier: vii, 68, 272, 318; on Lady Arthur Russell, 355n12; on Ethel Smyth, 7; on Woolf's diaries, 35, 229, 279, 305, 319; on *The Years*, 172
Bell, Clive, 176; and Lytton Strachey, 71; and war, 145, 221; Woolf's talks with, 30, 31; writings of, 166
Bell, Julian: death of, 229, 230, 231, 250, 252, 256, 304; talks of war, 147, 156, 164, 221, 226, 227–28, 247; Woolf's dream of, 256; writings of, 306
Bell, Quentin, vii–viii, 1, 7, 221, 224

Bell, Vanessa, 7, 353n5; art of, 36; children and, 226, 312; death of Julian, 229, 230, 254, 277, 304; early diary of, 18; and Roger Fry, 105, 106, 107, 139, 282, 304; and Spanish Civil War, 221, 226, 228, 304; and suicide, 308; Virginia's affection for, 224, 263, 322; Virginia's competition with, 86; Virginia's letters to and from, 166, 255; Virginia's visits to and with, 36, 71, 224, 254

Bendavid-Val, Leah, 357n15, 358n20

Bennett, Arnold, 26–27, 33, 34, 36; journals of, 117

Bennett, Gordon, 212

Benson, Stella, 85, 346n14

Berenson, Bernhard, 347n20

Beresford, John: edits James Woodforde's journal, 48, 343–44nn21–22, 344n24; and other diaries, 49; and the Woodfordes' popularity, 51–52

Berman, Jessica, 5, 337–38n3

Bernhardt, Sarah, 297, 299, 347n20

Berry, Mary Seaton, 332, 363n1

Best, Richard, 211

Betjeman, John, 269

Beyle, Marie-Henri. *See* Stendhal

Bibesco, Princess Elizabeth, 109

Binnie, Eric, 301

Birrell, Augustine, 136

Bishop of Chelmsford (Henry Wilson), 151

Bishop of Norwich, 50

Bishop of St. Davids, Wales (Basil Jones), 257

Bishop of St. Davids, Wales (Connop Thirwall), 260

Bishop of Wells (George Henry Law), 44, 45

Bishop of Wells (Edward Willes), 49, 51

Bismarck, Otto von, 109

Blackie, John, 184

Blackshirts, 101. *See also* Fascism; Nazis

Blodgett, Harriet, 337n4, 355n16, 355–56n19

Blunt, Wilfrid Scawen, 363n1; diaries of, 162, 172, 255, 332, 354n13; Charles Ricketts and, 360n8

Bodkin, Thomas, 218

Boer War, 65, 156, 345n33

Bonaparte, Napoleon. *See* Napoleon Bonaparte

Book-of-the-Month Club, United States, 81

Boswell, James, 10, 112, 267, 280, 313; Samuel Johnson and, 331, 338n7; *Journal of a Tour to Corsica*, 333; *Journal of a Tour to the Hebrides*, 331, 338n7

Bottomley, Gordon, 361n17

Bowen, Elizabeth, 310, 314, 319, 320

Bowlby, Rachel, 362–63n11

Boxall, Nelly: dismissal of, 87, 346n12, 347n15; speaks in Woolf's diary, 71; Woolf's struggles with, 11, 28, 82

Bradley, Katherine. *See* Field, Michael

Bradshaw, David, 101, 126

Bray, Mary (MacKenna), 211, 212, 218, 219. *See also* MacKenna, Stephen

Bréal, Edouard, 293

Bright, John, 184

British Book Society, 81

British Expeditionary Force, 254

British Labour Party, 5, 253, 362n2

British Legion, 254

British Museum, 298, 299

British Union of Fascists, 5, 101. *See also* New Party

Brittain, Vera, 7

Brontë, Charlotte, 203, 206, 207

Brook, Peter, 324

Brooke, Stopford, 292, 332

Brookes, Professor Francis, 98–99, 348n26

Brown, Ettie Meredith, 261–62

Browne, Sir Thomas, 291

Browning, Elizabeth Barrett, 57, 347–48n26; "Aurora Leigh," 93, 346n6; Michael Field and, 89, 93; and *Flush*, 74

Browning, Pen, 98, 347n20

Browning, Robert: and Michael Field, 93–94, 96, 97, 98, 99, 100, 347n20, 347–48n26; *Jocoseria*, 93

Buchan, John, 164, 254

Buchenwald, 287

Bulgákov, V. F., 240, 243, 245, 246. *See also* Tolstoy, Leo

Bülow, Chancellor Bernard von, 61, 65

Bülow, Countess Maria von, 60–61
Burke, Edmund, 310
Burne-Jones, Edward, 297, 299
Burney, Dr. Charles, 71
Burney, Frances ("Fanny"), 14; diaries of, 10, 71, 81, 113, 129, 130, 234, 254, 275, 328, 331, 338n7, 363n1; horse trope and, 7, 33, 222, 275, 280, 306; and Walter Scott, 280; scribbling and, 200; and Hester Thrale, 316
Burns, Robert, 19–20, 263, 267, 268
Burr, Anna Robeson, 126, 128, 137. *See also* James, Alice
Bury, Lady Charlotte, 118, 331
Bussy, Dorothy, 115, 117
Bussy, Janie, 103
Byron, Lord (George Gordon), 338n6; *Childe Harold*, 9–10; *Don Juan*, 338n6; funeral of, 207; war and, 227

Caesar, Julius, 109
Caliban, 96
Caligula, Emperor, 285
Calloway, Stephen, 301
Cambridge Anti-War Council, 109
Cambridge, Duchess of, 188
Cambridge University: Clark lectures, 76; and F. L. Lucas, 282–83, 284, 290; and Charles Ricketts, 361n15; Trinity College, 76, 180; Woolf's dislike of, 283, 318, 346n5, 356n6
Cameron, Julia Margaret, 178
Campbell, Mrs. Patrick, 5
Canterbury Cathedral, 268
Carlston, Erin G., 252
Carlyle, Jane, 179, 182
Carlyle, Thomas, 179, 181, 193, 196, 357n9
Carnera, Primo, 30
Carolyn, Princess of Wales (also Queen Caroline), 342n11
Carrington, Dora, 71, 72, 77–78, 346n5
Case, Janet, 230
Cavendish, Lady Frederick, 255, 335, 363n1
Cecil, Lord David, 30, 31
Cézanne, Paul, 256, 294
Chalmers, Anne, 333
Chamberlain, Neville: and Munich accord, 253, 287–88, 290; praises Mussolini, 5; protection of Poland, 272; resignation of, 302
Chambrun, Jacques, 274
Chapman-Huston, Major Desmond, 345n31, 345n34. *See also* Daisy, Princess of Pless
Chaucer, Geoffrey, 78, 161, 289, 319
Chavannes, Pierre Puvis de, 294, 300
Chavasses, Dr. H. S. and Mrs., 313, 321
Chekhov, Anton, 332
Chertkóv, V. G.: clashes with Countess Tolstoy, 236, 237, 238–46; early life of, 236; exile, 236; Aylmer Maude on, 246; Alexandra Popoff on, 358n19, 358n22; as Tolstoy's editor and publisher, 235, 236, 357n13, 358n19
Chesterfield, Lord (Philip Stanhope, 4th Earl), 285
Chesterton, C. K., 306, 314
Child, Miss, 270. *See also* Kilvert, Reverend Frances
Chilver, Richard, 227–28
Chopin, Frédéric, 355n8
Chorley, Miss, 205, 206. *See also* Weeton, Ellen
Churchill, Lady Randolph, 56
Churchill, Winston, 56, 162, 176; admires Mussolini, 5; opposition to Munich accord, 253, 362n2; as Prime Minister, 302, 310; Princess Daisy on, 65
Clark, Sir Andrew, 134. *See also* James, Alice
Clark, Sir Kenneth, 301
Clarke, Bessie, 128. *See also* James, Alice
Clarke, Stuart N., 138
Clarkson, Catherine, 338n12. *See also* Wordsworth, Dorothy
Cleopatra, 223, 272
Cleopatra's Needle, 222, 356n1
Clifford, Lady Anne: diary of, 37, 48, 71, 333, 342n9. *See also* Sackville-West, Vita
Clutton-Brock, Sheelah, 360n6
Cobbe, Frances Power, 90
Cobden-Sanderson, Thomas: friendship with Lord and Lady Amberley, 180; journals of, 12, 180, 333, 338n13; mystical beliefs of, 180; and Charles Ricketts, 360n8; Dorothy Wordsworth's journal and, 12

Cockerell, Sydney, 294, 361n15
Cole, Reverend William, 263, 334, 359n5
Colefax, Lady Sybil: model for Woolf's resurrection, 173–74, 175, 227, 251, 312, 317, 327, 354n4
Coleridge, Hartley, 18
Coleridge, Mary, 332
Coleridge, Samuel Taylor, 18, 21; illness of, 20; and Stephen MacKenna, 214; poems of, 19, 340n22; and Dorothy and William Wordsworth, 14–15, 18, 19, 20, 22, 268, 341n27
Coleridge, Sara, 306, 307, 308
Colt, Elizabeth, 193
Colum, Padraic, 211
Communist Party, 227
Congreve, William, 223, 228, 230
Cook, Thomas, 168
Cooper, Diana, 75
Cooper, Edith. See Field, Michael
Cooper, Emma Bradley, 88, 89. See also Field, Michael
Cooper, James, 88. See also Field, Michael
Cornwall, Miss, 262. See also Kilvert, Reverend Francis
Cornford, John, 226
Cornwallis-West, Constance ("Shelagh"), 60. See also Daisy, Princess of Pless
Cornwallis-West, George, 56. See also Daisy, Princess of Pless
Cornwallis-West, Mary ("Patsy"), 60, 62, 63, 64, 66. See also Daisy, Princess of Pless
Cornwallis-West, William ("Poppets"), 60, 62, 64. See also Daisy, Princess of Pless
Cory, William, 331
Cowper, William, 167
Creevey, Thomas, 334
Crespigny, Sir Claude de, 156
Crimean War, 158
Cuddy-Keane, Melba, 324, 325
Cummings, Bruce Frederick. See Barbellion, W.N.P.
Cunningham, Valentine, 3
Custance, Mrs., 51, 52, 55. See also Woodforde, Reverend James

Custance, Squire, 51, 52. See also Woodforde, Reverend James
Czar Nicholas II, 65

Dachau, 69
Daisy, Princess of Pless (Mary-Theresa Olivia Cornwallis-West), 345n31, 345n35; as battler, 59, 62–63, 67; and Winston Churchill, 65; descent from Henry III, 344n26; diaries of, 25, 37, 55–67, 334, 344n27; influence on *Flush*, 57, 67, 74, 346n4; and Kaiser Wilhelm, 345n30; relationship with husband, 57, 58, 59, 60, 61, 62, 64, 66–67, 344–45n30; and Vita Sackville-West, 55; and *Three Guineas*, 66; and *The Years*, 57–58, 59, 62, 64, 67, 344n28
D'Annunzio, Gabrielle, 347n20
Dante (Durante degli Alighieri), 135; André Gide reads, 350n23; the *Inferno*, 29; as support and inspiration for Woolf, 9, 29, 110, 150, 175
Darracott, Joseph, 301
Davies, Emily, 355n11
Davies, Margaret Llewelyn, 8, 278
Davies, Maurice Llewelyn, 278
Debenham, E. R., 216–17, 218–20, 356n21, 356n24
Degas, Edgar, 299
Delacroix, Eugène, 361n15, 363n1; diaries of, 117, 280, 326, 335
Deladier, Édouard, 287–88
De La Mare, Walter, 27, 315, 319–20, 339n14
Delaney, J.G.P., 301; on Ricketts' art, 294, 297; on Ricketts' and Shannon's art collection, 297; on Ricketts' cruel father, 296, 299; and Ricketts' death, 299; on Ricketts and Michael Field, 295; on Ricketts and Charles Holmes, 298; on Ricketts' journals, 298; on Ricketts' mother, 296; on Ricketts' theatre designs, 361n16; on Ricketts and war, 299; and the Vale Press, 360n10
De Quincey, Thomas, 15, 214, 339n16
Diary: collaborative diaries, 87–100, 88, 297; crossroads diaries, 210, 213, 220; daily diaries, 51, 151, 233, 269, 358n17; death and,

262–63; diary candor, 41, 85, 113, 116, 196, 210, 347n22; diary closure, 11, 38, 78–79, 110, 231, 290, 323, 324, 326; diary continuity, 3, 29, 78, 229, 250, 325, 347n15; diary ease, 78, 255; diary openings, 57, 78, 102, 129, 170, 171, 177, 222, 226, 250, 275, 284, 315–16, 318; diary specimen days, 8, 154, 165, 310, 311; discontinuity of, 324–25; fictive diaries, 118; fragility of, 41, 115, 191, 206, 262–63, 269–70, 273, 298, 301, 314, 318, 329; illustrated diaries, 41; journal-letters, 203, 204, 205, 207; loose-leaf diaries, 2, 6, 140, 223, 230, 250, 273, 303, 316, 318, 327; margin notes in, 33, 113, 125, 297, 347n15, 352n3; natural history diaries, 2; periodic diaries, 2, 29, 63, 112, 129, 165, 203, 212, 297; rereading of, 41, 113, 169, 196, 213, 233, 250, 269, 297, 347n15; travel diaries, 2, 34, 78, 102, 118–26, 149, 207, 208, 273, 274, 297, 298, 343n18, 352n2, 357n9; war diaries, 305; women and diaries, 11–23, 47, 49, 55–67, 87–100, 126–37, 168, 172, 177–89, 192, 193, 194, 195–98, 198–209, 231–48, 338n12, 343n19, 355n8, 355nn13–15
Dickens, Charles, 319
Dickinson, Emily, 183
Dickinson, Goldsworthy Lowes, 72, 88, 291
Dickinson, Violet, 161, 165–66
Dodds, E. R., 217–18, 220; on Captain MacKenna's diaries, 210; helps with Stephen MacKenna's Plotinus, 216, 220; on Stephen MacKenna's diaries, 210, 213, 215, 217, 219, 220; on Stephen MacKenna's early life, 210, 212; on Stephen MacKenna's talk, 211
Dodgson, Campbell, 165
Donne, John, 37, 71, 75. See also Clifford, Lady Anne
Donoghue, Emma, 88, 347n22, 348n27
Doolittle, Hilda. See H.D.
Dostoevsky, Fyodor, 347n15, 357n9
Douglas, W.H.D., 30, 31
Doumer, Paul, 68
Dryburgh Abbey, 254
Duckworth, George, 186, 312, 355n12
Duckworth, Stella, 18–19

Duke of York, 176
Duse, Eleonora, 297, 347n20

Eastman, Max, 139
Edel, Leon, 128, 133
Eden, Robert Anthony, 253, 362n2
Edward, Prince of Wales, 153, 190. See also King Edward VII
Eliot, George, 181, 352n36
Eliot, Maggie, 185
Eliot, T. S.: "East Coker," 315; egotism of, 85, 226, 312; essays of, 87; F. L. Lucas and, 283, 292; poems of, 274, 283, 339n14; shade cast by, 307, 315, 349n8; and war, 108, 145; Woolf diary portraits of, 28, 85, 307; Woolf's letters to, 100, 317
Eliot, Vivien, 28
Elliptical Club, 193
Emerson, Ralph Waldo, 128, 332, 351n31
Emmet, Ellie, 127. See also James, Alice
Emmet, Minnie, 128. See also James, Alice
English Kennel Club, 153
Epstein, Jacob, 139
Essex, Lord, 158
Esty, Jed, 270, 337n6, 353n5
Evelyn, John, 332, 363n1
Everest, Louie, 110, 256

Fascism, 146, 147, 324–29; in Britain, 5, 101; in Germany, 5, 68–69, 108, 109, 138, 145, 147, 168; in Italy, 111; in Russia, 68; in Spain, 221, 227; women and, 69, 145, 148. See also Nazis; Woolf, Leonard: *Quack, Quack!*
Fawcett Library, 101–02
Fearnley-Whittingstall, Reverend Herbert Oakes, 45–46
Ferdinand, Archduke Franz, 56
Fernald, Anne E., 338n6, 362n10
Field, Michael (Katherine Bradley and Edith Cooper), 347n19, 347n21, 347nn23–25, 363n1; *Anna Ruina*, 95; *Attila*, 92; *Bellerophôn*, 90, 93, 94; and *Between the Acts*, 69, 97; *Borgia*, 295; and Robert Browning, 93–94; joint diary of, 69, 85, 87–100, 131, 334, 347n20; in *Last Romantics*, 301; *Long*

Index 383

Field, Michael—*continued*
  Ago, 90, 94, 98; and George Meredith, 90–93; *New Minnesinger*, 89, 93; and George Moore, 94–95; *A Question of Memory*, 92, 96, 97; and Charles Ricketts, 97, 99, 294–95, 301, 347n20, 361n17; and John Ruskin, 89–90; *Stephania*, 92; and *Three Guineas*, 69, 99, 281; *The Tragic Mary*, 91, 92, 95, 294–95; and Oscar Wilde, 94, 95–96; *William Rufus*, 94; and *The Years*, 88, 99
Fisher, Herbert, 162, 354n14
Fitzgerald, Edward, 356n20
FitzPatrick, Lady Olivia, 61–62. *See also* Daisy, Princess of Pless
Flaubert, Gustave, 358n28
Flush (dog), 74
Forster, E. M., 145–46, 283
France, Anatole, 135
Franco, General Francisco, 272
Franco-Prussian War, 120, 124, 193
Franklin, Benjamin, 233
Freud, Sigmund, 276, 278
Fry, Margery: and Roger Fry's biography, 107, 139, 282, 307; old age mobility of, 362n4; Woolf's travel with, 71
Fry, Roger: and John Bailey, 166; as a battler, 255; death of, 102, 103, 104–05, 106, 108, 109, 110, 125, 126, 139, 140, 141, 142, 149, 349n9; and Michael Field, 88, 347n20; and André Gide, 110, 117, 249n11; and the Rev. Francis Kilvert, 266; and King's College, 283; letters of, 139, 352n3; F. L. Lucas on, 283, 291; model for Old Virginia, 26, 28, 72, 74, 102, 103, 104–05, 106, 107, 108, 109, 110, 139, 140, 142, 144, 149, 169–70, 174, 250, 255, 256, 275–76, 278, 279, 282, 304, 306, 317, 348n4, 349n9, 359–60n4; and Charles Ricketts, 293–94, 361n19; *Roger Fry: A Biography*, 3, 107, 115, 116, 117, 139–40, 141, 142, 251, 253, 254, 255, 256, 272–73, 275, 276, 282, 293, 294, 301, 303–04, 306, 307, 308, 310, 313, 314, 317, 352n3, 359n2, 359n4, 362n1; and Lytton Strachey, 71; Woolf's letters to, 100, 349n11, 352n1; writings of, 169–70
Furse, Katharine, 73–74

Gandhi, 30
Gardner, Major and Diana, 313, 319
Garibaldi, Giuseppe, 194, 210, 217, 353n12
Garnett, Constance, 232
Garnett, David ("Bunny"), 80, 232, 312
Garrett, Dr. Elizabeth, 182, 186, 226
Gatling gun, 193, 196
General Strike (1926), 277
George IV, King. *See* King George IV
George V, King. *See* King George V
Gérente, Alfred, 88
Gibbon, Edward: John Bailey writes on, 165; F. L. Lucas on, 285; Woolf's essay on, 223, 224, 227, 230
Gibbs, Frederick, 190
Gide, André, 350n20, 363n1; and Arnold Bennett, 117; and Roger Fry, 117; illness and, 111, 112, 131; journals of, 41, 102, 110–18, 129, 130, 131, 255, 280–81, 313, 320, 326, 334, 335, 350nn16–19, 350n21, 350n23, 350n24, 351nn25–27; and F. L. Lucas, 280–81, 282; movement and, 111; *Nouvelle Revue Française* and, 111, 349n13; and "Reading at Random," 117–18; and John Salter's diary, 153; and Lytton Strachey, 117; "Strait is the Gate," 118, 320; suicide and, 112, 113, 118, 320, 350n14, 350n18; and *Three Guineas*, 111, 118; and Leo Tolstoy, 233; voracious reading of, 110, 116, 117–18, 349n12, 350n23; and war, 117, 118; and *The Years*, 118
Gilbert, W. S., 297, 360n12
Giles, Dr., 262
Girton College, 183
Glendenning, Victoria, 171
Goebbels, Joseph, 324
Göering, General Hermann, 287
Goethe, Johann Wolfgang von, 12
Goldenweiser, A. B., 232, 239, 240, 246, 357n10. *See also* Tolstoy, Leo
Goldsmith, Dr. Oliver, 79, 82, 83, 85, 109
Goncourt brothers: collaborative diaries of, 83, 88, 99, 117, 297, 332, 350n16, 360n11; and André Gide, 250n16, 351n25; and Ivan Turgenev, 83
Gonne, Maud, 212

Gordon-Woodhouse, Violet, 30
Gorky, Maxim, 234, 357n14
Gosse, Sir Edmund, 162, 299, 347n20
Gottfried, Prince, 65
Goya, Francisco, 249
Grant, Duncan, 348n4; and Roger Fry, 107, 359n4; and suicide, 359n4; and war, 346n2; Woolf visits with, 71
Graves, Sally, 221, 227–28
Gray, Thomas, 96, 305
Grein, J. T, 95
Grey, Jane, 190–91
Grey, Sir Edward, 354n14
Grix's School, 151
Grote, George, 182
Grote, Harriet, 182, 355n8
Grüber, Ruth, 148
Guild of St George, 89
Gunn, Elizabeth, 15, 340–41n26
Gurney, Edmund, 132
Gwynne, Rupert, 70

Haig, Field Marshall Earl, 254
Hakluyt, Richard, 362n10
Hall, Edward, 355n17; and Charlotte Brontë, 203, 206; editing of *Journal of a Governess*, 199, 203, 204, 205, 207, 208, 209; and Weeton's egotism, 355n18; and Weeton's later life, 209
Hans Heinrich XV, Prince of Pless, 56, 65, 66; relationship with Daisy, 57, 58, 59, 60, 62, 66–67; and women, 60–61. *See also* Daisy, Princess of Pless
Harben, H. D., 334
Harcourt Brace, 102, 250, 362n1
Hardy, Florence, 53
Hardy, Thomas, 53, 71, 112
Harris, Alexandra, 1, 326
Harris, Lilian, 8
Harrison, George Bagshawe, 335
Harrow Debating Society, 190
Haskins, Mabel, 308
Hawarden, Miss, 209. *See also* Weeton, Ellen
Haydon, Benjamin Robert: journals of, 29, 333, 341n4; Keats and, 29

H.D. (Hilda Doolittle), 360n13
Heenan, John C., 155
Hemingway, Ernest, 265
Herbert, Philip, Earl of Pembroke, 281
Hercules, 171, 175
Hiemer, Ernst, 286
Higgenson, Thomas Wentworth, 183
Hinden, Dr. Rita, 313
Hitler, Adolf, 108, 109, 146, 221, 290, 306; ambitions of, 101; and Austria, 249, 252–53, 276, 285, 289; and Czechoslovakia, 249, 253, 272, 276, 287–88, 362n2; dictating European narrative, 249, 253, 286, 302, 304, 305; and Emperor Caligula, 285; and England, 273, 302, 305, 307–11; and France, 302, 305; Sigmund Freud on, 276; Roger Fry versus, 250, 255–56; and Joseph Goebbels, 324; Wyndam Lewis on, 24; F. L. Lucas on, 285, 286, 287–88; and Munich accord, 287–88; Nazi salute, 69, 147, 168; 1933 assumption of power, 68–69; and Poland, 272, 273; and Rhineland, 168, 174; Ernst Toller on, 146; Bruno Walter on, 86; and women, 68–69, 101; Woolf counter to, 69, 249, 250, 273, 324–29
Hoare, Lord, 45
Hogarth Press, 257, 281; aid to Woolf's art, 11; distracts from diary-keeping, 12, 170, 274; distracts from public art, 12, 28, 274, 317, 341n3; and *Goodbye to Berlin*, 325–26; lean years, 149, 169, 274, 304; and F. L. Lucas, 288; possible changes in, 84, 230, 231; profits, 221–22, 250; and *Roger Fry: A Biography*, 304, 307; Russian writers and, 12, 232, 357n14; George "Dadie" Rylands and, 282; sale of, 250–51; voice in cultural affairs, 111; and war, 254, 280, 317, 325–26; and *The Years*, 149, 169, 170–72, 174
Holland, Lady Elizabeth, 331
Holmes, Charles, 293, 294, 298
Holmes, Dr. Oliver Wendell, 188
Holst, R.N.R., 297, 298, 299
Homer, 285–86
Honorius, Emperor, 285
Hopkins, Gerard Manley, 263, 267

House, Humphrey, 268
Houseman, A. E., 292
How, Canon Walsham, 262. *See also* Kilvert, Reverend Francis
Hsieh, Lili, 326
Hughes, Arthur, 161
Hughes, Thomas, 161
Hugo, Victor, 194
Hussey, Mark, 337n5
Hutchinson, Barbara, 26, 75–76, 108
Hutchinson, Elizabeth (Wordsworth's niece), 267
Hutchinson, Mary, 26, 71, 75–76
Hutchinson, St. John ("Jack"), 75–76, 108
Huxley, Aldous, 34, 112, 117, 148–49, 350n15
Huxley, Thomas, 184
Hyndman, Tony, 226

Ibsen, Henrik, 357n9
Image, Selwyn, 294
Independent Theatre, 97
Ingelow, Jean, 89
International Writers Congress, 228
Isherwood, Christopher, 24, 221, 228, 250, 325–26

Jaccaci, A. F., 293
Jackson, Anna, 1
James, Alice: and Henri-Frédéric Amiel's diary, 352n36; and Maria Bashkertseff's *Journal*, 352n36; as battler, 127, 129, 130, 131, 132, 134, 137, 352n36; diary of, 102, 126–37, 334, 351nn32–35, 352n36; on George Eliot's *Journals*, 352n36; illness and death of, 126, 130, 131, 132, 133–36, 137, 351n34; and Charles Ricketts, 360n14; suicide and, 132–33, 136, 137; and *Three Guineas*, 128, 130–31; and *The Years*, 102, 127–28, 137
James, Henry (the novelist), 128, 130, 174, 322; friend of Leslie Stephen, 127, 351n30; and Alice James' diary, 126, 136; and Alice James' illness and death, 133, 134, 136–37
James, Henry (senior), 132
James, Rear-Admiral Bartholomew, 331
James, Robertson, 137
James, William, 128; and Alice James' diary, 132, 134, 135, 136–37
Jeans, James, 30
Jewsbury, Maria Jane, 339n19
Johnson, Dr. Samuel, 162, 316
Johnson, Esther ("Stella"), 53, 85–86, 347n16. *See also* Swift, Jonathan
Johnson, Miss Scott, 84. *See also* Hogarth Press
Johnson, President Andrew, 192
Jones, E.B.C. ("Topsy"), 360n6. *See also* Lucas, F. L.
Jones, Robert, 340n24
Jowett, Benjamin, 182, 192
Joyce, James, 211, 320, 340n25

Kaiser Wilhelm, 65, 156, 345n30, 354n14
Keats, John, 29, 105–06
Kelly, Ambrose, 212
Keppel, Alice, 56, 65, 68. *See also* King Edward VII; Sackville-West, Vita
Keynes, John Maynard: King's College and, 283; on World War II, 68, 108–09, 276–77
Killen, Glady Ellen, 349n7
Kilvert, Edward, 263
Kilvert, Reverend Francis: and *Between the Acts*, 249, 270–71; and Robert Burns, 263; diaries of, 249, 255, 257–71, 269, 280, 325, 335, 359n6; and Roger Fry, 266; and Hitler, 267; poems of, 261, 263; and suicide, 266; *Vicar of This Parish*, 269; and walking, 265, 268; and war, 264–65, 266, 267, 268, 270; and Parson James Woodforde, 257, 258, 259; and Dorothy Wordsworth, 258, 267–68; and William Wordsworth, 258, 267–68
Kilvert Society, 269
King Alexander of Jugosavia, 109
King Edward VII, 56, 65, 68. *See also* Edward, Prince of Wales
King Edward VIII, 176–77
King George IV, 270
King George V, 56, 65, 177
King of Sweden (Oscar II), 153
Kinnegad Slashers, 217
Kipling, Carrie Balestier, 174
Kipling, Rudyard, 5, 164, 177

Kitchener, Herbert, 354n14
Knight, William, 340n26
Koch, W. John, 67
Kolnai, Aurel, 290
Koteliansky, Samuel, 232, 357n10
Kübler-Ross, Elisabeth, 135

Labour Party. *See* British Labour Party
La Fontaine, Jean de, 8
Lamb, Charles, 17
Lamb, Henry, 71
Lamb, Mary, 17
Lane, Anthony, 351n27
Lansbury, George, 148
Latham, Richard, 207. *See also* Weeton, Ellen
Lawrence, D. H., 78, 267
League of Nations Union: calls for, 65, 194, 294; and Japan, 24; F. L. Lucas on, 287; Mussolini's defiance of, 138; Dr. Afred Salter and, 353n7
Leaska, Mitchell, 77, 346n11
Leavis, Q. D., 252
Lee, Hermione, 5, 272, 353n8; on Roger Fry, 349n11; on Adolf Hitler, 101, 302; on Ethel Smyth, 7, 97, 302; on Leonard Woolf, 24–25, 172; on Woolf's diaries, 1, 337n1
Leeds, Nancy, 66. *See also* Daisy, Princess of Pless
Lehmann, John, 37, 74, 250–51
Lehmann, Rosamond, 112, 117
Lejeune, Philippe, 2, 327
Lenare (photographer), 75
Leopardi, Giacomo, 350n23
Leopold X, 61
Levin, Susan, 19, 340nn21–22
Lewis, C. Day, 280
Lewis, Cecil: editing of Charles Ricketts' diaries, 293, 297, 298, 299, 300; Ricketts' letter to, 299; Ricketts' portrait of, 360n9; on Charles Shannon, 300
Lewis, Wyndham: attacks on Woolf, 105–06, 107, 108, 109, 140–41, 142; *Hitler*, 24
Lister, Joseph, 153
Llewelyn Davies, Margaret. *See* Davies, Margaret Llewelyn

Lochner, Louis P., 324
Lockhart, John, 11
London Society for Women's Service Marsham Street Library, 101–02
Longman, C. T., 263
Loring, Katharine Peabody: as Alice James' companion, 128, 130, 134, 135, 136, 351n34; and Alice James' diary, 129, 131, 136, 137
Lounsberry, Barbara: *Becoming Virginia Woolf*, 337n2, 338n7, 347n18, 351n31, 354n7, 360n11; *Virginia Woolf's Modernist Path*, 337n3, 341n4, 341n7, 342n9, 342n14, 347n16, 354n13, 360n8
Lowell, James Russell, 178–79, 231
Lucas, F. L. ("Peter"): and "Anon," 292, 308; on Caligula, 285; and Chaucer, 289; and Lord Chesterfield, 285; criticizes Jonathan Swift, 290; on Goldsworthy Lowes Dickinson, 291; "exhibits" mentally ill wife, 279, 289–90, 291, 300; on Fascist treatment of the Jews, 286–88; on Roger Fry, 289, 291; on Homer, 285–86; journals of, 116, 117, 273, 279, 280–81, 282–92, 335, 350n22; literary criticism of, 283, 292; praise of Desmond MacCarthy, 284, 290–91; praise of Samuel Pepys, 290; and Charles Ricketts, 300; on Sir Walter Scott, 289; and the Rev. John Skinner, 288; and Lytton Strachey, 291; and suicide, 290, 291–92; and *Three Guineas*, 288, 290–91; and World War I, 283
Lucas, Prudence, 279, 288–89, 291
Lucretius, 165
Ludendorff, General Erich, 138
Lynch, Colonel Arthur, 213
Lyttelton, Mary Kathleen, 166

Mabel (servant). *See* Haskins, Mabel
Maber, Richard, 269
Macaulay, Rose, 349n7
MacCarthy, Desmond, 211; and John Bailey, 166–67; Clark lectures and, 76; *Criticism*, 74; criticism of *Mrs. Dalloway*, 36; and F. L. Lucas, 284; *Portraits*, 74; praises T. S. Eliot, 315; war and, 108, 302; Woolf's criticism of *Drama*, 320

MacCarthy, Mary ("Molly"), 320
MacDonald, Ramsay, 24, 146
MacKenna, Captain Stephen, 210, 217
MacKenna, Robert, 210, 217
MacKenna, Stephen, 363n1; diaries of, 168, 175, 210–20, 328, 334; Irish independence and, 210, 214, 215, 217–19, 328; and *Three Guineas*, 168, 175, 217, 219, 220, 328; and Leo Tolstoy's diary, 246–47; translation of Plotinus, 210, 212–13, 214, 215–17, 218, 219, 356n21, 356n24; and war, 217, 218, 219, 220; and Wordsworth's *Prelude*, 211–12
MacLennan, Michael Lewis, 301
Mallarmé, Stéphane, 111, 211
Malraux, André, 350n24
Manchuria, 345n2
Manning, Cardinal Henry, 117
Mansfield, Katherine: death of, 85; ellipses of, 323; journal of, 12, 208–09, 333; mocks William and Dorothy Wordsworth, 12–13, 18; "public of two," 314; and Ellen Weeton, 208–09; Woolf's letters to, 100
Marbury, Elizabeth, 96
Martin, Kingsley: admiration for Leonard Woolf, 353n5; egotism of, 142; gossip of, 31, 176; prevents Woolf's writing, 142, 149, 311; on war, 227
Mary, Queen of Scots, 91
Matheson, Hilda, 306
Matisse, Henri, 166
Maud, Constance, 128, 130. *See also* James, Alice
Maude, Aylmer, 246, 247, 357n13, 358n19
Maupassant, Guy de, 118, 351n29; Joseph Conrad on, 351n28; death and, 120, 121, 122–23, 124, 126; and Alice James' diary, 137; Henry James on, 351n28; and "Professions for Women," 119; and Prometheus, 125; on solitude, 118, 120, 121–22, 123, 125; suicide and, 120, 122–23, 126; Tolstoy on, 118; travel diary, *Afloat*, 102, 118–26, 131, 334, 348n4; on war, 118, 120–21, 124, 126; *A Woman's Life*, 118, 125; and *The Years*, 102, 125–26
Mavourneen, Kathleen, 260–61. *See also* Kilvert, Reverend Francis
Mazzini, Giuseppe, 194

Meath, Countess Mary of, 333
Meek, James, 358n22
Meredith, George: and Michael Field, 90–93, 94, 100, 347n20; poem "Juggling Jerry," 173, 174–75, 227, 251, 317, 327; and *Three Guineas*, 91–92; treatment of Oscar Wilde, 299
Meredith, Mary, 266
Mérimée, Prosper, 285
Meryon, Dr. Charles, 313, 332
Metternich, Count (Paul Wolff), 56
Michelangelo, 300
Michelet, Jule, 311
Mikháylovna, Varvára, 237, 240, 241, 246. *See also* Tolstoy, Countess Sophia
Mill, Harriet Taylor. *See* Taylor, Harriet
Mill, John Stuart: death of, 194–95; mentor to Lord and Lady Amberley, 182, 184, 188, 192, 193, 194–95, 355n10; *On Liberty*, 179, 181, 278, 355n9; on new Reform Bill, 183–84, 186
Milne, A. A., 145
Milton, John, 49, 214
Mirsky, Prince (Dmitry Petrovich Svyatopolk-Mirsky), 68, 140–41
Mitzi (Leonard Woolf's marmoset), 147
Modernism, 3, 144, 283; formal experiment, 2, 325, 337n6; fragmentation and, 2, 324–25; nonlinear narration, 325; Woolf's modernist diaries, 2, 6, 70, 324, 328, 338n8
Moeller van den Bruck, Arthur, 290
Monkshouse, Mrs., 338n12. *See also* Wordsworth, Dorothy
Montaigne, Michel de, 72, 112, 116
Moore, G. E., 293, 302
Moore, George, 27, 174; and Michael Field, 94, 347n20
Moore, T. Sturge: and Michael Field, 88, 93, 96, 98 99, 100; and Charles Ricketts, 293–94, 295, 297, 298, 301, 361n17
Moorman, Mary, 240n26
Moreau, Gustave, 294
Morgan, John, 270
Morrell, Lady Ottoline, 71, 138, 210, 249
Morris, William, 297, 299
Mortimer, Raymond, 148–49
Mosley, Oswald, 5, 24, 101, 176

Mott, Lucretia, 188
Munich accord, 253–54, 255, 287
Museum of Oaklands, Chelmsford, 353n11
Musgrave, Archer, 353n12
Mussolini, Benito, 146, 252–53, 286, 290; and Abyssina (Ethiopia), 138, 148, 160, 162, 353n7; and Emperor Caligula, 285; invades Albania, 272, 276; and Munich accord, 287–88; praise for, 5; and women, 109; Woolf counter to, 69, 324–29

Napoleon Bonaparte, 108, 109
National Gallery, 256, 293, 295, 299, 361n19
National Joint Committee for Spanish Relief, 228
Nazis, 138, 168; persecution of the Jews, 221, 147; rise of, 5; Sterilisation Law, 68–69; and women, 68–69, 101, 348n1. *See also* Fascism
Nero (Carlyle dog), 179, 196
Nero (Emperor), 362n8
Nevill, Lady Dorothy, 331
Newman, Cardinal John Henry, 258
Newnham College, 88–89, 252
New Party, 5, 24. *See also* British Union of Fascists
Nicolson, Harold, 24, 176, 255
Nietzsche, Friedrich, 291, 357n9
Nin, Anaïs, 118
Noailles, Comtesse Mathieu de, 349n7
North, Cynthia, 306

O'Brien, Justin, 112, 349n13, 350n15
Ocampo, Victoria, 109, 348n3, 349n7
Oldfield, Sybil, viii, 345n33
Olympia Auditorium, 101
O'Neill, Arthur, 190
Onslow, Lord (William Arthur Bampfylde), 176
Orient Express, 78
O'Rinn, Liam, 211–12

Paganini, Niccolò, 120
Palmerston, Lord Henry, 191
Parnell, Charles, 109
Parnell, Katharine, 109

Pascal, Blaise, 116
Pater, Walter, 94
Pavlova, Anna, 30
Pearn, Inez. *See* Spender, Inez Pearn
Pearse, Patrick, 217–18
Pedder, Edward, 205, 206, 207. *See also* Weeton, Ellen
Pembroke, Henry, 10th Earl, 335
Pepys, Samuel: diary of, 7–8, 10, 117, 196, 254, 267, 280, 298, 331, 339n7; and Rev. Francis Kilvert's diary, 267; and London, 267; F. L. Lucas praise of, 290; Charles Ricketts and, 298
Perkins, A. F., 254
Peterloo Massacre, 180
Philippe, Charles-Louis, 111
Philipps, Wogan, 228
Phillips, Anne, 266
Pinker (dog), 8
Pless, Princess Daisy of. *See* Daisy, Princess of Pless
Plomer, William: as editor of Kilvert's diaries, 257, 258, 262, 263, 266, 267, 268, 269, 270; Woolf letters to, 257, 266, 359n7
Plotinus: MacKenna translation of, 168, 210, 212, 214–17, 219, 220, 356n21, 356n24; on war, 218
Poincaré, Raymond, 30
Pollard, Jane, 14
Ponsonby, Arthur, 232
Ponsonby, Dorothea, 232
Pope, Alexander, 341n27
Popoff, Alexandra, 358n19, 358n22
Powell, Anthony, 269
Price, Priscilla, 270
Pridmore-Brown, Michele, 325
Prince Albert, 190
Prince Alfred, 190
Princess Daisy of Pless. *See* Daisy, Princess of Pless
Prometheus, 175; and T. S. Eliot, 28; and *Jacob's Room*, 26; and Maupassant, 125; and Ethel Smyth, 36; and *The Waves*, 26, 36, 37; and World War II, 305; and *The Years*, 169, 172, 175, 198; and William Butler Yeats, 28

Proust, Marcel, 267
Pulitzer, Joseph, 212, 213, 214

Queen Alexandra, 56, 66
Queen Caroline, 270
Queen Marie of Romania, 109
Queen Mary, 65
Queen Victoria, 56, 64–65, 176, 190
Queen Wilhelmina, 302

Racine, Jean, 166, 350n24
Rau, Dr. Leo, 231
Rau, Petra, 69, 168, 221
Raverat, Jacques, 117
Read, Herbert, 307
Reischach, Count, 61
Réjane, Gabrielle, 297
Rembrandt, 293
Renan, Ernest, 110
Renard, Jules, 116, 117, 333, 351n26
Renoir, Pierre-Auguste, 256
Richardson, Dorothy, 340n25
Richmond, Bruce, 149, 165
Ricketts, Blanche, 296
Ricketts, Charles, 360n8, 363n1; and Michael Field, 97, 99, 273, 281, 293, 294–95, 301, 347n20; and Roger Fry, 293–94, 361n19; and Gilbert and Sullivan, 297, 360n12; and the Goncourt brothers, 297; and Charles Holmes, 293, 294, 298; Alice James and, 360n14; journals of, 99, 273, 281, 292–301, 335, 360n13, 360n15; in *Last Romantics*, 301, 361n19; loss of mother, 296, 363n1; and T. Sturge Moore, 293–94; and Charles Hazelwood Shannon, 293, 294, 295, 296, 361n19; and George Bernard Shaw, 292; and *Three Guineas*, 273, 281, 292, 296, 300, 360–61n15; and the Vale Press, 293, 295, 297, 360n10, 360n15; and war, 292, 297, 299–300, 301; and Oscar Wilde, 293, 295, 299, 300; and William Butler Yeats, 292, 293
Ricketts, Edward, 296–97
Ripper, Jack the, 30
Robeson, Paul, 228
Robins, Elizabeth, 347n20

Robinson, Henry Crabb, 12, 17–18, 22, 332, 341n27
Robson, Elaine, 280
Robson, William, 311
Rochefoucauld, Francois de la, 116
Rockefeller, J. D., 212
Rodin, Auguste, 212
Roland, Elizabeth Anne, 262–63
Rosenfeld, Natania, 249
Rossetti, Christina, 71
Rossetti, Dante Gabriel, 95, 295, 361n15
Rothenstein, William, 97, 99, 295, 347n20
Rothermere, Lady, 350n19
Rothschild, Alice de, 58
Rothschild, Baron (Sir Nathan Mayer Rothschild), 56
Rousseau, Jean-Jacques, 116
Royal Academy of Arts, 361n15
Royal Albert Hall, 101
Royal Irish Academy, 220
Rubens, Peter Paul, 300
Ruskin, John: and Michael Field, 89–90, 100, 347n20; and Stephen MacKenna, 212
Russell, Arthur, 185–86, 194
Russell, Bertrand: and *The Amberley Papers*, 168, 172, 177–98, 355nn10–11; on Lady Henrietta Stanley, 355n11; on Lord Amberley's writing style, 355n10
Russell, Flora, 355n12
Russell, Frank, 177, 186–87, 195
Russell, George Gilbert William ("Willy"), 193, 195
Russell, John (Lord Amberley): *Analysis of Religious Belief*, 180, 181, 197–98; and Thomas Carlyle, 193; and Thomas Cobden-Sanderson, 180; diaries of, 168, 172, 177–98, 334; and John Stuart Mill, 182, 192, 193, 194–95, 196, 278, 355n10; political career of, 189, 190, 191–93, 355nn14–15; and Sir Walter Scott, 180; and Leslie Stephen, 178, 180; and *Three Guineas*, 168, 178, 182–89, 193–94, 198; on war, 168, 193–94; on women's rights, 182, 184, 185, 186, 187, 188, 193
Russell, Kate Stanley (Lady Amberley): and Jane Carlyle, 179, 182; and Thomas Carlyle,

179, 181; and Thomas Cobden-Sanderson, 180; diaries of, 168, 172, 177–98, 226, 334, 355n8, 355n13–15; Thomas Wentworth Higgenson on, 183; and Oliver Wendell Holmes, 188; and John Stuart Mill, 179, 181, 182, 183–84, 188, 194–95, 278; and Lucretia Mott, 188; and Dr. Lucy Sewell, 188; and Elizabeth Cady Stanton, 189; and Leslie Stephen, 178; and Harriet Beecher Stowe, 189; and Helen Taylor, 182, 184, 188; and *Three Guineas*, 168, 178, 182–88, 193–94, 198; on war, 193–94; on women's rights, 179, 181, 182–89, 355n11
Russell, Lady Arthur (Laura), 185–86, 355n12
Russell, Lady Frances Elliot-Murray-Kynynmound: against Amberley's marriage, 181, 183, 191; and Amberley's diaries, 191, 195; and Kate Amberley's diaries, 196; critiques women's rights work, 186–88; raises Amberley children, 177, 354n6
Russell, Patricia, 178, 196
Russell, Prime Minister John (1st Earl Russell): and Kate Amberley's diary, 196; death of, 354n6; as Prime Minister, 177, 191–92, 193; and son (Lord Amberley), 180, 181, 182, 183, 190, 192, 193, 194, 195; and women's rights, 186, 187, 191
Russell, Rachel Lucretia, 188, 195
Rylands, George ("Dadie"), 282, 283, 353n5

Sackville-West, Edward ("Eddy"), 248, 359n2; diary of, 279, 325; writings of, 349n7
Sackville-West, Lady Elizabeth, 354n5
Sackville-West, Victoria (Vita's mother), 55
Sackville-West, Vita, 11, 280, 306; and *Between the Acts*, 270; *Diary of Lady Anne Clifford* and, 37, 38, 71, 342n9; distant relative of Lord Amberley (John Russell), 177, 354n5; distant relative of Princess Daisy of Pless, 25, 37, 55; *The Edwardians*, 11, 338n10; and *Flush*, 74; lack of ego of, 36; New Party and, 24; *Pepita*, 250, 270; relationship with Woolf, 24, 37, 140, 306, 320; and *A Room of One's Own*, 7; Woolf's letters to, 21, 37, 55, 56, 63, 74, 177, 232–33, 283, 345n32
Saint Paul, 90, 109, 110

Saint Raphael, 122
Saintsbury, George, 165
Salisbury Cathedral, 359n7
Salter, Dr. Alfred, 148, 159, 353n7
Salter, Dr. John, 363n1; diary of, 138, 148, 150–60, 164, 217, 334, 353n10; and *Three Guineas*, 157–58, 159, 160, 217; and *The Years*, 154, 159, 160
Salter, Laura Duke, 151–52, 154
Sand, George (Amantine Dupin), 355n8
Sands, Ethel, 221
Santayana, George, 307
Sappho, 90–91, 94
Sayers, Tom, 154
Schimmelpenninck, Marie Anne, 181
Schreiner, Olive, 96
Scipio (Publius Cornelius Scipio Africanus), 285
Scott, Sir Walter, 11; John Bailey and, 161; and *Between the Acts*, 280; John Buchan and, 254; and Fanny Burney, 280; diary of, 10, 180, 199, 254, 273, 280, 289, 313, 331, 335, 338n7; Michael Field and, 88; "Gas at Abbotsford," 280, 313; influence on Lord Amberley, 180; F. L. Lucas and, 289; meeting with Dorothy and William Wordsworth, 11–12, 20, 268, 340n23; and the Rev. John Skinner, 343n17; Woolf's visit to Dryburgh Abbey, 254; *The Years* and, 82, 340n23
Scottish Kennel Club, 153
Sélincourt, Basil de, 225
Sélincourt, Ernest de, 340n26
Seneca, Lucius Anneaus, 291, 362n8
Senhouse, Roger, 71
Sermon on the Mount, 234
Seward, William, 192
Sewell, Dr. Lucy, 188
Shah of Persia (Shahanshah), 153
Shairp, Principal, 340n26
Shakespeare, William, 18; *Coriolanus*, 309; and Michael Field, 90; *Hamlet*, 289; *Henry IV*, 187; *King Lear*, 43–44; *Macbeth*, 60, 84; *A Midsummer Night's Dream*, 259; *Othello* and the Tolstoy marriage, 238, 240; *The Tempest*, 96; Woolf and, 9, 87, 138, 306, 309, 319, 338n5

Shannon, Charles Hazelwood, 293, 294, 296, 361n15; diaries of, 297, 298; and Michael Field, 295, 347n20; and the Goncourt brothers, 297; and H.D., 360n13; illness of, 300; in *Last Romantics*, 301, 361n19; and Vale Press, 293, 295, 297, 360n10, 361n18

Shaw, Charlotte, 68

Shaw, George Bernard, 71, 100; and Michael Field, 346n20; model of vigorous old age, 73, 84–85; and Charles Ricketts, 292, 300, 361n16

Shelley, Lady Frances, 332

Shelley, Percy Bysshe, 37, 308

Sickert, Walter: as cosmopolitan, 83; and Michael Field, 347n20; and Ivan Turgenev, 83; Woolf's "Walter Sickert: A Conversation," 82, 83, 85, 88, 109–10, 223

Silenus, 96

Silver, Branda, 48

Simon, Lady Shena, 228

Simpson, Wallis, 176

Sinclair, Sir Archibald, 221

Sisyphus, 169, 175

Sitwell, Florence, 335

Sitwell, Osbert, 108, 349n7

Skinner, Anna (wife of John Skinner), 43, 47

Skinner, Anna (daughter of John Skinner), 40, 41, 43

Skinner, Fitz Owen, 43

Skinner, Joseph, 40, 41, 43, 47

Skinner, Laura: death of, 43, 47; diary of, 43, 47, 342–43n16, 343n17

Skinner, Owen, 40, 43, 47

Skinner, Reverend John: antiquarian researches of, 41, 43, 263, 342n15; diaries of, 25, 32, 34, 38–48, 71, 334, 342nn10–13, 342–43n16, 343n18, 359n5; and the Rev. Francis Kilvert, 263; possible bipolar disorder of, 44–45, 46; Sir Walter Scott and, 343n17; suicide of, 25, 32, 38–39, 44, 312; and Ellen Weeton, 204, 205; women and, 40, 342n11; and the Rev. James Woodforde, 45, 51

Skinner, Russell, 39, 41, 43, 44, 342n10

Skinner, Tertia, 43

Sleeman, J. H., 217

Smyth, Ethel, 85, 86, 317, 339n14; as battler, 7–8, 302, 327, 341n6; *Between the Acts* and, 7, 97; Boer War and, 345n33; diaries of, 10; "March of Women," 7, 87; model of valiant old age, 7–8, 26, 27, 37, 73, 86, 87, 273, 275, 279, 317, 327, 341n2, 347n17; *The Prison*, 7, 36; "Professions for Women" and, 33; and *A Room of One's Own*, 7; Woolf diary portraits of, 7–8, 70, 149; Woolf's effort to discipline, 30, 31, 36–37, 87, 347n17, 349n7; Woolf's letters to, 177, 251, 256, 279, 283, 318–19, 320, 346nn3–4, 347n17, 349n7, 349n9, 354n2; *The Wreckers*, 342n8; *The Years* and, 7

Snowden, Margaret ("Margery"), 7

Sonnenberg, Rhonda, 273

Soviet prison camps, 30

Spanish Civil War: and Julian Bell, 221, 226–31; early headlines, 30; fall of Barcelona, 272; fall of Madrid, 272; F. L. Lucas on, 287; Stephen Spender on, 226–27

Spencer, Herbert, 100, 347n20

Spender, Inez Pearn, 226, 273

Spender, Stephen: defends Woolf, 106, 107; ego of, 226; and war, 146, 226–27

Spinoza, Baruch, 359–60n4

Spiras, Mela and Robert, 276, 277

Spooner, Sarah, attempted suicide of, 54

Squier, Susan, 346n7, 356n1, 362n9

Squire, J. C.: John Bailey and, 162; on Stephen MacKenna, 210

Staël, Madame de, 200

Stalin, Joseph, 249, 252–53, 285; attacks Finland, 359n1; Woolf's counter to, 324–29

Stanhope, Lady Hester, 313

Stanley, Monsignor Algernon, 185. *See also* Russell, Kate Stanley

Stanley, Aunt Louisa: against women's rights, 185, 187, 188; and Jane Austen, 355n13; and Peterloo Massacre diary, 179–80; and Kate Stanley's marriage, 191; writing style of, 355n8

Stanley, Blanche, 178

Stanley, Edward, 2nd Baron Stanley of Alderley, 181, 185

Stanley, Henry M., 134
Stanley, Lady Henrietta, 194; encourages Lord Amberley, 182, 188, 191; founder of Girton College, 183, 355n11; restrictions on Kate, 181; supports Kate, 183, 188; writing style of, 355n8
Stanley, Lyulph, 181, 191
Stanley, Maude, 181
Stanton, Elizabeth Cady, 189
Stekel, Wilhelm, 289
Stella (Esther Johnson), 53. *See also* Swift, Jonathan
Stendhal (Marie-Henri Beyle): early journals of, 48, 333; and André Gide, 350nn23–24; loss of mother, 363n1; and Yeats and *The Waves*, 107
Stephen, Adrian, 18, 196, 272
Stephen, Ann, 306
Stephen, Judith, 252
Stephen, Julia, 13, 110, 139, 143–44
Stephen, Sir Leslie: John Bailey on, 166; Clark lectures, 76; diary of, 18–19; George Meredith and, 90; religious faith of, 180, 181; and Annie Thackeray, 178; and "Minnie" Thackeray, 178; Virginia's relationship with, 29, 47, 76, 143–44; and *The Years*, 143–44
Stephen, Thoby, 13; death of, 9, 18, 32, 166; and *Jacob's Room*, 21; and *The Waves*, 9, 21, 39
Sterne, Laurence, 328
St. Helier, Lady, 30
St. John, Christopher, 87
Stock, Aaron, 207, 209. *See also* Weeton, Ellen
Stock, Mary, 207, 208, 209. *See also* Weeton, Ellen
Stoddart, Sarah, 333
Stonehenge, 359n7
Stowe, Harriet Beecher, 189
Strachey, Alix, 147
Strachey, Colonel Richard, 181
Strachey, James, 71
Strachey, Lady Jane Maria, 179, 355n9, 355n11
Strachey, Lytton: and John Bailey, 166; Dora Carrington and, 346n5; and André Gide, 117; illness and death of, 38, 71, 72, 105, 107; King's College and, 283; F. L. Lucas on,

291; *Portraits in Miniature and Other Essays*, 74; *Queen Victoria*, 166; and Lady Hester Stanhope, 313; Woolf letters to, 19, 100, 165; Woolf's talks with, 30, 31
Strachey, Oliver, 71
Strachey, Ray, 101, 362n5
Strindberg, August, 234
Sturgeon, Flora, née Woolf, 278, 320
Suffragettes, 7, 58, 163
Suffragists, 7; Elizabeth Garrett, 182, 183; Lady Amberley, 179; Lady Strachey, 355n9. *See also* Russell, Kate Stanley
Suh, Judy, 324, 325–26
Sukotín, Mikhail Sergéevich, 239, 240
Sullivan, Arthur, 297, 360n12
Svyatopolk-Mirsky, Prince. *See* Mirsky, Prince
Swift, Jonathan, 363n1; *Journal to Stella*, 41, 53, 71, 113, 85–86, 117, 204, 333, 347n16; F. L. Lucas criticism of, 290
Swinnerton, Frank, 140–41, 142
Sydney-Turner, Saxon, 339n14
Symonds, Arthur, 347n20
Symonds, John Addington, 295
Synge, J. M., 211, 212, 356n20

Tagore, Rabindranath, 98
Tapsel, Thomas, 242
Tavener, Mary, 258
Taylor, Harriet, 179, 189. *See also* Russell, Kate Stanley
Taylor, Helen, 182, 184, 188, 189, 194. *See also* Russell, Kate Stanley
Tennyson, Lord Alfred, 190
Terry, Ellen, 316, 347n20
Thackeray, Annie, 178
Thackeray, Harriet Marian ("Minnie"), 178
Thackeray, William Makepeace, 181
Thomas, Daisy, 259–60, 261
Thomas, Mr., 259–60
Thompson, J. O.: as compiler of Dr. Salter's diaries, 150, 151, 152, 153, 155, 160
Thomsett, Annie, 6
Thrale, Hester, 316, 317
Tiresias, 94
Toller, Ernst, 146

Tolstoy, Annochka, 357–58n17
Tolstoy, Countess Sophia: *Autobiography* of, 232, 235, 238, 247; and Fanny Burney's diary, 234; and V. G. Chertkóv, 236, 237–41, 242–46, 358n18; copies *Anna Karenina*, 234; copies *War and Peace*, 234, 357n15; diaries of, 222, 226, 231–48, 335, 358nn17–18, 358n21; as editor and publisher of Tolstoy's works, 234, 235, 244, 247, 357n16, 358n19, 358n22; Aylmer Maude on, 246; and photography, 242–43, 358n20; Alexandra Popoff and, 358n19, 358n22; as property manager, 232, 234, 235, 242; suicide threats of, 234, 236, 237, 239, 241, 243, 245, 358n18
Tolstoy, Count Nikolai Ilyich, 233, 242, 357n11
Tolstoy, Ilya, 357n17
Tolstoy, Ivan, 232
Tolstoy, Leo, 363n1; *Anna Karenina*, 234, 237, 247; and V. G. Chertkóv, 235, 236, 237–38, 239–40, 241, 242–43, 245, 246, 357n13; *The Cossacks*, 232; *Criticism of Dogmatic Theology*, 235; *A Cycle of Reading*, 235; death of, 232, 235–36; diaries of, 117, 222, 226, 231–48, 326, 335, 357nn12–14, 358n19, 358n21; early life of, 233, 357n11; *For Every Day*, 235; André Gide and, 233; love letters of, 232; and Stephen MacKenna, 212; on Maupassant, 118; and photographs, 242–43, 358n20; self-condemnation of, 233, 245, 247; and *Three Guineas*, 247; on war, 234, 236, 247; *War and Peace*, 234; *The Way of Life*, 235; Woolf's admiration for, 232, 357nn9–10
Tolstoy, Leo Lvóvich, 236
Tolstoy, Masha, 234
Tolstoy, Sasha: copyist for Tolstoy, 234, 235, 239, 241, 245; and Countess Tolstoy's attempted suicide, 245; diarist, 246; and Leo Tolstoy's diaries, 240, 241, 242, 244, 245; and Tolstoy's flight, 245–46
Tolstoy, Sergius, 235, 237, 244, 246, 258n19
Tolstoy, Tatiána: copyist for Tolstoy, 235; diarist, 246; 1926 London lecture, 232–33; supports Leo Tolstoy, 240, 241, 242, 244
Tomlin, Stephen ("Tommy"), 36, 222, 225–26, 229–30

Treby, Ivor C., 347n19, 347n23
Tregoning, Angela, 269
Trench, Melesina, 331
Trevelyan, George, 162
Trevelyan, Robert C., 71, 293, 294, 348n6
Trinity College, Cambridge, 76, 180
Turgenev, Ivan, 82, 83, 85, 109, 347n15

Valentinian, Emperor, 285
Vale Press, 293, 295, 297, 360n10. *See also* Ricketts, Charles; Shannon, Charles Hazelton
Valéry, Paul, 115
Vanderbilt, Cornelius, 56
Vanhomrigh, Esther ("Vanessa"), 53, 85–86, 347n16. *See also* Swift, Jonathan
Vassar College, 183
Vaughan, Janet, 143, 145
Vaughan, Madge, 145, 166
Vaughan, William, 163, 354n15
Vaux, Mary James, 137
Venables, Mrs., 259, 260, 270
Venables, Vicar, 260, 262
Verlaine, Paul, 347n20
Victoria, Queen. *See* Queen Victoria
Vigny, Alfred de, 117, 313, 362n6

Walpole, Horace, 180, 359n5
Walpole, Hugh, 37, 303, 346n11
Walter, Bruno, 86
Walton, Izaak, 49
Ward, Mrs. Humphrey, 346n11
Warlock, Peter, suicide of, 30
Watry, Maureen, 361n18
Watson, William, 165
Watts, G. F., 96, 178, 347n20
Webb, Beatrice Potter, 14, 85; diaries of, 34, 63, 333; *My Apprenticeship*, 67, 333, 341n7; *Our Partnership*, 34; Woolf visit with, 34
Weeton, Captain, 199, 200, 208
Weeton, Edward, 199, 200
Weeton, Ellen, 363n1; diaries of, 168, 175, 198–209, 334; disastrous marriage of, 203; dislike of war, 208; ego of, 199, 201, 203, 204, 209; praise for, 355–56n19; as school mistress, 203, 355n17; and the Rev. John

Skinner, 204; and Jonathan Swift, 204; and *Three Guineas*, 168, 175, 198, 199, 200, 207–08, 209; and Dorothy Wordsworth, 199, 200

Weeton, Mrs., 199–200, 201, 202, 209

Weeton, Tom: education fund of, 200, 201–02, 209; ungrateful brother of Ellen, 201–02, 204, 205, 206, 209

Wells, Amy, 53

Wells, H. G., 53, 75, 174, 307

West, Margaret, 84, 230. *See also* Hogarth Press

West, Rebecca, 87, 147

Westminster Abbey, 299

White, Miss Betsy, 49, 50

Whitehead, Mrs., 203

Wigans, Horace, 192

Wigram, Ralph, 146–47

Wilberforce, Octavia, 222, 226, 317, 320, 322

Wilde, Oscar: and Michael Field, 94–96, 97, 100, 347n20; and Charles Ricketts, 293, 295, 299, 300

Wilhelm II, Kaiser. *See* Kaiser Wilhelm

Williamson, Henry, 335

Willingdon, Lord, 30, 31

Wilmot, Catherine, 332

Wilson, Jean Moorcraft, 362n7

Winkley, Miss, 207. *See also* Weeton, Ellen

Wishart (publishing house), 75

Wodehouse, P. G., 151

Wolff (dog), 57, 74. *See also* Daisy, Princess of Pless

Wollstonecraft, Mary, 21, 22

Women's Employment Federation, 101

Wood, Sir Evelyn, 156

Woodforde, Dr. R.E.H., 48

Woodforde, John, 54

Woodforde, Nancy: diaries of, 49, 343n19; and food, 52; relationship with James Woodforde, 49, 50, 52; in Woolf's Woodforde essay, 53–54, 55

Woodforde, Reverend Frank, 49

Woodforde, Reverend James: diaries of, 25, 45, 46, 48–55, 71, 333, 334, 343–44n21–25, 359n5; equable temperament of, 46, 49, 50–51, 343–44n20; illness and, 54; and the Rev. Francis Kilvert, 257, 258, 259; Parson Woodforde Society, 344n25; and *A Room of One's Own*, 54–55; and the Rev. John Skinner, 45, 51; suicide and, 54; Nancy Woodforde and, 49, 50, 52, 53

Woodforde, Reverend Samuel, 49

Woodforde, Robert, 49

Woof, Pamela, 16, 340n26

Woolf, Barbara ("Babs"), wife of Philip, 108

Woolf, Bella, 26

Woolf, Edgar, 353n5

Woolf, Flora. *See* Sturgeon, Flora

Woolf, Harold, 26

Woolf, Leonard: *Barbarians at the Gate*, 274; domestic interaction, 8, 35, 71, 72, 74, 75, 77, 81, 85, 107, 110, 138, 169, 174, 176, 224, 231, 277, 278, 279, 281, 289, 310, 311, 349n7, 352–53n5; Hogarth Press and, 11, 84, 111, 149, 169, 171–72, 174, 225, 230, 231, 232, 250–51, 254, 257, 274, 280, 281, 288, 304, 307, 313, 316, 317, 323, 325–26, 341n3, 357n14; illness of, 84, 231, 247, 250; King's College and, 283; *Nation & Athenaeum* and, 6, 11, 31; and old age, 74, 251; *Quack, Quack!*, 148; responses to Virginia's works, 37, 170, 171, 174, 175, 317; and Paul Robeson, 228; on George Bernard Shaw, 73; and Ethel Smyth, 70; and *Three Guineas*, 145, 252, 352–53n5; war and, 5, 24–25, 145, 147, 221, 227, 302, 305, 345–46n2, 352–53n5; *The War for Peace*, 302; *A Writer's Diary* and, 1, 321–22; writings of, 107; and *The Years*, 102, 169, 170, 171, 172, 174, 175

Woolf, Marie, Leonard's mother, 26, 71, 278–79

Woolf, Philip, 108, 353n5

Woolf, Virginia, 102–03; and Amiel's diary, 356n22; Byron and, 9–10, 338n6; concern with old age, 2, 7–8, 26–28, 72, 73–74, 75, 84, 106, 139, 174, 224, 251, 255–56, 277–80, 304, 309, 312–13, 314, 321, 362nn4–5, 362n7; dress and, 103; female support and, 2, 7, 11, 85, 314, 327; "fidgets" of, 327; Hogarth Press and, 11, 28, 35, 84, 111, 149, 169, 171–72, 174, 175, 225, 230, 231, 232, 250–51,

Woolf, Virginia—*continued*
254, 257, 274, 280, 281, 288, 304, 307, 317, 325–26, 341n3, 357n14; movement and, 111, 249, 250, 251, 254, 255, 278, 279, 282, 306–07, 308–10, 313, 314, 316, 318–19, 320, 321, 325, 329, 362n4, 362n7, 362n10; passion for reading of, 32, 79, 80–81, 84, 110, 125, 306, 310, 311, 312, 314, 316, 320, 327, 328, 349n7; reading notebooks of, 12, 21, 48; and Paul Robeson, 228; and Vita Sackville-West, 21, 55, 56, 63, 345n32; scrapbooks of, 5, 145; sensitivity to criticism of, 106; spontaneous invention of, 33; suicide and, 1, 4, 29, 30, 72, 78, 106, 118, 132, 143–44, 171, 173, 252, 253, 255–56, 305, 308, 312, 316, 346n5, 352n4, 359n4, 362n2; *Time* magazine cover of, 221; and walking, 14, 26, 78, 84, 110, 117, 224, 252, 265, 274, 282, 307, 309, 310, 311, 319, 321, 359n6, 362n10; Beatrice Webb and, 85

Woolf, Virginia, diaries of: bird tropes in, 8, 142, 173, 174–75, 227, 251, 303, 306–07, 308, 313, 317, 327; diary audience, 2, 6; diary candor, 85; diary closings, 11, 38, 78–79, 110, 231, 323, 326; diary continuity, 29, 38, 78, 229, 250, 316, 347n15; diary covers, 6, 25, 38, 70, 80, 103, 223, 250, 273, 281, 282, 314, 337n1, 341n1, 345n1, 346n8, 348n2, 352n2, 354n1, 356n2; diary credo, 146, 177–78, 251, 304, 338n8; diary ease, 78, 255; diary fragility, 1, 273, 314, 318, 329; diary graphs, 222, 225; diary length, 64; diary openings, 25, 70, 73, 78, 80, 102, 110, 170, 171, 177, 222, 226, 250, 275, 315–16; diary portraiture, 6–8, 26–27, 36, 73–74, 84, 142–43, 146–47, 149, 150, 170, 172–74, 175, 226, 278, 279, 325, 326, 327; diary purposes, 2, 3, 8, 12, 35, 38, 52, 53, 69, 71, 72, 74, 75, 76, 79, 80, 85, 105, 106, 107–08, 112–14, 116, 125, 129, 141, 143, 148, 149–50, 160, 168, 169, 171, 175, 223, 224, 225, 226, 228, 230, 247, 248, 251, 253, 255, 273, 275, 276, 278, 279, 281–82, 303, 305, 316, 320, 324, 325, 326, 327, 328, 347n15, 358n4; diary questions, 79, 82, 83, 86, 103, 150, 173, 230, 253, 277, 281, 314, 317, 326, 348n3, 353n9, 356n7, 359n3; diary rescue, 313, 322; diary signs of illness, 72–73, 106, 279, 313, 320–21, 359n4; diary structure, 2, 69–70, 78, 108, 326, 327; diary "tricks" to induce prose, 11, 70, 338n11; Elderly or Old Virginia, 2, 6, 31, 87, 103, 107, 125, 140, 149, 177, 209, 255, 279, 303, 312, 328, 347n15, 348n4; entry number, 2, 6, 8, 25, 69–70, 71, 80, 84, 103, 105, 139, 141, 142, 143, 145, 150, 169, 170, 223, 229, 252, 253, 275, 276, 277, 302, 303, 305, 316, 318, 324; horse tropes in, 7, 8, 25, 30, 32, 33, 34, 35, 36, 37, 76, 77, 86, 103, 105, 106, 107, 109, 139, 141, 149, 177, 225, 227, 251, 274, 275, 278, 279, 306, 310, 317, 338nn5–6; loose-leaf diaries, 2, 6, 140, 223, 230, 250, 273, 303, 316, 318, 327; margin notes, 33, 125, 347n15, 352n3; morning diary-writing, 2–3, 8, 25–26, 27, 33, 70, 71, 75, 80, 103, 108, 150, 169, 175, 229, 303, 358n2; natural history diary, 2; rereading of, 169, 250, 316, 317, 338n8, 347n15; specimen days, 8, 310, 311; travel diaries, 2, 34, 78, 102, 149, 273, 274, 352n2, 357n9; undated entries, 70, 229; water tropes in, 25, 28, 29, 33, 35, 36, 37, 38, 70, 71, 73, 76, 77, 79, 80–81, 82, 83, 84, 87, 103, 104, 118–19, 139–40, 143, 144, 145, 148, 172, 175, 223, 224, 228, 229, 230, 251, 252, 253, 254, 255, 273, 274, 276, 277, 281, 307–08, 309, 311, 312, 313, 314–15, 317–18, 320, 322, 341nn6–7, 346n9, 346n11, 346n13; *A Writer's Diary*, 1

—1897 (first extant) diary of, 1, 2, 12, 18–19, 127, 248, 324

—1899 Warboys diary of, 2, 15, 30, 118–19, 254–55, 308, 318

—1903 diary of, 2, 99, 129, 133, 143–44, 173, 309, 359n7

—1905 diary of, 2, 170

—1905 Cornwall diary of, 2, 14, 39, 72, 139, 175, 263

—1906–1908 Great Britain travel diary of, 2, 14, 127, 178, 359n6

—1906–1909 Continental travel diary of, 2, 198

—1909 diary of (*Carlyle's House and Other Sketches*), 2, 45

—1915 diary of, 2, 112, 279, 316, 321
—1917–1918 Asheham House natural history diary of, 2, 142
—1917–1918 Hogarth House diary of, 2
—1918 diary of, 2, 107, 140, 338n6, 338n8
—1919 diary of, 2, 6, 107, 146, 177–78, 211, 251, 328, 338n8
—1920 diary of, 2, 45, 77, 204
—1921 diary of, 2, 12, 80, 106, 125, 144, 169, 171, 175, 340n25
—1922 diary of, 2, 283
—1923 diary of, 2
—1924 diary of, 2, 38, 77
—1925 diary of, 2
—1926 diary of, 2, 186, 283, 338n5, 341n7
—1927 diary of, 2, 30, 140, 223
—1928 diary of, 2, 140, 223
—1929 diary of, 2, 6, 140, 223, 316, 360n6
—1929–1930 diary of, 2, 3, 4, 5–11, 29
—1930–1931 diary of, 2, 3, 4, 25–38, 70, 175, 345n1, 360n6
—1932 diary of, 2, 3, 4, 68 69–79, 325
—1933–1934 diary of, 2, 3, 4, 68, 79–87
—1934 diary of, 2, 3, 4, 102–10
—1935 diary of, 2, 3, 4, 135, 138–50, 326
—1936 diary of, 2, 3, 4, 168–77, 203, 354n1, 354n3
—1937 diary of, 2, 3, 4, 222–31, 250, 252, 278, 356nn4–5, 357n8, 359n3
—1938 diary of, 2, 3, 4, 250–56, 275, 277, 282, 285, 358n1, 358nn3–4, 362n2
—1939 diary of, 2, 3, 4, 273–82, 287, 288, 292, 359nn3–4
—1940 diary of, 2, 3, 4, 224, 292, 302, 303–15, 319, 321, 322, 362nn3–5, 362n8
—1941 diary of, 2, 3, 4, 110, 224, 302, 315–23, 324
Wordsworth, Dora, 339n19
Wordsworth, Dorothy, 26, 85, 338n13, 363n1; attention to women, 16–17; and Robert Burns, 19–20; and André Gide's diaries, 115; illness of, 17–18, 268; journals of, 6, 10, 11–23, 71, 150, 268, 333, 338n12, 339nn17–18, 340n22, 340–41nn26, 341n28; and the Rev. Francis Kilvert, 258, 267–68; *Lyrical Ballads* and, 16, 19; meeting with Sir Walter Scott, 11–12, 20; mocked in Katherine Mansfield's *Journal*, 12–13; poems of, 17–18, 22, 267; relationship with William Wordsworth, 12, 13, 14, 16, 17–19, 20–21, 22, 23, 267, 339n18, 340–41nn24–26, 241n28; and Henry Crabb Robinson, 12, 17–18; suicide and, 17; walking and, 14, 17, 18, 265, 268; and Ellen Weeton, 199
Wordsworth, Mary, 18, 19, 267, 339n20
Wordsworth, William, 21, 231, 338n13, 340n22; and Robert Burns, 19–20; criticized by F. L. Lucas, 360n5; "Graves of the Poets," 267; Rev. Francis Kilvert and, 258, 267, 268; *Lyrical Ballads*, 16, 19; Stephen MacKenna and, 211–12, 217; meeting with Sir Walter Scott, 11–12, 20; "Memorials of a Tour of the Continent, 1820," 338n12; mocked in Katherine Mansfield's *Journal*, 12–13; *Prelude*, 8, 9, 11, 29, 211–12, 339n14; relationship with Dorothy, 12, 13, 14, 16, 17–19, 20–21, 22, 23, 202, 268, 339n18, 340–41nn24–26, 341n28; Henry Crabb Robinson and, 12, 17; "Tintern Abbey," 267, 339n16; Woolf's admiration for, 339n14
Wright, Dr. Joseph, 151
Wyndham, George, 162

Yeats, William Butler, 328, 347n20; and Stephen MacKenna, 211, 220; model of vigorous old age, 26–28, 36, 73; poetry of, 339n14; and Charles Ricketts, 292, 293; on war, 108; and *The Waves*, 106–07; Woolf diary portraits of, 26–28, 36
Young, Arthur, 85, 334

BARBARA LOUNSBERRY is professor emerita of English at the University of Northern Iowa. She is the author of *Becoming Virginia Woolf: Her Early Diaries and the Diaries She Read* and *Virginia Woolf's Modernist Path: Her Middle Diaries and the Diaries She Read* as well as *The Art of Fact: Contemporary Artists of Nonfiction* and is coeditor of *Writing Creative Nonfiction: The Literature of Reality*.

www.ingramcontent.com/pod-product-compliance
Lightning Source LLC
Chambersburg PA
CBHW031425160426
43195CB00010BB/621